BEYOND CARNIVAL

WORLDS OF DESIRE
THE CHICAGO SERIES ON SEXUALITY, GENDER, AND CULTURE
A Series Edited by Gilbert Herdt

BEYOND CARNIVAL

Male Homosexuality in Twentieth-Century Brazil

~

JAMES N. GREEN

The University of Chicago Press / Chicago & London

JAMES N. GREEN is assistant professor of history at
California State University, Long Beach.

The University of Chicago Press, Chicago 60637
The University of Chicago Press, Ltd., London
© 1999 by James N. Green
All rights reserved. Published 1999
08 07 06 05 04 03 02 01 00 99   5 4 3 2 1

ISBN (cloth): 0-226-30638-0

Library of Congress Cataloging-in-Publication Data

Green, James Naylor, 1951–
    Beyond carnival : male homosexuality in twentieth-century Brazil /
James N. Green.
        p.   cm. — (Worlds of desire)
    Includes bibliographical references.
    ISBN 0-226-30638-0 (alk. paper)
    1. Gay men—Brazil.   I. Title.   II. Series.
HQ76.2.B6G74   1999
306.76′62′0981—dc21   99-28059
                                                           CIP

⊗ The paper used in this publication meets the minimum
requirements of the American National Standard for Information
Sciences—Permanence of Paper for Printed Library Materials,
ANSI Z39.48-1992.

To Moshé
and
in memoriam
J. Elliott Green, Jr.

CONTENTS

ILLUSTRATIONS

Figures

Maps

Tables

Acknowledgments

In many ways this book began twenty-some years ago during a six-year sojourn in Brazil, as I simultaneously witnessed the slow-motioned demise of the military regime and the birth of a gay and lesbian rights movement. The friends from that period became the mainstays of my life in Brazil when I returned in 1994 to carry out the bulk of the research for this project. Without the support of Edmea Jafet, Henrique Carneiro, Martinha Arruda, and her two marvelous children, Suiá and Yama, I never would have managed to survive that year. Other old friends who became new friends again must also be mentioned: Cristina Ribeiro, Ederzil Camargo, Edward MacRae, Gilda Penteado, Hélio Goldsztejn, Hilda Machado, Hiro Okita, Jean-Claude Bernardet, John McCarthy, Jorge Beloqui, Jussara Florêncio, Luiz Amorim, Luiz Mott, Marcelo Abboud, Marisa Fernandes, Paula Maffei, Ricardo Silva, Robson Camargo, Rosa Parolari, Rosely Aparecida de Moraes, Tony Panciarelli, and Veriano Terto Júnior. In innumerable ways they provided personal and logistic support to make my research possible.

A new generation of activists in the Brazilian gay, lesbian, and transgendered movement gave me invaluable assistance in establishing contacts and carrying out my work. They include Augusto Andrade, Cláudio Nascimento, Cláudio Roberto da Silva, David Harrad, Elias Ribeiro de Castro, João Vargens, José Edwardo F. Braunschweiger, Karim Aïnour, Luiz Carlos Barros de Freitas, Marcelo Ferreira, Rosana Zaiden, Toni Reis, and Wilson da Silva.

Fearing that the topic of my doctoral dissertation would engender obstacles in the Brazilian archives, I brought with me a vaguely worded letter of introduction about a study on Brazilian masculinity during the Vargas era. My anxieties melted as I met person after person who assisted me in *garimpando* (mining) for sources. In the Arquivo do Estado de São Paulo, Lauro Ávila Pereira and Daniela Palma introduced me to a friendly and professional group of archivists who include Ady Siqueira de Noronha, Maria Zélia Galvão de Almeida, and Rosimeire dos Santos. Laura Guedes and Georgina Kaufman of the National Archive pointed me in the direction of key documents and suggested alternative research strategies. The staff of the Edgard Leuenroth Archive / UNICAMP in Campinas showed endless enthusiasm and dedication in helping me utilize the materials held there. Ângela M. C. Araújo, Elaine Marques Zanatta, Miriam Manini, and Marisa Zanatta assisted me immeasurably and have all worked to develop an important gay and lesbian collection at that archive.

One of the most pleasurable and unexpected benefits of my research in Brazil has been the development of a new network of friends and scholars who have valued my work and supported it in a multitude of ways. They include Afonso Carlos Marques dos Santos, Beatriz Kushnir, Carlos Bacellar, Carlos Soares, Celeste Zenha, Cristiana Senetinni Pereira, Durval Muniz de Albuquerque Júnior, Iara Lis F. Stto. Carvalho Souza, João Roberto Martins Filho, Joana Maria Pedro, Jorge Schwartz, Marcelo Florio, Luciana Gandelman, Marcos Luiz Bretas, Magali Engel, Margareth Rago, Maria Clementina Pereira Cunha, Maria Izilda Santos de Matos, Mary del Priore, Olívia Gomes da Cunha, Paulo Roberto Ottoni, Sílvia Miskulin, Simone Martins, Tânia Pellegrini, and Zilda M. Grícoli Iokoi. José Carlos Sebe Bom Meihy and Rachel Glazer also gave me helpful comments on a paper based on my initial research given at the University of São Paulo.

Special recognition must be given to several people who passed away during the four years I have worked on this project. Adauto Belarmino Alves, Alcir Lenharo, Edwardo Toledo, James Kepner, João Antônio de Souza Mascarenhas, and Rick Turner all inspired me, and their spirit is embedded in this book. Two other individuals offered essential help in crucial aspects of my research. Agildo Guimarães provided access to the world of *Snob* and kindly put me in contact with his social network in Rio de Janeiro. In turn, José Fábio Barbosa da Silva generously gave me the original copies of his pioneering sociological study of homosexuality in São Paulo.

During my graduate studies in Latin American history at UCLA, Bebe Bernstein, Hien McKnight, Nina Moss, and Sheila Patel all helped me maneuver though bureaucratic obstacles and encouraged the progress of my studies. The generous support that I received from the UCLA Latin American Center, the Tinker Foundation, and the Pauley Fellowship allowed me to conduct my research in Brazil. John O'Brien and Walter Williams of the Center for Scholars in Residence located at the University of Southern California, in cooperation with the ONE Institute, a program of the International Gay and Lesbian Archives, offered invaluable assistance and provided a scholarly environment during the writing phase of the dissertation. The Ken Dawson Award from the Center for Lesbian and Gay Studies (CLAGS), a graduate program of the City University of New York, and a graduate student award from the UCLA Lambda Alumni Association supplied much needed financial backing during the final stages of finishing my dissertation, the core of this work. Moreover, Daryle Williams and Phyllis Peres, the directors of a 1998 National Endowment of the Humanities Summer Institute in Brazil, showed flexibility in organizing the program to allow me to tie together final elements of my research.

My doctoral committee, José C. Moya, Ellen C. DuBois, Ramón Gutiérrez, and Karen Brodkin, offered constant encouragement of my academic potential and recognition of the importance of gay social and cultural history. The members of the editorial board of *Latin American Perspectives,* especially Marjorie and Donald Bray, Fran and Ron Chilcote, and Timothy Harding, have been an essential force in shaping my academic career.

John D'Emilio, Donna J. Guy, Jeffrey Escoffier, Robert Howes, Daniel Hurewitz, Daniel Kiefer, and Robert Levine all offered careful and valuable suggestions about improving my manuscript. My editor Doug Mitchell and his assistant Matthew Howard of the University of Chicago Press have been impeccable in their attention to the entire production process. Carlisle Rex-Waller meticulously copyedited the manuscript, and Paulo Simões kindly proofread and corrected my Portuguese. I wish to thank Aureo Silva for his assistance in designing the maps of Rio de Janeiro and São Paulo. Sharon Sievers, the chair of the History Department at California State University, Long Beach, Karen Lau, the office manager, and my colleagues have been tremendously understanding of my efforts to be both a teacher and a scholar.

Three other individuals must also be mentioned. My mother, Miriam D. Green, has always urged me to fulfill my dreams and has given me endless love over the years. My sister, Marycarolyn G. France, provided the initial push for me to go back to graduate school and has remained a close and loyal friend. Finally, the most important acknowledgment goes to Moshé Sluhovsky, my partner, editor, and colleague. Without his intellectual, emotional, and logistical support through all phases of this project, it never would have happened.

Author's Note

All translations from Portuguese to English are mine unless otherwise indicated. My citations of Portuguese titles follow the originals, hence the
variant spellings of key terms.

MAP I   Brazil

INTRODUCTION

～

In 1938, the popular singer Carmen Miranda starred in the Brazilian motion picture *Banana da Terra*.[1] In the film, she played a baiana, a woman from the northeastern state of Bahia, who sang and danced with a small basket of fruit perched precariously on her head. Her cinematic performance was an exaggerated imitation of the traditions of Afro-Brazilian market women from Bahia.[2] Soon afterward, during the three days of the Carnival celebrations that precede Lent, hundreds of men took to the streets of Rio de Janeiro. Clothed in the billowing white hoop skirts and sparkling clean turbans of the famed Northeast women, these men exceeded Carmen Miranda's own parody of the *baiana*.[3]

The practice of cross-dressing had long been a part of Carnival festivities, as had been the appropriation by certain men of the Afro-Brazilian women's traditional garb during pre-Lenten festivities. However, these celebrants were not ordinary married men dressed in drag, flaunting jewelry and finery borrowed from their sisters, mothers, and girlfriends in order to engage in three days of uninhibited revelry.[4] Their colorful impersonations of the decade's most famous popular singer and her stylized costumes unequivocally exceeded carnivalesque male gender transgressions of the day. These *falsas baianas* (fake Bahian women) à la Carmen Miranda engaged in festive subversion that mimicked both normative gendered behavior and traditional cross-dressing during Carnival.[5] Their celebratory performance in the streets of Rio de Janeiro was a public affirmation of these men's own notions of masculinity and femininity, notions that both challenged and reinforced Brazilian gender norms of the first half of the twentieth century.[6]

Carmen Miranda's persona became one of the international symbols of

Brazil during World War II.[7] For decades thereafter, gay men in Brazil and the United States recreated the image of the extravagantly dressed Brazilian bombshell. Over the years numerous musical reviews have elevated Carmen Miranda to cult stardom, and she remains among the galaxy of Hollywood icons.[8] In 1984, more than forty-five years after Carmen Miranda's first film appearance as a bejeweled *baiana*, and after the star's male followers first took to the streets to imitate her, male street revelers in Rio de Janeiro still utilized her image to suggest gender ambiguity and a gay sensibility. During that year's celebrations, a group of gay men formed the Carnival group Banda de Carmen Miranda, a split-off from the famed Banda de Ipanema.[9] Organizing their own street celebration, they created hundreds of excessive costumed parodies of Carmen Miranda and paraded through the streets of the Ipanema neighborhood of Rio de Janeiro in pre-Lenten merrymaking. The revelry led by the Banda de Carmen Miranda has become an annual event within Rio's Carnival festivities, a critique of traditional gendered behavior, and a public forum for both humorous and serious manifestations of gay pride.[10]

If the outrageous antics of Carmen Miranda in her Hollywood films symbolized to United States and European audiences Brazilian femininity in the 1940s and 1950s, the tall, tanned, young, lovely, gently swaying girl from Ipanema fed international heterocentric erotic fantasies about tropical women in the early 1960s. She was soon followed by images of scantily dressed light-brown-skinned Afro-Brazilian women, used by governmental and other tourist agencies to promote Rio's Carnival festivities. In recent years bronzed Brazilian men have joined both plumed *mulatas* in sequined G-strings and camp Carmen look-alikes. A burgeoning gay tourist industry in the United States now prepares glossy brochures for middle-class gay globetrotters featuring Rio's "Mardi Gras" celebrations as a hotbed of sizzling sex and unabashed permissiveness.

As early as 1970, Pat Rocco, one of the pioneering Los Angeles–based gay porn filmmakers, used Brazilian Carnival as a backdrop for an erotic 16-mm production, *Marco of Rio*.[11] In an age before videos, Rocco's classic reached a rather limited audience. In the 1980s and 1990s, however, sexually explicit gay video productions became a multimillion-dollar industry, complete with skilled filming and computerized editing. Director-producer Kristen Bjorn internationalized the United States–based genre with slick flicks shot in Eastern Europe, Latin America, and other "exotic" places, including several titles set in Brazil. Bjorn's first action feature film, *Carnival in Rio* (1989), featured men who ran toward the "dark, clean-cut, large-built, uncircumcised and seemingly good-natured variety."[12] In Bjorn's and other U.S. and European gay porn films, the muscular *mulato* has replaced the camp Carnival queen as the erotic and exotic "other."

For many foreign observers, from Buenos Aires to San Francisco and Paris, these varied images of uninhibited and licentious Brazilian homosexuals who express sensuality, sexuality, or camp during Carnival festivities have come to be equated with an alleged cultural and social toleration for homosexuality and bisexuality in that country.[13] Apparent permissiveness during Carnival, so the stereotype goes, symbolizes a sexual and social regime that unabashedly accepts fluid sexual identity, including male-to-male sexuality.[14]

When Carnival costumes have been cast off and life returns to normal, a somewhat different picture regarding the acceptance and toleration of homosexuality in Brazil emerges. A May 1993 poll of a cross section of two thousand Brazilian men and women revealed persistent anxiety over homosexuality. While 50 percent confirmed that they had daily contact with homosexuals at work, in their neighborhood, or in the bars and clubs they frequent, 56 percent admitted that they would change their behavior toward a colleague if they discovered he or she was homosexual. One in five would drop all contact with the person. Thirty-six percent would not employ a homosexual, even if he or she were the best qualified for the position. And, of those interviewed, 79 percent would not accept their son going out with a gay friend.[15]

Homophobia manifests itself in more violent ways as well. For almost two decades, Luiz Roberto Mott, an anthropologist and the founding president of Grupo Gay da Bahia, the country's longest-surviving gay rights organization, has been collecting data about the indiscriminate murder of homosexual men, lesbians, and transvestites in Brazil. In 1996 he published the results of his research in conjunction with the International Gay and Lesbian Human Rights Commission in a volume entitled *Epidemic of Hate: Violations of the Human Rights of Gay Men, Lesbians, and Transvestites in Brazil*. That study revealed the shocking statistic that "a homosexual is brutally murdered every four days, a victim of homophobia that pervades Brazilian society."[16] Many of those killed are sex workers, transvestites, or gay men who have picked up someone for a brief sexual escapade and end up victims of robbery and then sadistic murders.[17] Unidentified groups or individuals commit most of these homicides. Only 10 percent of these reported crimes lead to arrests. In 1995, Toni Reis, the founding copresident of the Brazilian Association of Gays, Lesbians, and Transvestites noted that in his native city of Curitiba there had been twenty documented slayings of homosexuals over the previous ten years with only two convictions.[18] The late Adauto Belarmino Alves, the 1994 winner of the Reebok Human Rights Award, documented the killing in October 1994 of twenty-three homosexuals in Rio de Janeiro.[19] The U.S. Department of State 1993 Human Rights Country Report for Brazil also pointed to such violence: "There continues to be reports of murders of homosexuals. São Paulo newspapers reported that three transvestites were murdered on March 14; other reports claimed that 17 transvestites were killed in the first three months of 1993. One military policeman was charged in the March 14 killings and was awaiting trial at year's end. Homosexual rights groups claim, however, that the vast majority of perpetrators of crimes against homosexuals go unpunished."[20]

The case that most dramatically exemplifies the violence against homosexuals in Brazil involved the 1993 murder of Renildo José dos Santos, a local councilor from the municipality of Coqueiro Seco, in the rural northeast state of Alagoas. On February 2, 1993, the town council suspended him from that body for thirty days because he had declared on a radio program that he was bisexual. He was charged with "practicing acts incompatible with the decorum due his position and bringing the reputation of the Council into disrepute." When the period of his suspension expired and he was not reinstated, he sought a court order from a judge to permit him to return to the council. The next day he was kidnapped. His remains were discovered on March 16. His limbs and head had been dismembered from his body and the corpse burned. Although five men, including the mayor of the town, were arrested in the case, they were acquitted of any involvement in the murder. No one has been punished for this crime.[21]

In an update of Luiz Mott's 1996 report, Grupo Gay da Bahia documented 130 murders of gays, transvestites, and lesbians in 1997, recognizing that these statistics were incomplete because they lacked information from many of Brazil's states. Of the reported murders, 82 were gay men, 42 transvestites, and 6 lesbians.[22] As a result of these ongoing human rights violations, in recent years more than a dozen Brazilian gay men have requested political asylum in the United States based on sexual orientation.[23]

The contradictory images of permissive Carnival festivities and murderous brutality are startling, yet the tensions between toleration and repression, acceptance and ostracism are deeply embedded in Brazilian history and culture. Just as the pervasive myth that Brazil is a racial democracy obfuscates deep-seated patterns of racism and discrimination, so too the notion that "there is no sin below the equator" obscures widespread cultural anxiety about same-gender sexual activity in Latin America's largest country.[24]

Paradoxical phenomena regarding same-sex eroticism and bonding abound. João do Rio, a noted turn-of-the-century journalist from Rio de Janeiro, was widely known to enjoy sex with other men. Enemies attacked his effeminacy in the press. Yet an estimated one hundred thousand residents of Rio de Janeiro came out to mourn his death in 1921.[25] In more recent years, Dener and Clodovíl, prominent fashion designers; Clovis Bornay, the long-time champion of Rio's Carnival luxury costume contests; Rogéria, a drag queen famous in the 1960s and '70s; and the stunningly seductive transsexual Roberta Close all have become public personalities. These feminine and effeminate figures, who embody the opposite of normative behavioral traits of virility and masculinity expected of Brazilian men, have found widespread popular acceptance and circulate comfortably among elite social circles. Their effeminacy and outrageous behavior, however, serve as a foil, representing the amusing but inappropriate model, *not* to be emulated. Women may embrace these kinds of celebrities as long as their sons or boyfriends manifest no similar comportment. Likewise, men may find drag stars to be alluring figures because they perform as perfect imitations of pervasive masculine stereotypes of the ideal woman. Scandalous queens or buxom beauties may enjoy relative social acceptance, as long as they are *other* mothers' and fathers' sons. In many ways they reinforce rather than upset the rigidly defined gender system.

When a family does discover that a son is gay, parents and relatives might come to tolerate that fact as long as he is not overtly effeminate and people outside of the family don't know. Often times, a "don't ask, don't tell" policy is implicitly in place. It still is not unusual for a grown man to continue living at home, where he contributes to the family income and goes out with gay friends on the weekends but never mentions a boyfriend or the details of his social life to his family. If he moves out to set up his own apartment in order to have more freedom and independence, he might still assist in covering family expenses. Relatives learn to suspend the perennial questions about girlfriends or marriage prospects in order not to hear too many details that might break this silent family truce or threaten supplementary income provided by a single son. For so many other men, marriage and children, with homosexual escapades on the side, become the answer to constant social pressure to conform, have a family, and follow social norms.

Until recent years, when an emerging lesbian and gay political movement began to challenge pervasive stereotypes, the average Brazilian conflated male homosexuality with effeminacy. According to anthropologists, this prevailing notion is a result of a traditional, hierarchically structured Brazilian gender system that divides men who engage in same-sex erotic activities into two categories—the *homem* ("real" man) and the *bicha* (fairy). This binary opposition mirrors the dominant heterosexually defined gender categories of *homem* (man) and *mulher* (woman) in which the male is considered the "active" partner in a sexual encounter, and the woman, in being penetrated, the "passive" participant. Anthropologist Richard G. Parker has noted: "The physical reality of the body itself thus divides the sexual universe in two. Perceived anatomical differences begin to be transformed, through language, into the hierarchically related categories of socially and culturally defined gender: into the classes of *masculino* (masculine) and *feminino* (feminine) . . . Building upon the perception of anatomical difference, it is this distinction between activity and passivity that most clearly structures Brazilian notions of masculinity and femininity and that has traditionally served as the organizing principle for a much wider world of sexual classifications in day-to-day Brazilian life."[26]

According to this model, in traditional same-sex erotic activities, the *homem*, or in slang terms, the *bofe* ("real" man), takes the "active" role in the sexual act and anally penetrates his partner. The effeminate male (*bicha*) is "passive" and is anally penetrated. The latter's sexual "passivity" ascribes him the socially inferior position of the "woman." While the sexually penetrated "passive" male is stigmatized, the male who assumes the public (and presumably private) role of the *homem* who penetrates is not. As long as he maintains the sexual role attributed to a "real" man, an *homem* may engage in sex with other men without losing any social status.[27]

Sexual roles, therefore, are significantly more important than one's sexual partner. The role-based terms of *homem* and *bicha* define this sexual universe. Accordingly, two *homens* cannot have sex with each other, since one, supposedly, must take the role of the penetrated partner. Likewise, a sexual relationship between two *bichas* cannot be consummated because it is presumed that both partners expect the other to be the "masculine" penetrator. When first mapping out this gender system in Brazil, anthropologist Peter Fry asserted that it remained dominant not only in the poor and working-class neighborhoods of the Amazon region where he conducted research in the early 1970s, but throughout Brazilian society, coexisting and sometimes competing with other systems. Fry speculated that the *homem-*

bicha model still prevails in the north and northeast regions of Brazil, in rural areas, and among the poor in the country's large cities. In this regard, Candomblé, an Afro-Brazilian religious tradition involving spirit possession, has offered some degree of social space and a certain status in Brazilian society for many *bichas* from humble origins.[28] Candomblé is widely practiced among the poor of African origins, especially in the northeastern city of Salvador, Bahia. In recent years, many middle-class men and women also have joined the religion. As early as the 1940s, anthropologist Ruth Landes noted that many of the *pais de santo*, a term roughly equivalent to priest, within Candomblé were effeminate men or homosexuals.[29] More recently Patrícia Birman has studied the gender roles and homosexuality in Candomblé and Umbanda, a varient Afro-Brazilian religious tradition, in Rio de Janeiro.[30]

Fry also has argued that sometime in the 1960s a new sexual identity emerged. It first took shape among middle-class male homosexuals in Brazil's urban centers, and it was based on sexual object choice rather than gender roles.[31] Urbanization, the expansion of the middle class, an endogenous counterculture, changes in gender relations, and international gay cultural influences all contributed to the construction of this new identity, which was similar to the gay identity that developed in the United States in the 1930s and '40s.[32] According to Parker, the two patterns currently coexist in Brazil. Men of poor and working-class cultural backgrounds still model their sexual behavior along the traditional *homem/bicha* dyad, and urban middle-class homosexuals have in general embraced what is known as a gay identity.[33] Indeed, one must think of multiple homosexualities or sexualities since a form of bisexuality, the phenomenon of married men who have sex with other men yet maintain heterosexual relationships, also remains common.[34]

Since the late nineteenth century, when physicians, lawyers, and other professions in Rio de Janeiro began writing about same-sex eroticism, the tendency has been to emphasize what is presumably the most obvious marker of such behavior. Effeminate men who frequented public spaces, dressed flamboyantly, and adopted mannerisms and fashions associated with women thus figure prominently in this early literature. However, what *seems* to be the dominant sexual/gender system shaping society's understanding and construction of homosexuality is not the whole picture. Gender and sexual role behavior have been much more fluid and shifting among Brazilian men, even among those men whose primary sexual desire was toward men of the same sex. At the turn of the century, physicians, lawyers, and other professionals developed or confirmed their theories about homosexuality based on the characteristics and activities of the effeminate men they studied. The limited amount of the data they collected, however, at times contradicted their own writings on homosexuality. By reexamining the material they ignored, one can detect a much more variegated sexual system operating. This becomes especially obvious when reviewing medicolegal studies of the 1930s, when a richer cache of sources provides examples of people who did not fit the model or stereotype of the effeminate *bicha*, yet freely negotiated in a subculture already in formation.

As a foreign observer of Brazilian history and culture, one has to be especially careful to avoid creating a "we-they" dynamic when trying to understand the dominant paradigm at a given historical moment. It is too easy simply to note that the pervasive gender system operating in the United States is constructed differently from that in Brazil or Latin America and that the active/passive organization of sexual life described above varies notably from homosexual behavior in Western Europe and the United States. By operating with this bipolar framework, one can easily create a false "other" and thereby erase the complexities and inconsistencies of an overarching model. The same can be said about pointing to the development of similar constructions of homosexuality in Brazil and the United States in recent decades. In understanding the emergence of a new gay identity among urban middle-class Brazilians in the 1960s, it is also perhaps more accurate to state that there was a gap between representation and social experience. Men in the 1930s (and earlier) at times simply did not conform to the social representation and stereotypes of the active/passive binary. Certain men enjoyed multiple sexual experiences, including both being anally penetrated and penetrating others. The cultural changes in the 1960s merely provided a social context for multiple representations to coexist, and even to develop new space or value in the subculture.[35]

Furthermore, there are clear signs that a subculture of effeminate and non-effeminate men who desired and had sex with other men existed *prior* to the introduction of Western European medical ideas of homosexuality in the late nineteenth century. While members of the Brazilian elite received the latest foreign ideas about sexuality and social-sexual classifications relatively quickly and transmitted them to the public through the press and the interlocking relationships among doctors, lawyers, journalists, and other sectors of the elite, same-sex erotic subcultures and identities preceded these borrowed constructs.

Donna J. Guy pointed out in "Future Directions in Latin American

Gender History" that research about masculinity, homophobia, and the domination of heterocentric gender systems has lagged behind other areas of investigation on gender in Latin America.[36] Indeed, the literature on same-sex sexual behavior and attitudes about it in Spanish Latin America remains scant and focuses mostly on anthropological, sociopolitical, and literary studies.[37] In the field of history, there are a handful of articles about homosexuality, sodomy, and the Inquisition during the colonial period in Spanish Latin America and Brazil, and even fewer works on the nineteenth and twentieth centuries.[38] Nevertheless, Argentine writer Daniel Bao has looked at the construction of homosexuality in Buenos Aires over five decades. Bao has argued that between 1900 and 1950 a homosexual subculture developed where men maintained "meeting places, their own argot, fashion, and sexual tastes and customs."[39] He has posited that at the turn of the century other major Latin American cities that had contacts with the United States and Europe may have developed similar subcultures. Jorge Salessi also has documented the rise of this subculture of late-nineteenth- and early-twentieth-century Buenos Aires and has discussed the taxonomic elaboration of categories of homosexuality devised by the Argentine medicolegal profession to study and medicalize this phenomenon.[40] No similar substantive historical work has been done on other Latin American countries.

The initial studies of same-sex romantic and sexual relations in Brazil, as in Spanish Latin America, have mostly come from social scientists, specifically anthropologists, although in recent years scholars have branched out into history, film, and literature.[41] Peter Fry opened up the field with articles on the relationship between homosexuality and the Afro-Brazilian religion Candomblé, attempting to explain why so many cult leaders have been effeminate homosexuals.[42] Fry's writings outlining the Brazilian gender system have shaped the work of numerous Brazilian anthropologists and other scholars who have studied homosexuality over the last two decades.[43]

Another important contribution to the study of twentieth-century Brazilian homosexuality has been the work of anthropologist Carlos Alberto Messeder Pereira. He has examined the writings of doctors and criminologists within the context of the modernization of Brazilian society in the 1920s and '30s. Pereira argues that these professionals transferred the debate about homosexuality from the legal, religious, and moral realm to the sphere of medicine and claimed their right to control or cure manifestations of homosexuality.[44] More recently, the historian Talisman Ford, in

reviewing the works of these medical experts, has reasoned "that the popular, traditional understanding of sexuality, based on a gender hierarchy,
survived the introduction of a medical model because in Brazil the two were
not all that different."[45] Ford contends that sexologists in the 1930s selec-
tively adopted European theories that considered homosexuality pathological, while maintaining an analytical construct that presupposed the active /
passive dichotomy. She further argues that members of the medical profession failed to implant an ideology based on the Brazilian gender system
and, therefore, their efforts to regulate and discipline same-sex eroticism
failed. Historian Peter Beattie has contextualized same-sex erotic behavior
within a political rather than a medical context. He has suggested that rising nationalism and militarism in the late nineteenth century evoked a desire on the part of the Brazilian state to define appropriate masculine
sexuality and therefore repress "unnatural" same-sex behavior.[46]

My own research project acts as a bridge between historical analyses of
the medicolegal discourses of the 1930s and the anthropological studies of
contemporary Brazilian homosexuals. It brings to life the vibrant worlds of
men who have enjoyed social and erotic relationships with other men over
the twentieth century. It shows that a subculture similar to the ones that
flourished in New York and Buenos Aires at the turn of the century also
existed in Rio de Janeiro and in São Paulo. An important component of the
development of this homosexual subculture, I offer, has been the appropriation of urban space. While noted by a handful of geographers, sociologists, and anthropologists, the phenomenon has not been thoroughly
examined.[47] One important aspect of this question concerns the connection
between the occupation of public areas and the alleged traditional spheres
of Brazilian social life, namely the *casa* (home) and *rua* (street).[48] As we
shall see, greater male accessibility to the public social space, the *rua*, has
facilitated same-sex erotic encounters between men. However, the cultural
stigmatization of such activity has at times encouraged the creation of a
"counter-*casa*," a private space where men could interact freely that served
as an alternative to the traditional family. When identifiable gay bars
opened in the late 1950s and early 1960s in Rio and São Paulo, they acted
as such spaces, located between the private (*casa*) and the public (*rua*), protecting their patrons from an aggressive and hostile society. Similarly, Carnival balls served as a yearly opportunity for the private to become more
public.

Another aspect of this research project, the analysis of the ways in
which race and class affected men who enjoyed erotic activities with other

men, explains how different racial and class positionings structured Brazilian society. Same-sex erotic encounters often afforded an opportunity for cross-class and cross-racial interaction, but unequal economic means and social status also generated serious tensions and reinforced relative social and racial segregation. The degree of interclass mingling among men engaged in sexual liaisons with other men informs the parameters of economic and racial segregation in Brazilian society. This study may thus offer an additional means of understanding the contradictions undercutting the public image of Brazil as a racial democracy.

Additionally, this investigation sheds new light on the Brazilian family, viewed for so long as a rigid, monolithic legacy of the patriarchal colonial past.[49] As we shall see, some Brazilian families rejected and even hospitalized male members who strayed from accepted social norms of a heterocentric society, while other families maintained wayward sons within the fold. Still other men, either because of their marginality or distance from traditional familial support systems, built family-like alternative social networks and found economic and psychological support with friends who shared their sexual desires. Moreover, the migration patterns of homosexual men from the Northeast to Rio and São Paulo, or from the countryside to the city, challenge the standard model presented by sociologists and historians, according to which people relied primarily on kinship ties to move from one area of Brazil to another. For many young men who fled the control and condemnation of family, relatives, and small-town society to achieve urban anonymity in both cities, friendship based on shared identity and similar erotic experiences provided ties thicker than blood.

While ruminating over the appropriate title for this work, one scholar suggested that the subtitle should read: "Male Homosexuality in Twentieth-Century *Urban* Brazil" or "Male Homosexuality in Rio de Janeiro and São Paulo." Indeed, Brazil is a continent-size country with markedly diverse regional variations (see map 1). The population majority only tipped from rural to urban in the 1950s. Sexual and gender systems in small towns and rural areas operate within the context of different social, cultural, and economic structures. During the twentieth century, literally hundreds of thousands of young men who became aware of their sexual desires and fantasies for other men have left family and friends in the countryside to migrate to the capital of their state or to move to Rio de Janeiro and São Paulo. These cities have become two of the most important centers for emerging homosexual subcultures. This study weaves together the story of male homosexuality in both Rio de Janeiro and São Paulo rather than attempting to create a history of gay urban life throughout the entire country. I chose to focus almost exclusively on these two cities for several reasons. Popular Brazilian national stereotypes paint Cariocas, the inhabitants of Rio de Janeiro, as carefree and fun-loving people who live for the beach, beer, and Carnival. By contrast, Paulistas, residents of the city of São Paulo, are considered serious, hardworking, and entrepreneurial.[50] Yet the two cities share many characteristics not found in other Brazilian urban centers. São Paulo has been at the economic forefront of Brazil since the coffee boom at the turn of the century catapulted it to national prominence. By the end of World War I, São Paulo surpassed Rio de Janeiro in industrial strength.[51] In the 1950s, the city of São Paulo's population surpassed that of Rio de Janeiro, which has remained Brazil's second most important economic center and was the nation's capital until 1960.[52] Both cities have long competed with each other for eminence in cultural production and in academic excellence, drawing artists and intellectuals from the rest of Brazil. In certain ways Rio de Janeiro and São Paulo together shape many cultural standards for the entire country.

The experiences of homosexual men in both cities have been similar in numerous respects. Throughout the twentieth century and especially after 1930 when transportation improved, men moved relatively easily between the subcultures of Rio de Janeiro and São Paulo. The close communication between these two urban centers created similar cultural expressions, codes, slang, and sexual behavior. Differences between Rio de Janeiro and São Paulo, however, influenced some aspects of the formation of the homosexual subcultures. Afro-Brazilian traditions and culture have had more effect on Rio de Janeiro, while large-scale European and Japanese immigration to São Paulo created a different ethnic, social, and cultural mix. The easy access to beaches and the physical and sensual possibilities in these public spaces shaped the Carioca homosexual subculture. Carnival in industrious São Paulo remains a pale imitation of the festivities in Rio de Janeiro. Public manifestations of homosexuality as expressed through Carnival drag balls, street celebrations, samba schools, and fantasy costume contests have been more common in Rio de Janeiro than in São Paulo. Despite these and other differences, available historical sources in both cities allowed the rendering of a rich and textured social history. As George Chauncey has shown in *Gay New York*, imaginative detective work, painstaking patience, and a creative use of the archives can bring surprising results.[53]

It should be noted that throughout this study the existing historical records have revealed much more about the lives of poor, working-class, and lower-middle-class men who sought out sexual fulfillment in public places than they have about gay members of the upper class, who had the luxury of more circumspect lives. The lower one's economic or social status, the more vulnerable a person was to police harassment. In the 1920s and '30s, physicians and criminologists were interested in conducting their research on lower- and middle-class men because of popular eugenics theories that linked poverty, degeneration, violence, danger, and disorder. In general, men from the upper class could hide their sexual lives behind a veil of respectability. Given the hierarchical structure of class relations in Brazilian society, members of the elite who sexually desired other men have by and large remained protected from the inconveniences of police interference. A prestigious family name and adequate political and social connections could usually shelter a transgressive son or husband from public scandal. A comfortable income could also provide the necessary privacy for romantic or sexual trysts, and wealthier men could even discretely purchase sexual favors if that were necessary. Unless one fancied men from lower classes, sexual and social interactions could remain isolated in private parties and gatherings among peers, far from the plazas and parks where poorer homosexuals might congregate. Thus, this study has an inevitable bias toward men from the social sectors that make up the majority of the Brazilian population.

Keeping this in mind, a wide array of documentation does exist, although the raw data is rarely neatly cataloged under "homosexuality" in the indices of the National Archive in Rio de Janeiro or among police files or court cases in São Paulo. The impossibility of adequate access to police and court records in both Rio de Janeiro and São Paulo required alternative means of gaining an insight into official state policies for policing and controlling same-sex erotic encounters.[54] Medical records, depositions of transvestites who were arrested in downtown São Paulo, and clipping files from several Brazilian publications were among the archival sources used.[55]

Complete reliance on sources produced by the medical profession, the state, and mainstream media to document manifestations of homosexuality as well as notions of gender and masculinity in Brazil could present a highly distorted view of these subjects. Therefore, I sought information from another authoritative source, male homosexuals themselves. In seventy interviews, men ranging in age from thirty-five to eighty-five recounted their lives, their experiences, and their perceptions about same-sex romantic and sexual encounters from the 1930s to the 1990s. I made a conscious effort to ensure that the interviewees reflected a cross-section of Carioca and

Paulista society, representing a wide diversity in class origin, racial background, and political positions. The different personalities I talked with opened many divergent universes to view: the worlds of activists from the gay rights movement of the 1970s and 1980s; drag queens who attended the Carnival balls in the 1950s and 1960s; university intellectuals who consciously shunned gay political groups; sex workers; transvestites; and "ordinary" gay men who lived their lives and loves without an established connection to any of the political or social movements that had developed in the early 1960s and during the demise of the dictatorship from 1977 to 1985. Two generations of journals—informal, homecrafted productions in the early 1960s and movement-based publications such as *Lampião* from the late 1970s—offered yet another insight into the lives of Brazilian homosexuals, reflecting different moments in the development of varied homosexual identities.

Finally, this study relies on my own participation in the events surrounding the founding and the course of the politicized gay rights movement in the 1970s. During my time in São Paulo from 1977 to 1981, my role as an activist and a leader of the progressive wing of the movement during its controversial formative years placed me in the eye of a storm. Knowing my own proximity to the subject under investigation and my stake in the way this history is written has forced me to proceed cautiously.

In one significant way, the composite picture drawn from an array of sources suggested an alternative periodization for part of this social history of male homosexuality in twentieth-century Rio de Janeiro and São Paulo. Traditionally, historians of modern Brazil divide historical periods according to the major political changes in the different regimes over the last hundred years: the Republic (1889–1930); the Vargas years (1930–45); redemocratization (1945–64); the military dictatorship (1964–85); the return to democracy (1985–present).[56] But the notable social transformations in Rio de Janeiro and São Paulo that reshaped gender relations and the use of urban space required reaching back to before the Revolution of 1930 to explain the developments in Brazil from 1930 until the end of the authoritarian Estado Novo in 1945. Likewise, the political change in regime in 1964 had much less impact on the homosexual subcultures of Rio de Janeiro and São Paulo than did the restrictive measures of the first three years of the Médici government (1969–1972).

Thus, this book begins by examining Rio de Janeiro, at the time the nation's capital, during the period 1898–1920. These two decades marked the end of social and political turmoil following the overthrow of the monarchy and the establishment of a republican government in 1889. The sources about same-sex erotic sociability in Rio de Janeiro for the late nineteenth century and the first two decades of the twentieth were both qualitatively and quantitatively richer than material found in São Paulo for the same general time frame. Straying from traditional periodization, I chose to examine the period from 1920 to 1945 as a whole in order to include the impact of events in the 1920s on the changes that took place in Brazil after the Revolution of 1930.

Likewise, the approach to the post–World War II period varies from conventional timelines. I divided this period into two parts: 1945–1968, when a distinct, modern, urban subculture developed, and the post–1968 period, when social and culture changes reshaped the contours of that subculture. This work ends as the first wave of the Brazilian gay and lesbian movement emerged in 1978, a year that is also associated with the beginning of the slow transition from dictatorship to democracy.

Inspired by John D'Emilio's *Sexual Politics, Sexual Communities: The Making of a Homosexual Minority in the United States, 1940–1970,* this study began as an examination of the dynamics that led to the emergence of a politicized Brazilian gay and lesbian movement in the late 1970s.[57] However, it soon became apparent that any analysis of activism by homosexuals under the military dictatorship required a broader investigation into the formation of complex interlocking urban subcultures that developed over the twentieth century. It also quickly became clear that another goal, that of presenting a social history of *both* men and women who have sexual and romantic ties with members of their own sexes, was too ambitious. If source materials on male homosexuality in Brazil are relatively scant, primary and secondary sources on women who loved or had sex with other women are even more so. I also had much less access to the social networks of lesbians in Rio de Janeiro and São Paulo than to the gay male world. The two universes intersect at times, especially in some clubs and social circles, but remain largely autonomous. Moreover, the relative invisibility of lesbianism vis-à-vis male homosexuality requires different research strategies. Rather than attempting to encompass an extremely broad topic, I therefore chose to focus on male same-sex erotic, romantic, and social interactions.[58]

Although images of tropical licentiousness and debauchery may shape the reader's initial approach to the subject of Brazilian male homosexuality, this work proposes to look *beyond* the gender transgressions and public displays of sexuality that take place during Carnival in order to examine the broader social and cultural reality of male homosexuality in Brazil over the course of the twentieth century. Within this process, indeed, men who engage in erotic and romantic relations with other men have appropriated Carnival festivities to express their own notions of gender and to expand acceptable manifestations of sensuality and sexuality. But the success of their occupation of social space has been the product of a protracted contest that has lasted decades. Moreover, if drag queens imitating the banana-bedecked *baiana* have achieved an elevated status within the three days of pre-Lenten festivities in recent decades, the social position of Brazilian homosexuals during the rest of the year has been much less favorable. Coping with arrests and street violence, negotiating around family restrictions, developing alternative support networks, having sexual adventures, and maintaining relationships are only some of the many issues that ordinary homosexuals have had to address in their daily lives.

This study of men who have crossed sexual boundaries, in turn, reflects back on the overall framework of Brazilian social values and rules of acceptable behavior and reveals much about cultural definitions of masculinity and femininity. Thus, a history of homosexuality in Brazil is a history of men, women, and gender relations. The effeminate homosexual, or *bicha*, acts as a marker that differentiates between his own "deviant" behavior and "normal" masculine behavior of a "real" man. By the nature of its binary opposition to the norm, the social stereotype of the "passive" and womanly man defines the "active" and "virile" male. Contradictorily, however, the sometimes fluid nature of gender identification, as exemplified in Carnival celebrations, can also generate ambiguity that subverts Brazil's otherwise rigid hetero-dominant sexual system. This work seeks to untangle all of these ostensibly inconsistent and competitive constructs of gender and masculinity. It argues that behavior, activities, and images of men who have had sex with other men contributed to the formation of multiple gender identities assumed by Brazilian men. In examining the many ways in which men who engage in same-sex eroticism and bonding negotiated through a hostile society, this project also historicizes and contextualizes the growing visibility of homosexual men in Carnival celebrations and the seemingly unique Brazilian manifestations of gender ambiguity as exemplified in the striking phenomenon of the camp persona of Carmen Miranda and her male imitators.

CHAPTER ONE

~

Pleasures in the Parks of Rio de Janeiro
during the Brazilian Belle Époque,
1898–1914

As Brazil entered the twentieth century, Rio de Janeiro, nestled among towering granite hills and surrounded by a broad bay on one side and the Atlantic Ocean on the other, underwent remarkable transformations. For a decade after the abolition of slavery in 1888 and the declaration of the Republic a year later, the nation had been enveloped in political turmoil. According to one historian of this period, "[i]n 1898, with [President] Campos Salles' assumption of power and the reassertion of a calm dominated by the regional elites, the Carioca *belle époque* begins.* That year there was a noticeable change in the air which soon affected the cultural and social milieu. The revolutionary days were over. The time for stability and urban life of elegance was at hand again."[1]

While the urban elite looked forward to political and social stability, impoverished Afro-Brazilians continued to pour into the capital from the surrounding countryside and other states in search of employment. Likewise, as a part of the tidal wave of European migration to the Americas in the late nineteenth century, foreign immigrants, especially Portuguese, contributed to the city's dramatic growth. Between 1872 and 1890, Rio's population almost doubled, jumping from 266,831 to 518,290. Sixteen years later, in 1906, it had increased to more than 800,000, and by 1920, the capital had 1,157,873 residents.[2] During this period, men outnumbered women in Rio de Janeiro. In the 1890 census, the new republican government registered 238,667 males and 184,089 females residing in the nation's capital. Among the native-born population, there was a relative gender balance of

---

* A Carioca is a resident of Rio de Janeiro.

159,393 men to 151,428 women. However, among foreign immigrants, men surpassed women 79,374 to 32,561.[3] Amid the bustle of everyday life in Brazil's largest urban center, thousands of young, single men roamed the streets in search of work, entertainment, company, and sex.

Rio's demographic boom also placed enormous pressures on the city's infrastructure, housing supply, and public health. In 1902, the federal capital's mayor, Francisco Pereira Passos, with newly elected president Rodrigues Alves's backing, ordered a radical urban renovation project that would transform much of the city center. Rio was to be heralded as a tropical version of modern Paris.[4] Illuminated broad boulevards lined with fashionable beaux arts buildings replaced dark, narrow, crooked streets and modest structures. Public health officials campaigned to improve sanitation and eliminate yellow fever through a program that, among other requirements, involved the obligatory inoculating of the entire population. The municipal government condemned more than sixteen hundred buildings, including many tenement housing units, and forced almost twenty thousand poor and working-class residents of Rio, many of whom were Afro-Brazilian, to find new housing. Some moved close by, while many others were forced to relocate to outlying suburban districts to the north of the downtown area.[5] Although protests and riots against new public health, sanitation, and residential removal programs revealed a deep resentment toward the government's overall plan, officials carried on with determination. In 1906 they declared their project complete, and Rio de Janeiro soon became known as *a cidade maravilhosa* (the marvelous city).[6] The press boasted that the nation's capital had become a bourgeois urban public space comparable to any of Europe's modernized cities.[7]

The forced removal of poor inhabitants from some of the downtown districts and the new French-influenced architectural facades lining the city's main new thoroughfare, Avenida Central (later renamed Avenida Rio Branco) produced an environment more pleasing to Rio's elite. However, the renovation plan did not eliminate all overt evidence of chaos, poverty, and urban decay deemed inappropriate by Carioca high society. Prostitution continued in parts of the downtown area. Crime remained a threat to those who frequented the newly renovated areas of the city's center. Poor men and women, especially people of color, still peddled their wares on the streets. And men who enjoyed sex with men tenaciously clung to several sites in the city center that they had appropriated as public places to find sexual partners and socialize with friends.

The most noted urban space for male-to-male sexual encounters and socializing was Largo do Rossio,[*] a square at the edge of traditional down-town Rio de Janeiro. The area received a facelift at the time of the Pereira Passos urban reforms and has remained a location of homoerotic sociabil-ity from the late nineteenth century until recent years.[8] At the center of the Largo do Rossio stood a majestic statue of the Brazilian emperor Dom Pe-dro I (1798–1834).[9] His son, Dom Pedro II (1825–1891) had ordered its erection in 1862 to celebrate the fortieth anniversary of the declaration of Brazilian independence from Portugal. On March 30 of that year, amid fan-fare and fireworks, the emperor and his entourage dedicated the sixteen-foot bronzed likeness of independent Brazil's first ruler, mounted on a steed and clutching a raised scroll representing the nation's constitution. The equestrian statute, which weighed sixty tons, rested on a massive thirty-foot pedestal decorated with bronze figures symbolizing Brazil's major rivers and metal plaques inscribed with the names of the country's provinces.[10] The government subsequently ordered the landscaping of the square around the monument with trees, gardens, statutes, and benches, making it one of the downtown area's pleasant open spaces, as well as a public repre-sentation of Brazilian nationalist sentiments. Located immediately off the plaza was the São Pedro Theater, which hosted major cultural events for Carioca high society throughout the nineteenth century and helped to draw other entertainment venues to the square (see map 2).[11]

Soon after the statue of Emperor Dom Pedro I was erected, the site ful-filled another "less patriotic" function as a venue for homosexual interac-tions. So much clandestine sexual activity took place in the praça that in 1870 a city administrator sent a communiqué to the head of local govern-ment operations about the situation. He complained that the municipal guard in charge of making the rounds in the plaza gardens had "abandoned those same gardens for most of the day to the perversity of boys and ill-in-tentioned people."[12] His complaint had little effect, however, and the area continued to attract men who sought each other out for socioerotic ends. As a result, in 1878, the secretary of the court police had to take more dras-tic actions, "seeing how there are individuals who go there at late hours to practice abuses against morality, forcing this Division to have patrols in those gardens, impairing the police from being in other places."[13] He di-rected the four entrances to the gardens in the plaza's center to be closed every night at midnight. Two weeks later, in response to another complaint that, in fact, the square was not being closed down as ordered, a govern-

---

[*] The word *rossio* means a public square or open marketplace and is sometimes spelled *rocio*.

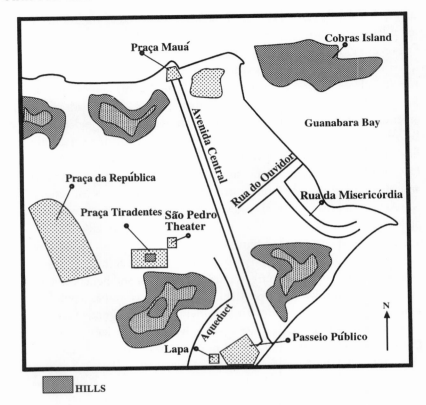

MAP 2   Rio de Janeiro, circa 1906

ment official assured the chief of police that the gardens were, indeed, being sealed off at night. Moreover, the night patrols issued a whistle warning to guarantee that no one would remain in the area past closing time.[14] Regardless of police surveillance and control of the area, men persisted in using the park as a venue for trysts with other men interested in sexual liaisons (see fig. 1).

Legal but Not Legal

During the post-1889 republican regime, homosexuality per se was not illegal. This had not been the case in colonial Brazil under Portuguese rule, when the law had defined sodomy as the anal penetration of a man or

FIGURE I   Praça Tiradentes, popularly known as Largo do Rossio, circa 1900. Landscaping and benches provided multiple opportunities for men to meet other men for sexual and romantic purposes in one of Rio de Janeiro's oldest cruising parks. Photograph by Marco Antônio Belandi, courtesy of the Arquivo Geral da Cidade do Rio de Janeiro.

woman. When two men were involved, the Office of the Holy Inquisition, which was installed in Portugal in 1553, as well as Portuguese legal codes, considered both the penetrator and the receptor to be sodomites. If found guilty of this offense, a person was subject to burning at the stake, and his or her property could be seized.[15] Between 1587 and 1794, the Portuguese Inquisition registered 4,419 denunciations. These included both those suspected of having practiced sodomy and those who provided confessions attesting to the fact that they had committed the "abominable and perverted sin." Of the total number, 394 went to trial. Thirty were eventually burned at the stake, 3 in the sixteenth century and 27 in the seventeenth century. Those not put to death could be sentenced to hard labor on the king's galley ships or to temporary or perpetual exile in Africa, India, or Brazil. Often these harsh punishments were enacted after the condemned had already suffered seizure of property and endured a brutal public whipping.[16]

In 1830, eight years after independence from Portugal, Dom Pedro I signed into law the Imperial Penal Code. Among other provisions, the new law eliminated all references to sodomy. The legislation was influenced by the ideas of Jeremy Bentham, the French Penal Code of 1791, the Neapolitan Code of 1819, and the Napoleonic Code of 1810, which decriminalized sexual relations between consenting adults.[17] However, article 280 of the Brazilian code punished public acts of indecency with ten to forty days' imprisonment and a fine corresponding to one half of the time served.[18] This provision gave the police the discretion to determine what constituted a public act of indecency. It also gave them the power to extort money from those threatened with arrest or detention.[19]

The 1889 republican government approved a new penal code in 1890 that maintained the decriminalization of sodomy. Although not explicitly punishing same-sex erotic activities, the new law sought to control such conduct through indirect means and restricted homosexual behavior in four distinct ways. Article 266 referred to "assaults on decency of a person of one or another sex through violence or threat with the goal of satiating lascivious passions or for moral depravation" and was punishable "by one to six years' imprisonment."[20] This article was usually applied in cases involving sexual relationships between adults and minors, including men with young boys.[21]

Adults engaging in sexual activities with other adults in a public setting could be charged under article 282, "Public Affront to Decency" (*atentado público ao pudor*). The crime was described as "assaults on modesty, offending propriety with shameless exhibitions or obscene acts or gestures, practiced in public places or places frequented by the public, and which without offense to the individual honesty of the person, assaults and scandalizes society."[22] It carried a prison sentence of one to six months. This provision, a revised carryover from the 1830 Imperial Penal Code, provided the legal basis for controlling any public manifestations of homoerotic or homosocial behavior. With catchall wording, the police or a judge could broadly define improper or indecent action and punish behavior that did not conform to heterocentric constructions.

Article 379, "On the Use of False Names, Fake Titles, or other Disguises," outlawed cross-dressing by prohibiting "disguising one's sex, wearing inappropriate clothes and doing so publicly to deceive."[23] The law carried a penalty of fifteen to sixty days' imprisonment. Although the police winked an eye at cross-dressing during Carnival, throughout the rest of the year, they could use this legal provision to arrest homosexuals who liked to wear clothes of the opposite sex.[24]

The fourth method for regulating public manifestations of homosexuality was to arrest a person for vagrancy. Article 399 of the 1890 Penal Code defined vagrancy as "leaving the exercise of a profession, employment, or any service in which one earns a living; not possessing a means of support and a fixed domicile in which one is residing; earning a living in an occupation prohibited by law or manifestly offensive to morality and propriety."[25] A penalty of fifteen to thirty days' incarceration could be imposed on anyone who happened to be arrested without work papers or who was engaged in male prostitution. The person also had to find gainful employment within fifteen days of his release.[26]

Together, these four provisions placed legal restraints on those who might congregate in public places in order to meet others interested in same-sex erotic activities. They gave the police the power to incarcerate arbitrarily those homosexuals who engaged in public displays of effeminacy, wore long hair, feminine clothing, or makeup, earned a living through prostitution, or took advantage of the cover of bushes or shrubs in shadowed parks to enjoy a nocturnal sexual liaison. Sodomy had been decriminalized in the early nineteenth century. However, criminal codes with vaguely defined notions of proper morality and public decency, as well as provisions that limited cross-dressing and strictly controlled vagrancy, provided a legal net that could readily entangle those who transgressed socially sanctioned sexual norms. Although homosexuality in and of itself was not technically illegal, the Brazilian police and courts had multiple mechanisms at their disposal to contain and control this behavior.

The Crossroads of Sin

On February 21, 1890, only three months after the overthrow of Emperor Dom Pedro II and the Brazilian monarchy, the new republican government changed the official name of the Largo do Rossio from Praça da Constituição (Constitution Plaza) to Praça Tiradentes in order to commemorate the upcoming centennial of the execution of Joaquim José da Silva Xavier, commonly known as Tiradentes.[27] This leader of a 1789 conspiracy against Portuguese imperial rule was tortured and executed near that site in 1792, and the rechristening of the plaza affirmed the antimonarchical sentiments of the new republican regime.[28] In spite of the official name change, the square remained Largo do Rossio in the imagination and common parlance of turn-of-the-century Cariocas and was still associated in the public's mind with same-sex sexual encounters.

Stately buildings, in the process of being remodeled in the latest French architectural style, surrounded Praça Tiradentes. Since the streets next to the park were also the termini of the streetcar lines that serviced the northern neighborhoods of the city, including the areas where many former downtown residents had been relocated as a result of urban renewal, this public space bustled with movement. The plaza's strategic location encouraged an eclectic combination of theaters, the brand-new motion picture houses, a concert hall hosting musical reviews and vaudeville performances, not to mention cabarets, popular cafés, and bars. Bourgeois Rio attended the elegant and spacious São Pedro Theater, while middle- and working-class customers had an array of cultural, culinary, libational, and sexual distractions close at hand.[29]

At the turn of the century, Pascoal Segreto, an Italian immigrant turned entrepreneur, built his entertainment empire at Praça Tiradentes. Among his investments was the Maison Moderne. This urban amusement park featured a mini–roller coaster, carrousel, Ferris wheel, and shooting gallery, with a small, partially open theater in the back and a café that served beer to working-class customers.[30] From this and several other modest entertainment establishments, Pascoal Segreto expanded his holdings by purchasing most of the public performance venues in the area around Praça Tiradentes. When he died in 1920, the humble immigrant, who had begun working as a shoeshine boy, owned most of the theaters and movie houses in the district, from the elegant São Pedro that billed top European talent to concert halls featuring the latest in risqué entertainment for the popular classes of Rio de Janeiro.[31]

Nestled among these establishments of public distraction in the vicinity around the plaza, one could find brothels and boardinghouses in buildings that had once served as expansive dwellings for elite families. The city's demographic imbalance in favor of single young men, especially immigrants, and the large number of poor women from the countryside and overseas favored this sexual traffic. Prostitutes ranged from high-class *francesas,* with the allure of their French origins, and recently arrived Jewish immigrants from Eastern Europe, known as *polacas,* to light-skinned Afro-Brazilian *mulatas.*[32] Middle- and upper-class men, engaging in fleeting bohemian forays in this demimonde, could mingle with prostitutes in popular establishments like the Stadt München bar and restaurant, and the Café Suiço, which were right off of the Plaza.[33] If not satisfied with the crowd in these meeting places, Carioca males could also wander a few blocks away to seek camaraderie or carnal pleasures in another vibrant center of nightlife in the Lapa neighborhood. Store clerks, students, and modest public servants who were unable to pay for the sexual services of women who boasted a French birthright could still find lower-class *polacas* and *mulatas* working near Praça Tiradentes.[34]

Although this was not the only prostitution zone in downtown Rio, the proximity of so many theaters, eating and drinking establishments, and popular entertainment venues provided plenty of customers for women in the sex trade, who serviced their clients in nearby bordellos or in the privacy of a rented room behind closed Venetian blinds. As has been noted, the Pereira Passos urban renovations of the century's first decade had been designed to modernize downtown Rio de Janeiro and place it on equal footing with European capitals. In spite of popular resistance, the government successfully forced many poor people, especially Afro-Brazilians, out of the downtown districts. However, regulation of prostitution in the area during the first two decades of the twentieth century remained sporadic.[35] Too many journalists, intellectuals, artists, and politicians from well-connected families procured women around Praça Tiradentes and other downtown sites for the police to operate effectively to rid the area of female prostitution.[36]

Amid the nightlife that surrounded the monument to Brazil's first emperor, in the darkened theaters under flickering lights of newfangled cinematographs, and on the benches and among the shrubbery in the park, men who sought out other men for sexual escapades took advantage of the loosened morals in this part of the city to procure pleasure for themselves. The mounted monarch continued to be a reference point for male-to-male sexual and social encounters. Rio chronicler Luiz Edmundo recalled a typical scene of 1901: "After eight at night lads with feminine airs, who spoke in a falsetto voice, bit on cambric handkerchiefs and laid their sheepish eyes on the manly and handsome statue of Mr. Pedro."[37]

Both the public spaces and the varied entertainment options offered ample opportunities for men to congregate with others of like-minded sexual and social affinities. The half-dozen theaters, countless bars, cabarets, and music halls also employed some of these men as actors, dancers, singers, waiters, and service employees. A favorite meeting place for this crowd was the Café Criterium, located immediately across from the park, where "actors and young lads with high-pitched voices who wore rice powder makeup and rouge" socialized.[38] One such painted youth who frequented the Largo do Rossio was José N., a nineteen-year-old Turkish-born street vendor. On April 13, 1905, his neighbor Baudilio G., a forty-five-year-old Spanish barber, was arrested for calling José N. a *puto do Largo do Rossio*.[39]

The police charged the barber with violating article 282 of the Penal

Code, "Public Affront to Decency." At the court hearing, Maria dos Anjos, a native of Portugal and washerwoman by profession, who lived across the street from the defendant, testified that at 10:30 that morning Baudilio G. had started fighting with the Turk, José N. She stated that the older man called him "a male whore, a depraved one, a male whore from the Largo do Rossio" and that these immoral words were heard by many people, including some young girls. Three other neighbors, both immigrants and Brazilian-born, repeated Maria dos Anjos's testimony.

Then the young Turk, who lived in the same building as the defendant, was asked to speak. He also confirmed the Portuguese washerwoman's version of events. Jose N. added that Baudilio G. had accused him of "taking his wife" and of "having makeup on his face." The defendant, Baudilio G., provided a different version of the verbal exchange. According to the Spanish-born barber, he had been angry with José, "for reasons of honor."[40] He further testified that he had indeed called José a *puto* because the Turk had rouge on his face. He added that the young man even had to go into the house to wipe it off. The barber was eventually acquitted of the charges.

Racial and national rivalries between immigrants and recently freed slaves in turn-of-the-century Rio de Janeiro constituted a conflict-laden backdrop to working-class social interactions.[41] This particular dispute, carried out in the public arena of a working-class neighborhood and involving Afro-Brazilians as well as Spanish, Portuguese, and Turkish immigrants, indicates that the accusation of being a *puto* could unite diverse groups against a common moral social enemy—the feminized man who allegedly worked as a prostitute. The record does not indicate definitely whether or not José, a recent immigrant who still signed his last name in the script of his native country in the police record, was in fact a *puto*, that is to say, that he earned money at the Largo do Rossio by having sex with other men. However, while Baudilio G. was formally charged with the offense of uttering the "indecent" word *puto*, the young street vendor was actually the one on trial. José's personal grooming and possible secondary source of income became the subject of public scrutiny. His use of rouge and other feminine markings represented inappropriate and immoral behavior that merited social condemnation. The resolution of the altercation exonerated Baudilio even though several witnesses, including the defendant himself, admitted that the barber had uttered the "indecent" expression. While using the word *puto* scandalized the neighborhood, being a *puto* was a much worse offense.

The term *puto*, the masculinized version of *puta*, or female prostitute,

was used in colonial Brazil and in Portugal to refer to "a boy who prostituted himself with the vice of sodomy or masturbation."[42] It was a popular version of the older term, *sodomita*, with its biblical origins, that was the
standard religious and legal way of describing persons who had anal sex
with persons of either sex in colonial Brazil. During the Brazilian belle
époque, the pervasive stereotype for men who had sex with other men emphasized their link to prostitution. Physicians, politicians, lawyers, intellectuals, and artists portrayed modern sodomites as effeminate men who
engaged in anal sex as passive partners and supported themselves as streetwalkers. As we shall see throughout this work, the connection between
prostitution, effeminacy in men, and homosexuality remained a powerful
representation of same-sex erotic behavior well into the second half of the
twentieth century, when alternative notions of sexual identity emerged that
challenged this dominant paradigm.

At some point in late-nineteenth-century Brazil, a new pejorative expression, *fresco* (fairy, faggot), which literally means someone (or thing)
that is fresh, came into popular use. Francisco José Viveiros de Castro, a
professor of criminal law at Rio de Janeiro's law school and a judge of the
High Court of Appeals of the Federal District, used the term in an 1894
volume entitled *Assaults on Modesty: Studies on Sexual Aberrations*. In his
chapter "Pederasty," he described Rio de Janeiro's *frescos*, referring to the
men who in the 1880s, during the last years of the empire, invaded the
masked Carnival balls at the São Pedro Theater in the Largo do Rossio:
"One of these *frescos*, as they are known in popular slang, became famous
using the name *Panella de Bronze* (Bronze Buttocks). He dressed admirably
as a woman, to the point of fooling even the most perceptive. They say that
he was able to acquire a fortune through his vile industry and that he had
so many visitors, people of high social position, that they had to request an
appointment beforehand."[43]

In turn-of-the-century Brazil, *fresco*, with the dual meaning of a fairy
or faggot and something fresh, became a common double entendre used to
poke fun at effeminate men or those assumed to engage in "passive" anal
sexual encounters with other men. Moreover, *frescos* were intimately associated with the Largo do Rossio. The term's multiple uses appeared in the
Dicionário Moderno, a slim tongue-in-cheek compilation of erotic and
pornographic slang, published in 1903: "*Fresco*—adjective meaning cool
weather, depraved due to modernization. Almost cold, mild, agreeable, that
which is not hot nor warm. That which is whimsical and breezy. One finds
them in the hills and in the Largo do Rossio."[44] Not only is a space associ-

ated with the *fresco*, but the figure evokes a relationship between social degeneration and modernization, as if the process of urbanization and the
transformation of traditional ways were to blame for same-sex erotic behavior. As we shall see, medical and legal professionals commenting on the
subject during this period drew similar parallels between homosexuality
and modernization.

The renovation of the Largo do Rossio during the urban renewal project at the beginning of the twentieth century provided one cartoonist the
opportunity to link *frescos* to the plaza. An ink drawing and a sardonic poem
entitled "Fresca Theoria (Requerimento)" (Fresh idea [or fairy's idea] [pe-
tition]) appeared in a 1904 issue of the magazine *O Malho*, which specialized in humor and political satire (see fig. 2). In the cartoon, a man in a
fashionable straw hat, flowery bow tie, short tight jacket, and busy close-
fitting pants stands with a buttock protruding, lending his figure an S-shape,
the classical pose of women in turn-of-the-century drawings. His index
finger is resting pensively on his chin as he ponders his new idea and the request that he is going to make to the city government. Behind him is a garden with the statute of Dom Pedro I in the background, an obvious
reference to the Largo do Rossio. Since the recent relandscaping of the park
had temporarily diminished access to the grounds for cruising and court-
ing, the protagonist, represented by the artist as a male prostitute, has found
himself out of work. The poem reads: "Given the cruel destruction / Of
the Rossio of my dreams / The unemployed Muse, / Although in gloomy
verses, / Will take a risk. / It is a rather hard shock / That constrains one's
freedom / In this ungrateful profession, / And from the mayor of the city
/ I require compensation."[45]

Not unlike the Spanish barber who accused José N. of wearing makeup
and being a "*puto* do Rossio," the author of this poem associates the square
with male effeminacy and streetwalking, as if sex between men could only
take place if an exchange of money occurred. In the cartoon, the fop even
considers petitioning the government for some type of financial support because of the temporary unavailability of the plaza. The stereotyped well-
dressed dandy, who lacks manly comportment and entertains foolish ideas,
is quickly identified with homosexual prostitution. Just as the working-class
neighbors of José N. linked his use of makeup to the Largo do Rossio and
male prostitution, one can assume that the middle-class readership of *O
Malho* understood the constellation of markers pointing to the ridiculed
figure of the *fresco*.

The conflation of particular forms of dress, prostitution, exaggerated

FRESCA THEORIA
(Requerimento)

— Ante a cruel derrocada
Do Rocio dos meus sonhos,
A musa desoccupada,
Embora em versos tristonhos,
Vai jogar uma cartada :

E' bem dura a collisão
Que me tolhe a liberdade
Desta ingrata profissão ;
E ao prefeito da cidade
Requeiro indemnisação !...

FIGURE 2   Cartoon portrayals of effeminate men, walking the street in search of sexual pleasures with other men, also linked them to Praça Tiradentes. Illustration from *O Malho* (Rio de Janeiro) 3, no. 93 (June 23, 1904): 31, courtesy of Biblioteca Nacional, Rio de Janeiro.

unmanly behavior, the term *fresco*, and the specificity of the Largo do Rossio as a privileged space for same-sex erotic adventures occurs in another cartoon from the same period also published in *O Malho* (see fig. 3). The drawing, entitled "Escabroso" (Unseemly) captures two men in conversation. One is a mature male, quite large, almost monstrous in size, with a goatee, walking cane, and a rough masculine appearance. The other figure, a man with a much smaller frame and a hint of a pencil mustache, is stylishly dressed with a flower in his lapel. He coyly looks downward and holds a Japanese fan in his left hand. A curled pinkie suggests effeminacy. His other

FIGURE 3   *Smaller Man:* "It's so hot. Neither cashew juice nor any other refreshment is enough, sir. I think that I go out every night in search of some place fresh [or cool]." *Larger Man:* "Won't the Largo do Rossio do?" Illustration by K. Lixto [Calixto Cordeiro], *O Malho* (Rio de Janeiro) 2, no. 20 (March 28, 1903): 14, courtesy of the Biblioteca Nacional, Rio de Janeiro.

hand caresses the edge of the fan. The more delicate man comments: "It's so hot. Neither cashew juice nor any other refreshment is enough, sir. I think that I go out every night in search of some place fresh [or cool]." To which his burly companion replies: "Won't the Largo do Rossio do?"[46]

Once again a play on words allows the cartoonist to portray commonly held social notions about the *fresco* and his territory. The corpulent, masculine gentlemen is capable of classifying his shy and demurring friend and relegating him to an appropriate urban territory where he can cool down while warming up with some sexual adventure. The artist operates on the assumption that the average reader will know the slang term for an effeminate man and thus understand the double meaning of his remark. Interestingly, this cartoon provoked comment in the pages of *Rio Nu* (Nude Rio), an erotic publication founded in 1898 that featured seminude women, piquant cartoons, short stories, and gossip columns.[47] Referring to the cartoon, the editor of the magazine commented: "Last Saturday *O Malho* carried a drawing showing an old man talking with a small elegantly dressed man with the airs of a little missy (of that kind from the Largo do Rossio)." After repeating the printed dialogue between the two figures, the editor sarcastically noted: "Well, *Malho*, you, who try to be a serious journal and say you are read by families, publish innocent items like this? If it were in *Rio Nu*, it would be pornographic, but in *Malho* it is humor."[48]

According to Cristiana Sunetinni Pereira, who has studied turn-of-the-century Brazilian pornography, *Rio Nu*'s editor used the cartoon to delineate the character of the journal in comparison to its competitors.[49] By imputing a hypocritical attitude to the editors of *O Malho* for publishing the drawing with its overt references to same-sex erotic behavior, *Rio Nu* effectively drew the limits between acceptable and unacceptable middle-class morality. In doing so, *Rio Nu* established its preeminence in the area of piquant journalism, and ridiculed its competitors for their middle-class moralism. Jokes about *frescos*, while appropriate in a magazine dedicated to pornographic humor, transgressed the boundaries of respectability when found in the pages of publications with a family audience, or at least so the editors of *Rio Nu* argued.

Putos and Pornography

Criticizing the slippery standards of their competitors did not preclude, however, the publishers of *Rio Nu* from promoting pornography designed to please an audience titillated by male-to-male sexual fantasies. Indeed, advertisements for the mail-order purchase of what appears to be the first Brazilian homoerotic pornographic story *Menino do Gouveia* (Gouveia's boy) appeared in the magazine in 1914. The fifteen-page booklet, divided into four chapters and complete with an illustration of two men engaged in anal intercourse, came out as the sixth in a series of sixteen *contos rápidos* (quick tales), which were likely produced to shore up the financial weaknesses of *Rio Nu*'s publishing house.[50] Interested buyers could purchase the slim volumes from newsstands and other distributors of the weekly erotic magazine for three hundred reis or receive them in the mail for five hundred reis, a modest sum at the time. The inexpensive booklets were thus accessible to anyone who earned more than subsistence wages. The exact circulation of these pornographic publications remains unknown, yet the mere fact that the sixth in this series tells the saucy tale of same-sex erotic delights indicates at least some market for their homoerotic content.

It seems likely that the anonymous author of *Gouveia's Boy* was a participant in the real-life sexual world of Rio's public parks. The remarkable similarity of elements in the story to contemporaneous and later accounts about the public life of Rio's homosexuals also lends value to the tale as a source for decoding the intricacies of homoerotic activities of *putos* and *frescos* in early-twentieth-century Rio de Janeiro. In keeping with the genre of pornographic literature, *Gouveia's Boy* is not a masterpiece of style or prose, yet the short story is written in a pleasant, positive tone, void of any underlying moralistic condemnation of sex between men.

The tale begins with the protagonist resting in bed with the author, whose pseudonym, Capadócio Maluco (Tricky Crazy One), implies uncontrolled debauchery. The author describes the boy, whom he has just penetrated for the second time, as a well-trained male prostitute with a soft voice, the characterization reinforcing the popular notion that effeminate men who had sex with other men were professional streetwalkers. The lad, Gouveia's boy, caresses his older partner's member as he relates the origins of his sexual desires: "I'll tell you. I take it from behind as a vocation. I was born that way as others are born to be musicians, soldiers, poets, or even politicians. It seems like when they were making me, at the moment of the last stab, my mother farted in such a way that all of my tastes are in the ass, and I also inherited the fact that I feel all of my pleasures in the rear."[51]

For the boy, "passive" sodomy becomes the essential component of his sexual pleasure. This innate desire manifests itself in early adolescence. Unlike other boys, who try to spy on nude women, he only wishes to see his uncle's penis. To achieve his voyeuristic ends, one morning he slips into the bathroom just as his uncle is preparing to take a shower. Revealing his tender ass to his uncle, the boy begs: "Uncle, do to me what you did to Auntie last night. Do it, yes?"[52]

His uncle, repulsed by the proposition, calls him a *puto* and expels him from the house. Dejected, the boy roams the streets of Rio de Janeiro in search of a man with a masculine presentation who enjoys sex with effeminate men. After hours of searching the public bathrooms of the city in vain for a suitable partner to satiate his urges, the boy comes to rest on a bench in the Largo do Rossio. There, an older man named Gouveia picks him up, takes him to the movies where he caresses the boy's penis, and then invites him to his room in the Lapa neighborhood for sex. At the end of the story, both the author and Gouveia endearingly call the youth a *puto,* as if the same-sex eroticism of effeminate young men and prostitution were synonymous. Both the storyteller and Gouveia are attracted to the feminine persona of the boy, who himself is only sexually fulfilled when his partners penetrate him (see fig. 4).

FIGURE 4   Illustration from *Gouveia's Boy* (1914), perhaps Brazil's first same-sex modern male pornography, courtesy of the Biblioteca Nacional, Rio de Janeiro.

In turn-of-the-century slang and in the language of this pornographic tale, Gouveia is a *fanchono*, the masculine man who desires sex with womanly men.[53] The eroticism of the piece arises from the sexual availability of the lad who actively seeks anal pleasure and permits himself to be treated as an object of desire by the *fanchono*. Thus, while gendered roles are present in the representation of the *puto* and the *fanchono*, both have same-sex desires that differentiate them from other men. Moreover, the *fanchono* is not merely a married man or a sexually frustrated bachelor out on the town picking up boys because women are not available. His sexual object choice is someone who, while feminized and younger, is not female. The *fanchono* is therefore part of the homosexual subculture, can navigate its sexual topography, and is an eager participant in social interactions with those who share similar desires. Yet, as we shall see, the *fanchono*, who was defined by his sexual role as the penetrator, was relatively invisible to the outside observers who described this world of *putos* and *frescos*. In part, this was likely due to the fact that his less feminized appearance and public performance permitted him to "pass." The *fanchanos'* apparent masculinity sheltered them from arrest and from the gaze of the physicians, lawyers, and other voyeurs who left most of the written documentation on same-sex eroticism in belle époque Brazil.

Although *Gouveia's Boy* is a fictional piece of pornography, the tale quite accurately maps the territoriality and sociosexual options available to most *putos*, *frescos*, and *fanchonos* in turn-of-the-century Rio de Janeiro. *Mictórios* (public urinals) in the city's plazas and parks offered anonymous venues to discover potential sexual partners. Among public spaces in the city, the Largo do Rossio provided special possibilities for new encounters. Just as Gouveia and the boy met in public plazas, resting on park benches afforded men open-ended opportunities to wait for prospective sexual companions. Escaping to a movie theater in the surrounding district furnished another discreet environment in which to engage in some sexual activities. Nearby boardinghouses or cheap hotels among the brothels surrounding the Largo do Rossio, in turn, became enclosed spaces to enjoy erotic passions more comfortably.

This widespread connection of the Largo do Rossio to homoerotic activities continued into the 1920s and '30s. A popular joke of the time confirms this lasting association. Referring to the balustrades that until 1902 surrounded the monument to Pedro I, the quip went as follows: "Do you remember Praça Tiradentes when it had a railing around it? / "Yes, I remember it." / "Oh, then you must be an old faggot (*viado velho*)."[54]

Sex and Sailors

The pornographic text and the expressions of popular humor described above emphasized and promulgated stereotypes of *frescos* as well-dressed, limp-wristed, womanly men who prostituted themselves to quench their sexual urges. Not all literary images, however, reproduced this cliché. In 1895, Adolfo Caminha, a young author, penned his second novel, *Bom-Crioulo*, which presented an alternative vision of same-sex eroticism in Brazil.[55] Without using the term, Caminha tells the story of a *fanchono* and his love for a pubescent boy. The novel portrays the life of a runaway Afro-Brazilian slave, Amaro, who has sought refuge as a sailor in the Brazilian navy. While at sea, tall and muscular Amaro meets and falls in love with Aleixo, a delicate blue-eyed, fair-skinned cabin boy. During shore leave, Amaro takes the boy to live in a rented room in Rio de Janeiro, where they engage in uninhibited sex. The love story, however, ends tragically. Carolina, their landlady and possibly a former prostitute, seduces Aleixo while Amaro is away at sea. In a passionate rage, Amaro then kills Aleixo for having betrayed him. This unique late-nineteenth-century romance from the naturalist literary school is one of the first novels with an explicit homosexual theme in Latin American literature.[56] Moreover, Caminha describes same-sex eroticism with unabashed frankness.

Bom-Crioulo is a complex novel that addresses multiple notions of both race and sexuality in turn-of-the-century Brazil.[57] The very title, which can be translated as either the "good black man" or "good nigger," alludes to the amiable qualities of the protagonist while perpetuating the pejorative stereotypes associated with Afro-Brazilians at the time.[58] But despite the racist sentiments sprinkled throughout the work, the author's depiction is ultimately a sympathetic one. Amaro, prisoner to his natural sexual inclinations as well as to his passion, is a noble and tragic hero.

Adolfo Caminha himself had a short and tragic life. Born in the northeast state of Ceará in 1867, he was orphaned at an early age and taken to Rio de Janeiro by an uncle, who enrolled him in the Naval School. He returned to his home state in 1887 as a second lieutenant and immersed himself in the intellectual and political life of Ceará. There he also embarked on a passionate love affair with the wife of an army officer. The resulting scandal led to his resignation from the navy. He returned to Rio de Janeiro in 1892 with his lover and worked as a low-level clerk to support his literary career. On January 1, 1897, he died of tuberculosis at age twenty-nine.[59]

Caminha wrote *Bom-Crioulo* only seven years after the abolition of

Brazilian slavery in 1888, and six years after military leaders overthrew the monarchy and established a republican government.[60] The novel is set both on the high sea and in Rio de Janeiro during an undefined year, perhaps sometime in the 1870s, when Emperor Dom Pedro II still reigned over the continent country. Indeed, movement and space are two important metaphors employed by the author. Amaro, the fugitive, moves from rural bondage to the open sea, where he achieves his freedom by reversing the course of his enslaved ancestors. As a sailor he is subjected to hard work and the brutal punishment of the whip, yet he savors his liberty. There, on a naval vessel, he also finds his sexual freedom, discovering his own desires for the innocent Billy Budd–like Aleixo. Although the pair consummate their affair on the high sea, they create a love nest in Rio de Janeiro in a rented room on Rua da Misericórdia, near the city's port. Shortly before arriving in the imperial capital, Amaro warns his young lover about the dangers of Rio:

> "But listen, don't you try to go running around with anybody else," Bom-Crioulo was saying. "Rio de Janeiro is a wicked, wicked city. If I catch you with somebody else, you know what's in store for you."
>
> The young lad chewed absent-mindedly on the tip of his blue calico kerchief with white spots, listening to the older man's promises, dreaming of a rose-coloured future in that oh so famous city of Rio de Janeiro, where there was a huge mountain called Sugar Loaf and where the emperor had his palace, a beautiful mansion with walls of gold.
>
> Everything took on exaggerated proportions in the imagination of this sailor-boy on his first trip. Bom-Crioulo had promised to take him to the theaters, to Corcovado (that was another mountain, from which you could see the whole city and the sea), to Tijuca, to the park called Passeio Público, everywhere. They were going to live together, in a room on Misericórdia Street, a room that would cost fifteen thousand reis a month, where there'd be a room for two iron beds, or maybe just one, if it were wide and spacious. Bom-Crioulo would pay for everything out of his own salary. They could live a peaceful life there.[61]

Rio de Janeiro offered the two anonymity, and a space away from intruding shipmates where they could carry out their passionate affair in solitude. Amaro, as an experienced sailor, could also teach the youth how to survive in the city. The cross-generational aspects of the relationship between Amaro and Aleixo seem to mirror notions of the Greek paradigm of homosexuality—which Caminha refers to on numerous occasions in the text—where older men seduce smooth-skinned boys for sexual pleasures, while at the same time providing them with fatherly guidance on the ways of the world. Indeed, it is not unlike the relationships described in *Gouveia's Boy*. Yet, Amaro's warnings about the dangers of Rio also reflect his own fear that some wealthier man might seduce his blond-haired cabin boy away from him. Their rented haven becomes the only site in Rio de Janeiro that they can enjoy together. Ironically, it is in that very space, which Amaro believes to be safe from the wickedness of the city, that his friend Carolina steals his love, thus provoking Amaro's downfall.

In many ways, Amaro does not conform to the predominant stereotype of the effeminate man, as portrayed by cartoonists and medical professionals in Brazil at the turn of the century. The Bom-Crioulo is a strong, virile figure whose masculinity is not questioned. As the penetrating partner in anal sex with the young cabin boy, Amaro is also similar to the *fanchono* Gouveia, who initiates and guides the sexual relationship. His homosexuality is driven by innate organic conditions over which he has little if any control. Yet despite Caminha's descriptions of the animalistic instincts driving Amaro's sexual desires, the protagonist is portrayed as a compassionate human being. As Robert Howes pointed out in an introductory essay to the 1982 English edition of the novel, Caminha, with "restrained dignity and seriousness," constructs Amaro as a "powerful, living character" whose love for Aleixo reflects his deep respect and caring for the lad.[62] On the other hand, Aleixo, as the object of sexual desire, is presented in less favorable terms. The delicate youth, who is innocently seduced into homosexual activities, shifts amorous allegiances when Carolina showers her attention on him. Unlike Gouveia's boy, Aleixo has no fixed sexual orientation. At the end of the tale, when Amaro kills him in jealous rage, the author creates sympathy not for the fickle lad but rather for the noble sailor whose passionate love brings his own death.

Although Caminha himself was not a homosexual, he nevertheless realistically described same-sex erotic behavior. He was able to do so, he admitted, because he had observed such activities while serving as an officer in the navy.[63] Peter Beattie, who examined court-martial cases involving sodomy in the Brazilian army and navy from 1861 to 1908, concluded that the details regarding homosexual interactions portrayed in the novel parallel the testimony given in actual legal hearings of the period. As in the novel, sexual roles between partners in the military characteristically tended to involve an "active" inserter in anal intercourse and a "passive" recipient. When the sex was consensual and those involved were convicted of committing sodomy, both partners were punished for the offense.[64] In other words, the military did not draw a distinction, at least when punishment was concerned, between the "active" and the "passive" participant in sexual intimacy. These sodomy trial records limit themselves closely to the events surrounding the sexual transgression. The incidents are also heavily filtered through the clerks whose task it was to summarize the testimony in technical or legal terms. From the court hearings, one cannot determine if these men participated in the sexual underworld of places like the Largo do Rossio or if they identified themselves as *fanchonos* or *frescos*.[65] Nevertheless, they confirm Caminha's literary description of at least one kind of sexual and romantic liaison among certain members of the navy.

Caminha's frankness and detachment about the subject of homosexuality shocked contemporary readers.[66] Negative reactions to his book provoked the author to pen a short response the following year entitled "A Condemned Book," which appeared in the literary magazine *A Nova Revista*. In his rebuttal to the unfavorable reviews of his work, Caminha characterized the public outcry as an "inquisitional act of the critics," and "perhaps the biggest scandal of the previous year." Caminha pointed to the hypocritical posturing of Carioca literary commentators who praised European writers such as Flaubert, Zola, Maupassant, and Eça de Queiroz, whose novels contained adultery, blasphemy, and immorality, yet condemned *Bom-Crioulo*: "Which is more pernicious: *Bom-Crioulo* in which homosexuality is studied and condemned, or those pages which are in circulation preaching in a philosophical tone the break-up of the family, concubinage, free love and all sorts of social immorality?"[67]

Caminha's public response to his critics indicates a familiarity with European literature on same-sex eroticism. Indeed, his use of the word *homossexualismo* in his 1896 defense of *Bom-Crioulo* was one of the first Brazilian literary applications of the term, coined by the Vienna-born writer Karoly Maria Benkert in 1869.[68] He pointed his detractors to the works of French and German physicians and psychiatrists who had written on the subject to show that his descriptions of Aleixo were not invented.[69] However, Caminha's apparent unfamiliarity with the rich homoerotic subculture of turn-of-the-century Rio de Janeiro (other than activities he had observed while serving in the navy) resulted in a unilateral portrait of same-sex romances as clandestine and cloistered affairs doomed to end in tragedy.[70]

Doctors, Lawyers, and Effeminate Men

Brazilian literary critiques of the homosexual content of Caminha's *Bom-Crioulo* ultimately based their arguments on an interwoven web of religious, legal, and medical discourses about same-sex eroticism that created a collective notion of the effeminate man as an immoral and degenerate being. While different authors articulated diverse theories about the origin, nature, and the appropriate attitude of the public and the state toward men who enjoyed sex with other men, the overall effect of these varied approaches nonetheless cast a negative light on those who engaged in this erotic activity. The Catholic Church still maintained that sex should be restricted to marriage and for the single purpose of procreation. While sexual activities between men were no longer punishable by death, sodomy was still considered a sin. The Brazilian state had decriminalized the practice at the beginning of the nineteenth century, but, nevertheless, the police discouraged homosexuality through the enforcement of other legal provisions prohibiting vagrancy and public displays of immodesty. Members of the medical profession wrote occasionally on the topic, combining traditional religious moral aversion to same-sex eroticism with theories that homosexuality was due either to physiological disorders or the lack of "normal" sexual outlets. These professionals also created a taxonomy that divided homosexuals into "penetrating" and "penetrated" individuals, although the criteria for these categories were shifting and inconsistent.

The medical literature produced in this period provides valuable insights into competing notions of the nature, causes, and manifestations of same-sex erotic behavior, the male sexual body, and its erogenous sites. The intention of the medical observers was to document a social problem, offer solutions that would improve the public health of the imperial (and later republican) capital, and create a growing role for medical professionals in maintaining public order and public health.[71] Their writings reveal the process by which moral arguments about the depravation of sodomy gave way to medical discussions about the pathology of pederasty.[72] Moreover, they provide an entry into the subculture of Carioca men who engaged in same-sex activities during the transitional period from empire to republic.

In 1872, Francisco Ferraz de Macedo, a medical doctor and pharmacologist, published a study entitled "About Prostitution in General and Particularly in Rio de Janeiro." The purpose of his treatise was to document the practice of prostitution in the imperial capital as a means of developing public health measures to contain the spread of syphilis. The volume included a detailed account of various kinds of same-sex erotic behavior practiced by *sodomitas* (sodomites) in Rio de Janeiro. Noting the prevalence of sodomites in the city, Ferraz de Macedo recorded: "We see devotees of that faction among all ages, be it through their passive role, active role, or mixed condition."[73] Ferraz de Macedo thus divided those he observed into multiple categories: the inserter in anal intercourse (*ativo*), the anally receptive person (*passivo*), or the person who enjoyed both forms of sexual pleasure (*mixto*, mixed), at times penetrating and other times being a receptor.[74]

Ferraz de Macedo considered the inserter in anal intercourse as much a sodomite as the receptive partner. In this respect, he followed the traditional view of the Catholic Church and the Portuguese state during the colonial period, as well as the de facto prosecution policies in the Brazilian army and navy during the empire. The sexual act marked *both* participants as sodomites. Ferraz de Macedo, however, went further in defining these men by analyzing their desires and self-presentation. According to the physician, the "active" sodomite was more difficult to identify than the "passive" sodomite because the former tended to look and act like any other man while the latter was effeminate. Both, however, clearly belonged to the Carioca subculture. Moreover, the "active" sodomite some times initiated sexual encounters through a *cantada*, that is, words or gestures indicating sexual interest. He might strike up a conversation with an unknown youth in a public place, shower attention on him, offer him tickets to the theater, and ultimately seduce him. In this regard, the relationship remained hierarchical and imitative of gender relations and courtship behavior between men and women, but both "active" and "passive" men, as well as those who had assumed more fluid sexual roles, were considered to be a part of the sodomites' world of desires.[75]

Although trained as a physician, Ferraz de Macedo did not offer any medical explanations for the origins of sodomy, nor did he consider the practice to be pathological, as European experts were beginning to maintain as early as the 1850s.[76] Rather, he ascribed the prevalence of the behavior to improper moral upbringing: "Since a boy who has received paternal virtues and advice, corroborated by his teachers who educate his spirit . . . will never turn toward the black sin; he will never be interested in or confused by the whirlwind of sodomites; he will never be found in Rio de Janeiro mixed up with the multitude of male prostitutes."[77] Morality rather than medicine is the appropriate means to stop this "aberration of nature."

Observing that sodomites proliferated throughout Rio de Janeiro, Ferraz de Macedo noted that they were more frequently found in the Sacramento district (where the Largo do Rossio was located) and other parts of the city center. He also recorded that many Carioca property owners profited considerably by renting rooms at all hours of the day and night to serve people who wanted to engage in "hedonistic acts." Soldiers, businessmen, and artists made up the largest portion of *ativo* sodomites. The practice was widespread among the military "due to the soldiers' time-restraints and lack of other means." Presumably, their restriction to the barracks or the ship made access to women difficult. The physician also argued that the hierarchical nature of the armed forces sanctioned the domination of enlisted men. Officers could order a lower-ranking person to participate in same-sex erotic activities without consent.[78] The observation that military personnel engaged in male-on-male sexual activities owing to the unavailability of women and to the controlled nature of barracks life implied that sexual desire was divorced from any romantic or long-term attachments. The soldier, presented with female company, would supposedly abandon the sodomitic behavior that circumstances had forced upon him.

Ferraz de Macedo extended his theory beyond the example of the military to argue that sodomy was a result of circumstances rather than inclination in other sectors of Brazilian society as well. He reported that some artists and men employed in commerce chose same-sex activities because of their "horror of syphilis" and the high prices charged by prostitutes. Even if one took the doctor's word at face value and agreed with him that the cost of a harlot were excessive, the physician still gave no explanation of how engaging in same-sex activities protected one from syphilis. His logic reflected the medical assumption current at the time that female prostitutes, as the principal repositories of sexually transmitted diseases, were primarily responsible for infecting the male population.[79] If two men had sex together, he seemed to argue, they could not spread syphilis or other sexually communicable illnesses. The physician's reduction of the sexual desire of the *sodomita ativo* to particular situations also failed to explain his own observations that "mixed" sodomites freely passed from one sexual role to another. Were these men, who enjoyed multiple pleasures of the body, inherent or circumstantial sodomites? The fact that they were both *ativo* and *passivo* suggests that these men's desires were more complex than those explained by the physician. If a *sodomita ativo* chose another man for a sexual partner because no woman was available, why would he also seek other forms of sexual enjoyment unless he derived pleasure from the experience?

Ferraz de Macedo's admission that he only observed *sodomitas passivos* might explain the confusing paradigm he established in describing the gender systems of these Cariocas.

The physician came up with a number of characteristics that he used to identify the *passivos*. In presenting them, he also conflated prostitution with effeminacy and with what he assumed to be the sodomite's sexual position in intercourse. "[I]f we see a young boy with a serious, serene walk, with short steps accompanied by movements of the trunk and the superior members, with legs a bit open and the toes pointed outward; in short, if we see a boy imitating the walk of a lady (that is, a prostitute), [a boy] who has studied the semi-lascivious movements of the body in the mirror and has put them into practice when he walks by with the objective of exciting and attracting the looks and desire of the passerby, we can suspect that it is an infamous boy that is going by."[80] Elsewhere in the text, Ferraz de Macedo referred to the professional male prostitute as *o bagaxa*, presumably another slang term. (*A bagaxa* meant female prostitute. By attaching the masculine article to this feminine noun, the expression conveys the notion of a feminized male prostitute). Ferraz de Macedo described *o bagaxa* as having an "effeminate, sweet, and pleasant way of speaking" and flamboyant style of dress. In the eyes of the physician, the allure of these streetwalkers was their imitation of the feminine—the provocative walk, the sweet, high-pitched speech, and the meticulous manner of dressing. Their womanly carriage and demeanor suggested seductiveness and desirability. Devoid of virility, they became the objects of masculine lust. Their cross-gendered behavior makes sense only within a bipolar construction of sexuality. Their femininity implied their sexual passivity as outlets for other men's desire, whether or not their actual erotic conduct conformed to the physician's speculation as to the nature of their sexual activity. As substitutes for syphilitic and high-priced whores, their bodies provided pleasures comparable to those of unavailable women.

Ferraz de Macedo further recognized that, not unlike prostitutes, these men possessed their own slang and signals to execute a *cantada*, a seduction. They managed to identify themselves to others in urban spaces through their conversations, hand gestures, and their "lack of serenity and circumspection."[81] While assuming a feminized appearance, these men still enjoyed masculine privileges. Like female prostitutes, they could frequent the streets, parks, and places of entertainment unaccompanied, at a time when most young women remained under strict family surveillance in order to protect their "purity." One could find them in the billiard halls, bars, and cafés, in the public *praças* (plazas) sitting on stone benches or joking and smoking in groups of two or three. They enjoyed strolling in public places more than any other activity, especially along the busy walkways, at church processions, in front of theaters, and during pilgrimages.

Much like the *francesas,* the refined and sophisticated French courtesans who offered their sexual services to members of the Carioca elite, these men possessed an elegance and style that suggested imitation of, if not membership in, the privileged class of Rio's high society. They made a point of dressing up, especially when frequenting the theater. They wore well-tailored jackets, pants made of fancy fabric that accentuated their form, fine polished boots, elaborately embroidered shirts, silk handkerchiefs (generally red or blue), and silk cravats. They perfumed their hair and donned tall white hats. Gold watch fobs and chains hung from their vests. They used expensive walking sticks, wore kid gloves, and smoked Havana cigars.[82] Ferraz de Macedo's descriptions of the most elegant and enchanting male prostitutes of Rio de Janeiro paint a portrait of Carioca swells. It is not clear how Ferraz de Macedo managed to leap to the conclusion that Rio de Janeiro's dandies were all sodomites, and prostitutes to boot. Surely not all of the finely dressed youth of the imperial capital engaged in same-sex erotic activities, as Ferraz de Macedo would lead us to believe.

These tropical fops were not the only *sodomitas passivos* described. The physician also included in this category street urchins, whose sexual activities allowed them to survive on the charity of the more fortunate. Poverty and the lack of opportunity, not innate effeminacy, were the forces that drove these boys to grant sexual favors in exchange for small gifts, a meal in a hotel, or a place to sleep at night. Excessive elegance and unmanliness, at least to the observing physician, implied a willful disposition toward homoeroticism. Poverty, like the unavailability of women and concerns for personal hygiene, resulted in unfortunate but forgivable forays into this "depraved" world, or so Ferraz de Macedo maintained.

When he completed his medical thesis in 1872, Ferraz de Macedo was hopeful about the possibility of eliminating, or at least diminishing, the number of men engaged in this behavior: "When the panic terror of the existence of syphilis among the public prostitutes stops invading the youth of Rio de Janeiro; when the immense number of feigned clandestine prostitutes no longer exists, so that they are forced to come public; when, as a consequence, the number of disguised concubines decreases and the number of prostitutes increases, certainly society will be disillusioned and one more step toward civilization will be taken; and it is incontestable that the terrible serpent of sodomy will have been seriously wounded." The physician's proposal to eliminate this "plague" that infected the social body of Rio de Janeiro involved police regulation of male and female prostitution, as well as public education of the lower classes, which, in the opinion of Ferraz de Macedo, were the social sectors most involved in this vice. For, as the eminent doctor observed, "rarely does one find among the group of proponents of the nefarious sin any illustrious man of careful upbringing."[83]

Ferraz de Macedo's sweeping generalizations about the absence of sodomites among the well-bred citizens of Rio de Janeiro is, of course, contradicted by his own detailed descriptions of the dandies that dallied outside the theaters or cruised the public parks. Indeed, one is never quite sure if he is describing elegantly dressed male prostitutes or simply upper-class sodomites. If the men he portrayed, whether streetwalkers or not, were not born of families from the city's elite, surely they aspired to such social status and dressed accordingly. Ferraz de Macedo's social position as a medical doctor in imperial Brazil placed him, too, among the men "of careful upbringing." His denial that sodomites belonged to "decent" society may reflect his own class prejudices. His documentation, however, exceeded his definition. The social markers that he recorded—fashions, codes, patterns of sociability and territoriality—revealed something quite different. Ferraz de Macedo's treatise on prostitution presents us with further evidence that as early as the 1870s a discrete subculture had developed in Rio de Janeiro involving much more than sexual encounters. Male-to-male sexual and social bonding were visible enough to provoke extensive comment on the part of at least one physician. The men he observed had created a unique world based on a common identity, dressing a certain way, communicating with similar codes and gestures, and meeting on the streets and in the public parks of Rio de Janeiro.

Red Ties, Rouge, and Pearl-Colored Makeup

In 1894, four years after the Largo do Rossio was rechristened Praça Tiradentes, and the year Adolfo Caminha finished writing *Bom-Crioulo*, Francisco José Viveiros de Castro wrote *Assaults on Modesty: Studies on Sexual Aberrations*. Viveiros de Castro, as mentioned previously, was a professor of criminal law in Rio's School of Law and a judge on the High Court of Appeals for the Federal District. His work included a chapter on pederasty, in which he wrote about same-sex sexual activity between adults.[84] Two decades previously, Ferraz de Macedo had offered moral explanations for why men engaged in sodomy. Viveiros de Castro argued that inversion was a medical problem, and unlike Ferraz de Macedo, who based his thesis on the observation of Cariocas, Viveiros de Castro derived most of his information from European sexologists. He even admitted in his chapter on pederasty that the material he presented was in large part a translated summary of Dr. Julien Chevalier's *Inversion of the Sexual Instinct from the Medico-Legal Point of View* (1885) and of Albert Moll's *The Perversions of Genital Instincts* (1893). Although not offering original theoretical contributions to the study of homosexuality, the Brazilian jurist was clearly aware of the latest European medical idea about *invertidos* (inverts), even employing that term which had only recently come into use in France.[85] However, Viveiros de Castro did not present just one clear medical theory about homosexuality. Rather he offered the reader a potpourri of explanations about the nature and causes of sexual inversion, citing an array of physicians, sexologists, and psychiatrists with divergent and contradictory views. These ranged from the idea that sexual inversion was congenital, pathological, and hereditary to the theory that it was an acquired behavior.

In addition to supplying his readers with a compendium of imported medical constructions about men who enjoyed same-sex erotic behavior, he also described spaces where men gathered in Rio de Janeiro: "The Largo do Rossio was in the old days famous for being a place where at night passive pederasts got together to wait for those who desired them. They groomed themselves in ways so that they could be easily recognized. They used very short jackets, silk scarves hanging from their pockets, very tight pants designed to fit the form of their thighs and buttocks. They approached the passersby asking for a match to light a cigarette in a sweet voice with provocative and lascivious body movements. During Carnival they dressed as women and invaded the masked balls in the São Pedro Theater."[86] Viveiros de Castro's depictions of the people who frequented the Largo de Rossio in "the old days" resembles both Ferraz de Macedo's portrayal of the well-dressed, unmanly men who walked the streets of Rio in the early 1870s looking for sexual partners, and the turn-of-the-century cartoon representations of *frescos*. Once again, their tailored clothing and gentle demeanor suggested sexual availability. Flowing scarves appear to have been a sign of femininity as well as a code of approachability. Carnival provided the opportunity to defy social mores in a public space by openly cross-dressing at masquerade balls when legal restrictions against such behavior were temporarily suspended.

Viveiros de Castro's ultimate message to the reader was contradictory. When it came to the issue of whether or not the pederast should be punished, the jurist clearly argued with a certain amount of compassion. Using German physician Albert Moll and the German-Austrian psychiatrist Richard von Krafft-Ebing to back up his position, Viveiros de Castro insisted: "When it has to do with Urnings,* that is individuals touched by congenital or psychic inversion, punishment would be a true cruelty, because they cannot abandon their inclinations, which are an integral element of their personality."[87] On the other hand, he spent a large amount of his chapter describing "three notable cases of pederasty in this city that have been studied scientifically by competent observers."[88] These individuals were quite different from the *frescos* who invaded Carnival balls in the Largo do Rossio. The first involved a man who had lived an isolated existence with two male servants with whom he had sexual relations, and who was eventually committed to a mental asylum. The second case included a lengthy story about an young clerk in a dry goods store who had had a sexual relationship with the shop owner. Discovering that his employer intended to marry a young woman, the clerk brutally killed his former lover in a jealous fit. The third case documented the rape and murder of a four-year-old boy by an older man. These stories hardly evoked empathy for Carioca pederasts, but rather reinforced the idea that men involved in same-sex relations were mentally ill, impassioned murderers, or child molesters. Expressing compassion for degenerate, effeminate pederasts while propagating stereotypes of murderous maniacs would remain a potent combination in the writings of other physicians, jurists, and criminologists well into the twentieth century. Viveiros de Castro's work is significant, however, because it represents one of the first attempts by Brazilian professionals to move beyond a moral analysis of same-sex eroticism to analyze the possible medical, biological, or psychic causes for the behavior. *Assaults on Modesty: Studies on Sexual Aberrations* is a transitional treatise between traditional religious and moral condemnations of sodomy and the medicalization of the pederast.

A decade later, in 1906, another Carioca doctor, José Ricardo Pires de

---

* The term Urning (sometimes translated as Uranian) was coined in Europe in the 1860s to refer to the theory that a man who felt sexual attraction for another man was actually a "woman trapped in a man's body."

Almeida, published a lengthy monograph on homosexuality in Rio de Janeiro, entitled *Homosexuality (Libertinage in Rio de Janeiro): A Study of the Perversions of Genital Instincts.*[89] Although ten years earlier both Viveiros de Castro and Adolfo Caminha had used the term *homossexualismo* in passing to refer to same-sex erotic behavior, the word now seemed more widely used by the medical profession as a synonym for Urning. However, "pederast" still remained the most commonly employed expression to refer to same-sex sexual activities between adults. Pires de Almeida confirmed both Ferraz de Macedo's and Viveiros de Castro's descriptions of the homoerotic sexual topography of Rio de Janeiro: "Until ten years ago, Urnings engaged in lascivious pleasures in boardinghouses, establishments that rented rooms by the hour, and private homes. . . . [A]ll of these *rendez-vous* [lodgings] were generally known by the police who tolerated this masculine practice that took place in the light of day and the dark of night."[90] Pires de Almeida's assertion that same-sex eroticism remained unchecked by the police seems to indicate that since under the 1890 Penal Code homosexuality, like female prostitution, was not illegal per se, the authorities had broad leeway in controlling its public manifestations. Unlike female prostitutes, who periodically had to contend with cleanup campaigns promoted by police chiefs, transgressive men seem to have faced less frequent and predictable regulation of their behavior.[91]

Just as Ferraz de Macedo had in the late nineteenth century, Pires de Almeida closely associated homosexuality with prostitution, observing that "[male] prostitution exists in all countries and in all civilizations; but, one can state that until fifty years ago, it was nowhere more ostensibly common than in Rio de Janeiro."[92] Following a line of argument similar to that of Ferraz de Macedo, Pires de Almeida restated the demographic and functionalist contention that same-sex erotic encounters resulted from the lack of available females. He insisted that by the turn of the century male prostitution had diminished in Rio de Janeiro as a result of the growing number of female streetwalkers. After Abolition in 1888, he explained, the number of female prostitutes had increased, especially among immigrant women, because slave women were no longer readily available for sexual use.[93]

Although one of the goals of Pires de Almeida's work was to document libertine behavior in turn-of-the-century Rio de Janeiro, his individual profiles of pederasts, a term he used to refer to any man, *ativo* or *passivo*, who had sex with other men, focused on personalities from the days of the empire. Contradicting Ferraz de Macedo's contention that homosexual behavior did not occur among Rio's elite, Pires de Almeida observed that "active and passive pederasts" existed in all social classes, including in the monastic orders, among the high army and naval officers, judges, public officials, the diplomatic corps, and regular clerics. By listing these examples, he argued that the ruling class was not immune to this "moral perversion."[94] He described in some detail the scandalous behavior of a prominent politician in the imperial government and a brigadier general in the imperial army. These comments, as well as his remarks about police "toleration" under the empire, may also have been a veiled republican criticism of the decadent nature of the recently overthrown monarchy.

In his treatise, Pires de Almeida presented brief sketches of several colorful and exotic members of the lower classes in late-nineteenth-century Rio de Janeiro. One of them, who called himself Traviata, was known for his flamboyant attire. He commonly wore a long Mexican jacket with a velvet collar, trousers the color of rosemary flowers, a red tie, a white scarf hanging from his pocket, low-cut polished shoes showing silk stockings, and a straw hat with a blue ribbon around it. He was an accomplished milliner, designing and decorating ladies' hats for the city's leading clothiers. Locks of curly black hair and a black mustache accented his large-cheeked face, which was always painted with rouge and pearl-colored makeup. He preferred to go out late at night to the Largo do Rossio or the Passeio Público, another popular public park in Rio de Janeiro. An accomplished singer with a contralto voice, he reportedly excelled at performing the part of Violetta in Verdi's *La Traviata*, hence his adopted name. The physician noted that he shared the typical gait of most "Urnings," swinging his hips and emphasizing his buttocks.[95] In using this terminology, as well as citing the works of Moll, Krafft-Ebing, Chevalier, and Tardieu, the author showed familiarity with the most up-to-date European theories by leading sexologists, including the notion that "Urnings" were neither male or female but rather members of a "third sex," whose feminine soul is trapped in a man's body. However, he described Traviata as both an "active and passive pederast," contradicting his own construction of the "typical" Carioca homosexual as a feminine and exclusively receptive male. Just as Viveiros de Castro had done a decade before, Pires de Almeida introduced and repeated European notions of homosexuality, but his own impressionistic accounts of same-sex eroticism in Rio often contradicted the foreign theories so faithfully reproduced.

Pires de Almeida described another nineteenth-century figure, an Afro-Brazilian street vendor named Athanasio, who sold sweets in the Largo do Rossio and the surrounding area. Like Traviata, he engaged in both inserter and receptive anal intercourse. His dress, reflecting the lower social status of a free black man, was less extravagant than that of white Cariocas of the period. He wore white or yellow rough cotton pants with legs that were gathered at the ankles, a loose shirt with an open collar and rolled up sleeves, and he was always barefoot. He lived on what was then Rua dos Ciganos, next to the Largo do Rossio, and it was said that he received private visitors at his home, from simple clerks to imperial senators.[96] Although some of the clerks who visited Athanasio may have been of African or of mixed racial origins, the imperial senators were obviously from the country's white elite. The fact that this street vendor attracted men of different classes and races to his humble dwelling indicates that same-sex erotic encounters, like heterosocial liaisons between female prostitutes and middle- and upper-class men in Brazilian society, provided a moment where class and racial barriers were transgressed. Anthropologist and historian Luiz Mott has documented homosexual encounters between masters and slaves and among men of different social classes as early as the colonial period.[97] Pires de Almeida's evidence indicates that these kinds of trysts continued into the late nineteenth century. Moreover, although these cross-racial and cross-class sexual affairs involved men with different positions of power, these differences did not seem to have been manifested in their sexual practices. Athanasio's willingness to penetrate or be penetrated demonstrates that a given performance in bed was not linked to a person's low social status. Coercion may have occurred between officers and enlisted men, but social superiority did not always imply sexual domination nor did it suggest an automatic reversal of class or racial power dynamics during sexual liaisons.

Even though Pires de Almeida diverged from Ferraz de Macedo's observations by describing "pederasts and Urnings of all classes, categories, and conditions," he did concur with late nineteenth-century observers about the spaces they occupied—"entrances of theaters, cafés, restaurants, billiard halls, doorways of convents, the stairways of the churches, the trees around Campo de Santana [a much larger park near Praça Tiradentes], the bath houses, and the basements of theaters." He noted that they socialized in groups of two or three or cruised the streets alone. They engaged in witty humor to tease each other and used their associates as intermediaries to make contacts with prospective partners.[98] They dressed elegantly, hiding their real age with youthful clothes, and used red ties as a coded indication of their sexual proclivities, a practice that seems to date back to the mid-nineteenth century in Brazil.[99]

In *Gay New York*, George Chauncey documents how the "fairies" of New York wore red ties, plucked their eyebrows, used rouge, and wore powdered makeup in the 1910s, '20s and '30s "to signal their anomalous gender status."[100] These same styles were prevalent in Rio de Janeiro at the turn of the century, and equally common in São Paulo in the 1930s, as we shall see shortly. There is no evidence that there was either a diffusion of these practices from New York and Europe to Brazil through informal networks or any other kind of international interchange among men who adopted these styles, as plainly occurred in the globalization of U.S. and European gay culture from the 1960s on. One must therefore question why such similar behavioral patterns and even color-coded signs of availability developed on the two continents at the same time. The red tie was likely used as eye-catching neckwear that could be spotted easily by interested passersby on a crowded street. Moreover, the color has traditionally been associated with prostitution, seduction, and sensuality in Mediterranean, Iberian, and northern European societies. In Brazil, newspapers and magazines and the American films shown in movie houses portrayed images of feminine beauty, style, and fashion that were imitated by women. It seems quite possible that effeminate men may have appropriated some of these gendered representations to express their own notion of what was aesthetic and seductive.

Although Pires de Almeida's 259-page treatise on homosexuality and libertinism in Rio de Janeiro often meanders away from the main subject, his ultimate analysis of the nature and treatment of men who manifested same-sex erotic desires presented most of the arguments that later Brazilian professionals would use to describe "the degeneration of the sexual instinct." The physician held that homosexuality either could be congenital or the result of improper upbringing. Contradictorily, he maintained on one hand that the "typical passive pederast" was an effeminate man, but on the other admitted "there is no external manifestation of the pederast that indicates or denounces his perversion." However, he also suggested that other European experts might find a link between homosexuality and physical traits. In this regard, he cited the work of Italian criminologist Cesare Lombroso, whose anthropometric studies of the relationship between the physical characteristics of the body and "degeneration" would become the basis of studies in Brazil in the 1930s.[101]

Pires de Almeida even engaged in modest polemics with the European masters, again revealing his confusion about whether or not one could detect physiological differences in pederasts. For example, he cited Ulrichs, who argued that Urnings, like women, were unable to whistle and had great difficulty in learning how to do so. Then he referred to Moll's interviews with large numbers of Urnings in which he found that they could indeed whistle like "normal men." Here, Pires de Almeida offered his contribution to the debate. He suggested that Moll's observations had been partially correct and partially wrong, since only "passive pederasts" are unable to whistle.[102] Silly as his assertion was, Pires de Almeida was attempting to enter the European debate about pederasts' biological and psychological characteristics. In seeking qualities that distinguished the Urning from "normal" men, Pires de Almeida, like Viveiros de Castro before him, was participating in the medicalization of the homosexual, that is, creating and describing a distinct category of men with unique physical and pathological traits.

A more significant divergence from Moll's theories was the Carioca physician's assertion that there was an essential difference between the nature of the "active" and "passive" pederast. Pires de Almeida insisted that the conflation of these categories into a single homosexual being was problematic.[103] As we shall see, Brazilian physicians and other professionals studying same-sex eroticism would resist abandoning a model that distinguished between the "active," masculine-acting person engaging in sexual activities and the effeminate man associated with the "passive" role in sex.

Regardless of Pires de Almeida's overall views about the degeneracy of same-sex erotic behavior, he, like Viveiros de Castro, argued against the idea that all homosexuals should be hospitalized or incarcerated, pointing rather to clinical treatment of this "inversion" through "moral education." He readily admitted, however, that a person who was born a homosexual or had practiced homosexuality for an extended period of time would likely become immune to such moral treatment, and he suggested that the close monitoring of child-rearing practices in order to catch the degeneration before it advanced too much. The ambiguity of his approach reflected the overall confusion among turn-of-the-century physicians about the etiology of homosexuality and, therefore, about the appropriate way to "treat" it.

João do Rio and the Capital's Enchanting Streets

In many ways, the public forms of sociability employed by *frescos* and described by these physicians and lawyers paralleled normative heterosocial interactions among the middle and upper classes during the Brazilian belle époque.[104] Prior to the first decade of the twentieth century, the Carioca

elite frequented Rua do Ouvidor, a narrow, half-mile-long street in downtown Rio lined with shops offering the latest in London and Parisian styles
and other European luxury goods.[105] The 1905 inauguration of Avenida
Central, the crown jewel of the Pereira Passos urban renovations, shifted
fashionable social interactions to that wide boulevard. Later known as the
Rio Branco, Avenida Central connected to Avenida Beira-Mar and thus also
linked up with the southern neighborhoods bordering Guanabara Bay. In
these three sites, well-to-do pedestrians displayed their most fashionable
foreign attire by strolling along the streets à la *flâneur*.

The art of *flânerie*, or *footing* as it was alternately called, involved meandering through the city to see and to be seen. Stopping to greet acquaintances, gossip with friends, or window shop reflected a privileged social
status. Wealth and certain professions enabled upper- and middle-class men
to spend leisure time in these seemingly purposeless excursions. While
poorer classes frequented the same city streets, their movements were
linked to the necessities of work. The *flâneur*, on the other hand, had the
time and resources to enjoy the finer aspects of the modern city at a casual
pace. Properly accompanied middle- and upper-class women could also
partake of this leisurely activity, as broad paved sidewalks replaced narrow
pothole-ridden streets and inadequate passageways.[106]

John Otway Percy Bland, a British traveler through South America
during World War I, described these tranquil promenades in downtown Rio
de Janeiro:

> When, after the hour of the siesta, the wives and daughters of the people don
> garments of respectability and take the air *en famille* in the Avenida [Central]
> or in the public gardens, the general absence of all apparent motive in their
> movements also reminds one of the contemplative East. Men and women
> alike walk the street like somnambulists; the women's faces generally wear a
> stolidly detached expression, emphasized by the conventional decorum,
> which in public ignores the existence of the other sex and feigns not to hear
> its Rabelaisian quips. The men either saunter along or stand in groups, pat-
> ting each other affectionately on the back and discussing local politics with
> much wealth of gesture, complacently blocking the footpath. The Avenida
> after four o'clock is a place for conversation rather than for locomotion; Eu-
> ropeans and other foolish people in a hurry, generally hire a taxi.[107]

Although Bland captured the slow-paced rhythm of Brazilian *footing*, his
outsider status probably kept him from noticing other interactions going on
concurrently with the aloof dismissal by proper women of masculine at-
tentions and the preoccupation with politics by expressive men.

Weaving along these fashionable spaces, young men and "decent" women could flirt with each other when appropriately accompanied or chaperoned. Friends could pass on the latest gossip or introduce an unattached cousin who might be visiting from the countryside or another city. Men who sought out other men for sexual adventures in public parks or along the fashionable avenues of downtown Rio could easily blend into the milling crowd of people browsing by store windows, stopping at cafés to discuss politics, or pausing at confectioneries for sweets. Just as two female friends might shop on Rua do Ouvidor and concurrently see which young lawyers or businessmen were out and about, or two students from the School of Medicine might sip coffee while seeing which attractive daughters of the Carioca elite were enjoying some fresh air, so too *frescos* used this public forum to seek out new partners and adventures. Moreover, because men had considerably more freedom to occupy the streets than did women, it would not be unusual at all for a single man to meander back and forth between the Largo do Rossio and Avenida Central or to wait patiently on a park bench for a young lad to join him, as did our fictional character Gouveia. While well-bred women would not venture out unaccompanied after sunset, *frescos* could readily roam the streets and parks of downtown Rio looking for sexual adventures well into the night.

Perhaps no one personified both the *flâneur* and the Carioca dandies described by Ferraz de Macedo, Viveiros de Castro, and Pires de Almeida better than did the journalist, social critic, and writer, Paulo Alberto Coelho Barreto, commonly known as João do Rio, one of his noms de plume.[108] This belle époque literary figure wrote eloquently about the art of *flânerie* in a collection of essays entitled *A alma encantadora das ruas* (The enchanting spirit of the streets), which was originally published in 1908. In the introduction to the book, he described what it was to *flaner*, or stroll: "To *flaner* is to be a vagabond and reflect, to be a fool and comment, and have the virus of observation linked to that of vagrancy. To *flaner* is to go about in the morning, during the day, at night."[109]

João do Rio's definition of *flânerie* was somewhat different from the aimless strolling of Carioca high society down Rua do Ouvidor or Avenida Central. His willingness to explore the city's poor neighborhoods was a far cry from promenading in fancy attire in exclusive downtown areas. His interest in investigating the city's exotic and dangerous spots at all hours of the day and night as a modern-day roving reporter, however, produced imaginative vignettes of everyday life in turn-of-the-century Rio. Yet João do Rio's urban meandering can be read as something more than the inquisitiveness of a correspondent seeking the next interesting story for an eager readership. João do Rio's decided sexual taste for other men leads one to speculate about multiple meanings behind his celebration of the art of metropolitan strolling. While little is known about the particulars of his erotic adventures, his nocturnal wanderings through Brazil's capital in search of innovative journalistic material may have also afforded him the opportunity to enjoy the sexual company of the sailors, soldiers, and common people who were the subjects of his articles and essays.[110]

One 1907 newspaper essay about urban parks and gardens reveals all too well his understanding of the potential varied uses of public places: "Isn't the garden a revival of the ancient forests filled with drunken revelers and satyrs," he wrote. "One can see nervous subjects, cautiously entering, twirling their mustaches, approaching one and then another, circling like vultures, murmuring proposals that makes one shiver, and going into the shadows where one can do anything." He went on to comment that "the police find the greatest licentiousness in the parks, reminiscent of Tiberian orgies." While João do Rio was rarely so explicit in his description of same-sex erotic activities in his writing, this passage captures the excitement and tension of sexual encounters in public places. When someone entered these "guardians of sensuality," as he called them, these places seem to receive that person with the nervous smile of an old satyr, and the night watchman, understanding what takes place in their domain, would always comment to another guard: "That goat is up to something." Finally, João do Rio wrote, "at the end of the evening, when the signal is made that the park's gates are to be closed, while most people push and shove to leave, exhausted as if they had just finished a long trip, those lingering behind take advantage of the relative solitude, and the garden convulses in a supreme spasm."[111]

Contemporary readers may find the notion of anonymous public sexual encounters in gardens, parks, cinemas, or restrooms totally alien to their life experiences. Yet for many *frescos* and *fanchonos* who had to hide their sexual desires from family, friends, and employers, these chance erotic liaisons constituted one of the few means to meet potential partners. Most men who lived with their families, parents, or relatives, or who perhaps shared a room in a boardinghouse, didn't have the option of organizing a tryst in their home. They could rent a room in a rundown hotel or other establishment that catered to prostitutes and men intent on sharing a bed for several hours or the night. Not everyone, however, was willing to run the risks involved in registering one's name with the proprietor and possibly becoming the victim of disapproval, scorn, or even blackmail.[112] For some, these public spaces became a necessity for sexual ful-fillment. For others, the challenge of the hunt, the inherent eroticism of seduction, the thrill of the quick encounter with danger at one's heels all added to the pleasure of the park. The genius of João do Rio's journalism was his ability to write about this hidden underworld and describe what today is called cruising in such a way that the average turn-of-the-century bourgeois newspaper reader probably did not understand the subtext, yet it would be apparent to those familiar with the alternative world operat-ing in these public spaces.

João do Rio was born in Rio de Janeiro to a middle-class family in 1881. He gained literary prominence at age twenty-three through a series of jour-nalistic reports about Afro-Brazilian and other non-Catholic religious prac-tices in the nation's capital.[113] His willingness to comb the city's hillside slums and visit poor and working-class suburbs in order to provide sensa-tionalist accounts of the capital's demimondes also revolutionized Carioca journalism, and he is credited with being Brazil's first modern reporter. During his lifetime, he produced more than 2,500 newspaper articles, short stories, and essays on urban life.[114] At age twenty-nine, João do Rio won election to the Brazilian Academy of Letters, a honor he campaigned to re-ceive with single-minded determination.

His meteoric rise to the highest-ranking literary circles was not as easy as his youth suggests. Indeed, youth was one of several obstacles João do Rio faced in his pursuit of literary honor. His racial heritage was another count against him: his mother was of Afro-Brazilian origins. Furthermore, he was principally a journalist and reporter, as opposed to a novelist or poet. None of these elements was an automatic barrier to the closed circle of Brazil's *letrados*. After all, Machado de Assis, the founding president of the Brazilian Academy of Letters, was himself a *mulato* of humble origins, and other journalists had been admitted to the society prior to João do Rio's election. Nevertheless, racism among the elite, the notion that success based on journalism did not quite match other literary endeavors, and his youth made his entry into the hallowed halls of high culture complicated. More important, however, was the fact that he was known to be a *fresco*. Accord-ing to one biographer, Brazil's senior literary figure Machado de Assis and the eminent statesman Barão do Rio Branco organized a faction to block João do Rio's election to the Brazilian Academy of Letters on two occa-sions because of his moral turpitude.[115]

After elaborate campaigning on his own behalf, however, João do Rio was admitted to the prestigious association with his third nomination.

Emílio de Meneses, an important member of the capital's literary circles, allegedly composed a couplet that revealed some degree of public disdain for the young author. Once again playing on the double meaning of *fresco* as an effeminate homosexual and as something cool, the verse went: "Predicting the coming heat / The Academy, which worships the cold, / Not being able to buy fans / Opened its doors to João do Rio."[116]

The writer Lima Barreto was another of João do Rio's literary adversaries. He not only considered João do Rio to be morally depraved, but he also resented the fact his rival had entered the academy while his owns efforts to be elected met with failure.[117] Lima Barreto parodied the author and journalist in his 1909 novel *Recordações do escrivão Isaías Caminha* (Memoirs of the notary public Isaías Caminha). João do Rio becomes Raul de Gusmão, a "talented lad" who is seen entering a cheap hotel with a naval gunman. In the story the rumor then spreads that the youth paid to have sex with the marine.[118] João do Rio was reportedly outraged by this caricature of his personal life and told Lima Barreto so in no uncertain terms. In private correspondences relating the event to friends, Lima Barreto was every bit as bitter and unkind to João do Rio as in his published work.[119]

On numerous other occasions throughout his professional career, João do Rio's enemies linked him to commonly understood public symbols of homosexuality in order to discredit his reputation. One such reference appeared in the premier issue of *O Gato* (The cat), a magazine of satire and humor first published in 1911. A full-page cartoon portrayed João do Rio and Olavo Bilac, Brazil's leading poet of the late nineteenth century, admiring a statute of the Roman emperor Heliogabalus in a museum. Bilac's index finger touches the muscular marble figure's prominently protruding buttock while João do Rio gazes down at the nude's genital area from the front. One comments: "Superb, isn't it?" The other replies: "It would be delicious if all men were like that!" (see fig. 5). The author of the sketch implies that both writers' sexual interests lean toward men, with Bilac perhaps more interested in penetrating a given partner and João do Rio enjoying a man's phallus. Whether Olavo Bilac, the author of Brazil's "Hymn to the Flag" actually sexually desired other men remains unclear. Bilac's biographers insist that his lifelong bachelor status was the result of a failed love for a young woman early in life that soured his desire to marry.[120] He certainly did not generate the animosity and criticism that João de Rio received, whereby the journalist was repeatedly accused of being a "passive pederast." Even if the cartooned innuendoes about Bilac were baseless, this representation of two prominent members of the Carioca *literati* reveals the

— Soberbo, heim!
— Que delicioso seria se todos os homens fossem assim!

FIGURE 5 João do Rio (*right*): "Superb, isn't it?" Olavo Bilac (*left*): "It would be delicious if all men were like that!" Cartoon by Seth [Álvaro Marins], *O Gato* (1911), courtesy of the Biblioteca Nacional, Rio de Janeiro.

vulnerability of public figures suspected of harboring sexual desires for other men.

One favorite means to attack João do Rio was to rechristen him João do Rossio, thus associating him with the *frescos* who frequented the Largo do Rossio. In 1920, the year before his death, for example, a government official, angered by João do Rio's editorial stand on the issue of Portuguese fishing rights off the coast of Brazil, accosted him in a restaurant with the query: "Is Madam the traitor Joãozinho do Rossio?" This public insult to his honor was followed by a leaflet criticizing his position in the controversy. Referring to João do Rio, who was at the time the director of the newspaper *A Pátria* (The Fatherland), by his real name and calling him an "invert" (*invertido*), the anonymous author of the pamphlet declared that "João do Rossio" had "founded a journal called *Pátria* which should be called *Mátria* because in matters that have to do with Paulo [Barreto], everything is feminine." The handbill went on to warn that "the poor and persecuted Brazilian fishermen . . . know how to kill fish and also know how to kill traitors and passive pederasts."[121]

João do Rio dressed meticulously in elegant attire, complete with a hat, monocle, and a walking cane.[122] He embodied the cultural aspirations of the Brazilian elite, who fastidiously imitated Europe's latest styles in order to be "á la mode" or "up to date," as they would say in borrowed French and English. He became an ardent admirer of Oscar Wilde and translated his play *Salomé* into Portuguese. In fact, in his essays, short stories, and columns, João do Rio freely mimicked the latest Continental literary ideas and fashions and recycled them in Brazil to an amused upper-class audience.[123] While João do Rio played the part of the sophisticated Europeanized fop to exaggerated perfection in public, he remained discreet about his private life in Brazil.[124] Europe, it seems, provided a more favorable environment for unsanctioned licentious behavior, and one of the few times João do Rio explicitly revealed that he had experienced amorous emotions was in a personal letter describing a 1910 trip to the French Riviera: "This blue coast! Oh, how would it be to have money and never leave here, to love, love, love. The love of these rich people who have nothing to do takes on unheard of proportions. . . . There is something for all tastes . . . and with a naturalness."[125] Indeed, for Brazilian men with homoerotic tastes and sufficient economic resources, Europe, and especially Paris, became a refuge, far from the watchful eyes of the family circles that demanded respectability, marriage, and children. Emílio Cardoso Ayres, the well-known caricaturist from a traditional clan in the northeastern state of Pernambuco, also chose Europe for his amorous escapades with other men, tragically committing suicide in a hotel in Marseilles under ambiguous circumstances in 1916.[126]

Perhaps João do Rio's own concern for personal circumspection in Brazil explains why a known *fresco* who conformed to all of the stereotypes of the effeminate dandy managed to rise to the heights of Brazilian society. As long as João do Rio praised and reproduced the norms valued by Brazil's upper classes, he remained their darling. In his work on turn-of-the-century Rio de Janeiro, historian Jeffrey Needell echoes this observation. João do Rio, he argues, "wrote about the Carioca elite's own world, not as it was, but as the elite *wanted* it. In the fantasies thus created of the Carioca *belle époque*, he helped make the Carioca elite self-conscious, and delightedly so. Moreover, by making elite culture and society the center of his flattering attention, he helped to legitimize it."[127] When he challenged a popular view, as in the case of his editorial stance in favor of Portuguese fishing interests in Brazil, this curtain of toleration fell, and he was left vulnerable to all of the prevalent social stereotypes and prejudices regarding *frescos*.

In short, the apparently frivolous fop could enjoy fame and fortune as long as his personal life remained discreet, unmentioned, and unrecorded and his public positions uncontroversial. The same could be said of other celebrated literary figures, such as Olavo Bilac and Mário de Andrade, whose sexual and amorous encounters with other men remain clouded in mystery and protected by national myths to this very day. As we shall see, the pattern of social toleration of flamboyant and effeminate figures who reproduced the cultural status quo will persist throughout the twentieth century. Haute couture designers, fashionable hairdressers, and famous drag stars who have conformed to normative notions of the feminine find a protected niche among the elite as long as they seem to reinforce the traditional representations of the feminine or the effeminate.

The portrait of the superfluous and foppishly elegant *fresco* described by Viveiros de Castro and Pires de Almeida at the turn of the century, and personified by João do Rio, continued in the public imagination into the 1920s. A 1925 cartoon of two meticulously attired men mirrors this stereotype (see fig. 6). The pair are apparently meandering with a purpose. One, a walking cane in hand, with delicate features, plucked eyebrows, and a hint of eye makeup, comments to his fastidiously dressed friend: "They say that Diogenes looked for a man with a lantern." To which his stylish companion replies: "Nonsense. For that, we don't need a lantern."[128]

— Dizem que Dio-
genes procurava um
homem com uma lan-
terna...
    — Que bobagem!
Nós para isso não pre-
cisamos de lanterna.

FIGURE 6   *First man:* "They say that Diogenes looked for a man with a lantern." *Second man:* "Nonsense. For that, we don't need a lantern." Cartoon by Alvarus [Álvaro Cotrim] (1925), courtesy of Celeste Guimarães Zenha.

Like cartoons published two decades earlier, the reference in this draw-ing to cruising, to the street as an arena of sexual desire, conveys a clear message. The delicate features of the characters and their attention to fash-ion feminize them. Yet even as womanly men they operate in male-domi-nated space—the street—where they are free to locate and seduce a man. The author of the drawing and the reading public, who are presumably aware of the codes and behavior of these men, can easily identify them as *frescos* or *putos,* and therefore find humor in the piece.

Much of the description about aspects of the lives of sodomites and pederasts in late-nineteenth- and early-twentieth-century Rio de Janeiro relies on the gaze of observing physicians, cartoonists, and novelists from "Rio *antigo*" (old Rio) rather than on the "authentic" voices of the men themselves. A broad picture of homosocial / sexual life in Rio de Janeiro can, nonetheless, be constructed. At the end of the empire and during the first decades of the Republic, there was a vibrant social world of men who creatively used public space, often also occupied by prostitutes and bo-hemian figures, to enjoy their passions and pleasures. Some adopted clothes and styles that signaled their sexual preferences and projected feminized images to broadcast their availability for sexual and social interaction with other men. Although some of these men's gendered personas and physicality drew from commonly held notions of womanly behavior and performance, their self-presentation did not mean that they necessarily engaged in the receptive sexual behavior that was traditionally associated with feminized men. Others retained a masculine image, but they, too, did not necessarily always conform to the socially ascribed role as penetrator when engaging in sexual activity. Among some, sexual roles were quite fluid, and their uses of the body for pleasure cannot be neatly categorized. Racial and class differences were also not necessarily barriers to social and sexual interactions. These men's clothes, customs, and codes indicate that they had formed a common social identity linked to their sexual behavior. Objects of derision by the medical profession and society in general, they nevertheless demonstrated a surprising resilience in maintaining multiple forms of sociability while defying the normative behavior of Brazilian society.

CHAPTER TWO

～

Sex and Nightlife,

1920—1945

Perhaps the best view of Rio de Janeiro is from atop Corcovado, the hunchbacked mountain that provides a panoramic perspective of the Atlantic Ocean, Guanabara Bay, and the chain of hills that surrounds the city. A hundred-foot-high Art Deco rendering of Christ the Redeemer, with arms outstretched to create an image of both the cross and divine protection over the city, crowns Corcovado, one of Rio's highest peaks. The statue was originally conceived as a national monument to commemorate Brazil's one hundred years of independence from Portugal, but centennial celebrations came and went in 1922 without the money to start construction. On October 12, 1931, the statue was finally inaugurated (see map 3).[1]

Looking down onto Rio de Janeiro that October day in 1931, one would have seen another granite escarpment to the south of Corcovado. This is Sugarloaf Mountain, which divides Guanabara Bay and the Atlantic Ocean. Curving along the coastline to the west lies the three-mile-long Copacabana Beach, with the internationally famous Copacabana Palace Hotel, opened in 1923, topping the skyline. At the end of the beach lies Fort Copacabana, the site of the 1922 *tenentes* (lieutenants') rebellion against the old republican government. Further west, one could observe the white sandy beaches of Ipanema and Leblon, which in the 1930s, like Copacabana, were still lined with elegant summer homes and only a scattering of apartment buildings.

Gazing down from Corcovado to the north, one could catch a glimpse of the Quinta de Boa Vista, the former imperial palace and gardens. Casting one's eye to the northeast, one would view the downtown area, with the *cidade velha* (old city) bisected by Avenida Rio Branco. Rio de Janeiro's

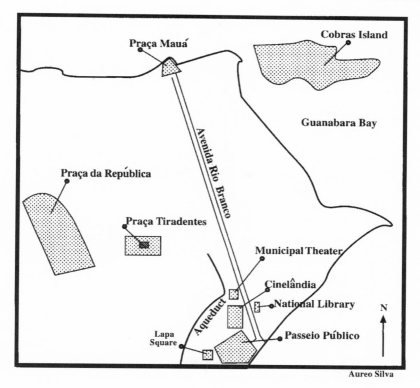

MAP 3 Rio de Janeiro, 1932

broadest street at the time began at the Praça Mauá, where in the 1930s most foreign tourists disembarked from luxury ocean liners, and ended at the Guanabara Bay at Avenida Beira-Mar. Wide pavements of small black and white stones laid out in mosaic designs bordered the hundred-foot-wide boulevard. Brazilwood trees lined its middle corridor.

Since the 1910s, Floriano Peixoto Plaza, abutting Rio Branco Avenue in downtown Rio de Janeiro, lay at the geographical center of Brazilian culture and politics. The Municipal Theater, modeled after the Paris Opera House, dominated the northern side of the *praça*. Directly behind it was the majestic Naval Club. Across the street from the Municipal Theater stood the National School of Fine Arts, and next door was the National Library, both buildings constructed with belle époque grandeur. South of the National Library, the Supreme Court presided, and beyond that lay the Military Club. Further down the street, the Senate sat in the Monroe Palace, an exact reproduction of Brazil's pavilion at the 1904 Louisiana Purchase

Exposition.[2] Completing the quadrangle surrounding the plaza, to the southeast of the Municipal Theater, stood the Municipal Council. Across from it was the Cinelândia district, financed and constructed by the Companhia Cinematográphica do Brasil and inaugurated in 1925 on the site of the old Ajuda Convent. There, tall office and apartment buildings housed groundfloor cafés, restaurants, confectionery shops, and luxurious movie theaters, such as the Odéon, Império, Glória, Pathé-Palácio, and Capitólio.[3] In 1928, a reporter for the *Jornal do Brasil* commented on the changes that had taken place in downtown Rio de Janeiro: "Avenida Rio Branco and Cinelândia seem to me to be like Times Square in a robust miniature transplanted from the great Yankee metropolis. The well-maintained gardens and parks remind me of those in Washington, New York, Paris and London; none of these centers has a plaza that is as beautiful as the Floriano Peixoto Plaza with its surroundings and sumptuous background."[4] A decade later, Hugh Gibson, the U.S. ambassador to Brazil, described Cinelândia in a similar fashion: "The district is brightly illuminated at night, and the parks and trees stand out clear as day. The Brazilians sometimes refer to it as 'the little Broadway,'—which is rather flattering for Broadway."[5]

This stately grouping of Parisian-inspired edifices with their eclectic beaux-arts facades awed Brazilians and foreign visitors alike.[6] The inviting physical space was the setting for a sophisticated and cosmopolitan society. At the same time, it became new territory for a less visible world. Just as during the turn-of-the-century, in the midst of this bustling city center, homosexual men flirted, gossiped, socialized, and enjoyed cultural activities with one another without attracting much notice. In the evenings, they lingered by lampposts, paused on park benches, exchanged longing glances, and then retired to the shadows of a building or to a rented room in the redlight district of the nearby Lapa neighborhood or the boardinghouses around Praça Tiradentes, never disturbing the surface of Rio's glittering social life. While the park surrounding the imposing statue of Emperor Dom Pedro I continued as a public space for homosexual liaisons, the beautiful central plaza facing the Municipal Theater became a new locus for homoerotic interactions. The area attracted not just the privileged few who prided themselves for having European elegance so close at hand, but Brazilians of all social classes, racial backgrounds, and ethnic origins. Here, men with sexual desire for other men could interact, establish new friendships, and procure sexual partners.

One of the thousands of young men who found their way to Rio de Janeiro from the countryside in the 1930s was a twenty-year-old *pardo* (brown-skinned) waiter.[7] Leonídio Ribeiro, the medical criminologist whose writing about the waiter has allowed us a glimpse into his life, only identified the young man by his initials, H.O. The young man, whom I shall call Henrique, had migrated to Rio from another state and worked serving meals at a downtown boardinghouse. On December 6, 1936, he was picked up by the police.

This was not Henrique's first arrest. He had been detained around midnight several months earlier. On both occasions, he stated that he hadn't understood why the police had stopped him. The evening of his second arrest, he had left his job at the boardinghouse and walked with some friends to the Olímpio Theater. But, Henrique insisted, they were not engaged in any illicit behavior. "A police car passed and picked us up. They brought us here to be examined," he stated to the officer who took his deposition at the police station. During the police investigation, Henrique admitted that he had no interest in women and had been attracted to men since he was thirteen, when he had had sex with a soldier in a movie theater. He also admitted that he liked to be anally penetrated and preferred young boys as sexual partners. In Rio de Janeiro, when he picked someone up, they would go to a lodging house for sex. Henrique would receive a thousand reis from his evening's companion, which amounted to 10 percent of his monthly salary. However, Henrique insisted that he wasn't a professional prostitute because he held down a regular job. Unlike other people without fixed employment who, in a given evening, had sex with four or five men, Henrique stated, he didn't stay with more than one man a night.

Before coming to Rio de Janeiro the year before, the young migrant explained, he had *not* gone out at night looking for adventures. (There was likely no overt homosexual subculture in the rural-based state of Espírito Santo from which he had come.) After arriving in the federal capital, however, he met other people with the same sexual inclinations and enjoyed taking walks at night with them. Perhaps trying to establish his moral character, he explained to the police that he avoided certain places, such as the Central Train Station. Soldiers congregated there, whom other young men solicited for sex, but Henrique insisted that he did not participate in those activities. Noting the effect of police surveillance on his and his friends' sexual activities, he reported that "before the police initiated a campaign of repression against them last year, they had stayed on the sidewalk of Rua São Pedro, adjacent to Praça Tiradentes, where the rooms they visited were also located, so that you only had to walk a little bit in order to pick up someone with ease."

Using Freudian terminology, but not following Freud's own understanding of homosexuality, Dr. Ribeiro considered Henrique to be "within the group of individuals of complete and permanent declared homosexuality whose libido is frankly inverted from the beginnings of their sexual activity." Noting the recalcitrant posture of these men, Ribeiro wrote in a somewhat obscure fashion: "We know that they are homosexuals . . . who are fully aware of their inversion. Social morality has made a mark on these individuals. However, their humiliation is at times annulled by their consciousness about the normality and even the excellence of their deviations." He then pointed to the fact that "they do not possess the social inhibition that in other inverts buries their abnormality in their subconscious. They act in their instinctual life with natural freedom and at times even cynicism."[8] In other words, many young homosexuals not only accepted their sexuality but were rather self-affirming about it.

This report on Henrique's arrest reveals significant information about same-sex erotic behavior in Rio de Janeiro in the 1930s. A subculture existed in the federal capital in the 1930s, just as in the late nineteenth and early twentieth century. Middle and lower-class men still gathered in downtown Rio looking for sexual partners, whom they would take back to rented rooms. Recent migrants to the city, upon meeting others who shared their desires, were integrated into a new social world where they quickly familiarized themselves with Rio's sexual topography. Movie theaters, train stations, and certain streets were among the multiple sites where they could meet other men, but they always had to be careful to avoid arrest. Some men frequented all of these places. Others, like Henrique, considered certain locations to be places where morally or socially inferior men congregated for social and sexual liaisons, and avoided them. Some men supported themselves by charging for sexual encounters; others accepted gratuities but relied on other employment for survival. Still others had sex without any financial compensation. Some adopted a defiant attitude toward social reprobation and considered their sexuality normal if not something unique and special, and they exercised great liberty in expressing it. Ribeiro's observations reveal the existence of a multifaceted, self-affirming, and self-conscious subculture in Brazil's major urban centers in the 1930s.

Significant transformations occurred in Brazil between 1920 and 1945. During these two and a half decades, Rio de Janeiro and São Paulo—the economic, political, and cultural centers of Brazil—became the battlegrounds for contested notions of national identity and divergent visions of the political and economic future of the country. The events that took place during this period and the disputed ideological and social constructions of the nation, race, cultural identity, and gender shaped both a nascent urban homosexual subculture and a medicolegal discourse about it. The following two chapters examine the relationship between two related developments: the growing visibility of male homosexuality in Brazil's two most important urban centers and the increase in writings about homosexuality by physicians, criminologists, and jurists. This chapter explores the physical urban spaces appropriated by homosexuals and describes the social interactions within this subculture. Chapter 3 surveys the reaction to this increasingly visible world by the medical profession, criminal anthropologists, and the state.

Changes in Brazilian Society and Culture

Urbanization and industrialization after World War I had a tremendous impact on men, women, the family, and gender relations in Brazil. Migration, immigration, and urbanization crowded hundreds of thousands of people (a majority of whom were male) into the country's major cities. The population of Rio de Janeiro jumped more than 157 percent between 1900 and 1940, expanding from 691,565 inhabitants to 1,764,141.[9] The increase for São Paulo was even greater. In 1900, the city had 239,820 inhabitants. By 1920 that figure had increased 141 percent to 579,033, and in the next two decades the population increased another 131 percent to 1,326,261.[10]

Before the war, the majority of working women employed outside their homes in nonagricultural sectors worked in domestic service. But between 1920 and 1940, the number of poor women employed in this area dropped to approximately 35 percent of all working women. Other lower-class women found jobs in manufacturing, especially textile production, and in the service sector, as salesclerks, office workers, and telephone operators. Significantly, during this period increasing numbers of middle-class women left the cloistered domestic sphere to join poor women as wage earners in providing for their own or their family's income needs. This shift in the profile of female wage earners was due in part to steep inflation and its effect on the household budget, an expanding consumer market based on industrial production, and an increased demand for women to fill service-sector jobs.[11] As a result of these changes, more middle-class women became public employees, schoolteachers, nurses, and professionals, upsetting the notion that women's primary social function was to be wife, mother, and guardian of a stable household. Whereas in the past only poor women had to balance their lives between their family and their need to obtain income by working outside of the home, now more middle-class women had to confront the contradictions between economic necessities and professional achievement on the one hand, and traditional social norms that had placed restrictions on their participation in the workforce on the other.

Both imported Hollywood films and Brazilian women's magazines glamorized modern, independent women and promoted cultural values that further encouraged women to assume a more public profile. The new women had a new look. However, "changes in fashions triggered widespread uneasiness about the apparent 'masculinization' of women and 'feminization' of men."[12] New closely cropped hairstyles for women provoked comments in cartoons and magazine articles that one could no longer distinguished a person's gender by traditional standards. During the belle époque, dandies may have suggested the emasculation of certain men. Now the differences between the sexes seemed to be doubly blurred.

All of these transformations challenged the entire gender system, especially as it was structured for middle-class women. At the same time, long-standing moral, religious, and social values pressured women to conform to their traditional roles. According to historian Susan Besse, "[r]apid change generated so many conflicting messages that men and women frequently expressed anxiety over how to adjust their values to new realities and how to define proper behavior in light of new necessities and opportunities. Women who failed to acquire a lacquer of modernity suffered ridicule and social ostracism, while those who took to heart messages that communicated the possibility and desirability of women's social, economic, and sexual emancipation were either regarded as immoral or stereotyped as ugly old battle axes. Women were expected to cultivate an outward appearance of modern sophistication while carefully preserving the 'eternal' female qualities of modesty and simplicity. They were to be both symbols of modernity and bastions of stability against the destabilizing effects of industrial capitalist development, shielding the family from 'corrupting' influences."[13]

The tension between the traditional organization of Brazilian institutions and society and the changes brought by urbanization, modernization, and industrialization manifested itself in other arenas. The 1920s and '30s witnessed a growing intervention by Brazilian physicians, jurists, and criminologists in social issues ranging from the "hygienic" function of the mother in the family to the relationship between race and crime. Social and moral concerns, these professionals argued, were not matters for the police or the church but problems to be addressed by science and medicine. With this argument, they pushed for greater influence in setting government policies and shaping public opinion. One measure of their success was the way eugenics theories imported from Europe and the United States in the 1920s and '30s were adapted to Brazilian circumstances. While contested by some physicians and other professionals, these theories dominated the thinking of the Brazilian League for Mental Hygiene and influenced leading criminologists and social anthropologists of the day.[14]

During these same years, Brazil went through a cultural renaissance that included the birth of the modernist movement and new debates on race and nationhood. Symbolic of these developments were two events that bridged a decade. In 1922, during the Modern Art Week in São Paulo, organized to celebrate the one hundredth anniversary of independence from Portugal, a group of young artists and intellectuals issued a manifesto challenging the nation to turn inward to discover the "authentic" cultural roots of Brazil. Among the innovative tenets of the movement was the idea of *antropofagia*, or the cannibalization of European culture and its reinvention within the Brazilian context. By questioning the Eurocentric orientation of cultural consumption by the middle and upper class, the movement promoted a turn to Brazilian motifs in art, architecture, literature, and music. Further reassessments about the nature of Brazilian national identity took place after the 1933 publication of Gilberto Freyre's landmark historical and sociological study, *The Masters and the Slaves*. Freyre argued that modern Brazil had been forged through the mixture and synthesis of the African, Indian, and European races and cultures.[15] This celebration of the positive aspects of miscegenation in the formation of the Brazilian nation met resistance from eugenicists, physicians, criminal anthropologists, and sectors of the elite who maintained the superiority of European influences.[16] Both the modernist movement's and Freyre's emphasis on Brazil's rich cultural and social legacy provided important ideological underpinning for nationalist sentiments that counterbalanced the Eurocentric and at times racist positions of many middle- and upper-class professionals.

These developments, namely, modernization, urbanization, and the increased medicalization of social issues, all took place in the midst of political instability that continued uninterrupted throughout the 1920s and '30s. In 1917 and 1919, anarchists and socialists led two general strikes in São Paulo. Labor unrest made it clear that industrialization and urbanization would not come without social instability. During the 1920s, young army officers staged a series of unsuccessful revolts against the government and articulated a vague program in opposition to the ruling oligarchy and in favor of reforms in the electoral process. The formation in 1927 of the electoral coalition known as the Bloco Operário e Camponês (Workers' and Peasants' Bloc), led by the newly formed and already outlawed Communist Party, added to the elite's anxiety about a restless working class.[17]

In 1930, the Brazilian economy took a tailspin as coffee prices crashed with the onset of the Great Depression. That same year, Getúlio Vargas, the unsuccessful presidential candidate and former governor of Brazil's southernmost state, Rio Grande do Sul, headed a military revolt that catapulted him into the presidency and ended the thirty-five-year political hegemony of the states of São Paulo and Minas Gerais. The internal political conflicts that ensued—the rebellion of the state of São Paulo against the central government in 1932, the failed communist insurrection of 1935, the aborted fascist coup d'état in 1938—increased concerns about the stability of the entire political and social order. The political result of this tumultuous period was the establishment in November 1937 of the authoritarian Estado Novo (New State) headed by President Vargas. The new regime quickly moved against all opposition from the left and far right, concentrated powers in the presidency, expanded the centralizing role of the state in economic and social affairs, and remained in power until the end of World War II.

How did men who developed sexual and romantic ties to other men negotiate through this whirlwind of change? How did they construct notions of gender and identity? In short, what was life like for the homosexual men who frequented the cafés, cinemas, and streets of downtown Rio de Janeiro and São Paulo?

Observing Homosexuals

Soon after Getúlio Vargas seized control of the national government in the Revolution of 1930, Baptista Luzardo, Rio de Janeiro's new chief of police, called on Leonídio Ribeiro, then a faculty member of the School of Medicine, to become the director of the Institute of Identification of the Federal District Civil Police.[18] According to Ribeiro's memoirs, "I was forced, then, to heed his appeal, based on the arguments that the Revolution needed the collaboration of apolitical technicians to carry out the work of renovating the methods of public administration in Brazil."[19] Ribeiro's task was to devise a system that would permit the new government to issue a national identification card. His role as an "apolitical" physician provided the aura of a "citizen above suspicion" to carry out this assignment. In this position, Ribeiro immediately initiated a flurry of activities. He organized the National Congress on Identification and published a magazine on the subject. He brought international experts to Brazil and held training sessions with police captains and commissioners from Rio de Janeiro, São Paulo, and Belo Horizonte. He also set up the Laboratory of Criminal Anthropology to carry out scientific experiments on civil and criminal identification.[20]

Ribeiro's efforts received international recognition. In 1933, the Italian Royal Academy of Medicine awarded him the Lombroso Prize for a three-volume report of his research in Brazil, which he duly accepted in a ceremony held in Turin in 1935. Ribeiro's prizewinning work included the results of scientific research carried out at the Institute of Identification on four diverse topics: the pathology of fingerprinting, Guarani Indian blood types, Afro-Brazilian criminal biotypes, and the relationship between male homosexuality and endocrine malfunctioning. Ribeiro recycled the main points of his study in a dozen articles published between 1935 and 1938.[21] He then compiled all of his material in *Homosexualismo e endocrinologia* (Homosexuality and endocrinology), which appeared in Brazil in 1938 and was translated into Italian and issued in Rome in 1939 and in Milan in 1940.[22] Ribeiro, who had a long and illustrious career as a member of Brazil's intellectual elite, held steadfastly to the validity of the results of his research until his death in 1976.[23]

To carry out his 1932 study, Ribeiro solicited the support of Dr. Dulcidio Gonçalves, an official of the Rio de Janeiro police force, who brought a "precious contingent" of 195 "professional" homosexuals to the Laboratory of Criminal Anthropology to be photographed and measured to determine if there were any relationship between their sexuality and their physical appearance.[24] What exactly Ribeiro meant by "professional" homosexuals is not entirely clear. Some of the men he observed might have been earning extra pocket money while working at another job during the day, as was the case with "Henrique."[25] Others might actually have been earning a living through prostitution. Many of the men picked up by the police in downtown Rio were probably socializing with friends or looking for prospective sexual partners with no thought of financial gain, but their interaction with other men in an area of the city where male-to-male eroticism was common automatically lumped them into the category of "professional" homosexuals.[26] Perhaps Ribeiro's notion of "professional"

TABLE I.   Profession of Homosexuals Studied by Ribeiro, Rio de Janeiro, 1932

Profession	Number	Percentage
Domestic professions	84	43.07
Commerce/sales	34	17.43
Tailors	17	8.71
Workers	16	8.2
Other professions	44	22.56
TOTAL	195	100

SOURCE: Leonídio Ribeiro, *Homosexualismo e endocrinologia* (Rio de Janeiro: Livraria Francisco Alves, 1938), 108.

referred to the fact that these men dedicated much of their free time to seeking out same-sex sexual partners, or that their lives revolved around their erotic desires.

Ribeiro's own statistics support the fact that most of those arrested were gainfully employed. A breakdown of their professions reveals a variety of occupations (see table 1). The large number employed in domestic services (43 percent) seems to confirm eyewitness observations made in the 1930s that many effeminate homosexuals worked in serving and cleaning positions in brothels and boardinghouses. While it is possible that some of these domestic workers may have provided sexual services alongside their domestic chores, many others (34 percent) labored in factories, sales, and sartorial activities. It is impossible to know exactly what Ribeiro's team meant by the category "other professions." If the term referred to white-collar or middle-class occupations, such as government employees, it still represents only 22.5 percent of the total number of those arrested, indicating that more than 75 percent of the young men picked up by the Carioca police came from poor or working-class backgrounds.

One should not assume that Ribeiro's subjects necessarily represented a random sampling of Rio de Janeiro's male homosexual subculture. His information, while offering a snapshot view of this world, remains skewed. Based on the criminologist's own assertion that his research subjects were "professional" homosexuals, it is possible that the police only targeted flamboyant or obviously effeminate men walking the streets of Rio de Janeiro in the known cruising areas. The overrepresentation of such men in the criminal records indicates that they were more likely to get arrested. The arrest of such men, in turn, would have conformed to social stereotypes that equated homosexuality with effeminacy. It is also probable that few middle- or upper-class men ended up in Ribeiro's final research sam-

TABLE 2.   Racial Makeup of Homosexuals Studied by Ribeiro, Rio de Janeiro, 1932

Race	Number	Percentage	Percentage according to 1940 Census
White	119	61.05	73.11
Mixed race	67	34.35	16.52
Black	9	4.60	10.07
TOTAL	195	100	100

SOURCE: Leonídio Ribeiro, *Homosexualismo e endocrinologia* (Rio de Janeiro: Livraria Francisco Alves, 1938), 107; Instituto Brasileiro de Geografia e Estatística, *Recenseamento geral do Brasil (1° de setembro de 1940)*, part 16, *Distrito Federal* (Rio de Janeiro: Serviço Gráfico do Instituto Brasileiro de Geografia e Estatística, 1951), 6.

ple. Those who might have been caught in a police roundup would have had the necessary money, connections, or social position to avoid incarceration. Taking these considerations into account, and noting that the pool of men studied came mostly from poor, working-class, and lower-middle-class backgrounds, one can still observe interesting patterns.

The racial makeup of those arrested, while mirroring census figures for Rio de Janeiro in general terms, shows more diversity than appears in the overall population (see table 2).[27] Ribeiro's statistics show that more than 60 percent of the detained homosexuals were white, and only 4.6 percent were identified as black. Ribeiro's team classified more than one third as *mestiços*, that is, as having a mixed racial background.

Racial identity in Brazil has long been complicated to codify for several reasons. Historically, there has been a cultural propensity for people to "whiten" themselves, that is, to dissociate themselves from darker-skinned members of the population, thus gaining a higher social status.[28] Moreover, the methodology of the census itself was problematic. We do not know the criteria that Ribeiro and his assistants used in determining racial categories. If they relied on the arrested person's own interpretation of his racial identity, the statistics would likely reflect the same whitening bias inherent in the census figures.[29]

Furthermore, in the 1930s, many intellectuals still maintained that it was in Brazil's best interest to have a whiter population. Given Ribeiro's own theories about the links between race and criminal behavior, it is as possible that his laboratory engaged in "de-whitening," a conscious or unconscious distortion that involved classifying men as coming from a mixed racial background when they themselves may have identified as white. Associating deviance with race and implying that dark-skinned people were

TABLE 3.   Age Range of Homosexuals Studied by Ribeiro, Rio de Janeiro, 1932

Age	Number	Percentage
20 or under	74	37.94
21 to 30	99	50.76
31 to 40	20	10.25
Over 40	2	1.02
TOTAL	195	100

SOURCE: Leonídio Ribeiro, *Homosexualismo e endocrinologia* (Rio de Janeiro: Livraria Francisco Alves, 1938), 107.

more likely to be homosexuals than were people from European backgrounds coincided with popular eugenics theories that emphasized the degenerate nature of certain races. The underrepresentation of white men in the group as compared to the overall population may have also been the result of the fact that middle- and upper-class men could have more easily avoided arrest. Conversely, the smaller number of black men may reflect a lesser degree of accessibility to the central areas of Rio de Janeiro where homosexuals socialized and, in this case, were arrested.

Of the 195 homosexuals studied, 183 admitted that they were homosexuals, while 12 denied the fact. More than 98 percent (193) were single, and only 2 were married. The age distribution of those arrested points to the youthful composition of the crowd that cruised the streets of Rio de Janeiro in the 1930s (see table 3). On the other hand, the fact that almost 40 percent of the men were twenty or younger may merely indicate that the youth involved in the downtown street scene were more vulnerable to arrest. This also may explain why almost all of those arrested were single. According to the 1920 census of Rio de Janeiro, 18 percent of men between ages sixteen and twenty-nine were married. The number increased to almost 24 percent by 1940.[30] One can only assume that married men who enjoyed sex with other men were more discreet and avoided being arrested for their "vice" in downtown Rio de Janeiro or could use their married status to differentiate themselves from others at the time the police were rounding up their subjects for this investigation.

Effeminate and "Real" Men

Ribeiro's statistical studies did not detail the life stories of the 195 individuals arrested. However, the few biographies he recorded of individuals such as Henrique indicate that these men still seemed to conform to hegemonic gender norms operative at the turn of the century. These norms divided sexual activities in traditionally gendered terms. One was either a "real" man, who assumed the penetrating role during sex, or the penetrated, "passive," and feminine receptor. Yet, as we shall see, the sexual practice of many men was much more complex than this prescribed model. Some men engaged in both "active" and "passive" sex, and thus undermined the dominant paradigm with its implicit logic of a bipolar dyad that structured sexual relations. Other "real" men did not linger in the homosexual subculture and left little information about their own notions of desire and sexual identity. More can be said about the effeminate men, who assumed a more visible profile in this urban demimonde.

Ribeiro detailed the life of one of these men, M.S., known by the feminine nickname "Marina."* According to Ribeiro, Marina had already expressed preferences and attitudes associated with girls, such as playing with dolls and enjoying domestic chores, at a young age. When he was sent to a boarding school at age twelve, he already felt strong attractions to other boys. His first sexual experience was with a school inspector, who penetrated him anally. A few years later, Marina left his family in the northern part of Brazil, moved to Rio de Janeiro, and found a job in a theater review as a dancer and member of the chorus. In Rio he met a man of a higher social status, and they initiated a six-year relationship in which Marina adopted the traditional role of a woman. He kept the household, had a wardrobe full of women's clothes, and assumed what Ribeiro considered a feminine persona: "the pleasure to serve, dedication, the spirit of sacrifice, passivity, and a sense of dependence."[31] The relationship fell apart, however, when Marina's "active partner," as Ribeiro described him, decided to get married to a woman. Marina became so severely depressed about his lost love that his former partner had to reassure him of a lasting friendship through frequent telephone conversations and long sentimental walks. He even passed by Marina's house in a car with his fiancée at his request.

In portraying the feminine personality of Marina, Ribeiro describes him as a "woman trapped in a man's body." This was precisely the way some men made sense of their attractions to other men in the rigidly gendered system of this period. Born with male genitals but sexually attracted to other men, some thought that their essence, soul, spirit, or mind was, in

---

* I have retained the gendered pronouns consistent with a person's sex unless that individual specifically uses the markers of the opposite sex when describing him / herself. I will also indicate a person's nickname or assumed persona by placing it in quotation marks the first time that it is mentioned.

fact, feminine and wrongly incarcerated in a male body.[32] Neither his probable Catholic upbringing, the social milieu of his background in rural Brazil, nor the medical profession offered Marina an alternative model of how to construct his sexual and social identity. His desire to serve, to assume the traditional role of woman in the relationship, seemed to be the only available option.

Other men from this period echoed this pervasive but not exclusive notion that same-sex relationships could only develop when the strictly divided roles of "active" manly men and "passive" feminine men were played out. Since the voices of these men were filtered through the optics of physicians who considered homosexuality a deviation, one must examine these medical and sociological reports cautiously. Nevertheless, they provide valuable clues about the lives of these men and how they constructed their gender identity.

In 1938, a group of students from the Institute of Criminology studied the "customs, habits, nicknames and slang" of homosexuals in São Paulo. Among the material collected by these field researchers was a five-page autobiography written by Z.B.G., known by the nickname "Zazá."[33] According to this story, Zazá (like Marina) comes from the countryside to the big city in 1928 to find work. And like Marina, he is first seduced by an older man and assumes the passive role in their sexual encounters. Traveling back and forth between Rio de Janeiro and São Paulo, he works as a male prostitute and provides sexual favors for "active pederasts." In using this expression, Zazá, of course, is repeating a term originally introduced into Brazil through nineteenth-century medical discourse. By the 1930s, "pederast" had become widely employed as one of several expressions to refer to men who had sex with other men. Whether Zazá actually used the term or it was "translated" from another word by the criminology students who eventually published the report, it nevertheless indicates that feminized men were not the only participants in the subculture that Zazá described. According to the narrator of this tale, men who took the "active" role in same-sex encounters sought out men rather than women, and paid for sex with them. This contradicts both medicolegal and popular constructions of what constituted normative homosexual behavior.

In 1935 Zazá falls in love for the first time. He dramatically remembers the affair: "I began to love a brown-skinned boy, with cute black eyes. And my passion grew! I was totally in love. Love is such a sublime thing. But what love, what craziness I had for him. So much jealousy! Even of his shadow. If I fought and broke up with him, it was only for a few hours because I couldn't stand the separation and soon would run back and beg him not to leave me. I would die if he were to leave me."

Zazá, like a prostitute dependent upon her pimp, supports his lover financially and even sleeps with other men whom he otherwise would have rejected so that his "man" will not lack bread to eat. However, just as Marina loses his "real" man, a "real" woman takes Zazá's partner away from him. Zazá suffers so much that he has to leave São Paulo, and he moves to the port city of Santos to forget his love. There he meets the second passion of his life: "A friend of mine told me that one passion kills another. That's what happened to me. One night, in a bar I noticed a guy who was staring at me as if I were a person he already liked. He later came up to me, politely offering his company and then his love." The affair revives Zazá: "We dated as if I were a young girl. I woke up every day to the honk of the horn of his truck because we didn't live together at the time."

Again, the relationship ends when Zazá's man leaves him for a woman. So Zazá finds a third man to live with. But after a time his second love reappears and starts following Zazá around, saying that he regrets their breakup. He also confesses that he can't get used to women. When Zazá tells the man that he no longer loves him, his pursuer pulls a knife. Zazá dramatically remembers: "At this very moment my current 'friend' came by. They got into a fight. Fortunately no one was wounded and only because of this did he stop bothering me."

The altercation transforms our narrator: "This was a memorable day for me. I could love, and I was also loved. And loved by two people because I loved only the third and was loved by him; and, the second, who still showed signs that he loved me, was so humiliated that he tried to kill me. *Senti-me mulher!* (I felt like a woman!) I don't know how to explain it. It seems to me that love between men is more violent that the love between a man and a woman; that is, when a *passivo* and *ativo* like each other, it is more than that of a man and a woman." Zazá not only identifies with the active / passive, male / female construct, but he feels that when two men engaged in such a relationship, the intensity and passion were, in fact, superior to the traditional heterosexual norm.

Following this dramatic event and a rite of passage from a "dating girl" to a "total" woman, Zazá finally finds domestic bliss. "My third love insisted on living with me as if I were a real woman: he bought cooking utensils, an iron, etc. In short, I cooked and washed as if I were a good and devoted wife." Zazá even gave up prostitution because his "husband" didn't want to share Zazá's body with others. However, this relationship also ends, and Zazá laments his fate: "I am twenty-four years old and I think that I am aging before my time due to the times I have been unjustly imprisoned and the crazy and rampant loves that I have had so that I could follow my destiny and feel what other women feel, that is, the pleasure of feeling the male member, something which I still love as I love my freedom."

Zazá's confessional tale is reminiscent of romantic pulp fiction or Hollywood B-movies of the period. The story is simple and the plot line predictable. A poor innocent country boy comes to the big city, is seduced by an older man who offers him a few presents and promises him the world. He loses his virginity and virtue and becomes a fallen man (in the imagination of Zazá, a fallen woman). The seduction scene could have come out of any Harlequin romance: "[O]ne night he grabbed me and frenzily kissed my virgin mouth, giving me the impression that everything would melt inside of me. In the heat of passion, in feeling his hot lips pressed against mine, I surrendered my body and soul, and he used my still young flesh in the way he wanted. I could have resisted for more time without doing this crazy thing. . . . But his kiss on my mouth . . . I felt incapable of defending myself from his clutches." The memories of his first passion linger even when Zazá returns to his hometown of São Carlos in the hinterlands of the state of São Paulo and is unable to have sex because he is surrounded by his family. "I didn't forget, however, that emotional pleasure, the pleasure of a man who satiated my flesh, and I was satiated with that member which had already stained the morality of a young boy."

Back in the big city and no longer pure and innocent, Zazá, the fallen heroine, now assumes a new destiny, that of the vamp, femme fatal, and streetwalker. "I became vain, even going so far as to think of myself as a woman. I plucked my eyebrows, powered my face, used lipstick, and went out onto the streets to pick up men who would go after me. Not just one. There were many." The transformation is complete. From innocent young boy he has become a painted woman with throngs of "real" men falling at his feet desirous of his feminine form.

Then comes a handsome lover, followed by another, and finally a knife fight between number two and number three. Zazá, now a medieval princess, watches over two knights flashing their lances (or knives, or phalluses) in a battle for their loved one's affection. The dispute for Zazá's hand elevates him to the status of wife as number three, the victor, sweeps Zazá away to their domestic castle where he becomes queen of the house: "It was my best 'friendship' in which I found the most happiness and in which I was more of a woman. I washed, cleaned, ironed and enjoyed as much happiness as possible because I foresaw that so many good things at the same time would naturally not last forever."

The end, too, is predictable. It is not the happy ending of most Hollywood films, but the tragic operatic finale of the lonely discarded woman, old before her time, paying for her sins. Paying for the sins of his ancestors, too, for Zazá recalls or invents an aristocratic past, which adds to the drama of his denouement: "[F]or they were barons and baronesses, while I am simply a helpless *passivo* with no hope that I won't be rejected. I am Zazá of the hot or cold nights of dear São Paulo."

Like many literary works, this one concludes with a dedication as well as a disclaimer. "I apologize to the psychiatrist for the numerous mistakes and the bad Portuguese used in this stupid and quick summary of my inglorious past. I hope that your studies go well and that you graduate without having to repeat a year." Zazá's narrative, appropriately, finishes with the words in English that closed all Hollywood movies in the 1930s: The End.

It is too easy to dismiss this story as a poor imitation of a second-rate romance that ends in self-effacing tragedy within the social constraints structured by heterosexual norms. The narrative is so melodramatic and seems so consciously fashioned to appeal to its public, in this case the inquiring eye of criminology students, that one might question Zazá's rendition of his life, just as one must look skeptically at Ribeiro's and other physicians' observations of Brazilian "pederasts." It is certainly possible that this overdrawn story is a creation for Zazá's own self-understanding, and that only through creating himself as a heroine can disparate events form a coherent account of his life. Certainly there is a confessional tone to Zazá's chronicle, as if he hopes the students of criminology in receiving the tale will understand and perhaps accept him because he has suffered so much. This story, be it an accurate autobiographic account or a fictitious rendering of a wished-for past, nevertheless suggests that Zazá and other men like him ultimately found ways to adjust to their own sexual desires and fashion their lives accordingly. The internalized self-loathing of a maladjusted "pederast" whose happiness seems ephemeral is combined with a combative spirit imbued with ingenuity, bravery, and perseverance. Zazá, like other effeminate men, assumed his identity as a "woman" with a large dose of self-confidence. While his narrative is laced with references indicating that he at times felt that his pederasty was deplorable, the overall tone of the autobiography is passionate and optimistic. Zazá's tale emphasizes that the hero(ine) has rightly lived out his destiny of feeling the physical, emotional, and spiritual pleasures of a woman.

This narrative also indicates that sexual roles among men who had sex with other men were far more complex that Zazá's understanding of his own identity, and that transgressions of the bipolar construct of *passivo/activo* or *fresco/homem* were as problematic for Zazá as homosexuality itself was for the medical observers who documented his life. Zazá expresses his own confusion and anxieties in an anecdote in his narrative. One day he decides to seek out the man who had initiated him into sex, or as he states, had "vaccinated my flesh with pederasty, disgrace, and dishonor." Surprisingly, when the man becomes aroused, he asks Zazá to penetrate him. Zazá is aghast that a "real man" who had seduced him also enjoys "passive" sex: "He cynically grabbed my member, got it hard and then demanded that I put it in his anus. I came inside of him and was dumbfounded when I realized that I had surrendered to a man who was not completely macho and was, in fact, passive, like me. Understand these men, I thought." Zazá's first sexual partner, the man whom he had fantasized about when he returned to his family in São Carlos, no longer fit into the neat social categories as either an exclusively "active" or "passive" sexual performer. He was no longer the macho "real" man of Zazá's desires. The encounter challenged basic assumptions about the supposed natural essence of the "passive" womanly man that Zazá had adopted as an integral component of his persona. He attempted to comprehend how a macho and virile "active" man could succumb to the pleasures of anal penetration and, therefore, reach beyond the "real" man/*fresco* paradigm to more fluid notions of sexual identity. One is left with the impression that Zazá was unsuccessful in the task of conceiving an alternative way of defining gender roles.

Names and Name Calling

Sometime in the 1920s, or even earlier, the term *viado* (faggot, fairy) joined the epithets *puto* and *fresco* in popular parlance as another belittling word for effeminate men who had sex with men. The term comes from the word *veado*, which is a male deer, but it acquired another pronunciation in street parlance, perhaps to distinguish the pejorative term from any reference to the animal.[34] How the term *viado* developed is clouded in mystery. One theory holds that the expression originated in 1920s Rio when a police commissioner ordered the arrest of all the homosexual men cruising in a given park (some versions name Praça Tiradentes, others the nearby Praça da República). His subordinate attempted to carry out the assignment, but he reported back to his superior admitting failure. He explained that when the arresting officers tried to apprehend the young men, they ran away like deer. The incident is said to have been covered and popularized in the press and indeed has become a gay folk myth.[35]

An example of the pejorative power of the term can be found in the records of the Pinel Sanatorium in São Paulo. On August 10, 1937, the family of Bernardino de C.A., a forty-three-year-old government worker from the city of São Paulo, committed him to the sanatorium because he was hallucinating.[36] According to the medical record, Bernardino lived alone, drank a lot, and enjoyed the city's red-light district. He was shy, but frequently would fall passionately in love with young girls, although always from a distance. At one point, he became enamored of a female prostitute who lived with another man. Bernardino was so in love with her that, afflicted and drunk, he sought out the woman's lover and tearfully confessed his passion for the streetwalker. He then managed to arrange a secret sexual liaison with her, but failed to maintain an erection and have an orgasm. The experience traumatized him, and he began to question his own masculinity. The examining physician, who recorded his story about two weeks after Bernardino had been admitted to the mental hospital, reported: "He began, then, to fear that his loved one thought he acted that way because he was an invert. This idea tormented his mind day and night." Bernardino started to imagine that people on the street knew that he was a *pederasta passivo* (passive pederast) and that the boyfriend of his unrequited love was spreading rumors of his questionable masculinity. The report continues: "[H]e began to hear voices that reached his room from the street, and which distinctly offended him, calling him the name of a certain animal, the symbol of the *invertidos*."

That animal, of course, was the *veado*. Bernardino's anxiety about the possibility that he was homosexual and that the entire society knew it drove him nearly mad. Upon allegedly hearing passersby calling him a *viado*, he sought out relatives to lodge a complaint on his behalf with the police about the "antisocial attitudes" of the pedestrians of São Paulo. Alarmed at his behavior, they took him to a physician, who recommended Bernardino's hospitalization. Diagnosed with schizophrenia, withdrawn and depressed, Bernardino remained in this private hospital a little less than a month. When he was released, the releasing physician commented in the medical record that owing to his excessive drinking, Bernardino's mental problems would probably return.

There is no indication that the hospital attempted to address Bernardino's anxieties about his sexuality and masculinity. This case, however, reveals the psychological and social mechanisms that imputed homosexuality to impotence and sexual malfunctioning. Being called a *viado* challenged Bernardino's masculinity, questioned the core of his identity, and evoked a maddening fear of rejection and marginality. Perhaps, Bernardino had, in fact, repressed homoerotic desires that led him to project his own insecurities onto others, making them the accusers of what he himself felt. We will never know. Regardless of his sexual proclivities and anxieties, the fear of being named a *viado* drove him close to insanity and revealed the power behind the expression and its implications for Brazilian men.

The word *viado* is so pejorative that alternative symbols are sometimes used to avoid the term. For example, the illegal numbers game, the *jogo do bicho* (game of the animals), which dates back to the turn of the century, uses the numbers one to twenty-five as possible bets. Each number is assigned to an animal, and twenty-four is the deer, or *veado*. Thus, if you want to insinuate that a person is a homosexual, you can use the number twenty-four and call the person *vinte e quatro*. This numerical value has such negative associations that some people will use the expression three times eight in order to avoid using the number twenty-four.[37]

Another term for effeminate men who had sex with other men, *bicha* (fairy, faggot), evolved in the 1930s.[38] While it has many other meanings, including intestinal parasite, it remains today the most common way to speak pejoratively about a gay man. As with the word *viado*, there are conflicting versions as to its origins as derisive slang.[39] A 1939 study of the social activities, customs, habits, nicknames, and slang of homosexuals in downtown São Paulo headed by Dr. Edmur de Aguiar Whitaker included a list of vernacular expressions used by the young men. Among the annotated argot were three references to the term. *Bicha* was defined as a passive pederast. *Bicha sucesso* meant a passive pederast who led the good life. *Bicha bacana* referred to a pederast with monetary resources.[40]

Was *bicha*, then, a word created by these men themselves or did it originate outside their society as an epithet designed to question masculinity and impute effeminacy?[41] One explanation for the origin of the term as an endogenous expression of the homosexual subculture is that it was a clever adaptation of the French word *biche*, a doe, a female deer. It seems plausible that the men who frequented this subculture simply made a playful twist on *viado*, adding a touch of sophistication by using a French term. Moreover, *biche* was also used in France as a term of endearment for a young woman.[42] Thus, young homosexuals might have invented a new use of the word *bicha* both as a play on words and to make light of the stinging term *viado* by adopting it as an affectionate expression to refer to other effeminate men.

Alternatively, one of some twenty-one definitions of the Portuguese word could indicate the etymology of this expression. A *bicha* also means an irritated or angry woman, and in the Northeast it is also a synonym for a streetwalker.[43] In a world of painted men and women, where joking and teasing were commonplace, it is plausible that effeminate male prostitutes could have referred to their friends and associates as *bichas* (angry women) when the latter were teasingly or actually upset. In fact, the meanings attendant on the appropriated French word *biche* may have combined with the more explosive local definitions to create a slang term laced with European sophistication.[44] Whatever the actual origin, both of these hypotheses link the expression to the social milieu from which it appears to have originated, namely the demimonde of prostitutes, pimps, rogues, and petty thieves.

Widespread use of *bicha* as a derogatory label seems to have occurred only in the early 1960s, when it began to compete with *viado* as a common way of inflicting verbal injury by outsiders. While it is perhaps impossible ever to discover the exact origin of the expression, the fact that the word *bicha* likely evolved out of the world of effeminate men and street hustlers in the 1930s adds to its symbolic potency. The voyage of the expression is revealing. Generated from within a subculture, the term was later appropriated to demean the same people who may have created it. Transmitted from a colorful semi-clandestine world of hookers and hustlers into a larger universe, it returned as an instrument of aggression, hostility, and marginality.

Like the earlier use of *fresco* and *puto*, the terms *viado* and *bicha* also served to define socially appropriate and inappropriate masculine sexual behavior. The image of the *bicha* as the limp-wristed, swishy queen became the foil that confirmed the masculinity of the heterosexual Brazilian male. The *bicha*'s transgression of gendered demarcations and the ambiguity of feminine behavior in a male body also provoked masculine anxiety and aroused the fear that the feminine in the "other" might also be in oneself. As we shall see throughout this work, images of the *bicha*, *viado*, pederast,

and homosexual become major elements in structuring the cultural definitions of Brazilian masculinity and gender.

The Bars and Cabarets of Lapa

In the 1930s, the homoerotic topography of Rio de Janeiro stretched in a
semicircle from Praça Floriano Peixoto and the Passeio Público in Cinelândia, through the bohemian and working-class neighborhood of Lapa, to
Praça Tiradentes. The two ends of this sweeping arch-shaped area, namely,
Cinelândia and the former Largo do Rossio, provided public venues for homosocial and homosexual interaction. In boardinghouses, tenement buildings, brothels, and rooms rented by the hour, Lapa offered still more private
spaces for intimate interactions, both heterosexual and homosexual. Lapa's
bars and cabarets were also sites used by men who were looking for "fast"
women and a good time as well as men desirous of sex with other men.[46]
Public employees, journalists, middle-class professionals, bohemian intellectuals, and adventurous young men from traditional families mixed freely
with small-time crooks, thieves, gamblers, pimps, *frescos*, and whores. Literary figures from the modernist movement, artists, and rising stars in
Brazilian intellectual circles, such as Jorge Amado, Cândido Portinari,
Sérgio Buarque de Holanda, and Mário de Andrade, came to the bars and
cabarets of Lapa to mingle with important names in Brazilian popular music—Noel Rosa, Cartola, Nelson Cavaquinho, Chico Alves—and hear
their latest musical compositions.[46]

   The relatively lax social environment of Rio de Janeiro's bohemian
quarter did not necessarily mean that men who sexually desired other men
were free from social hostility, or that they automatically felt comfortable
in openly expressing their homoerotic interests while carousing in Lapa or
in the surrounding districts. Mário de Andrade, a founding member of the
modernist movement and one of Brazil's most celebrated twentieth-
century authors, moved from São Paulo to Rio de Janeiro in 1938 to live in
the neighborhood of Glória, adjacent to Lapa. It was no secret among the
modernist literati in São Paulo that Mário de Andrade was a homosexual.
Indeed, the author severed contacts with Oswald de Andrade, another ti-
tan of the movement, in 1928 after Oswald, using a pseudonym, published
a reference to Mário in the *Diário de São Paulo* as "our Miss São Paulo,
translated into the masculine."[47] However, Mário de Andrade led a discreet
private life while living in Rio from 1938 to 1941, and it seems that rumors

of his sexual proclivities did not reach the ears of some of his new friends and companions in the nation's capital. Moacir Werneck de Castro, a member of a group of young Carioca bohemians who socialized with the famous Paulista writer, later recalled that he and his cohorts had no idea that Mário de Andrade had led a double life or was a homosexual. The author of the Brazilian masterpiece *Macunaíma* would spent endless hours with this new generation of aspiring writers and intellectuals of the *Revista Acadêmica* (Academic magazine), savoring their company but apparently never initiating any sexual contacts with his youthful colleagues. Yet in retrospect, when learning about Mário de Andrade's homoerotic desires, Werneck de Castro could see the profoundly homosexual content of some of his writing.[48]

Other artists, composers, and writers who frequented these bohemian sites in Rio in the 1930s and '40s achieved a relative acceptance within their social milieu while carefully guarding the secrets of their sexual desires from a wider audience. Such was the case with the singer Chico Alves, who had a "preference for boys" and who, according to one contemporary witness, didn't even bother to hide the fact that he had had sexual escapades with men in public places. The popular singer Jorge Goulart recalled how people protected the myth surrounding Chico Alves: "In our group Chico's sexual habits were openly discussed, they said that he was a *fanchono*, that he like to have sex with boys. I mentioned this fact to some people; the subject is taboo. They wouldn't allow the myth to be touched, or rather the myth couldn't stand information like that, as if it were the worst thing imaginable."[49] Alcir Lenharo, a historian of Brazilian popular singers of this period, explained that while members of a given group of Carioca bohemians might have been protective of the public image of a fellow artist or drinking partner, shielding knowledge of his homosexuality from the outside world, within their own social network, they would themselves subject the *fanchono* to ridicule and discrimination.[50]

Madame Satan, the Black "Queen" of Brazilian Bohemia

Aspiring artists and writers may have had to protect their public image and suffer the malicious comments of their contemporaries, but not all bohemian *fanchonos* hid their sexual desires from public scrutiny. Among the many colorful figures who frequented this area of Rio in the 1930s was "Madame Satã" (Madame Satan), an Afro-Brazilian who had killed more

than one man on the streets of Lapa with the deft use of his knife. His story
in some ways parallels the lives of many other young migrants who came
to Rio de Janeiro from the countryside and the Northeast in the 1920s and
'30s. Yet in other ways he stands apart from other homosexuals as a *bicha*
willing to defend himself by any means necessary against his aggressors.
Madame Satã never tried to hide the fact that he liked sex with other men.
Unlike Mário de Andrade or other prominent figures in the arts and letters,
Madame Satã came from a humble background and lived a modest life without guardians dedicated to protecting his reputation. However, because he
became a folk figure of sorts, his life has been better documented than the
lives of other young men who were observed by the investigative physicians and students of criminology of the 1930s, or the countless others who
have disappeared from the historical record.

Madame Satã was born João Francisco dos Santos on February 25,
1900, in the town of Glória do Goitá in the hinterlands of the northeastern
state of Pernambuco, one of seventeen sisters and brothers.[51] His mother,
a descendant of slaves, came from a humble family. His father, the offspring
of a former slave and a son of the local landed elite, died when João Francisco was seven. The next year, with seventeen mouths to feed, his mother
swapped her young child to a horse trader in exchange for a mare. Within
six months, João Francisco had managed to escape from this harsh appren-
ticeship by running away with a woman who offered him work as a helper
in a boardinghouse she planned to set up in Rio de Janeiro. Madame Satã
later summed up the change: "I stayed with her from 1908 to 1913 and the
difference between Dona Felicidade and Lareano [the horse trader] is that
I took care of the horses for him the whole day long and for her I washed
dishes and cleaned the kitchen, carried the prepared meals and did the shopping at the São José Market located at Praça XV. It was a full day's work. I
had no rest. I didn't earn anything. I didn't go to school, and I received no
affection. I was a slave just the same without anything a child needs."[52]

At age thirteen, João Francisco left the boardinghouse to live on the
streets and sleep on the steps of the tenement houses in Lapa. For six years
he worked at odd jobs in and around the neighborhood, from carrying gro-
cery bags from the market to selling pots and pans door to door. At age
eighteen he was hired as a waiter at a brothel, known as Pensão Lapa, the
Lapa Boardinghouse. Madames of brothels commonly hired young homosexuals to work for them as waiters, cooks, housekeepers, and even as part-
time prostitutes if a client so desired. Since many of these young men had
assumed certain traditional feminine mannerisms, it was assumed that they

could easily and efficiently perform domestic chores and live among prostitutes without creating sexual tension. Their marginalized, anomalously gendered identity comfortably coexisted with the *francesas* (French prostitutes), *polacas* (Eastern European Jewish prostitutes), and *mulatas* (women of mixed European and African descent) who worked at the many bordellos that operated in Lapa.

"Kay Francis," another young migrant from Pernambuco, had adopted the name and persona of the American film star after seeing one of her movies in his home state capital of Recife in the mid-1930s. Very effeminate and without any schooling or special skills, he recalled his experiences of looking for employment after arriving in Rio in the late 1930s: "I needed a job and my friends told me to go to see Madame X at a house of prostitution. Lots of young *bichas* worked at the brothels all over Lapa and Mangue. They would clean and cook. The madames liked them because they weren't interested in the prostitutes. When Madame X looked at me, she said that I was too nice a boy to work for her, and she got me a job as a servant in a house, so I never ended up working in whorehouse nor did I become a prostitute."[53]

Kay Francis was sent away from Lapa to avoid its corrupting influences. João Francisco, however, remained there among the winding streets, the one- and two-story buildings with their large portals and a honeycomb of rooms and apartments, and the corner bars where men gathered to drink beer and *cachaça* (a potent sugarcane rum). In this milieu, young João Francisco became a *malandro* (a rogue) and petty hustler. According to Moreira da Silva's definition in *O último malandro* (The last rogue), a *malandro* is a "cat who eats fish without having to go to the beach to catch them."[54] An old-time waiter from a Lapa bar described the Carioca rogue in more colorful terms: "A *malandro* in the old days, a real, authentic *malandro* was a man who was to a certain degree honest, full of dignity, conscious of his profession. He was always clean, wearing silk shirts with rhinestone buttons, a white tie and shoes with Mexican heels. He wore an expensive Panama hat. His fingers were full of rings."[55] João Francisco himself defined a *malandro* as "a person who joined in the singing, frequented the bars and cabarets, did not run away from a fight, even when it is with the police, did not turn anyone in, respected others, and used a knife."[56] In Rio de Janeiro where unemployment was high and poverty widespread among the lower classes, the *malandro* survived by gambling, hustling, pimping, stealing, composing samba songs, or running some small-time racket. His image suggested masculinity and virility. His weapon, the knife, was ever

ready to seal the fate of someone who had offended his honor, cheated him
in cards, or betrayed his trust. The *malandro* has become so much a part of
Brazilian popular imagination about Rio de Janeiro, that he is an obligatory
figure among the Carnival characters in every samba school parade competition.

   While João Francisco maintained the image of the virile *malandro* when
frequenting Lapa's nightlife, he continued to work in the kitchen during the
day. In 1928 he found employment as a cook's helper in another boardinghouse, where he met a young actress who enjoyed his imitations of Carmen
Miranda and other female stars.[57] Through connections, she got him a job
in a show at Praça Tiradentes, where many musical reviews were staged.
He had a small part where he sang and danced, wearing a red dress with his
long hair falling down over his shoulders. His artistic career, however, was
aborted by an incident that challenged his masculinity and created a myth
around him, a myth that subverted the popular image of the passive and
helpless homosexual.

   Years later, Madame Satã was interviewed by a journalist for a dramatized memoir of his life. According to this account, written in the 1970s,
one evening after the show João Francisco returned to his room in Lapa.[58]
It was late at night, and he decided to eat at the corner bar. While he was
drinking *cachaça* and waiting for his meal, a local policeman came into the
bar. Noticing João Francisco dressed in a fine silk shirt, stylish pants and
sandals, the night patrolman confronted him aggressively.[59] "*Viado*," he
called out. João Francisco ignored his epithet, so the man repeated it. "Is it
Carnival time, *viado?*" Again no reply from João Francisco. "Well, is it or
isn't it Carnival, faggot?" João Francisco remained silent, and so the guard
approached him and shouted: "*Viado vagabundo*" (shiftless faggot). "I just
came from work," João Francisco finally replied. The night guard retorted:
"Only if your work was getting fucked or robbing others." The name-
calling escalated into an altercation. João Francisco went to his room, which
was nearby, and returned with a gun.

   "So the faggot has returned?" the night guard challenged. "Your
mother!" shot back João Francisco. "I'll hit you for that," the guard threatened. "Try it," responded João Francisco. "And you are going to sleep in
the police station." "With your mother," answered João Francisco. A fight
ensued. João Francisco pulled his gun and shot the night patrolman dead.
Sentenced to sixteen years in prison, he was released after serving two years
based on an appeal that he had fired in self-defense. The incident and his
time in jail launched him definitively on his career as a *malandro*. His fame

as a tough, no-nonsense cop killer permitted him to work "protecting" local bars for a service fee. His reputation also provoked many confrontations with the police, who hauled him into the precinct station more than once in retaliation for the shooting of an officer of the law. Between 1928 and 1965, he spent more than twenty-seven years in prison.[60]

Although he projected a tough-guy image, his assumed name, Madame Satã, undercut the traditional association of *malandro* with manliness, evoking a figure at once mysterious, androgynous, and sinister. João Francisco dos Santos came to the name quite accidentally. In 1938 some of his friends convinced him to enter the costume contest during the Carnival ball held at the Teatro República near Praça Tiradentes. The event, promoted by the Carnival street group Caçadores de Veados (Deer [or Faggot] Hunters), was an opportunity for homosexuals to dress up in fancy drag costumes for Carnival revelry. According to Madame Satã, "it was really a contest that attracted tourists from all parts of Brazil and foreign countries. Everyone applauded a lot, and the *bichas* who participated won good prizes and got their pictures in some newspapers and became famous."[61]

João Francisco created a sequined-decorated costume inspired after a bat from the northeast of Brazil, and won first prize—an Emerson radio and a wall hanging. Several weeks later, he was arrested with several other *bichas* while strolling in the Passeio Público, the park adjacent to Cinelândia where homosexuals cruised. When the booking officer at the police station asked all of the *bichas* to give their nicknames, João Francisco stated that he didn't have one. He feared that the arresting officer would recognize him as a *malandro* and give him a hard time. Suddenly the police official remembered that he had seen João Francisco at the fantasy costume contest during Carnival. Associating the costume with the principle actress in a recently released American film with the Brazilian title *Madame Satã*, which was having a successful run in Rio de Janeiro at the time, he inquired: "Weren't you the one who dressed as Madame Satã and won the *bichas'* contest at the República this year?"[62] João Francisco had been rebaptized.

As soon as the *bichas* arrested with João Francisco were released, the story spread throughout the city. The nickname stuck, although at first João Francisco wasn't sure he liked it: "I didn't want to have the nickname of a *bicha* because I thought it would be too much of an announcement of who I was, and I got into a lot of trouble. I even hit some of the first people who called me Madame Satã. But this only made things worse. . . . And so slowly I got used to it. Later, comparing my nickname to those of others, I saw that my nickname was much more beautiful. It was distinguished."[63]

Madame Satã projected multiple, apparently contradictory images. He identified himself as a brave *malandro* who was willing to fight and even kill to defend his honor. Yet he was a self-declared *bicha*. In a 1946 court case when Madame Satã was arrested for disorderly conduct after he had been refused entrance to the Cabaret Brasil because he was improperly dressed, the police commissioner painted a detailed description of the infamous *viado:* "He is a person of above average height, rather robust and black; he dresses modestly and appears to be in good health. He is very well known in the jurisdiction of this police station, since he frequents the Lapa Plaza and its surroundings. He is a passive pederast, he shaves his eyebrows and adopts feminine ways even altering his own voice. Nevertheless, he is an extremely dangerous person since he doesn't even respect the police authorities. He has no religion. He smokes, gambles and gets drunk. His education is rudimentary. He is single and has no prodigy. He is always seen with pederasts, prostitutes and other people of low social status."[64] While Satã didn't wear rice powder makeup and rouge like Zazá and so many other *bichas*, he did alter his eyebrows to suggest a feminine look. And though the police commissioner was wrong about his gambling habits, he did capture the enigmatic combination of Madame Satã's image as a "queen" with an "altered" voice and his reputation as one of Rio's most dangerous criminals.

Satã was proud of his ability to wield a knife and win a fight, two marks of a *malandro*'s bravery and virility. Yet he openly admitted that he liked to be anally penetrated, a sexual desire that was socially stigmatized and the antithesis of manliness represented by the penetrating knife blade. While the popular respect usually afforded a *malandro* was linked to his potency, masculinity, and his willingness to die for his honor, Madame Satã simply contradicted the stereotype. He was aware of the anxiety his persona provoked, especially among the men who picked fights with him:

They couldn't get used to my bravery because I was a known homosexual. They thought that they wouldn't lose [a fight] with me and that is why they were always trying to provoke me and beat me up. On the other hand, the newspapers always emphasized my exploits precisely because I was a homosexual. What was I supposed to do? Become a coward just to satisfy these people? Let them do with me what they do to all of the other *bichas* who are beat up all the time and are arrested every week only because the police believed that *bichas* should be hit and should do the cleaning in the police stations? And for free. No, I couldn't go along with that vexatious situation. I thought that there was nothing wrong with being a *bicha*. I was one because

I wanted to, but that didn't make me any less a man because of it. And I became a *bicha* willingly, and I was not forced by others.[65]

Many different themes are woven into this statement. Madame Satã clearly identified as a *bicha*, a man who "performed" as a woman in bed: "I began my sex life at age thirteen when the women of Lapa organized bacchanals in which men, women, and *bichas* participated. . . . I was invited to some and functioned as a man and as a *bicha*. I liked being a *bicha* more and that is why I became a *bicha*."[66] He not only identified with being a *bicha*, he was proud of it. It was common practice for the police in Rio de Janeiro and São Paulo to round up homosexuals in the downtown areas and detain them for several weeks so that they could use their services to clean up the police stations. Unlike other *bichas*, who would be routinely arrested for allegedly violating article 282 of the criminal code (public assault on decency) or article 399 (vagrancy) so that the police could get them to perform domestic chores at the precinct stations, Madame Satã refused to submit to such humiliation and abuse. His rebellious attitude outraged his enemies and the police and made good copy in the press precisely because he did not conform to the standard stereotype of the homosexual.

The myths surrounding Madame Satã's prowess and bravery grew with time and even followed him into prison, where he retained widespread respect even though he was a *bicha*.[67] One memorialist, remembering the bohemian life of Lapa, related another story about the black homosexual *malandro*, portraying him as an indomitable superhero unwilling to submit to police control: "It was said that five cars from the emergency unit went to Lapa just to arrest Madame Satã. The minute they saw him, one of the officers shouted: 'Madame, get into the car and don't even scratch or you will take lead.' To which he responded, calmly: 'You can have them send more cars. Five isn't enough to pick me up.' And they had to ask for help and three more cars. And even then they had to tie him to a handcart in order to take him off to jail."[68]

Madame Satã remained defiant and proud into his old age. A journalist interviewing him in the 1970s became tongue-tied upon meeting the epic figure and only managed to address him as "Madame." "Do you want to offend me?" Madame Satã inquired. The journalist replied that he didn't and asked why. To which Satã responded: "Because my name is Satã. Your mother's a madame."[69]

What did this larger-than-life figure have in common with the thousands of young men who found their way to Cinelândia in Rio de Janeiro or similar cruising grounds in São Paulo? Despite the fame surrounding the personality he had created, Satã lived and died a poor man.[70] Like Zazá and so many others who supported themselves in prostitution or other low-paying jobs traditionally occupied by women, poverty and social marginality relegated Satã to Lapa, a rundown neighborhood, filled with brothels and bars. Satã, like Henrique and thousands of other effeminate men, could only find "legitimate" work in boardinghouses, bars, or bordellos. In a society where family and personal connections were often the path to employment, homosexuals, commonly ostracized by their relatives, had few other options. While Madame Satã's life as a *malandro* distinguished him from most other *pederastas* of Rio de Janeiro and São Paulo in the 1930s, he shared with them a carefree self-acceptance of his sexual desires. And like the man who deflowered Zazá, he transgressed the assumptions and associations of femininity and passivity that supposedly defined *bichas*.

Parks and "Pederasts" in São Paulo

Like Rio de Janeiro, the city of São Paulo went through striking changes in the first third of the twentieth century. In the 1880s, São Paulo was still a provincial town, but by the turn of century, the state of São Paulo already produced more than 65 percent of the nation's coffee and attracted hundreds of thousands of European immigrants who came to work in the coffee fields.[71] Many workers quickly gravitated to the capital, which became a bustling metropolis of multiple nationalities. A German traveler, commenting on the city's ethnic diversity in the first decade of the twentieth century, noted: "São Paulo is not a Brazilian city of 450,000 inhabitants but an Italian city of 100,000, a Portuguese city of maybe 40,000, a Spanish city of equal number, a small German city of about 10,000 inhabitants, with few of its advantages and many of its disadvantages. There are even 5,000 Syrians who alone have three newspapers in Arabic; some 1,000 French, Russians, Japanese, Poles, Turks in addition to the English, Scandinavians, and Americans in unknown numbers due to inaccurate statistics. The rest, perhaps a third of the total, must be Brazilian."[72] Like Rio de Janeiro, São Paulo also attracted hundreds of thousands of migrants from the hinterlands of the state and the impoverished Northeast. By the 1930s, it had already become the most important industrial center of nation.[74]

This rapid demographic growth provoked a corresponding physical expansion of the city. At the turn of the century, the downtown district was located in a triangular area set on higher ground, surrounded by ravines and two small riverbeds. Government buildings, the law school, banks, businesses, small workshops, and offices were crowded together in this historic city center. In 1892, the city built a hundred-meter bridge, the Viaduto do Chá, which spanned one of the ravines, the Vale do Anhangabaú, and provided easier access for trams, carriages, and pedestrians from the city's expanding periphery to the downtown area.[74] The viaduct also opened up a new commercial and residential district, where the Paulista elite constructed elegant homes and erected the belle époque-styled Municipal Theater, inaugurated in 1911. This elegant edifice became the centerpiece of bourgeois cultural life in São Paulo (see map 4).

City planners then set their eyes on improving the Vale do Anhangabaú. They wanted to integrate the ravine into overall urban renewal projects. In May 1911, Joseph Antoine Bouvard, the honorary director of architectural, urban, and circulation services of Paris, submitted a report to the city fathers of São Paulo, presenting his vision of the new urban space: "[T]he need to create free and unencumbered spaces, planted areas and air reservoirs must be always kept in mind. The number of inhabitants will

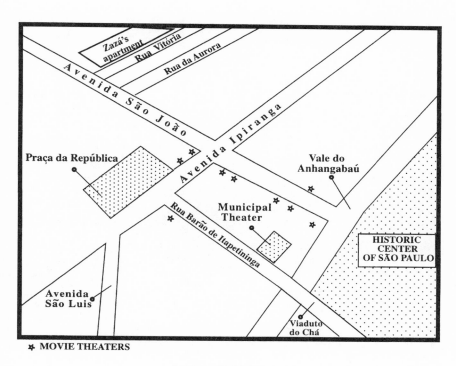

✳ MOVIE THEATERS

MAP 4   São Paulo, 1930

grow, population density will increase, as will the number of constructions; buildings will become taller and taller and, therefore, open spaces will be ever more necessary; public squares, gardens and parks will be a must."[75] The Vale do Anhangabaú was transformed into what for a time was called the Central Park of Brazil, an overenthusiastic comparison since the Paulista park was significantly smaller than the one in New York. However, the park's sweeping sidewalks and open spaces, dotted with trees, shrubs, and benches, did offer a terraced expanse at the foot of the Municipal Theater (see fig. 7).

The area quickly became a meeting ground for men interested in same-sex erotic activity. The park was located within walking distance of cheap hotels and rented rooms, and in the 1930s, by numerous movie theaters that also served as semipublic venues for homosexual activities. Brothels, boardinghouses, and tenement buildings sprang up in the areas nestled between the historic and new city centers and the residential neighborhoods beyond them. Nearby Paissandú Square attracted a bohemian crowd much like Lapa in Rio de Janeiro.[76] Propriety and impropriety, bourgeois respectability and erotic homosociability coexisted precariously in this urban landscape.

Another cruising area in São Paulo was Avenida São João. The avenue radiated out from the historic center and Anhangabaú Park through a com-

FIGURE 7   The Vale de Anhangabaú Park in downtown São Paulo was a favorite site for same-sex cruising and socializing in the 1920s and 1930s. Photograph courtesy of the Arquivo do Estado de São Paulo.

mercial center to residential neighborhoods. In the mid-1930s, entrepreneurs began to build a string of luxury movie theaters along the avenue near the downtown area. By 1945, São João was known as the Cinelândia of São Paulo, with six of the city's ten most important theaters dotting the thoroughfare.[77] Immediately beyond this entertainment area was a "transition zone" between the city center and the surrounding residential neighborhoods.[78]

In a 1935 economic and social study of the utilization of Avenida São João, Lucila Herrmann described the zone: "It is an area of great material mobility, movement, changes in residency. . . . Individuals in this area don't feel trapped by economic ties (real estate property, stable employment, etc.). Only the prostitutes, we can say, find affinity and a professional center there. But they do not have the freedom to choose as do other social groups because they are constantly controlled by the *polícia de costumes* (vice squads) and are frequently forced by the authorities to move to other zones. [The people living in this area] don't have social ties (family, relatives, social relations, a sense of neighborliness, human respect, associations, etc.); and, therefore, they feel more independent to move around." While Herrmann may have underestimated the social cohesion and solidarity of the prostitutes of the area, she pointed out an interesting connection between mobility and social tolerance. Noting that the district contained a mosaic of religions, cultures, political ideas, nationalities, colors, and races, Herrmann argued that this diversity, coupled with a disposition for mobility, created a "mental propensity toward a rapid acceptance of innovation and a minimum fixation on taboos, conventions, and common moral codes."[79] This may be one of the reasons why young homosexuals gravitated to the area. Prostitutes, stigmatized and marginalized by Paulista bourgeois culture and morality, would logically identify with, or at least show less hostility toward, *bichas*, who also faced social prejudice and had a pariah status.

Mapping the sexual topography of the area is somewhat problematic. According to Herrmann's analysis of census statistics for the area around São João Avenue, 32 percent of the population were foreigners, 52 percent men, 72 percent single adults, and only 6 percent of the residents were children.[80] Of course, not all of the single men were homosexual nor all of the single women prostitutes, but the small number of children and the high percentage of single adults is consistent with the 1938 study by the team of students from the Institute of Criminology of the State of São Paulo who examined the "customs, habits, nicknames and slang" of homosexuals in

São Paulo. Most of the homosexuals interviewed lived in this zone. "Gilda de Abreu," Zazá, and "Tabu" all rented modest rooms in the same building on Rua Vitória. Gilda and Zazá lived alone while Tabu shared quarters with a friend, "Preferida." Gilda also rented a room up the street where he took his paying partners for sex. "Damé," a tailor by trade, occupied a more comfortable apartment nearby. He made clothes exclusively for prostitutes, and also sublet furnished rooms in his apartment to female streetwalkers.[81]

São João Avenue and the Anhangabaú Park were not the only public places where homosexuals congregated in downtown São Paulo in the 1930s. Another site was the elegantly landscaped Praça da República, located near both the bordellos and the bourgeois shopping area along Barão de Itapetininga Street.[82] On the other side of the historic city center, the park known as the Jardim da Luz and the public bathroom in the adjacent Estação da Luz also attracted heavy traffic in men seeking sexual contacts with other men.[83] Amid the crowds of passengers coming and going, one could loiter in the park across from the train station without attracting too much attention from the police. The restroom in the São Paulo train station, as in the Central Terminal in Rio de Janeiro, provided a somewhat dangerous but promising location for identifying other men interested in sex. Lingering at a urinal, touching or stimulating one's genitals, and conveying other signals of interest and availability became a quick and anonymous means of attracting a potential sexual partner. Public restrooms offered easy accessibility to a large number of men in a relatively private space for quick erotic contacts.[84] Men who did not identify themselves as homosexual yet who enjoyed homoerotic activities could find willing partners in this venue.[85] Cheap hotels and brothels that surrounded the train station then afforded a more private site to enjoy mutual desire.

Movie Theaters and Movie Stars

Sexual encounters in public parks and bathrooms ran the risk of police arrest for "public assault on decency." Therefore, men also appropriated a more discreet public site to meet potential partners. The darkness of the cinema house, the focused attention of the audience on the silver screen, and the luxurious and expansive multiple waiting rooms, hallways, and bathrooms typical of the modern movie palaces provided an ideal location for same-sex erotic adventures. One could escape from work for an hour or two during the day and engage in a clandestine and anonymous liaison in this dimly lit space. For the "real man" who enjoyed sex with a *bicha*, for the person with ambivalent or confused feelings about sex with other men, and for the person not yet acculturated to the sexual topography of Rio de Janeiro or São Paulo, movie theaters became exemplary spaces to engage in covert sexual activities. Because they were located near the areas where many of the men lived, the movie houses of Cinelândia in Rio de Janeiro and the elegant new theaters near Avenida São João in São Paulo became preferred homosexual venues. Movies were also one of the most popular forms of entertainment for low-income people.[86] The relatively cheap admission price made movie theaters one of the most accessible semipublic places for men with few economic resources to have sex with other men.

Henrique mentioned that his first same-sex erotic activity had taken place in a movie theater.[87] "Jurema" admitted that he sometimes went to the movies to pick up "active" partners. In the darkness of the theater he would *fazer crochet* (literally, "do crochet"), that is, reach out and touch another man's crotch to show he was interested in sex.[88] These anonymous sexual encounters could end in mutual masturbation, in intercourse if conditions permitted, or at a cheap hotel outside of the theater.

Homosexuals, however, did not only go to the cinema for sex. Brazilian, American, and European movies played an important role in their lives in other ways. Kay Francis, who was born João Ferreira da Paz in the small town of Agua Preta in the backlands of the state of Pernambuco in 1912, grew up in abject rural poverty. In 1932, he had moved to Recife, the capital of the state, to work as a house servant. He went to the cinema quite frequently and became fixated on Kay Francis, one of Hollywood's most highly paid stars of the 1930s. Sixty years later he still built his persona around this 1930s actress. Remembering the magic of her image projected onto the silver screen, he explained: "I wanted to be just like her. She was so glamorous. So I began to imitate her."[89] For the next half century, whenever he had the opportunity, João Ferreira da Paz became Kay Francis. During Carnival, at friends' parties, and later at drag contests in Rio de Janeiro in the 1950s, he transformed himself into a dazzling copy of the Hollywood screen star. The Brazilian Kay Francis explained that his U.S. counterpart captured his imagination because she had suffered so much in her movie roles yet always remained elegant and glamorous.

Movie magazines, such as *A Cena Muda* (The silent scene) and *Eu Sei Tudo* (I know it all) and popular illustrated weeklies such as *O Cruzeiro* closely followed the lives of Hollywood movie stars, as well as the lives of Brazilian radio singers and actresses. These publications set standards for fashion, makeup, and hairstyles, all of which were closely imitated by their readers. Movies and magazines provided the opportunity to develop a more intimate relationship with the representations of feminine beauty, style, and grace they brought to life. The photographic eye of the students of the Institute of Criminology captured this relationship between young homosexuals and famous models and actresses. Thus, among the modest decorations in Zazá's sparsely furnished room they observed four framed photographs of female stars hanging on the walls over the bed. A pile of women's magazines lay stacked on the floor. Damé's more elegantly decorated room, filled with a queen-size Turkish bed covered by a lace bedspread, also contained nicely framed pictures of movie stars, both male and female, along with portraits of members of his family.[90]

Notions of the feminine ideal, of course, differed. Pernambuco-born Kay Francis looked toward Hollywood. The cross-dressing prostitute Gilda de Abreu fashioned himself after a national female star, whose name she appropriated. "Lena Horne," a friend of Madame Satã's, chose the African American singer and actress as a model.[91] Kay Francis identified with the pain and suffering of the aristocratic women played by her Hollywood double. Gilda de Abreu applied her meticulously painted lips according to her idol's cosmetic choices.[92] One can imagine that Lena Horne took pride in identifying with a famous film star and female singer of African ancestry. Romantic male actors could also provoke fantasy and sexual desire. Alfredinho, for example, fell in love with the strong, masculine actors in the movies he had first seen as an adolescent.[93] Because of the popularity of the silver screen during this period, these cinematic representations, both imported and Brazilian, became powerful reference points for Carioca and Paulista homosexuals as they shaped and reinforced standards of masculinity and femininity.

Boardinghouses and Brothels

While the street offered various opportunities for sexual adventure as well as a venue for socializing and popular entertainment, an apartment or rented room could become a refuge from social censure and police harassment.[94] In the confines of a modestly furnished room or in a well-decorated apartment, these men provided each other with moral support and companionship. They could invite friends over to gossip, exchange clothes, and plan an evening's outing. They could also experiment with putting on makeup or wearing women's garments. Gilda preferred visiting friends to spending too much time on the street, where he was teased and tormented. In the privacy of his room, he was free to wear a low-necked evening gown that left his body feeling naked. "Conchita," while relatively discreet in public, preferred to dress as a woman in the room that he rented in a boardinghouse. In pictures taken by the students of criminology, Zazá dressed for the camera in an evening gown. His friend Tabu modeled in women's undergarments.[95] These men created their own *casa* (home) and network of friends, which oftentimes supplanted the support system of the traditional Brazilian family.

Housing was a problem for men with limited economic resources, who maintained distance from their families, or who simply wished to live close to the Anhangabaú Park and other downtown cruising areas. As São Paulo grew and middle- and upper-class families moved further away from the city's center, older large houses were converted into *pensões* (boardinghouses) or *cortiços*, residences broken up into individual dwelling units in which entire families might occupy a room or two.[96] These spaces offered inexpensive lodging for families who had recently migrated to São Paulo as well as for single men and women.

Most *pensões* were sex-segregated to protect the "morality" of young working girls, living in the big city far away from families and relatives. However, many boardinghouses for women served as covers for brothels. In 1934, for example, the São Paulo police registered 283 such houses throughout the city.[97] Thus, as a means of clearly maintaining the moral propriety of an establishment, the manager of a "decent" *pensão* for women would not let men visitors into the boardinghouse unless closely supervised. Likewise in *pensões para cavalheiros* (boardinghouses for gentlemen) female visitors were not allowed. This practice of male-only housing, however, provided a convenient cover for young men who wanted to escape the watchful eye of their families, neighbors, and others. Since it was not unusual for two or more men to share a room in a *pensão,* a landlady was less likely to question two males seeking joint lodging, especially if neither were excessively flamboyant or feminine. Such was the case of two young schoolteachers who fell in love and moved to a rented room in the working-class neighborhood of Braz in 1935.[98] Other buildings, known as *rendez-vous* or *hospedarias,* provided cheap rooms for both homosexual and heterosexual sexual liaisons. This is the type of establishment to which Henrique took his sexual partners in Rio de Janeiro.[99]

Working for a Living

A person from a humble background, with no support from his family and who acted too effeminate, had few employment options. Many men, there-

fore, took jobs in boardinghouses, where they could assume roles traditionally assigned to women as cooks, waiters, and cleaners. In Rio de
Janeiro, both Madame Satã and Henrique supported themselves this way.
Others found work as assistants in one of the many brothels that served the
growing male population of São Paulo. "Flor de Abacate" worked as a
cleaning person in one such establishment. On occasion, owners of other
houses of prostitution would contact him for sex with a customer who
didn't want to be seen picking up another man on the street.[100]

Male prostitution, as a source of income, was not a lucrative profession
for effeminate men. Gilda boasted to the inquisitive students of the São
Paulo Institute of Criminology that while working as a clerk in Rio de
Janeiro, he had done quite well, owning an apartment with luxurious accommodations, several suits, and a radio. Whether this story of economic
success was true or not, in São Paulo Gilda had gone through hard times
while working as a male prostitute. He nevertheless insisted that he did not
want to change his life because he loved "pederasty."[101]

Tabu also worked as a prostitute. He had come to Rio de Janeiro from
Bahia at the age of sixteen with a Portuguese man who supported him until the man's company transferred him back to Portugal. While in Rio de

FIGURE 8   Tabu and Zazá, two Paulista homosexuals interviewed by medical students in the
1930s. Reprinted from *Arquivos da Polícia e Identificação* 2, no. 1 (1938–39), between 250 and 251.

Janeiro, the police arrested Tabu, and he was photographed as one of the subjects in Leonídio Ribeiro's 1932 study of homosexuality. He then moved to São Paulo where he supported himself by picking up men and taking them to a room he rented exclusively for his paying partners. Tabú's friend Zazá also worked as a male prostitute in a *hospedaria* (see fig. 8). Dozens of other homosexuals also resided in this boardinghouse. Some were old and infirm and lived off the charity and generosity of other renters.[102]

Sex with male prostitutes ran risks for "real" men, who might find themselves involved in a setup known as *conto do suador*, literally, "the story of one who sweats." The medicolegal expert Edmur de Aguiar Whitaker described what could happen: "A passive pederast invites a given individual who he accidentally meets on the street to engage in homosexual practices with him and takes him to his room (or to the room of a friend). With the previous agreement of other friends, one of them hides in the room under a table covered with a cloth that is long enough to cover the furniture down to the floor. The victim puts his clothes on a chair near the said table which is between the chair and the bed. He lies down with his head toward the table. While he engages in homosexual practices, the hidden individual examines his wallet and removes its contents. Only later does the victim discover the robbery since the wallet was put back in the pocket."[103] Whitaker reported the case of a twenty-three-year-old tailor from São Paulo who received a six-month sentence for a *conto do suador* robbery. On July 13, 1934, the young man had invited another man, referred to as B. de G., to the residence of two friends. While the young tailor had sex with the victim, his two friends stole his wallet. Afterward, the three split the money. Two were caught by the police soon thereafter, while the third escaped to Rio de Janeiro.

Another convicted thief, E.L., worked as a waiter in São Paulo. He was nine years old when he first had sex with another male. At age seventeen he engaged in anal sex for the first time. His father discovered his activities and forced him to marry. After begetting two children, he left his wife to seek a male partner. Between 1935 and 1937, the police arrested him nine times for robbery and pederasty. He spent time in the state penitentiary for a 1935 conviction of *conto de suador*. E.L. explained that he and a friend had robbed the man he had had sex with because they had been unemployed at the time.[104]

These stories reveal two aspects of the marginality of the homosexual subculture as it is unveiled in the documents. On one hand, social ostracism pushed many into urban areas teeming with illicit activities. Difficulties in finding employment led some to prostitution and petty theft. Getting paid to have sex with a man and then stealing his wallet was, for at least a few, part and parcel of scraping together a living, particularly in the 1930s, when the Brazilian economy was still suffering the effects of the worldwide depression. On the other hand, those who sought out sex among the brothels and boardinghouses in the downtown areas of the city also faced danger if they relied on sex with a male prostitute or a new acquaintance as a means of satiating erotic desires. Moreover, many victims of the *conto de suador* could not go to the police because it would mean explaining how they had found themselves in such a compromising position. Thus, married men and those who feared exposure of their homosexual trysts were particularly vulnerable when they dared to spend an hour or a night with a painted man.

A Hint of Rice Powder, a Touch of Rouge

Gilda de Abreu, who fashioned his persona after the famous Brazilian film star of the 1930s, lived near the brothels, cinemas, and cruising grounds of the Vale do Anhangabaú. A migrant from the northeastern state of Bahia, Gilda had first moved from his hometown to Rio de Janeiro at age seventeen. During the day, he worked as a clerk in a store. At night, he went out to find male sexual partners. At age eighteen he decided to give up "the life" and find a girlfriend, but he returned to same-sex relations two years later because he realized that he preferred sex with men. Moving to São Paulo in the early 1930s, he supported himself working as a prostitute. Gilda lived in a modest room. The furniture consisted of a bed, a rough table, and a chair. On the wall there were pictures of movie stars and a few wall pegs to hang his clothes. For entertainment, he went out to the movies or to visit other homosexuals in the neighborhood. He preferred not to walk on the street during the day because he had plucked eyebrows, and long hair in the style of a woman. He also walked in an effeminate way. His exaggerated way of dressing was generally noted and caused scandals, catcalls, bad names, and run-ins with the police. Around six in the evening, he would have dinner and then go out to Anhangabaú Park to find "active" partners.[105]

The use of suggestive feminine fashion, makeup, plucked eyebrows, and nonmasculine nicknames was common among *bichas* in the 1930s. The adoption of a female nom de guerre, such as Gilda, Zazá, Tabu, Marlene, Conchita, and Damé, as well as other traditional gendered indicators, expressed the pervasive notion that homosexuals were cross-gendered beings. For those who worked as prostitutes, traditional female fashion markings

served as a signal of sexual availability. For those who found other types of
employment that permitted some degree of gender transgression in dress
and appearance, unconventional self-presentations helped define an identity that corresponded to Brazilian society's standard portrayal of women.
These pervasive feminine representations also implied a light-hearted, exaggerated, satirical mimicry of the qualities these effeminate men actually
possessed or thought they should possess. However, for those men who had
to hide their sexual desires most of the time, an evocative nickname shared
among friends or a discreet layer of rice powder and a touch of rouge applied just before a Saturday night stroll through the Anhangabaú Park provided a suggestion of the feminine while preserving an overall masculine
representation.

Cross-dressing in public constituted a violation of the criminal code
until 1940. Appearing on the street in drag or in excessively feminine apparel and makeup could provoke an arrest and an extended stay in jail.
Therefore, many men wore masculine attire but subverted it to imply feminine fashion. Gilda, for example, would wear a short suit jacket with a tight
waist. Zazá, when dressed in a suit, also favored an exaggerated style. He
used a short jacket and high-waisted pants that were narrow in the hips and
wide in the hem. Describing Conchita, a tailor by profession, the students
of the Institute of Criminology noted that his raiment and personal grooming were less flamboyant than his friends', with only one slight exception:
"His style of dress, unlike other pederasts that hang around the Anhangabaú Park, reflects a certain amount of good taste, following the fashion without exaggerating. He dresses well and with sobriety. He doesn't use
makeup or pluck his eyebrows, merely applying a light layer of rice powder on his face." Damé, who like Conchita worked as a tailor, also dressed
in suits with a masculine cut and without an exaggerated style. He admitted, however, that he wanted to dress in women's clothes, but did not do so
in order to avoid embarrassing his family. We don't know if Conchita used
a hint of powder to suggest identification with the feminine, sexual availability, or both. However, when pressed with the question of why Kay
Francis and her friends in Rio de Janeiro liked to wear rouge, rice powder,
and makeup on the streets in the 1930s, he replied more pragmatically: "It
made me look good."[106]

The fear of losing one's employment or having problems with neighbors also motivated many young men to exercise caution in their behavior
and dress. Jurema, a nineteen-year-old office worker, had run away from
his parents' house in order to have more freedom. He lived with a friend

near the downtown area. However, no one at his office or in his apartment building knew that he was a "pederast" nor did he want them to know. Jurema dressed according to the latest fashion without any exaggerated flares, and he did not use make-up. Nor did he dress up as a woman, because the first time he had done so, he was arrested by the police and spent time in jail.[107] Feminine markers, of course, could result in social ostracism, especially if a person lived with family or relatives. Conchita, whose parents resided in the port city of Santos, left home so as not to cause problems with his family.

Unconventional dress could even lead to hospitalization in a mental institution. The father of a twenty-nine-year-old lawyer from Rio de Janeiro committed his son to the Pinel Sanatorium, a private mental hospital in São Paulo, because the young man was "excessively concerned about his looks," spent "four or five hours in the bathroom 'fixing himself up,'" and "stayed out late at night." According to his medical report in the mental hospital file, the young lawyer used lipstick, a toupee, and shaved the hair on his chest and abdomen. The administering physician ordered electroshock treatment for six weeks in order to correct his behavior.[108]

Not all men who openly admitted their sexual attraction to other men used feminine markers to identify themselves to potential partners. Alfredinho, who had a masculine nickname and worked as a printer, dressed in ordinary men's clothes and did not use any makeup. He came into contact with the interviewers through an accidental meeting at the house of a friend who lived in the red-light district. Single and twenty-four years old at the time he was interviewed, he lived with his family in the working-class neighborhood of Braz. Alfredinho reported that he didn't attempt to pick up *ativos* on the streets because he came from "an honest family" and had many acquaintances who, presumably, might recognize him. Because the Anhangabaú Park was known as a public venue for *viados*, Alfredinho did not wish to risk being seen there; it would only cause tensions with his family and friends.[109]

Men like Alfredinho, who enjoyed sleeping with other men yet did not conform to common stereotypes of effeminate "pederasts," are only rarely represented in accounts of the homosexual subculture of São Paulo in the 1930s. It is possible to speculate that such men were relatively few. However, it is more likely that homosexual men like Alfredinho, who did not dress effeminately and who avoided those areas of the city where they might be recognized and associated with "immoral and improper" behavior, were generally invisible to outsiders, who sought obvious markers to identify "pederasts" in places where they reputedly congregated. Indeed, Alfredinho only appears in the 1939 study by chance and not because of any systematic sampling done by the students of criminology. Given the amount of evidence available, it is impossible to reconstruct an accurate profile of all of the types of men who engaged in homoerotic activities during this period. Neither is it possible to develop a precise assessment of the relative proportion of those whose behavior, identity, and social life conformed to patterns more similar to Gilda's than to Alfredinho's. The historical documents at hand, however, do at least reveal that the constructions of gender identity, sexual behavior, and social interactions were much more variegated and complex that the Brazilian social scientists of the 1930s would lead the reader to believe.

Although Brazilian popular notions of gender transgression divided men into "passive," effeminate *bichas* and "active," "penetrating," "real" men, individuals in the 1930s did not neatly conform. First of all, why did some "real" men prefer *bichas* to women? One possibility might have been that morally upright women were not easily available for sexual pleasures. With a premium placed on a woman's virginity, some "real" men might have been forced to seek out effeminate men as temporary sexual replacements. Francisco Ferraz de Macedo in 1872 explained the proliferation of sodomy in imperial Rio de Janeiro using that logic. Why, then, did *ativos* choose Zazá or Gilda de Abreu over a female prostitute who lived in the same neighborhood? Male prostitutes seemed to earn about the same as female prostitutes and maintained a similar precarious standard of living, and therefore it would not have been cheaper for a financially strapped man to choose a *bicha* over a woman.[110] Nor is there any indication that the men who sought out male prostitutes were particularly poor. If that were the case, the allegedly common crime of *conto do suador* would have been a highly unprofitable endeavor for those who entertained male clients. I would argue instead that some "real" men discovered a special attraction to men with soft features, plucked eyebrows, and rouged cheeks, that their desire stretched beyond the pragmatic necessity of obtaining a body, any body, to penetrate for sexual pleasure.

The logic behind the notion of the universality of the "real" man/ *bicha* paradigm also implies the inviolability of the "active" sexual role of the "real" man. Even though some "real" men might have chosen males over females because of specific desires attached to men's bodies as opposed to women's bodies, these "real" men, so the argument goes, still performed the role of penetrator. Once again, reality proves richer than the construct.

"Flor de Abacate" lived with a truck driver for two years and then with a lieutenant in the Special Police. Presumably, his two lovers were "real" men who penetrated him sexually. However, when interviewed by the students from the Institute of Criminology, Flor de Abacate was living with and presumably having sex with a female prostitute.[111] Zazá was shocked when his first sexual partner later wanted to switch roles and be penetrated instead of taking the role of penetrator. Alfredinho surprised the investigating students because although he began his same-sex erotic activities penetrating his partners, he soon permitted others to penetrate him. Alfredinho's situation was described in the following terms: "We should note that when he entered this milieu, he did so as an active pederast; he even got venereal disease twice by maintaining relations with passive pederasts. He continued to frequent the milieu and later with time he inverted and became passive. The most interesting characteristic of this pederast is the circumstance of being passive and active at the same time. He frequently maintains sexual relations with women like any normal man. . . . Yet he says that when he sees a strong, good looking lad he likes to have relations with him."[112] Madame Satã also created social anxiety because he didn't neatly fit popular notions of "appropriate" sexual behavior of *bichas*. He was aggressive and violent, two markers of masculinity, yet he openly admitted his desire to be penetrated by other men.

Because the criminologists, physicians, psychiatrists, and jurists who investigated and wrote about homosexuality in the 1930s based their thinking on the overarching theory of the immutability of the active / passive, *homem / bicha* model, they usually failed to take notice of men who didn't fit into the mold of the effeminate male. The men who were vulnerable to arrest and the disciplining power that resulted from the medicolegal observations conducted under police supervision were visible precisely because they transgressed gender norms. By circulating in areas of the city where homosociability could result in same-sex erotic liaisons, by exhibiting signs of effeminate behavior, or by engaging in public sexual acts, Ribeiro's subjects became the objects of "scientific" investigation regarding homosexuality. The results of his study are predicated on examining those who to some degree already conformed to a preconceived notion of homosexual behavior. In the next chapter, we will examine the ways in which the predisposition on the part of professionals to think in gendered terms shaped the official discourses about homosexuality and the actions of the state.

CHAPTER THREE

～

Control and Cure:
The Medicolegal Responses

On January 16, 1935, police officers escorted Napoleão B., a twenty-five-year-old single man and a teacher by profession, to the Pinel Sanatorium in São Paulo.[1] When admitted to the hospital he was in sound mental health, although he was a bit agitated because his father had ordered him committed. According to the physician's entries on the admission forms, Napoleão, with the aid of his sister, had founded a private school that had prospered. Several months prior to Napoleão's hospitalization, he had dispensed with his sister's services and begun to rely solely on the advice of another teacher, João Cândido F., age twenty-eight, who assisted him in running the school. Soon thereafter Napoleão moved out of his parents' home to share a rented room with João Cândido in a working-class neighborhood of São Paulo. Suspecting that their son had been engaging in homosexual practices with João Cândido, Napoleão's parents had him committed.

Unlike most records from this mental hospital, which only contain the case history, psychiatric observations, and results of medical tests, Napoleão's folder includes three handwritten letters. The first is dated January 25, 1935, nine days after the police brought him to the hospital, and is addressed to João Cândido. The hospital intercepted the letter, which was never delivered. It reads in part, "Friend and brother F.: Don't give up hope, please understand that everything that is happening is due to my family. Don't let anyone take over the administration of the school. I have given you the necessary authorization. You should run it, whatever happens." Napoleão then went on to give his friend some advice about getting legal assistance and paying the school employees. He continues: "F., I miss you so much that I can't stand it, but I have the courage to suffer and fight come what may. Only death will separate us. [Signed in English] Your, your brother and friend. Napoleão. Send my regards to everyone." He then adds in Portuguese: "Don't telephone or send letters here because if they discover that people outside of the family know I am here they will send me to some other place. Don't even tell anyone the manner in which your received this letter."

Although his correspondence was intercepted, Napoleão managed to hire a lawyer, who sued his father to obtain Napoleão's release. According to a newspaper account of the trial, Dr. Antônio Carlos Pacheco e Silva, in his capacity as the director of the sanatorium, testified on behalf of the family and defended the medical necessity of Napoleão's hospitalization.[2] The judge threw out the patient's petition to be released, and Napoleão remained in the hospital for another seven months.

The last entry in his medical records hints that Napoleão, after losing the legal battle with his family and the hospital, entered a mild state of depression: "At first he rebelled against his hospitalization. Seeing, however, that his efforts and those of the friend who was interested in his release brought no results, he adjusted to the situation. Other than a certain apathy and indolence there is nothing else to be said about his stay in the Sanatorium other than that he said that he regretted his conduct and was willing to change after returning to normal life."[3] Ironically, Napoleão was released on September 7, 1935, Brazilian Independence Day. We do not know if he went back to his friend João Cândido or if he tried to "change." Perhaps pressures exerted on him by his family, society, and the state weighed too heavily on him, and he abandoned his relationship with his "friend and brother."[4]

Napoleão and João Cândido's ordeal is emblematic of the different ways in which the medical profession, legal and psychiatric institutions, the family, and social pressures came to bear on men who engaged in homosexual practices in the 1930s and 1940s. Traditional moral codes, backed by the Catholic Church, condemned homosexuality. Professional experts considered same-sex erotic behavior to be pathological, requiring medical or psychological assistance to modify the conduct and cure the individual. Many family members attempted to repress and control what they considered inappropriate and embarrassing behavior of relatives who engaged in "perverse" sexual relations. When they failed, they sometimes resorted to the intervention of the state. The police, courts, and the medical profession acted in a concerted manner to contain and control this "deviancy." Presumably, these institutional pressures to discourage homosexual activities served to discipline and demoralize some individuals who ended up retreating into heterosexual "normalcy." Others, however, like Napoleão and João Cândido, attempted to resist, if only for a time. Still others seemed to have gone through their hospitalization relatively unchanged and continued to express their homosexual desires during their confinement and after they were released "uncured."

The Medicolegal Preoccupation with Homosexuality

The crisis in the political regime in the 1920s, coupled with problems related to urbanization, industrialization, modernization, and after 1930, the Depression, all provoked a sense of turmoil in Brazilian society. General strikes, labor unrest, the rise of communism and fascism, the shifting position of women, debates about race and nationhood, discontent among young military officers and sectors of the middle class, and the rise of Vargas to power in 1930 were merely some of the manifestations of the conflicts straining the fabric of Brazilian society. Although the increasing visibility of a homosexual subculture in Brazil's largest urban centers might have gone unnoticed by many people living through these trying times, it nevertheless provoked interest and alarm among members of the medicolegal profession. The young men from the downtown areas of Rio de Janeiro and São Paulo studied by Ribeiro, Whitaker, and other physicians and criminologists represented uncontained sexuality. The effeminate manners of many of these men and their apparent unwillingness to conform to traditional representations of masculinity upset normative gender roles. Moreover, new European theories about the origins of homosexuality suggested that these men's behavior was due to congenital hormonal imbalances. Just as the Brazilian social body of the 1920s and '30s was "out of control" with political and social unrest, so, too, it seemed, was the physical body of the homosexual, whose malfunctioning hormonal system caused immoral and degenerate behavior and whose comportment defied established standards of masculinity and femininity.

Throughout this period, those who studied the apparent increase in manifestations of homosexuality offered various means to contain or cure sexual "perversion," including an expanded role of the state in responding to this social pathology. The positivist tradition in Brazil, which emphasized applying "science" to further social progress while at the same time maintaining an orderly society, supported the state's intervention in solving social ills.[5] Accordingly, this philosophy, which still served as the ideological framework for most professionals in the 1920s and '30s, legitimized the role of physicians, jurists, and criminologists in their attempts to discover and study illnesses as well as propose cures as a means of promoting a vigorous and healthy nation. The positivist tradition also served as a backdrop to debates about race, eugenics, gender roles, the place of women in Brazilian society, and the causes of homosexual degeneration.

Within this context, proposals by eugenicists for prenuptial examinations and for restrictions on immigration based on racial selection, as well as campaigns against alcoholism, emphasized the beneficial role of the state in controlling social degeneration. In her study of eugenics in Latin America, Nancy Leys Stepan argues that soon after the 1917 general strike, in which forty thousand workers paralyzed the city of São Paulo, Brazilian medical doctors made the first formal call for eugenics as a "suprapolitical, medical path to ease the social tensions within a rapidly growing, urban population. . . . The threat of urban unrest called into question the adequacy of old-style, laissez-faire liberalism for solving social problems and suggested new roles for the state in regulation of relations between workers and owners and even in intervening directly in social life."[6]

Although not all of the professionals who studied homosexuality backed the array of proposals presented by the eugenics movement in Brazil, they shared the perspective that the medical and legal professions as well as the state should play an increased role in addressing social problems. As far as many upper and middle-class doctors and lawyers were concerned, communists, fascists, criminals, degenerate blacks, immigrants, and homosexuals had to be contained, controlled, and, in the case of homosexuals, cured if possible. The 1930s, therefore, became a testing ground for how best to purify the Brazilian nation and heal it of its social ailments.

In this chapter, I examine the different theories about homosexuality discussed among the small number of physicians, jurists, psychiatrists, and criminologists who expressed concern about the manifestations of same-sex erotic activities in Brazil's urban centers. I then explore the various methods proposed to contain, control, and cure this social ill. These suggestions were offered by more than a dozen doctors and other professionals and published in over thirty books, pamphlets, and articles from the late 1920s until the end of the 1930s. Their authors did not share a monolithic view about the origins, expressions, and possible cures of same-sex erotic behavior. However, their overlapping training in law, medicine, psychiatry, and criminology supports viewing their work as a whole within the broader interdisciplinary context of medicolegal investigations and discourses. Many held multiple positions as university professors and directors of government institutes or agencies while also maintaining private practices, all of which provided income.[7] Their training in medicine and law, and sometimes in both fields, placed them among a small elite of middle- and upper-class professionals who relied on family ties, patronage, and personal loyalty to their mentors as vehicles to establish and advance their careers.[8] This small circle of physicians, lawyers, criminologists, and psychiatrists interacted in the same medical schools and professional organizations and published articles in the same handful of journals on subjects related to crime, sexuality, law, and medicine.[9] Their writings on homosexuality, while divergent in many details, were ultimately similar in their overall approach to the subject. The consolidation of the authoritarian Estado Novo (1937–45) under Getúlio Vargas coincided with a marked decline in these professionals' publishing on the topic. The chapter ends with some suggestions about why intellectual production by these "experts" in homosexuality diminished by the early 1940s.

Everywhere and Growing in Numbers

The men who wrote about same-sex eroticism in the 1920s, 1930s, and early 1940s universally agreed on one premise: homosexuality has existed throughout history in all social classes and in all societies.[10] Their cursory histories of homosexuality usually included a theory that God had annihilated the biblical city of Sodom because its inhabitants had engaged in the "nefarious sin" and a mention that the "vice" had been widely practiced in Greece and Rome, although adamantly condemned by St. Paul and the early Christians. Some writers pointed to the licentious nature of different Brazilian indigenous groups at the time of the Portuguese arrival in 1500 as proof of widespread manifestations of sodomy in different cultures.[11] Authors sometimes referred to famous political and military leaders, such as Julius Caesar and Frederick II of Prussia, and to artists, such as Michelangelo and Shakespeare, as examples of eminent homosexuals from the past. Oscar Wilde was also a favorite figure mentioned, perhaps because he symbolized the "modern" homosexual in the imagination of sexologists, physicians, and criminologists. One author even wrote an extensive treatise on Wilde, linking his large body to endocrine imbalances and homosexuality.[12]

It should be noted that the intellectuals writing about homosexuality in the 1930s did not cite Gilberto Freyre's work about the legacy of the colonial past in the formation of Brazilian sexuality. Although Freyre only wrote occasionally about homosexuality in his own work, he mentioned the phenomenon of "effeminate or bisexual men" and "inverts" among Brazilian natives. He also referred to acts of sodomy committed by Europeans in colonial Brazil as part of a larger argument about the licentious nature of the Portuguese colonizers.[13] Perhaps his work was ignored because *Casa grande e senzala* (The Masters and the Slaves) came out in 1933 at a time when Brazilian medicolegal professionals looked to Europe for their intellectual inspiration. Moreover, one of the theses of Freyre's work, the positive contributions of African culture to Brazilian society, ran counter to racist assumptions still held by some of these authors.

Freyre's work, nevertheless, concurred with the principle argument of the Brazilian "experts" on the subject of sexual "inversion." Homosexuality was universal, transhistorical, and according to a number of physicians who wrote on the subject, growing at an alarming rate. For example, Dr. Viriato Fernandes Nunes presented a thesis entitled "Sexual Perversions in Legal Medicine" to the São Paulo School of Law in 1928 in which he emphasized the increasing visibility of men who engaged in sexual activities with other men. "*Invertidos,*" he argued, "come from all ages and classes. This depravity is very prevalent and seems to become more and more widespread."[14] Leonídio Ribeiro, summarizing European studies and theories on homosexuality, regarded it as a global phenomenon and noted that "the number of individuals of all social classes who present disguised or evident manifestations of sexual perversions has increased everywhere."[15]

Afrânio Peixoto, a public health specialist and a leading figure among the educated elite who ran the medical schools, mental institutions, criminology labs, and various related professional societies, commented on the increasing visibility of homosexuals in the introduction to Estácio de Lima's 1935 volume, *A inversão dos sexos* (The inversion of the sexes). After recounting the story of Sodom and Gomorrah, Peixoto stated that the world was very different in 1935: "Some things, however, have changed, not only in science but in life. Based on statistics from England, France, Germany, and the United States, it is calculated that the number of inverts is ten percent of men (masculine inversion is easier to verify, more frequent, more declared) or five percent of the population. Therefore, the world would have today, if there are two billion inhabitants, one hundred million inverts. . . . This number is not arbitrary, since the most honest or the least hypocritical of those people, the North Americans, speak of six million in a population of 120 million, unfortunate as it is for doctors, sociologists and moralists."[16] Curiously, Peixoto failed to make the corresponding calculations for Brazil. (If his statistics are correct, there would have been 88,207 homosexual men in Rio de Janeiro and another 66,881 in São Paulo at the time of the 1940 census.) Indeed, none of the physicians or criminologists studying homosexuality in the 1930s actually attempted to make a precise or even rough estimate of the number of "inverts" in the country. Even though the "experts" proved cautious in offering exact figures, they were almost universally emphatic that the number of these "diseased individuals" was rising.

Interestingly enough, the Catholic Church seemed removed from this debate on homosexuality. Although physicians and jurists quoted the Bible to contextualize sodomy, and cited church fathers to preach the immorality of sexual activities between men, they concurrently insisted that the legal and medical profession—and not the church—should be the arbiters of how to understand and treat this sexual deviancy. The Catholic Church's silence regarding an issue that was so hotly debated among certain professionals might have had more to do with the status of church-state relations in the 1920s and the '30s than with any lack of concern for issues related to homosexuality. After the establishment of the Republic in 1889 and the separation of the Catholic Church from the state, Brazil's dominant religious institution went through a process of internal readjustment. Catholicism was no longer the official state religion, and the church lost status, privileges, and benefits from republican disestablishmentarianism.

After the end of World War I, the church hierarchy began a concerted campaign to restore the union of church and state. Symbolic of their efforts was the dedication in 1931 of a statue of Christ the Redeemer high atop Corcovado, overlooking and presumably protecting the nation's capital, and by extension, all of Brazil. Cardinal Dom Sebastião Leme of Rio de Janeiro officiated at the ceremony and used the occasion to warn the new Vargas regime to heed the strength, power, and influence of the church. Over the next decade the Catholic prelate would obtain most of his goals—the prohibition of divorce and the recognition of religious marriage by civil law; the permission to have religious education in public schools during school hours; and state financing of church schools, seminaries, and hospitals.[17] The cardinal's campaign involved the large-scale mobilization of the faithful through myriad church-sponsored organizations.[18]

During this political and social offensive, the Catholic Church chose not to attack homosexuality. Even Father Álvaro Negromonte's widely sold book, *A educação sexual (pais e educadores)* (Sex education for parents and educators), mentioned lust, masturbation, and other sexual vices, but not homosexuality.[19] Perhaps Negromonte, the director of religious teaching for the Archdiocese of Rio de Janeiro, thought that it was best not to expose parents, educators, or curious children to such immoral practices. But while the church leadership chose not to engage in the debate with the physicians and jurists who argued for a "scientific" rather than religious or moral approach to understanding homosexuality, their active participation was, in fact, not necessary. Medicolegal professionals themselves insisted in one paragraph of their writing that homosexuality should no longer be considered a vice or a sin, and in the next they admonished parents to provide good moral upbringing to avoid manifestations of the perversion in their children. The age-old Catholic notion of the immorality of "the love that dare not speak its name" was so internalized among the upright middle- and upper-class doctors, lawyers, and other professionals that it remained an underlying assumption in their work, and their scientific and medical discourses were sprinkled with traditional Catholic moral teachings.

If Catholic doctrine was not the explicit reference point for those who wrote on homosexuality, European scholars certainly were. Just as Viveiros de Castro and Pires de Almeida at the turn of the century based their ideas on European medical literature, so, too, the Brazilian physicians and criminologists who wrote on the subject in the 1920s, '30s, and '40s, summarized theories imported from France, Germany, England, Spain, and occasionally the United States. As historian Nancy Leys Stepan has noted, Latin Americans, including Brazilians, looked to European thinkers and "embraced science as a form of progressive knowledge, as an alternative to the religious view of reality and as a means of establishing a new form of cultural power."[20] These appropriations related to new research being conducted in Europe and the United States in endocrinology and hormonal functioning in the 1920s and '30s, as well as general theories about eugenics, criminal behavior, and social deviancy.[21] Two international figures in particular stand out in this regard as exerting the most influence in shaping Brazilian notions about homosexuality and its relationship to race, gender, criminality, and biology. They were Cesare Lombroso, the Italian criminologist, and Gregório Marañón, a professor at the University of Madrid.

Cesare Lombroso (1836–1909), one of the pioneers in the field of criminal anthropology, defended the theory of the born criminal, *delinquente nato*, whose weakened nervous system predisposed him to engage in degenerate behavior, which included mutilation, torture, homosexuality, and the tattooing of the body.[22] Lombroso and his followers used phenotypes to determine criminal degeneracy. His work influenced Ribeiro, who employed Lombroso's anthropometric techniques to measure the body parts of the 195 men arrested in Rio de Janeiro in 1932 in order to prove the link between hormonal imbalances and homosexuality. As was mentioned in chapter 2, Ribeiro received the Lombroso Prize in 1933 for his criminal-anthropological investigations, including his 1932 study of Carioca homosexuals.

The other influential international figure was Gregório Marañón (1887–1960), a professor of medicine at the University of Madrid who penned the introduction to Ribeiro's 1938 work, *Homosexualismo e endocrinologia*. Marañón's own masterwork, *La evolución de la sexualidade e los estados intersexuales* (The evolution of sex and intersexual conditions), was published in Spain in 1930, and in English translation two years later. He also wrote a summary of his theory about intersexuality for the Brazilian medicolegal journal *Arquivos de Medicina Legal e de Identificação*, where so many articles on homosexuality appeared in the late 1930s.[23] Arguing that homosexuals possessed both masculine and feminine characteristics because of an endocrine imbalance, Marañon offered a biological explanation for homosexuality. The term "intersexual" described this liminal positioning between the two sexes. Marañon, however, recognized that this condition was merely a predisposition toward homosexuality. Exogenous factors, such as religion and ethics, could moderate or annul it.[24] By suggesting that it was possible to change one's homosexual condition, Marañón created a space for the intervention of the church rather than medicine as a possible vehicle for the recuperation of the intersexual. In this respect his theories, and those of many of his followers in Brazil, looked to science without abandoning more traditional notions of how to contain manifestations of deviant behavior. Although biology played a significant role in the making of the intersexual, morality, ethics, and sexual restraint might prove sufficient to overcome physiological deficiencies.

Marañón's ideas about the endocrinological origins of homosexuality were adopted by most other Brazilian physicians and criminologists writing on the subject in the 1930s. Among them was Afrânio Peixoto, a leading forensic physician, who argued for another term, *missexual*, because of the mixture of the masculine and feminine he diagnosed in these "abnormal" and "degenerate" beings.[25] Despite such niceties of definition, there were not actually any substantive differences in the various terms employed by these physicians to describe homosexuality. Both the intersexual and the missexual were persons whose malfunctioning biological makeup had produced both masculine and feminine sexual characteristics, with the resulting erotic desires for the same sex. The term inversion emphasized the sexual-object choice of the individual; intersexual and missexual explained the biological causes of this disorder. Peixoto and other physicians also agreed with Ribeiro and Marañón that external, nonbiological factors could affect homosexual behavior and even modify the sexual desires of a given individual. Thus the cure, while primarily biologically based, might also involve psychological and moral efforts, that is to say, physicians, psychologists, *and* the church.

The theory of the biologically degenerate nature of homosexuality and the notion that those who suffered from this organic defect possessed a mixed and undefined sexual identity held disconcerting implications for physicians, who, in general, were members of Brazil's elite and defenders of the moral order.[26] As anthropologist Carlos Alberto Messeder Pereira has noted, "the categories of 'missexualidade' or 'intersexualidade' point basically to the 'mixture,' 'the confusion' of masculine and feminine characters, which should be separate. Even the category 'sexual inversion' points to something that is 'out of place'—inverted. Thus, when the medicolegal profession employs these categories in the 1930s, their main concern is the need for a 'correct ordering,' or 'putting things in their correct places.'"[27] The ambiguous nature of the intersexual or missexual's biological makeup and his inverted sexual desires also destablized gender categories. Homosexuality, as conceived by the physicians and criminologists, upset notions of proper gender roles. Most of the individuals they observed had feminine behavior that was considered part and parcel of their disorder. These "passive pederasts," as they continued to be called, engaged in sexual acts associated with traditional notions of feminine "passivity." Understanding the exact causes for this biological degeneration and possibly finding a cure for the disorder would also mean the correction of improper comportment. Men behaving in womanly ways could once again be returned to appropriate masculinity.

Sizes and Shapes

Not satisfied with merely repeating European theories, Leonídio Ribeiro also attempted to verify them by conducting research on Brazilian subjects.

The political and administrative requirements of the new regime headed by Getúlio Vargas facilitated his study of "deviant" behavior along the lines suggested by Lombroso and Marañón. This was partly the result of the reorganization of the federal police in the nation's capital, an element of Vargas's overall strategy of modernizing and centralizing governmental power, as well as controlling rebellious workers and the restless underclass. After 1930, government-issued identification cards and employment passbooks assisted employers and the police in keeping track of anarchist and socialist labor agitators, undisciplined employees, and vagrants.[28] Improved fingerprinting methods aided the accurate identification of citizens and immigrants alike. Perfecting blood-type tests and "discovering" the links between race and criminality offered more "scientific" means to contain and control an unruly urban population. The research conducted by Leonídio Ribeiro, as the director of the Department of Identification of the Federal District Civil Police, was part of this effort. His study of the 195 homosexuals arrested by the Carioca police in 1932 used modern criminological methods to identify Brazilians with "pathological deviations" and cure their inappropriate, antisocial sexual activities. Whereas turn-of-the-century studies of same-sex erotic behavior in Rio de Janeiro had relied on the personal, anecdotal observations of physicians and jurists, Ribeiro used his position and the power of the police to obtain a sizable sampling for his investigation.[29] The increased influence of the state in the 1930s aided his efforts to identify, classify, and possibly cure them.

In order to carry out his study, Ribeiro employed the same anthropometric system of categorizing body types that he had previously used in examining thirty-three blacks and mixed-race men convicted of murder (see fig. 9).[30] His classification scheme measured the trunk of the body in relationship to the arms and legs of the individual and offered three general groupings—normo-linear (normal), brevi-linear (short), and longi-linear (long)—with subdivisions in each group. Ribeiro found that 54.61 percent fell within the longi-linear group; 5.12 percent were brevi-linear; and 38.46 percent were normo-linear. Isolating individual physical characteristics and comparing them to a "normal" standard, he came up with a series of "abnormalities" among the men he observed (see table 4).[31] Ribeiro never described the prototypic homosexual based on the results of his measuring efforts, but it would appear to have been an underweight young man of normal height with longer than normal arms and legs, and a shortened thorax. Ribeiro also never explained the actual relationship between these characteristics and homosexuality. Presumably, bone development was linked to

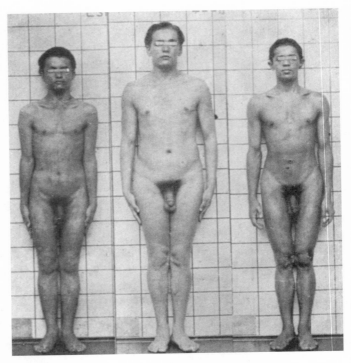

FIGURE 9   Line-up of Carioca homosexuals "with feminine aspects." Reprinted from Ribeiro,
Homosexualismo e endocrinologia (1932), between 104 and 105.

the hormonal system, yet Ribeiro failed to make this connection explicit.
Ribeiro's scientific reasoning was itself more circular than linear. His logic
was simple: these are the physical characteristics of almost two hundred declared homosexuals; the most common phenotype noted therefore represents the physical attributes of the typical homosexual.

To further link the physical characteristics he observed with the supposed endocrine imbalances in his subjects, Ribeiro also examined the distribution of body, pubic, and head hair, arguing that secondary sexual
characteristics served as an excellent means of identifying hormonal mal-
functions, and, therefore, homosexuality. According to Ribeiro, Marañón
had found feminine hair distribution in 75 percent of the homosexuals he
examined. Using Marañón's criteria, Ribeiro compared the shape of his
subjects' pubic hair to what he considered to be the masculine ideal, hexag-
onal-shaped hair growth covering the stomach, thighs, and the area between the scrotum and the anus.[32] His findings, however, did not live up to

those of his mentor (see table 5). Most of the men Ribeiro studied had "normal" body hair distribution (60 percent) or no body hair at all (37 percent). A mere 3 percent had "abnormal or exaggerated" body hair. Moreover, only 18.46 percent had "feminine" triangulated pubic hair.

As if to compensate for inconclusive statistical findings, Ribeiro provided numerous lineup shots of nude men with captions that pointed to their "feminine forms and physiognomy, with pubic hair distributed in a triangular shape."[33] He also published photographs of subjects who lacked pubic hair, but then went on to point out that these men normally shaved it off. Ribeiro did not comment on why the men engaged in this practice, but it may be the reason why he found nearly 20 percent of the men with triangulated pubic hair. Perhaps some homosexuals in the 1930s shaped or shaved off the hair around their genitals to evoke the image of seductive women, just as they used a bit of rouge or makeup to suggest the feminine. Whereas this explanation points to the conscious construction of an effeminate persona through the use of physical markings associated with women, Ribeiro suggested that the distribution of body hair represented an essential and inherent biological characteristic of the homosexual.

Without presenting any quantitative data to back up his conclusions, Ribeiro argued that other physical characteristics caused by endocrine malfunctioning were also linked to homosexuality. They included gynecomastia (the abnormal enlargement of the breast in a male), "feminine distribution of body fat," wide hips, and enlarged genitals. Ribeiro illustrated his assertions through a series of photographs, although in some cases his criteria and definitions had no relationship to the point he was trying to make. For example, four photographs of male genitals were captioned as "different passive pederasts with exaggerated development of the

TABLE 4. Physical Characteristics of Homosexuals Studied by Ribeiro, Rio de Janeiro, 1932

Physical Characteristic	Percentage with Characteristic
Excessive superior members (arms)	62.05
Excessive inferior members (legs)	59.4
Deficient abdomen	69.23
Deficient thorax	52.82
Deficient trunk of the body	63.58
Normal height	74.74
Deficient weight	70.61

SOURCE: Leonídio Ribeiro, *Homosexualismo e endocrinologia* (Rio de Janeiro: Livraria Francisco Alves, 1938), 106–7.

TABLE 5.   Secondary Sexual Characteristics of Homosexuals Studied by Ribeiro, Rio de Janeiro, 1932

Type of Hair[a]	Number	Percentage
Masculine distribution	177	90.76
Feminine distribution	18	9.23
Body hair		
Normal distribution	117	60.00
No body hair	72	36.92
Abnormal or exaggerated	6	3.07
Pubic hair		
Masculine distribution	91	46.66
Intermediate distribution	58	29.74
Feminine distribution	36	18.46

SOURCE: Leonídio Ribeiro, *Homosexualismo e endocrinologia* (Rio de Janeiro: Livraria Francisco Alves, 1938), 108.
[a]In his report, Ribeiro never fully explained the significance of head hair other than to note that baldness was considered to be a sign of virility.

penis." In another section of his work, the subjects of the same four photographs were described as "homosexuals showing the normal or exaggerated development of their external organs." One is at a loss to determine which of the four examples of male genitals is normal and which is exaggerated in size.[34] In addition to ignoring or falsely presenting his own empirical evidence, Ribeiro never addressed the contradiction in his argument that both feminine characteristics and "oversized" sexual organs, presumably due to some endocrinal excess, were signs of homosexuality.

To argue his thesis, the criminologist then presented another conclusion based on Marañón's work, again unsubstantiated by the data. "In two-thirds of the cases studied by us, there was at least one sign of disturbances of an endocrine nature, revealing alterations of the genital and adrenal glands."[35] In other words, homosexuality could be traced to biological abnormalities in a majority of the subjects observed. In another part of his study on homosexuality, Ribeiro acknowledged theories that pointed to exogenous factors. Failed love affairs, poor moral upbringing, separation of the sexes in schools, and overprotective mothers were among the factors Ribeiro mentioned.[36] But after a nod to pyschology and environment, Ribeiro always returned to his biological explanation: "Even though some of the arguments presented by the psychoanalyst are to a certain point acceptable, the theory which has gained more and more ground affirms that in the majority of cases of sexual inversion there is an organic cause or predisposition which can be provoked, favored or aggravated by environmental influences."[37] As this statement makes clear, Ribeiro was not a strict biological determinist. He recognized other factors that could influence homosexual behavior. The "essential" homosexual, however, was a man whose hormonal chemistry dictated his sexual desires. External factors might strengthen or attenuate homosexual tendencies, but the disordered body was the ultimate cause of this degeneration.

In short, other than the finding that 56 percent of the men examined had longer than "normal" arms and legs, Ribeiro's investigation provided little morphological evidence of any links between hormones and homosexuality. Indeed, his entire research model was seriously flawed because he did not conduct a control study on two hundred declared heterosexuals to verify his results. Nor did Ribeiro provide adequate explanations as to why 34 percent of the men he measured showed no observable physiological manifestations of homosexuality. Nevertheless, over the next decade, more than a dozen physicians and criminologists cited Ribeiro's study without ever questioning his dubious statistical findings, inconsistent logic, and unscientific procedures. His theories, research methods, and analysis became the model for other mini-research projects conducted in Brazil, especially in São Paulo, which in turn influenced further thinking and writing about the subject. One such study was conducted by Edmur de Aguiar Whitaker, a psychiatrist working for the anthropology laboratory of the São Paulo police department's identification service.[38] Following Ribeiro's methodological approach of using arrested subjects for his study, Whitaker examined eight homosexuals, again without a control group. All eight men were diagnosed with "secondary feminine sexual characteristics," such as triangulated pubic hair and a wide pelvic structure. Whitaker further reported that most were psychopaths (without explaining how he reached that conclusion), with limited or normal intelligence. He conceded, however, that "in addition to endogenous degenerative disorder, this abnormality can be, in its exogenous form, the result of an unbalanced personality [or] a poor adaptation to one's environment." Whitaker recommended a correctional medical cure without specifying what that might entail.

Race, Crime, and Homosexuality

When Dr. Viriato Fernandes Nunes argued in his 1928 legal essay that the moral perversions of homosexuality, masturbation, sadomasochism, and

bestiality "violently attacked social norms," he referred to two widely publicized sex crime cases of the previous year: the alleged killing of three
young boys by Febrônio Índio do Brasil and the purported slaying of four
youths by Prêto Amaral.[39] Both men were of African heritage, and both
cases involved rape and the sadistic murder of the victims. Linking homosexuality to sadism, Dr. Nunes emphasized the threat that homosexual
"perversion" presented to society. Unable to control their sexual impulses,
he argued, "degenerate" figures such as Febrônio Índio do Brasil and Prêto
Amaral, and by extension all homosexuals, posed a serious danger to
Brazil's social fabric, to the family, and to the proper ordering of gendered
relationships. The subtext of Nunes's thesis also evoked racial anxiety,
namely, the ominous image of dark, sinister forces preying on the purity of
innocent, white Brazilian youth.

Unlike Ribeiro and other physicians who wrote about homosexuality
in the 1930s, Nunes did not argue that it was based on inherent biological
factors. Rather, he pointed to the social impact of the behavior. Loyal to
the positivist tradition still influential in Brazilian intellectual circles, Nunes
acknowledged that "the punishments which in former times castigated perverts such as Prêto Amaral and Febrônio Índio do Brasil were excessively
rigorous and without any scientific basis." Comparing them to punishments
of his day, Nunes assured his readers that progress had been achieved: "Society benefited very little from the elimination of these criminals. They
should be removed and regenerated if possible. Today, with modern therapeutic processes, with the study of psychoanalysis, one can restore the
psychiatric balance that these perverts lack. And when that is not achieved,
the criminal will be detained but with comfort and humanity while unable
to commit other offenses." On a practical level, Nunes pointed to the proposed establishment of São Paulo's Manicômio Judiciário, an asylum for the
criminally insane, as the privileged place to achieve this goal. He argued
that its location next to the Juquery State Mental Hospital, either as an independent hospital or as a dependency of the state hospital, would facilitate its objectives.[40]

The writings of the late 1920s and the 1930s never drew an explicit link
between race and homosexuality, but the connection was embedded in the
underlying themes of the text. The choice of certain figures to symbolize
the excesses of the "perversion" relied on pejorative cultural stereotypes
about nonwhite Brazilians held by many in the medicolegal profession as
well as among sectors of the intellectual elite in general.[41] The works of
Leonídio Ribeiro and Antônio Carlos Pacheco e Silva exemplify this ap-

proach. While Ribeiro only used a page or two to describe "Marina," "Zazá," and "H. de O," he devoted an entire chapter of *Homosexualismo e endocrinologia* to the celebrated case of Febrônio do Brasil.[42] Readers of his book could extract only an extremely limited vision of the lives of ordinary homosexuals in the 1930s, a vision probably distorted by the physician's own prejudices. But they received voluminous information about an alleged murderer and rapist of innocent children.

Ribeiro's interest in Febrônio Índio do Brasil was not merely didactic. He had a personal stake in the case. Ribeiro was one of three criminologists who testified at the trial on behalf of the defense and argued that Febrônio was insane and therefore should be sentenced *ad vitam* to the Manicômio Judiciário. From Ribeiro's perspective, the case took on a broader significance as a study of how society should deal with homosexuality that degenerated into insanity. In an unusual twist, Ribeiro linked homosexuality and sadism and noted that "the known cases of sadism do not occur among excessively masculine individuals, as is the popular notion, but rather among those of effeminate organization, such as the Marquis de Sade."[43] To prove his point, Ribeiro feminized the infamous symbol of sadism and presented a detailed account of his life, emphasizing Febrônio's long arrest record. The physician culminated his account with the accusations that Febrônio had attracted several youths to deserted places where he tortured, sexually molested, and then killed them.

Ribeiro's description of Febrônio begins by defining him racially: "Febrônio is a dark *mestiço* whose characteristics [are a result] of the crossing of *caboclo* [in this case, Indian] with *prêto* [black]." In the medical language of the 1920s and '30s, influenced as it was by eugenics theories, Febrônio's racial mixture implies degeneration. Three lineup photographs of Febrônio accompanying the chapter seem to have been carefully placed in the volume to substantiate Ribeiro's theory of the link between homosexuality and hormonal disorder. The caption reads: "Homosexual—sadist, Febrônio, author of three homicides by strangulation, besides other crimes, showing signs of endocrine disturbances."[44] Paradoxically, as in the lineup shots of the 195 homosexuals mentioned earlier in this chapter, it is difficult for the observer to note any difference between Febrônio's appearance and that of any other average naked man of his age. Once again, to compensate for the inconclusive proof presented in the book's images, Ribeiro relies on captions to contradict his visual documentation.[45]

Antônio Carlos Pacheco e Silva, the director of the Juquery State Mental Hospital in São Paulo and an eminent professor of clinical psychiatry at both the University of São Paulo and Paulista medical schools, similarly used images of race, crime, and sadism to create the specter of the homosexual as a danger to society. In a chapter titled "Constitutional Psychopaths: Atypical States of Degeneration" in his 1940 award-winning book, *Psiquiatria clínica e forense* (Clinical psychiatry and forensics), Pacheco e Silva outlines and defines an array of sexual perversions.[46] He lists these perversions as sadism, masochism, necrophilia, bestiality, exhibitionism, homosexuality, frigidity, nymphomania, satyriasis, and onanism. To illustrate these degenerate behaviors, he provides four examples. One is a two-paragraph description of a man who molested the corpse of a six-year-old girl. A second example of sadism and necrophilia involves a thirty-two-year-old *pardo* (person of mixed blood) who had sex with and then strangled a young boy.[47]

Two other cases receive more prominent treatment in the chapter. One describes a lesbian, photographed both in a dress and in men's clothes. Pointing out that Ribeiro's study only refers to men, Pacheco e Silva explains how he and his colleagues discovered their subject: "A curious case of feminine homosexuality, which is the origin of this study, recently passed through the Psychiatric Clinic of the Medical School of the University of São Paulo. It is interesting in multiple ways. . . . It proves that cases of feminine sexual inversion also deserve to be explained in detail in light of modern endocrinological learning."[48]

On numerous occasions, the author states that the subject, referred to only as E.R., is "sick." One gets the impression that his aversion to her was linked to the fact that she shamelessly cross-dressed, assumed a traditional masculine identity, and aggressively sought out female sexual partners. While E.R. was not accused of any criminal offense, the fact that she was black stood out. Her two portraits are prominently placed in the text, and she is described by reference to her race several times. We are told that she only liked white women. As one of only a few examples of female homosexuality portrayed by medicolegal professionals in this period, the emphasis placed on her race conveyed a subtext that linked darker-skinned people to perversion.[49]

E.R. was not involved in criminal behavior, but Pacheco e Silva's fourth example, J. A. Amaral, was. The joint presentation of the two subjects offered a unified discourse: nonwhites were inclined to homosexuality, degeneracy, and even criminality. Throughout his case study, J. A. Amaral is referred to as "Prêto Amaral" (Black Amaral), a pejorative nickname that referred directly to his dark skin. Amaral's first alleged victim is also discussed in racialized terms. "He was a white boy, fair, [with] green eyes, brown hair, looking fourteen years old." The image is clear: a black man, a *prêto*, had seduced, raped, and strangled an angelic boy. Two large mug shots captioned "O Prêto Amaral" accompany the case study, as if to emphasize the point. The section on "hereditary background" stresses the murderer's African origins: "His parents were born in Africa—the father in the Congo and the mother in Mozambique. They came to Brazil as slaves and here were bought by the Viscount of Ouro Preto." His physical examination also highlights his race: "This is an individual whose color is black, but is of a physiognomic type rare in his race. The nose, far from being flat, is aquiline and slightly curved."[50]

Pacheco e Silva describes the alleged seduction, murder, and molestation of four young victims. He then cites European authorities—Von Krafft-Ebing, Forel, and Lombroso—to explain Amaral's sadistic and necrophilic behavior. Finally, he argues for isolation in a mental hospital rather than incarceration: "It is to the asylum and not to prison that these obsessive impulsive people should be sent, and the hideous character of the crimes committed by some of them should not be separated from the pathological nature of the act. It is rare for sexual perversion to be the only syndrome in these degenerates."[51] Like Nunes in 1928, Ribeiro and Pacheco e Silva a decade later argued for a "modern," scientific, and "humane" treatment of "perverts" who had committed other crimes. However, just as Ribeiro pointed to the homosexual acts of Febrônio as a way of linking homosexuality to criminality, so Pacheco e Silva connected sexual acts with murder and pathological behavior.

Why were the "scientific" observations and research results of Ribeiro, Pacheco e Silva, and other medicolegal professionals so readily accepted by their colleagues without any criticism of their obviously faulty methodology and flawed logic? In part this had to do with the nature of investigations related to race and crime at the time. Many Brazilian intellectuals wholeheartedly embraced eugenic notions of the inferiority of certain races and the degenerate nature of certain social types, especially when the proponents of these theories were European. Moreover, the system of patronage and the hermetic character of this area of study discouraged criticism of mentors, sponsors, and colleagues. Rather than recognize and confront the inconsistency in European or Brazilian theories or research methods regarding crime, race, or homosexuality, a small circle of intellectuals praised each other's work, wrote glowing introductions to each other's monographs, and cited each other's "findings." The culture engendered within this interlocking web of Brazilian professionals discouraged critical reflections on the research results, whether it related to identifying degeneracy or offering an antidote for the sickness of homosexuality.

Curing the Disease

The "enlightened" perspective offered by Ribeiro and others suggesting a biological cause for the origin of homosexuality started to shift the issue away from the traditional moral teachings of the Catholic Church into the realm of science and medicine. Afrânio Peixoto, who was one of Ribeiro's mentors, emphasized this point: "It is not a sin, a crime, or a vice to be punished, but an organic deviation, an internal malformation, to be diagnosed, recognized, and corrected. Not religion nor law, which have no place here, but hygiene, medicine, surgery, perhaps, to restore the deviant man, [and] the perverted woman to their normal health. It is no longer a matter, as in ages past, of expelling the leper or syphilitic from the city for fear of being contaminated, but rather of isolating them in hospitals where they can get treatment and become healthy. Neither hostility nor law will correct sexual inversion. It should be treated by appropriate means."[52]

Ribeiro reiterated Peixoto's call for shifting the rehabilitation of homosexuals away from religion to medicine. Ribeiro's chapter "Homosexuality in Light of Medicine" in *Homosexualismo e endocrinologia* underlined the essential role he believed physicians should play: "In the last century the problem of homosexuality began to be studied by doctors and psychiatrists interested in discovering its causes so that jurists and sociologists could modify existing legislation that had been based on empirical notions and other prejudices, and if possible treat it through scientific means." Ribeiro then indirectly challenged Catholic doctrines, which considered homosexuality a moral transgression. He also opposed those who argued that, as a social crime, inversion should be duly punished: "The practices of sexual inversion can no longer be considered a sin, vice, or crime, since in most cases it has been shown to involve sick or abnormal individuals who should not be punished since they need treatment and assistance above all else." Homosexuality among men, Ribeiro argued, was beyond the individual's control because a malfunctioning endocrine system impelled this deviant behavior. Physicians should treat these innocent casualties: "Medicine has freed crazy people from prisons. Once again, it will save these poor individuals from humiliation, many of whom are victims of their degeneration and abnormalities for which they are not responsible."[53] In other words, homosexuals should be pitied for their malady, and the responsibility of medicine should be to find a way to cure them of their diseased condition.

The essential problem for those who pointed to science and medicine to reduce the number of homosexuals was their inability to offer an actual "cure" for the behavior. In the chapter "Medical-Pedagogic Treatment," Ribeiro speculated on two possible courses of action: proper upbringing and education first and, if that proved unsuccessful, testicle transplants. When defending surgical therapy, Ribeiro cited experiments in which testicles and ovaries were transplanted into a single animal. He optimistically stated that "the so-called 'experimental hermaphrodite' reveals the true path to the medical treatment of sexual inversion cases."[54] Ribeiro then proceeded to suggest human testicle transplants as the preferred therapeutic treatment. Indeed, he even contemplated the possibility of animal donors. Moreover, citing Marañón, he emphasized the importance of performing this surgery on children when they reached puberty, before their perversions had become firmly established.

Because most physicians and lawyers conceded that manifestations of homosexuality could also be based on nonbiological factors, they inevitably retreated to psychological, moral, and behavioral suggestions as the alternative solution to stemming its rise. Lacking definitive evidence or concrete methods for medical remedies, these professionals slid back into the myriad theories and proposals borrowed from traditional Catholic moral teachings and ideas of European sexologists. In 1928, for example, Nunes pointed to the deep psychological roots of inversion, "From childhood they are more troubled than other children: they are well-mannered, delicate, and reveal feminine attitudes and aptitudes in all of their actions. Their interest is in pleasing other boys and young men. At a later age and with better reflection and wiser judgment, they note how ridiculous their inversion is; and, if they have any moral force left, they try to correct it. Others, however, who are impotent, dominated, and defeated by their inversion, continue to practice their perverted love and do so as naturally as if they were carrying out a morally equivalent noble action."[55] Although Nunes essentialized inversion and attributed it exclusively to effeminate boys, he recognized, that adults had two different approaches to dealing with their same-sex sexual desires. While some were unable to restrain their passion and embraced their sexuality, others managed to overcome their "perversion" through moral will. Ribeiro also emphasized moral will and proper upbringing as means to avoid homosexuality, especially among children.

The question of "nurture versus nature," regarding the causes and therefore the treatment of homosexuality became a concrete political question by the end of the 1930s. Growing concern among the medical and legal professions about homosexuality and its ever more visible manifestations inspired proposals to reformulate the penal code. As has been mentioned, homosexuality per se had not been a criminal offense since the enactment of the Imperial Penal Code of 1830. After the formation of the Estado Novo in November 1937, jurists in charge of rewriting the Brazilian code of 1890 considered including a provision, initially suggested in 1933, that would have penalized homosexual acts between consenting adults with up to one year in prison. Although the provision was omitted from the final draft, the debate about the law reveals the divergent ways professionals approached this social issue.[56]

Reeducation or Criminalization?

In July 1938, Aldo Sinisgalli, one of the students from the Institute of Criminology of São Paulo who had interviewed eight homosexuals in the Vale de Anhangabaú the previous year, presented two papers on homosexuality at the First Paulista Congress of Psychology, Neurology, Psychiatry, Endocrinology, Identification, Criminology, and Legal Medicine. Sinisgalli's first exposition outlined the intellectual debate about homosexuality in Brazil.[57] In a companion paper, he summarized his conclusions on how to solve the "problem." In a style reminiscent of a political manifesto, he called for the arrest, confinement, treatment, and cure of all Brazilian homosexuals:

> Homosexuals, pederasts, are not normal men.
> As abnormal people, they need adequate treatment.
> Punishment, reclusion in prisons is unjust because it does not bring minimal practical results.
> Letting pernicious elements free is dangerous and prejudicial to society.
> Thus, an institute for pederasts is necessary.
> In the institute for pederasts, they will be treated, reeducated.
> A professional selection will be made, granting the inverts relative freedom.
> We propose a legal mechanism permitting the confinement of pernicious pederasts to the social environment of this institute.
> In this way, we will benefit society and the inverts.
> In this way, we will resolve scientifically and humanely this social problem.
> In this way, I am certain, we will glorify our country and our people.[58]

His presentation was made eight months after the establishment of the authoritarian Estado Novo government, and the ideological undertones of his declaration echoed the nationalistic rhetoric promoted throughout the 1930s as Vargas moved toward greater state control over citizens' lives in the hope of solving the nation's problems.[59] Sinisgalli's logic was simple. Homosexuals were degenerates whose mere incarceration would not eliminate their abnormality. A "scientific" procedure had to be established to cure their perversion. A state-run institution with the power and the necessary trained professionals to achieve this goal needed to be set up. The prestige of the nation and its people was at stake in this endeavor. In other words, the state, rather than the family, should assume the responsibility of controlling and curing this "pernicious element" of Brazilian society.

The discussion following the paper's presentation provoked a serious debate about the means to achieve Sinisgalli's ends. Dr. J. Soares de Melo, a professor of the São Paulo School of Law, pointed out that while Sinisgalli's idea was laudable, the state could not arbitrarily confine homosexuals because current legislation did not punish homosexuality. If one wanted to arrest a person, he pointed out, it would require the "legal inventiveness" of charging him with corruption of a minor or carnal violence. Homosexuals who had not committed either of those crimes could not be detained. Soares de Melo therefore proposed a change in the law in order to make homosexuality a criminal act. Pointing to Nazi Germany, the eminent law professor noted: "In European capitals like Berlin, violent measures have been taken to stop the wave of corruption that has spread there. It would be strongly advisable that in any future Penal Code of the country there were mechanisms that punished all forms of homosexuality regardless of the modality in which they are expressed."[60]

Sinisgalli responded by arguing that confinement as punishment would neither help society nor cure the homosexual. Rather, an institute to treat pederasts would both remove them from society and rehabilitate them. He added that the institute he proposed would not be designed for criminally insane homosexuals, who should be sent to the Manicômio Judiciário. Ribeiro de Godoy concurred with Sinisgalli. He argued that since homosexuality was a psychological depravation, it required a medical cure and not criminal detention.[61]

As was suggested earlier, the issue of the criminalization of homosexuality was not merely an academic debate restricted to a professional association of criminologists and physicians.[62] In May 1938, when the members of the São Paulo Society of Legal Medicine and Criminology discussed the issue, Francisco Campo, the justice minister of the newly established Estado Novo regime, appointed a noted jurist, Professor Alcântara Machado, to draft a new penal code. During the deliberations of a commission created to reformulate Alcântara Machado's draft, a proposal was introduced to criminalize homosexual acts. Under the heading "Homosexuality," article 258 provided: "Libidinous acts between individuals of the masculine sex will be repressed when they cause public scandal, imposing on both participants detention of up to one year."[63] The suggestion was to expand the scope of article 282, "Public Assault on Decency," which prohibited "shameless exhibitions or obscene acts or gestures practiced in public places or places frequented by the public" and carried a prison sentence of one to six months.[64] Significantly, for the first time since sodomy was decriminalized in the early nineteenth century, this proposal made an explicit reference to same-sex erotic activities by placing this paragraph of the code under the rubric "homosexuality." Moreover, unlike previous provisions prohibiting public assaults on decency, the punishment of acts that caused public scandal would have included private activities that came to public attention.[65]

Another significant proposal for the new criminal code was a clause that sustained the positions of Ribeiro and other medicolegal professions regarding the medical treatment of homosexuals. The draft law read: " In dealing with pathological or degenerative abnormal [people], the judge may, based on a medical expertise, substitute the sentence for security measures appropriate to the circumstances."[66] Ribeiro hailed this provision as a sign of the "degree of its author's culture" because it allowed the judge, based on adequate consultation with the medicolegal profession to "substitute prison with hospitalization."[67] Ribeiro, however, overlooked the fact that the draft applied to any libidinous acts performed by men that caused public scandal. The proposal actually would have given the court system expanded authority to detain people for extended periods of time, if, in the eyes of medical authorities, they deserved special measures of control.

Article 258 was struck from the last set of proposals for the 1940 Penal Code. The final draft relied on a streamlined version of the article in the 1932 Consolidated Codes that prohibited obscene acts in public, increasing the maximum punishment from six months to a year. Since the internal governmental discussions about whether or not to include an explicit reference to homosexuality never reached a public forum for debate, we don't know why the jurists in charge of reformulating the criminal code decided not to include the draft proposal. Nor does Ribeiro explain why the commission chose to reword the draft article and eliminate any specific reference to male homosexuality or to the expanded power of judges to hospitalize "pathological or degenerative abnormal" people.[68] During the Estado Novo, Vargas disbanded the Congress; and, therefore, the new criminal code was approved by executive decree. Apparently, those within Vargas's government who made the decisions about what ended up in the final version of the law considered that the existing web of legal, social, moral, and medical constraints on homosexuality was adequate to address this social "ill." Nor were judges granted extra legal power to sentence homosexuals to mental institutions, as Ribeiro had hoped. Nevertheless, precedents were already firmly in place that permitted family members of homosexuals in collaboration with physicians and psychiatrists to commit relatives who engaged in perverse sexual activities to mental hospitals.

Mental Institutions and Social Control

As has been pointed out, the increased interest in homosexuality by prominent members of the medical profession in the 1920s and '30s had a different impact on different segments of Brazilian society. Individuals from lower classes and with darker skin were more vulnerable to arrest for vagrancy, prostitution, or charges of public indecency than were middle-class homosexuals. The latter faced a different form of social control. With no medical cure in sight, middle-class families, when confronted with a member whom they suspected of being an "invert," often sought another avenue of assistance. If mental hospitals could not cure a person's homosexual behavior, they could at least provide a place to contain wayward relatives and control that behavior.

One of the institutions that families turned to was the Juquery State Mental Hospital, located near the city of São Paulo. Founded at the turn of the century as a "modern" mental asylum, Juquery was considered a model for similar hospitals throughout the country. Maria Clementina Pereira Cunha's study of Juquery provides helpful insights into the policies and practices of physicians who treated people considered mentally ill or insane. Cunha argues that the asylum used the authority of "science" and the guise of offering both a "cure" and "assistance" to achieve a political goal. Its objective was "to legitimize the exclusion of individuals or social sectors that did not totally fit within the penal apparatus; to permit the confinement and perhaps the regeneration of individuals resistant to the

disciplines of work, the family and urban life; to reinforce socially important roles for the protection of order and discipline by medicalizing deviant
behavior, such as sexual perversions or vagrancy, and permitting its reclu-
sion to be read as an act in favor of the insane person and not against him
or her."[69]

Homosexuality fell within the category of sexual perversions, and confinement was the principle therapeutic method utilized to "cure" this deviation. Under its first clinical director, Dr. Francisco Franco da Rocha, who
ran Juquery from 1896 until his retirement in 1930, the mental asylum
served as a repository for homosexuals placed there by their relatives.[70] For
example, Archangelo L., a seventeen-year-old cobbler from São Paulo, was
committed to the hospital on March 30, 1908, by his parents. The asylum's
physician diagnosed his condition: "Excessive development of the virile
member. Since sixteen, he is a passive pederast. He never practiced normal
coitus with a woman."[71] Associating physical degeneracy with the moral
degeneracy of homosexuality, Archangelo was described as having "badly
shaped ears" and an "asymmetrical head." Yet he showed no signs of mental illness other than the diagnosis of being a "passive pederast." In fact, in
his interview, the young shoemaker proceeded rather cautiously in an attempt to protect himself from the intrusive questioning of the alienist, as
reflected in the doctor's own notes: "[H]e has an exact notion of time, space
and surroundings. He responds well although his answers take a while, since
the patient tries to hide most of the truth in relationship to his life, but he
is easily betrayed by disguised and well-asked questions."

Another patient, José P., a single forty-year-old from São Paulo, was
hospitalized in November 1920. His diagnosis also linked his physical characteristics to moral degeneration. Here, however, feminine characteristics, rather than "oversized" genitals, signaled perversion. "Physically and
morally he looks like a woman: high voice, lack of hair on his legs and
body, the disposition of the Venus Mound, his way of walking." Clearly,
José P. was confined because he manifested effeminate behavior. José, like
Archangelo, offered resistance to his forced hospitalization. He consistently
demanded to be released from the asylum and was so adamant about his desire to leave Juquery that the medical staff labeled it an *idéia fixa* (fixation)
that "constituted his only line of reasoning."[72]

Despite their utilization by middle-class families, by the 1930's public
institutions such as Juquery had developed a reputation for offering less
than adequate services. The hospital served all social classes, but poor
people, especially those of African and mixed racial backgrounds, soon

constituted a large percentage of its population. The development of a network of private institutions then supplanted the hospital as the privileged location to place a "mentally ill" relative. Even families with modest economic resources preferred these private sanatoriums, because they assumed their relatives would receive better care there without having to have contact with indigent and lower-class patients.[73]

One of these new private hospitals, the Pinel Sanatorium, located on the outskirts of São Paulo, was inaugurated in 1930 under the direction of Dr. Antônio Carlos Pacheco e Silva, who played a pivotal role in the development of psychiatric care in São Paulo. In 1930, Pacheco e Silva also succeeded Dr. Francisco Franco e Rocha as the director of the Juquery State Mental Hospital, simultaneously administering both institutions during the 1930s. The same year that Vargas came to power in the Revolution of 1930, the new government appointed Pacheco e Silva to head the Department of General Assistance to Psychopaths, which was charged with defining official policy on mental health. In addition, Pacheco e Silva founded and served as president of the Paulista League for Mental Hygiene, an organization that promoted eugenics in Brazil. In light of Pacheco e Silva's influence in the psychiatric field, his administration of the two most important psychiatric institutions in the state of São Paulo can reveal a great deal about the standards and methods of psychiatric care afforded homosexuals in the 1930s and '40s.

On January 30, 1931, Manoel de O. brought his twenty-year-old son, Adalberto, all the way from Uberlândia in southern Minas Gerais to the Pinel Sanatorium in São Paulo.[74] The admitting physician recorded both that Adalberto was a "sexual invert" who had contracted syphilis through anal intercourse and that he was in full agreement with the young man's hospitalization. However, the doctor's notes on Adalberto's psychic condition revealed a more complex scenario. Adalberto admitted to the doctor that he had engaged in passive anal sex over the last four years, but against his own will and only to annoy his father, with whom he did not get along. He stated that he had had only five sexual partners during that time. The youth related that he always tried to be caught in the act by his father in order to demoralize him. Adalberto insisted that he had not enjoyed passive sex and was not, in the words of the physician, "constitutionally an invert." He expressed anger toward his father because the man had wanted to leave Adalberto in the asylum for more than a month. To get even, the lad boasted he would continue to engage in anal intercourse in front of his father with the sole purpose of demoralizing his family. The physician was not convinced by Adalberto's story and concluded that he was, in fact, a sexual invert without any additional mental disturbances "who used the excuse of getting revenge on his father in order to hide his perversion."

If the professionals at Pinel were correct in concluding that Adalberto enjoyed homosexual encounters, then his version of events reveals contradictory sentiments: both a lively sense of survival and possible feelings of self-hatred and denial. Faced with a hostile society that condemned and at times punished homosexuality through confinement in mental institutions, Adalberto attempted to defend himself by constructing a story that legitimized his sexuality by attributing it to a mere act of revenge. His denial of any desire related to his sexual behavior, however, failed to convince the physicians or his father to authorize his release. After forty days of confinement, Adalberto took matters into his own hands and escaped from the hospital.

Another recalcitrant son detained in the Pinel Sanatorium was Sydney da S., a fifteen-year-old from São Paulo.[75] His father noted on the admissions questionnaire that since his son had reached puberty and begun to grow rapidly, he had showed "a certain mental imbalance of reduced proportions." Moreover, he entered the sanatorium looking pale and run-down, a condition his father attributed to excessive masturbation. Although the family stated that he had not been violent, nor had he entertained ideas of suicide, the boy did laugh for unknown reasons, especially when he heard "spicy" conversations. When asked if the son had performed inappropriate or immoral deeds, his father wrote that he had been violent and gross with members of the family and had committed a minor theft, although, to the best of his father's knowledge, he had not engaged in any immoral acts. Medical observations completed two weeks after his confinement on August 1, 1933, present a somewhat different picture. Sydney, it seems, stole small objects from the house, sold them, and then squandered the money. When caught, he staged "theatrical" scenes and feigned suicide, especially when alone at home with his mother and sisters.

Sydney quickly adjusted to life within the institution. He made friends among the other patients and was affectionate toward the male nurses. He was, in fact, too affectionate for the observing physician, who noted that he was exorbitantly expansive and sought to hug effusively both patients and the male staff. Several days after entering Pinel, Sydney was caught by an employee while attempting to engage in passive anal sex, presumably with another patient. He showed no remorse or shame for his actions, "facing the incident with a certain naturalness" that annoyed the supervising physician. Sydney was diagnosed as "a child with an atypical state of degeneration, carrying the physical signs of hereditary syphilis," although his record did not contain the results of any medical tests to merit that conclusion. What therapeutic methods were employed on Sydney is unclear from the surviving records. All we know is that on December 31, 1933, his family removed him from the hospital "much improved."

It appears that Sydney's confinement to Pinel had more to do with his family's inability to control the wild behavior of an adolescent than with any other psychiatric problem. He easily adapted to his new environment, making friends and seeking emotional support. Although his father saw his masturbation as the source of his unbalanced comportment and declining health and the physician viewed his homosexual encounter as a manifestation of degeneration, the youth seemed to adjust to his own sexuality in a spontaneous and natural way reminiscent of the homosexuals interviewed in downtown São Paulo in the late 1930s.

Controlling Wayward Fathers

In "Priests, Celibacy, and Social Conflict: A History of Brazil's Clergy and Seminaries," historian Kenneth P. Serbin explains how the Brazilian Catholic hierarchy went to great lengths in the 1930s and '40s to hide priests' sexual adventures from public scrutiny.[76] Transferring recalcitrant clergy from one seminary or pastoral duty to another rather than disciplining them was one of the favored tactics employed to cover up potential public scandals. For example, one priest of the Vicential order at a seminary in São Luis, Maranhão, who had a long history of involvement with young seminarians in the early 1930s, was relocated to Fortaleza to avoid problems with the congregation.

Other priests were not so lucky. Macario S., for example, a German-born priest, entered the Pinel Sanatorium on September 12, 1930, as the result of an incident in which one of the boys with whom he maintained sexual relations threatened to denounce him. From a letter found in his file and written shortly after his confinement, it appears that the priest had suggested going to the mental asylum in order to extricate himself from a potential scandal.[77] The medical admission records indicate that the priest had engaged in homosexual activities over many years: "He is a priest from the São Bento monastery. He came to Brazil many years ago. In Germany he had engaged in homosexual practices. For this reason he was surrounded by rigorous vigilance in the first period after he arrived in Brazil. Slowly, however, he won over the confidence of his superiors so that recently he has enjoyed considerable freedom. He assiduously engaged in the occupation of teaching poor boys (day laborers and seamen's apprentices), and with this pretext he had the opportunity to engage in sexual perversion that had been latent for some time but had never disappeared."

Although the interviewing physician noted that the patient was "perfectly oriented" about his relationship to the outside world, Macario did seem anxious. The priest reported that he was upset because he did not possess the peace of mind for spiritual tranquillity. He also admitted that he had "broken the rules of good morality through sinful thoughts and acts that he had practiced." It appears that he quickly realized his suggestion of voluntary confinement was a miscalculation. He communicated to the physician that he feared he would only get worse in the sanatorium and end up "crazy," spending the remaining days of his life in Juquery State Mental Hospital. Macario furthermore reported that he had already undergone extensive treatment for syphilis, a disease he picked up in a restroom in Poço de Caldas, a city in the state of São Paulo. Evidently, news of his infectious ailment had already spread through the sanatorium, and the priest complained that in the dining hall everyone looked at him with repugnance.

Although the abbot may have thought that committing a wayward priest to Pinel would solve a thorny problem, Macario did not adjust to his confinement peacefully. Two and a half months after entering the institution, the priest penciled a letter to the abbot. Because it was written in German, someone in the hospital duly translated the correspondence and saved it in his dossier. In the epistle, Macario explained that owing to the circumstances surrounding his confinement he had lost all the respect that should be afforded to a man of the cloth: "I have been here for ten weeks and my situation has become unbearable. Everyone knows why I am here, and for that reason I am the target of mockery and scorn. I am forced to listen to the most vile obscenities and jokes. I am the cause of scandal and disgust. . . . I am unable to speak a single word about God or religion to any of the patients. Nor can I interact with anyone. As far as everyone is concerned, I am scandalous. It is getting worse every day, and I can do nothing to fix it. I am lost for now and for eternity. How horrible!" The priest's ostracism reflects both the deeply embedded nature of social prejudice against homosexuality and the ability of other patients to appreciate the irony of a man supposedly above moral reproach violating the church's teachings about celibacy and proper sexuality. Macario's syphilitic condition merely added to his pariah status.

Having initially suggested the mental institution as a way of escaping punishment, Macario now begged for mercy and compassion from God and the abbot: "O my God, show clemency to me so that through my regret and penitence I can return to thee and repair for the rest of my life the scandal which I caused." He then proposed that the abbot send him to a monastery in Sorocaba, near São Paulo, or to Germany, where he could receive consolation and spiritual assistance. "It seems as if I have lost all faith in God and all love of God and those near him. All religious feelings have died in me. I am only able to pray with great effort. My God, what a horrible end to my life as a priest." Macario's plaintive letter to the abbot revealed a deep spiritual crisis. He recognized that according to church teachings he had committed mortal sins and feared that further confinement in the mental institution, a virtual purgatory, was only preparation for the pains and torments of hell. Spiritual regeneration may have been his goal, but the priest also offered practical arguments to obtain succor. Whereas ten weeks earlier, Macario had suggested a medical "cure" to avoid a monastic scandal, now he recognized that the physicians could not alter his sexual desires: "The doctors also say that it is time to remove me so that I can recuperate in another calm and quiet place. I know that this is not the place to calm my soul. The experience of almost three months has shown me that I cannot achieve [peace] here, and that the torments of one's conscience cannot be cured by medical means. . . . For the love of God, get me out of here and send me to Sorocaba until your Excellency can definitively decide my future. Don't abandon me. Save me from this horrible situation." Complaining that he had been in the hospital without mass, confession, or absolution, the priest begged the abbot to release him before Christmas. Evidently, his superior heeded his request, and Macario left Pinel on December 6, 1930.[78]

In this case, as in others, the Catholic Church, like stalwart middle-class families, used mental institutions such as Pinel as repositories for those who could not contain their homosexual desires. If modern sanatoriums offered a cover for "insane" relatives, removing them from attics and the embarrassing gaze of neighbors, so too could they serve as confinement for moral transgressors. Since prevailing medical diagnoses considered homosexuality a disease, it was justifiable to sequester a relative in a mental institution if family pressures failed to change his ways. Curing a patient's homosexuality was, alas, a different matter altogether.

Shock Treatment

In the early 1930s, physical confinement was the principal "therapeutic" means for controlling homosexuality. From what one can glean from the medical records, physicians at Pinel Sanatorium did little else to modify the behavior of Napoleão, Adalberto, Sydney, Macario, or others similarly detained. A stay of weeks or months in the hospital was meant to alter a person's deviancy and set him on a righteous moral path to heteronormalcy.

By the end of the 1930s, more interventionist medical treatments were prescribed. Dr. Pacheco e Silva, who continued to direct both the state-run hospital and the private mental asylum, enthusiastically adopted new therapeutic techniques applied in Europe and the United States.[79] Physicians at Pinel began using "convulsive therapy" (*convulsoterapia*) and insulin injections to "cure" what was considered schizophrenic behavior. Convulsive therapy consisted of injecting the drug cardiazol into a patient in increasingly larger amounts to provoke epileptic seizures.[80] Insulin therapy (*insulinoterapia*) relied on the application of insulin to cause a hypoglycemic shock, which put the patient in a coma. This technique was used to treat both schizophrenia and general paralysis.[81] Low-level electroshock aversion therapy to treat homosexuality was first used in the United States in 1935. In 1941, Dr. Pacheco e Silva added electroshock therapy to the list of treatments used at Pinel. Experiments similar to those carried out at Pinel on Brazilian "inverts" were also applied at state mental hospitals in the United States by 1941, revealing how up-to-date Pacheco e Silva was with methods being used in the United States at the time.[82]

Among those at Pinel who received shock therapy was a patient who believed that others called him "faggot" behind his back and another whose anxieties about his effeminate behavior and physical characteristics prompted the psychological diagnosis of schizophrenia.[83] In still other cases, physicians apparently employed these new therapies to discipline men who manifested no "abnormal" psychic behavior other than suspected homosexual tendencies.

One patient diagnosed as schizophrenic and submitted to shock treatment was Armando de S. O. Filho. Described as an intelligent young man with artistic gifts, especially for literature and music, the twenty-five-year-old publicist was first admitted to Pinel on October 29, 1939.[84] Armando had married at age nineteen and was insanely jealous of his wife, whom he accused of having illicit affairs. After one particularly violent altercation with her, Armando's family took him to a beach resort near São Paulo to rest. There he developed the fear that his voice had changed and that he was becoming a "sexual invert." Moreover, Armando thought that everyone noticed this fact and that people spoke behind his back about the transformation. Armando's family decided to hospitalize him. Confined for six months, he was released in April 1940, only to be admitted a year later for further "treatment," which now included electroshock and convulsive therapy.

While Armando was uneasy about his sexual identity, his family's anxiety that their son had become an invert was the driving force behind his hospitalization. During his first stay in Pinel in 1939, before electroshock therapy had become common, it appears that the medical staff engaged in no curative therapy, and that confinement alone was presumed to regenerate him. Once shock therapies had been introduced, however, they became the favored corrective measures for deviant sexual behavior. Although it is not clear if Armando had ever engaged in homosexual activity, his own anxiety about the possibility of becoming an invert clearly played a part in provoking his severe nervous breakdown. He was not the only person confined at Pinel because of a breakdown linked to fears of becoming a homosexual. On March 11, 1940, the brother of Mario B. brought the thirty-four-year-old single bank worker from Rio de Janeiro to the São Paulo hospital.[85] In the admittance form under "other information," Mario's brother noted: "Recently he imagined that he was a homosexual and because he was considered crazy as a result, he wanted the bank to hospitalize him." The admitting physician elaborated on the case, noting that Mario had always had a strong imagination, was sensitive and very emotive. In 1935, he had become depressed because he felt that he had failed in supporting his brothers and feared that he was a homosexual. He was initially placed in a mental hospital in Rio de Janeiro, where he was diagnosed as schizophrenic and underwent insulin therapy followed by convulsive therapy, neither of which "produced the expected results." At Pinel the staff repeated insulin therapy, which provoked two comas but did not change the patient's psychic condition. Rediagnosed as "constitutionally schizophrenic with a rapid evolution toward complete dementia," Mario remained in the institution for four years. In December 1941, his father authorized electroshock therapy. His record, however, does not indicate whether or not this treatment was administered.

Since most medical folders contain few details about patients' lives from their own perspectives, it is impossible to know whether these patients had ever engaged in homosexual activities. According to his brother,

Mario's fears that he might be homosexual and his feelings of inadequacy about fulfilling filial obligations had provoked his mental crisis. But it is equally possible that the family's own anxieties about his possible homosexuality led them to remove him from home and place him in the hospital to be "cured."

Insulin and electroshock therapy were used on homosexual patients even when there was no diagnostic hint of schizophrenic behavior, and the intent seems to have been to discipline rather than cure. Thus, Octávio Barros de O., a twenty-year-old student from Rio de Janeiro, spent a year in the Pinel Sanatorium.[86] The supervising physician's notations indicate that Octávio had no psychological problems, but the student was somewhat withdrawn and gave the impression that he had some fear of persecution. The physician also mentioned that Octávio had spent three months in the Botafogo Sanatorium in Rio de Janeiro, where he had undergone insulin and convulsion therapy, for which he showed a total horror. (Octávio's disdain for the medical treatments in Rio de Janeiro might explain his persecution fears.) His medical record is silent about who committed him to the mental hospital or about the treatments he received during the year he spent at Pinel. It did mention, though, his continued sexual desires: "During his stay in the Sanatorium, the patient continued to present signs indicating the lowering of his ethical feelings, making it necessary to watch over him constantly, given his homosexual tendencies." Much to the chagrin of his physician, he left "without showing major changes in his mental state," from which we can assume his homosexual tendencies remained intact.

Another victim of shock "treatments" was Renato E. de A.[87] The twenty-nine-year-old bachelor, a lawyer by profession, was born and raised in Rio de Janeiro. His father, Dr. Bernardino E., who was probably a lawyer himself, brought his son to Pinel, a long day's journey, on June 15, 1943. According to the physician's diagnosis, "the patient is calm, oriented and conscious. We do not note any kind of psychological disorder. He was brought to the Sanatorium due to the irregular behavior that has gone on for some time now. He manifests very accentuated homosexual tendencies. From his own external habits we see that the feminine instinct dominates him: he uses lipstick, a hairpiece and shaves his thorax and abdomen, etc."

Renato, it seems, was already integrated into the life of Carioca homosexuals. He had adopted the use of makeup and shaved his body hair. His metamorphosis alarmed his father, who worried about his son's indifference to his profession and his fixation on appearance. In the admission form, Renato's father noted that his son had no desire to work, had developed a tendency to lie, and had manifested mental problems since age nine. In an uncommonly detailed addendum to the admission form, he outlined background information on his son:

> The patient, being hospitalized, has presented abnormalities since approximately age eight or nine.
>
> A. Infancy: in school he avoided socializing with other boys; during recreation he stayed to himself since he greatly disliked all masculine games and exercises.
>
> B. Adolescence: for unjustified reasons he stopped going to classes during the last year of school; and had to take exams in the second semester.
>
> C. Youth: tremendous indolence: no aptitude for work, excessive preoccupation with his beauty. For hours, four or five, he remained in the bathroom "fixing himself up." He went out late at night and slept during the day.

According to his father's description, Renato's homosexuality stemmed from his indifference to masculine activities—sports, study, a professional career, and hard work. Rather than following in his father's footsteps as a lawyer, Renato ignored proper bourgeois behavior and led a bohemian life. His excessive attachment to personal grooming confirmed his father's fears that his son's early feminine behavior had evolved into unabashed homosexuality.

While the physicians at Pinel did not think that Renato suffered any observable mental disorder, they nevertheless ordered what had become standard medical treatment for diagnosed schizophrenics. Between June 29 and August 10, 1943, Renato received electroshock therapy eleven times. A month later, he was permitted to leave the institution once a week for day trips or walks, and he was released nine months after his initial hospitalization. Unfortunately, the medical record does not reveal the physicians' diagnosis of Renato's condition when he left Pinel. Had he, like Napoleão eight years before him, acquiesced to his family's desires that he abandon his "degenerate" behavior? Had eleven sessions of electroshock therapy dissuaded him from at least manifesting his desires and sexual identity in order for the treatment to cease? Did Renato return to his bohemian lifestyle, or did he conform to his father's desires to practice law and become a stalwart member of society? While we may never know the results of the Pinel Sanatorium's preferred treatment in the early 1940s, Renato's case makes it clear that electroshock therapy had become more than a means of startling paranoid schizophrenics out of autistic stupor. The treatment inflicted on Renato for his unconventional behavior may have passed as a cure, but it was in fact a punishment. In dealing with manifestations of homosexuality among middle-class men, the medical profession's solutions, just like the arbitrary arrests of lower-class and dark-skinned men, did not achieve the expected results. Homosexual behavior continued unabated.

The Estado Novo and the Body, 1937–45

Most historical works on the Estado Novo emphasize the centralization of political power and the restructuring of class relations during this period.[88] Other historians have examined the regime's political ideology, showing how the Estado Novo relied on authoritarian practices that were part of Brazilian traditions, but were now modernized and incorporated as propaganda and educational vehicles for Vargas's policies.[89] The growth of the state's power in the regulation of ordinary life, from Carnival parades to trade unions, has been widely documented. Alcir Lenharo has noted that "the broad project of the reordering of society—corporatism—was supported entirely in the image of the organic nature of the human body. The parts that composed society were thought of in the same way as the relationship among the organs of the body: integrated and without contradictions. The objective of the project, therefore, aimed at neutralizing the foci of social conflicts and making the classes (organs) in solidarity with each other."[90] Dissolving political parties, outlawing strikes, and maintaining strict press censorship, all were parts of the reordering of the political body.

The physical body itself was not left out of this reconstruction of the Brazilian nation. New magazines entered the market, emphasizing health, hygiene, and physical education. The government promoted the "new" masculinity, which idealized strength, youth, and power. One physical education magazine summarized this ideal: "The new Physical Education should form a typical man who has the following characteristics: figure thinner than fuller, graceful muscles, flexibility, light-colored eyes, agile, . . . sweet, happy, virile, . . . sincere, honest, pure in acts and thoughts."[91] Schools and factories became sites of group exercises, sports, and marching. Brazil's entry into World War II in 1942 only accelerated this process, as production became militarized. On May Day that year, Vargas proclaimed to a crowd of industrial workers that "in the end, we are all soldiers of Brazil."[92]

Paradoxically, just as the Brazilian physical body was taking on such importance, there was a noted decline in writings about homosexuality by medicolegal professionals. Several hypotheses might explain the decrease in intellectual production about the subject. First of all, one must remember that most of the theoretical work about homosexuality had been borrowed from Europe and, to a much lesser extent, from the United States. With the European continent in turmoil during the 1930s and the world at war in the '40s, Brazil did not have easy access to new writings that could have added to the literature at hand or inspired further intellectual production. Second, no immediate medical cure accompanied the main endogenous medical explanation for homosexuality, namely, hormonal imbalances. Testicle transplant therapy did not become a popular treatment; indeed, there appears no indication that Brazilian physicians ever attempted to test this possible remedy. Marañón's and others' theories on "intersexuality" and "missexuality," based on erroneous understandings of embryo development, had become discredited. Moreover, Brazilian physicians did not have the resources to establish laboratories to conduct their own research in endocrinology or biochemistry.[93] Most reputable intellectuals began to abandon eugenics theories, especially those regarding racial issues, by the 1940s, partially because of the association of these ideas with Nazi Germany. Writers, such as Gilberto Freyre, who had redefined the contribution of Africans to Brazilian culture, began to assume a prominent role in national intellectual debates, further discrediting eugenics ideas.[94] After a decade of intense discussion, writing, and "research," homosexuality as a topic of debate among medical and legal professionals retreated into the margins.

In less than two decades, homosexuality had been extensively studied, classified, and pathologized. Although this process had begun in the late nineteenth century, the consolidation of the role of the medical and legal professions under the Republic (1889–1930) and during Vargas's rule (1930–45) vis-à-vis the state facilitated the "medicalization" of the homosexual. Medicolegal professionals won the campaign to have more jurisdiction over the subject, although they had to share their authority with the police and the state. Under the Estado Novo, the governing elite decided not to establish a specific hospital to cure homosexuality or pass a law explicitly naming homosexuals in crimes against public decency. It was not necessary. The sick social body of the previous two decades was becoming robust with the exercise, regimentation, and discipline of the new order. Emphasis was placed on a healthy, positive image of Brazilian society, discarding the notion of degeneration that had aroused such concern in the past.

This did not mean, however, that the writings of the medicolegal profession on homosexuality faded into obscurity. The ideas and theories developed during the 1930s were popularized in the 1940s through sexual manuals, which reached broader sectors of Brazilian society. According to Celeste Zenha Guimarães, who has researched the "myths" of homosexuality, "from the 1930s on, there was an expressive dissemination of this kind of product [vulgarized sex manuals] which increased even more in the 1940s. These compendiums presented in accessible language the concepts already analyzed, such as making the population fear engaging in certain acts as well as in having contact with the 'physical and moral types' described in the treatises of legal medicine and psychopathic forensics."[95]

Ultimately, the writings of physicians and other professionals dovetailed with these popular manuals on sex, which reinforced long-held traditional views about homosexuality. Although Brazilian experts constantly cited European theories, they tended to adapt the models they borrowed to prevalent Brazilian notions of sexuality and popular ideas about same-sex sexual activity. Talisman Ford has argued that Brazilian sexologists deemphasized the importance of classifying homosexuals based on their sexual-object choice, which was a key component of the European medical construction of the homosexual by the turn of the century. Instead, Brazilian writers focused more on specific gender-based behavior and hierarchical sexual roles in categorizing homosexuals. Thus, according to most European sexologists, a man was a homosexual if he had or desired to have sex with another man, regardless of the specific fantasies or practices carried out in bed. Innate characteristics, whether congenital or acquired, produced a unique being, the homosexual, with a unique essence. In anal intercourse, both the man penetrating and the man being penetrated were, therefore, considered homosexuals. As Ford points out, Brazilian physicians and other observers reframed European theories of homosexuality along lines that conformed to popular assumptions that associated male homosexuality with effeminacy and passive anal sexuality. Brazilian writers acknowledged the existence of "active," as well as "passive" pederasts, as had Viveiros de Castro and Pires de Almeida at the turn of the century, but the emphasis was on the individual who conformed more closely to traditional representations of women in Brazilian society, namely, the effeminate man who to all appearances was anal receptive in sexual intercourse. The "active" partner presumably possessed masculine characteristics and therefore did not have the same fixed homosexual essence typical of the effeminate man. This adaptation of European theories to local understandings of same-sex eroticism may explain why the model of the homosexual based on sexual-object choice did not become a pervasive construct in Brazil in this period, as Ford has suggested.[96]

"Passive pederasts" and effeminate men, indeed, were the main focus of Brazilian writing and research. In part this was due to their greater visibility in the urban landscape of Rio de Janeiro and São Paulo, as well as their vulnerability to police harassment, arrest, and at times "scientific" research. With plucked eyebrows and rouged cheeks, they simply did not melt into the crowd. But as we have seen in the chapter 2, the actual sexual practices of the alleged "passive pederasts" was more complicated than the models that the sexologists brought to their investigations. The "inconsistency" in the sexual behavior of certain individuals in regard to "active" and "passive" intercourse often defied the "Brazilian" paradigm that defined and categorized same-sex comportment.

Equally important, however, in measuring the influence of European theoretical models as screened through Brazilian sexologists on the construction or reconstruction of popular conceptions of homosexuality is the actual effect that these medicolegal professionals had on the day-to-day lives of men engaged in same-sex erotic activities or on the population at large. Although the stated goal of many writers on the subject was to educate society about this social disease, much of their material was written in professional journals directed to the police, criminologists, and physicians. Their ideas about homosexuality certainly influenced the medical and legal professions, as well as criminologists, and thus had an impact on patterns of "treatment." But, there is no indication that these publications reached broad audiences. Thus, the effect of their writings on most homosexuals was indirect at best.

More widespread propagation of their theories and ideas through sexual education manuals tended to water down the enlightened elements in their proposals for the treatment of homosexuality. The new, popular publications about sex often combined synthetic summaries of the theories of European and Brazilian sexologists with moralistic and religious statements that associated homosexuality with vice and corruption. One such book, *Psicoses de amor* (Love psychoses) by the prolific sexologist Hernâni de Irajá, was already in its fourth edition in 1931, with four more editions out by 1954. Literary and scientific circles regarded the work of its author highly. A front-page article in the popular magazine *Fon-Fon*, for example, heralded Irajá as one of the most important intellectuals of the day and the book as "a notable work about the subject of the pathology of love."[97] Illustrating the chapter entitled "Homosexuality: Sexual Inversion" was an ink drawing of ghoulish figures whose fingernails and teeth dripped with blood. Skeletal heads and suffering men crowded together to convey the message that homosexuality led straight to hell. The author left no room for doubt about his views on the subject: "Homosexuality is love or the practice of sexual acts between individuals of the same sex. Morally and physically wasted individuals in the state of total corruption and decadence try to relive numbed sensations with new and strange pleasures. From hence comes the vice of pederasty."[98] Regardless of the efforts of Ribeiro and others in the medicolegal profession to present a less moralistic and more "scientific" view of homosexuality, this perspective remained dominant in popular literature well into the 1970s.

CHAPTER FOUR

～

New Words, New Spaces, New Identities, 1945–1968

The demise of Getúlio Vargas and the authoritarian Estado Novo at the end of World War II opened up a nineteen-year period of democratic governments.[1] This era ended with the military coup d'état of March 31, 1964. Four years later, in 1968, massive student demonstrations and widespread opposition to the generals in power provoked a power shift within the military. In late 1969, hard-liner General Médici rose to the presidency. The regime closed Congress and jailed thousands of dissidents. Press censorship increased, and opposition was silenced.

In the two and a half decades between 1945 and 1969, mass migration to Brazil's major metropolises tipped the demographic balance from rural to urban. In 1950, 64 percent of all Brazilians lived in the countryside, and the remaining 36 percent resided in cities. Ten years later, this number jumped to 45 percent, and in 1970, 56 percent of the population lived in urban areas. Rio de Janeiro and São Paulo continued to draw the largest numbers of rural migrants, especially hundreds of thousands of peasants who left the drought-ridden Northeast to seek employment in the Southeast. Many of these migrants found their way to the factories of São Paulo, which became the major force behind the entire country's industrialization.[2]

Post–World War II economic prosperity produced an expanding market and a growing urban middle class. National industries provided a broad array of commodities ranging from steel to household appliances and other mass-produced consumer items at affordable prices. As a result of closer ties forged with the United States during World War II, American industrial and cultural production flooded the Brazilian market, and in the late 1950s European automobile manufacturers joined U.S. corporations in setting up plants in the Greater São Paulo area. Propelled by the radio, the printed media, and television, Brazil quickly became a mass-based consumer society. In the late 1940s, the country entered the golden age of radio, as the airwaves linked the sprawling continent-nation. Radio singers became national idols, adored by millions. In 1951, Brazil was the fourth country in the world to install television, and by the end of the decade TV had outpaced radio in shaping public attitudes and standardizing language and culture. Newspapers, magazines, foreign movies, and American comic books informed readers of the latest fashions, styles, and cultural shifts from New York, Hollywood, Paris, and Rome.

Constructions of appropriate gender roles shifted in a contradictory manner during the first part of this period. Rigidly defined gender norms that had been encouraged under the Estado Novo began to bend as more middle-class women entered the labor force, completed secondary education, and sought university degrees. Yet these same women were still expected to be virgins when they reached the altar, and obedient and submissive wives after marriage, cradling and nurturing families that were ultimately ruled by men. A double standard that sanctioned sexual promiscuity among men but expected moral purity among women still prevailed. By the end of the 1960s, however, cultural changes began to challenge these values and weaken traditional sexual roles.[3]

During these twenty-five years, there were also significant alterations in the composition and the development of the male homosexual subcultures of Rio de Janeiro and São Paulo. New notions of sexual and gender identity emerged and challenged the prevalent bipolar dyad of "real" men and effeminate *bichas*. Nightlife options expanded and exclusively gay bars opened. Homosexuals occupied new areas of Brazil's major cities. Fan clubs for popular radio singers served as another means of creating community and integrating men into this burgeoning subculture. The attendance at the annual Miss Brazil beauty pageants offered a forum for public display of camp, as well as the opportunity to measure and challenge traditional notions of feminine glamour, beauty, and fashion. Despite the opposition of certain "macho" men who tried to drive the *bichas* off the sands, a section of the popular Copacabana Beach in Rio de Janeiro became homosexual territory. Carnival balls catering to homosexuals received extensive press coverage, while glamorous cross-dressers emerged from these drag balls to perform in mainstream theater productions that attracted a wide audience. A group of homosexuals in Rio de Janeiro began to put out a newsletter, *O Snob*, filled with gossip, camp humor, and self-affirmation. The paper, in turn, inspired thirty similar publications throughout the country. Within these social networks, some even dreamed of an "imagined community" of homosexuals who would unite in an effort to change social hostility toward them.[4] These developments, which totally reshaped the urban gay subcultures of São Paulo and Rio de Janeiro, are the focus of this chapter.

"Whoever gets to know Copacabana, doesn't want to live anywhere else"

In 1952, Agildo Guimarães moved from Recife, the capital of the northeastern state of Pernambuco, to Rio de Janeiro. More than forty years later, he recalled that while living with his family in Recife, he had become seriously depressed. He went through an emotional crisis during which he couldn't stop crying. His family did not know what to do with him, and he did not have the courage to tell his mother that he wanted to leave home and move to Rio. Agildo found it unbearable to continue living in a hostile environment where he was constantly pressured to have a girlfriend and eventually get married. Moreover, the word had gotten out that he was a *bicha*. This bothered his boyfriend, a "real" man and certainly *not* a homosexual, who did not like the fact that rumors of their relationship were circulating throughout the neighborhood. Letters from a friend, a corporal in the army who was stationed in Rio de Janeiro, telling Agildo how exciting that city was only increased the youth's desire to leave his hometown. Finally, he discussed the matter with his family, who agreed to let him go, and he embarked for the nation's capital in 1952.[5]

During this same period, Carlos Miranda, who lived in Campos, a city in the state of Rio de Janeiro, also faced a crisis with his family. His brother knew that Carlos had sex with other boys and thought that this behavior brought shame on the family. When Carlos broke up with a boyfriend, he, like Agildo, sank into a state of depression. As luck would have it, a doctor who had lived openly as a homosexual in Rio de Janeiro began treating him. The physician convinced Carlos's family that by allowing the youth to travel to Rio de Janeiro on weekends his health would improve. After a few excursions to the nation's capital, Carlos, too, decided that Rio was his salvation, and he moved there in 1954.[6]

João Antônio Mascarenhas passed through Rio de Janeiro in 1950 on his way to Europe. He was a law student from the southern state of Rio Grande do Sul, and his family was financially comfortable. It was February and Carnival time, so he decided to go to the drag ball at the João Caetano theater at Praça Tiradentes, a ball that was attended almost exclusively by homosexuals. Men danced together, hugged each other, and ended up having sex in the midst of revelers. Ever since he had first gone to a Carnival ball at age seventeen in his home state, João Antônio had seen men dressed as women in the festivities, but never had he experienced anything like that Carnival ball in Rio de Janeiro. He also ended up moving to the nation's capital.[7]

All three men were attracted to Rio de Janeiro because they discovered the gay subculture that thrived there. Moving to the city meant obtaining freedom from family supervision, control, and pressures to marry and have children.[8] Rio de Janeiro possessed an energy that was enchanting, and all three quickly settled into life in the *cidade maravilhosa*. João Antônio, with a law degree in hand, quickly found work in the federal bureaucracy. Agildo, who had fewer economic resources, stayed with a close friend of the family's until he could find employment and, eventually, a tiny apartment in Copacabana. Carlos rented a room in a house in Copacabana and ultimately set up his own apartment in that neighborhood.

Throughout the 1940s and '50s, Lapa, Cinelândia, and Praça Tiradentes continued as territories frequented by men seeking sex with men. However, the city's most vibrant nightlife had shifted to Copacabana, which became *the* place to live (see map 5). Nossa Senhora de Copacabana Avenue, which cut through the long narrow neighborhood set between green-covered granite mountains and a white-sanded beach, boasted new cinemas and fancy boutiques. Even though the casinos had been closed by law in 1946, Rio's high society gathered in Copacabana's other elite watering holes. The Copacabana Palace Hotel attracted celebrities from around the world, and its Golden Room booked the country's top artists.[9]

The fascination with Copacabana was widespread, and many from Rio de Janeiro's middle class aspired to take up residency there. Real estate speculators crammed building after building into the neighborhood. While the upper middle class and wealthy could afford spacious oceanfront apartments, most residents tended to live in smaller apartments or studio singles, known as *caixas de fósforos* (matchboxes).[10] Copacabana became a predominantly middle-class neighborhood, although many who identified themselves as such struggled hard to maintain a household there.[11] Towering apartment buildings replaced the elegant summer beach houses of Rio's well-to-do families. Nestled on the ground floor of some of these buildings were tiny, noisy nightclubs known as *inferninhos* (little hells), where one

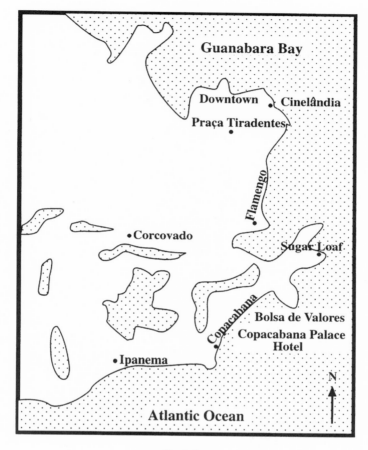

MAP 5   Rio de Janeiro, 1960

could hear the most recent musical arrivals from the United States or popular Brazilian performers.[12] Alternatively, from the late '50s on, one could
go to a more quiet nightspot in the neighborhood to catch the latest bossa
nova tune.[13]

Middle-class homosexuals, or those who aspired to that lifestyle,
sought out Copacabana because it offered a privileged space for entertainment, cruising, and socializing. Others, with fewer resources, chose boardinghouses or shared apartments in neighborhoods between Copacabana
and the city center. While, in general terms, a class division separated those
who frequented Copacabana from those who preferred the center and the
pleasures of Cinelândia, for example, there was no strict social segregation

between the two locations. Men from poor backgrounds seeking upward mobility gravitated toward Copacabana. Middle- and upper-class homosexuals who liked "real" working-class men, soldiers, and sailors often sought them out in downtown cruising areas. Cinelândia also had an abundant number of cinemas, which continued to shelter sexual encounters. In the late 1950s, Sérgio, who lived in a northern suburb of the city, went to a downtown movie one day and discovered a world of easy sex. He especially enjoyed going to Cinema Passatempo, which showed continuous newsreels, shorts, and cartoons and was designed for people who had an hour or two to kill downtown.[14] During Carnival, homosexuals from all over the city converged on Cinelândia, where many of the street festivities took place, and nearby Praça Tiradentes, where the drag balls were held. Because Cinelândia was near the commercial, governmental, and financial centers of the city, all sectors of the population crisscrossed the area for work as well as for pleasure. In the cinemas, cafés, and cruising areas, homosexuals of all social classes took advantage of long lunch hours or after-work beers to socialize, make new friends, and find sexual partners.[15]

Although Copacabana, with its beachfront properties and breathtaking views of Rio's surrounding mountains, had a worldwide reputation as a modern, exciting place to live, it also had its detractors, who criticized its inhabitants' fast living and sexual permissiveness. A 1952 article in *Manchete*, a photo-news magazine with a national circulation, warned Brazilian tourists about the dangers of the area. The journalist's sordid vision of life in Copacabana focused on homosexuality as one of the neighborhood's many vices. In rather circuitous language, he wrote: "On the streets of Copacabana, unprepared tourist, you will find types that will surprise you. Vice, mainly sexual, freely dominates the scarcely illuminated apartments. A multitude of asexuals, professional addicts, and victims of glandular disorders confront each other, attack each other, fighting collectively for the same objective. . . . It doesn't require more than a week to understand how true the statement of [Police] Commissioner Padilha is: 'The majority of Copacabana lives off sex.'"[16] The vice-ridden figures with glandular disorders were, of course, homosexuals, who, the author argued, lived mostly as prostitutes or hustlers.

Writing a year later about the neighborhood's clubs, another journalist portrayed a decadent city with "all kinds of nightclubs, including existentialist and semi-existentialist ones." The reference to the potentially subversive and dangerous new philosophical import from Paris was hardly subtle. The journalist then made clichéd comparisons to the Left Bank scene: Dark and smoke-filled bars attracted "the most consummate scoundrels, easy women, leftovers from the world war, attractive men who live off their looks, perverts, and homosexuals."[17] In spite of this dismal portrait of Copacabana, it was precisely the modern and bohemian image of the beachfront city with its glamorous nightspots and easy sex that attracted so many people, foreign tourists and native Brazilians alike. It was also one of main reasons why so many homosexuals chose to live and have fun there.

Places where homosexual men could socialize in Copacabana abounded in the 1950s. Open-air cafés lined the broad black and white mosaic stone sidewalks that curved along the oceanfront of Avenida Atlântica. One could pause at the Alcazar, where men dressed as women paraded in their fancy costumes during Carnival, and where quick sex was always to be found in the bathroom. Stopping for a beer or dinner at any of the local restaurants or cafés also offered an opportunity to cruise other men and possibly find a sexual partner. These establishments did not purposefully cater to a homosexual clientele, and sometimes owners or managers were hostile toward customers who behaved flamboyantly. Fearing that too many effeminate-acting men might give a place a "bad" reputation and result in a drop in business from heterosexual couples and families, most businesses imposed strict norms on their customers that prohibited any public manifestations of affection between men and discouraged "camp" behavior. Nevertheless, gay men appropriated different cafés and restaurants in Copacabana as sites for socializing until they were driven out by antagonistic proprietors.[18]

Young homosexuals, dressed to the nines, also spent endless hours walking in groups of two and three up and down Nossa Senhora de Copacabana Avenue, window-shopping for the latest fashions (see fig. 10). Pausing at clothing displays or strolling leisurely along this avenue provided ample possibilities to catch the glance of someone "interesting" or to see who else was out on the town.[19] Because men had more freedom than women to stay out on the town into the early morning hours, the midnight sessions at the Rian and Copacabana Metro movie theaters were always packed with small groups of young men. They were there to enjoy the latest film from Hollywood, but many also went to late-night movies to meet other men with similar sexual, social, or cultural interests. It was during one such evening's outing that Carlos Miranda met Peres, the founder of Turma OK, a social network of gay men that functioned in the late 1950s and throughout the '60s. Carlos's new acquaintance introduced him to a circle of friends and to a rich social life. "[Peres] used to organize a small group of friends in his apartment every week where we would get together and listen to music, talk, and sip on a drink because there were no bars

FIGURE 10   Agildo Guimarães and friends during a night out, cruising on Avenida Nossa Senhora de Copacabana, Rio de Janeiro, 1957. Photograph courtesy of Agildo Guimarães.

or discotheques for us at the time. And that's how the Turma OK came about."[20]

As Carlos rightly recalled, in the early and mid-1950s just as there were no cafés and restaurants that catered exclusively to a homosexual clientele, places for men to spend an evening out together were nowhere to be found. Men who wished to go to a nightclub or bar to interact somewhat openly with other homosexuals had to "occupy" a given establishment until they were pressured to leave by patrons, bouncers, manager, or owner. In 1952, one popular meeting spot was A Tasca. A journalist described it as Copacabana's "newest sensation" and noted that homosexuals were among those who enjoyed the new nightclub: "All sexes [were there]. Feminine, masculine and undefined."[21]

However, the homosexual takeover of a bar or a club could be ephemeral, as João Antônio Mascarenhas discovered. While still living in Rio Grande do Sul, he read an article by Ruben Braga in a popular magazine. Braga, a famous journalist who chronicled Rio's nightlife, had described a nightspot patronized by homosexuals. João Antônio recalled: "He said it was on Ronaldo de Carvalho street next to the Lido Plaza at [Lifeguard] Post 2, that it was named Aquário [Aquarium], and that he had seen men whispering to each other and holding on to each other. It caught my attention. The next time I got to Rio I went looking for it, but I couldn't find it. I guess it must not have lasted long."[22] Another journalist explained the demise of Aquário as being the result of the "excess of delicate specialization that made it the target of [Chief of Police] Padilha's fury."[23]

Similarly, for a short period of time, Carioca homosexuals chose Posto 5, a small, dark nightclub that featured live entertainment, as a favorite meeting place.[24] Likewise, Scotch Bar, located on Nossa Senhora de Copacabana, was partially "taken over" by discreet upper- and middle-class homosexuals in the late 1950s. Vítor, who lived in Rio de Janeiro at the time, described Scotch Bar as having plaid wallpaper and fine leather chairs. He remembered it as one of the most elegant bars that Copacabana had ever had. Although the owners of Scotch's were known to be hostile to their new patrons, homosexual men insisted on frequenting the bar. A tense truce between the bar owners and customers permitted the tenuous "occupation" of this chic establishment for several years.[25]

By the early 1960s, some nightclub entrepreneurs realized that there was a market for places that catered exclusively to homosexuals and began to change policies that had discouraged a gay clientele. This was in part due to the fact that the critical mass of homosexuals coming to Copacabana had become large enough to sustain a number of gay-identified establishments. Homosexual visibility became less and less of a novelty as Carnival drag balls received widespread press coverage, gained an international reputation, and enjoyed relative tolerance from both the public and the police. Social and sexual mores also loosened in the 1960s, permitting a more liberal attitude toward sexuality in general. All of these factors contributed to the growth of places where homosexuals might congregate more freely. By 1964, Copacabana could claim over a half dozen nightspots servicing mostly gay customers, including Alcatraz, Alfredão, Dezon, Stop, Sunset, and Why Not? Some only remained open for a season, but others became part of Carioca homosexuals' social scene. Thirty-five years later, when asked about which establishment was Rio's premier "gay" bar, many gay men seemed to recall Alfredão as the first club that catered exclusively to homosexuals and managed to survive more than a short time.[26]

Bichas and Beaches: Defending New Territory

While many came to Copacabana for its nightlife, its beautiful beach also attracted men from all over the city and country. By the mid-1950s, homosexuals had staked out an area in front of the Copacabana Palace Hotel that they called "Bolsa de Valores," after the stock exchange, referring to the quality of cruising and flirting that took place there (see fig. 11). Carlos Miranda, who started going to the Bolsa in 1954, didn't know when people first came up with that name. "When I asked [why it was called that], they told me that the Bolsa de Valores is where you showed yourself to be valued (valorizar). A place for valorization, to show your body."[27] Carlos also wasn't sure why homosexuals had chosen that specific spot to congregate. He speculated that because the Copacabana Palace Hotel was such a large, visible structure, it was an easy landmark for people to use as a reference point. Perhaps the young homosexual men also hoped to catch a glimpse of Yves Montand, Nat King Cole, Marlene Dietrich, Rock Hudson, or Rita Hayworth, who were among the countless international guests and performers entertained by playboy owner Jorge Guinle in the elegant hotel.[28]

Writing in 1958 about gay beaches for *One Magazine*, the pioneering journal of one of the first homophile organizations in the United States, Frank Golovitz observed: "There's a lot of difference between a gay bar and a gay beach. For one thing the beach is more truly 'gay' and in a much

FIGURE 11   Agildo Guimarães and friends at the Bolsa de Valores, the gay beach located in front of the Copacabana Palace Hotel, Rio de Janeiro, 1957. Photograph courtesy of Agildo Guimarães.

healthier sense. And although some are 'on the make,' the percentage isn't as high as in the bars. Nor is the tension. With rare exceptions, a beach is out in the open. . . . [I]t is probably the only place where large mixed groups of homosexuals can be freely observed 'acting natural.' And class boundaries fall away even more at the beach than in other sectors of gay life."[29] Copacabana's gay beach had similar characteristics. "We would meet our friends there," Carlos recalled. "We weren't outrageously effeminate, but our clothes were more daring."[30] The Bolsa de Valores also facilitated integration into the homosexual subculture of Rio de Janeiro. One could gossip, flirt, make plans for the evening, and meet new friends. People from different social backgrounds who shared common sexual desires could interact more freely than in pricey establishments that de facto excluded those of modest means. Newly arrived migrants from other parts of Brazil could be warned about the latest cruising area where the police were shaking down homosexuals caught in compromising situations. In short, the Bolsa became an integral part of the sexual topography and social lives of Carioca homosexuals.

However, not all open homosexuals liked to go there, especially those interested in finding a "real" man who did not assume a homosexual identity. Moreover, despite a certain social leveling of beach life, the middle-class aura surrounding Copacabana still prevailed. Rivas, an Afro-Brazilian worker, for example, preferred a section of the Flamengo Beach, which was closer to downtown. "I didn't go to Copacabana (I still like Flamengo). There were more *bofes* ["real" men] than in Copacabana, and it was humbler and more pleasant."[31] Rivas preferred the company of Brazilians of modest origins. Just as some men sought out "real" men in downtown Rio de Janeiro, he found that Flamengo Beach also offered more fertile cruising grounds for masculine, working-class men who might be willing to have sex with a *bicha*.

The concentration of mostly effeminate men at the Bolsa in Copacabana provoked a response from the "macho" neighborhood youth who used the same area for their own socializing and leisure activities. Carlos remembered one specific day in 1954 or '55, soon after he had arrived in Rio: "There were attacks, and they threw sand at us. They even brought a banner to the beach one day that said: '*Bichas* Get Out of Here.'"[32] According to Carlos, neighborhood boys stuck the painted cloth banner into the sand as a warning that homosexuals were not welcome anymore in front of the Copacabana Palace Hotel. Their hostilities, however, backfired. The sand that they threw at the *bichas* got all over the families who were sitting nearby. Protective mothers, angry that their children had also been showered by sand, began defending the besieged homosexuals. They argued that those under attack hadn't been bothering anyone. They even threatened to inform the boys' parents, since they all lived close by and knew each other. The aggression stopped, and the Bolsa de Valores remained a social meeting ground for homosexuals.[33]

The attacks on the beach were not the only occasions when homosexuals who lived or socialized in Copacabana suffered aggression from men who disapproved of or who were threatened by their sometimes flamboyant and effeminate behavior. João Baptista remembered a term used by homosexuals to describe gay-bashing of the early 1960s: "When there was a group of guys who would beat up homosexuals, we would say 'There's going to be a *revertério*' [the change from a good to a bad situation], or, 'Be careful, so-and-so is *revertério*.'"[34] Carlos Miranda recalled another slang term used right after Alfred Hitchcock's film *The Birds* was released in 1963: "There was a lot of harassment. People would surround homosexuals and bother them, so we called these guys *os pássaros de Copacabana* (the birds of Copacabana).[35] While João Antônio was never personally beaten up, he also remembered street violence against homosexuals: "There was a group of a half dozen middle-class boys who hung out at Miguel Lemos Street and Nossa Senhora de Copacabana and attacked people for the simple fact that they had an effeminate appearance."[36] When asked if the police ever intervened to defend homosexuals being physically assaulted, Riva scornfully replied, "Not at all! They were too busy blackmailing *bichas* in the movie theaters."[37]

In fact, police harassment was a constant problem for Carioca homosexuals in the 1950s and '60s, and their archenemy was Police Commissioner Raimundo Padilha, who waged a campaign to "clean up" the downtown, a campaign that included detaining homosexuals. Baptista recalled: "You couldn't stand around in one place or the police would come by and arrest you."[38] Riva remembered going downtown to the Iris Movie Theater for a sexual escapade. After having an erotic encounter with a man in the balcony, his furtive partner pulled out a police badge, took him to a police van, and held him for several hours. When the police officer realized that Riva did not have any money to offer as a bribe, he was released. Others were not as lucky. Police sweeps through the downtown areas where homosexuals gathered were commonplace. Usually those arrested were booked for vagrancy if they could not show that they were gainfully employed. Those who did work might have to pay a bribe to be released without further complications. The possibility that the police might contact a person's family about a son, brother, or father picked up in a downtown cruising area was a sufficiently effective threat to enable authorities to extort a small sum from detainees. Not all those arrested, however, could afford that means of gaining freedom. Many had to suffer the indignation of several hours' or days' incarceration, although one group of fourteen homosexuals arrested in 1953 managed to break out of their cells and stage a near-successful escape from detention.[39]

In spite of police surveillance and arrests, homosexuals not only tenaciously held on to the urban sites so essential for public sociability, but they expanded these spaces throughout the decade. Beaches, bars, restaurants, and cafés became "liberated zones," where men had a bit more freedom to interact with friends and new acquaintances. These places became key to the formation of an urban subculture that would become increasingly visible through the 1950s.

Beauty Pageants, Muscle Men, Radio Stars, and Fan Clubs

The beaches, bars, and streets of Copacabana were not the only new spaces appropriated by homosexuals. The Miss Brazil beauty pageant, held at the Maracanãzinho auditorium north of downtown, was also contested territory throughout the 1950s. This annual event attracted homosexuals from all over Rio de Janeiro. While bathing-suited beauties paraded around below, some campy men would imitate them in the upper seats, to the amusement of other homosexual men in the audience. Riva reminisced nostalgically: "When there were contests at Maracanãzinho, the Miss Brazil contest or Miss Rio de Janeiro, we would go and expose ourselves to danger. There were *lots* of *bichas*. It was beautiful inside. It was simply marvelous. But when it was over, the guys would persecute us, throw stones at us; it was horrible. But the next year, we would be there again. We dressed differently, a lot of red, a lot of tight pants. At the time the contests were in the winter, and in our sweaters we were scandalously beautiful. No one dressed as a woman. That happened only at Carnival balls."[40]

The Miss Brazil contests provided many self-identified effeminate homosexuals with a collective experience. The events became public venues for those who wished to parade and camp about their own sense of femininity. The pageant contestants also served as role models for those who identified with the traditional notion of feminine beauty. For others, it was a social occasion to see friends, show off one's latest sartorial acquisitions, and perhaps even catch a "real" man who had come to see the women, but could be convinced to leave with a *boneca* [doll, effeminate homosexual].[41]

If some Carioca homosexuals sought out sexual partners among the crowds of men admiring Brazilian bathing beauties, others enjoyed erotic pleasures through muscle magazines and bodybuilding contests that became popular in Brazil after World War II. Brazil even had its own publication dedicated to the subject, *Força e Saúde* (Strength and health), first issued in 1947 and supplemented by *Músculo* (Muscle) in 1953.[42] *Músculo*, a slick thirty-six-page monthly produced in Rio, prominently featured the bulging biceps of João Baptista, Brazil's contribution to the international bodybuilding circuit. The magazine also revealed the near perfect bodies of foreign champions, including Steve Reeves, Mr. Universe 1950, who would go on to a career playing Hercules in Italian B-movies.[43] João Baptista, Brazil's muscled star, never made it to the silver screen, but he was the fifth runner-up in the 1950 Mr. Universe competition held in Paris and fourth runner-up two years later in London. Dubbed the "Brazilian Apollo" by the photo-magazine *Manchete*, in the early 1950s he could be spotted on the beaches of Copacabana working out or simply flexing his muscles for camera lenses and delighted crowds.[44]

During the 1950s in the United States, certain gyms and beaches were locations where men attracted to muscular men either worked out or lingered in order to enjoy the visual beauty of these athletes' well-defined bod-ies.[45] The same was true in Brazil although bodybuilding remained a much less popular sport than soccer, the national obsession.[46] Since Brazil did not produce any male pornography in the 1950s and the importation of foreign materials was difficult, these muscle magazines provided the next closest al-ternative. Pumped-up bodybuilders in skimpy, tight-fitting bathing suits and revealing posing straps offered erotic stimulation for an interested read-ership. Moreover, because the magazine could be ordered by mail, men could receive it all over the country.

Jim Kepner, a pioneering leader of one of the United States's first gay rights organizations, recalled that sometime in the early 1950s the editors of *One*, the Los Angeles-based One Institute's homophile publication, re-ceived a copy of a Brazilian bodybuilding magazine with an accompanying letter. According to Kepner, the sender apologized for the modest quality of the magazine, but explained that it was the only publication of its kind for homosexuals in Brazil.[47] Indeed, a subtext lay beneath the surface of the neatly designed Brazilian bodybuilders monthly, and the most visible man-ifestation was a series of illustrations by Jean Boullet, a popular French artist of the 1950s, who painted nude and near-nude men with clear homo-erotic overtones. In 1952, after taking fourth place in the Mr. Universe con-test, João Baptista slipped over to Paris where he modeled for Boullet. Soon thereafter, the owners of *Saúde e Força* and *Músculo* offered the magazines' readership the possibility of receiving a photo of Baptista along with four-teen etchings of the Brazilian national champion "in athletic poses" created by the "existentialist French artist." Several articles promoted the offer, in-cluding one showing the Brazilian Apollo signing copies of the sales item and informing readers that mail-order purchases to admiring fans all over the country had already been pouring in.[48]

Boullet chose to portray Baptista as a Greek or Roman archer. He wears nothing but a short leather codpiece loosely held together by leather thongs hugging his hips. A buckled strap crosses over his perfectly shaped chest to secure a quiver that is slung over his back. Baptista holds a bow in one hand and reaches for an arrow with the other, emphasizing his biceps. His face—stylized lips, nose, eyebrows, and hair—recalls that of a classic Greek statue or perhaps Michelangelo's David.[49] Boullet's renderings of Baptista were not the only illustrations that appeared in the publication. The editors also published the work of another French artist, George Quaintance, en-titled "Cave Man," which appeared on the back cover of one issue. Here again, the homoerotic subtheme is transparent. A muscular man wearing

what appears to be a fur posing strap lifts a heavy stone club to kill a fero-
cious mountain lion.[50]

The publishers of *Força e Saúde* and *Músculo* even attempted international marketing of their publications by submitting a nude picture of João
Leal Filho, the Brazilian national bodybuilding champion in 1949–50, to
the United States muscle quarterly *Physique Pictorial*, where it appeared in
the fall 1954 issue. Leal Filho, who trained at the Força e Saúde Gym in Recife, was shown in the shower, discreetly posed to avoid exposing his genitals. For a U.S.$1.00 American readers could request a sample copy of the
Brazilian publication, mailed directly from Rio de Janeiro.[51] Although few
foreigners may actually have sent off for a copy of *Força e Saúde* in order
to enjoy the muscular beauty of João Leal Filho, the editors of these Brazilian magazines understood the publications' dual audiences. Those Brazilians who bought *Músculo* and *Força e Saúde* merely to keep up on the latest
news of the national bodybuilding organization, which was headed by the
editors of the magazines, may have missed the eroticism of these artistic
contributions and seminude pictures, but homosexuals bought the publications for their gorgeously muscled men. The magazines offered an exciting
stimulus for solitary sexuality under the cover of a sport's publication, and
they were one of the few ways that isolated individuals far from Rio or São
Paulo might have ongoing access to soft athletic porn.

Admiring muscular men might have occupied the free time of many
Caricoca homosexuals, but it was not the only pastime that interested members of this urban subculture. In the early '50s, like the Miss Brazil beauty
pageants, the studios of Rádio Nacional, a government-owned radio station broadcasting from Rio de Janeiro to the rest of the country, became
occupied territory.[52] Gay men flocked to the studio auditoria to listen to
their favorite female singers—the elegant, sophisticated, and sensual Marlene, the virtuous and pure Emilinha Borba, the tragic Nora Ney, and the
suffering Dalva de Oliveira, to mention just a few.[53] They bought these
singers' records, and joined their fan clubs. According to Alcir Lenharo, the
author of *Cantores de rádio* (Radio singers), fan clubs served a social function, channeling the public's desire to have access to the radio stars. A court
of admirers surrounded a given singer. In exchange for paying monthly
membership dues, fans could follow the star's career, praise her, defend her
against her detractors, and feel close to her. The fan became a member of
the celebrity's intimate family. Rio de Janeiro, where most of the radio divas lived, also afforded devotees the real possibility of approaching their
idols. The singers received their admirers, accepted their gifts, attended

events organized in their honor, and nurtured the relationship between celebrity and adoring followers.[54] Lenharo argued that the relationship between gay fans and female singers was not so much an identification with the individual drama or history of a particular singer, but rather a sharing of the star's fame. Entering the radio station where a famous singer performed, attending live broadcasts to cheer a favorite and jeer her rival, and participating actively in a fan club were all opportunities to develop personal contacts and connections with these women at a moment when modern mass culture was developing in Brazil. Through actively involving oneself in the life of a given radio singer, a fan, in this case a young homosexual, would symbolically enter into the world of fame and fortune of that personality.[55]

Most young homosexuals had their favorite radio star. The reasons for being an unconditional supporter and member of the fan club of a given singer were as varied as the multitude of images projected by the different radio stars and encouraged by the administration of Rádio Nacional.[56] Baptista, for example, preferred Marlene because she projected the image of one of the most elegant women in the country. She introduced new hairstyles, brought back the latest fashions from Paris, and, according to Baptista, even introduced the style of women wearing pants, which resulted in three months suspension by Rádio Nacional.[57] Lenharo identified with Nora Ney because of her deeply tragic and emotional musical style, which paralleled her real life. He also admired her political commitment to left-wing causes.[58] Everyone, moreover, had an opinion about the public rivalry between Marlene and Emilinha, a feud promoted by the heads of the radio station to encourage active involvement of the public in the lives and careers of these performers. The drama of their ongoing dispute fueled the passions and interests of their followers, who even resorted to violence against defenders of their rival.[59]

Attending live performances at the radio station or fan club events brought homosexuals into close contact with others who shared the same passions and interests. Friendships were formed, and those unaware of the homosexual topography of Rio de Janeiro or São Paulo were initiated into a subculture through these contacts. Ricardo, for example, a young boy from a poor family, began attending recordings in São Paulo. He slowly became aware that there were other young men in the audience like himself, and he eventually made friends with several who took him to the cruising areas of downtown São Paulo. Likewise, Luiz joined a fan club in São Paulo which corresponded with members in Rio de Janeiro. His new friends introduced him to places where homosexuals congregated in Rio de Janeiro and São Paulo, and a new world opened up for him.[60] In short, fan clubs and attendance at radio broadcasts, and later on, TV performances, provided a sense of family and belonging for many homosexuals. The singers became symbolic maternal figures, who graciously received gifts such as domestic appliances and household items from their adoring fans.[61] The social cohesion forged in the clubs and in the audience, as well as the collective adoration of their idols, aided many homosexuals in coping with the isolation that social hostility so often forced upon them.

Cruising São Paulo

In the post–World War II period, homosexual territories and forms of sociability in São Paulo expanded considerably just as they had in Rio de Janeiro. During the Estado Novo, the governor of the state of São Paulo had passed a decree confining prostitution to Bom Retiro, a neighborhood of Jewish merchants and small businesses near the central train station. This effort was part of a larger campaign to clean up the downtown area and regulate the behavior of women of the night. More than 150 brothels and 1,400 women were crowded into a small section of that neighborhood, where they could be monitored by the police and health officials.[62] As a result of greater police control of the downtown district, homosexuals, who had shared much of the same territory as prostitutes in the 1930s, were forced to shift their own cruising areas from the Anhangabaú Valley to Dom Pedro Park on the opposite side of the raised land that marked the core of historic São Paulo.[63] However, this confinement was relatively short-lived, and thirteen years later, in 1953, a new decree eliminated the previous restriction of prostitution to a specific area of the city. Brothels, rooms rented by the hour, and street prostitution proliferated once again throughout the central area of the city. As in previous decades, many of the sites utilized by prostitutes overlapped with the new cruising areas appropriated by homosexual men.

In 1958, José Fábio Barbosa da Silva, a young sociologist, decided to write his master's thesis about homosexuality in São Paulo.[64] Barbosa da Silva approached the subject quite differently than had the medical writings of the 1930s, which classified homosexuality as a sickness. Influenced by sociologists in the United States, the young academic conceptualized homosexuals as a minority group with a distinct subculture. For his study, Barbosa da Silva asked seventy men to complete an extensive questionnaire about their lives and the ways they dealt with their homosexuality. He selected mostly middle-class men as informants and avoided both male hustlers and flamboyant, effeminate homosexuals. There are obvious problems with using Barbosa da Silva's research results to draw any definitive conclusions about the makeup of the Paulista homosexual subculture in the 1950s. His sampling was narrow and mostly involved discreet-acting middle-class men. The study, nevertheless, is an important source for reconstructing the ways some males who engaged in same-sex eroticism organized their lives in relationship to their sexual desires.[65]

As part of his research project, Barbosa da Silva asked his seventy informants, ranging in ages from seventeen to forty-seven with an average age of twenty-six, to answer eighty-two questions. They included issues involving their first homosexual experiences, the process of meeting other homosexuals, the kinds of friendships and partners they maintained, and the ways in which individuals dealt with their family and society in relationship to their sexuality. The sociologist provided only a few quantitative results in his analysis of the responses to his queries, which are nonetheless quite revealing. For example, almost all of the respondents reported that their first homosexual encounter took place between the ages of eight and twelve. This data reveals a continuity in the practice of same-sex eroticism among young boys that had been reported in late-nineteenth-century literary works such as Raul Pompéia's *O Ateneu* (The Atheneum), in Gilberto Freyre's accounts of rural life in early-twentieth-century northeastern Brazil, and in anthropological studies of contemporary Brazilian sexual systems.[66]

Among the seventy men surveyed, 10 percent considered themselves "active" and 63 percent "passive." Barbosa da Silva classified the remaining 27 percent as "duplo," meaning that they both penetrated and were penetrated in anal intercourse. Adding together the number of men who either exclusively or at times assumed the "active" role in penetrative sex, the total is 37 percent.[67] Since popularly held stereotypes imagined that men who identified as homosexuals preferred to "take it" from "real men," this figure is particularly significant. Even with Barbosa da Silva's exclusion of "effeminate" men from his sampling, who presumably would have been more likely to admit preferring "passive" anal intercourse, the number of "active" individuals, all of whom considered themselves homosexuals, is relatively high. This 37 percent figure reveals a dissonance between popular images and real practices. It may also suggest a shift in the way certain men constructed notions of their own sexual desires. Identifying as a homosexual did not automatically mean that a person engaged in one single kind of sexual activity. Rather, some men seemed to have operated comfortably within a social milieu that was not exclusively divided between those who identified as "active" and those who saw themselves as "passive" in their erotic preferences.

Barbosa da Silva's study also indicates a correlation between the discreet comportment reported by many of his informants and their class background. Although they were part of the homosexual subculture of São Paulo, middle-class men with good jobs and family reputations to protect many times chose more circumspect behavior to avoid damaging their social status. One respondent to Barbosa da Silva's questionnaire suggests this relationship: "Taking into consideration the reaction of society in general to homosexuality (repugnance and contempt), ostentatious behavior and scandalizing others can only be negative . . . (in the form of greater repression). . . . I think discreet behavior is a thousand times more preferable. I have always tried to hide (to a certain degree) my homosexuality due to relationships within the general society and for economic reasons. I was threatened with job loss due to my homosexuality." Another informant pointed to the same phenomenon: "There are people who try never to let it be known that they are homosexuals, and they act as if they are well-adapted to society. They do this for economic reasons or because they feel ashamed and guilty, but mainly because of the way that society has contempt for homosexuals. These people place a lot of value in what others think, and due to these circumstances, real or imaginary, they live a double life."[68]

In addition to explaining the socialization process of Paulista homosexuals, Barbosa da Silva also mapped the urban territory they occupied. During the day, this area was the center of São Paulo's commercial and business district, but in the evening it became home to a bustling nightlife. Barbosa da Silva explained the attraction of this area for homosexuals: "This entire pleasure zone . . . comes alive at sundown and finds greatest movement on Saturday nights and on the eve of holidays. The reduction of sanctions, the concentration of groups of men looking for sexual pleasures and entertainment are basic factors that serve as catalysts for homosexual groups."[69]

Barbosa da Silva described the main cruising area as the convergence of São João and Ipiranga Avenues, which formed the shape of a large T (see map 6). Avenida São João, the top of this T, was the thoroughfare that

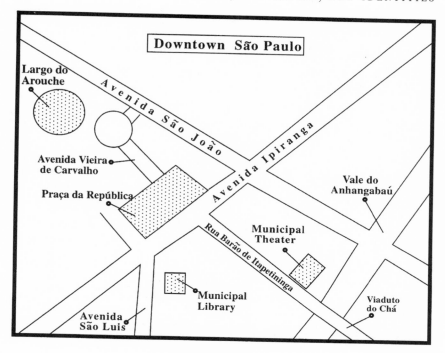

MAP 6   São Paulo, 1960

connected the Vale de Anhangabaú, the traditional cruising area of homosexuals in the 1930s, with the expanding city center. As in previous decades, the movie theaters along this avenue, such as Art-Palácio, Oasis, Marabá, and Cairo, offered a sheltered space where men could escape work for an hour or so and find a partner for a furtive sexual encounter. To one side of Avenida Ipiranga, which intersected São João and formed the base of the T, lay Praça da República. The public bathrooms in this lushly landscaped park provided another venue for sexual liaisons for office boys and business executives alike. According to Barbosa da Silva, the restrooms in other miniparks scattered throughout the downtown area—Largo do Arouche, Largo de Paissandú, and Ramos de Azevedo—were also used as meeting places for quick sexual interactions, as were those in the bus and train stations.[70]

Paulista homosexuals adapted the Brazilian tradition of *footing* to this urban landscape. In *footing,* a typical practice of small-town Brazil, groups of young men and women meandered in opposite directions around the main plaza in order to flirt, gossip, and choose a desired boyfriend or girl-friend. In São Paulo, homosexuals strolled around downtown blocks in a similar manner. One favorite route went from the Bar do Jeca, at the corner of São João and Ipiranga Avenue, down Ipiranga to the Praça da República, alongside the park, and back to São João Avenue.[71] This form of cruising took place individually or with small groups of friends who would walk and talk together, all the while remaining aware of potential sexual partners coming in the opposite direction.

Barbosa da Silva analyzed how many men, who, because of social sanctions had to be discreet while cruising, still managed to communicate their availability: "It is through certain peculiarities of behavior—such as gestures, ways of speaking or walking, the company one is with, the clothes . . . that attract attention so that homosexuals can identify each other."[72] The young sociologist noted the tacit understanding that the identity of those circulating in the city's center would remain within this homosexual world. While individuals might have gossiped about others who were seen cruising in the downtown area, that information was not passed on to outsiders.[73] Clóvis, who frequented the downtown area in this period, recalled this same group solidarity: "At the time, the groups of *bichas* were very tight and not loose-knit as they are today. They went to each others' apartments a lot. From time to time they went out for a walk together to São Luis Avenue, Galeria Metrópole. There was more interaction among people; they would visit each others' houses, organize fun and games."[74]

For many homosexuals, one of the attractions of the downtown area was the availability of "real" men. Their challenge was to *conquistar* (seduce) these randy men by paying for a few drinks or sweet-talking them into engaging in a sexual escapade.[75] In this reversal of traditional gender roles, the allegedly "passive" homosexual became the person actively pursuing a sexual liaison. The "real" man, on the other hand, assumed the role of the one conquered, who, so it would seem, only reluctantly engaged in sex with a *bicha*. Thus, a given person who identified as a homosexual and desired "real" men had to develop a degree of personal assertiveness in order to be a successful seducer. This sexual dynamic in which the homosexual had to take the initiative contributed to the formation of an identity imbued with a self-confidence that countered social stereotypes of the pathetic and passive *bicha*.

Getting a person to agree to have sex was only one step in the seduction process. Then one had to negotiate a place to go. Many homosexuals who lived in small apartments in the downtown area were able to bring friends or sexual partners back to their residences. Others, who lived with their families or with friends who didn't know they were homosexual, had to seek public accommodations. Clóvis recalled, "There weren't specific hotels for gays as there are today. You had sex in makeshift hotels that were also used by heterosexuals. Cheap hotels always let two guys stay the night, even spend the weekend. I remember that on 7 de Abril Avenue there was a little hotel called São Tião where we could go very discreetly and stay there with a guy."[76]

As was the case in Rio de Janeiro, São Paulo did not have bars that catered to an exclusively gay clientele in the 1950s. Homosexuals shared spaces with others who sought out the nightlife this downtown area offered. The Paribar, the Barbazul, and the Arpège, bars located near the Don José Gaspar Plaza surrounding the Municipal Library, served a diverse clientele. Outside tables in some establishments gave them the air of Parisian cafés.[77] Students, intellectuals, and theater people sat at Paribar, a sidewalk café, where they discussed socialist politics, existentialism, or literature. One of the intellectuals who frequented the area in his youth recalled this period in the 1950s: "Our bars were syncretic and ignored any kind of specialization, something that developed in the mid-60s (to my surprise when I returned after being abroad for two years) with bars like Ferros [a lesbian bar] and Redondo, which were frankly corporative in nature. Arpège was the opposite [of Paribar]. Unlike the others already mentioned, it was not a Parisian-style bar. It was a luncheonette, but it went to the extreme in the social osmosis that we have referred to. In addition to those who used the [municipal] library, there were artists, journalists, university students, and all imaginable kinds of political, cultural or simply sexual dissidents."[78] According to Barbosa da Silva's field notes, for a short period of time in the late 1950s one bar, the Anjo Negro (Black Angel), catered to a homosexual clientele and even had a drag show, but it was soon shut down by the police. Another establishment, Nick's Bar, which provided food and beverages to patrons of the Teatro Brasileiro de Comédia (Brazilian Comedy Theater), then became a favorite hangout for many homosexuals who gravitated to the more tolerant company of intellectuals and artists, where they could interact and discreetly cruise potential partners. Similarly, João Sebastião Bar attracted an "exotic" crowd that included homosexuals.[79]

The parks, plazas, public restrooms, cafés, and restaurants where Paulista homosexuals congregated were sites where men from somewhat different social classes could mingle. Those who earned a small salary could slowly nurse their beer while socializing with friends. Those with more disposable income could organize a group of friends to enjoy a night out on the town that might include dinner at a good restaurant in the area and then a promenade to seek out "new" young men for a sexual liaison. Middle- and upper-class homosexuals, who preferred a more discreet life, organized dinner parties and social gatherings among their friends as an alternative to going to the downtown gay cruising area, where they might be seen and identified as homosexuals. Darcy Penteado, an artist who participated in one such social group in the 1950s and '60s, explained that more economically privileged homosexuals preferred such circles, where they could discuss art, theater, literature, and music in a close environment. "Of course, there was also a lot of *frescura* (camp)."[80]

In the mid-1960s, the construction of a large downtown shopping mall, the Galeria Metrópole, afforded homosexual men a new space for social interaction. Clóvis recalled the structure: "It was built as an architectonic, urban space. When it was still under construction the *bichas* already said: 'We're going to invade that space, it is going to be ours; there will be a whole pack of *bichas* in that *galeria*.'"[81] The Galeria Metrópole became the hot spot of gay São Paulo. With its movie theaters, bars, nightclubs, bookstores, and escalators, it was ideal for cruising. Like the area surrounding the Municipal Library, only meters away, it became the common meeting ground for poets, artists, intellectuals.[82] A relative degree of toleration toward homosexuals in this area of the city center, however, did not necessarily mean that homosexuals had achieved social acceptance in the 1950s and '60s. Bohemian intellectuals in downtown São Paulo may have shared space with "sexual dissidents," but hegemonic opinion still considered homosexuality to be perverted, decadent, and unnatural. One merely had to step a few yards from the Paribar or Galeria Metrópole into the Municipal Library and read the literature there on homosexuality to realize how little positive material was available to the public at the time.

Libraries and Books

In 1956, Max Jurth, a member of the French homophile organization Arcadie, visited Brazil.[83] One of Jurth's interests was examining the literature on homosexuality in Brazil's public libraries, and he conducted a miniresearch project at the Municipal Library in São Paulo.[84] He posited the simple question: "What would a law or medical student find on the subject?" He discovered that in the main catalog his hypothetical student would have been sent from the word "homosexuality" to the subject heading "sexual aberrations." There he would have found a German edition of Magnus Hirschfeld's work, *Die Homosexualität des Mannes und des Weibes* (Homosexuality of men and women, 1914) and the 1883 French edition of P. Garnier's *L'onanisme seul ou à deux* (Onanism alone or with another). The Municipal Library also held a copy of the 1922 volume by Portuguese author Arlindo Camillo Monteiro, *Amor sáfico e socrático* (Sapphic and Socratic love). Only two Brazilian publications were listed in the card catalog: Edmur de Aguiar Whitaker's "Estudos biográficos dos homosexuais de São Paulo" and a work by Sílvio Marone entitled *Missexualidade e arte*, published in 1947.[85] Thus, in the early 1950s in modern industrialized São Paulo, the central public library provided little information about homosexuality for those who did not read a foreign language. Books about sexual education, such as the previously mentioned work by Hernani de Irajá, *Psicoses de amor*, which included a chapter about homosexuality, continued to be published. However, they were superficial and moralistic repetitions of the writings of the 1930s and were of questionable scientific merit. The works of Ribeiro, Whitaker, Sinesgalli, Peixoto, and Marañón still provided the framework for the medicolegal profession's view of homosexuality, and therefore shaped the thinking of most would-be jurists and physicians who studied the topic in medical or law schools.

The situation was not much better regarding the belles-lettres. Daniel Franco, an activist in the São Paulo gay rights movement of the 1970s, noted the lack of material about homosexuality in the 1950s: "Until recently there wasn't gay literature in Brazil. The little that existed was imported, since no Brazilian author dared to ruin his name in such a risky business. One could read *Corydon* by Gide or *The Banquet* by Plato, or *The Confusion of Sentiments* by Stefan Zweig."[86] But, as we shall see, despite these difficulties, some novels with gay themes were available.

In particular, both Franco and Jurth mentioned one new work, Jorge Jaime's *Homossexualismo masculino* (Masculine homosexuality).[87] According to the book's introduction, Jaime originally presented the work in 1947 as a seminar paper for a class in legal medicine while earning a law degree from the National Law School in Rio de Janeiro. A second edition, published in 1953, was a reprint of Jaime's medicolegal treatise with an additional 140-page novel, *Lady Hamilton*, which, in the form of a diary, described the life of Paulo, a homosexual.[88]

One is immediately struck by the design of the book's cover, which is reminiscent of European and American homoerotic art of the 1950s and

'60s (see fig. 12). A very handsome fair youth dominates the space, staring out innocently, or perhaps romantically into the distance. Hovering over him to the left is an equally attractive older man with a mustache. His gaze suggests protectiveness and affection for the younger man. The image does not communicate degeneration, sickness, or perversion, but rather a wholesome relationship between the two men. As a marketing tool, the cover no doubt attracted many Brazilian homosexuals, who probably thought that they would find a positive treatment of the subject. Alas, they must have been disappointed.

FIGURE 12   Cover of *Homossexualismo masculino*, Jaime Jorge's 1953 treatise on male homosexuality in Brazil.

In the introduction to the work, Jaime explained how he had conducted extensive research to obtain the information contained in his essay and novel: "I did 'field research,' I visited the bacchanals of pederasts, I went to observe them in the wings of theaters, in the rehearsals in the casinos. They have a closed society which is difficult to get to know and which is very dangerous to invade. I tried to get their confidence and some showed me their diaries, intimate letters and told me their sad stories." The eleven letters that he published as part of this volume in fact captured the complexity of the lives of different homosexuals in Rio de Janeiro in the late 1940s, from men in love with soldiers to the lively correspondences of young homosexuals relating their travels abroad. However, the overarching tone of Jaime's work is condemnatory, exuding self-righteous pity and pious forgiveness: "Miserable wretches. Unfortunate ones, they only adore machos and fall in love with them. Forgive them, they are sick; they know not what they do."[89]

Homossexualismo masculino in essence presented the same medicolegal arguments that Ribeiro, Marañón, Sinesgalli, and Whitaker had defended a decade and a half earlier. Homosexuality was caused by hormonal disorders, and pederasts were criminals. Jaime spoke in no uncertain terms: "Sodomy has brought and will always bring with it the germs of sickness, tragedy, and crime. Don't been fooled, young adolescents. When they speak to you of 'a celestial happiness,' of an 'immortal pleasure,' don't believe them. I have seen the other side of 'Socratic Love,' and I assure you that it is horrendous, monstrous."[90]

Yet the sympathetic treatment of the book's cover and several of Jaime's proposals, including increased penalties to punish the extortion and blackmail of homosexuals and to crack down on police abuses, were somewhat at odds with the moralistic character of the work as a whole. It was these positive proposals that probably found resonance among some of its Brazilian homosexual readers and won the French homophile's praise: "Jorge Jaime, who, according to what we are led to believe, is not a homophile, defends Rio's homosexuals against certain abuses that the police are used to inflicting upon them with no legal basis. They are sometimes arrested in cruising places, taken to the police station, and there, after being insulted and humiliated, are abused by the policemen, who submit them to the passive role."[91] Moreover, in the section of the book entitled "Homosexuality and Law," Jaime made the startling proposal that homosexuals should be granted the right to marry: "There are millions of inverts who live maritally with individuals of the same sex. If marriage were granted between men, it would not create any monstrosity; rather it would only recognize a legal state, a de facto state. Illegitimate children for the longest time were also not afforded any legal protection. The Law didn't recognize them, didn't acknowledge their existence. Today, in spite of all of the pressure of the Church, they are a reality and have equality with legitimate children. The legal union among the sick is a right denied only by dictatorial countries. If lepers can marry each other, why should pederasts be denied that right? Only because normal people are repulsed by an act of this nature."[92]

Jaime defended his proposal with a curious logic. He argued that marriage between homosexuals would reduce exploitation of young men, blackmail, and male prostitution. Moreover, the public act of marriage would communicate the abnormality of the couple and would also prevent innocent young women from marrying homosexuals. In a liberal tone he wrote: "The Urning is only happy when living with men who satisfy his instincts. And many men feel happier when they have relations with Urnings than with women. Then, why not protect them legally? The Law was put on Earth to regulate reciprocal interests. Today, more than in any other time, the concept of the family has evolved a lot and now 'happiness is happier than morality.'" However, in the next sentence Jaime undercut all of his tolerance with a simple question: "But can there really be happiness when there are anal fissures and liquids containing gonococcus?" He then went on to argue, as the medical and legal professionals had insisted fifteen years before, that Brazil needed special hospitals to treat homosexuals and special clinics to reeducate them. His "modern" and "enlightened" outlook advanced very little from those of the past generation of writers on the subject.[93]

If readers of *Homossexualismo masculino* still had any doubts about the "monstrous" and "perverted" nature of homosexuality after reading Jaime's sixty-five-page medicolegal tract, they could then go on to the author's novel, *Lady Hamilton*, the second part of the compilation. Jaime made his intentions perfectly clear in the introduction to his narrative. "*Lady Hamilton* is no masterpiece of literature. If it has no value as a literary work, it at least has value as a descriptive document of all of the degrading horrors that millions of pederasts who live on the face of the earth suffer. Let the grammarians and stylists become horrified with so many wrongly placed pronouns, but let the legislators become enlightened when they make laws for the sexually sick so that they know their involuntary weaknesses, so that they pity these unfortunate sick ones—such was my goal in getting out this work."[94]

Jaime was honest about the literary merits of his fiction. *Lady Hamilton* is an exceedingly melodramatic and contrived story of the life of Paulo, a homosexual. Like Lady Hamilton, the lover and wife of Lord Admiral Nelson, whose life story was told in the popular 1941 movie *That Hamilton Woman,* Paulo rises to richness and fame and then plummets into poverty and degradation. The novel follows Paulo through sundry improbable situations in which he falls in love with numerous masculine men, who rarely respond positively to his affections. He passes through the nightspots of Rio de Janeiro frequented by homosexuals, participates in wild orgies organized by foreigners and Brazilians, takes on as lovers American sailors stationed in Rio de Janeiro during World War II, travels to New York, where he becomes a famous ballet dancer and millionaire, and ends up bankrupt and alone in Rio de Janeiro. His sister comes to live with him, and Paulo falls in love with his sister's boyfriend. Paulo seduces the boyfriend, who later regrets his actions and attacks Paulo, calling him a *puto* and a *viado*. In the final chapter, Paulo has become a drug addict and a leper. He eventually goes out and hangs himself, but his bad luck is not yet over. His body falls from the rope and is found covered in mud.

It seems that Jaime intended to convey a single message: homosexuality leads to death and destruction. Ironically, in the effort to drive his message home, he presented details about the lives of homosexuals that a reader interested in the work because of its cover or title could appropriate to construct a positive sense of homosexuality. A young man struggling against his own sexual desires toward other men certainly would find in the book a confirmation of all the social, moral, and religious objections to homosexuality. At the same time, he could discover clues about the semi-clandestine homosexual subculture of Rio de Janeiro and São Paulo, the names of bars, popular meeting places, and current slang, all of which might offer assurance that he was not alone in his sexual feelings.

Jaime continued to dwell on the subject of homosexuality in a 1957 collection of poems entitled *O monstro que chora* (The monster who cries) dedicated to "all the monsters who love and cry."[95] A series of poems tell the fable of Robert, who meets a monster with human emotions. The monster is a metaphor for homosexuality. Another poem in the collection indicates that Jaime maintained contact with Rio's homosexual subculture throughout the 1950s. "Cartões postais" (Post cards) mentioned several cruising places in Copacabana that were popular in the late 1950s, as well as some of the bars frequented by homosexuals. Part of the poem, a conversation between two gay men, reads:

Shall we go to "Tasca" or to "Follies"?
—O.K.! All right!
— "O.K." No. "Bolero."
Happy contented pederasts
On the beach of dreams.
A good macho,
Just can't be found![96]

Looking back at Jaime's work from the perspective of an activist in Brazil's gay rights movement, Franco wrote: "This work, which made the pretense of being scientific, was highly prejudicial for the readers of the period, since in seeking to defend gays, he treated them as crazy or depraved, recommending the hospital or the sanatorium instead of prison. That tragic essay belongs to gay folklore and can only be read today as a joke."[97] But while his work reinforced hegemonic notions of the homosexual as lonely and sick, Jaime's treatise, novella, and poems nevertheless captured real moments in the lives of Rio de Janeiro's homosexuals. Through the letters, references to meeting and cruising places, and vignettes about *bichas* in Cinelândia, homosexuals could catch life-affirming glimpses of others like themselves. Just as Radclyffe Hall's *Well of Loneliness* enjoyed widespread lesbian readership from the 1920s and '30s all the way to the '50s and '60s, despite the desolate and depressing elements of its story, so, too, Jorge's work may have provided certain consolations to homosexuals, who otherwise had to look far and wide to find themselves depicted in print, positively or negatively.

Another work dealing with homosexuality is Mário de Andrade's short story "Frederico Paciência," written in 1924 and revised many times before its posthumous publication in 1947.[98] The story describes the romantic friendship of two students (presumably one being the author) who drift apart without consummating their desires other than through furtive kisses and affectionate embraces. The narrator expresses relief that the friendship has dissolved and the two are separated by distance, implying that now he does not have to face his own homosexual feelings for Frederico Paciência. Although the protagonist is not a sick and pathetic figure, he nevertheless leaves the reader with the impression that it is far better to repress homoerotic feelings than to express them openly. In many ways, this short story parallels the real life of Mário de Andrade, who also attempted to contain his sexual desires for other men and shrouded his personal life in a veil of secrecy.

Not all literary production about homosexuality was so dismal. In 1951,

Paulo Hecker Filho, a writer from the southern state of Rio Grande do Sul, published the novella *Internato* (Boarding school). The story describes the life of Jorge, who falls in love with Eli while attending a boarding school.[99] Eli, popular among his classmates, is famous for seducing both women and younger boys in the school. One Saturday evening, after leaving a party drunk, Jorge takes Eli to a whorehouse where he engages in oral sex with his object of desire, even though Eli has gonorrhea. When Jorge returns to the boarding school on Monday afternoon, the news of his affair with Eli has spread through the institution. Alfredo, Jorge's roommate and whose sister Jorge has been dating, immediately attacks him, beating him to the ground and pelting him with epithets—*nojento* (disgusting) and *fresco* (faggot). Publicly humiliated, bloodied and beaten, Jorge, however, is not a tragic figure like Paulo in *Lady Hamilton*, who, defeated, commits suicide. Hecker rescues his protagonist from moral degradation and gives him self-respect: "Like a shout, pride sets him on his feet. And with his lips dripping blood and his face tear-streaked and dirty, he defies the boys who are watching him, the whole school, the whole world; he accepts his fate and runs to meet it, going toward the solitary trees in the distance. No one follows him. There's deep silence."[100]

Jorge and Eli are both expelled from the school. Because Eli maintains his status as a virile male by being the "active" partner in sexual liaisons with other males, he is judged less harshly than the more passive Jorge. Eli's castigation also ends up being less severe: "The principal felt it was his duty to moralize. But the case was so clear-cut, and Jorge's attitude so adamant, that he was cut short at the onset and was able to communicate little more to him than the sentence of expulsion for the two of them. Eli's punishment was naturally lighter, and a month later, at his family's insistent request, he was readmitted." The story ends simply: "Jorge packed his bags and went home by train the same night. He would return to being just his mother's son. Would he return?"[101]

The last phrase of the novella—"Would he return?"—left Jorge's life for the reader to shape. The ambiguous phrasing presented multiple possible outcomes. Would he return home to the protection of his mother and family? Would he turn his back on his romantic and sexual feelings for other men? Or would he leave home to find a new life in a distant city like Rio de Janeiro or São Paulo? His future, while uncertain, did not automatically leave the reader with a sense of hopelessness. In this respect, it was one of the few literary works about homosexuality in the early fifties that did not end in tragedy and despair.

Social Networks as Alternative Families

Had Jorge traveled to Rio de Janeiro or São Paulo in the mid-1950s, as his real-life fellow *gaúcho* (native of Rio Grande do Sul) João Antônio Mascarenhas had, he could have joined a rich social life of supportive homosexuals, who would have willingly guided him through life's storms and stresses. The public realm of homosexual sociability, which included street cruising, drag balls, the beach, and Miss Brazil beauty pageants, was a major part of these men's lives, but the building blocks of the subculture were the groups of friends (*turmas*) who provided an alternative family for homosexuals facing a hostile society. The traditional extended family offered most Brazilians their primary support network. This was especially true for migrants to the large urban centers, who sought out relatives to facilitate their transition to urban life through temporary housing, job leads, and moral support. Many homosexuals who arrived in Rio de Janeiro or São Paulo as family outcasts, or who simply moved out of their homes to enjoy more personal freedoms, relied heavily on constructed families of other homosexuals as they faced similar problems.

In his master's thesis chapter entitled "The Socialization of the Homosexual," Barbosa da Silva published an excerpt from the diary of one of the men he interviewed in his research project. The passage illustrates the isolation that many homosexuals felt before finding friends who shared their sexual desires: "I have never felt so alone. . . . Will this loneliness always be a stigma in my life? Do I have something intrinsic in me that repels other people? If they keep 'hating me for no reason,' I will go crazy. I am so sad that I'm capable of doing something so that they would hate me for a good reason. Here I am in my room. Forgotten, sad, humiliated."[102] Likewise, Anuar Farah, who came to Rio de Janeiro from Campos in 1962, experienced extreme isolation before finding a network of friends. "People sought out a family," he remembered. "I arrived here all alone, and I felt the need to have a family here. People came to Rio crying out for a family."[103]

Barbosa da Silva also explained how membership in a social group helped create and reinforce a homosexual identity: "To the extent that the homosexual manages to make contact with other people in society who are similar to him, he tends to face his option differently. It comes to mean the personal affirmation as a homosexual, linking the individual more and more to the category."[104] Thus, the *turma* acted both as a support network and a means to socialize individuals into the subculture, with all of its codes, slang, public spaces, and assumptions about homosexuality.

Turmas formed around class or regional affinities and common interests. Thus, Ricardo brought together a *turma* with others who wanted to do amateur theater. Luiz created a social circle with other homosexuals who belonged to the same fan club of an Italian popular singer. Agildo's social network produced a newsletter written by the members of his group and distributed in Cinelândia and the Bolsa de Valores. Carmen Dora Guimarães's study of a group of middle-class homosexuals who all came from Belo Horizonte to Rio de Janeiro in the early 1970s exemplifies the confluence of class and regional solidarity in the formation of a homosexual *turma*.[105]

Jorge Jaime published a series of letters in *Homossexualismo masculino* from members of a *turma* in Rio and their friends who had traveled to the United States after World War II. The correspondences record the way in which homosexuals negotiated between life in their social network and the outside world. They developed a complex private idiom, which employed coded language, camp humor, double entendres, and fictitious girlfriends to communicate about their romances, friendships, and adventures. The letters also offer a glimpse through the eyes of participants into the differences between gay life in the United States and Brazil in the late 1940s.

In 1947, Robert, the Brazilian-born son of British citizens, wrote to his best friend Alfredinho in Rio de Janeiro about life in Chicago, where he had moved after the war to work for an export company: "Every day that passes, I get to know more about the city and LIFE in the United States. I already have numerous friends; and Bob, Tim, Jack and Joe are all good friends." The twenty-two-year-old then went on to depict his social life: "The 'night-clubs' for *entendidos* are always full, and if there is one good thing in this world, it is Saturday night in one of these places. What a life, my old friend, what a life!"[106] In describing the homosexual nightclubs of Chicago, Robert used the word *entendido,* a slang term that literally means "one in the know." The word was used as a coded expression among homosexuals. It identified individuals (as homosexuals) and places (where they congregated) while keeping others (presumably those not in the know) from understanding the actual content of the reference.[107]

That same year, Armando F., another Brazilian, sent his impressions of New York to his friend Rodrigo, who lived in Rio de Janeiro. He described a passionate affair with his new American boyfriend, Fred, who after having declared his eternal love to the young Brazilian, took him out to celebrate. "We went to 'Macdouglas Tavern', an *entendissimo* [very *entendido*] bar, only for men and very elegant people so that he could tell the boys that we loved each other, and from that moment on, we were going to be exclusive with each other."[108]

In these letters, Robert and Armando developed code words to communicate with each other to prevent outsiders from understanding their secret language and their double lives. Similarly, in real life, it was necessary to hide one's true self, since overt displays of effeminate behavior or references associated in the popular culture with homosexuality would have resulted in social stigmatization, barriers to employment, and embarrassment to "respectable" families. Among friends in closed *entendido* circles, however, camp humor, parodies of heteronormative behavior, and the playful regendering of names provided relief from the pressures of having to conform to strict social standards. Both Robert and Armando carefully employed code words and freely switched gender markers to recount their adventures in order to hide the fact that they belonged to a homosexual subculture. Undoubtedly they feared someone would find their epistles and realize that they were homosexuals. While the letters provided a vehicle for mutual support and affirmation of their homosexual lives, their discovery could have led to a family scandal, expulsion from home, or even hospitalization. Yet their literary ploys are so obvious as to suggest that they were designed as much to undercut the rigid social norms with which Robert and Armando were expected to conform as to hide their sexual desires and social networks. Perhaps because the language in the letters was so transparent, Robert counseled caution about letting the correspondence be read by others. A postscript advised: "Tear up or burn this after reading it."[109] Fortunately for us, Alfredinho did not heed Robert's suggestion.

Modifying gendered designations was a favored way of upsetting traditional social roles as well as disguising real identities. Yet in these letters, at least, it proved quite unconvincing as a means of achieving discretion. Robert, for example, admitted to Alfredinho that he had not visited Tancredo, a mutual Brazilian friend. "First because my 'wife' (who took me to New York) didn't want to; and secondly, even if [he] did, I don't have the address of 'Madame.'"[110] When Robert referred to his male romantic partner as his wife, he was probably not commenting on sexual positions in bed or even on their social roles in the relationship. Rather, he parodied conventions that defined couples in heteronormative terms. He hardly performed subterfuge, though, by attempting to conceal the fact that his "wife" was a male. Had he been serious about deceiving a nosy reader, he would have chosen the word *namorada* (girlfriend) to hide his activities. Nor did he make any effort to disguise the fact that Tancredo, with a masculine name, had a feminine nickname, "Madame."

Other parts of Robert's letter also indicate that the language, while coded, could be easily understood by any but the most innocent and naive. For example, Robert asked about life in Rio de Janeiro: "I would like to know how 'Gilbertina' is. Has she divorced Eddie yet?" The feminization of Gilberto into the improbable woman's name Gilbertina lent camp humor to the letter. No doubt Gilberto's friends called him by this nickname in Rio de Janeiro. Attributing marriage to the relationship between Gilberto and Eduardo playfully mimicked socially defined expectations about permanent heterosexual relationships, yet Robert jokingly undermined the reference to marital stability by questioning the longevity of the romance. Moreover, when Robert referred to Eduardo as "Eddie," an increasingly common practice of appropriating English words in Americanized post–World War II Brazilian culture, he likely did so to project a cosmopolitan and sophisticated persona.

In his letter, Robert asked for accounts of the nightlife in Rio de Janeiro, especially a bar in Copacabana patronized by sailors, prostitutes, and homosexuals during the war: "Send me news of Rio, of the *frequentadoras* [female clientele] of Bolero, and of your intellectual and 'sportive' activities." Again by using the feminine gender marker to describe his friends, Robert both communicated and hid direct references to the semi-clandestine homosexual world of Rio de Janeiro. The references to "sportive" activities served as a thinly disguised allusion to sexual escapades. In this respect, Robert documented a stark contrast between the development of public homosexual life in Brazil and in the United States. Whereas he was able to visit exclusively gay "nightclubs" (presumably bars) in Chicago and New York, neither Rio de Janeiro nor São Paulo had equivalent spaces in the late 1940s and early 1950s. Bars, such as the Bolero, in Copacabana, received a mixed crowd, in which homosexuals mingled with sailors, prostitutes, and others seeking pleasures of the night. But even without nightclubs for *entendidos,* homosexuals managed to create a rich and creative social life in the *cidade maravilhosa.*

Robert ended his epistle with a humorous and lighthearted greeting to his friends. Assuming the air of a film star, he dramatically promised: "I'll answer all the letters that are sent by my fans, and I will supply color photos, autographed, and in the nude." Once again, the posture of glamour and sophistication served to affirm the lives of these men in comparison to a mundane, heterosexually defined society, which presumably lacked the urbane flair of their homosexual subculture.

In a second letter, written in the spring of 1947, Robert continued to describe gay life in the United States. He referred to an affair in the feminine: "I had lots of fun in Miami with a beautiful 'American woman,' a 'real marvel,' 'ten stars.' She slept with me in the Colonial Hotel and I almost died of fatigue and excesses. My God, what a night, wow!"[111] While a casual reader might have read the letter as a typical correspondence between two young men talking about their female conquests, other references reveal the hidden meanings behind gender-marking twists: "Chicago is simply marvelous, filled with 'marvels.' There are so many [marvels] that one doesn't know what to choose. I have had a lot of fun, and I go out almost every night to dinners, bacchanalian parties, theaters, and 'nightclubs.' I have already had a half-dozen adventures, but I'm still not engaged, since I want to choose well before marrying." Using the ambiguous term *maravilhas* (marvels), which in Portuguese could refer to a man, a woman, or an object, Robert was able to let his friend know without being explicit that he enjoyed affairs (*aventuras*) with other men, although he was not yet ready to settle down with any particular person. Although Robert used innuendoes to communicate information to his friend in Rio de Janeiro, he didn't bother to hide the fact that effeminate gay men (*loucas*) lived in the same building with him in Chicago: "The place where I live is a kind of Bolero hotel, full of *loucas*, and almost always there is some little diversion to distract us."

Robert admitted that building a social network of friends was crucial for surviving as a homosexual in the United States in the early 1950s. This was equally the case in Brazil, where small groups of friends were the foundations of the subculture. Public spaces, such as parks, cinemas, beaches, and certain streets provided opportunities to meet friends, make new acquaintances, and find sexual partners. However, these forms of sociability were mediated by police harassment and public hostility. Thus, as Clóvis remembered, private venues for social interactions played a crucial role in the lives of Paulista and Carioca homosexuals.

Intimate Parties and Newsletters

Among the many *turmas* that formed to provide support and sociability for their members in the 1950s was a group made up of northeasterners from Pernambuco, Sergipe, and Rio Grande do Norte, along with natives of the city and state of Rio de Janeiro. The northeasterners came from different social backgrounds, but they faced a common difficulty in adapting to life in Rio de Janeiro. The members of the *turma* would gather in someone's apartment for small parties, where they would occasionally organize playful spoofs of fashion shows and beauty pageants. These were discreet affairs. Those attending such gatherings knew that they had to enter and leave the host's apartment building without raising the eyebrows of the doorman or nosy neighbors. During the impromptu games or after amateur performances in someone's apartment, everyone knew not to clap, for it might draw attention to the festivities from nearby residents, who then might call the police to complain about loud and "immoral" behavior. Instead, as Agildo Guimarães recalled of parties he attended, guests might snap their fingers to express their approval of a particularly good "show."[112]

One such party, hosted at the house of "Edmea" in late June or early July 1963, included a "Miss Typical Costume" contest, where different *bonecas* (effeminate men) dressed in clothes representing regional parts of Brazil (see fig. 13). A jury made up of *bofes* ("real" men) selected by the "hostess" picked the winner. Agildo Guimarães, who felt that the jury's choice was inappropriate, decided to put together a simple, two-paged typed newsletter protesting the results. "The 'hostess' committed two errors," he wrote, "(1) she selected a jury that was supposed to know the sub-

FIGURE 13   Members of the *O Snob* social network during the Miss Traje Típica contest in Rio de Janeiro, 1963. Photograph courtesy of Agildo Guimarães.

ject, (2) she promised to put people on the jury who were *bofes* and outside the group. If they were unknown, it wasn't to all of the contestants."[113]

Agildo named his modest publication *O Snob* (The snob), because, as he explained later, the expression was "much in use among *bichas* at the time."[114] What started as a playful protest would see ninety-nine regular issues and one "retrospective" issue between July 10, 1963, and June 1969, when *O Snob* shut down because of the political climate surrounding the hard-line military government of General Médici. From a minimalist blue-inked newsletter with simple line sketches of female fashion models, *O Snob* became a thirty- to forty-page publication, featuring elaborate drawings, gossip columns, short-story contests, and interviews with the famous drag stars of the day. The members of the social network that put out *O Snob* distributed it among friends and acquaintances in Cinelândia and Copacabana, at times asking for a contribution to defray costs, other times giving it away free. Although *O Snob* was not the first of this homecrafted genre to appear in Rio de Janeiro, it was the most long-lasting and influential and inspired the appearance of more than thirty similar publications between 1964 and 1969, not only in other parts of the city, but throughout the state and in the rest of the country.[115] The pages of *O Snob* provide a unique entry into the world of *bichas, bofes, bonecas,* and *entendidos.* The journal is especially valuable for the varied notions of gender it portrays, the disputes that emerged over them, and its perspective on politics in the 1960s (see fig. 14).

In 1963, the year *O Snob* began publishing, Brazil was in turmoil with a wave of strikes, in which workers made both economic and political demands. Agrarian reform and more governmental control of multinational companies and capital were two burning issues of the day. The editorial of the first issue of *O Snob* announced modest goals for the publication and located the journal clearly in the center of political extremes: "Presenting our little journal: Finally we are launching the first issue of our journal. The journal of our group. To make comments about parties, gossip, the latest news. We don't intend to have a large circulation or compete with *O Globo* or *Última Hora* [mainstream dailies]; and, as we are neither left or right, it is better to stay in the middle (*no meio*). It will have millions of defects and errors. We apologize. And if you want to write, you can send [articles] to the editorial staff or to the headquarters of our club."[116]

Agildo's positioning of the journal was also a play on words, since as well as "middle" *meio* also means "milieu," in this case the homosexual subculture. The use of the double meaning of the term reflected a desire on the

FIGURE 14   Cover of issue 95 of *O Snob*, honoring founding editor Agildo Guimarães, Lady
Gilka Dantas, 1968. Illustration courtesy of Agildo Guimarães.

part of the editors to produce a fun gossip sheet, filled with campy humor
and information about the members of the *turma* without involving itself
in the polarized political disputes of the period. In the first year of publication, the journal made only one political reference to current events, a passing mention that five members of the group had joined the national bank
workers strike.[117] The editors of *O Snob* did not, however, comment on the
March 31, 1964, military takeover in which President João Goulart was
overthrown. Indeed, it seems that the generals' rise to power in 1964 had

no direct impact on the lives of many young homosexuals, except perhaps those with direct links to the Brazilian nationalist-populist movement or to the left. Although word later got out that the Ministry of Foreign Affairs had dismissed some low-level public servants accused of being homosexual, there appeared to be no generalized persecution of homosexuals during the first years of military rule.[118] With or without the military in power, life seemed to go on as usual for this group of young men.

As the editorial also made clear, Agildo thought of his literary production as a modest newspaper from the first issue. *O Snob* defined itself as "A news journal for *entendido* people. A journal for the right crowd. A journal for you who have good taste."[119] The title word "snob," which had entered the Brazilian vocabulary at the turn of the century, had the same meaning as its English equivalent. The phrase "right crowd," an inadequate rendition of the Portuguese original, *gente bem*, referred to people with good taste, style, or money. The title and slogan conveyed a consistent message throughout the journal's six-year run. *Bonecas* had style, grace, personality, a sense of fashion, and good taste that set them above the rest of society. They were aware of their superior sensibility and flaunted it. Effeminate men possessed qualities that should be acknowledged and affirmed. This attitude was similar to that expressed by the slogan "Gay Is Good," developed by the gay liberation movement in the United States in 1969, and it is significant that such a self-affirming motto was adopted by the authors of *Snob* six years prior to the creation of the American slogan.[120]

In his research, Barbosa da Silva documented the lives of middle-class Paulista homosexuals who preferred to remain discreet about their private lives. They identified as homosexuals, but did not necessarily conform to the stereotype of the effeminate *bicha*, nor did they engage exclusively in "passive" intercourse. In contrast, the members of the *O Snob* group organized their notions of gender and homosexuality along the lines of the *boneca/bofe* duality. *Bonecas* sought out *bofes*, or *rapazes* (boys, guys), as their partners and companions, knowing that most of their "husbands" would eventually leave them for marriage and children. *Bofes* did not consider themselves to be homosexuals, and *bonecas* only pursued "real" men. In these social networks, intimate parties organized by groups of *bonecas* would always include young "real" men who ended up having sex with the *bonecas*.[121]

Comparing the findings of Barbosa da Silva in São Paulo with the voluminous records of the interactions of the *bonecas* of the *Snob* group, one notes the complexity of sexual identities that coexisted within the homo-sexual subculture of Brazil's two major urban centers. To a large extent the *boneca/bofe* construct predominated among men from poor and working-class origins, whereas many middle-class homosexuals no longer embraced a structuring of sexual roles that mimicked normative heterosexual gender behavior. This is not to say that all men from modest backgrounds adapted to the predominant *boneca/bofe* dyad or that all middle-class men rejected it. But one can note a differentiation developing in this period along class lines. Less can be said about the *bofes* who shared this world with *bonecas* and other homosexuals, yet presented themselves as essentially and ulti-mately heterosexual.

Some *bofes* had female girlfriends, with whom they had sex. Ramalhete explained why these *bofes* enjoyed sex with *bonecas* when sex with a woman was available to them: "Some women didn't like to suck, didn't want to be [anally] penetrated. A *bicha* had sex on her mind. She'd do anything. These men fell into their hands."[122] However, according to *bonecas* interviewed many years later, most *bofes* did not have sexual intercourse with women because of the strict moral codes that valued feminine virginity. Although restrictions on the sexual activities of middle-class women might have been more firmly in place than they were for those from poorer family back-grounds, the "ideal" woman, regardless of her race or social class, was ex-pected to remain "pure" until marriage. José Rodrigues recalled: "Many men would go out with their girlfriends, get really excited and then arrive at the *bicha's* house all hard and ready to fuck."[123] These men enjoyed the company and sexual pleasures of *bonecas*, but they often shunned them in the street to avoid public knowledge of their escapades. Even though their role as sexual penetrators assured them of their masculinity and made them the object of desire of *bichas*, they attempted to confine their adventures to these closed social circles.[124]

Within this world of *bofes* and *bonecas*, the thought of two *bichas* hav-ing sex together was as repugnant to *bonecas* as was the aversion of the ma-jority of the population to homosexual behavior in general. When two men actually acknowledged that they were both homosexual and wanted to have sex with each other, it was incomprehensible to many *bonecas*. Agildo Guimarães recalled the reaction among his group of friends when people discovered that two newcomers to their circle, who everyone had thought of as *bofes*, were having sex together: "The division between the *ativos*, the *bofes*, the men, and the *passivas*, the *bichas*, was a question of upbringing. A *bicha* was a *bicha* and a *bofe* was a *bofe*, and a *bofe* couldn't be a *bicha*. But we knew a couple who were both *bofes*. It was a scandal. It was absurd. The *bicha* has to always be passive. Doing what they were doing was horrible."[125]

Agildo himself lived for many years with an army paratrooper named Chico Dantas, and he assumed the nickname Gilka Dantas because he considered himself married to his *bofe*. He described other kinds of arrangements:

> In some *bicha/bofe* relationships, the couple got together only on weekends. Or they got together at night or went to a friend's house or to a hotel for sexual relations. Most didn't live together, but when they did, the *bicha* was the housewife. The *bofe* did the man's jobs, fixing things. The *bicha* didn't because he didn't know how to or because he just let the *bofe* do it. The *bicha* cooked and cleaned the house. Some *bofes* who weren't really *that bofe* lived with a person many years. Other bofes got married [to women], and only had sexual relations [with *bichas*] from time to time. Either they liked the person or liked having the sexual relationship. I think that they had homosexual tendencies, but due to society they were afraid to admit it.[126]

Although rigid sexual roles ruled the household and the bed, as Agildo readily admitted, not everyone conformed to the model. Yet those who ended up maintaining a long-term relationship without marrying, were "not *that bofe*," since assuming a homosexual identity meant that you were not a "real" man. Masculinity was the essence of being a *bofe*. Femininity was the essence of being a *bicha* or a *boneca*. The term "homosexual," to the extent that it was used by this social network, referred to *bichas* and *bonecas*, not to *bofes*. However, as we have seen from the sociological sampling conducted by José Fábio Barbosa da Silva in São Paulo in this same time period, the homosexual universe was not simply made up of self-defined *bonecas* and masculine-identified *bofes*. Some men who considered themselves homosexuals did not necessarily identify with the flamboyant *boneca* persona. A large percentage of Barbosa da Silva's survey sample engaged in both "active" and "passive" sexual activities. In short, the array of ways in which people organized their sexual lives reveals a much more complex sexual system than the one promoted by the *Snob* audience.

Among the constellation of subgroups within the homosexual world of Rio de Janeiro and São Paulo were older men who were known as *tias* (aunties). The term usually referred to middle- or upper-class men who had a certain financial security that allowed them to support a younger man in exchange for sexual services. During the 1950s and '60s, younger *bichas* and *bonecas* who sought out *bofes* or *rapazes* might have bought them a drink, lent them spending money, or housed them for a few days, but they generally did not have the financial resources to support a *bofe* in exchange for his sexual services. Such agreements were more typical of the relationship established between many *tias* and younger boys.[127] In a collection of short stories published in 1975 entitled *Os solteirões* (The bachelors), Gasparino Damata, a Brazilian journalist and writer, captured the lives of the *tias* and their relationship to young boys. Poverty, unemployment, and lack of opportunities for so many younger men provided *tias* with numerous possible partners. Damata's short story, "O voluntário" (The volunteer) describes another prototype figure, the macho male who never marries, likes to penetrate young boys, and dislikes *bichas*. Although this type is harder to find in documents of the period, Damata's literary portraits of homosexual life in Rio de Janeiro in the early 1960s ring true and one can assume that he was writing from personal knowledge.[128]

While discreet middle-class homosexuals, macho bachelors, and financially comfortable *tias* were all figures within this urban universe, the *O Snob turma* was largely composed of *bichas*. Those involved in relationships brought their *bofes* to social events. A few *tias* came to some of their parties. *Rapazes* (guys) floated in an out of the group. *Bonecas*, however, ran the show.

Beauty Queens, Other Royalty, and Their Husbands

The pages of *O Snob* allowed the *bonecas* in the group to express in writing a part of their persona that they often had to conceal in everyday life. An article about one of the members of the *turma*, Ozório, also known as "Tatiana," described the daily contradictions that the *bonecas* faced: "He, like all of us, lives in two worlds. The real, the life out there, and the illusionary inner life of our marvelous and enchanting little world. In this world of fictitious beauty, Tatiana Koseiusko, descendant of the Russian Imperial house, now dethroned and cast out, is a great lady."[129] Indeed, the pages of *O Snob* were filled with news and gossip about ladies, marquises, and assorted royalty. The *bonecas* also drew pictures of each other with up-to-date hairstyles and elegant gowns. While their coiffeurs and clothes changed from puffy bouffants and Jacqueline Kennedy gowns in 1963 to the Twiggy-look and miniskirts in 1968, the attraction to and the imitation of the feminine remained constant. One satirical short piece in the journal summed up the relationship between the *bicha* and the *bofe* in "The *Bicha's* Ten Commandments":

1. Love all men.
2. Never remain alone.
3. Kiss all *bofes*.
4. Don't think about the future.
5. The more intimacy in bed the better.
6. Always pretend that you love only one.
7. Never forget the *bofe* who got married.
8. Avoid talking about money.
9. Don't like *mariconas* (faggots).
10. Only marry for an hour.[130]

According to this author, the *bicha* was not just any woman, but the hardened femme fatale with many lovers and no obligations. Nor did she like her fellow "sisters," as the admonition about *mariconas* revealed. In fact, throughout the pages of *O Snob*, there remained a constant tension between "bitchiness" and sisterhood. *Bichas* wrote endless columns praising other journals and *bonecas* of the Carioca subculture. However, competition and the desire of different *bonecas* to remain at the center of attention often divided the group.[131] Given the constant external social pressures on the *bonecas*, the group's internal squabbles over personal glory and self-affirmation were understandable. Group divisions were minimized through the moderating influence of Agildo Guimarães, the journal's unassuming but charismatic founding editor, who remained a key figure in maintaining the group's social cohesion and the publication's relatively long life.[132]

A New Identity Emerges

As early as 1966, the *bicha/bofe* model received severe criticisms from at least one of the members of *O Snob*. Hélio, known as Gato Preto (Black Cat), considered himself to be a homosexual but not a *boneca*. He valued the supportive family network of *O Snob* and played an active role in nurturing the *turma* and the publication.[133] At the same time, however, he consistently questioned the rigid social and sexual roles assumed by the *bonecas*. In fact, he had changed his nickname from Pantera Rosa (Pink Panther) to Gato Negro precisely to affirm the notion that one didn't have to be effeminate to be a homosexual. Gato Preto summarized his thinking in an article published in the last issue of the journal in June 1969:

Bonecas will always be a poorly made caricature of women, since biologically they are male and will continue to be; and certain tics and mannerisms
that the *bonecas* adopt to be feminine end up being clownish. "They"* even
invent [the idea] that women in order to be women have to be just like
"them." And for this reason, [the *bonecas*] like so few [women]. Being a
woman is something completely different from what I see around here. The
bonecas end up creating laws of femininity that not even real women recognize. Look at your mothers. Would you like to be like them or like Danuza
Leão [a Brazilian sex symbol]? Which of the two is more of a woman? Oh,
it is the woman with whom you identify more closely. . . . If homosexuality
is only camp, great, but it also shows that the effeminate are a minority. They
seem more numerous exactly because they become caricatures and call
everyone's attention to themselves.[134]

Hélio was influenced by the incipient youth movement in Brazil, which
questioned traditional social and moral values, such as premarital virginity
for women and the hierarchical nature of Brazilian society. Through a column in the paper, he brought these ideas into the *turma*. He went so far as
to suggest that instead of publishing so many sketches of elegant and sophisticated women, representing a idealized vision of the group's members,
O Snob should publish nude male drawings and photographs: "Everyone
knows very well that for an *entendido* it is more pleasurable to see nude men
than feminine drawings at gala night affairs. And if there are respectable
magazines that only show nude women, why can't we show men?"[135]

Anthropologists who have written on homosexuality in Brazil have
noted the emergence in the 1960s of a new middle-class gay identity. One
of the indications of this development, according to these authors, was the
popularization of the term *entendido*. The word had been around for a while
to describe a certain type of gay man. Thus, Carmen Dora Guimarães, in
her pioneering anthropological study of a group of fourteen homosexuals
in Rio de Janeiro in the early 1970s, noted: "Even though it is still used by
some in the network, for the majority the term *entendido* is old-fashioned
and defines a kind of homosexual of the traditional middle class who is '*en-
rustido* [closeted, discreet], who lives two lives.'"[136] Edward MacRae in his
anthropological work *A construção da igualdade* (The building of equality),
which examined the group Somos, Brazil's first gay rights organization,
founded in the late 1970s, has argued that the *entendidos*, as a distinct social
group among Brazilian homosexuals, developed in São Paulo in the late

---

* Gato Preto used *elas*, the feminine pronoun, to refer to the *bonecas* in his article.

1960s.[137] Another anthropologist, Peter Fry, has likewise described the emergence of the *entendidos* among the middle classes of Rio de Janeiro and São Paulo in the late 1960s.[138] Their periodization is supported by the recollections of gay men who frequented the São Paulo nightlife in the early 1960s that the term *entendido* was first used in that city in 1964–65 among the theater crowd.[139] According to anthropologists, the *entendido* rejected pejorative, gendered terms, such as *viado, louca,* or *bicha,* as well as flamboyant behavior. Rather, the *entendido* preferred a term of self-identity that reflected a more guarded public persona. In addition, MacRae has suggested that the *entendido* adopted new "egalitarian" sexual behavior that did not imitate the active/passive, male/female dyad associated with traditional, hierarchical *homem/bichas* interplay.[140]

Thus, although the term *entendido* had its origins in the 1940s (or even earlier), as the letters published in Jaime Jorge's *Homossexualismo masculino* indicate, the meaning and usage of the word, seemed to shift in the 1960s. In addition to remaining an expression used almost exclusively by homosexuals as a code word that did not contain the sting of *viado* or even *bicha,* it was employed by Hélio as a synonym for a homosexual who did not assume a specific masculine or feminine gender role. Others in the group, however, used the term more generically as a polite expression for *bichas.* This was its meaning as it appeared in *O Snob's* masthead, as well as in an article published in 1967 promoting the idea of holding the First Congress of *Entendido* Journalists, which would unite all of the mini-publications produced by Brazilian *bonecas.*[141]

Agildo's recollections of the negative reactions provoked by the participation of a *bofe* couple in the group and the constant battle that Hélio waged with the *bonecas* of *O Snob* about gender roles exemplify this contested territory throughout the 1960s. The tension was between *pintosas* (obviously effeminate men) and those who considered themselves to be homosexuals with a more masculine identity. Barbosa da Silva's research even excluded the former because they were too flamboyant and ostentatious and chose instead to interview middle-class men who would have undoubtedly referred to themselves as *entendidos.* Class differentiation among the men who moved in the world of *bichas, bofes, tias,* and *entendidos* was not automatically a determining factor in shaping one's sexual identity, but it nevertheless could have an impact on the ways in which people presented themselves and negotiated both their subculture and the society at large.

Dissident Voices and Evolving Politics

Just as some men within the *O Snob* social network began to question normative homosexual identities, in the late 1960s scattered individuals within the Catholic Church also challenged moral teachings regarding homosexuality. Critics, however, raised their reservations within the framework of overall policies that still considered same-sex eroticism as an unnatural act. Internal church discussions in the wake of Vatican II and the growing strength of the supporters of liberation theology in Brazil created a climate that permitted at least one Catholic intellectual to consider a new approach to homosexual behavior. In 1967, Jaime Snoek, a priest and trained Catholic theologian born in Holland but residing in Brazil since 1953, wrote an article about the topic in *Revista Vozes*, a "Catholic cultural magazine." Snoek estimated that 4 to 5 percent of the male population and 2 to 3 percent of the female population was homosexual. In a reference to homophile organizations in Europe and the United States, he recognized that "in some countries this minority group has managed to organize in a common effort for their emancipation."[142] From a humanistic point of view, Snoek acknowledged that homosexuals were a significant minority who were forced to live a clandestine and marginal life and had a suicide rate five times higher than heterosexuals. He also asserted that "homophilia cannot be considered a sickness. It becomes an illness when a person is not integrated and open (*assumida*)" and suffers because of his sexuality.[143] As a professor of moral theology and seminarian, Snoek counseled understanding on the part of priests and recommended a series of liberal guidelines from the Pastoral Institute of Holland, which included discouraging marriage as a solution and supporting stable "homosexual friendships" based on fidelity.[144]

Snoek remained, nevertheless, an isolated voice of toleration within the Catholic Church, and others criticized his positions directly and indirectly. In a 1969 column in the prestigious daily *Jornal do Brasil*, Dom Marcos Barbosa answered a young man's query about homosexuality with a veiled reference to Snoek's views, condemning the theologian for his support of "certain illicit unions."[145]

Although debates within the Catholic Church about homosexuality did not result in any significant changes in its policies or approaches to the topic, at *O Snob* Gato Preto's questioning of prevalent constructions of homosexual identity was soon reflected in the journal's content. Clau Renoir, who became *O Snob*'s editor in 1969, explained the innovations in the publica-

tion: "1969 seems to be a year of novelties. At least for us, of *Snob,* many
new things will happen in the course of the year. We initiate a more adult
journal where the chronicles, poetry, articles of real interests, short stories,
and healthy social columns without gossip, which by the way has been abandoned for some time by our columnists, and the omission of drawings of
feminine figures . . . will show that we are now revealing who we truly are.
We are near the twenty-first century, two steps from the moon, and we can't
allow people with certain fantasies to remain stationary a century behind
the times. We know that we will be criticized initially, but we will fight so
that everyone will follow us in our march toward progress, as eternal pioneers."[146] A subsequent issue announced *O Snob's* "New Phase." The cover
drawing, instead of portraying a beauty queen, showed two nude men making love (see fig. 15). Although the political situation cut short this new experiment in journalism, a transformation had taken place among many of
the *bichas* and *bonecas* of *O Snob.*

Prior to 1968, the members of the *turma* who wrote articles for *O Snob*
only rarely commented on political topics, even those related to homosexuality. Several issues of the publication brought international news of the
legislation liberalizing the legal status of homosexuality in Britain, as well

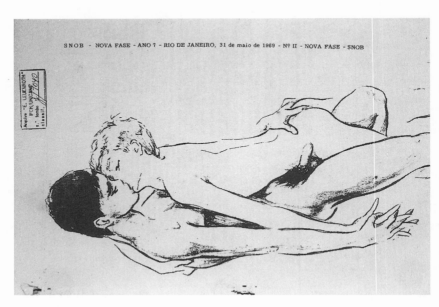

SNOB - NOVA FASE - ANO 7 - RIO DE JANEIRO, 31 de maio de 1969 - Nº II - NOVA FASE - SNOB

FIGURE 15   Cover of final issue of *O Snob* (May 1969), reflecting the shift in notions of gender
among Brazilian gay men. Illustration courtesy of Agildo Guimarães.

as comments expressing the hope that the winds of change for homosexuals would come to Brazil.[147] The student, youth, and revolutionary movements that swept the world in 1968, however, clearly influenced the group, and the journal reflected the changing mood evident in Brazil. Throughout that explosive year, practically every issue of *Snob* carried an editorial or article referring to the Vietnam War, student demonstrations in Paris, the hippie movement, and international and Brazilian student protests. Yet the writers for the journal had not become political activists, and the juxtaposition of the news of the day with gossip of the group revealed that world and national events, with rare exceptions, seemed somewhat distant to these *bonecas*. Claudia Renoir's "Social Column," whose title was a play on words that conflated political social events and *boneca* social events, reported on politics and "socializing" in the same paragraph: "World attention is turned toward Paris where the peace negotiations for Southeast Asia are taking place. But the Vietcong, in ignoring the agreement, have waged the biggest battle of the Vietnam War by attacking the city of Saigon. And in that same Paris, students clash with police during demonstrations about the state of French education. However, one of the most important events of this beginning of May was the visit made to Bahia by Gilka Mina [Agildo Guimarães], Sandra Cavalcante and Altair. And the journal *Subúrbio a Noite* sponsored a gala event in the salons of the suburban organization."[148] For this *boneca*, the trip of *O Snob's* founding editor to the Northeast and a party organized by another friendship network in the northern suburb of Rio were as newsworthy as student protests, wars, and politics.

Some members of the *turma*, however, were willing to articulate political views. In an interview, Gato Negro harshly criticized the military.[149] Founding editor Agildo Guimarães also clearly positioned himself in favor of student protests. In an article about seven recent special events in his life, he wrote a poetic account of the March of 100,000 in Rio de Janeiro on June 26, 1968, a protest against the military government:

> At a late hour in the afternoon the people fill Rio Branco Avenue with banners, signs, slogans and that locomotive desire to move forward, to change what is wrong. And the cries of Freedom, Freedom echo by a thousand mouths at the same time, and a thousand multiplied by a thousand as the transcendental echo goes on to infinity. That emotional sensation [comes] when we feel the brotherhood of an ideal in a totality never imagined, the shivers throughout our body, the tears that come to our eyes, and that strange feeling that we are not alone. The desire to go on shouting, shouting, marching, marching. And when everything is over, and when we go

home, we are sure that life has to change. . . . The planted seed has to grow and bear fruit. That which is brought to us must be passed on. It cannot stop.[150]

Neither Hélio nor Agildo had direct contacts with leftist or student activists in the political movement against the military dictatorship. However, their consciousness of their own marginal status as homosexuals, combined with a certain tendency to see themselves as intellectuals, drew them to these protests.

Another contributor to the journal, inspired by the recent student demonstrations, imagined a protest march by *bichas* and *bonecas*. Written at the end of March 1969, the parody captured a scene remarkably similar to actions organized by the gay liberation movement around the world shortly thereafter. Titled "Protest," the story began: "In reaction to the current situation that has become unbearable, a system was set up to defend the rights for freedom of the gay world." The article then went on to imagine a mass meeting where it was decided that everyone would march with banners and placards to the president's summer residence to demand that the government take the necessary measures "in favor of the civil rights of the Brazilian *boneca*." Glamorous protest banners in Gothic letters were prepared for the march. One slogan comically counterpoised condemnation of Rio de Janeiro's homophobic police commissioner with praise for a drag entertainment star: "Down with Padilha. Long Live Rogéria." Another said: "Prohibit Sexual Promiscuity between Men and Women," while a third campy banner read: "In the Parties of Itamaratí [Ministry of Foreign Affairs], We Want to Go as *Travesti* [in drag]."[151]

The political climate of 1968 also encouraged the editors of *O Snob* to propose the coordination of efforts among different publications produced by groups of *bonecas* through the establishment of the Associação Brasileira da Imprensa Gay (Brazilian Association of the Gay Press, ABIG).[152] Several journals in Rio de Janeiro made this proposal a reality in early 1969 by holding the association's first meeting, which, in keeping with *O Snob*'s tendency toward hyperbole, was called the ABIG Congress. The participants elected a president and held an awards banquet. But the military dictatorship's harsh policies in 1969 quickly intimidated such efforts, and the nascent organization never advanced beyond this incipient stage.[153] Another frustrated project of 1968 involved the formation of a center, christened Shangri-lá in the hopes of its becoming a special, almost magical place where the group could socialize. Agildo proposed the idea of this alterna-

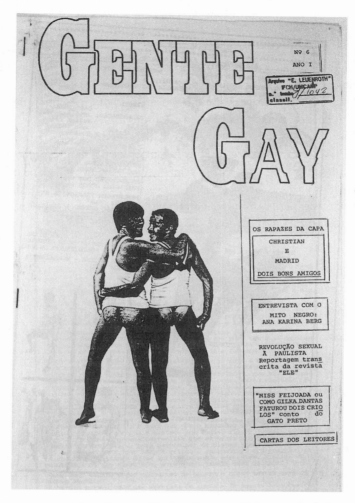

FIGURE 16   Cover of *Gente Gay,* one of the first efforts to publish a mass-circulation gay publication in the early years of political liberalization under the military dictatorship in 1976. Illustration courtesy of Agildo Guimarães.

tive social space for conferences, theater productions, readings, and film showings, but the changing political situation discouraged this plan as well.[154]

   O Snob ceased publication in mid-1969. Hélio (Gato Preto) recalled that paranoia had spread through the group. The members usually distributed the journal in cruising places and among friends. With a wave of arrests and torture of oppositionists, many supporters of *O Snob* feared that their journal might be confused with the left-wing "subversive" publications.[155] Agildo later recalled that many of the group's members also drifted away because more gay bars opened up in the late 1960s. With additional entertainment options available to members of the group, *O Snob's* function as a social network diminished. Instead of attending intimate parties with friends, many preferred to go out to nightclubs.[156]

The journalistic efforts of several members of the group, however, were revived in 1976 as the country began to see a liberalization of the political climate (see fig. 16). In that year, Agildo, Anuar, Hélio, and other former collaborators of *O Snob* founded *Gente Gay* (Gay people), the first of a wave of new publications that marked the beginning of a politicized gay and lesbian rights movement in the country.

CHAPTER FIVE

~

The Homosexual Appropriation
of Rio's Carnival

A year before Carmen Miranda inaugurated her new film persona as a singing *baiana* to her Brazilian fans, Hugh Gibson, the United States ambassador to Brazil in the mid-1930s, published a traveler's account about aspects of life in Rio de Janeiro. Gibson's 1937 travelogue offered readers an appreciation of the "mysteries of Rio," the "beauties of the place," and "the charms of the people."[1] The ambassador was an amateur photographer, and his chapter on Carnival contains two images that he took during the celebrations. One captures revelers crowded into convertibles and slowly moving down the city's main thoroughfare as part of pre-Lenten festivities. The other photograph is captioned "Negro Carnival Club" (see fig. 17). Twenty-nine people push their way into the black and white photo. A plumed fan serves as an umbrella hovering over the crowd. Most of the faces seem to be those of men dressed in exotic women's costumes. The style is Oriental and Roman, with beaded halters covering chests to evoke the image of breasts. Rich, shining material suggests wealth and luxury. Most men are decorated with jewelry. Strings of pearls, large dangling earrings, and elaborate headgear proclaim style, affluence, elegance. Yet there is an artificial aspect to their attire that reveals the humble origins of the revelers. Carefully plucked eyebrows, rouged cheeks, and painted lips fail to hide square jaws and the masculine features of some. Other men manage to convey a softer, feminine look. They are posed and clearly self-conscious of their stylized appearance. The two figures in the foreground lounge seductively in front of the camera. The men in drag smile directly into the camera and seem to be enjoying themselves more than the few men in masculine attire, a policeman, a man dressed in a sailor's cap, and a Roman soldier.

FIGURE 17   Carnival club, Rio de Janeiro, circa 1937. Reprinted from Gibson, *Rio de Janeiro*
(1937), 145.

Ambassador Gibson did not provide his readers with any more information about these male Salomes and Scheherazades caught by his lens.
Perhaps they were simply invisible to an eye that marveled at interracial
mixing in pre-Lenten festivities yet did not perceive the cross-gendered
content of Carnival. Perhaps Gibson's own sense of propriety and morality censored any comment on the distinctive presentations of these men.
Whatever the reason for Gibson's silence, cross-dressing men, like the ones
he so carefully—or perhaps unintentionally—documented, have become
a prominent part of Rio de Janeiro's Carnival. Their presence during the
pre-Lenten celebrations reinforces the image that Brazil is a haven for sexual renegades and transgressors of conventional gender roles. This unilateral notion obscures the fact that for much of the twentieth century, bold
public manifestations of gender role reversals were temporary and confined
to the celebratory moment. "Jurema," a young office worker living in São
Paulo in the 1930s, discovered this hard fact when he decided to experiment
with wearing women's clothes in public. Because it wasn't during Carnival
time, the police arrested him.[2] "Flor de Abacate," who also lived in São
Paulo in the '30s, admitted enjoying cross-dressing, but would only do so

publicly during pre-Lenten celebrations when the police would not bother him. While most transgressive behavior was permitted during Carnival, it was only allowed for three or four days of the year. During the other 362 days, one had to remain within the boundaries established by society, especially the gender boundaries, or pay the consequences.

Many foreign tourists and observers of Brazilian culture who have enjoyed Carnival in Rio de Janeiro assume that the current prominence of gay men throughout the festivities is a time-honored tradition. This is not the case. The homosexual appropriation of space during Carnival celebrations has been a long and protracted process. Mainstream Brazilian society has accommodated itself uneasily and unevenly to the expansion of homosexual territories within pre-Lenten festivities. Public and official responses have shifted between acceptance and repression, between curiosity and disgust. At the turn of the century, homosexual men "invaded" masked balls in feminine attire. They also organized groups of cross-dressers who participated in street revelries. By the 1940s, drag balls emerged as the privileged place for public performances of the inversion of gender representations. Throughout the 1950s, the prominence of these balls increased, as events organized exclusively for the homosexual subculture grew in number, size, and visibility. While participants in street revelries also engaged in cross-dressing, drag balls were the primary sites within the rule of misrule where one could transgress norms of masculinity and femininity without concern for social hostility or punishment. By the mid-1970s, drag balls had become an integral part of Carioca Carnival. They attracted extensive and positive media coverage and an international host of participants. Concurrently, luxury costume contests at the government-sponsored "official" Carnival ball held at the Municipal Theater became another venue for homosexual men. Their creations became the epitome of the sumptuous Carnival *fantasia* (costume). As the official samba school parades became a multimillion-dollar international tourist extravaganza in the 1960s and '70s, homosexuals also played a key role in designing and participating in this Carnival event.

The appropriation and transformation of Carnival, in turn, has had an important impact on the overall standing of homosexuals in Brazilian society. Although drag balls and drag queens popularized unilateral images of homosexuals as transvestites and perfect imitators of feminine beauty, press coverage of these events increased the public's awareness of important elements of the homosexual subculture. The attraction of international celebrities to these affairs further legitimized these balls and contributed to the expanded social toleration toward homosexuality. In this chapter I examine three realms of Rio's Carnival occupied by homosexuals—street revelry, Carnival balls and costume competitions, and samba school parades—to illustrate this ongoing and evolving appropriation and subversion of Carnival festivities.

Performance as Inversion and Reproduction

Brazilian anthropologist Roberto Da Matta, using both Mikhail Bakhtin's theoretical framework for the analysis of early modern popular European culture and Victor Turner's approaches to understanding public rites, argues that Brazilian Carnival is a celebration in which ordinary people, through the inversion of roles and the rule of misrule, can temporarily infuse egalitarian values into a rigidly structured and hierarchical society.[3] Da Matta emphasizes the inversion during Carnival of the two principal spheres of Brazilian life, namely the *casa* (home) and the *rua* (street). During Carnival, the unpredictable dangers of the street become the domain or home of the reveler. Free from the restrictions and rules of family life, one can enjoy an unbridled sensuality and sexuality. Everything is permitted. For three or four days during the year, Da Matta maintains, a poor black domestic servant can dress as a courtier or noblewoman to become the queen of the samba school parade. During that same street celebration, the maid's white middle-class employer may choose to rent a costume and parade seminude in the same samba school. Casting off bourgeois morality during Carnival, the usually proper and staid *madame* feels free to project an image of sexuality and impropriety. Da Matta argues that Carnival is also the one moment during the year when people are allowed to cross class lines to express *communitas*.[4]

Dividing Brazilian life into the *casa* and the *rua*, or private and public spheres, and then pointing to Carnival as an annual event in which these realms are inverted, offers a neat overarching framework for analyzing Brazilian culture, but it obscures important social realities. Historian Sandra Lauderdale Graham employs this construct to describe the social interactions in the Brazilian capital during the nineteenth century, but she observes a twist in the inversion of the commonly held notion of "safe" home and "dangerous" street for urban slaves. For those in forced servitude, the streets of Rio provided a freer space to socialize and interact than the confines of their masters' households, not just at Carnival time, but throughout the year.[5] Similarly, in her work on the history of Rio's Carnival, Maria Clementina Pereira Cunha has emphasized the ways in which pre-Lenten festivities are less an inverted mirror of the Brazilian social structure and an expression of communal egalitarianism than a moment in which different social classes express and play out social conflicts. Commenting on the turn-of-the-century Carnival antics known as the *entrudo,* in which people from different social classes engaged in raucous street battles with buckets of water and scent-filled wax balls, Cunha argues: "The celebration becomes a virtual war because it reveals and multiplies daily tensions: being an occasion to invert, strip bare, and play with daily life, it exposes [life's] open wounds without hiding behind day-to-day masks."[6]

Likewise, cross-dressing during Brazilian Carnival is more than a simple inversion of gender roles and socially defined dress codes. Indeed, the phenomenon reflects deeply embedded social tensions. Heterosexually identified men may borrow their wives', girlfriends', mothers', or sisters' gowns, jewelry, and makeup to dress as women for a day of revelry and engage in a playful exploration of their own notions of gender, but this foray into the feminine is temporary. Their transgression is limited to society's superficial markers of gender. In donning feminine apparel, they are not signaling an inversion of their sexual identity or their role as "real" men. Despite their feminine representation, they remain the masculine "active" partner in intercourse. To make that perfectly clear and in order to avoid any confusion about their everyday sexual identity, these men usually maintain an element of the masculine in their performance—a beard, a hairy chest, unshaven legs. After Ash Wednesday, they return to their family and friends, daily routine, and socially appropriate comportment and dress.

In contrast, for many Brazilian homosexuals Carnival, rather than being an act of inversion, provides the opportunity for an *intensification* of their own experiences as individuals who transgress gender roles and socially acceptable sexual boundaries the entire year. Da Matta's notion of inversion in the use of the street thus only applies in relative terms to homosocial and homosexual activities, because for men engaged in such behavior the street is a privileged public space throughout the year. During the four days of Carnival, members of this subculture merely transform the streets into a *more* public arena. What has been discreetly hidden in myriad daily exercises in obfuscation becomes an open performance without the social sanctions. Even those homosexuals who do not ordinarily identify with a feminine persona may choose to explode in an outlandish mimicking of the womanly during Carnival as if to challenge 362 days of con-

tainment within strict confines of appropriate masculine and feminine behavior.

For other homosexuals, cross-dressing during Carnival is also less an
inversion than an attempt to conform to femininity. By assuming the garments, makeup, and personas of women, these men attempt to live out their
own feminine fantasies and desires by meticulously imitating the social
norm. Carnival provides them with a broader stage than that of intimate
parties among supportive friends. Dressed as women, some men proclaim
to Brazilian society that they are more feminine and ladylike than women
themselves. Kay Francis, according to her own testimony, anxiously
awaited Carnival because the celebration provided her with the opportunity to transform herself into a better Kay Francis than the star herself.[7]
Thus, while sartorial inversion implies reversal of the status quo, it also
works to reinforce pervasive standards of the feminine, and therefore, the
masculine.

Although some men may attempt to achieve perfect imitations of glamorous and beautiful women, another form of cross-dressing during Carnival contains an element of playful parody, designed less to pass as and more
to mimic and exaggerate femininity. Common portrayals include men costumed as pregnant brides, or as femmes fatales with oversized breasts and
buttocks. Through outlandish imitations of women, these male revelers
bring an element of camp to their embodiment of the feminine. David
Bergman has suggested common characteristics of camp that seem to ap-
ply to the performances of these Brazilian men during Carnival, including
exaggerated, artificial, and extreme style; tension with popularized, commercial, or consumer culture; positioning outside of mainstream culture;
and affiliation with homosexual culture or self-conscious eroticism that
questions the naturalization of desire.[8]

The epitome of Brazilian camp performance during Carnival has been
the multiple variations on the images of Carmen Miranda, dressed in the
garments of the *baianas,* the Afro-Brazilian women from the northeastern
state of Bahia. The *baianas'* attire, complete with turban, bared midriff, and
layered, billowing skirts, has been an important element in Carnival street
parades since the early twentieth century. Men donned the same garb during Carnival even before Carmen Miranda's first film performance as a *baiana* in 1938, but *bichas* quickly picked up the camp element in Miranda's
representation, with her excessive amounts of jewelry and eclectically decorated turbans.[9] It should be noted, however, that cross-dressing men's exaggerated replication of Miranda's own appropriation of the *baiana,* that

is, the imitation of an imitation, usually ends up erasing the Afro-Brazilian elements in the performance. The parody of the parody, while representing the epitome of camp, becomes oblivious to its origins. Just as the United States ambassador artfully photographed a "Negro Carnival Club" without noticing or daring to comment on its cross-gendered content, so too Carmen Miranda and her imitators have ended up eliminating the roots of their creation. Similarly, camp imitations of women, with exaggerated costumes, excessively padded body parts, and humorous antics, can ultimately reinforce traditional gendered stereotypes, diminishing or erasing the parody's effectiveness as a critique of rigid social norms.

The *communitas* experienced by homosexuals during Carnival celebrations is also different from the cross-class commonality that Roberto Da Matta and others describe. In the 1950s, *bichas* reported anticipating and savoring the four days of Carnival *loucura* (craziness) because they could join their friends in the streets or in Carnival balls and become caught up in the fever of the moment. Their *communitas* came from the feeling of group solidarity while parading in outlandish costumes through the streets of Rio or from the excitement of being crowded onto a dance floor with hundreds if not thousands of other homosexuals. In this semipublic and semiprivate space, social hostility toward their sexual comportment seemed remote and the pleasure of the moment was a comforting respite from their daily lives. In this way, they were not a part of the generalized *communitas* that Da Matta has ascribed to Carnival. On the contrary, their experiences during these festivities largely reinforced their *difference* from the other revelers. The existence during Carnival of multiple "communities" with unique characteristics can strengthen rather than weaken social barriers. Thus, at least as it applies to the homosexual presence in these celebrations, the idea that social differentiation simply melts away during Rio's Carnival into a pervasive spirit of *communitas* is somewhat illusory.

A Brief History

Pre-Lenten Mardi Gras festivities in Rio de Janeiro can be dated to the seventeenth century, when people engaged in a raucous street celebration known as *entrudo*, in which revelers threw water basins and buckets filled with lemon scented water on each other.[10] In 1604 the governor of Rio de Janeiro tried to outlaw this ritualized street fighting because it had become too violent, but the tradition resisted official prohibitions. Throughout the colonial period, Carnival remained a festival enjoyed particularly by the poor and lower classes. Slaves and freed persons, blacks and *mulatos,* celebrated the holiday by parading through the streets, imitating and satirizing the clothes, gestures, and airs of the elite. The *entrudo* continued as playful street fighting, at times escalating into more aggressive confrontations in which urine and feces were substituted for lemon-scented water. Over the years, authorities attempted to control the activity on numerous occasions by issuing edicts prohibiting its practice, usually to no avail.[11]

In imperial Brazil (1822–89), the Carioca elite sought to clean up and refine Carnival celebrations. They organized sophisticated masquerade balls similar to ones popular in Europe at the time. The immediate precursor to the first masked Carnival ball took place on January 22, 1840, at the Hotel Itália in the Largo do Rossio. The dance was so successful that it was repeated the next month during Carnival. Newspaper advertisements announced the event as a "Masquerade Ball, like the ones they hold in Europe on the occasion of Carnival." The gala affair's popularity sparked a new tradition in Brazilian pre-Lenten celebrations.[12] In 1932, the government of Rio de Janeiro began sponsoring a masquerade ball at the Municipal Theater, which was attended by the Carioca elite. The event, which included a luxury costume competition, evolved over the years into the most prestigious of several balls attended by Brazilian high society and the international jet set.[13]

Street Carnival took on new forms with the introduction of clubs, first organized in the 1850s, that paraded through the streets in costumes. Revelers marched behind floats presenting allegoric scenes, accompanied by drums and music. By 1900, the police had licensed more than two hundred such Carnival clubs. In the first decade of the twentieth century, a musically based street celebration, known as the *rancho,* developed in Rio de Janeiro. Groups of people, mostly of poor and Afro-Brazilian origins, danced in the street, accompanied by musical bands and choruses that sang *rancho* tunes. During the same time period, costumed revelers of means organized motorcades in convertibles and drove up and down Rio's main avenue. Known as the *corso,* this tradition began in 1907 when the daughters of the president of the Republic rode along the recently inaugurated Avenida Central before stopping to watch the Carnival celebrations. Car owners immediately adopted the practice, which began to disappear after 1925 when the streets became glutted with automobiles.[14]

In 1917 the hit song "Pelo Telefone" (Over the telephone) popularized samba, and the new musical genre and dance style, rooted in Afro-Brazilian traditions, soon permeated Carnival celebrations.[15] *Escolas de samba* (samba schools) evolved in the late 1920s and early 1930s when poor people, again mostly of Afro-Brazilian origins, many of whom lived in Rio de Janeiro's hillside slums, organized groups that paraded together during Carnival to the syncopated rhythm of samba tunes.[16] In the early 1930s, the government of Getúlio Vargas intervened in these spontaneous celebrations and established regulations to recognize them as official events. Through the Commission of Tourism, the government granted subsidies to the Carnival schools, awarded prizes in a competition to determine the best school, and established an entire program of Carnival activities for the city of Rio de Janeiro.[17] By the late 1960s, the samba school parades had became ostentatious extravaganzas, with lavish floats carrying bikini-clad beauties in dazzling costumes, all vying for first place in the government-sponsored competition. As a result of this commercialization of Carnival, the female, dark-skinned samba-school participant, wearing sequined and plumed outfits and moving sensually and frenetically to the samba beat, has come to represent what has been billed as "the Greatest Show on Earth."[18]

Street Carnival Merriment

In 1930 Antônio Setta, who was known as A Rainha (the Queen), and some of his friends organized the Carnival street group Bloco Caçadores de Veados (Deer Hunters). The name played on the term *viado*, the pejorative expression for an effeminate homosexual. Made up mostly of transvestites dressed in luxurious costumes, the Caçadores de Veados group attracted large crowds, who enthusiastically applauded the *frescos'* elegant attire.[19] Madame Satã, who participated in this *bloco* in the 1930s, remembered how he and his friends paraded through the streets of Rio de Janeiro in plumes and sequined gowns, flaunting a self-conscious elegance and femininity. They also basked in the applause and recognition of the beauty of their creative and luxurious apparel.[20] Carnival street revelers took advantage of the suspension and inversion of strict social rules to engage in cross-dressing and gender parodies (see fig. 18). In the case of Caçadores de Veados, the organizers and participants both absorbed and made a jest of aggressive terminology usually employed against effeminate Brazilians and those who enjoyed sex with other men.[21]

Cross-dressing during Carnival, however, did not necessarily mean that those who engaged in gender-bending were homosexuals or condoned

FIGURE 18   Street Carnival celebration, Rio de Janeiro, 1932. Photograph courtesy of the
Museu da Imagem e do Som, Rio de Janeiro.

same-sex eroticism. An example both illustrates the relative nature of Carnival permissiveness and the social limitations placed on certain behavior.
In 1941, the Cordão da Bola Preta (Black Ball Club), one of Rio de Janeiro's
traditional groups that organized both balls and street festivities, decided to
satirize a standard Carnival figure, the Rei Momo (King of Farce), a jovial
and robust character who opened the city's pre-Lenten festivities. Offering
their own version of the King of Carnival, the Cordão da Bola Preta
announced the crowning of the Queen of Carnival, the Rainha Moma.
Anointed Her Majesty Federica Augusta, the Lioness-Hearted, this festive
royal figure was, in fact, a male member of the club dressed as a woman.
The Cordão de Bola Preta's internal discipline and morality, however,
made it clear that although one of their associates could cross-dress as Her
Majesty Federica Augusta, the club did not permit homosexuality among
its members. The eulogistic history of this Carnival association documents
this point clearly. A young bohemian from a good family applied for membership in the club. When one of the club's directors checked his address,
he discovered that it was a house where homosexuals lived. He reported his

findings to the club and argued that the lad should be rejected because he was likely to be a homosexual. "Under no circumstances could 'pederasts' join the Club," the association's chronicler explained. The rejected applicant appealed the decision and brought one of his girlfriends to the meeting. She testified that her lover was, in fact, not a "pederast." After he further explained that he only rented a room in the house in order to "rest" there, the directorate approved his application.[22]

The club permitted the Rainha Moma to parody the King of Farce because rules of masculinity and femininity were only temporarily suspended. A "real" man could dress as an empress to mimic one of Carnival's traditions; a pederast could not. Likewise, "real" men were permitted to parade dressed as pregnant women, brides, or prostitutes in this traditional Carnival street group because their gender transgression was limited and defined in time. Ash Wednesday brought order to a world turned upside down during Carnival. Gender representations were neatly re-encased in predetermined modalities. A pederast signified disorder that reigned throughout the entire year, and such a breach of the dominant paradigm was simply not sanctioned, as least within heterosexually defined groups like the Cordão da Bola Preta. Although some Carnival street groups such as Caçadores de Veados included and even encouraged the participation of *bichas*, others, reflecting pervasive social norms, had explicit policies to exclude their presence.

Invading Space

At the turn of the century, Dr. Viveiros de Castro remarked in *Assaults on Decency: Studies on Sexual Aberrations* that men dressed as women invaded masquerade balls during Carnival celebrations (see fig. 19).[23] Although cross-dressing and gender-bending expanded from the street to closed spaces, the masquerade ball was a contested territory. In the 1930s, for example, Madame Satã attended a Carnival ball at the República Theater located near Praça Tiradentes, where he entered a costume contest organized by the Bloco Caçadores de Veados.[24] While many homosexuals attended these balls, dressing in women's attire for the occasion, the event was not promoted as a drag ball. For example, in 1938, the year Madame Satã won a prize for the costume that would later give him his nom de guerre, the *Jornal do Brasil* published advertisements announcing four nights of Carnival celebrations at the theater where Satã competed with his *fantasia*. Although

FIGURE 19   Carnival cross-dressing, Rio de Janeiro, 1913. Photograph courtesy of the Museu da Imagem e do Som, Rio de Janeiro.

the announcements for the ball included mention of prizes for the best costume, there was no indication that men dressed in effeminate attire would be competing for the prizes.[25] More likely, word of mouth guided homosexual men to those places where they would be relatively free to arrive in drag and parade around in their creations.

Praça Tiradentes and the theaters surrounding the park became the favored location for Carnival festivities where cross-dressing was permitted but not necessarily promoted. Because the plaza had been a traditional cruising site for homosexuals, significant numbers of men who engaged in homoerotic activities still socialized with friends and met sexual partners there. Many of these men lived in nearby Lapa and worked in the theaters and cinemas in the area as dancers, actors, costume assistants, designers, attendants, and ushers.[26] Changes in Rio de Janeiro's nightlife in the 1930s and '40s further added to the attractiveness of the plaza as a place to congregate and attend public entertainments. In 1939, Walter Pinto, the "Ziegfeld of Praça Tiradentes," took over the management of the Recreio Theater and revitalized the musical reviews performed there. This form of entertainment, known as *teatro de revista*, was a mixture of vaudeville, operettas, circus acts, and political cabaret. Women in sequined gowns, ostrich feathers, and revealing costumes attracted a wide audience, ranging from members of the Carioca elite to the expanding middle class. In order to compete with the luxurious floor shows at the Copacabana Palace Hotel, the Atlântica Casino (also in Copacabana), and the Urca Casino (from which Carmen Miranda had catapulted to fame in New York and Hollywood that same year), Pinto offered double the salaries for chorus girls and went to Europe, Cuba, and Japan to seek new stars.[27] The outlawing of gambling in 1946 also contributed to the rejuvenation of Praça Tiradentes as the entertainment center of the city. As the casinos shut down, show business entrepreneurs trimmed their acts and moved them to the theater district. Praça Tiradentes became associated with glitzy glamour and risqué shows. Not surprisingly, during the four days of Carnival festivities, the theaters and cinemas were used to host Carnival balls.

Homosexual men attended the Carnival balls in the theaters near Praça Tiradentes in growing numbers in the 1940s. In 1948, during one such ball, held at the João Caetano Theater at Praça Tiradentes, Dercy Gonçalves, a star of the *teatro de revista* who specialized in comedy laden with sexual innuendoes, improvised a costume contest for young men who had come to the ball in drag. A few men, dressed as *baianas*, participated in the event. The costume competition was a success. Having received the sanction of a stage celebrity, the tradition of organizing costume contests for men in drag quickly became an institutionalized part of Carnival festivities.[28] What had started in the early 1930s as a homosexual penetration of a clearly heterosexual space became, fifteen years later, part and parcel of carnivalesque celebrations.

Carnival Queens and Drag Balls

In the early 1950s, the tactic of appropriating space in Carnival balls and organizing groups that paraded in women's clothes during street revelry yielded to something new. Entertainment entrepreneurs began to target homosexual men for the costumed balls, advertising their presence at the events and encouraging the attendance of drag queens. The desire of certain businessmen to tap into this particular market was due in part to the growth in the homosexual subculture in Rio de Janeiro in the post–World War II period, as well as to the economic expansion that broadened the middle class and increased its buying power. As a result, one could choose among several Carnival balls directed toward a homosexual audience. The most expensive tickets were for the ball held at the João Caetano Theater. Men from lower social classes, who could not afford to attend that *baile*, went instead to Carnival celebrations at the Recreio Theater or the República Theater, where Madame Satã had won the best prize for his sequined bat costume in 1938.[29]

Cross-dressing was not obligatory at the events. Indeed, based on the examination of photos taken inside the balls in the 1950s, most men did not dress in costumes at all.[30] Among those who chose to dress up for the occasion, a good number stuck to masculine vestments—the manly uniforms of sailors, the billowing pirate shirts of buccaneers, or the togas of Roman soldiers. These costumes had a touch of daring and flamboyance but remained within the boundaries of masculine propriety. Likewise, some men dressed as women not to equal beauty queens, chorus girls, and femmes fatales, but rather to make fun of rigid social rules of gender through effeminate gestures, makeup, and clothes. However, drag queens in sequins and feathers remained the featured attraction. Nevertheless, the growing success of these balls cannot be attributed solely to the license of men dressed as women. In 1950, for example, a young woman, Elvira Pagã, participated in a pre-Carnival parade through the streets of Copacabana clad only in a matador's cape and a golden-colored bikini. Her scant costume created a sensation. The next day she was invited to participate in the first contest for the Carioca Queen of Carnival. She won, and a freer Carnival dress code was established.[31]

In 1951, the costume competition at the João Caetano Theater ball received city government funds set aside for pre-Lenten festivities. The event also began to attract a national audience, as men from all over the country came to the capital to attend the ball and enter the costume competition. That year there was a tie for first place, when a contestant from São Paulo dressed as "Ziegfeld Follies" split the prize with a young man from the southern state Rio Grande do Sul, who appeared as Iemanjá, the Afro-Brazilian goddess of the sea. The second place went to a youth who had traveled all the way from the northeastern state of Rio Grande do Norte and spent over Cr 70,000 on his costume, no small sum at the time.[32]

Prior to the 1950s, newspapers and magazines either employed heavily coded terms to describe balls where homosexuals dressed in drag or simply ignored them entirely in their Carnival reporting. For example, during the 1938 Carnival coverage, the Rio-based *Jornal do Brasil* published a photograph that showed what appeared to be a group of men in drag at a ball. The caption called them "The 'Who Are They?' Group." The journalist or editor who wrote the copy for the photo alluded to the ambiguous image projected by this group of men, who obviously stood out from the rest of the Carnival revelers and attracted the photographer's attention. But the newspaper still used *eles* as the male gender marker when referring to "them."[33] *Manchete,* a picture-news magazine similar to *Life, Look,* or *Paris Match,* which was launched in 1952, did not mention the drag balls or the homosexual component of Carnival festivities in its extensive coverage of that year's celebrations. In 1953, however, *Manchete* wrote about the drag balls and the prevalence of *travestis* (transvestites) in Carnival celebrations. The term *travesti* quickly became a code word used by the press to refer to all homosexuals. Those newspapers and magazines that noted the presence of *travestis* made a clear distinction between Carnival cross-dressing by heterosexual men, who used borrowed dresses for a temporary gender transgression, and the effeminate men who dressed as women to express their "real" identity. Through this press coverage, homosexuality was linked to effeminacy and cross-dressing, as personified in the *travestis* attending a Carnival drag ball. As a result, Carioca journalists writing for nationally distributed publications contributed to the construction of the stereotypical image of the Brazilian homosexual.

Although a majority of those who attended the balls in the 1950s and '60s did not cross-dress or wear any evident markers of effeminacy, the press nevertheless singled out outlandishly attired men for featured photo opportunities. In doing so, they projected the impression that these balls were almost exclusively frequented by *travestis.* For example, a 1953 article entitled "Types of Carnival" included several pictures of men dressed in women's clothes. One was of a bikini-clad man wearing a costume suggestive of a *baiana* and dancing on a little stage on the back of a pickup truck. The caption read: "This one was influenced by the beach and the *teatro de revista* in conceiving his type [personage]. It is the *travesti* dressed for the occasion, who doesn't go anywhere without a moving stage." Another photo showed a wigged man clad in an evening gown dancing at a ball. The accompanying caption affirmed: "The *travesti* is very common; there is always an influx of them. This year in Rio the República Theater was their headquarters. Indescribable balls, unique in the Americas."

During that same Carnival of 1953, Evaraldo de Barros, a journalist from the daily *Última Hora,* wrote an exceptionally perceptive piece about homosexual men dressed in drag, whom he referred to as the *falsas baianas* of Brazilian Carnival. The article's subtitle summarized the journalist's argument: "Rich Costumes in the Most Original Balls of Rio—João Caetano and Carlos Gomes are their Domains—They Live for the Moment and Are Not Existentialists. During the Year They Wear Masks."[34] Barros then went on to explain how "they" (using feminine gender markings) celebrated Carnival: "Everything about them is false. Their hair, their beautiful bust, their mother-of-pearl or tanned skin, their dresses, their names, the story of the proper family (that mustn't know that "she" is there). In short, their sex is a product of a fervent imagination. The *falsas baianas,* harem women, Spanish ladies, cancan girls, dolls, and ballerinas are still paradoxically the only real thing in the Carnival balls of the João Caetano and República Theaters or perhaps in all of Rio's Carnival."

At a time when Jean Paul Satre's philosophy was the rage among young bohemian intellectuals from Copacabana and Ipanema, this journalist, contradicting the title of his own article, insisted that the true practitioners of existentialism were the young men who shed their inhibitions, family prohibitions, and social sanctions to live for the moment in pre-Lenten merriment. He also recognized the psychological role that Carnival played in the lives of these men, who joined together from all social classes to have fun at the balls: "Enthusiastically expressing feelings repressed during the rest of the year, doctors, lawyers, waiters from the boardinghouses in the Lapa and the Canal Zone, diplomats, journalists, salesmen, in short, representatives of all social classes appear in very expensive costumes belonging to the fragile sex. And the ball is a show to see."

In fact, the drag balls held in the theaters and movie houses in and around Praça Tiradentes were probably the most socially integrated Carnival events in Rio de Janeiro in the 1950s. Both the effeminate and the discreet, both the outrageous and those fearful that their family would be upset if they knew of their attendance, showed up at Praça Tiradentes during Carnival. Those who earned meager wages carefully saved up to purchase their tickets. Revelers of all social strata intermingled on the dance floors to the syncopated rhythms of the latest Carnival hits. In contrast, as a rule the Carioca elite attended only the official ball at the Municipal Theater or festivities at the Copacabana Palace Hotel and other exclusive parties. The middle class and the poor also participated in different and socially separate Carnival costume balls and dances. While all social classes went to watch the Carnival parades of the samba schools going down Avenida Rio Branco, those who danced in the schools were generally the poor from the *favelas* or working-class neighborhoods. In the 1950s, the middle class (and the poor) looked on from the streets or stands, and the elite gazed on the festivities from carefully isolated and protected areas. In the 1960s, members of both the middle class and the elite began to attend samba school rehearsals and participate in the parades, but this had been less common in the 1950s.[35]

In comparing the "Ball of the *Falsas Baianas*" to those of the elite and the "traditional" Carnival celebrations, Barros noted that the affairs at Praça Tiradentes were much tamer and more civilized. He also pointed out that the civility of participants was at times spiced with humor, campy comments, and friendly viciousness: "The beauty and richness of the costumes rivals that of the best balls of high-class people. The order, energy, respect, and the lack of fights, or even simple act of urinating, contrasts shockingly with what one sees in the so-called 'carnivalesque societies.' And those who attend the balls at the João Caetano are so well bred. Although they are all transvestites—even their names [are transformed], the treatment is always friendly: 'How elegant Madame Mon Amour is!' 'That's so nice of you, dear. How can this tired old Chinese Pagoda costume compete with your beautiful Spanish Lady, adorable Margot?'"[36]

Barros was quick to point out that the "tired old Chinese Pagoda costume" cost "Mon Amour" twenty-five thousand cruzeiros, a small fortune at the time. He also reminded the reader that not all the *falsas baianas* who went to the costume balls dressed in luxurious costumes. And while he reinforced the notion that these affairs were almost exclusively attended by drag queens, he nevertheless captured the spirit felt by many homosexuals who saw in Carnival, and especially the costume balls, a special moment in the year's cycle. For many, it was the only time that they could express different notions of gender from those imposed on them by society: "At the end of the show when Carnival is over, the *falsas baianas* begin the real Carnival. They fasten onto their faces a mask of disdain for everything that surrounds them; they bury themselves in their offices, clinics, businesses, boarding houses, etc. They begin the struggle for the next Carnival . . . penny by penny, in order to arrive at the time when they can take off the mask that they use throughout the year and unfurl their expensive costumes."[37]

José Rodrigues, a native of Recife who came to Rio de Janeiro in 1952, recalled how he and his friends celebrated Carnival in the 1950s: "When Carnival arrived, the three days were crazy. We went out in the morning to spend the day in the street festivities of the Bloco dos Sujos [the Group of Dirty-Ones, a modern-day variation of the *entrudo*]. We'd be with one group and then join another. At three-thirty or four o'clock we'd come home and dress up as women. Everyone invented a costume. We'd go downtown again where we would dance, sing, and play. Then we would come back home, take a shower, and dress to go to the balls at the João Caetano. . . . We didn't work, sleep, or eat for three days. For us, Carnival was important because we could dress up, wear makeup, and look beautiful, something you couldn't do during the rest of the year."[38]

While flamboyant drag queens reigned at the João Caetano and the other balls that had a distinctly homosexual profile, they also attended other pre-Lenten festivities where the tactic of invading balls continued. One popular event was the Artists' Ball, sponsored by people in the theater and the arts. Since it took place the week before Carnival, the press covered it as the celebration that launched the season. However, because it was not an "official" *travesti* ball, one journalist explained that the costume cross-dressing was not caused by sexual "deviation" but rather was the result of liquor or *lança-perfume* (an ether that people sniffed in a handkerchief to achieve a temporary feeling of euphoria): "Some took advantage of the Carnival party to liberate themselves and came clearly as *travestis*. But one doesn't need to go to Freud for a convenient explanation. Limitless carnivalesque exaltation, *lança-perfume*, and whiskey end up being the real factors responsible for many things that take place."[39]

Because no pictures of men dressed as women accompanied this photojournalistic account of the Artists' Ball, one does not know if the author chose not to see homosexuality where it "did not belong." Perhaps he did indeed observe heterosexual men playfully clad in borrowed feminine raiment. The coverage of the Baile dos Artistas by *Manchete* in 1954 leads one to surmise that some journalists, like the U.S. ambassador to Brazil in the 1930s, either had an uncanny inability to see what was there or believed it was inappropriate to comment on what they saw. That year, Brazil's most popular photo magazine published a color spread of the Artists' Ball.[40] One picture showed three men in Carnival costumes. The first was wearing black tights with strings of sequins over his chest, a fancy mask, and a big flowing cape. The second wore white Bermuda shorts with a puffed-sleeved Cuban blouse tied at the midriff. He was also masked and held either a purse or a fan. The third man was dressed in black tights, a large cape, and a red mask with feathers. They evoked a traditional feminine aura, yet there was no reference in the text of the article describing these men as *travestis*. Possibly, this was due to the fact that they were not dressed up as showgirls, *baianas*, or divas. Their decidedly flamboyant costumes did not completely transgress gender boundaries. The press associated gorgeous drag queens with homosexuality, but they did not identify all cross-dressers as homosexuals. Those, such as the participants of the Cordão da Bola Preta whose conduct was not outrageously feminine, could pass as "normal" men on a Carnival fling. Likewise, homosexuals cross-dressing in locations not associated with the *travestis* could at times be viewed as "ordinary" men simply flirting with the feminine for a day or so. However, if someone's performance suggested a more permanent identification with the other gender, then that cross-dresser became suspect.

By 1956 the drag balls had become elaborate affairs. Costumes were increasingly ostentatious and expensive, and some contestants needed three or four assistants to help them make their grand entrance.[41] The balls also began to attract members of Brazilian high society and a few international guests. As a result, the press gave more coverage to the events, which were gaining in status as a Carnival landmark. Literary twists indirectly communicated the content of the festivities. Journalists referred to the delicate nature of the participants in the costume contests to imply that they were like women: "Monday's exhibition at the João Caetano is traditional. This year, it inspired more interest, and gave the impression of surpassing previous years. The theater was completely filled, and the extravagant party went through the night. Among the spectators one could see many society people, brought in perhaps by the strange curiosity of seeing close up the more inverted than entertaining show, which attracts Cariocas, Paulistas, Brazilians in general, and foreigners. The golden peacock was the most popular costume. Five of them got their multicolored feathers mixed up in the hall. A veritable crowd greeted them along the walkway when the costume contest took place. There was fainting and swooning, which is very natural and understandable in that kind of party."[42] The reporter carefully distanced the members of the Brazilian elite who attended this drag party from other revelers. Curiosity and the fame of the *baile* brought them there, he emphasized, and not any common bond with the "inverted" men dressed as women. Once again, however, this representation of the Carnival balls at Praça Tiradentes erased the vast majority of the participants in the event. As far as the journalist covering the celebration was concerned, crossdressers performed and the elite watched. Those homosexual men not dressed in glittery gowns yet attending the ball were notably absent from any descriptions of the night's festivities.

While thousands of homosexuals rubbed shoulders with a scattered number of members from the Brazilian elite who visited the drag balls at

Praça Tiradentes, the bulk of high society, elegantly clothed in tuxedos and formal evening gowns, attended the official Carnival ball at the Municipal Theater eight blocks away. Just as feathered peacocks elicited applause from fellow *travestis* and others assembled at the drag balls, so, too, at this grand ball homosexual men wore extravagant costumes. They were dressed, however, in masculine attire, as emperors, knights, and kings in elaborately designed apparel and paraded in the luxury costume contest, to the acclaim of all. The pioneering personality in this effort was Clóvis Bornay, a public employee who worked in the National Historical Museum in Rio de Janeiro. He began his second vocation as a competitor in Carnival costume contests in 1937. Many years later, he recalled the beginning of his career: "When I was old enough to go to the Municipal Theater I showed up in a costume that I designed titled the "Hindu Prince," taking advantage of some crystal prisms from a lamp that had been left in the basement of my house. My first appearance in public was so successful that I made it a habit for thirty-one consecutive years."[43] Crystal prisms evolved into sequins and silks and increasingly ostentatious and elaborate outfits. While a daring costume for a "real" man might be a Roman toga or a foray into femininity in his wife's dress, Bornay and the men who followed him in the luxury costume contests chose more and more flamboyant expressions of elegance, at times outdoing the women competing for the best female costume. Indicating his dedication to the event, Bornay explained: "Instead of buying a car, I spend my savings on costumes and continue to take the bus."[44] Bornay chose the sparkling grandeur of kings and emperors as sartorial themes to express his belief that men, too, could be peacocks.

In 1956, the grand prize for the most sumptuously costumed male went to Zacarias do Rego Monteiro, dressed as an elegant Pierrot.[45] In the women's contest, the award-winning raiments, "The Royal Butterfly" and "The Trojan Horse," were created by Aelson Novoa Trinidade, a fashion designer who was known to be gay and who also made costumes for musical variety shows.[46] The most ostentatious, glamorous, and glittering costumes were all created by homosexuals, yet gender roles at this official gala celebration were rigidly enforced.[47] As far as Brazilian high society was concerned, at "respectable" Carnival events, men could only represent masculine figures, and women likewise had to dress in women's costumes. Although nontraditional gender representations found expression in the creativity and luxuriousness of the displays, among the Brazilian elite, decorum and discretion enveloped homosexuality. Among working-class and middle-class celebrants at Praça Tiradentes, flamboyant cross-gendered behavior was a featured attraction. In both balls peacocks reigned, but at the Municipal Theater they were required to remain, at least formally, macho.

Negative Reactions

In 1957, a shift occurred in the coverage of the drag Carnival balls. Whereas in previous years the newspapers and magazines had made joking and mildly pejorative comments about the *travestis* who went to the balls, the reporting about the Meninas do Paraíso (Girls of Paradise) Ball at the João Caetano Theater was aggressively hostile. One journalist for *Manchete* wrote: "Ever since the law permitted it, morality has been shoved aside and the scandalous and shameful Monday ball at the João Caetano Theater has taken place. [It is] a veritable parade of aberrations, abnormalities, and moral cripples which should make the authorities blush. In order for our readers to have an idea of what happens at the party of the so-called 'Girls of Paradise' you should know that photographers were not allowed to enter so the shamefulness was not graphically documented. Our photographers worked at the entrance of the João Caetano catching snapshots that we bring to the readers' attention to show how right we are in being indignant. Another of our intentions, the main one, is to try to attract the attention of [morally] upstanding [people], so that we can see that from here on this repulsive thing does not repeat itself."[48]

The moralistic tone of the article revealed a rejection of any overtly homosexual participation in Carnival. Yet the captions that accompanied the photos covering the ball contained a mixed message. One alluded to the police barricades set up to maintain order at the entrance to the event and read: "Here opinions are divided. It's a man. No, it's a woman. It was a woman. Yes, there was a wire barrier and bravery between the photographers and the 'girls.'" A picture of a man dressed as a showgirl of the 1910s was captioned: "Sometimes the costumes, one cannot deny it, were fancy and in good taste." On one hand the article exuded moral superiority, yet these comments were undercut by a begrudging respect for the style of those who faced hostile crowds in order to attend the event. Valéria Lander, who first participated in a Carnival costume ball in 1934, remembered the violence unleashed against the drag queens in 1957. "You know, it wasn't as easy as today. We were stoned on the street. It was horrible. We had to get out of our cars and run to get into the ball or we would have been beaten, and they would have destroyed our costumes."[49]

Journalistic accounts provide no explanation as to why the public and the press were so hostile to that year's Carnival ball when they had not been so in the past. The visibility of the balls, encouraged, no doubt, by prominent coverage in the country's leading photo magazine over the preceding three years, had attracted large crowds of curious onlookers. Some came to be amused by the *viados* in colorful costumes who paraded at the entrance to the ball. Many in the crowd were sympathetic spectators or homosexuals themselves. Still others, apparently threatened by such overt manifestations of gender blurring, pelted cross-dressers with stones as they entered the theater housing the pre-Lenten festivities. *Manchete*'s moralistic coverage may have simply reflected the views of a particularly religious editor or journalist who abhorred homosexuality rather than indicating some overall trend on the part of the press against public displays that deviated from traditional heteronormative behavior. Similarly, the physical violence against those attending the ball may have been the result of a backlash by members of the public opposed to such daring and open transgressive performances, which seemed to be more in evidence in each succeeding Carnival.

Regardless of one's interpretations about the reasons for an increase in public disdain for the drag balls, this Carnival territory of homosexuals and cross-dressers clearly remained a contested semipublic space through the late 1950s. While revelers may have experienced *communitas* in the protected environment of the theaters, surrounded by other men who shared their erotic desires and similar day-to-day survival experiences, sectors of the Brazilian press and the public remained uneasy about the ambiguous gender slippage and sexual pleasures that they believed took place at these sites. Indeed, the vacillating and sometimes hostile positions of the press, the public, and the police toward these Carnival balls and overt manifestations of homosexuality throughout the 1950s and 1960s reveal the ongoing tension between a traditional religious morality that found same-sex eroticism to be abhorrent and unnatural and a more tolerant, if begrudging acceptance of *bichas* and *travestis* as inevitable, relatively harmless figures within the Carnival landscape.

As a result of the disturbances at the 1957 balls, the following year the city government shut down the costume contest and policed these Carnival events, presumably to avoid a repeat of the jeering crowds and stone throwing. In spite of this increased official control and the continued animosity of some onlookers, the *bailes* were held on three consecutive nights before Shrove Tuesday. Ironically, *Manchete,* which had initiated the campaign to discredit the balls the year before, made an about-face and denounced the very yellow journalism that it so recently had encouraged. The journalist covering the Baile do Arco-Íris (Rainbow Ball) reported that it was spirited in spite of the hostile crowd that loomed outside. "At the moment the [costume] parade has been prohibited and the ball, previously rather spontaneous and very crowded, has been regulated by the city government with guards in profusion and a crowd jeering those who enter costumed. It was, however, a rather lively, orderly ball with the least number of fights (or drunks), and the presence of foreign diplomats and families. The bad Carioca press who went there to exploit it in an unseemly way is at fault for the immense number of people who entered while being jeered, hiding their faces with masks."[50]

Although *Manchete* had abandoned its most vicious attacks on manifestations of homosexuality, the populist daily *Última Hora* maintained a moralistic posture both against this gender transgression and any other pre-Lenten public behavior that shocked "good morals and propriety." In an article entitled "From Revelry to Exaggeration: Excesses that Stain Carioca Carnival," the newspaper criticized "scenes that stained one of the Carnivals that had once been the best in the world." The article criticized manifestations of both homo- and heteroerotic behavior associated with many Carnival balls as well as the audacious representations of drag queens, including pictures to underscore its points. One showed a man lifting up a woman and kissing her on the thigh. Presumably, the shot symbolized the licentious permissiveness of modern Carnival festivities. Another picture presented the image of two men, one in an imitation leopard-skin swimming suit, with matching gloves and hat. The caption read: "Scenes of authentic debauchery. . . . Gestures and attitudes which are absolutely not in agreement with the healthy traditions of Rio's Carnival."[51]

While the editors of *Última Hora* nostalgically reinvented a past when decency reigned during Carnival celebrations, they also promoted that year's international guest, Rock Hudson. The Hollywood heartthrob of the 1950s had just separated from his wife after a two-year marriage. Neither the Brazilian journalists nor most of Hudson's fans seemed to know that he had been pressured into marrying his agent's secretary in 1955 to quell an increasing number of rumors spreading throughout Hollywood about his homosexuality.[52] As 1958's most famous Carnival visitor, the press photographed Rock Hudson with Brazilian starlets, beauty queens, and other eligible female members of the city's high society. Journalists even speculated on a possible romance between Hudson and Brazilian actress Ilka Soares since the pair were inseparable during the star's ten-day stay in Rio.[53] Rock Hudson attended multiple Carnival celebrations, including the Gala Ball in the Municipal Theater with its famous luxury costume contest. During the masked ball held at the Gloria Hotel, a photographer caught him laughing with his Brazilian entourage. At some point in the evening someone placed a silk sash over Rock Hudson's muscular chest. Embossed over the two-toned ribbon in Gothic letters was the phrase "Princess of Carnival" (see fig. 20). Few people probably understood the irony of the image when it appeared in *Manchete*'s 1958 Carnival coverage. To the public, Rock Hudson represented raw masculinity and heterosexuality. Yet, in hindsight, this portrait captures the contradiction that shaped Rock Hudson's life.[54] As long as Hudson's homosexuality remained discreet and he projected a masculine persona, his career as a Hollywood sex symbol was assured. Likewise for many Brazilian homosexuals, especially those from the middle and upper class, social survival has meant hiding their homoerotic desires and practices from their family and employers, and even inventing fictitious girlfriends, or fashioning lives of subterfuge through marriages of convenience. Although Carnival may have been the opportunity for many gender-bending drag queens and other homosexuals to ignore "good morals and propriety," defy rules of "appropriate" public behavior, and explode in erotic frenzy on the dance floors among thousands of like-minded souls, not everyone who coveted sex with other men would take advantage of the sexual and social opportunities this pre-Lenten celebration offered.

A New Era in Carnival Celebrations

Despite jeering crowds, canceled competitions, and hostile journalism, the balls attended by drag queens and other homosexuals grew in number. By the early 1960s, one of these balls, the Baile dos Enxutos (Ball of the Shapely Men) had become a Carnival institution. The event—whose name was a twist on the slang term *enxuta*, which referred to a beautiful and shapely woman—would be held almost every year for the next two decades.[55] The press also began to acknowledge the increasing importance of homosexuals in Carnival celebrations. Coverage continued to vacillate

FIGURE 20   Rock Hudson, "Princess of Carnival," surrounded by admiring socialites and celebrities at the Gala Ball during 1958 Carnival in Rio de Janeiro. Photograph courtesy of *Manchete*.

between denigration and jocular admiration for the balls. In a special Carnival edition, *Manchete* summarized: "Of the eight hundred balls that take place in Rio, from a week before and during the three days of Carioca Carnival, four stand out: the Artists' [Ball] in the Gloria Hotel on Fat Thursday; the one at the Copacabana Palace Hotel on Saturday; the traditional Gala Ball at the Municipal Theater on Monday; and the Transvestites' Ball, also on Monday, at the João Caetano Theater. Of the four, the one at João Caetano, internationally known, is perhaps the least well attended, but due to the tremendous abundance of transvestites (now called *enxutos*) coming from all states, Argentina and Chile, it is the most sought after."[56] Articles popularized the term *enxuto*, making it, along with the word *travesti*, a journalistic synonym for a male homosexual. Reporters also referred to the overrepresentation of "the Third Force" in Rio's Carnival, a play on words alluding to homosexuals as a third sex. Even though the costume competition had been prohibited for three years running, presumably because its contestants had evoked such public interest and some popular hostility, the balls held at theaters near Praça Tiradentes were filled with hundreds of ostentatiously dressed boys in rich and witty costumes, who were joined by thousands of other Carnival revelers (see fig. 21).[57]

In 1961, as the novelty surrounding the daring raiment of certain drag queens faded and *travestis* became simply another Carnival spectacle, costume competitions were reintroduced, but without the traditional walk-way parading. Drag queens wearing high-heeled shoes and elaborate headdresses spent the evening modeling their sequined and feather-laden gowns in the entranceways to the theater holding the ball. A panel of judges then interviewed the contestants, awarding the three finalists gold medals. That year, the person who came in fourth, while not receiving a trophy, was contacted by an entertainment entrepreneur after the ball to work on a Panamanian cruise ship.[58] *Última Hora*, the first Brazilian newspaper to reach a mass audience through the use of sensationalist coverage, now publicized the Baile dos Enxutos and informed its readers of the prizes awarded to the three best dressed contestants.[59] The editorial shift in the coverage of this event may have reflected a general change in public response to these *bailes*. The ever-increasing publicity about the balls during the 1950s had encouraged the large number of voyeurs who crowded outside theater entrances to watch the parade of elaborately costumed queens. As security measures limited the outbursts of violence that accompanied these grand entrances and as the uniqueness of the events wore off, a more tolerant attitude toward the *bailes* evolved. Perhaps economic considerations also motivated

FIGURE 21 *Travesti* contestant for costume competition during Carnival celebrations at the João Caetano Theater, Praça Tiradentes, Rio de Janeiro, 1957. Photograph courtesy of the Arquivo do Estado de São Paulo.

the editors of *Última Hora* to modify the tone of their coverage, for in 1962, the organizers of the Baile dos Enxutos placed a one-eighth page advertisement in successive editions before and during Carnival. In the ad, an ink-penned bikini-clad woman, with long-sleeved black gloves and a feathered tutu, announced the four-night Carnival event.[60] While a female figure was chosen for the promotion, the drag content of the affair was clear from the its cross-gendered name. Two elements in the advertisement revealed the way in which the ball had become incorporated into Carnival celebrations. First, the large and important Antártica soft-drink company was an official sponsor of the event. Second, the same ads announcing the Baile dos Enxutos also informed readers of a matinee children's Carnival at the same theater. The *enxutos* had become somewhat respectable, at least during Carnival. That year an international audience of *alegres rapazes* (gay [happy] boys) flocked to the balls from Argentina, Uruguay, and Chile.[61]

Contradictorily, at the same time that the balls were achieving a relative respectability, the government once again placed restrictions on the event, presumably to avoid hostile reactions from those who disapproved of men dressing up in drag.[62] To circumvent this rule, competitors in the costume show were not allowed to enter the Recreio Theater in full regalia. Instead, they had to bring the headdresses, gowns, high heels, and feathers unassembled, and mount their extravagant showpieces only when they were inside the theater. A panel of judges, made up of Walter Pinto and other prominent figures in Brazilian show business, presided over the evening.[63]

The competitions were not the only reason so many homosexuals packed into these balls. The collective experience of thousands of dancing revelers singing the same Carnival tunes, which they had learned from their favorite radio singing stars, created a sense of unity and community in this special space where one could be free to camp, flirt, and simply have fun.[64] Moreover, the structure of the multitiered theaters provided options for licentiousness. Ângelo, who consistently participated in Carnival celebrations, remembered the drag balls in the early 1960s: "There was a hierarchy of sexual escapades. On the first floor everyone danced and nothing happened. On the second floor only a little bit took place. On the third floor, which was a balcony, it was an orgy."[65]

Inevitably, the police made arrests during the four days of pre-Lenten debauchery, and the *travestis* of the Baile dos Enxutos and other drag balls were a favored target. Although erotic behavior taking place within the confines of the ballroom or balconies escaped close police surveillance, "scandalous" public displays could attract official responses. At the 1964 ball, for example, the military police leveled billy clubs at some who attempted to enter the Recreio Theater, arresting anyone who protested police abuse.[66] When detainees were released on Ash Wednesday still dressed in Carnival garb, they would often continue to celebrate by performing impromptu shows on the stairs of the police station. After newspapers began to cover this event, it became a popular place to gather for those looking for one last festive moment before Carnival was over. Crowds would gather to await this demonstration of outrageous camp, and the men who had been denied the opportunity to display their costumes during the drag balls found a daytime venue and a cheering audience to enjoy their antics. In making light of their arrests and playing to the crowd, these men mimicked the stereotypical image of the drag queen, transforming the situation into a site of performance and defiance. They then paraded through the city as a *banda* (street group), calling themselves "What Am I Going To Tell Them at Home?"[67]

The Bailes dos Enxutos and the steps in front of the police headquarters were not the only places where costumed beauties displayed their elaborate raiment. Men dressed as women also paraded throughout other parts of the city in gowns, bathing suits, and even bikinis to show off their costumes.[68] One popular outdoor café in Copacabana, the Alcazar, became a favorite spot for cross-dressers to model their elaborate costumes and perform mock "marriages" with male bystanders. Informal rules of Carnival permissiveness permitted the "girls" to camp around and express themselves in public in ways not permitted throughout the rest of the year, but at times the police were also called in to establish "morality" and order.[69] If an altercation broke out, authorities inevitably hauled away the men in drag, who would join the ranks of the "What Am I Going To Tell Them at Home?" contingent leaving the police headquarters on Ash Wednesday.

In 1964, Jorge Goulart's recording of "Cabeleira do Zezé" (Zezé's Long Hair), which alluded to the homosexual presence during Carnival, became a hit tune. The song, an immediate Carnival classic, went as follows:

> Look at Zezé's long hair.
> Do you think he is?
> Do you think he is?[70]

When this composition was played during Carnival balls, the following two beats were then filled with the word *bicha*, shouted loudly and festively by the dancing crowds. Although heterosexual revelers chanted the refrain and added the term *bicha* as a pejorative reference to effeminate men, those who attended the Carnival balls at Praça Tiradentes shouted the same filler as a playful affirmation of their sexual identity.[71] The song continued:

> Do you think he is bossa nova? Do you think he is Moslem?
> He seems to have gone astray [*transviado*].
> But I don't know if he is.
> Cut his hair. Cut his hair.

The lyrics have multiple meanings. Bossa nova, of course, refers to the "new style" Brazilian music that was popular in 1964, but here the term also implies homosexuality. *Transviado* signifies a person gone astray. The title of the movie *Rebel without a Cause*, for example, was translated as *Juventude Transviada*, literally, "youth who had gone astray." In the early 1960s, young people who imitated new fashions and styles were called *juventude transviada*. The word is also a play on the term *viado*, the pejorative term for homosexuals, and is close to the word *travesti*, providing another association with homosexuality. The author of this Carnival tune, João Roberto Kelly, was the entrepreneur who popularized the professional drag show *Les Girls* that same year. Given Kelly's close links to the homosexual subculture of Rio de Janeiro, one can assume that he intentionally employed double entendres in the lyrics. Moreover, crooner Jorge Goulart, who recorded the hit song, while not a homosexual, appeared as an honored guest at the drag balls in the early 1950s, making him a friend of the subculture.[72] In subsequent Carnivals, the song continued to evoke multiple meanings. It retained its pride-laden content for gay revelers, while also serving as a vehicle for Brazilians who retained a hostile attitude toward homosexuality to make fun of effeminate men. This song is still sung at Carnival balls and in street parades with the same contradictory utilization and subversion of the negative term *bicha*.

By 1966, two rival balls, the Baile dos Enxutos and the Baile das Bonecas (Dolls' Ball), attracted members of the Brazilian elite and a growing international audience. Ângelo Ramos, the third-place winner in the costume competition at the Baile dos Enxutos, held that year at the São José Cinema instead of the traditional Recreio Theater, lamented that his native country of Venezuela did not host a ball "so overflowing in sensitivity."[73] *Última Hora* continued to carry advertisements announcing the Baile dos Enxutos. A quarter-page ad showed an androgynous figure in high heels, net stockings, and plumed headdress. A limped wrist emphasized the fact

FIGURE 22   Advertisement for "Dolls" Carnival Ball, Rio de Janeiro, from *Última Hora* (Rio de Janeiro), February 4, 1966, 7. Illustration courtesy of *Acervo Última Hora*, Rio de Janeiro, Arquivo do Estado de São Paulo.

that this was a drag ball (see fig. 22). More than six thousand people attended the *baile*. The press also covered the Ash Wednesday event when the "What Am I Going to Tell Them at Home?" group, now numbering seven hundred, poured out of the police station. Dozens of photographers and cinematographers registered this final Carnival show "as *travestis* calmly paraded down President Vargas Avenue, transforming it into the scenery from a Fellini film."[74] Taking advantage of the presence of the press, "Miriam," "Elisabete," and "Betty Davis," who had come especially from São Paulo to celebrate Carnival in Rio de Janeiro, complained that they had spent a fortune on their costumes, "but the police don't care about this and took them to the District [police station]." "Ângela" and "Sandra Dee" also complained that they had been detained at the door of the São José Cinema and taken off to jail. Perhaps, having arrived late, they had not managed to enter the ball and had caused a commotion at the door. More likely, moralizing police arbitrarily rounded up these outrageously dressed queens and took them to the station as a way of restricting their flamboyant public performances.

The year 1968 was special for Rio de Janeiro's drag balls. Two different balls sold out during the four nights of Carnival. The events enjoyed widespread popularity, and the police did not interfere in the celebrations. In spite of the military's takeover of the government four years earlier, 1968 began with widespread popular hopes that the regime would loosen its grip on Brazilian society.[75] A reporter for *Última Hora* noted that "this year the *enxutos* could celebrate in all of the balls. In a sign of the times, for the first time, there was real freedom."[76] Significantly, Soares, a six-time, prize-winning drag queen, organized her own event that year, an event that was to become the first drag ball organized by *enxutos*. Soares proudly pointed out that her friends could freely attend the festivities at the Copacabana Palace Hotel, the Municipal Theater, and the Canecão, where people in the past had not always accepted *travestis*. "We spend the entire year doing shows of *travestis;* we can say that currently that there are no longer any female stars, only men. Rogéria [a drag entertainer] is a star of Carlos Machado's [a nightclub entrepreneur]. This is an advance. Next year we hope that in addition to the Recreio and the São José, there will be a greater number of balls dedicated to the *enxutos*. We are working hard for this."[77] The social tolerance reflected in the proliferation of drag queens, who could now comfortably attend all the major Carnival balls, was in part linked to a general opening in Brazilian society in 1968. At the same time that drag queens like Rogéria and Valéria headlined at *teatro de revista* performances and worked in high-class nightclubs, many segments of society were starting to question the military dictatorship's rule. Students protested the generals' policies. Artists and writers challenged censorship. National and international musical and cultural currents encouraged the emergence of countercultural movements such as *tropicalismo* that were imbued with antiauthoritarian sentiment. For much of that year, it seemed the regime's days were numbered.

A Temporary Turn for the Worse

In early 1969, the military responded to the massive social mobilizations of the previous year with a clampdown on all opposition to the government. This included, among other measures, increased censorship and the silencing of all dissent. Strict moral codes accompanied the new Médici government's social policies. These affected public displays of homosexuality and especially the *bailes* directed to a homosexual audience. The balls took place, but their organizers had to present a much more muted profile. As a result, neither *Manchete* nor *Última Hora*, which had covered the balls favorably in recent years, mentioned them in their reports of Carnival in 1969 and 1970. The ads that appeared in 1969 for the balls at the Rival Theater merely showed the dancing women used in the Baile dos Enxutos ads over the previous decade, while the title of the ball was omitted from the promotion.[78] Those who had consistently attended the balls could find out when and where the events were held by recognizing the same ad design, but censorship or self-censorship eliminated any written references to *bonecas* and *enxutos*.

New government policies did not just target the drag balls. Federal censors also intervened in one of the most important *bailes* of the Carioca elite, held at the Copacabana Palace Hotel. According to the foreign press, which published news that went unreported in Brazil, less than twenty-four hours before the gala was scheduled to take place, federal officials "ordered a complete cover-up of 240 paintings depicting the motif of the ball—a young couple making love." To avoid shutting down the Carnival celebration, organizers had to have black paper discs pasted over the parts of the paintings that offended government censors. Furthermore, on February 12, 1970, the military government issued a new edict declaring prior press censorship. Article 1 of the decree clearly set down the new guidelines: "The distribution of books or periodicals in national territory will be subordinated to the prior verification of the existence of material offensive to morality and propriety." This government oversight of the printed media dampened all coverage of events that might be considered offensive to the generals' notions of decency.[79]

In 1971, as a result of a new government policy that explicitly prohibited *travestis'* participation in Carnival events, promoters barred many cross-dressers from entering their organized festivities. In explaining the ban on cross-dressers and drag balls, Edgar Façanha, the director of the Division of Censorship and Public Entertainment, clarified the government position: "Homosexuals cannot be prohibited from entering public balls, as long as they behave appropriately." He admitted that new restrictions on Carnival festivities were really designed to do away with the drag balls: "The purpose of the police is to not allow balls exclusively for *travestis*, whatever the name of the ball or wherever it takes place."[80] In other words, the government recognized that prohibiting homosexuality throughout the entire society was an impossibility. Instead, they chose to focus on erasing any public manifestations of visible effeminacy, as symbolized in the performances of *travestis* during Carnival. Presumably discreet homosexual behavior was tolerated while flamboyant public gender-bending was not.

The government's moralistic policies did not stop at attempting to prohibit the drag balls. They also canceled the male luxury costume contest held at the Municipal Theater. This prohibition was directly related to a clampdown on other "inappropriate" public manifestations of homosexuality. A journalist filed a news dispatch with *Veja* magazine, Brazil's equivalent to *Time*, explaining the situation: "The prohibition of the male costume competition at the Municipal Theater is strictly linked to the policy of removing homosexuals from television. It is a measure that comes from high government levels. It is a fact easily verified, that everyone agrees with, but that no authority has the courage to admit. No one, evidently, admits that they give in to pressure."[81] Presumably, by filming the contestants who were widely assumed to be *enxutos*, the televised coverage of the event would have promoted homosexuality. Several months later, the government backtracked on its decision to prohibit drag balls, but did not retreat on its resolve to cancel the officially sponsored luxury costume contest at the Municipal Theater.[82] The director of the Division of Censorship and Entertainment made it clear that the government's policy reversal on drag balls was to prevent *travestis* from spreading throughout the city's Carnival clubs and making it difficult for authorities to control them.[83] The *bonecas* responded with what was reported as the wildest drag balls ever, which included topless drag queens bearing their hormonally enhanced breasts.[84]

In 1974, as the new government of General Geisel initiated a policy of controlled political liberalization, drag queens and *travesti* balls re-exploded onto the Carnival scene. Liza Minelli, at the zenith of her career as an international celebrity, attended one of the balls, lending it additional prestige.[85] Two years later, in 1976, more than three thousand revelers attended that Carnival season's largest drag ball, leaving hundreds more waiting outside in the vain hope of joining the party. Among the waiting crowd was

Raquel Welsh, who did finally manage to get in. It is intriguing to specu-late whether she was almost denied admission because she had blended too easily into the crowd of shapely *bonecas*.[86] By the mid-1970s, these *bailes* had become a permanent part of Rio's Carnival festivities.[87] Several moved to new venues in more upscale theaters and nightclubs away from Praça Tiradentes, which had fallen into urban decay. Drag queens also brought a campy touch to the Banda de Ipanema, a street Carnival group that paraded through the beachfront upper-middle-class neighborhood of Ipanema, while others participated in the Baile da Paulistinha, a Carnival street party held in the downtown Lapa neighborhood.[88]

As a result of the increasing amount of publicity that the Carnival drag balls received, the public image of the homosexual became intimately tied to that of the Carnival drag queen. The readers of mass-audience maga-zines and newspapers were now accustomed to pictures of flamboyant effeminate men during Carnival, even though the majority of those who attended the *travesti* balls dressed in traditional male garb. To many Brazil-ians, homosexuals were those men who dressed in feathers, sequins, and a wig, and who made a grand entrance into the Baile dos Enxutos or the Baile dos Travestis. The words *travesti* (transvestite), *boneca* (doll), and *enxuto* (shapely male) had joined *viado* (faggot) and *bicha* (fairy) as popular terms synonymous with homosexuality. While visibility bred familiarity and a de-gree of social tolerance, cross-dressing and its association with homosexu-ality crystallized into an amusing sideshow during Carnival celebrations, although a prominent and permanent one.

Cross-Dressing Year Round

Carnival balls were not the only events that popularized the association be-tween homosexuality and the men who appeared in public as women. In 1963, Jacqueline Deufresnoy, a French entertainer who had undergone a sex change after working as a cross-dresser under the stage name Coccinelli, arrived in Rio de Janeiro. The Carioca press played up the fact that Coc-cinelli, who was blond, buxom, and bikini-clad, had once been Jacques Charles, a recruit in the French army during the Algerian War. Now she was the epitome of sensuality and feminine beauty. While in Rio de Janeiro, Coccinelli teased journalists as she sunbathed at the Copacabana Palace Ho-tel and informed them that she would perform in one of Carlos Machado's shows, dancing, singing, and stripping to the tune of U.S.$10,000.[89] The male-dominated press treated Coccinelli as a "real woman" because she closely conformed to the traditional masculine fantasies of the perfect female: she was shapely, coquettish, sexual, and even maternal. Accompanied by her "husband," she lamented to reporters: "My dream is to be a mother. That is what would make me a really happy woman. I have fame and fortune; now I want a child."[90] The front-page coverage of Coccinelli's visit to Rio de Janeiro carried a subtext: Transvestites, and by extension all homosexuals, including transsexuals, would be tolerated if they conformed to male stereotypes of properly gendered women. As long as they were glamorous, sexy, and sophisticated women who aspired to heterosexual respectability, they could find a niche in Brazilian society.

Soon after Coccinelli captured the imagination of journalists and the public, Brazil produced its own Coccinellis, as drag shows moved from gay nightclubs to mainstream stage venues. The drag stars of the mid-1960s did not have to undergo sex changes to provoke curiosity and win fame. Their performances, which were directly influenced by Carnival drag balls, provided another opportunity for contact between the homosexual subculture and the broader public. In occupying a unique space within urban popular culture, they further reinforced the traditional image of the homosexual as an effeminate man who desired to dress as a woman, perhaps even to become one. But, like Carnival drag queens, these performers won benign public toleration of more overt manifestations of effeminacy among men.

In early 1964 "Stop," one of the few gay nightclubs in Rio de Janeiro, featured a show titled *The International Set,* starring cross-dressers who had achieved prominence in the Carnival drag balls. Stop was located in the Galeria Alaska in Copacabana, an area that had become a cruising zone for homosexual men. Unlike drag shows performed in gay bars earlier in the 1960s, where lip-synching amateurs dressed in fancy gowns imitated famous divas, this production was more professional. It attracted an upper-class audience and received notice in the press.[91] *Les Girls,* a second show performed at Stop later that year, became an overnight sensation. The plot of *Les Girls* was simple. It took place in the office of a psychiatrist, who listened to the problems of beautiful women, who were, of course, all men in drag. Between scenes, the audience witnessed the transformation of the male nurse José Maria into Maria José. The cast sang, danced, and paraded around in elegant costumes. The drag queens assumed their roles as women with perfection, and the metamorphosis of José Maria affirmed the aspirations of men who wished to dress as women. *Les Girls* toured in clubs in São Paulo, and eventually traveled to Uruguay. Just as a non-gay audience had visited Praça Tiradentes to observe Carnival drag balls, now those interested in seeing these new shows went to the main homosexual cruising area of Copacabana. As one reporter wrote: "The success was such that in less than three months 'they' [in the feminine] changed all of the costumes (the ending is an authentic fashion show, and one of the best) and added new numbers, always drawing incessant applause from the public, which is slowly losing its fear of Galeria Alaska. The house is always filled."[92] According to people who saw the production, it rivaled the big-budget shows that catered to Rio de Janeiro's international tourist market.[93]

Between 1965 and 1967, there was an explosion of drag shows running throughout the year. (As we have seen, this expansion took place while the military consolidated its rule over the country. Yet until 1969, the armed forces seemed more interested in eliminating political opposition to their rule than in controlling public manifestations of homosexuality). Most of the drag shows during this period were performed in the Praça Tiradentes theater district, alongside the bump-and-grind productions and risqué musical reviews that were popular at the time. They played in similar venues in São Paulo and other major cities throughout the country. Some productions were built exclusively around a cast of elegant drag queens, while others featured drag performers as part of the show. With titles such as *Bonecas de Mini Saia* (Dolls in Miniskirts, 1967) and *Les Girls em Alta Tensão* (High-Tension Girls, 1967), the shows reflected the changes in fashions and sexual mores of the period. Other shows, such as *Boas em Liquidação* (Good Women on Sale, 1965), *Bonecas em Quarta Dimensão* (Dolls in the Fourth Dimension, 1965) and *Agora É Que São Elas* (Now It Is Them, 1967), emphasized the novelty of these new stage acts.[94]

Men dressed as women on the Brazilian stage were not new. Since the turn of the century, most *teatro de revista* shows had at least one skit where an actor cross-dressed. Stage and screen stars, such as Grande Otelo, Oscarito, and Colé, invariably wore wigs and skirts for comic effects.[95] In the 1930s, Madame Satã attempted a stage career performing as a woman. In the 1940s, Carlos Gil delighted audiences with humorous imitations of Carmen Miranda and other famous artists in small theaters in Copacabana and Praça Tiradentes. A revival of *teatro de revista* at Praça Tiradentes in the 1950s continued the tradition (see fig. 23). The novelty of the mid-'60s was the appearance of men as beautiful and elegant women, not merely as comic parodies of the opposite sex. The new male showgirls projected an image of being "more female" than the female stars. Rogéria, one of the stars of these drag shows, personified this new performance style. She became an

FIGURE 23   Cross-dressing in a vaudeville musical theater review in the 1950s. Photograph
courtesy of Banco de Imagens AEL / UNICAMP.

international celebrity, and eventually achieved top billing at Parisian
nightclubs. Her career symbolizes the way in which cross-dressing and gender notions specific to the homosexual subculture of Brazil extended beyond Carnival drag balls and gay nightclubs to reach a new public.[96]

Rogéria was born some time between 1943 and 1946 as Astrolfo Barroso Pinto.[97] When he was quite young, he discovered the homosexual subculture of Rio de Janeiro's Cinelândia: "Every *boneca* [girl] makes her
debut, and so as not to be an exception I also made mine in Cinelândia. I
confess that I don't regret it. I lost all of my repression there, and I did
everything I wanted to do. Cinelândia wasn't that bad; it just had a reputation. Many good people from Copacabana came to have their little encounters there secretly, since they knew they could find there that which
every day became more and more scarce: MEN."[98]

When he was sixteen, Astrolfo went to the República Theater near
Praça Tiradentes to watch the grand entrance of the *travestis* during the
Carnival drag balls. "I saw Sophia arrive; she was beautiful, and how she
camped it up, how she was applauded. I thought to myself: 'Will I some day
be as successful as she is?'"[99] Since Astrolfo was underage, he couldn't en-

ter the theater that year, but during subsequent Carnivals he transformed himself from a pimply makeup artist, working for low wages at a local television station, into Rogéria, a glamorous queen of Rio's Carnival. As a result of Rogéria's popular new look, she was invited to join a drag show, and from there it was a short way to a show at the Stop in 1964. "In the first show I did," she explained, "I explored the business of the *transformista** a lot. A good wig, legs exposed, and there you have it."[100] She toured with Les Girls in Brazil, and then was featured in Carlos Machado's Las Vegas-style productions. Following an intensive schedule of shows in nightclubs and gay bars, she traveled to Luanda, Angola. After performing in Africa for a little more than a year, she moved on to Barcelona, where she stayed with Coccinelli, whom she had met in Rio de Janeiro. Armed with a letter of recommendation from Coccinelli, Rogéria went to Paris, where she eventually rose to stardom at the nightclub "Carrousel." In 1973, she returned to Brazil, an international star.[101]

According to Rogéria, her family accepted her transformation rather quickly. Rogéria recounted her mother's reaction: "There was a period when I began to say: 'Mamma, life has changed. Now I get up, sleep, dress, and comb my hair as a woman.' Mamma didn't understand and thought that I had gone through an operation. She began to write: 'My daughter, why didn't you tell me before?' 'But mamma, I didn't have an operation.' I only added: 'The day that I have an operation you will be at my side.' . . . But even so, I am a woman, inside, mentally, and I want to be called SHE. And the first two days when my mother arrived, she switched back and forth between 'he' and 'she.' Then one day she took the boat between Rio and Niterói with me. From that day on when she saw the men look at me with admiration for being a woman, 'she' won out."[102]

Rogéria's success was based on the ability to conform to ideal standards of feminine beauty and attractiveness. She recounted an anecdote about her grandfather: "The nice thing is my grandfather who is almost ninety. When I entered [as a woman], he was surprised, seeing that big blond entering with dark glasses, very feline. . . . He looked at me and said: 'Now you are no longer my grandson, now I have a beautiful granddaughter.'"[103] It's not important whether Rogéria was engaging in myth building or accurately retelling the way her family so warmly embraced their new-found daughter and granddaughter. The significance of her stories lies in the manner in

---

* A *transformista* literally means one who transforms him / herself. It implies performance and not necessarily a personal identification with the new persona.

which the *travesti* gained familial and social legitimacy: It was her beauty, glamour, and desirability that led her mother and grandfather to accept her. According to her self-fashioning, it is likely that had Rogéria been ugly, awkward, and artistically unsuccessful, her family's response might have been less tolerant. Other motivations may also have been at play. Alcir Lenharo has observed that many Brazilians accept their homosexual relatives if the latter provide significant economic support to their families. Life stories of homosexuals and *travestis* published in newspapers and magazines confirm this relationship between reluctant toleration of an effeminate or cross-dressing son and the economic support they provided to their relatives.[104]

Young men like Astrolfo who reshaped their gender identity and created personas like that of Rogéria (and even managed to make a living out of their transformation) did so to conform to traditional notions of femininity. The *travestis* who attended the Bailes dos Enxutos, as well as drag show performers such as Rogéria, associated glamour, feminine seduction, shapely bodies, and meticulously made-up faces with their sexual desires. In attempting to create representations of the ideal woman, they incorporated and sometimes even exaggerated the social stereotypes associated with the gender they embraced.

Although only a minority of Brazilian homosexuals dressed up in drag for Carnival or in jest during intimate private parties, the newly won prominence of drag queens in the entertainment world provided tremendous pride for many who were a part of the homosexual subculture of Rio de Janeiro. Homosexuals who did identify as *bonecas* looked to these famous *travestis* as role models to be emulated. The readers and collaborators of *O Snob*, for example, followed the rise in the careers of different drag queens. They printed "exclusive" interviews with Rogéria, Marquesa, and Soares, three of the most prominent *travestis* in Rio de Janeiro at the time.[105] *O Snob* also reported news of drag shows. One issue, for example, proudly informed the readers that Marquesa had sent the journal a program of the *Les Girls'* show, then touring in Uruguay, and a postcard, which read: "I am here in Montevideo after a glorious season in Punta del Este. The show has pleased [the audience] a lot, and we have filled both the theater and the club every night. We receive *O Snob* thanks to the goodwill of Manequim, and thus I (in fact all of us) can quell our longings for Rio which are enormous. I hope that you are enjoying good health and of course are surrounded by *bofes*. Accept a warm hug from your friend, Marquesa." Thus, even as the *bonecas* of *O Snob* eulogized the successful careers of the drag queens who had broken into show business, the stars did not forget those who had supported them. Marquesa praised the journal for its efforts to report news of gay life in Brazil: "While I was out of the country, I kept up with the gossip in Rio through *O Snob* and I showed it to the Uruguayan *bonecas*, who thought it was a wonderful idea to launch a gay journal."[106]

By 1969, the novelty of drag shows had worn off, and the number of productions declined. Moreover, the moralistic ideology of the Médici government discouraged such outrageous performances, and, indeed, the military expanded censorship rules to include theater pieces that dealt with homosexuality. However, an imperfect imitation of these cross-dressers multiplied on the streets of Rio and São Paulo as more and more men dressed as women to work as prostitutes. Whereas in the 1960s, *travestis* could be seen only during Carnival or within the confined spaces of gay clubs or drag shows, by the 1970s, there was a proliferation of transvestites pounding the sidewalks of Rio, São Paulo, and other major cities offering sexual favors for cash. The press's promotion of drag queens, greater visibility of *travestis* during Carnival celebrations, the androgynous look that pop cultural figures introduced into Brazilian fashion and comportment, and a generalized loosening of strict codes of dress and behavior had created a new climate. Year-round public cross-dressing, while not accepted, became much more prevalent.

Samba School Parades

In the December 31, 1968, edition of *O Snob*, one of the columnists discussed plans for 1969. Instead of suggesting the usual February ritual of attending one of the drag balls, he presented alternative ideas: "And Carnival, everyone, how will it be? The best plan is to go out of town or join one of the samba schools."[107] Newly imposed government restrictions on cross-dressing coincided with a new phenomenon in Carnival activities. Ever since the early or mid-1960s, samba school parades, which had been mostly made up of the Afro-Brazilian residents of Rio de Janeiro's *favelas* (hillside slums) and poor neighborhoods, were inundated with middle-class people who wanted to parade with the schools.[108] *Bonecas* joined this movement and participated enthusiastically in the design and production of costumes and floats for the parade. This is not to say that *bichas* from humble or even middle-class backgrounds had not been a component of the samba school productions prior to the 1960s, but a number of factors augmented their profile within this Carnival activity. Ângelo, a homosexual who began to parade with a samba school in the late 1960s, explained the reason why so many *bichas* sought out the venue for Carnival revelry: "It was the costumes, the dazzle, the brilliance, and the happiness that was inside us."[109] For many homosexuals, parading with the samba schools became one of several Carnival activities that they engaged in during the three days preceding Ash Wednesday. It was not uncommon to join a samba school one day, attend at least one drag ball, participate in informal, playful street festivities, and hook up with one of the *bandas* (organized street groups).[110]

The commercialization of the samba school parades in the late 1960s and early 1970s, fueled by color television coverage and the international tourist trade, encouraged increasingly ostentatious productions.[111] Homosexuals participated actively in all aspects of the parade, from creating the spectacular visual effects associated with the processions to joining a given *ala*, or section, to samba down the avenue in a luxurious costume.[112] Ramalhete pointed out the division of labor within the samba schools: "The president of the samba school is a *macho;* most who develop the story line are gay. [The gay person] is the one who works with the visual aspects, the scenery, the costumes. The machos build the floats; the one who uses the hammer is a man. The gay comes up with the ideas, puts it all together, and works out the small details. Many of the men work as carpenters, but they are all directed by gays."[113] Ângelo and João Baptista, who closely followed the developments in the samba school parades over the 1960s and '70s, echoed Ramalhete's observations about the homosexualization of Carnival. Both pointed to the samba school artistic director Joãozinho Trinta, whose extravagant productions won multiple first prizes in the 1970s. "He's openly gay and without a doubt, he brings his sensibility and feminine side to Carnival," observed João Baptista.[114]

While Ângelo, João Baptista, and Ramalhete all essentialized homosexuality by ascribing to it an innate artistic and creative sensibility, their observations about the proliferation of homosexuals in the production of the samba school spectacle remain poignant. As the yearly competition demanded increasing amounts of sparkle, glitter, and ostentatious luxury, many homosexuals, who had broken the social taboos prohibiting men from wearing flamboyant vestment, stepped forward as *destaques* (special features) of the parades. Clóvis Bornay and other champions of the Municipal Theater's male luxury costume competition, took prominent positions on the floats, dressed in all of their regalia. They were eventually joined by male drag stars, who outdid each other in aspiring to be the queens of Carnival.[115] The esthetic standards set by *travestis* in the Baile dos Enxutos and more discreet homosexuals in the luxury costume contest had become the norm for successful samba school productions.

By the 1970s, the space for *bichas* and *bonecas* within Carnival had been secured. From the surreptitious occupation of masquerade balls, to the creation of their own space in the Baile dos Enxutos, to participating in the design and orchestration of the internationally renowned samba school parades, homosexuals carved out and defended their position within Carnival celebrations. As we have noticed, the process of overcoming opposition to their participation in pre-Lenten activities was uneven. It relied in large part on the humor and determination of the *bonecas*, who insisted on their legitimate place within the spectrum of Carnival celebrations. Their ability to jest about the treatment they received from the police by forming the Ash Wednesday parade "What Am I Going to Tell Them at Home?" turned the distasteful experience of arrest into a moment of camp humor. It may not have eased official government control of Carnival activities, but it offered a unique resistance to hegemonic paradigms. By breaching traditional norms of respectability through outrageous and humorous behavior, homosexual revelers also widened cultural notions of normative femininity and masculinity. And above all else, their infusion of extravagant and luxurious costumes, floats, and decorations into Carnival's visual scenery transformed the spectacle. While one cannot attribute all of the changes in the samba school parades in the 1970s to those who enjoyed close contacts with the homosexual subculture, the connections and influences of gay artistic directors, costume designers, and visual artists remain apparent in the rich spectacle. Aspects of camp were thoroughly integrated into the parades' content. The peacocks of the Baile dos Enxutos, once laughed at and dismissed, ended up symbolizing an important aspect of Rio's Carnival experience. Their prominence in certain Carnival balls, in street revelries such as the Banda de Carmen Miranda, as well as in key elements of the samba school parades has made these pre-Lenten festivities the most visible marker of gay life in Rio de Janeiro. The appropriation of aspects of Rio's Carnival, in turn, has had an impact on the lives of many Carioca homosexuals throughout the rest of the year.

CHAPTER SIX

~

"Down with Repression:
More Love and More Desire,"

1969–1980

The year 1968 began with student protests against the military dictator-ship and with a growing sense of optimism concerning the possibility of a return to democratic rule.[1] It ended with harsh governmental decrees—known as the Institutional Acts—which included the closing of Congress, the suspension of constitutionally guaranteed rights, and the re-vocation of many elected officials' mandates. Additional restrictive mea-sures followed in 1969. The arrest and torture of government critics became commonplace.[2] In response, members of several left organizations who hoped to topple the military government stepped up their guerrilla warfare activities. After the unified commandos of two such groups kidnapped the U.S. ambassador to Brazil in September 1969, the generals authorized the banishment of government foes and the death penalty for subversive ac-tivities. The next month the military reopened a purged Congress in order to install hard-line General Emílio G. Médici as president. Fear and pes-simism descended upon the country. Indicative of the dismal assessment of the political situation shared by many opponents of the regime, four of the most popular young singers and songwriters of the 1960s—Caetano Veloso, Edu Lobo, Gilberto Gil, and Chico Buarque de Holanda—left for exile in Europe.

Brazil's 1970 World Cup soccer victory in Mexico encouraged a eu-phoric wave of nationalism that was orchestrated and promoted by the mili-tary regime.[3] Government propaganda, encapsulated in a slogan originally borrowed from the United States, "Brazil: Love It or Leave It," emphasized patriotism, order, and national progress. Concurrently, Médici initiated an energetic campaign promoting the economic, political, and social achievements obtained under military rule. The economic progress cited by government defenders included an expansion of exports, increased trade with Japan, the building of car plants and paved roads, lower interest rates, and new credit agreements with the United States.[4] Indeed, during the period of the Brazilian "economic miracle" (1968–73), yearly growth rates reached 11 percent. The military's economic model and financing policies favored income concentration in the urban middle and upper classes and provided an expanding market for domestic durable goods. Many within these middle sectors, in turn, supported the military. The standard of living for the working class and poor dropped in this period, but strict government controls on union activity prevented an organized response.[5]

One apologist for the regime, comparing the violence in Vietnam, Northern Ireland, and the United States to the situation in Brazil, praised the security and stability created by the government's policies: "Brazilians are revitalizing themselves with summer vacations. . . . The general atmosphere is sun and sand. Millions are touring the country from one end to the other on paved highways in cars produced in Brazil. The world seems to be at war, but Brazil is at peace. A taxi driver, interpreting the common person's philosophy of these clear and sunny days, makes the comparison when he hears the news: 'Instead of killing each other like those Irish, we are dancing and singing during Carnival.'"[6] While small groups of leftist urban guerrillas continued to battle the military, by the end of 1972, most of the organizations that promoted armed struggle had been dismantled by the government, and their members were either killed, in jail, or in exile. Médici's policies were not restricted to neutralizing the violent opposition to his rule. The military also imposed stricter censorship regulations, which expanded government control of the press, radio, television, and the arts.[7] Having achieved social, political, and economic stability, Médici appointed General Ernesto Geisel, the director of the state-owned oil company, to succeed him in 1974.

The astronomical increase in oil prices after the 1973 embargo by the Organization of Petroleum Exporting Countries undermined all of the regime's plans. With low oil reserves and burgeoning foreign debt payments, inflation rose dramatically. Sectors of the middle class that had supported the dictatorship during the period of economic prosperity now joined much of the working and poorer classes in voting for the only legal opposition political party, the Movimento Democrático Brasileiro (Brazilian Democratic Movement). The opposition's surprising advance in elections for federal and state legislative seats at the end of 1974 forced Geisel to rethink his strategy for political control. Soon thereafter, he initiated a gradual policy of democratization, which would eventually return the country to civilian rule. Contradictorily, he continued censorship, removed certain politicians from office, and ordered the arrest and torture of some opponents.[8]

In this period, both the progressive wing of the Catholic church and various leftist currents, operating underground, engaged in organizing efforts among the poor and working class in urban and rural settings alike. Their efforts would soon bear fruit. A multitude of social movements developed, demanding democracy, improved working conditions, and a better standard of living. More militant labor activists began to gain control of many of the important unions in the country's industrial centers. They demanded wage increases to make up for a loss in their purchasing power, and an end to government interference in union affairs.[9]

In 1977, massive student mobilizations challenged the dictatorship. In subsequent years, workers in the greater São Paulo area went on strike to protest government economic policies and demand better wages and working conditions. The opposition again did well in the 1978 elections, picking up more support from all social classes dissatisfied with military rule. Grassroots social movements multiplied, and alternative newspapers critical of the regime sprouted up everywhere. A feminist movement also emerged in this period, as did black consciousness groups, which organized in the country's major cities.[10]

The feminist challenge to patriarchy, rigid gender roles, and traditional sexual mores, initiated a discussion within Brazilian society that dovetailed with the issues that the gay movement raised from 1978 on. Gay activists and many feminists saw themselves as natural allies against sexism and a macho-dominated culture. Sonia Alvarez, a political scientist who has studied Brazilian feminism, explains the dynamic around the development of the movement: "Women's organizations flourished in the more flexible political climate that prevailed in Brazil after the mid-1970s. The growing involvement of women in a variety of opposition struggles soon gave rise to new, gender-based political claims. Early organizational efforts among women in São Paulo were isolated and diffuse. The military regime's deliberate demobilization of the population placed severe constraints on their further development. However, political decompression and the proclamation of International Women's Year in 1975 (itself partially a response to the growing international women's movement) abruptly expanded the *opportunity space* available for women's mobilization even when other forms of political protest were significantly restricted by government repression and censorship."[11] After the government initiated its policies of gradual liberalization in 1974–75, working-class women came together in grassroots community-based organizations to demand improvements in urban services and child care facilities. During the same period, human rights activists, women who had been involved in underground leftist organizations, and female intellectuals formed middle-class feminist groups. In 1976, former student activists and university women from São Paulo founded the first self-proclaimed feminist Brazilian journal, *Nós Mulheres* (We women).[12]

In the early years of the women's movement, most activities centered around the support of organizing efforts in poor and working-class neighborhoods and in the movement to obtain amnesty for all imprisoned and exiled opponents of the regime. Class-based issues took priority over gender-specific questions. Alvarez notes that, by 1978, a transformation had taken place in this perspective: "Over time, most feminist groups increasingly framed their political claims in both class- *and* gender-specific terms, refusing to subordinate one struggle to the other and proclaiming that gender struggle was an integral and inseparable component of general social transformation; a struggle that, some argue, only women, the direct victims of gender oppression, could lead."[13]

Like feminists, homosexuals took advantage of the same "opportunity space" to break ground for the building of a gay movement. In 1978, a dozen intellectuals from Rio de Janeiro and São Paulo founded *Lampião da Esquina,* a mass-circulation monthly tabloid directed at a gay audience. Several months later, a group of men in São Paulo formed Somos (We Are), the country's first gay rights organization.[14]

The 1978 São Paulo strike wave of auto- and metalworkers added fuel to the movement to democratize the country. Faced with mounting opposition from all sides, Geisel's handpicked successor for the presidency, General Figueiredo, accelerated the process of liberalization, which ultimately resulted in the military's stepping down in 1985.[15]

In this chapter, I examine two developments that took place under military rule. I first detail the lives of Brazilian gay men between 1969, the worst moment of military rule, and 1978, when *Lampião da Esquina* and Somos were founded. During these ten years, the urban space for homosexuals expanded significantly. Bars, discotheques, and saunas proliferated. This development was part of the generalized phenomenon of increased consumer opportunities among the urban middle class. *Travestis,* working as prostitutes, flooded the downtown areas of Rio de Janeiro and São Paulo, and *michês* (male hustlers) also became more visible on the streets of both cities. Police responded with periodic mass arrests. In the cultural arena, pop singers, such as Ney Matogrosso and Caetano Veloso, projected an androgynous image and hinted at their bisexuality or homosexuality. These social and sexual changes predated the emergence of a politicized gay movement in Brazil—the second major focus of this chapter. Many converging factors facilitated the rise of this movement: the social space won by *bichas* and *bonecas* during the 1960s, the diffusion of ideas from the international gay movement, the development of an indigenous Brazilian critique of machismo and homophobia, and the influence of the leftist political and social movements on key activists. The emergence of a gay political movement was also the result of the consolidation of a new gay / *entendido* identity. I explore the interplay of all othese forces in the crucial period prior to the movement's birth.

Bars, Discos, and Saunas

The repressive measures taken by the military to stamp out "subversion" had a discouraging effect on homosexual sociability between 1969 and 1972. The military police conducted downtown sweeps of Rio de Janeiro and São Paulo (see fig. 24). The police arbitrarily stopped people to see if their papers were in order, and suspicious individuals could be arrested for questioning.[16] Clóvis, who still cruised the downtown area in the late 1960s, recalled the effect of the generals' "revolution" on homosexuals in São Paulo: "The military coup of 1964 took time to be felt where we hung out; 1966–67 was the height of Galeria Metrópole [shopping mall]. The revolution of 1964 didn't have an immediate effect on people until after AI-5 [Institutional Act Number 5] in 1969. Then there was a massive *blitz*. They closed the three gates of the Galeria Metrópole, arrested everyone, and took them off in police vans and a bus. This decreased the number of people who went there, and the Galeria Metrópole went down hill."[17]

Comar, at the time a set designer working in the theater in Rio de Janeiro, remembered: "Nineteen sixty-nine to 1972 was a horrible time with a lot of persecution, not so much of gays as such but definitely in the theater with censorship."[18] Government measures created a climate of caution if not fear in the homosexual subculture. The editors of *O Snob* and the rest of the home-crafted *boneca* publications *O Snob* had inspired shut down be-

FIGURE 24   Arrest of homosexualis in Cinelândia, Rio de Janeiro, 1969. Photograph courtesy of *Acervo Última Hora*, Arquivo do Estado de São Paulo.

cause of the new political situation.[19] The extent of social control, however, never reached the level of Argentina's during the military dictatorship (1976–83), when gay establishments were subjected to intimidation and closures.[20] Brazilian places of entertainment, both gay and straight, operated relatively freely from 1972 on. Modern gay saunas, such as For Friends in São Paulo and the Ipanema Sauna in Rio de Janeiro, provided new venues for same-sex erotic encounters. Discotheques attracted a large clientele. Two of these popular nightclubs, Sótão in Rio de Janeiro and Medieval in São Paulo, became among the hottest spots of the cities' nightlife. Although the police harassed club owners on occasion, money slipped under the table kept law enforcers at bay. This contradiction between the overall political climate and the extension of gay space is counterintuitive. We would expect a right-wing military government, which censored plays that were "subversive" or violated "morality and propriety," also to close down gay clubs. This, however, was not the case.

Some historians have explained that the regime, in fact, had a clear political goal in maintaining a relatively free and open public sphere, as long as it was devoid of activities critical of the dictatorship. These historians have also argued that the Brazilian military utilized popular entertainment, like soccer and Carnival, as escape valves for the pent-up frustration of the working masses. These two popular pastimes, so the argument goes, dissipated opposition to the regime.[21] Was the government's relative laissez-faire regarding discotheques and other gay establishments designed to neutralize a potentially politicized constituency? This hardly seems the case. In the early 1970s, "Gay power," as the international movement was labeled in the press, seemed another remote and exotic phenomenon of the United States and Europe and clearly removed from the concrete concerns of the Brazilian authorities.

Moreover, if the government censored "immoral content" in artistic productions, why did it permit homosexuals to congregate in bars and baths? The answer lies in the scope of control that the military was able to impose on Brazilian society. Censorship disputes of the 1970s were conducted largely within the confines of literary and artistic expressions that the military deemed a direct challenge to the policies of the regime or to public morality. In this regard, the social territory of steam rooms and dance floors was relatively insignificant. Furthermore, the previous two decades had witnessed increased tolerance for manifestations of homosexuality, as long as they remained in enclosed spaces and escaped from these semi-clandestine venues only once a year during the pre-Lenten festivities of Carnival. Likewise, drag shows staged in theaters in Copacabana or Praça Tiradentes posed no overall threat to moral propriety.

Although, on the whole, gay entertainment and leisure spots were not harassed by the regime, some non-carnivalesque displays of effeminacy by men prompted outcries from conservative sectors of the society. In 1972, for example, the Censorship Council for Juvenile Affairs of Belo Horizonte, the capital of the important state of Minas Gerais, demanded that two fashion designers be banned from television. Their "lack of manly firmness and masculinity," argued the censors, "left much to be desired in the moral education of infants and youth."[22] Even a major Carnival tradition, the male luxury costume contest, did not escape the efforts of conservative elements in the government to erase images of effeminate men from the mass media.[23] From 1973 on, however, it became harder to maintain restrictions on these and similar public manifestations of "unmanly" behavior, as a multitude of more demanding issues began to challenge the military's grip on Brazilian society. Ultimately, the regime would lose the battle because of its own weaknesses and its essential indifference concerning issues of private conduct.

After 1972, entrepreneurs took advantage of this opening for homosexual sociability and offered a growing number of options for middle-class gay consumers, whose disposable income had increased in the period of the "economic miracle." The Sótão Discotheque in Rio de Janeiro's Galeria Alaska, and Medieval, located near São Paulo's modern high-rise financial district on Paulista Avenue, attracted an upper-middle-class clientele, who could afford the steep cover charges for an evening of dancing, shows, and fun. While these were the top-of-the-line discotheques, many others also opened and served a socially diverse array of patrons. Zig-Zag in Rio de Janeiro and Nostro Mundo in São Paulo were two of many such clubs that attracted a broad spectrum of homosexuals.[24] These clubs provided a year-round meeting place for friends and potential partners. The non-Brazilian music they played and the foreign gay tourists who visited them strengthened links to the latest trends in the international gay subculture. Just as Carnival balls created a space where individuals could dance to music with a homosexual subtext and feel a collective affirmation of their identity and sexuality, so too these nightclubs contributed to a level of cohesion among homosexuals from diverse backgrounds.[25]

The most sophisticated and elite gay nightclubs were not necessarily dens of libertine debauchery. Just as in the United States and Europe, the best gay discotheques of Rio de Janeiro and São Paulo became popular places, frequented by both gay men and trend-conscious nonhomosexuals. During the mid-1970s, for example, Rio de Janeiro's famous discotheque Sótão, located in the center of the gay nightlife district in Copacabana, prohibited men from touching each other while they danced.[26] John McCarthy, who had lived in Rio de Janeiro since the early 1970s and later became an activist in the gay and lesbian movement, explained:"[Sótão] became international and chic. I think that [the owners] didn't want it to become too gay. That is, it was in their interest for it to be a gay place because that brought in money and gave [the disco] a certain charm. But they didn't want to frighten [straight] patrons who brought prestige to the house."[27]

Discos were not the only social meeting places for homosexuals. Movie theaters continued to provide opportunities for erotic encounters.[28] The Primor, a large old movie theater in downtown Rio de Janeiro, was a popular place for anonymous sexual liaisons. Men of all social classes, from office boys to business executives, took advantage of the dark corners and mostly empty seating to engage in orgiastic activities, while "staircases and balconies became runways where *travestis* improvised shows."[29] The owners, administrators, and employees of these movie houses usually ignored the activities that took place in their establishments because the patronage provided significant income, especially for the more rundown places in downtown Rio de Janeiro and São Paulo.[30]

Many other meeting places for homosexuals opened in this period. Whereas in the 1960s both urban centers had only a couple of saunas and steam baths where men could come for sexual adventures, by the 1970s these cities boasted world-class establishments.[31] Anthropologist Dos Santos has argued that "the actions that take place in the saunas of Rio, Belo Horizonte, New York, London, or Amsterdam are not substantially different, although there are at times immense distances in the degree of openness and in the ways things take place."[32] Like movie theaters, many of the saunas were places where men from all social classes could meet and where married men could come and engage in anonymous same-sex activities. Other saunas opened outside the city center, where the lack of public transportation made them less accessible to people without cars or money for a taxi. Moreover, the higher admission fees to these establishments excluded lower-class patrons. These saunas, along with some clubs that also opened outside the cities' centers, catered to middle- and upper-middle-class customers, further diversifying consumer options.[33]

Urban territories also expanded. In the 1960s, homosexual spaces were concentrated in Copacabana, Cinelândia, and Lapa in Rio de Janeiro, and in parts of downtown São Paulo. In the 1970s, entrepreneurs inaugurated bars, restaurants, clubs, and saunas in the more affluent beachfront neighborhood of Ipanema in Rio de Janeiro. Likewise, gay Paulistas could frequent establishments in middle-class areas of the city, as well as near the new financial district along Avenida Paulista. Separate spaces for lesbians also opened in this period. In São Paulo, for example, lesbians frequented and then "took over" Ferro's restaurant, which became the first public meeting place for women interested in same-sex sexual relationships in that city.[34]

Beaches continued to be a popular place to meet. In addition to using the Bolsa de Valores in front of the Copacabana Hotel, gay men began to concentrate on other beaches. On one occasion in 1972, the police arrested twenty-five *travestis* using women's bikinis on the Flamengo Beach near the downtown area. According to military police spokesmen, men dressed in women's clothes had engaged in "performances" to the amusement of Sunday beachgoers. Several complaints by bystanders resulted in arrests.[35] The audacity and openness with which these men offered public displays of camp evoked amusement and toleration, but also provoked restrictions. Gay men also occupied territory on Ipanema Beach. The newly appropriated space lay adjacent to a dune that had become a meeting place for members of the counterculture. The heterogeneous young crowd of hippies, artists, intellectuals, and musicians exhibited a tolerant attitude toward homosexuality. Just as in the mid-1950s, the conquest of new territories and the defense of old ones involved confrontation and sometimes violence, but the trend was toward expansion, not contraction.[36]

Travestis and Male Hustlers

Another significant transformation in the urban homosexual landscape of the early 1970s was the increased visibility of *travestis** and *michês* (male hustlers) on the streets of Rio de Janeiro and São Paulo.[37] The trend reflected the growing commercialization and commodification of sex in Brazilian society. The economic prosperity of the middle classes afforded more people more opportunities to purchase sex. At the same time, the expanding poverty of the lower classes, who were, on the whole, excluded from the benefits of the "economic miracle," forced some into prostitution

---

* In the 1970s, the term *travesti* developed a connotation so inextricably linked to prostitution that I have chosen not to use the English word transvestite, which simply implies cross-dressing.

as a source of income. Moreover, employment discrimination against very effeminate men channeled some into the profession.[38]

Many of the *travestis* who worked as streetwalkers wore tight miniskirts, low-cut blouses, high-heeled shoes, net stockings, and carefully coiffed wigs. Others teased their own hair to suggest a fashionable look, but wore simple women's skirts and jackets. Still others donned blue jeans and revealing tops to attract male customers. As in previous generations, they assumed women's names—"Vera," "Nadie," "Shirlene," "Marcia."[39] However, unlike the *bichas* who had traded sex for money near the Vale de Anhangabaú in the 1930s, many, if not most, now turned to science to enhance their looks and ingested or injected hormones to develop breasts.[40]

Several changes in Brazilian society may help explain the phenomenon of a visible increase in the number of cross-dressers working as prostitutes in the 1970s. Dress codes for men and women slackened, as unisex styles blurred distinctions between masculine and feminine wear. Women could appear in public in jeans and more revealing clothes, while men could adopt more androgynous styles without severe social stigmatization. The drag shows in gay clubs that became so popular in the mid to late 1960s promoted the mystique of the captivating man dressed as a woman. Drag stars like Rogéria, who used their sexual appeal to seduce the male public, aroused curiosity about what a liaison with a *travesti* could be like. It is likely that they contributed to the creation of a market for streetwalkers who provoked clients with the message: "Try it, you'll like it." The increase in the number of *travestis* in public places was also a democratization of the phenomenon of the drag star: hundreds if not thousands of men who could never become successful on stage had the opportunity to become financially solvent on the street. The growth of the market was such that, by the late 1970s, Brazil began to export *travestis* to Europe, first Spain and France and then Italy.[41] Whereas at the beginning of the decade social mobility or economic gain for some effeminate men meant moving to Rio de Janeiro, São Paulo, or another major Brazilian city, by the end of the decade ambitious *travestis* dreamed of Paris or Rome.[42]

Prostitution itself was not a criminal offense in Brazil. However, the police could use charges of vagrancy, disturbing the public peace, or conducting obscene acts in public to control prostitution by cross-dressers. The most commonly used charge was vagrancy.[43] Arrested *travestis* were required to prove that they were gainfully employed. If they could not provide work papers, duly signed by a legitimate business or employer, the *travestis* had thirty days to find employment. If they were arrested again without fulfilling this requirement, they were subject to up to three months imprisonment under article 59 of the criminal code.[44] *Travestis* who were legally registered and employed and who in addition to their job also worked part time in prostitution could still be charged with public indecency or public disorder.

Guido Fonseca, who in 1976–77 was the police commissioner of the Fourth District, which covered much of São Paulo's downtown area where prostitution was common, explained that the policy was designed to drive *travestis* off the streets: "Even if [a *travesti*] stayed in jail only four or five days, he suffered losses because he then didn't earn money to pay rent or make a payment on a car. He would begin to realize that what he was doing didn't provide enough to earn a living. He would either leave the area of the Fourth District and work in another area, where there wasn't any repression, or he could get a job and make a living from another profession."[45] As part of the campaign to control the proliferation of *travestis* in São Paulo, Fonseca ordered a special file to be made for each cross-dresser who was arrested for vagrancy, disturbing the peace, or indecent public acts. After police sweeps and arrests, the *travestis'* pictures were taken and personal information was carefully noted. This allowed the police to keep detailed records of the *travestis'* activities. The files could also be used to identify *travestis* accused of robbing or extorting their johns.

More than three hundred of these files have survived. According to an analysis of one hundred files, seventy-five of the arrested men were between the age of eighteen and twenty-four. Almost a quarter were natives of the city of São Paulo, while another 15 percent came from state of São Paulo, and the rest hailed from other parts of the country. Of the total, fifty-nine came from urban areas and forty-one from rural Brazil. While their declared professions varied, thirty-four stated that they were hairdressers. Most of the others performed work traditionally associated with women: they were manicurists, cosmeticians, dressmakers, and window dressers. Only 11 percent declared that they had no profession.[46] Comparing the salary most *travestis* declared that they earned from other employment with the amount obtained on the street, one can understand the economic forces that pushed people into prostitution. The majority earned at least twice their "professional" salaries by selling their bodies.[47] Fonseca admitted the irony of the police's policy whereby those who could prove they had "legitimate" employment, even if it provided them with less than a subsistence wage, could not be charged with vagrancy, whereas a person earning a much better living by prostitution alone could be jailed for three months.[48]

As the number of male streetwalkers increased, so did the demand. This raises an interesting question about the behavior of Brazilian men who had sex with *travestis*. These men were not looking for female sexual partners, and they consciously chose men dressed as women, when female prostitutes were readily available. Even more surprising, Fonseca recalled, most of the arrested *travestis* had claimed that, during their sexual encounter, the majority of their clients wanted to be anally penetrated. Valéria, an elegant transsexual who worked the streets near the Hilton Hotel in downtown São Paulo in 1975, echoed this assertion. As a transsexual, Valéria did not have the necessary endowments to please many of her customers: "Almost all of the men I go out with want me to be active with them. But you know . . . it's impossible. I have everything that a woman has, so I can't. I have lost many clients because of this, but what am I going to do?"[49] The vast majority of *travestis*, however, had not undergone sex changes and therefore could attend to the needs of their clientele.

Asked if this claim about the role of the *travesti* in the sexual liaison might be mere bravado, aimed to provoke the listener as well as to invert a commonly held assumption, Adauto B. Alves, who helped found the First National Gathering of *Travestis* in Rio de Janeiro in 1993, rejected that possibility: "Most *travestis*' clients desire a person who looks like a woman, but acts like a man in bed."[50] According to Alves, those *travestis* who have sex-change operations find that prostitution as a source of income can drop dramatically as a result. This pattern, if true, subverts the stereotype that the *bicha* or effeminate man is always penetrated in sexual relations. The man as a "woman" becomes a "man" in bed, while the allegedly masculine partner seeks out a substitute woman to experience sexual pleasure in ways traditionally ascribed to effeminate men. Several possible explanations for this phenomenon can be posited. Fonseca speculated that *travestis* were popular because many of their johns were not heterosexual, but rather discreet homosexuals who did not want the night porters in their buildings to see them entering their apartments with a male sexual partner.[51] Others might have been unable to break away from the traditional male / female role model, which required a defined masculinity and femininity in sexual encounters. Or perhaps some men simply enjoyed the pleasure of an androgynous experience.

Just as cross-dressers became more visible in the mid-1970s, so did male hustlers, popularly known as *michês*. As in previous decades, it was not uncommon for young men, generally from poor or working-class families, to live off *tias* (aunts), older gay men.[52] The older man provided the youth with gifts, a place to stay, and spending money in exchange for sex. It was the young man's masculinity that made him attractive to the *tia*, and the youth generally made it clear that he preferred women and would eventually marry. By doing so, he reaffirmed his virility, and maintained the older man's attraction. In the early 1970s, the number of *michês* had become so widespread in Rio de Janeiro and São Paulo that the phenomenon began to receive attention in the press.[53] Reporting about male hustlers increased after the murder of Fred Feld, an American pianist who worked in Copacabana nightclubs. Feld invited twenty-two-year-old Anival Fonseca back to his luxury apartment adjacent to Galeria Alaska. When the two entered into a dispute about how much Feld was willing to pay, Anival struck and killed the performer. Returning to the area several days later to continue hustling, he was apprehended by police.[54]

Commenting on the murder a week later to a local journalist, Paulo, a homosexual who lived near Lapa, explained the dependence of many middle-class *bichas* on male hustlers, and the precarious life that many *entendidos* lived: "Violence, robbery and the exploitation of *entendidos* is routine for us. A day doesn't go by without a friend having a tragic story to tell. And these guys like the one who killed Fred Feld don't only hang around places frequented by marginal characters and the unemployed." Describing how well-dressed, smiling, and accessible hustlers had spread throughout the Zona Sul, the southern wealthy part of Rio de Janeiro, the journalist observed: "They are always planning how to rob a *bicha*. There are *bonecas* who only realize this when they are faced with danger." Paulo himself admitted that at the end of the evening, when there were few paying *entendidos* left on the street looking for a hustler, he would offer one of the *michês* a place to stay for the night in exchange for sex. Underlining the economic content of the transaction, he lamented that he generally could not afford to pay for sex: "I don't have the money to support one by giving him . . . clothes, money, food."[55]

Anthropologist Sérgio José de Almeida Alves, who interviewed forty-one *michês* in the mid-1970s, concluded that, with two exceptions, none of the men considered themselves to be homosexual. While they liked their work, they did not link their sexual activities with other men to homosexual desire or identity. Most insisted that financial necessity motivated them, although a few admitted that they would have sex with a given person without charging if they liked the person's looks.[56]

The dynamics of the relationship between *bichas* or *tias* and *michês* was a complicated power game. Older boys and young men, who were driven by poverty or who were willing to trade their bodies for easy money, used their youth and their ability to project raw masculinity to attract older men. In exchange, they received financial compensation and, at times, entry into a social world otherwise inaccessible. The crossing of class lines brought sexual excitement, but at times it could also mean physical danger.[57] In acting out the sexual fantasy of masculinity and femininity, the two players, in fact, engaged in another variation of the *bicha/bofe* dyad. The *tia/ miché* and the *bicha/bofe* relationships both reflected polarized notions of gender.

Cultural Transformations and Androgynous Figures

When the opposition movement failed to topple the government in 1968, only a minority of politicized students opted for armed struggle and underground opposition to the military dictatorship. The systematic arrest and torture of members and supporters of the left had a chilling effect on people who had participated in the upheavals of 1968 or who feared that the long arm of repression would reach them. The dissolution of *O Snob* in 1969 was merely one of many examples of caution and even paranoia that overtook those who did not support the military government or who belonged to marginal segments of society. Alternative avenues of legal protest were largely cut off. Opposition artists, writers, and musicians had to contend constantly with the censor, who vetoed works for their political and moral content.

The late 1960s and early 1970s were years of social as well as political upheaval. International countercultural ideas had filtered into Brazil and influenced many urban middle-class youth.[58] Among the new challenges to hegemonic social values were the use of drugs, a rejection of the consumer-based society that the government's policies encouraged, and the destabilization of sexual codes, especially the issues of premarital female virginity and normative heterosexuality for both women and men. Theater groups such as Teatro Oficina confronted middle-class audiences with sexually explicit scenes that had managed to pass the censors.[59] Singers such as Caetano Veloso, Maria Bethânia, and Gal Costa—leading figures in the musical movement known as *tropicalismo*—projected unabashed sensuality in their performances and were rumored to have had homosexual affairs.[60] All of these developments helped to create a climate favorable to the questioning of traditional notions of gender. In the early 1970s, the unisex image that Caetano Veloso and others had popularized in 1968 was taken much further by other artists, the most notable being the theater group, Dzi Croquettes, and the singer Ney Matogrosso. Both used gender-bending and androgyny to shake up standard representations of the masculine and feminine. Their shows reflected a broad social acceptance among middle-class audiences for provocative portrayals of gender roles and identities.[61]

Dzi Croquettes, formed in Rio de Janeiro in 1972, brought together the enthusiasm of a group of amateur artists and the professional expertise of Lennie Dale, an American Broadway dancer residing in Brazil.[62] Unlike the drag performers of Praça Tiradentes, who sought classical feminine beauty, grace, and style in their portrayal of women, the fourteen cast members of Dzi Croquettes dressed in a mixture of masculine and feminine attire. Baritone-voiced men decorated with glitter and makeup projected their virility despite, or perhaps because of, feminine accoutrements.

An observer of their work remembered a typical scene: "In an explosion of music, shouting, flashing lights and frantic movement, the stage is taken over by harem women, leading ladies, widows, clownlike prostitutes, Pierrots, and rumba dancers: it is the Dzi Croquettes family. You can tell them apart by their makeup, costumes, and gestures. They have one thing in common—an undifferentiated masculine and feminine image. Large eyelashes, exaggerated lipstick, and sparkling glitter forming psychedelic designs splotch their faces and bodies. [They] have beards, mustaches, and hairy chests. Their delirious clothes include lamé dresses, sequined and fringed bathing suits, frayed ballet leotards, combinations that don't fit together, extravagant hats, wigs, . . . soccer socks held up with ladies' garters, high-heeled shoes, or heavy boots with legging."[63]

The group's camp humor inverted all standards of normative sexual roles, upsetting traditional gender markings and representations of masculinity. Their gender-blending sexual message promoted the idea that their external images were superficial anomalies. The fluidity with which they assumed masculine and feminine personas, Dzi Croquettes seemed to say, was possible precisely because human beings possessed characteristics of both sexes within themselves. The refrain of one song pronounced that, in spite of the apparent "otherness" of their representations, they were no different from the members of the audience: "The marvelous presence of Dzi Croquettes, citizens, made in Brazil! I've already warned you, we're people computed just like you!"[64]

Dzi Croquettes emphasized sexual freedom. Their androgynous representations and a phrase used in their shows—"everyone should be able to have sex with whomever they want"—provoked the question of their sexual identity. While they were effeminate, they also projected masculinity, so according to traditional standards, they were not exactly *bichas*. Nor were they *travestis*, since the actors made no attempt to replicate the standard presentation of feminine beauty. In trying to reconcile the group's ambiguous images, which defied classification, the press invented new phrases to describe them, such as *travesti sem bichismo* (drag without faggotry) and *travesti sem cara de homosexual* (transvestite without appearing to be homosexual). The media finally settled on the term "androgyny."[65] Dzi Croquettes played with these journalistic inventions by responding: "Deep down [the terms] are the same thing: a *travesti* is a *bicha* from the lower classes; now an androgynous person is the son of someone in the military."[66] While appearing to be merely a humorous commentary, the troupe's observation was quite poignant, for portrayals of homosexuality in the press were indeed class coded. Middle- and upper-class men who transgressed gender boundaries were ascribed an androgynous persona, while the poor or working-class men who cross-dressed were *travestis*, a term that increasingly associated with prostitution, street life, and marginality.

Dzi Croquettes played to packed audiences in Rio de Janeiro and São Paulo in 1973 and 1974 and then toured Europe, returning to Brazil in 1976. During their first two years on stage, they attracted a large number of dedicated fans, many of whom were homosexual. The success of the troupe's productions can be attributed to their ability to express openness about sexuality and their critique of rigid gender categories. Just as the drag shows of the 1960s represented an affirmation of the *bicha*, Dzi Croquettes' performances in the early 1970s captured a new identity in formation. A subtext of the group's shows argued that a man could sexually desire other men and assume both an effeminate and masculine sexual identity. In the absence of a gay movement and with few other vehicles to express this viewpoint, the impact of Dzi Croquettes became all the more important.

Ney Matogrosso, a rock musician who often performed songs in falsetto, had a similar influence on the changing conceptions of appropriate masculine behavior in Brazil in the early 1970s.[67] As lead singer for the band Secos e Molhados,* which burst onto the music scene in 1973, Ney used dramatic makeup and exotic costumes to convey the same androgynous image that had made Dzi Croquettes so popular in the theater that

---

* The name literally means wet and dry, but is also the term for dry goods.

same year. Citing Degard Morin's *Mass Culture in the Twentieth Century*, one journalist for the youth culture weekly *Pasquim* explained to his readers why Ney evoked such a strong reaction from a diverse audience that ranged from middle-class grandmothers to hippies: "Androgyny as it is presented by some international pop groups allies itself with a natural eroticism of mass culture. . . . [Morin] concluded that 'using desire and dreams as ingredients and means of playing the game of supply and demand, capitalism, rather than reducing human life to materialism, fills it with dreams and diffuse eroticism.' These dreams and diffuse eroticism have to show up somewhere, and I am very tempted to believe that at the moment Secos e Molhados fulfills both obscure needs."[68] Indeed, Ney Matogrosso projected a new androgynous sexuality that appealed as much to women as it did to homosexual men.

The singer left Secos e Molhados in 1975 and launched his career as a soloist. Bare-chested and covered with strings of beads, he would strut around the stage in feathered headpieces, or perform a striptease with the use of mirrors, stopping short of nudity to avoid problems with the censors. Invariably people asked the question, "Well, is he or isn't he?" for it remained incomprehensible to think that a heterosexual man would perform such flamboyant antics. The doubt in the public's mind came from the fact that Ney Matogrosso never lost a traditionally masculine flair while presenting an outrageous stage persona. In a 1978 interview with the Brazilian edition of *Interview* magazine, he clarified his sexual orientation unequivocally and declared that he was gay. His statement about homosexuality in the three-page article resulted in an official government investigation of the journal to determine whether or not it had violated the press law by publishing material that offended "morality and propriety."

As a rising rock superstar, Ney Matogrosso's openness about his sexuality offered a new model to many homosexuals. He spoke proudly about the way he provoked desire among both women and men: "Now I perceive that when women realize that I am a homosexual they go crazy with desire for me. A macho man doesn't know how to give pleasure. He fucks, comes, and gets off. Because I am a homosexual, I know how to caress a woman, because I like to be caressed. And when I am in bed with a man, I am not a woman, I am a man."[69]

Ney's notion of masculine virility in bed, however, did not preclude behavior traditionally associated with women. In another section of the interview, he explained how he promoted his feminine attributes: "For example, sensibility is only permitted for women. Emotion [means] woman.

Making oneself beautiful. Woman. I am a person who has emotion and sensibility and I am proud not to hide it. I show it. Now if this is feminine by [social] standards, I don't give a shit."[70] While Matogrosso's stage persona did not meet with universal acceptance, his audacious behavior was one of an array of cultural manifestations that helped expand toleration for homosexuality.

During this period books and plays with homosexual themes appeared in increasing numbers, skirted the censors, and at times presented a positive image of the homosexual.[71] Several theatrical productions of the late 1960s and early '70s depicted the ways in which homophobia destroyed people's lives. Walmir Ayala's 1965 play *Nosso filho vai ser mãe* (Our son is going to be a mother) portrays the story of a young man who confronts social prejudice after he has articulated his desire to get pregnant. His challenges to dominant heteronormative values, however, result in his mother's decision to commit him to an asylum.[72] The following year, Nelson Rodrigues, one of Brazil's most important modern playwrights, published *O Beijo no Asfalto*. The play describes the story of a man seen kissing a youth moments before the latter dies in a fatal car accident. This incident unleashes a chain of events that leads to the loss of the man's job, his wife, and eventually his life.[73] While the protagonists in both plays suffer from social prejudice, the authors' intentions were to elicit the audience's compassion and sympathy for their plight.

In 1971 the off-Broadway hit *The Boys in the Band* (1968) played in Rio de Janeiro. According to Sylvio Lamenha, writing in the counterculture publication *Já:* "It is a play that is worth seeing a second time for the courage in dealing with the subject, for the quality of acting, and for the good theatrical climate. This is especially so in a moment when there is practically nothing else to see and enjoy. And after all, guys, I am also a member of the band."[74] While today's critics may find that *The Boys in the Band* presents stereotypical caricatures of homosexuals and ends on a needlessly tragic note, at the time the presentation by and about homosexuals was a refreshing novelty on the stage, as Lamenha pointed out.

More significant, perhaps, was the 1974 production of Fernando Mello's *Greta Garbo, quem diria, acabou no Irajá* (Who would have guessed that Greta Garbo would end up in Irajá), a box-office success. The play portrays the life of Pedro, an *entendido* who falls in love with Renato, a penniless youth fresh from the countryside. The two meet in Cinelândia. The first act revolves around the innocence of the youth and Pedro's unsuccessful attempts to seduce him. Renato ultimately returns to his hometown, much the wiser after his stay in Rio. Before his departure, Pedro gives Renato a parting kiss. The comic element in this play involves Renato's naiveté. The youth is unaware of the slang and the ways of Carioca homosexual subculture. The audience was either already "in the know" (*entendido*) or became more familiar with gay life in Rio de Janeiro through watching the play.[75] *Greta Garbo* ran for several years and became as popular with broad audiences in its time as *Les Girls* had been a decade earlier.

Several literary works of the late 1960s and 1970s also had an impact on the changing notions of homosexuality in Brazil. The 1967 anthology *Histórias do amor maldito* (Stories of damned love), edited by Gasparino Damata, collected thirty-five short stories by Brazilian authors, all containing sexual themes ranging from adulterous love affairs to homosexuality.[76] The book made available selections from earlier works with homosexual themes, such as *Bom-Crioulo* and *Internato*, which had been out of print for some time. Damata's own collection of short stories, *Os solteirões*, published in 1976, included realistic tales of hustlers, *tias*, *bichas*, and a novelty: masculine-identified men who only slept with young virile boys.[77]

Another author, Aguinaldo Silva, drew on his experience as a criminal reporter to create realistic portraits of urban corruption, violence, and decay. His 1975 novel *Primeira carta aos andróginos* (The first letter to the androgens) detailed the cruising activities of a *bicha* in a Carioca cinema. Darcy Penteado's work, *A meta* (The goal), which came out the following year, was widely promoted in the press.[78] The volume, a collection of short stories capturing various aspects of life in the homosexual subculture, was a hard-hitting statement in favor of homosexuality. Its cover was no less audacious. It showed a handsome muscular man, shirtless, his blue jeans provocatively half-unbuttoned. The photograph was a homoerotic portrayal of the image of the "gay macho" that had become popular in the United States and Europe. The subtext seemed to be that homosexuals are not all effeminate *bichas* or womanly *travestis*. Moreover, one of the short stories was a thinly disguised autobiographical account of the author's numerous homosexual escapades. Penteado, a famous set designer and portrait artist of the Paulista upper class, used the promotion of his book to talk about his own sexual identity as a gay man and about the need to organize a movement in Brazil. His "coming out" had a profound impact. One journalist, writing about the sexual revolution in São Paulo, commented: "Since the day that Darcy Penteado decided to announce his homosexuality publicly with his autobiographical book *A meta*, gay power in São Paulo has not been the same."[79] While previously the public assumed that many homosexuals were fashion designers, artists, Carnival luxury contest winners, performers, and famous hairdressers, Penteado's willingness to discuss his sexuality unabashedly offered a new image of the "out" homosexual. His posture provided many homosexuals with an important example to follow. However, the receptivity of middle-class audiences to beautiful *travestis*, androgynous performers, plays with homosexual themes, and the writings of an emerging gay literati notwithstanding, popular attitudes toward homosexuality were slow to change.

Access to Information

In spite of government censorship during the 1970s, bits and pieces of information about the rise and growth of the international gay and lesbian movement found their way into the Brazilian press. While articles about Brazilian homosexuality ranged from hostile to sympathetic, depending on the newspaper, international news, though infrequent, tended to present a positive picture of the gay and lesbian movements abroad. The articles informed the readership of protests, legal cases, and activities designed to expand democratic rights for gays and lesbians in the United States and Europe.[80] For example, in 1969, *Jornal da Tarde,* an afternoon daily from São Paulo, carried a Reuters piece on "gay power" in San Francisco. *O Globo,* one of Rio de Janeiro's largest-circulation newspapers, ran a short Associated Press story about a 1970 New York march organized by the Gay Liberation Front. The next year, the prestigious *Jornal do Brasil* published a brief article on an Italian gay rights group, as well as a report on the second annual gay and lesbian protest parades in New York.[81] Over the next few years, the country's leading newspapers picked up other international news items that further informed their readers about efforts of gay and lesbian groups to demand same-sex marriages and to eliminate the American Psychiatric Association's classification of homosexuality as a sickness. *Jornal do Brasil* also carried a story about the activities of the Argentine Homosexual Liberation Front, the only South American gay rights group that existed at the time.[82]

The alternative press, which managed to skirt censorship restrictions, criticized the military dictatorship, and had a targeted readership of students, intellectuals, and young people in general, occasionally provided information about political and cultural changes taking place abroad.[83] Yet, as was the case in the mainstream press, the references were sparse and intermittent. An exception to this rule was the short-lived journal *Já* (Right now), a split-off from the popular alternative weekly *Pasquim*.[84] Based in Rio de Janeiro, *Já* appeared on newsstands during the second half of 1971 but closed after only a dozen issues. The weekly ran a column entitled "Gay Power," a series of brief notes and news items, which were collected and signed by Sylvio Lamenha. Whether or not this was the columnist's real name, it marked a contrast to the articles written for *O Snob* and similar handcrafted productions whose journalists had represented their public persona in the feminine. A clenched fist clutching a bouquet of wild flowers served as the column's logo, as if to suggest both political militancy and countercultural values. "Gay Power" carried vignettes about famous Brazilian and European homosexuals, recommended books and plays that portrayed homosexuality in a positive light, and conveyed news about the beginning of a gay political movement in Europe. The column also printed information about gay bars in Rio de Janeiro and São Paulo. The last column before the journal closed down carried a two-page banner headline in English entitled "Gay Liberation Front," reflecting the influence of the international movement. While the journal did not manage to survive the year because of competition from *Pasquim*, the column, which was the first of its kind, marked a new, open approach to homosexuality.[85]

Even drag stars on the rise were influenced by the international movement. In 1971, Aguinaldo Silva interviewed the famed cross-dresser Rogéria. The interview was conducted by mail because Rogéria was still on tour in Africa. Asked about the "gay revolution," Rogéria mentioned the United States–based Mattachine Society and criticized the organization for preaching the superiority of homosexuality. "[Homosexuality] is about being equal, and having the same rights," she explained. When queried about whether or not she would participate in "Gay Power Liberation" if asked to do so, the Brazilian drag queen replied: "I was always a militant. When I get up on the stage and evoke emotions from the audience, I am showing how much humanity exists inside of me, in my art. Many homosexuals are militants, each in his field, principally in art. The day a black *bicha* shows up who is a great soccer player, he will be applauded in Maracanã [Stadium] with tremendous fondness. People always have this reaction when they are face to face with a homosexual and note his humanity. Homosexuals are a repressed minority, but there is a fundamental difference. It is possible to destroy other minorities, racial minorities for example. The homo minority is indestructible. You would have to eliminate all men and women to get rid of homosexuals."[86] Rogéria's language was notably political. She cate-

gorized homosexuals as an oppressed minority, and preached self-affirmation as means of coping with discrimination—two basic elements of the
international movement. The article presented her as an articulate and sensitive person, and a strong political role model for the *bonecas* who had already been emulating her grace and style.

The journal *Pasquim*, which published the interview with Rogéria, had
an uneven track record when it came to dealing with homosexuality. The
country's largest circulating counterculture newspaper, the journal used humor to criticize the military dictatorship and conservative social mores. Sexual innuendoes, irreverent criticism of many traditional middle-class social
conventions, and the prolific use of photographs of seminude women placed
the editors in a continuous battle with government censors. *Pasquim*'s per-
sistence in opposing the military's restrictions on its publishing endeavor
garnered it considerable prestige and a large national readership. The journal had a clear Carioca appeal. It promoted the easygoing lifestyle of middle-class residents of Rio de Janeiro's *zona sul* (southern zone), especially
the oceanfront neighborhood of Ipanema. Beach life, beer, and beautiful
women were glorified as the ideal aspirations of all Brazilian men.[87]

When the journal carried an article about a drag queen like Rogéria,
who emulated traditional feminine beauty, the tone was usually lightly sar-
castic but nevertheless respectful.[88] The transformation from male to female did not upset the traditional representations of gender, and the
conventional heterocentric and male-dominated discourse of the journal
remained secure. Homosexuals such Madame Satã also won the respect of
Pasquim. The tabloid encouraged a cult image of the *malandro* from Lapa,
described as a *bicha brava* (a brave faggot) who "fought like a man" and
would kill to defend his honor.[89] Again, gender roles were not threatened
by Madame Satã's persona. But effeminate men, who neither managed to
transform themselves into perfect imitations of female models nor exuded
masculine virility, did not fare well in the pages of the journal. Many issues
contained pejorative jokes about *bichas*. In fact, *Pasquim* historian José Luiz
Braga argues that the journal popularized the expression throughout the
country.[90] The headline on the cover of one issue, for example, announced
in large type "TODO PAULISTA É BICHA" (All Paulistas are faggots). In small
type, squeezed in between the phrase "All Paulistas" and "are faggots," was
the modifying explanation "who don't like women." In an inside article, hu-
morist Millôr Fernandes explained that sales had dropped and so the editors had come up with the inflammatory banner to attract attention to the
journal.[91] *Pasquim*'s writers held nothing sacred in their humorous critiques

of middle-class Brazilian life, politics, and the military, but homosexuals and early feminists, like Betty Friedan, who visited Brazil in 1971, were easy targets for this haven of countercultural male chauvinists. Although *Pasquim* remained a symbol for criticism of the social status quo, the journal only reluctantly changed its coverage after the feminist and gay movements had marked their place on the cultural and political landscape in the late 1970s.[92]

Pasquim's writers may have offered negative or stereotypical portrayals of homosexuals, but by the mid-1970s other journalists began presenting alternative and more positive images. In February 1976, a young journalist named Celso Curi started a daily column for the São Paulo edition of *Última Hora*. The column was entitled "Coluna do meio" (Middle column), a double play on words referring to a soccer term and the homosexual *meio* (milieu). Celso's articles were an immediate success and boosted the journal's circulation.[93] The column included commentaries on international and national gay personalities, and news of gay bars and nightclubs in Rio de Janeiro and São Paulo. Letters poured in from homosexuals all over Brazil enthusiastically praising Celso for his courage in writing the column. A personal ads section called "Correio elegante" (Elegant post) was especially popular.[94] The column became a clearinghouse for thousands of homosexuals throughout the country who wished to connect with each other. Celso Curi became an overnight celebrity in the gay subcultures of Rio de Janeiro and São Paulo. The following year, the editor of one alternative gay paper called him the "first spokesperson for Brazilian homosexuals."[95]

The success of Curi's column encouraged other journalists to follow suit. In 1977, Glorinha Pereira, a former model and owner of both a gay sauna and nightclub in Rio de Janeiro, penned a column titled "Guei,"* which appeared in the *Correio de Copacabana*, a neighborhood weekly with a circulation of fifteen thousand. Antônio Moreno ran a column that same year called "Tudo entendido" (Everything understood)," which appeared in the Carioca daily *Gazeta de Notícias*.[96] The mainstream press also reported on the gay subcultures of Rio de Janeiro and São Paulo, informing their readers about the diversity of bars, saunas, discotheques and minipublications that existed in 1976 and 1977.[97] These articles usually presented homosexuality in a positive light. Reporters offered textured

---

* The transformation of the English word "gay" into the Portuguese phonetic spelling *guei* appeared in 1977 and was promoted by linguistic purists but eventually fell out of use.

descriptions of gay life, including nonstereotypical anecdotes about individuals. The new coverage of the 1970s stood in stark contrast to that of the previous decade.

Independent Gay Journalism

In December 1976, inspired by the efforts of Celso Curi and a few other journalists, Anuar Farad, Agildo Guimarães, Hélio Fonseca, José Rodriques and other former writers and readers of *O Snob* decided to produce their new publication, *Gente Gay*. They realized that the political climate was propitious. Dozens of alternative journals negotiated around government censors and found their way to newsstands. Cautious about complications that might arise if they submitted a journal with explicitly gay-themed material to the censor, the group opted to continue their practices of the 1960s and circulate *Gente Gay* informally. By adding a simple statement, "for internal circulation," the editors of this new publication calculated that they would be protected from any violation of the press law.

The title of the journal reflected a change in the language of the subculture. By 1976, the English term "gay," which had been familiar to Carioca and Paulista homosexuals for more than a decade, had entered the popular lexicon. After the media had used the expression "gay power" to refer to the movement in the United States and Europe in the early 1970s, it was no longer a discreet code word, as the term *entendido* had been. *Gente Gay* maintained many elements of *O Snob*, but there were cosmetic improvements in its physical appearance and a marked change in the content. While *Gente Gay* was still typewritten, photocopying had replaced the mimeograph machine. Drag queens remained cover girls (this time with photos instead of sketches), but the editors placed male nude frontal shots, clipped from international gay publications, throughout the issues. Whereas the contributors to *O Snob* had used female pseudonyms to protect their anonymity and to play with their identification as *bonecas*, now the list of editors and writers included many people's real names. Anuar recalled the initial fear about revealing their names: "We were really 'out'— look, you can't imagine the fear we felt . . . , but we used our names."[98] Once the founders of the journal got over their initial trepidation, they even published snapshots of parties organized by the group. One could clearly identify people's faces, and names appeared below their images in neatly placed captions.

The content of many articles in *Gente Gay* also changed. The familiar style of gossip and internal news of the group continued, but the journal now also carried information about the international gay movement. One issue, for example, published impressions of a reader's visit to the United States. The article included an extensive report on bars in Detroit, Washington, D.C., and New York, as well as news about the Gay Liberation Front at Wayne State University in Detroit.[99] The editors reported on transformations that were taking place in the Brazilian subculture, and informed their readers of recently published fiction with explicit homoerotic themes. One issue reproduced a lengthy article about artist and writer Darcy Penteado, who had come out publicly the previous year.[100] All the while, the editors maintained their camp humor and still paid attention to *bonecas*. The same issue that profiled Darcy Penteado also featured an interview with Veruska Donayelle, who had been elected Miss Press by members of *O Snob* ten years earlier. Now with perfect makeup and long hair, she posed seminude, her hormone-induced breasts exposed. Whereas in the 1960s, the members of *O Snob* who identified with the feminine could only suggest their affinities by cross-dressing at Carnival or wearing a dress during a discreet party, a decade later they could use hormonal therapy to live out their fantasies year round.

Gente Gay received such a positive reception that the editors decided to have it printed professionally. This ambitious plan, however, proved to be the journal's downfall. The editors lacked experience in administrating a larger-circulation newspaper. They published two issues of a thousand copies each, but could not recoup the significantly greater costs of a printed publication. Furthermore, the decision to expand *Gente Gay*'s circulation was taken at precisely the same time that a group of journalists and intellectuals with years of professional experience launched the monthly *Lampião da Esquina*, distributing ten thousand copies of the first issue of the monthly throughout Brazil. The competition totally undermined the efforts of *Gente Gay*'s editors to go forward with their project.[101]

In São Paulo, two other journals directed at a gay audience were launched in 1977. The first, *Entender* (Understand), drew its title from the slang term *entendido*. Beginning as a homecrafted product much like *Gente Gay*, and coming out once a month, by the end of the year it was printed in tabloid format. The journal contained news of the bars and cruising areas in São Paulo and Rio de Janeiro, and even published advertisements for some of the gay saunas. Like *Gente Gay*, it folded because it could not maintain a large enough circulation to finance itself. Likewise, *Mundo Gay:*

O Jornal dos Entendidos (Gay world: The journal of *entendidos*) had a short life. It too carried advertisements for businesses, bars, and services and was distributed at newsstands, and it too had stopped circulating by the year's end.[102]

These first attempts at producing gay newspapers failed for a number of reasons. The editors lacked the journalistic and administrative skills necessary to manage a large-scale enterprise. They did not know how to distribute their product widely. With limited sales and little reserve capital, the editors did not have the resources to improve the graphic quality or sustain publication until the readership increased. The journals' collaborators were not seasoned journalists, but enthusiastic novices who did not have reputations, beyond circles of friends, that could increase interest in the papers. Nevertheless, the efforts to create these newspapers mirrored a shift among many homosexuals. More individuals were willing to be open about their sexual orientation in print. Furthermore, the increasingly favorable political climate encouraged an optimism about the possibility of achieving what had been thought impossible until even recently, namely, to establish some kind of "gay power" in Brazil.

The Consolidation of a New Identity

By the 1970s, a distinct new identity had taken hold within the homosexual subculture of Rio de Janeiro and São Paulo. This process had begun gradually in the 1950s and '60s and reflected an uneven and combined interaction of multiple factors. Expanded public space for homosexual sociability increased the opportunities for people to interact with others who shared their identity. Influences from the sexual revolution of the late 1960s and the international gay movement offered different ways to think about sexual roles and positioning vis-à-vis hegemonic models and helped people to become more open about their sexuality. New, less rigidly gendered masculine role models, as exemplified by prominent artists and performers, offered options other than the *bicha/bofe* dyad. Newspapers, plays, and literary works provided new vehicles to discuss homosexuality. Columnists like Celso Curi, and ephemeral alternative publications, such as *Gay Society, Entender,* and *O Mundo Gay,* promoted this new identity.

As has been mentioned previously, anthropologist Peter Fry and others have pointed to the use of the word *entendido* by homosexuals in Rio de Janeiro and São Paulo in the 1960s as an indication of the prevalence of this new identity. They have argued that the *entendido* was less attached to hierarchical gender roles and adopted the concept of a more egalitarian relationship with sexual partners. Moreover, the "active" (penetrating), "passive" (penetrated) sexual relationships themselves became more fluid. Fry has located this change within the context of major social transformations of the middle and upper classes in the large urban centers, the same transformations that would also produce new identities for women during the same period.[103]

However, Barbosa da Silva's research among Paulista homosexuals seems to indicate that these changes in identity began in the 1950s and merely increased in intensity in the 1960s and '70s. Moreover, the choice of the term *entendido* as the prototypical symbol to represent this transformation obscures aspects of the phenomenon described. In the 1960s, the expression *entendido* had multiple uses and connotations, not just the meaning Fry has ascribed to it. For members of *O Snob,* the term was a synonym for a *boneca* or *bicha,* that is, a person attracted to "real" men. Clóvis, in reminiscing about Paulista life in the early 1960s, recalled that the term *entendido* was used by the theater crowd in 1964–65 as a less harsh term for a homosexual.[104] Moreover, the word *entendido* was rejected by the first Brazilian gay groups as too representative of the "closeted" homosexual. Many early activists preferred to use the word *bicha* within the groups to extirpate its pejorative meaning.[105] By the 1980s, most activists and the majority of the subculture had adopted the word "gay" as a term of self-identification for their sexual persona. Even then, gay retained multiple meanings. Ramalhete, who had been sexually active in the Carioca subculture since the 1950s, considered the term to be a modern version of *bicha.* He retained the gendered dyad, which now was *homem* ("real man") and "gay" instead of *bofe* and *bicha.*[106] Terminology aside, the new identity that Fry and others have accurately described was clearly gaining ground. Many members of this urban subculture placed less emphasis on sexual roles within a relationship and adopted the notion that both partners were homosexual. Moreover, self-acceptance seemed to become more pervasive. Even as early as 1968, a feature article on homosexuality in the magazine *Realidade* reported that none of the men interviewed considered their sexual orientation to be a sickness, although letters to the editor in response to the report repeated moral condemnation of the practice.[107] In 1977, the psychiatrist Flávio Gikovate also noted this phenomenon: "Until about five years ago, I had several homosexual clients who sought a 'cure,' that is, they wanted a treatment for what they considered to be sick behavior. . . . In the last few years, I have only worked with homosexuals for other reasons. That is, people no longer look for a 'cure.'" Although the predominant medicolegal discourse continued to maintain that homosexuality was pathological behavior, fewer homosexuals were seeking medical or psychiatric treatment.[108]

Agildo Guimarães recognized the change in his own conception of sexual roles and behavior: "Before [in the '50s and '60s] everyone was either *bicha* or *bofe*. Afterward, we began to discover that you could have sex with someone and play the active role in bed. You didn't have to be a *bicha* in bed. Things changed a lot in the 1970s."[109] While Agildo could not articulate the reasons for this shift, his journalistic endeavors, *O Snob* and *Gente Gay*, suggest some contributing factors. In the rigidly gendered cultural environment of the 1950s, the socialization of homosexuals into the subculture reproduced the normative gender system. The *bichas* and *bofes* of *O Snob* paralleled the dominant paradigm. As this hegemonic construct began to bend in the 1960s, new ways to fashion one's sexual identity seemed possible. International and national role models offered alternative examples of creating new kinds of relationships and new types of sexual activities. *Bichas* discovered, as Agildo himself reported, that sexual roles could be fluid. While the content of *Gente Gay* at times reflected the more traditional language of *bonecas* and adherence to the *bicha/bofe* dyad, it also contained elements of the new. Masculinity was no longer divorced from homosexuality. Instead of being "either/or," one could be both. This is not to argue that one sexual system replaced the other. The emergence of the new model coexisted with the *bicha/bofe* polarity. The process began in the urban middle class, while homosexuals from rural areas and lower classes, with less access to alternative models, tended to reproduce the *bicha/bofe* construct.

Coming Together

In 1976, João S. Trevisan, a São Paulo writer who had lived in the United States in the early 1970s and was in contact with the San Francisco Bay Area gay liberation movement, attempted to form a discussion group on homosexuality among university-educated Paulistas. According to Trevisan: "There were never more than a dozen at the meetings, all young men. Some came with vague liberal and assertive propositions, while the thoughts and feelings of others were hampered by the ideology of the old left. We tried to study some texts. However, the participants, who were very reticent about the experiment, were paralyzed by feelings of guilt—even when they had been humiliated by their [left-wing] party comrades for being homosexuals. The big question that they asked themselves, frequently heard in gay groups in the movement's first phase, was 'Is it politically valid for us to discuss sexuality, something generally considered secondary given the situation in Brazil?'"[110] The group Trevisan organized failed to coalesce and fell apart after a short time. Trevisan would remain a consistent critic of any leftist influence in the Brazilian gay movement. In his analysis of the consciousness-raising group, Trevisan identified an important source of tension that was to continue and ultimately divide the first successfully organized group in São Paulo: while one perspective within the group favored a movement that focused only on gay issues, another trend defended alliances between gay groups and other social movements, including sectors of the left.

Trevisan and other homosexuals who had reservations about the left were justified in many of their concerns. The Brazilian Communist Party was the hegemonic leftist organization until the early sixties and had tremendous influence among Brazilian intellectuals and artists. It maintained the traditional Stalinist position that homosexuality was a product of bourgeois decadence. The Communist Party was fractured by the 1962 Sino-Soviet dispute and post-1964 internal fights about whether or not to support armed struggle against the dictatorship, but the ideological aversion to homosexuality remained a constant in all of the organizations that emerged out of the Partidão (the big Party).[111] Many militants or supporters of the left suffered social ostracism when they came out to their comrades about their own sexual desires. The negative experiences of Aguinaldo Silva, an editor of Lampião, with the Communist Party and other sectors of the left in the 1960s, for example, led him to criticize any relationship of leftist organizations with the incipient movement.[112] Herbert Daniel, who joined a guerrilla group in the 1960s, found that the homophobia within the organization was intolerable.[113] Fernando Gabeira, although himself not gay-identified, criticized the antifeminist and antigay position of many leftist organizations, which he experienced while living among the exile community in Europe after he had been banished from the country for being involved in the kidnapping of the United States ambassador in 1969.[114]

Trevisan's group only stayed together for a few meetings, but a second attempt at forming a politically focused gay group took place in Rio de Janeiro at about the same time. On July 1, 1976, an activist distributed an invitation in some gay meeting places and to the press announcing a social gathering of the União do Homossexual Brasileiro (Union of the Brazilian Homosexuals), which was to be held three days later in the gardens of the Museum of Modern Art. The leaflet read in part:

> *Day of the Homosexual*
> ... On this occasion, besides socializing, we will have the opportunity to get to know the profile of the struggle that we are involved in for the rights of the Brazilian homosexual for a dignified and respectable life. Come and bring your lover. If you are a poet, bring your poetry. If you are a musician (composer) bring your work. If you are a supporter, bring your smile and an embrace for an unattached friend. Long live the Union of the Brazilian Homosexual. For better opportunities and equal opportunities. Long live July 4. Happiness. Love. Respect.[115]

It is possible that the anonymous author of the leaflet scheduled the event on July 4 because this date was close to the Stonewall commemorations, which were celebrated in the United States and other parts of the world around June 28. The invitation used language reminiscent of the student movement, which had emerged from underground activity the previous year, but the slogans had a less confrontational thrust. The tone of the leaflet communicated both caution and a desire to create a movement built on equality and mutual respect.

On July 4, as reporters gathered to cover the event, eight arrest vans and seventy men from the General Department of Special Investigation surrounded the museum. Individuals who might have approached the area to attend the meeting no doubt were discouraged by such a daunting police response.[116] The gathering did not take place, and the effort to mobilize Rio de Janeiro's homosexuals failed. The official reaction to the attempt to organize a gay activist group indicated that the government still viewed any political or semipolitical public events as potentially subversive. While homosexuals could congregate in the discotheques on Saturday night, coming together in a public space to demand political goals, such as equality, dignity, and respect, was a challenge to the regime. In the early days of political liberalization, democratic activities of this sort were still blocked before they had any chance of success.

A year later the political climate had improved significantly. In late 1977, Winston Leyland, the editor of the San Francisco–based Gay Sunshine Press, came to Brazil to collect material for an anthology of gay Latin American literature. João Antônio Mascarenhas, who hosted him in Rio de

Janeiro, took advantage of Leyland's visit to organize a series of interviews with the press, in which the publisher talked about the international gay rights movement. The press coverage was extensive and extremely positive.[117] Leyland's visit catalyzed the group of intellectuals who met with him. They decided to form an editorial collective and publish a newspaper for homosexuals that would be a vehicle for discussions on sexuality, racial discrimination, the arts, ecology, and machismo. The editorial of the first issue, entitled "Out of the Ghetto," began: "Brazil, March 1978. Favorable winds blow in the direction of a degree of liberalization on the national front: an election year, the press reports promises of a less rigid Executive, there is talk of the formation of new political parties, of amnesty; an investigation of the proposed alternatives indicates even an 'openness' in Brazilian discourse. But why a homosexual journal?" The editors then argued for the need to break out of the isolation of the restrictive ghetto in which Brazilian homosexuals circulated as well as to break down the social stereotypes associated with homosexuality.[118] Aguinaldo Silva, the leading force behind this effort, explained the plan for the new journal as a response to the difficult problems that homosexuals faced: "[A] majority of homosexuals, trying to navigate through repression, lead an 'abnormal' life, because one cannot lead a normal life in a semi-rotten society like ours. But at least they try to live exactly like other people—that is, 'fighting' to survive on a day-to-day basis."[119]

The newspaper was named *Lampião da Esquina*. The title, which literally meant "lantern, or lamppost, on the corner," suggested gay street life. It also referred to a historic personage, Lampião, a Robin Hood figure who had roamed the Brazilian Northeast in the early twentieth century. The editorial board of *Lampião* included well-known names from academic circles, such as anthropologist Peter Fry and Jean-Claude Bernadete, who worked in film studies. Painter and writer Darcy Penteado joined the monthly, as did activist intellectuals such as João Antônio Mascarenhas and João S. Trevisan. Several professional journalists also brought important practical experience in newspaper production to this new endeavor. With capital raised by a fundraising letter sent to "friends and friends of friends," *Lampião* started with a circulation of more than ten thousand per issue and was sold in newsstands all over the country. The tabloid-sized paper published short stories, essays, news of the international gay and lesbian movement, information about bars and cruising sites, and notices of events that might interest a gay readership. With experienced writers and financial resources, the editors produced a quality journal. Although *Lampião* initially presented itself as a journal that would bring together women, blacks, the ecology movement, and homosexuals, it remained largely directed to a male homosexual audience. It did, however, run feature interviews with figures who discussed the feminist movement, the black consciousness movement, lesbianism, and other social and cultural issues that were debated in Brazil at the time.[120]

The first issue of *Lampião da Esquina* came out in April 1978. The cover story featured an article about Celso Curi, the pioneering gay columnist for *Última Hora*. The previous year, the military government had charged Curi with violating article 17 of the press law. Among the charges leveled against the young journalist were the following: "In a continuous manner between February 5 and May 18, 1976, he offended public morality and propriety in the 'Coluna do Meio,' whose name left no doubt as to the subject dealt with, [namely] homosexuality which is clearly praised; [he also] defended abnormal unions of members of the same sex, even promoting them through the section 'Correio Elegante.'"[121] The editors of *Lampião* used the first issue of the paper to defend Curi and to argue that the case against him dramatized the need to have an organized movement, whose goal should be to defend individuals against arbitrary antigay actions by the government and to fight homophobic attitudes in Brazilian society in general.

Soon after *Lampião* appeared on newsstands across the country, a dozen gay men in São Paulo organized a group that evolved into Brazil's first lasting and successful gay liberation organization. The group initially called itself Núcleo de Ação pelos Direitos dos Homossexuais (Action Nucleus for Homosexuals' Rights), and in its first stage it acted as a consciousness-raising group like the one that Trevisan had organized in 1976. It later developed subgroups, which carried out activities ranging from political campaigns to discussion sessions. During the first six months of the group's existence, its size remained small, consisting of fifteen to twenty individuals, mostly men. Membership remained fluid as people moved in and out of the small organization.

As 1978 came to an end, the group's name became a heated topic of debate. Did the name, Action Nucleus for Homosexuals' Rights, discourage new members from joining the group because of its bold political agenda? Some members speculated that the activist tone of the group's name was the reason why only a dozen people came to a given meeting. Others suggested that people were afraid to join a semisecret group. Some proposed changing the name of the group to Somos (We Are), in homage to the short-lived publication put out by the Argentine Homosexual Liberation Front, which came to life in Buenos Aires in 1971 and disappeared in 1976 during the long night of the military dictatorship. Others wanted a name that clearly expressed the purpose of the organization and offered the suggestion Grupo de Afirmação Homossexual (Group of Homosexual Affirmation). Designations that included the word "gay" were roundly rejected because, participants argued, they imitated the movement in the United States.[122] The consensus was that a unique Brazilian movement needed to be forged. The borrowing of foreign terms, it was reasoned, might jeopardize this effort. The group finally reached a compromise and renamed itself Somos: Grupo de Afirmação Homossexual.

On February 6, 1979, Somos members attended a public debate at the University of São Paulo. The event was part of a four-day series of discussions on organizing Brazil's "minorities"—women, blacks, Indians, and homosexuals. The program on homosexuals featured a panel of speakers, including editors of the journal *Lampião* and members of Somos. More than three hundred people packed the auditorium to attend the roundtable talk, which turned into a "coming out" event for the Brazilian gay and lesbian movement. The discussion following the panelists' presentations was electric, as charges and countercharges between representatives of leftist student groups and gay and lesbian speakers crisscrossed the assembly room. For the first time, lesbians spoke openly in public about the discrimination they encountered. Gay students complained that the Brazilian left was homophobic. Left-wing students who defended Fidel Castro and the Cuban Revolution argued that fighting against specific issues, such as sexism, racism, and homophobia, would divide the growing movement against the military regime. They maintained that people should unite in a general struggle against the dictatorship.[123] The first controversy in the emergent Brazilian gay rights movement was dividing along the same lines that had paralyzed Trevisan's discussion group two and a half years earlier. Over the next year as new groups sprung up both in São Paulo and in other cities, gay and lesbian activists would continue to debate whether to build an autonomous movement independent of the social forces mobilized against the military regime or to forge links with these new social movements.[124] As a result of debates and discussions surrounding this and other issues related to homosexuality, initiated in large part by gay and lesbian activists, psychiatrists, sexologists, and academics began publishing more favorable material about same-sex relations in the press and in professional journals.[125] Instead of relying on the medicolegal writings of the 1930s and '40s, these authors in general presented the idea that homosexuality was merely one of many different possible sexual behaviors and not pathological.[126]

With Somos's new public profile and the formation of similar groups around the country, the Brazilian government moved against *Lampião*. Since August 1978, the paper had been the subject of a police inquiry on a charge of offending "public morality." A leaked government document revealed that the military intended to shut down the publication either through a provision of the press law or a financial audit. In early 1979, the military accused *Lampião* editors of committing offenses against "morality and propriety" that could result in imprisonment for up to a year. Intellectuals, cultural and artistic figures, the journalists' union, and the Brazilian Press Association denounced the government's measures. Somos members, in one of the their first acts of political activism, formed a committee in defense of *Lampião* that circulated a petition protesting the military's action. Eventually, the dictatorship ended the financial audit and dropped charges against the editors of the gay press.[127]

In April 1980, activists from eight groups met in São Paulo for the First National Gathering of Organized Homosexual Groups. A thousand lesbians and gay men packed the Ruth Escobar Theater near downtown São Paulo to attend an indoor closing ceremony of the event. Several weeks later, on May 1, International Workers Day, a contingent of fifty openly gay men and lesbians marched together with hundreds of thousands of other Brazilians through the downtown working-class neighborhood of São Bernardo in the nation's industrial center. They had come to support a general strike of São Paulo–area unionists, whose work stoppage had provoked a government-ordered state of siege by the Second Army. The gay and lesbian activists marched behind a banner boldly demanding: "Stop Discrimination against Homosexual Workers." A leaflet distributed by the contingent linked the struggle of the strikers with that of the oppressed (blacks, women, and homosexuals), pointed to instances of job discrimination, and called on the unity of the working class to end such practices.[128] When the contingent moved into the local soccer stadium to participate in the rally at the end of the march, thousands of bystanders welcomed them with applause.

Despite the fact that a sector of the gay and lesbian movement was beginning to build links with the left and other forces opposed to the military regime, the state apparently paid little attention to the movement after it failed to shut down *Lampião*. A survey of the files of both Rio de Janeiro's and São Paulo's Delegacia de Ordem Política e Social (DOPS), the political police charged with the surveillance of "subversive" elements, reveals that this repressive apparatus, at least, largely ignored gay and lesbian activists. The DOPS files, opened to researchers in 1994, contain documents of some of *Lampião*'s editors, but they relate to those individuals' links to left organizations in the 1960s or to the movement against the dictatorship in the 1970s without any reference to the person's homosexuality or to gay and lesbian activism.[129] Perhaps the political police were too involved in keeping up with the explosive dynamic of the labor movement, which was threatening to topple the military's plans for a gradual liberalization, to follow closely a movement still small in numbers and without a clearly articulated political agenda. In examining the police files of this period, one also gets the impression that the infiltrators and informants who supplied information to DOPS could barely follow the array of demonstrations, protests, public meetings, student organizations, and strikes that characterized the period. Whatever the reason, the newly formed gay and lesbian movement seems to have been largely overlooked by the repressive arm of the state.

If the political police had have been closely accompanying the moves of gay and lesbian activists, they would have noted the fallout from the participation of fifty members and supporters of Somos in the May Day protests. The decision to march in the May 1 demonstration had not been unanimous, and it further increased the growing tension within the nascent movement. That issue, and the larger debate over whether or not to work with sectors of the Brazilian left, soon divided Somos irreparably. A minority, who were opposed to any collaboration with leftist forces, left Somos and formed another group, Outra Coisa (Something Else).

While the division in the emerging movement was fiercely debated in the pages of *Lampião*, a police roundup of more than fifteen hundred gay men, transvestites, and prostitutes in downtown São Paulo designed to "clean up" the area reunited the divergent forces. On June 13, 1980, five hundred people gathered on the steps of the Municipal Theater, a traditional free-speech area, to protest the arrests that had taken place the previous month. As a light mist began to fall, activists called for the removal of the police chief and urged the rally to march through the streets of São Paulo. After a number of brief speeches by Darcy Penteado and other public figures, the crowd wove through the center of São Paulo protesting the arbitrary arrests and chanting: "Abaixo a Repressão, Mais Amor e Mais Tesão" (Down with Repression, More Love and More Desire). A movement had been born.[130]

Conclusion

~

Gay tourists visiting Rio de Janeiro today for Carnival celebrations would be disappointed by a visit to Praça Tiradentes, the historic cruising ground where Carioca men have sought same-sex erotic adventures since at least the 1870s. The bronze statue to Emperor Dom Pedro I still graces the center of the square, but most of the surrounding belle époque buildings have either fallen into disrepair or have been replaced by ugly modern structures. The city government has erected a metal fence around the plaza to prevent homeless people from sleeping there at night. Few trees or other greenery decorate the desolate open space. Across from the João Caetano Theater a handful of *travestis*, who have clearly seen better times, lean against lampposts and stand in doorways soliciting customers in the middle of the day. Masses of poor and working-class people move quickly around the plaza to catch buses or to shop in the jumble of stores selling cheap clothes and other inexpensive consumer items. Several rundown turn-of-the-century hotels still offer rented rooms by the hour for furtive sexual liaisons; but other than the *travestis* clustered on one street corner, few signs of the plaza's past as a site of homoerotic interactions remain. Riotour, the government agency promoting tourism, does not even direct gay visitors to Praça Tiradentes in its Carnival brochures. This official state body does refer to the presence of homosexual men in Rio but points gay tourists to the middle- and upper-class neighborhoods of Copacabana and Ipanema and mentions several different gay balls to choose from among the array of celebrations taking place during Carnival. If Praça Tiradentes was once a singularly privileged place for homoerotic adventures, now Rio de Janeiro boasts dozens of bars, restaurants, and clubs that service a gay clien-

279

tele in several neighborhoods throughout the city. The former Largo do Rossio is a faint memory of the past, but gay life is alive and well, even serving as an attraction for the international tourist industry.

Likewise, if one were to meander through São Paulo across the bridge that links the historic center to other parts of the downtown area, the Anhangabaú ravine below the pedestrian walkway would hardly seem to be a site that once hosted nocturnal rendezvous of *bichas* and their willing partners. Several generations of urban renovations have stripped the rolling landscaped park of of its former beauty and elegance. Just as Praça Tiradentes is no longer fixed in the popular imagination as a public space where men engage in "immoral acts" with each other at night, so too Anhangabaú Valley is not even remembered by middle-aged gay Paulistas as a traditional cruising ground.

The relocation of public spaces appropriated for homoerotic sociability, however, is not merely a function of urban decay and the emergence of new, more modern sites that can accommodate a middle-class gay consumer-oriented crowd. Rather, the marked expansion of homosexual topography reflects a much more open and visible presence of gay men in both Rio de Janeiro and São Paulo. Although clearly delineated gay neighborhoods have not developed, many different sites in both cities have become meeting spots for homoerotic encounters. These public social spaces have been essential for the development of multiple forms of same-sex erotic sociability throughout the twentieth century. Even though the most obvious function of these places has been to facilitate encounters of men seeking sexual partners, they have served a variety of other purposes as well. During the twentieth century, park benches in the Vale de Anhangabaú and Cinelândia, sections of the beaches of Copacabana and Ipanema, Miss Brazil beauty pageants, the auditoria of Radio Nacional, numerous Carioca and Paulista movie houses, and Carnival celebrations have provided endless opportunities for men to meet other men, not just for sex but to build networks of friends and acquaintances. These ties have provided *bichas, bonecas, entendidos,* and other gay men support systems essential for survival in a society that has been hostile to men—effeminate or otherwise—who did not conform to heteronormative social and sexual expectations.

As suggested throughout this work, men who sought out sexual relationships with other men have had to negotiate around the Brazilian family structure, which despite modernization and urbanization remains the mainstay of Brazilian society, providing significant support for its members and cushioning them from harsh economic and social realities. For many, the tension between belonging to a semi-clandestine sexual and social subculture on one hand and maintaining a close relationship to one's family on the other has been solved by leading a complex double life. The hostility of family members toward manifestations of effeminacy, the discovery by relatives of one's secret life, or the fear of revelation have all prompted an array of responses. Many young men moved out of their parents' homes before marrying or relocated in large urban centers to escape the day-to-day control of their families without having to cut off ties with relatives. Rather, they sought ways to keep unsupportive or hostile family members at a distance. The alternative family structures and support networks these young men created as they integrated into the homosexual subcultures of Rio and São Paulo became the fundamental means by which many managed to survive and thrive without close family ties. Over the years, these alternative families have grown into a community, which now offers gay men in Rio de Janeiro and São Paulo a variety of social options and support mechanisms ranging from bars and clubs to newspapers, magazines, and activist organizations.

Significantly, and as we have seen throughout this study, a same-sex erotic subculture existed in Rio de Janeiro prior to the invention of the term homosexual and the importation of European medical models that cataloged sexual "pathologies" and "deviant" behaviors. For much of the twentieth century, the dominant gender paradigm that shaped this subculture organized itself along traditional notions of appropriate masculine and feminine comportment. Nevertheless, it is important to point out that the fluidity of sexual desires, identity, and erotic practices transgressed the norms that divided same-gender sexuality along active/passive lines and that is commonly ascribed, incorrectly, to same-sex behavior prior to the 1960s and gay liberation. Long before the term came into widespread use in the 1980s to signify sexual practices by two men who did not identify with the *bicha*/"real" man construct, people were building "gay" relationships. Multiple sexual systems have coexisted and interacted throughout much of the century, and historians should beware of identifying the allegedly more egalitarian model of same-sex activity with progress.

This work ends with the emergence of a Brazilian gay and lesbian rights movement at the end of the 1970s. The history of that movement has yet to be written. Yet one observation about the politicized movement is in order. Suggesting the course of historical events that *might have* taken place is a risky enterprise. It nevertheless seems clear that had the Brazilian military government not unleashed a wave of repression, expanded censorship, and restricted fundamental democratic rights in late 1968 with the imposition of Institutional Act No. 5 and other measures, a politicized gay and lesbian rights movement may well have emerged in the early 1970s. Such a movement developed in Argentina with the founding of Nuestro Mundo (Our World) in November 1969 and the Argentine Homosexual Liberation Front in 1971. Likewise, gay and lesbian rights groups formed in Mexico and Puerto Rico, two other semi-industrialized and semi-urbanized countries, in the same period. Although these organizations were influenced by the international lesbian and gay movement that developed in the United States and Western Europe in the 1970s, they remained rooted in and were shaped by their particular national realities. Certainly the conditions were ripe in Brazil by the late 1960s for similar developments. Urbanization, modernization, and industrialization had contributed to the formation of vibrant subcultures in Rio de Janeiro, São Paulo, and other major cities. Same-sex erotic sociability took place in multiple sites, from public spaces in parks, cinemas, and other cruising areas to gay-oriented businesses, bars, and clubs. The process of the formation of distinct identities within these subcultures included numerous cultural expressions, among them the publication of home-crafted newsletters, an increasingly visible presence during Carnival, and a myriad other manifestations of collective interactions. Moreover, in spite of government censorship, the countercultural influences that permeated the youth and student movements in the 1960s encouraged a limited discussion in society and in the media about sexuality, gender roles, and homosexuality. Even with the military's draconian measures, publications in the early 1970s managed to write about "Gay Power" and suggest avenues for the political organization of homosexuals. When the military regime resolved to head off a social explosion by implementing a gradual process of political liberalization in the mid-1970s, groups immediately came together to challenge hegemonic notions of homosexuality as perverted and sick behavior. Although the groups that formed in the late 1970s onward have not developed into mass movements, they have managed to provoke national debates on issues such as domestic partnership benefits, civil marriage, and social violence against homosexuals.

Given the fact that Brazil has long been a Catholic country, one might ask why the church has not played a more aggressive public role in opposing manifestations of homosexuality over most of the twentieth century? In part this is due to the fact that until recently, no social actors had articulated a position that homosexuality was a positive and healthy form of sexuality. Physicians and other medicolegal experts who published extensively on the subject in the 1930s and early 1940s, as well as sexologists and psychologists who continued to write about homosexuality in the post–World War II period, relied on Catholic teachings about the immorality of same-sex eroticism as a backdrop to their arguments for more "tolerant" social attitudes toward the depraved individuals about whom they wrote. Confessors instructed their parishioners about the sinfulness of homosexuality, reinforcing pervasive social norms and encouraging deep feelings of guilt among adolescents and adults who felt sexual desire toward people of the same gender. Priests who were caught transgressing church rules were quietly disciplined and removed from positions before public scandals might erupt. Traditional Christian teachings condemning homosexuality as sinful or immoral permeated Brazilian society and remained the hegemonic discourse until gay and lesbian activists, along with a few psychologists and sexologists, challenged this predominant perspective in the late 1970s.

In recent years, the dramatic growth of Evangelical and Pentecostal forms of Christianity has injected a new player into Brazil's religious landscape. The fundamentalist beliefs of these Protestant groups have strengthened the traditional antihomosexual discourse of the Catholic Church. In the late 1980s, Evangelical Christian legislators united with those who espouse established Catholic teaching against homosexuality to oppose a constitutional amendment prohibiting discrimination based on sexual orientation. In the 1990s, this coalition continued to block legislative proposals in favor of domestic partnership benefits. The Afro-Brazilian religion Candomblé seems to have provided the only alternative spiritual, social, and religious environment for homosexuals until the recent formation of gay religious groups. Pioneering research by anthropologists about homosexuality and Candomblé needs to be supplemented by further investigation in order to understand the historical roots and factors that have contributed to its apparent toleration toward homosexuality.

Just as influential as the Catholic tradition, the overall racial hierarchy of Brazilian society has defined the contours of the urban subcultures described throughout this study. Overlapping racial and class cleavages characteristic of the general society have also been reflected in the social interactions of Brazilian homosexuals. While middle-class men of European ancestry may have enjoyed temporary sexual liaisons with lower-class men of mixed racial or African backgrounds, these relationships tended to be organized around economic and social status and power. Thus, a comfortably positioned Paulista might hire a male hustler from a working-class family for a night of sex, but the social gulf between them would likely preclude a lasting relationship. If the mutual exchange of sex for financial support proved agreeable for a period of time, the hierarchical class dynamics would almost inevitably persist despite the intimacy of the two individuals. The pervasive national beliefs that Brazilians are not racist and that the country is built upon the foundations of a racial democracy merely submerge any recognition of the ways that skin color can determine social positioning. Although sexual and social interactions between members of different racial and socioeconomic groups have occurred, sharp class divisions and a racial hierarchy have precluded substantial integration.

As more gay-oriented consumer options became available in the 1960s and '70s, the social and economic tensions within the homosexual subcultures of Rio de Janeiro and São Paulo merely mirrored general social trends. Currently, mostly white, middle-class homosexuals have more access to the new moneyed gay economy and can enjoy the wide range of social options available, while Brazilians of lower-class backgrounds, many of whom are of African descent, still find themselves with far fewer opportunities to circulate in the gay world. Whereas middle-class men can develop a certain autonomy from the restrictive aspects of family life, poorer Brazilians still rely much more on the family structure to survive, although the pressure to marry and have children remains a constant on members of all social classes.

In June 1995, over three hundred delegates representing gay and lesbian groups in sixty countries of Asia, Europe, North America, Central America, the Caribbean, and South America gathered in Rio de Janeiro to attend the week-long Seventeenth Annual Conference of the International Lesbian and Gay Association (ILGA). Marching along Atlantic Avenue, the boulevard that borders the shining white sands of Copacabana Beach, delegates and two thousand gay and lesbian supporters ended the convention by celebrating the twenty-sixth anniversary of the 1969 New York Stonewall Rebellion, the beginning of gay liberation in the United States. A 25-foot-wide yellow banner demanding "Full Citizenship for Gays, Lesbians, and Transvestites" led the parade. A contingent of women followed, carrying signs advocating "Lesbian Visibility," which drew applause from observers. Drag queens teased and flirted with onlookers from atop a pink-hued "Priscilla" school bus and two large sound trucks, lent by the bank workers' union. Many participants dressed in carnivalesque masques and costumes. A 125-meter-long rainbow flag billowed in the wind. At the end of the march, people tearfully sang the national anthem and lingered until a light rain dispersed the crowd.

In August 1964, "Gigi Bryant," one of the members of the social network that edited *O Snob,* concluded a seven-part series on the "art of cruising." In one of her articles, she described Maracanãzinho, the large arena where events such as Holiday on Ice and the Miss Brazil beauty pageant took place. After ridiculing members of the groups who had attended shows there, Gigi joked that "since the faggot top-set is converging on Maracanãzinho, it's likely to become the social center of various social classes in the future." What's more she teased, "Indeed, it is very possible that in better days the First Festival of *Entendidos* will take place there with representatives from other nations converging on our country. That would generate lots of publicity and be a grand utopia."[1]

In 1964, Gigi's predictions were good for a laugh. Yet thirty years later, her remarks have proved remarkably prescient.

Notes

Introduction

1. A *banana da terra* is a large banana from northeast Brazil. In this film Carmen Miranda first appeared in a costume that would be her trademark, singing "O que é que a bahiana tem?" (What is it that the Bahiana woman has?). The film premiered in the Metro-Passeio Movie House in downtown Rio de Janeiro on February 10, 1939, immediately before Carnival festivities of that year.

2. For an analysis of the Afro-Brazilian influences on Carmen Miranda's performances, see Zeca Ligiéro, "Carmen Miranda: An Afro-Brazilian Paradox" (Ph.D. diss., New York University, 1998).

3. Martha Gil-Montero, *Brazilian Bombshell: The Biography of Carmen Miranda* (New York: Donald I. Fine, 1989), 152–53.

4. See Roberto DaMatta, *Carnivals, Rogues, and Heroes: An Interpretation of the Brazilian Dilemma,* trans. John Drury (Notre Dame: University of Notre Dame Press, 1991), 85–87; the chapter "The Carnivalization of the World," in Richard Parker, *Bodies, Pleasures, and Passions: Sexual Culture in Contemporary Brazil* (Boston: Beacon Press, 1991), 136–64; and chapter 5, "The Homosexual Appropriation of Brazilian Carnival."

5. Geraldo Pereira's popular song "Falsa baiana" distinguished the "real" and the "false" *baiana* by the former's ability to samba in such a way that she left everyone desiring her. The *falsa baiana* provoked no such response. The ambiguity of gender blending during Carnival and the erotic pleasures derived from the knowledge that a man is dressed as a sexually provocative woman is discussed in chapter 5. Based on pictures of Carnival cross-dressing in the 1920s and '30s, the *falsa baiana* seemed aimed more at camp-laced gender parody than at an attempt to evoke sexual desire.

6. Sherna Gluck helped me clarify this contradictory phenomenon.

7. During World War II, Hollywood movie moguls, with the backing of the Roosevelt administration's Good Neighbor Policy, used the Brazilian singer to repackage and market a mythical image of Latin American women and culture in the name of garnering support in Latin America and among North American audiences for the United States government's war policies. For an overview of Hollywood's treatment of Brazil in this period, see Sérgio Augusto, "Hollywood Looks at Brazil: From Carmen Miranda to Moonraker," in *Brazilian Cinema,* ed.

Randal Johnson and Robert Stam (New York: Columbia University Press, 1995), 51–61; Allen L. Woll, *The Latin Image in American Film* (Los Angeles: UCLA Press, 1977); and Martha Gil-Montero's discussion about the role of Carmen Miranda in the plans of the Motion Picture Section of the State Department's Office of the Coordinator of Inter-American Affairs in *Brazilian Bombshell*, 110–26.

8. To cite one example, the San Francisco *Beach Blanket Babylon* production features characters who mount on their heads ever higher, gaudier, and more comical fruits and other objects in turbans and wigs in a direct reference to the Miranda look. While the production has attracted a large gay following in its more than twenty-year run, it is also popular among a wider audience. The City of San Francisco has even named a small street in honor of this camp theater review.

9. The Banda de Ipanema, founded in 1966, was one of several attempts in the post-1964 military coup d'état period to revitalize street Carnival and return to the practice of street revelry. The *banda* organizers would choose a given year's theme song and hire a percussion band to lead thousands in slow syncopated sambaing through the streets of Ipanema, the upper-middle-class neighborhood and home of bossa nova as well as Brazilian bohemia from the 1950s through the 1970s. The Banda de Carmen Miranda split from the Banda de Ipanema in 1984. See "Ipanema cria Banda Carmen Miranda," *O Globo* (Rio de Janeiro), December 15, 1984, 12.

10. In June 1995, lesbian and gay activists gave this carnivalesque tradition a more political focus by organizing the March for Full Citizenship. Using Brazilian Carnival music and motifs, more than two thousand people paraded along Copacabana's Avenida Atlântica for the closing event of the Eighteenth Annual Conference of the International Gay and Lesbian Association, held that year in Rio de Janeiro. To long-time organizers involved in the lesbian and gay rights groups since the early 1980s, the march symbolized the maturation of the movement and the wedding of the political with the festive in a typically Brazilian combination (Marisa Fernandes, Luis R. B. Mott, Wilson da Silva, interview by author, tape recording, Rio de Janeiro, June 25, 1995). Likewise, Brazilian camp has permeated the gay movement in the United States. AIDS activists in San Francisco, for example, have embraced the image of Carmen Miranda, complete with exaggerated platform shoes, gaudy jewelry, and improbable headdresses, to parade through the city's gay neighborhoods as "Condom Mirandas," distributing foiled prophylactics to amused and bemused passersby.

11. Pat Rocco, *Marco of Rio*, 16 mm, Bizarre Productions, Los Angeles, 1970.

12. Kristen Bjorn, *Carnival in Rio*, Kristen Bjorn Productions, Miami Beach, 1989. Other Bjorn films set in tropical Brazil include *Tropical Heat Wave* (1990), *Jungle Heat* (1993), *Paradise Plantation* (1994), *A World of Men* (1995), and *Amazon Adventure* (1996).

13. An excellent example of the conflation of Brazilian homosexuality with Carnival in Rio de Janeiro is Júlio Gomes, *A homossexualidade no mundo* (Lisboa: by the author, 1979), 153–92.

14. See Parker, *Bodies, Pleasures, and Passions*, 85–95 and 136–64. At least one empirical study conducted in 1973 indicated that Brazilians were less tolerant about homosexuality that popular images might indicate. Interviewing 112 students in the northeastern city of Campina Grande, Paraíba, the study found that Brazilians were more prejudiced against homosexuality than Canadians and assigned much higher probabilities to a "feminine" male being homosexual than the Canadian subjects did (John Dunbar, Marvin Brown, and Sophie Vuorinen, "Attitudes toward Homosexuality among Brazilian and Canadian College Students," *Journal of Social Psychology* 90 [1973]: 173–83).

15. According to the poll, in the Northeast the level of nonacceptance of a son going out with a gay friend increased to 87 percent ("O mundo gay rasga as fantasias," *Veja*, 12 May 1993, 52–53).

16. Luiz R. B. Mott, *Epidemic of Hate: Violations of the Human Rights of Gay Men, Lesbians, and Transvestites in Brazil* (San Francisco: Grupo Gay da Bahia / International Gay and Lesbian Human Rights Commission, 1996), 1.

17. A case study of several of these murders that took place in São Paulo is Antônio Sergio Spagnol, "O desejo marginal: Violência nas relações homossexuais na cidade de São Paulo" (master's thesis, Universidade de São Paulo, 1996). For a journalistic account of the 1987–88 wave of murders of homosexuals in Rio de Janeiro and São Paulo, see Márcio Venciguerra and Maurício Maia, *O pecado de Adão: Crimes homossexuais no eixo Rio–São Paulo* (São Paulo: Ícone, 1988). For other examples of violence against gay men in Rio de Janeiro in the late 1960s and '70s, see also Luiz Carlos Machado, *Descansa em paz: Oscar Wilde* (Rio de Janeiro: Editora Codecri, 1982).

18. Toni Reis, interview by author, tape recording, Curitiba, Paraná, January 20, 1995.

19. Adauto Belarmino Alves, interview by author, tape recording, Rio de Janeiro, July 18, 1995.

20. U.S. Congress, House, Senate, Committee on Foreign Relations and International Relations, *Country Reports on Human Rights Practices for 1993*, prepared by the Department of State. 103d Cong., 2d sess., Joint Comm. Print, 1994, 376.

21. U.S. Congress, House, Senate, Committee on Foreign Relations and International Relations, *Country Report on Human Rights Practices for 1996*, prepared by the Department of State, 105th Cong., 1st sess., 1997, Joint Comm. Print, 372–73; U.S. Congress, House, Senate, Committee on Foreign Relations and International Relations, *Country Report on Human Rights Practices for 1995*, prepared by the Department of State, 104th Cong., 2d sess., 1996, Joint Committee Print, 1996, 348; U.S. Congress, House, Senate Committee on Foreign Relations and International Relations, *Country Reports on Human Rights Practices for 1993*, prepared by the Department of State, 103rd Cong., 2d sess, 1994, Joint Committee Print, 376; Amnesty International USA, *Breaking the Silence: Human Rights Violations Based on Sexual Orientation* (New York: Amnesty International Publications, 1994), 13–14; Dignidade, Grupo de Conscientização e Emancipação Homossexual, *News from Brazil*, no. 2 (June 1994): 2–3; "Reclamando nossos direitos," *Jornal Folha de Parreira* (Curitiba) 3, no. 25 (May 1995): 2.

22. Grupo Gay da Bahia, "Violação dos direitos humanos e assassinato de homossexuais no Brasil—1997," *Boletim do Grupo Gay da Bahia*, no. 37 (January / February 1998): 32–48.

23. Brazilian Marcelo Tenório, at the time a thirty-year-old house painter living in San Francisco, was the first person to be granted political asylum in the United States for fear of persecution based on sexual orientation (James Brooke, "In Live-and-Let-Live Land, Gay People Are Slain," *New York Times*, August 12, 1993, 3).

24. The debate about whether or not Brazil is a racial democracy has a long history reaching back to the 1930s. Giberto Freyre's classic work, *Casa grande e senzala* (1933) subsequently published in 1946 in English as *The Masters and the Slaves: A Study in the Development of Brazilian Civilization* (Berkeley: University of California Press, 1986), challenged dominant notions of the Brazilian elite about the inferiority of African-Brazilians and people of mixed racial descent. Freyre argued that the legacy of colonial patterns of miscegenation engendered social toleration among those of African, Portuguese, and Indian backgrounds that was quite different from forms of racial discrimination he observed while studying in the United States in the 1910s and 1930s. Freyre also insisted that the sensuality, licentiousness, and promiscuity of Portuguese male colonists that led to sexual liaisons with African and indigenous women set the patterns for libertine elements in contemporary Brazilian culture. In conflating racial toleration and sexual dissoluteness, he outlined the framework for most of the commonly accepted assumptions in Brazil about the national attitudes toward race and sex. Since the 1960s, scholars have meticu-

lously criticized Freyre's notions of the Brazilian propensity for racial toleration, yet his theories about sexual permissiveness have received much less questioning. See Jeffrey D. Needell, "Identity, Race, Gender, and Modernity in the Origins of Gilberto Freyre's *Ouvre*," *American Historical Review* 100, no. 1 (February 1995): 51–77. For a discussion of late-nineteenth- and early-twentieth-century Brazilian elite notions of race, see Thomas E. Skidmore, *Black into White: Race and Nationality in Brazilian Thought* (Durham: Duke University Press, 1993), and Dain Borges, *The Family in Bahia, Brazil, 1870–1945* (Stanford: Stanford University Press, 1992). Among the works challenging Freyre's thesis about racial toleration in Brazil are Carl N. Degler, *Neither Black nor White: Slavery and Race Relations in Brazil and the United States* (Madison: University of Wisconsin Press, 1971); Robert Edgar Conrad, *Children of God's Fire: A Documentary History of Black Slavery in Brazil* (Princeton: Princeton University Press, 1984); George Reid Andrews, *Blacks and Whites in São Paulo, Brazil, 1888–1988* (Madison: University of Wisconsin Press, 1991); and Pierre-Michel Fontaine, ed. *Race, Class, and Power in Brazil* (Los Angeles: Center for Afro-American Studies, 1985). Emília Viotti da Costa perceptively explains how the myth of racial democracy found resonance among the Brazilian elite and even Afro-Brazilians in the 1930s and '40s and points to reasons why there was a shift in perceptions in Brazil from the 1960s on. See Emília Viotti da Costa, "The Myth of Racial Democracy: A Legacy of the Empire," in *the Brazilian Empire: Myths and Histories* (Chicago: University of Chicago Press, 1985), 234–46.

25. João Carlos Rodrigues, *João do Rio: Uma biografia* (Rio de Janeiro: Topbooks, 1995), 255.

26. Parker, *Bodies, Pleasures, and Passions*, 41. Much of Parker's theoretical models have been inspired by the pioneering work of Peter Fry, a British anthropologist and longtime resident of Brazil who initiated the academic study of homosexuality and Brazilian gender systems in the mid-1970s. See Peter Fry, *Para inglês ver: Identidade e política na cultura brasileira* (Rio de Janeiro: Zahar Editores, 1982); and Peter Fry and Edward MacRae, *O que é homossexualidade* (São Paulo: Editora Brasiliense, 1983). See also Richard Parker, *Beneath the Equator: Cultures of Desire, Male Homosexuality, and Emerging Gay Commmunities in Brazil* (New York: Routledge, 1999).

27. See Michel Misse, *O estigma do passivo sexual: Um símbolo de estigma no discurso cotidiano* (Rio de Janeiro: Achiamé, 1979). Anthropologist Steven O. Murray has questioned the assertion that as long as "real" men don't transgress their ascribed gender role, they maintain their social status. He argues that forays into same-sex sexual activities by men who take the penetrating role may not be as sanction-free as some have observed. See "Machismo, Male Homosexuality, and Latin Culture," in *Latin American Male Homosexualities*, ed. Stephen O. Murray (Albuquerque: University of New Mexico Press, 1995), 59.

28. Fry, "Homossexualidade masculina e cultos afro-brasileiros," in *Para inglês ver*, 54–86. A version of this chapter was republished in English as "Male Homosexuality and Spirit Possession in Brazil," *Journal of Homosexuality* 11, no. 3–4 (summer 1986): 137–54. It was also reproduced as "Male Homosexuality and Afro-Brazilian Possession Cults," in Murray, *Latin American Male Homosexualities*, 193–220.

29. An account of her anthropological research on Candomblé with only passing remarks about effeminate men's role in the religion can be found in a reprint of her 1947 published study. See Ruth Landes, *The City of Women* (Albuquerque: University of New Mexico Press, 1994). Her documentation of homosexuality and Candomblé were presented in Ruth Landes, "A Cult Matriarchate and Male Homosexuality," *Journal of Abnormal and Social Psychology* 34 (1940): 386–97. For a contemporary anthropological account of Candomblé in which homosexual men are among the adherents to the religion, see Jim Wafer, *The Taste of Blood: Spirit Possession in Brazilian Candomblé* (Philadelphia: University of Pennsylvania Press, 1991).

30. Patrícia Birman, *Fazer estilo criando gêneros: Possessão e diferenças de gênero em terreiros de umbanda e candomblé no Rio de Janeiro* (Rio de Janeiro: Relume Dumará, EdUERJ, 1995).

31. Fry, "Da hierarquia a igualdade: A construção histórica da homossexualidade no Brasil," in *Para inglês ver*, 87–115.

32. George Chauncey, *Gay New York: Gender, Urban Culture, and the Making of the Gay Male World, 1890–1940* (New York: Basic Books, 1994), 358–61.

33. Richard G. Parker, "Changing Brazilian Constructions of Homosexuality," in Murray, *Latin American Male Homosexualities*, 241–55.

34. Richard Parker, "After AIDS: Changes in (Homo)sexual Behaviour," in *Sexuality, Politics, and AIDS in Brazil*, ed. Herbert Daniel and Richard Parker (London: Falmer Press, 1993), 100.

35. A discussion with John D'Emilio helped me clarify this point.

36. Donna J. Guy originally presented this essay as a paper to the Conference on Latin American History of the American Historical Association in January 1994. It was subsequently published in *Americas* 51, no. 1 (July 1994): 1–9.

37. The anthropological study of lower-middle-class Nicaraguan families after the Sandinista revolution by Roger N. Lancaster, *Life Is Hard: Machismo, Danger, and Intimacy of Power in Nicaragua* (Berkeley: University of California Press, 1992), explores notions of homosexuality and that country's gender system. A collection of articles in Murray, *Latin American Male Homosexualities*, focuses on the construction of multiple homosexual and same-sex erotic identities in Mexico and Peru among both the indigenous populations and Spanish-dominated cultures. Jacobo Schifter has written several works on homosexuality in Costa Rica. They include *La formación de una contracultura: Homosexualismo y SIDA en Costa Rica* (San José, Costa Rica: Editorial Cuaycán, 1989), and *Lila's House: Male Prostitution in Latin America* (New York: Harrington Park Press, 1998).

See also Barry D. Adam, "In Nicaragua: Homosexuality without a Gay World," in *If You Seduce a Straight Person, Can You Make Them Gay? Issues in Biological Essentialism versus Social Constructionism in Gay and Lesbian Identitites*, ed. John P. De Cecco and John P. Elia (Binghamton: Harrington Park Press, 1993), 171–80; Lourdes Argüelles and B. Ruby Rich, "Homosexuality, Homophobia, and Revolution: Notes toward an Understanding of the Cuban Lesbian and Gay Male Experience." *Signs: Journal of Women in Culture and Society* 9, no. 4 (summer 1984): 683–99; Hilda A. Hidalgo and Elia Hidalgo Christensen, "The Puerto Rican Lesbian and the Puerto Rican Community." *Journal of Homosexuality* 2, no. 2 (winter 1976–77): 109–21; Carlos Jáuregui *La homosexualidad en la Argentina* (Buenos Aires: Ediciones Tarso, 1987); Marvin Leiner, *Sexual Politics in Cuba: Machismo, Homosexuality, and AIDS* (Boulder: Westview Press, 1994); Ian Lumsden, *Homosexuality: Society and the State in Mexico* (Toronto: Canadian Gay Archives, 1991), and *Machos, Maricones, and Gays: Cuba and Homosexuality* (Philadelphia: Temple University Press, 1996); Rafael L. Ramírez, *Dime capitán: Relexiones sobre la masculinidad* (Río Piedras: Ediciones Huracán, 1993).

David William Foster's *Gay and Lesbian Themes in Latin American Writing* (Austin: University of Texas Press, 1991) presents an overview of homosexuality in literature. Foster has also edited *Latin American Writers on Gay and Lesbian Themes: A Bio Critical Sourcebook* (Westport, Conn.: Greenwood Press, 1994). This work contains 130 entries by sixty scholars who examine the literary production of writers with a professed gay or lesbian identity, those who have written on gay or lesbian themes, and authors whose work reflects a gay or lesbian sensibility. See also David William Foster and Roberto Reis, eds. *Bodies and Biases: Sexualities in Hispanic Cultures and Literatures* (Minneapolis: University of Minnesota Press, 1996). The anthology edited by Emilie L. Bergmann and Paul Julian Smith, *Entiendes? Queer Readings, Hispanic Writ-

ings (Durham: Duke University Press, 1995), has collected articles that deal with Spanish Latin America and Latinos living in the United States. See also Robert Howes, "The Literatures of Outsiders: The Literature of the Gay Community in Latin America," *Latin American Masses and Minorities: Their Images and Realities*, Seminar on the Acquisition of Latin American Library Materials 30 (1987): 288–304, and by the same author, "Literature of the Contemporary Brazilian Gay Community: A Review," *Modernity and Tradition: The New Latin American and Caribbean Literature, 1956–1994*, Seminar on the Acquisition of Latin American Library Material (1996): 126–38.

38. Rudi C. Bleys, *The Geography of Perversion: Male-to-Male Sexual Behavior outside the West and the Ethnographic Imagination, 1750–1918* (New York: New York University Press, 1995); Serge Gruzinski, "Las cenizas del deseo: Homosexuales novo hispanos mediados del siglo XVII," in *De la santidad a la perversion, o de porque no se cumplia la ley de Dios en la sociedad novohispana*, ed. Sergio Ortega (Mexico City: Enlace / Historia, 1985), 255–81; Clark L. Taylor, "Legends, Syncretism, and Continuing Echoes of Homosexuality from Pre-Columbian and Colonial México," in Murry, *Latin American Male Homosexualities*, 80–99; and Richard Trexler, *Sex and Conquest: Gendered Violence, Political Order, and the European Conquest of the Americas* (Ithaca: Cornell University Press, 1995).

See also Patricia Aufterherde, "True Confessions: The Inquisition and Social Attitudes in Brazil at the Turn of the Seventeenth Century," *Luso-Brazilian Review* 10, no. 2 (1973): 208–40; Lígia Belini, *A coisa obscura: Mulher, sodomia, e inquisição no Brasil colonial* (São Paulo: Editora Brasiliense, 1987); Luiz R. B. Mott, "Relações raciais entre homossexuais no Brasil colonial," *Revista Brasileira de História* 10 (1985): 89–102; Luiz R. B. Mott, "Escravidão e homossexualidade," in *História e sexualidade no Brasil*, ed. Ronaldo Vainfas (Rio de Janeiro: Graal, 1986); and Luiz R. B. Mott, *O sexo proibido: Virgens, gays, e escravos nas garras da inquisição* (Campinas: Editora Papirus, 1989).

39. Daniel Bao, "Invertidos Sexuales, Tortilleras, and Maricas Machos: The Construction of Homosexuality in Buenos Aires, Argentina, 1900–1950," in De Cecco and Elia, *If You Seduce a Straight Person*, 208.

40. Jorge Salessi, "The Argentine Dissemination of Homosexuality," in Bergmann and Smith, *Entiendes?* 49–91. See also Jorge Salessi, *Médicos, maleantes, y maricas: Higiene, criminología, y homosexualidad en la construcción de la nación Argentina, Buenos Aires, 1871–1914* (Rosario: Beatriz Viterbo, 1995).

41. Studies on homosexuality in literature and film include Luiz Gonzaga Morando Queiroz, "Transgressores e transviados: A representação do homossexual nos discursos médicos e literários no final do século XIX, 1870–1900" (master's thesis, Universidade Federal de Minas Gerais, 1992); Sapê Grootendorst, "Literatura gay no Brasil: Dezoito escritores brasileiros falando da temática homo-erótica" (manuscript, University of Utrecht, Holland, 1993); Antônio do Nascimento Moreno, "A personagem homossexual no cinema brasileiro" (master's thesis, Universidade Estadual de Campinas, 1995).

42. Fry, *Para inglês ver*, 54–86.

43. Fry's theories are presented in Fry, *Para inglês ver*, and Fry and MacRae, *O que é homossexualidade*. Many of Fry's students have produced important anthropological studies about homosexuality in Brazil. They include Carmen Dora Guimarães, "O homossexual visto por entendidos" (master's thesis, Museu Nacional, Rio de Janeiro, 1977), a study of a social network of fourteen gay men in Rio de Janeiro in the early 1970s; MacRae, *A construção da igualdade*, an anthropological analysis of Somos, Brazil's first gay rights organization; Nestor Perlongher, *O negócio do michê: Prostituição viril em São Paulo* (São Paulo: Editora Brasiliense, 1987), an examination of male hustlers; and Veriano de Souza Terto Júnior, "No escurinho do cinema . . . :

Socialidade orgiástica nas tardes cariocas" (master's thesis, Pontífica Universidade Católica do Rio de Janeiro, 1989), an examination of homosexual sex in Rio's cinemas. Parker, *Bodies, Pleasures, and Passions*, also relies on Fry's pioneering work.

44. Carlos Alberto Messeder Pereira, "O direito de curar: Homossexualidade e medicina legal no Brasil dos anos 30," in *A invenção do Brasil moderno: Medicina, educação, e engenharia nos anos 20–30*, ed. Micael M. Herschmann and Carlos Alberto Messeder Pereira (Rio de Janeiro: Rocco, 1994), 88–129.

45. Talisman Ford, "Passion in the Eye of the Beholder: Sexuality as Seen by Brazilian Sexologists, 1900–1940" (Ph.D. diss., Vanderbilt University, 1995), 179.

46. Peter M. Beattie, "Asking, Telling, and Pursuing in the Brazilian Army and Navy in the Days of *Cachaça*, Sodomy, and the Lash, 1860–1916," in *Rethinking Gender and Sexuality in Latin America: An Interdisciplinary Reader*, ed. Donna J. Guy and Daniel Balderston (New York: New York University Press, 1997), 65–85.

47. The pioneering work in mapping homosexual spaces in Brazil was an article by José Fabio Barbosa da Silva, "Aspectos sociológicos do homossexualismo em São Paulo," *Sociologia* 21, no. 4 (October 1959): 350–60. This young sociologist charted the cruising areas of downtown São Paulo. Following up on his work, Perlongher in *O negócio do michê* updated Barbosa da Silva's sexual topography in the 1980s. Sara Feldman, "Segregações espaciais urbanas: A territorialização da prostituição feminina em São Paulo" (master's thesis, Universidade de São Paulo, 1988), plots the physical space occupied by female prostitution in São Paulo. Rogério Botelho de Mattos and Miguel Ângelo Campos Riberio look at both male and female prostitution in "Territórios da prostituição nos espaços públicos da área central do Rio de Janeiro (Rio de Janeiro, 1994). More recently, historian David Higgs has mapped same-sex eroticism among men in Rio de Janeiro. See David Higgs, "Rio de Janeiro," in *Queer Sites: Gay Urban Histories since 1600*, ed. David Higgs (London and New York: Routledge, 1999), 138–63. David Bell and Gill Valentine's recently edited collection, *Mapping Desire: Geographies of Sexualities* (London: Routledge, 1995), presents an international perspective on studies of the nature of place and notions of space as they relate to pleasure, desire, and sexuality.

48. Anthropologist Roberto DaMatta employs the framework of *casa* and *rua* to chart present-day Brazil's social spheres. See Roberto DaMatta, *Carnivals, Rogues, and Heroes: An Interpretation of the Brazilian Dilemma*, trans. John Drury (Notre Dame: University of Notre Dame Press, 1991).

49. Gilberto Freyre in *The Masters and the Slaves* argues that the plantation-based patriarchal family has remained the model for family structure and functioning into the twentieth century. This perspective was repeated in the article by Antônio Candido de Mello e Souza, "The Brazilian Family," in *Brazil: Portrait of Half a Continent*, ed. T. Lynn Smith (New York: Dryden Press, 1951), 291–312. Mariza Corrêa challenges this vision in "Repensando a família patriarcal brasileira [notas para o estudo das formas de organização familiar no Brasil]," in *Colcha de retalhos: Estudos sobre a família no Brasil*, ed. Mariza Corrêa (São Paulo: Editora Brasiliense, 1982), 13–38. In the essay, she maintains that while the patriarchal family may have been the dominant model, it was only one among many contesting forms of social organization. For a synthesis of the different interpretations of the family based on Freyre's work, see Borges, *The Family in Bahia*, 4–6, 46–47.

50. Joseph A. Page, *The Brazilians* (Reading, Mass.: Addison-Wesley, 1995), 12. Page codifies these regional clichés, which are among the first stereotypes one hears upon arriving in Brazil.

51. Warren Dean, *The Industrialization of São Paulo* (Austin: University of Texas Press, 1969), 13.

52. In 1950 the population of the Federal District (Rio de Janeiro) was 2,241,152, and that of the city of São Paulo was 2,227,512. In the 1950s, São Paulo's population soared passed that of the nation's capital (Instituto Brasileiro de Geografia e Estatística, *Recenseamento geral do Brasil [1° de Julho de 1950]: Sinopse preliminar do censo demográfico* [Rio de Janeiro: Serviço Gráfico do Instituto Brasileiro de Geografia e Estatística, 1951], 2).

53. Chauncey, *Gay New York*, 365–72.

54. The National Archive in Rio de Janeiro has perhaps a hundred thousand (mostly uncataloged) court cases filed alphabetically by first name. Arrest and booking records were unavailable when I conducted the bulk of my research in 1994–95. Police and court records in São Paulo are not indexed, and the archives are inaccessible to researchers at this time.

55. Unfortunately, two of the older and more important newspapers of Rio de Janeiro and São Paulo, the *Jornal do Brasil* and the *Estado de São Paulo*, do not have working indices readily available to the public.

56. José Maria Bello, *A History of Modern Brazil, 1889–1964* (Stanford: Stanford University Press, 1966); Thomas E. Skidmore, *Politics in Brazil, 1930–1964: An Experiment in Democracy* (New York, Oxford University Press, 1967); Donald E. Worcester, *Brazil: From Colony to World Power* (New York: Charles Scribner's Sons, 1973); E. Bradford Burns, *A History of Brazil*, 2d ed. (New York: Columbia University Press, 1980); Thomas E. Skidmore, *The Politics of Military Rule in Brazil, 1964–85* (New York: Oxford University Press, 1988); Lincoln de Abreu Penna, *Uma história da República* (Rio de Janeiro: Nova Fronteira, 1989); Ronald M. Schneider, *"Order and Progress": A Political History of Brazil* (Boulder: Westview Press, 1991); and Boris Fausto, *História do Brasil* (São Paulo: EDUSP, 1994).

57. John D'Emilio, *Sexual Politics, Sexual Communities: The Making of a Homosexual Minority in the United States, 1940–1970* (Chicago: University of Chicago Press, 1983).

58. For works on lesbians in Brazil, see Belini, *A coisa obscura;* Tamara Teixeira de Carvalho, "Caminhos do desejo: Uma abordagem antropológica das relações homoeróticas femininas em Belo Horizonte" (master's thesis, Universidade Estadual de Campinas, 1995); Maria Luiza Heilborn, "Dois é par: Conjugalidade, gênero, e identidade sexual em contexto igualitário" (Ph.D. diss., Museu Nacional, Universidade Federal do Rio de Janeiro, 1992); Miriam Martinho, "Brazil," in *Unspoken Rules: Sexual Orientation and Women's Human Rights*, ed. Rachel Rosenbloom (San Fransisco: International Gay and Lesbian Human Rights Commission, 1995), 18–22; and Luiz R. B. Mott, *O lesbianismo no Brasil* (Porto Alegre: Mercado Aberto, 1987); Denise Portinari, *O discurso da homossexualidade feminina* (São Paulo: Editora Brasiliense, 1989).

Chapter One

1. Jeffrey D. Needell, *A Tropical Belle Époque: Elite Culture and Society in Turn-of-the-Century Rio de Janeiro* (Cambridge: Cambridge University Press, 1987), 19. Needell argues that the Brazilian belle époque began in 1898 with renewed national political stability under President Campos Salles, spanned the first decade and a half of the twentieth century, and ended in 1914 with the onset of World War I.

2. Directoria Geral de Estatística, *Recenseamento geral da República dos Estados Unidos do Brasil em 31 de Dezembro de 1890, Distrito Federal* (Rio de Janeiro: Imprensa Nacional, 1895), lxxiii; Directoria Geral de Estatística, *Recenseamento do Rio de Janeiro realisado em 20 de Setembro de 1906* (Rio de Janeiro: Imprensa Nacional, 1907), 180–261; Directoria Geral de Estatística, *Recenseamento do Brazil realisado em 1 de Setembro de 1920: População do Rio de Janeiro (Distrito Federal)*, vol. 2 (Rio de Janeiro: Imprensa Nacional, 1923), xxvi.

3. Directoria Geral de Estatística, *Sexo, raça, e estado civil: Nacionalidade, filiação, culto,*

e analphabetismo da população recenseada em 31 de dezembro de 1890 (Rio de Janeiro: Imprensa Nacional, 1898), 30–31.

4. The overall project, which also included the modernization of the capital's port, involved the collaboration between Lauro Müller, the minister of transport and public works and Rio's mayor, Pereira Passos. Engineer Paulo de Frontin designed and coordinated the construction of Avenida Central, the new boulevard that cut through downtown Rio, while public health specialist Oswaldo Cruz directed a campaign to rid the city of the plague, smallpox, and yellow fever. Georges Eugène Haussmann's urban reforms of Paris in the 1860s heavily influenced this team directing Rio's renovations (Needell, *A Tropical Belle Époque*, 31–51).

5. Oswaldo Porto Rocha, *A era das demolições: Cidade do Rio de Janeiro, 1870–1920* (Rio de Janeiro: Prefeitura da Cidade do Rio de Janeiro, Secretaria Municipal de Cultura, Departamento Geral de Documentação e Informação Cultural, Divisão de Editoração), 69, 77–78.

6. The term *cidade maravilhosa* was coined by Coelho Neto in an article entitled "Os sertanejos" (Backland dwellers) that appeared in *A Notícia* (Rio de Janeiro), November 29, 1908, 3.

7. The following sources treat various aspects of Rio de Janeiro's turn-of-the-century urban transformations: Maurício de Almeida Abreu, *Evolução urbana do Rio de Janeiro*, 2d ed., (Rio de Janeiro: IplanRio / Zahar, 1988); Jaime Larry Benchimol, *Pereira Passos, um Haussmann tropical: A renovação urbana da cidade do Rio de Janeiro no início do século XX* (Rio de Janeiro: Secretaria Municipal de Cultura, Turismo, e Esportes, Departamento Geral de Documentação e Informação Cultural, Divisão de Editoração, 1992); José Murilo de Carvalho, *Os bestializados: O Rio de Janeiro e a república que não foi* (São Paulo: Editora Schwarcz, 1987); Lia de Aquino Carvalho, *Habitações populares* (Rio de Janeiro: Prefeitura da Cidade do Rio de Janeiro, Secretaria Municipal de Cultura, Departamento Geral de Documentação e Informação Cultural, Divisão de Editoração, 1995); Sylvia F. Damazio, *Retrato social do Rio de Janeiro na virada do século* (Rio de Janeiro: EdUERJ, 1996); Teresa A. Meade, *"Civilizing" Rio: Reform and Resistance in a Brazilian City, 1889–1930* (University Park: Pennsylvania State University Press, 1997); Roberto Moura, *Tia Ciata e a Pequena África no Rio de Janeiro* (Rio de Janeiro: Prefeitura da Cidade do Rio de Janeiro, Secretaria Municipal de Cultura, Departamento Geral de Documentação e Informação Cultural, Divisão de Editoração, 1995); Needell, *A Tropical Belle Époque*, and "The Revolta Contra Vacina of 1904: The Revolt against 'Modernization' in Belle-Époque Rio de Janeiro," *Hispanic American Historical Review* 67, no. 2 (May 1987): 233–69; Marco A. Pamplona, *Riots, Republicanism, and Citizenship: New York City and Rio de Janeiro City during the Consolidation of the Republican Order* (New York: Garland, 1996); Rocha, *A era das demolições;* Giovanna Rosso Del Brenna, ed., *O Rio de Janeiro de Pereira Passos: Uma cidade em questão II* (Rio de Janeiro: Editora Index, 1985); Nicolau Sevcenko, *A revolta da vacina: Mentes insanas em corpos rebeldes* (São Paulo: Editora Brasiliense, 1984).

8. The area surrounding the plaza was originally known as Campo dos Ciganos (Gypsies' Field). In eighteenth-century Rio de Janeiro, when Portuguese law prohibited gypsies from residing within the city, this field, outside municipal limits, served as a place for them to camp. As Rio expanded, the city government put the land to other uses. Around 1780, the municipal council set up an open marketplace in the area and gave it the name Largo do Rossio.

9. In 1807, Dom Pedro I's father, Dom João VI, fled to Rio de Janeiro with the Portuguese royal family and a large entourage to avoid capture by Napoleon's troops, which had invaded the Iberian peninsula. In 1815, while residing in Rio de Janeiro, which had become the capital of the Portuguese empire, Dom João VI elevated Brazil to the status of kingdom. He returned to Portugal in 1821, leaving his son Dom Pedro I in Brazil as prince regent. A year later, Dom Pedro I declared Brazilian independence and received the title of emperor. He reigned from 1822

to 1831, when he abdicated and returned to Portugal, leaving his five-year-old son Dom Pedro as heir to the throne. Dom Pedro II ascended the throne in 1840. For a biography of Dom Pedro I, see Neill Macaulay, *Dom Pedro: The Struggle for Liberty in Brazil and Portugal, 1798– 1834* (Durham: Duke University Press, 1986).

10. *Diário do Rio de Janeiro*, March 31, 1862, 1; Iara Lis F. Stto. Carvalho Souza, "Pátria Coroada: O Brasil como corpo político autônomo, 1780–1863" (Ph.D. diss., Universidade Estadual de Campinas, 1997), 436–55. I thank Iara Lis Carvalho Souza for sharing her work with me.

11. In 1811, the court hairdresser, Fernando José de Almeida, raised funds to build the Teatro São João on the site. The theater was inaugurated on October 12, 1813, and was dedicated to Dom João VI, then crown prince of Portugal, in celebration of his birthday. On February 26, 1821, in response to popular pressure in favor of a constitutional monarchy in Portugal, Dom João VI's sons, Dom Pedro and Dom Miguel, stood on the veranda of the theater and in the name of their father, the king of Portugal, Brazil, and Algarves, swore to defend the constitution that the Portuguese constituent assembly was preparing to write. The next year, the government renamed the Largo do Rossio "Praça da Constituição" (Constitutional Plaza) in honor of the event. When the Teatro São João burned down in 1824, Fernando José de Almeida got permission to build another one on the same site, which he named the Imperial Teatro de São Pedro de Alcântara in homage to the recently proclaimed Brazilian emperor Dom Pedro I. The theater later became known simply as Teatro São Pedro (Augusto Maurício, *Algo do meu velho Rio* [Rio de Janeiro: Livraria Editora Brasiliana, 1966], 75–80).

12. Arquivo da Cidade do Rio de Janeiro, códices 15.4.29, April 9, 1870, 29.

13. Arquivo da Cidade do Rio de Janeiro, códices 15.4.29, no. 5841, August 26, 1878, 14.

14. Arquivo da Cidade do Rio de Janeiro, códices 15.4.29, September 10, 1878, 15.

15. Article 13 of the 1603 Philippine Code, "Of those who commit the sin of sodomy and with animals," stated:

Anyone, regardless of their rank who in any way commits the sin of sodomy, will be burned until they have turned to ashes so that there will never be any memory of their body or grave, and all of their property will be confiscated by the Crown of the Kingdom if they have descendants, and in the same way their children and grandchildren will be lose their rights and become as infamous as those who commit the crime of treason.

1. And this law also extends and applies to women who commit the sin against nature with one another and in the same way that we have said about men.

2. Likewise any man or woman who has carnal relations with an animal will be burned until they have turned to dust.

However, for that condemnation their children and descendants will not lose their rights or become infamous nor will they be harmed concerning succession or other matters if they have the right to inherit.

3. And the persons who commit the sin of sensuality with others of the same sex will be seriously punished by being sent to the galleys and other extraordinary penalties according to the mode and the perseverance of the sin.

See José Henrique Pierangelli, *Códigos penais do Brasil: evolução histórica* (Bauru, São Paulo: Jalovi, 1980), 26.

16. Luiz R. B. Mott, "Pagode português: A subcultura gay em Portugal nos tempos inquisitoriais," *Revista Ciência e Cultura* 40, no. 20 (1988): 121–23.

17. Ibid., 8. On the French precedents, see Marc Daniel, "Historie de la législation pénale française concernant l'homosexualité," *Acadie* 96:618–27 and 97:10–29.

18. Pierangelli, *Códigos penais do Brasil*, 259–60.

19. For a detailed study of the police of imperial Rio de Janeiro, see Thomas H. Holloway,

Policing Rio de Janeiro: Repression and Resistance in a Nineteeth-Century City (Stanford: Stanford University Press, 1993).

20. Pierangelli, *Códigos penais do Brasil*, 299.

21. For example, in 1890, José Antônio de Oliveira was accused of molesting young boys who came to his home to learn to read (Arquivo Nacional, 028C 1890 7H.163). In 1891, twelve-year-old José Edmundo accused Antônio Francisco Vieira Rodrigues of anally penetrating him while the former worked as a house servant for the latter (Arquivo Nacional, 029 1891 MV.18). In 1906, Ambrosio Roque de Belém, age nineteen, was convicted of "assault on decency" on ten-year-old João Batista da Conceição (Arquivo Nacional, 040 1906 T8 2021).

22. Pierangelli, *Códigos penais do Brasil*, 301.

23. Ibid., 314.

24. Gualater Adolpho Lutz, "Auto-acusação, homossexualismo, e transvestitismo: Contribuição à prática da criminologia psicanalítica" (medical thesis, Faculdade Nacional de Medicina, Universidade do Brasil, Rio de Janeiro, 1939), 199. Lutz analyzed the psychological makeup of a young man who engaged in cross-dressing and confessed to a murder that he had not committed. In this case, police did not prosecute the cross-dresser because he was emotionally unbalanced. "Jurema," one of nine homosexuals interviewed by students of the Institute of Criminology in 1938 or 1939 reported that he didn't like dressing up as a woman in public because the first time he had done so, he had been arrested by the police. Another informant, "Gilda de Abreu," preferred not to walk in the streets because he plucked his eyebrows, kept his hair long in the style of a woman, and walked in an effeminate way. His dress was generally noted and caused scandals, catcalls, bad names, and run-ins with the police (Edmur de Aguiar Whitaker, Eddi Kraus, Magino Roberto de Oliveira, and Aldo Sinisgalli, "Estudo biográfico dos homossexuais [pederastas passivos] da Capital de São Paulo: Aspectos da sua atividade social, costumes, hábitos, 'apelidos,' 'gíria,'" *Arquivos de Polícia e Identificação* 2, no. 1 (1938–39): 244–62.

25. Pierangelli, *Códigos penais do Brasil*, 316.

26. Madame Satã, the famous black homosexual and rogue figure of the Lapa neighborhood of Rio de Janeiro, related how he and his homosexual friends were arrested on numerous occasions in the 1930s for vagrancy. See Sylvan Paezzo, *Memórias de Madame Satã, conforme narração a Sylvan Paezzo* (Rio de Janeiro: Lidadora, 1972), 61–65.

27. Vivaldo Coaracy, *Memórias da cidade do Rio de Janeiro*, 3d ed. (Belo Horizonte: Itatiaia, 1988), 71–104; Maurício, *Algo do meu velho Rio*, 73.

28. Historians do not agree on the exact location of his execution, but it was not in the Largo do Rossio.

29. Evelyn Furquim Werneck Lima, "Arquitetura do espetáculo: Teatros e cinemas na formação do espaço público das Praças Tiradentes e Cinelândia, Rio de Janeiro, 1813–1950" (Ph.D. diss., Universidade Federal do Rio de Janeiro, 1997), 112–25. For a history of *teatro de revista*, the vaudeville theater reviews that were popular during the turn of the century, see Roberto Ruiz, *O teatro de revista no Brasil: Do início à primeira guerra mundial* (Rio de Janeiro: INACEN, 1988).

30. "A Maison Moderne," *O Malho* (Rio de Janeiro) 3, no. 95 (July 9, 1904): 10.

31. Regina Nóbrega, "Tudo começou com 'seu' Paschoal," *Lampião da Esquina* 3, no. 36 (May 1981): 15; Neyde Veneziano, *O teatro de revista no Brasil: Dramaturgia e convenções* (Campinas: Editorial da Universidade Estadual de Campinas, 1991), 38–42. For a history of vaudeville entertainment in Rio de Janeiro, see Salvyano Cavalcanti de Paiva, *Viva o rebolado! Vida e morte do teatro de revista brasileiro* (Rio de Janeiro: Nova Fronteira, 1991). For a study of the impact of Brazilian cinema on turn-of-the-century Rio de Janeiro, see Vicente de Paula Araújo, *A bela época do cinema brasileiro* (São Paulo: Editora Perspectiva, 1976).

32. On the *francesas*, see Needell, *A Tropical Belle Époque*, 171–73. For a study of *polacas* and Jewish prostitution in Brazil, see Beatriz Kushnir, *Baile de máscaras: Mulheres judias e prostituição, as polacas e sua associações de ajuda mútua* (Rio de Janeiro: Imago Editora, 1997); Jeffrey Lesser, *Welcoming the Undesireable: Brazil and the Jewish Question* (Berkeley: University of California Press, 1995); and Lená Medeiros de Menezes, *Os estrangeiros e o comércio do prazer nas ruas do Rio, 1890–1930* (Rio de Janeiro: Arquivo Nacional, 1992). An examination of prostitution in nineteenth-century Rio de Janeiro is Luiz Carlos Soares, *Rameiras, ilhoas, polacas . . . a prostituição no Rio de Janeiro do século XIX* (São Paulo: Editora Ática, 1992).

33. For a survey of Rio de Janeiro's cafés during the belle époque, see Danilo Gomes, *Antigos cafés do Rio de Janeiro* (Rio de Janeiro: Livraria Kosmos Editora, 1989).

34. Coaracy, *Memórias da cidade do Rio de Janeiro*, 97.

35. Marcos Luiz Bretas, *Ordem na cidade: O exercício cotidiano da autoridade policial no Rio de Janeiro, 1907–1930* (Rio de Janeiro: Rocco, 1997), 198–204.

36. Sueann Caulfield, "The Birth of Mangue: Race, Nation, and the Politics of Prostitution in Rio de Janeiro, 1850–1942," in *Sex and Sexuality in Latin America*, ed. Donna J. Guy and Daniel Balderston (New York: New York University Press, 1997), 88–92.

37. Luiz Edmundo, *O Rio de Janeiro do meu tempo* (Rio de Janeiro: Imprensa Nacional, 1938), 1:151–52.

38. Gomes, *Antigos cafés do Rio de Janeiro*, 108.

39. Arquivo Nacional, 039 1905 T7.492.

40. The court record reveals little about the alleged breach of honor committed by the young street vendor against the affronted barber for the supposed taking of the older man's wife. Baudilio's public questioning of José's masculinity was, no doubt, taken as a legitimate way of defending one's honor. This justification for Baudilio's immoral utterances, however, may have been a last minute defense to excuse his conduct.

41. Sidney Chalhoub, *Trabalho, lar, e botequim: O cotidiano dos trabalhadores no Rio de Janeiro da belle époque* (São Paulo: Editora Brasiliense, 1986), 38.

42. *Diccionário da lingua portugueza recopilado dos vocabulários impressos até agora e nesta segunda edição novamente emendado e muito accrescentado por Antônio de Maraes Silva Natural do Rio de Janeiro offerecido ao muito alto e muito poderosos Principe Regente N. Senhor. Tomo Segundo F–Z* (Lisbon: Lacédina, 1813).

43. Francisco José Viveiros de Castro, *Atentados ao pudor: Estudos sobre as aberrações do instinto sexual*, 3d ed., rev. and enl. (Rio de Janeiro: Livraria Editora Freitas Bastos, 1934), 222. This work, originally edited in 1894 was republished in a 1934 expanded edition based on the manuscripts left by the author.

44. "*Fresco.*—Adjetivo arejado de modernização depravada. Quase frio, ameno, suave, que não tem calor nem quenturas. Que faz frescuras, que tem o sopro da brisa. Encontra-se muito nos morros e no largo do Rossio" (Bock [J. Brito], *Dicionário moderno* [Rio de Janeiro: Editora Rebello Braga, 1903], 39; reprinted in Dino Preti, *A linguagem proibida: Um estudo sobre a linguagem erótica* [São Paulo: T. A. Queiroz, 1983], 270).

45. "Ante a cruel derrocada / Do Rossio dos meus sonhos, / A musa desocupada, / Embora em versos tristonhos, / Vai jogar uma cartada: / É bem dura a colisão / Que me tolhe a liberdade / Desta ingrata profissão; E ao prefeito da cidade / Requero indenização!" *O Malho* (Rio de Janeiro) 3, no. 93, (June 23, 1904): 31.

46. "Mas que calor tem feito! Não há cajuada, nem refrescos que cheguem . . . seu comendador! Calcule que todas as noites levo . . . à procura de algum lugar em que possa haver fresco. / O largo do Rossio não serve?" (K. Lixto [Calixto Cordeiro], *O Malho* (Rio de Janeiro) 2, no. 20 (March 28, 1903): 14.

47. Cristiana Sunetinni Pereira, "Um gênero alegre: Imprensa e pornografia no Rio de Janeiro, 1898–1916" (master's thesis, Universidade Estadual de Campinas, 1997). I thank Cristiana Senetinni Pereira for graciously sharing her masters' thesis with me.

48. *Rio Nu* (Rio de Janeiro), April 1, 1903, quoted in Pereira, "Um gênero alegre," 39.

49. Pereira, "Um gênero alegre," 39–40.

50. Ibid., 229.

51. Capadócio Maluco, *O menino do Gouveia*, Contos Rápidos no. 6 (Ilha de Vênus: Editora Cupido, [1914]), 3.

52. Ibid., 7.

53. *Fanchono* was a popular term for sodomite in the sixteenth-century. See Luiz R. B. Mott, *O Sexo proibido: Virgens, gays, e escravos nas garras da inquisição* (Campinas: Editora Papirus, 1989), 14; Wayne R. Dynes, "Portugayese," in *Latin American Male Homosexualities*, ed. Stephen O. Murray (Albuquerque: University of New Mexico Press, 1995), 261. Over time, the term has shifted meaning, originally signifying an effeminate man who had sex with other men and eventually coming to mean a masculine homosexual who enjoyed penetrating other men. For example, an 1849 dictionary published in Portugal considered the word "obscene" and defined *fanchono* as "one who gives libidinous passion to someone of their sex; effeminate" (Eduardo de Faria, *Novo diccionario da lingua portugueza*. [Lisbon: Typographia Lisbonense, 1849], 3:12). In *O menino do Gouveia*, the author refers to Gouveia as a *fanchono*. A quarter of a century later, the word was defined as "a lascivious man who seeks sensual pleasures with individuals of the same sex; an active pederast." The same dictionary defined the feminine form of the word, *fanchona*, as a robust woman with virile aspects and habits or predilections of the masculine sex." See Laudelino Freire, ed., *Dicionário da língua portuguesa* (Rio de Janeiro: A Noite Editora, 1941), 3:2484. Ascribing masculine content to the term when referring to both men and women reflected not only the transformation of this epithet from its original use referring to the effeminate, but also to the fact that both the homosexual subculture and Brazilian society at large acknowledged the identity of the "virile" and "masculine" homosexual who enjoyed sex with other men.

54. Nestor de Holanda, *Memórias do café Nice: Subterrâneos da música popular e da vida boêmia do Rio de Janeiro* (Rio de Janeiro: Conquista, 1970), 166.

55. Adolfo Caminha, *Bom-Crioulo* (Rio de Janeiro: Prefeitura da Cidade do Rio de Janeiro, Secretaria Municipal de Cultura, Turismo e Esportes, Departamento Geral de Documentação e Informação Cultural, 1991). An English version is *Bom-Crioulo: The Black Man and the Cabin Boy*, trans. E. A. Lacey (San Francisco: Gay Sunshine Press, 1982).

56. David William Foster, *Gay and Lesbian Themes in Latin American Writing* (Austin: University of Texas Press, 1991), 10.

57. Cf. Peter Fry, "Léonie, Pombinha, Amaro, e Aleixo: Prostituição, homossexualidade, e raça em dois romances naturalistas," in *Caminhos Cruzados: Linguagem, antropologia, e ciências naturais* (São Paulo: Editora Brasiliense, 1982), 33–51; and Elias Ribeiro de Castro, "No limiar do permitido: Uma introdução ao espírito carnavalesco do romance de Adolfo Caminha" (Universidade de São Paulo, 1997).

58. The term *crioulo* has a variety of meanings, including one referring to anyone, either of European or African decent, born in the Americas. However, *crioulo* is often used in a less than respectful way to refer to a person of Afro-Brazilian origins.

59. Saboia Ribeiro, *Roteiro de Adolfo Caminha* (Rio de Janeiro: Livraria São José, 1957), 84–85.

60. Caminha's strong republican sentiments reverberate throughout the novel. His vivid descriptions of the extensive use of the whip as punishment are also an indictment of the navy, which forced him to resign as a result of the amorous scandal in Ceará.

61. Caminha, *Bom-Crioulo: The Black Man and the Cabin Boy*, 52–53.

62. Robert Howes, introduction to *Bom-Crioulo: The Black Man and the Cabin Boy*, 15–16.

63. Adolfo Caminha, "Um livro condenado," *A Nova Revista* (Rio de Janeiro) 2 (February 1896): 41. I thank Robert Howes for obtaining a copy of this article for my use.

64. Peter M. Beattie, "Asking, Telling, and Pursuing in the Brazilian Army and Navy in the Days of *Cachaça*, Sodomy, and the Lash, 1860–1916," in *Rethinking Gender and Sexuality in Latin America: An Interdisciplinary Reader*, ed. Donna J. Guy and Daniel Balderston (New York: New York University Press, 1997), 72, 73–84. Of the ten cases cited by Beattie in his article, those enlisted men and noncommissioned officers convicted of committing consensual "immoral acts" with other men received sentences ranging from one week to six months. In one case where force was involved, the perpetrators received a four-year sentence, the maximum time allowed for that crime under the military penal code, and the victim was not convicted of any offense.

65. Alhough I did not have the opportunity to examine these cases directly, Peter Beattie kindly shared his observations about the filtered nature and the technical tone of these military proceedings.

66. Maria Letícia Guedes Alcoforado, "Bom-Crioulo de Adolfo Caminha e a França," *Revista de Letras* (São Paulo) 28 (1988): 85–86.

67. Caminha, "Um livro condenado," 42. The translation of this quote is from Robert Howes's introduction to *Bom-Crioulo: The Black Man and the Cabin Boy*, 14. Caminha's ironic and bitter tone toward his detractors appears to be more than the defensive positioning of an author who has received bad reviews. It also likely reflected his contempt for social norms, which resulted in his ostracism from Ceará society following his adulterous affair. His relatively sensitive and somewhat sympathetic portrayal of Amaro might also stem from these experiences.

68. David F. Greenberg, *The Construction of Homosexuality* (Chicago: University of Chicago Press, 1988), 409. It seems that the first use of the term homosexual in Brazil was by Viveiros de Castro in his 1894 work, *Assaults on Decency: Studies on Sexual Aberrations* (Viveiros de Castro, *Atentados ao pudor*, 217–20).

69. Caminha cited Dr. Ambroise Tardieu, *Etude médico-légale sur les attentats au moeurs* (1857); Dr. Albert Moll, *Les perversions de l'instinct génital* (1893); and Richard von Krafft-Ebing (Caminha, "Um livro condenado," 41).

70. *Bom-Crioulo* was not the only novel to portray homosexuality in the first years of the Republic. Several other literary works that described same-sex eroticism during the late empire and in the first years of the Republic also maintained the notion that the behavior was immoral and unnatural. For example, in 1885 the physician Ferreira Leal published, *Um homem gasto* (The spent man) about the decline and fall of a man from the Brazilian elite (Ferreira Leal, *Um homem gasto: Episódio da história social do XIX seculo. Estudo naturalista por L.L.*, 2d ed. [Rio de Janeiro: Matheus, Costa, 1885]). Three years later, Raul Pompéia published *O Ateneu* (The Atheneum), which portrayed same-sex activities among Carioca students in a private school in Rio de Janeiro. See Raul Pompéia, *O Ateneu* (São Paulo: Editora Ática, 1991). In addition, the Portuguese novel, *O Barão de Lavos* (1891), which chronicled the decadent life of a Portuguese nobleman with same-sex erotic desires, was circulated in Brazil and known to Caminha (Abel Botelho, *O Barão de Lavos (pathologia social)* [Porto: Imprensa Moderna, 1908]). For a discussion of turn-of-the-century literary and scientific portrayals of homosexuality in Brazil, see Luiz Gonzaga Morando Queiroz, "Transgressores e transviados: A representação do homossexual nos discursos médico e literário no final do século XIX, 1870–1900" (master's thesis, Universidade Federal de Minas Gerais, 1992).

71. Many historians of Brazil have argued this point in specific analyses of different professions and institutions that "modernized" during this period. See, for example, Dain Borges, *The*

Family in Bahia, Brazil, 1870–1945 (Stanford: Stanford University Press, 192), 85–111; Sueann Caulfield, "In Defense of Honor: The Contested Meaning of Sexual Morality in Law and Courtship, Rio de Janeiro, 1920–40" (Ph.D. diss., New York University, 1994); Jurandir Freire Costa, *Ordem médica e norma familiar* (Rio de Janeiro: Edições Graal, 1979); Maria Clementina Pereira Cunha, *O espelho do mundo: Juquery, a história de um asilo* (Rio de Janeiro: Paz e Terra, 1986); Magali Engel, *Meretrizes e doutores: Saber médico e prostituição no Rio de Janeiro, 1840–1890* (São Paulo: Editora Brasiliense, 1988); Martha de Abreu Esteves, *Meninas perdidas: Os populares e o cotidiano do amor no Rio de Janeiro da belle époque* (Rio de Janeiro: Paz e Terra, 1989); Talisman Ford, "Passion in the Eye of the Beholder: Sexuality as Seen by Brazilian Sexologists, 1900–1940" (Ph.D. diss., Vanderbilt University, 1995); Micael M. Herschmann and Carlos Alberto Messeder Pereira, "O imaginário moderno no Brasil," in *A invenção do Brasil moderno: Medicina, educação, e engenharia nos anos 20–30*, ed. Micael M. Herschmann and Carlos Alberto Messeder (Rio de Janeiro: Rocco, 1994), 9–42; Margareth Rago, *Os prazeres da noite: Prostituição e códigos da sexualidade feminina em São Paulo, 1890–1930* (Rio de Janeiro: Paz e Terra, 1991); Simon Schwartzman, *A Space for Science: The Development of the Scientific Community in Brazil* (University Park: The Pennsylvania State University Press, 1991); Nancy Leys Stepan, *Beginnings of Brazilian Science: Oswaldo Cruz, Medical Research, and Policy, 1890–1920* (New York: Science History Publications, 1981).

72. In this respect, the "pathologizing" of pederasty or homosexuality in Brazil beginning in the late nineteenth century parallels the process in Europe described by Michel Foucault. See *The History of Sexuality: An Introduction*, trans. Robert Hurley (New York: Vintage Books, 1990), 1:42–43.

73. Francisco Ferraz de Macedo, "Da prostituição em geral e em particular em relação ao Rio de Janeiro" (medical thesis, Faculdade de Medicina da Universidade do Rio de Janeiro, 1872), 115.

74. Throughout this work, the terms *passividade* and *actividade* refer to anal penetration or receptivity and not to a generalized agency or lack thereof.

75. Ibid., 118–19.

76. For example, French physician Bénédict A. Morel wrote *Treatise on Degenerations* in 1857, which presented same-sex sexuality as a degenerative condition. That same year, forensic medical expert Ambroise-Auguste Tardieu published *Medicolegal Study of Assaults on Decency*, which argued that sodomites were exclusively "active" or "passive" and that among the "passive" pederasts, effeminacy and other physical characteristics could easily identify them. These works shaped French cultural anxieties about same-sex erotic relationships for the next half century (Vernon A. Rosario, *The Erotic Imagination: French Histories of Perversity* [New York: Oxford University Press, 1997], 72–75).

77. Ferraz de Macedo, "Da prostituição em geral," 120.

78. Ibid.

79. Engel, *Meretrizes e doutores*, 71–102.

80. Ferraz de Macedo, "Da prostituição em geral," 116.

81. Ibid., 117.

82. Ibid., 116–17. Jeffrey Needell has pointed out in private correspondence with the author that if Ferraz de Macedo were indeed accurate in his description that some of these men wore tall white hats, they would have stood out notably in the landscape of Brazilian upper-class public sociability.

83. Ibid., 120–21.

84. Viveiros de Castro's use of the term "pederast" to refer to those men who engaged in same-sex activity conformed to the meaning it had assumed among sexologists in Europe at the

turn of the century. In the mid-nineteenth century, Johann Ludwig Casper, a forensic medical expert, had borrowed the term "pederasty" from the classic Greek for "boy-love." Yet by the late nineteenth century, the word had become confused with the Latin *paedicatio*, which meant anal intercourse, and was used to signify that sexual activity rather than the sexual desires of adults for children. See Hubert Kennedy, "Karl Heinrich Ulrichs: The First Theorist of Homosexuality," in *Science and Homosexualities*, ed. Vernon A. Rosario (New York: Routledge, 1997), 30.

85. Arrigo Tamassia, an Italian forensic doctor, coined the term invert (*inversione dell'instinto sessuale*). Neurologists Jean-Martin Charcot and Valetin Magnan, neurologists, borrowed the concept to describe the case of a French man in 1882 (Rosario, *The Erotic Imagination*, 70). In addition to Chevalier and Moll, Viveiros de Castro mentions virtually all of the European sexologists who had written on homosexuality, including Richard von Krafft-Ebing, Karl Heinrich Ulrichs, and Ambroise-Augustine Tardieu. Viveiros de Castro also advised the reader that Adolfo Caminha was writing *Bom-Crioulo*. He might very well have discussed these works with Caminha or supplied the novelist with copies of writings by Tardieu, Moll, Krafft-Ebing that Caminha cites in his defense of *Bom-Crioulo*.

86. Viveiros de Castro, *Atentados ao pudor*, 221–22.

87. Ibid., 233. The term Urnings was invented in the 1860s by Karl Heinrich Ulrichs, a lawyer and writer from the kingdom of Hanover, who considered men who had sexual and romantic attractions to other men as "the third sex." The word is a reference to Aphrodite Uranus in Plato's *Symposium* (Kennedy, "Karl Heinrich Ulrichs," 26–29).

88. See Viveiros de Castro, *Atentados ao pudor*, 235–45.

89. José Ricardo Pires de Almeida, *Homosexualismo (a libertinagem no Rio de Janeiro): Estudo sobre as perversões do instincto genital* (Rio de Janeiro: Laemmert, 1906).

90. Pires de Almeida, *Homosexualismo*, 73.

91. Bretas, *Ordem da cidade*, 176 n. 9.

92. Pires de Almeida, *Homosexualismo*, 49–50.

93. Ibid., 50–57.

94. Ibid., 77.

95. Ibid., 78–81.

96. Ibid., 80.

97. Luiz R. B. Mott, "Relações raciais entre homossexuais no Brasil colonial," *Revista Brasileira de História* 10 (1985): 89–102.

98. Pires de Almeida, *Homosexualismo*, 78–82.

99. According to Pires de Almeida, Brazilian playwright Martins Pena's comedies of the 1840s contain references to the use of red ties by effeminate men (ibid., 82). I was, however, unable to find any such reference in Pena's work, although the author employed cross-dressing in the staging of his plays.

100. George Chauncey, *Gay New York: Gender, Urban Culture, and the Making of the Gay Male World, 1890–1940* (New York: Basic Books, 1994), 54.

101. Pires de Almeida, *Homosexualismo*, 184, 191. See chapter 3 of this work, "Control and Cure: The Medicolegal Responses," for more information on the influence of Lombroso on Brazilian medical theories of homosexuality.

102. Ibid., 81–82.

103. Ibid., 165.

104. To a great extent, the medical and legal professionals who documented Carioca dandies and *frescos* engaged in a selection process whereby descriptions of homosexuality were filtered through their own class prejudices. Although Ferraz de Macedo, Viveiros de Castro, and Pires

de Almeida describe in detail some members of Rio de Janeiro's popular classes who engaged in same-sex eroticism, one ultimately can deduce much less about homosexual behavior among the vast majority of poor and working citizens of the capital than among the privileged classes during the Brazilian belle époque. The general social conditions of the overwhelming majority of Rio's population can be found in June E. Hahner, *Poverty and Progress: The Urban Poor in Brazil, 1870–1920* (Albuquerque: University of New Mexico Press, 1986); Esteves, *Meninas perdidas;* Rachel Soihet, *Condição feminina e formas de violência: Mulheres pobres e ordem urbana, 1890–1920* (Rio de Janeiro: Forense Universitária, 1989); and Damazio, *Retrato social do Rio de Janeiro.*

105. Jacomino Define, "A Rua do Ouvidor," *Kosmos* (Rio de Janeiro) 2, no. 1 (February 1905): 37–39; Needell, *A Tropical Belle Époque,* 164–66. See also Joaquim Manuel de Macedo, *Memórias da Rua do Ouvidor* (Brasília: Editora Universidade de Brasília, 1988), and Danilo Gomes, *Uma rua chamada Ouvidor* (Rio de Janeiro: Prefeitura da Cidade do Rio de Janeiro, 1980).

106. Rosa Maria Barboza de Araújo, *A vocação do prazer: A cidade e a família no Rio de Janeiro republicano* (Rio de Janeiro: Rocco, 1995), 326–28; Fantásio [pseudonym], "O namoro no Rio de Janeiro," *Kosmos* (Rio de Janeiro) 3, no. 7 (July 1906): 43–45.

107. John Otway Percy Bland, *Men, Manners, and Morals in South America* (New York: Charles Scribner's Sons, 1920), 51.

108. I have gathered information on João do Rio from the following sources: Gilberto Amado, *Mocidade no Rio e primeira viagem à Europa,* 2d ed. (Rio de Janeiro: Livraria José Olímpio Editora, 1958), 44–65; Raúl Antelo, *João do Rio: O dândi e a especulação* (Rio de Janeiro: Livrarias Taurus-Timbre Editores, 1989); Gentil Luiz de Faria, *A presença de Oscar Wilde na belle-époque literária brasileira* (São João do Rio Preto, São Paulo: Pannartz, 1988); Renato Cordeiro Gomes, *João do Rio: Vielas do vício, ruas da graça* (Rio de Janeiro: Relume Dumará, 1996); Raimundo Magalhães Júnior, *A vida vertiginosa de João do Rio* (Rio de Janeiro: Civilização Brasileira, 1978); Ignácio de Lyra Neves Manta, *A arte e a neurose de João do Rio* (Rio de Janeiro: Francisco Alvarez, 1977); Needell, *A Tropical Belle Époque,* 207–25; João Carlos Rodrigues, *João do Rio: Uma biografia* (Rio de Janeiro: Topbooks, 1996); and Carmen Lúcia Tindó Secco, *Morte e prazer em João do Rio* (Rio de Janeiro: Livraria Francisco Alves Editora/ Instituto Estadual do Livro, 1978).

109. João do Rio [Paulo Barreto], *A alma encantadora das ruas* (1908; Rio de Janeiro: Secretaria Municipal de Cultura, Departamento Geral de Documentação e Informação Cultural, Divisão de Editoração, 1995), 5.

110. Jean-Claude Bernardet inspired my initial interest in João do Rio through a similar reading of the author's nocturnal meandering.

111. João do Rio [Paulo Barreto], "A fisionomia dos jardins," *Gazeta de Notícias* (Rio de Janeiro), July 20, 1907, 2.

112. João do Rio captured the danger of police raids on boardinghouses or cheap hotels in another journalistic piece, entitled "Sono calmo" (Calm sleep), which appeared in a collection of his articles in *A alma encantadora das ruas,* 119–24.

113. The articles were published as *As religiões do Rio* (Paris: Garnier, 1904).

114. João Carlos Rodrigues, *João do Rio: Catálago bibliográfico, 1899–1921* (Rio de Janeiro: Prefeitura da Cidade do Rio de Janeiro, Secretaria Municipal de Cultura, Departamento Geral de Documentação e Informação Cultural, Divisão de Editoração, 1994).

115. Rodrigues, *João do Rio,* 59.

116. Magalhães, *A vida vertiginosa de João do Rio,* 126. The original reads: "Na previsão de próximo calores / A Academia, que idolatra o frio, / Não podendo comprar ventiladores / Abriu as portas para o João do Rio."

117. Monteiro Lobato, one of Lima Barreto's defenders, responded to the author's despondency over his failure to be elected to Rio's highest literary club because of his bohemian drinking sprees by attacking João do Rio: "You cannot enter the academy because of the 'impropriety of your downtown life;' nevertheless, the Academy admits the flagrant impertinence of a J[oão] do R[io]" (quoted in Needell, *A Tropical Belle Époque*, 223).

118. Lima Barreto, *Recordações do escrivão Isaías Caminha* (Rio de Janeiro: Livraria Garnier, 1989), 100.

119. Lima Barreto, *Um longo sonho do futuro: Diários, cartas, entrevistas, e confissões dispersas* (Rio de Janeiro: Graphia Editorial, 1993), 214.

120. See Raimundo Magalhães Júnior, *Olavo Bilac e sua época* (Rio de Janeiro: Companhia Editora Americana, 1974), 84–91; and Fernando Jorge, *Vida e poesia de Olavo Bilac* (São Paulo: Livraria Exposição do Livro, n.d.), 97–136, 150–62, 306–12.

121. Rodrigues, *João do Rio*, 243, 245.

122. Ibid., 38.

123. For details of João do Rio's promotion of Oscar Wilde in Brazil as well as his relationship to French literature and culture see, Faria. *A presença de Oscar Wilde na belle-époque literária brasileira*, 1988.

124. One of the few times João do Rio referred to male homosexuality in his writings was in a short story, "Impotência" (Impotence), written when the author was only eighteen and published in the newspaper *A Cidade do Rio* (Rio de Janeiro), August 16, 1899, 2. The story describes the unrealized homoerotic desires of an aging man.

125. Letter to Irineu Marinho, February 28, 1910, quoted in Magalhães, *A vida vertiginosa de João do Rio*, 153.

126. Gilberto Freyre, *Order and Progress: Brazil from Monarch to Republic* (Berkeley: University of California Press, 1986), 352; Herman Lima, *História da caricatura no Brasil* (Rio de Janeiro: José Olympio, 1963), 3:1289–98; Ingrid Elizabeth Fey, "First Tango in Paris: Latin Americans in Turn-of-the-Century France, 1880 to 1920" (Ph.D. diss., University of California, Los Angeles, 1996), 280–81.

127. Needell, *A Tropical Belle Époque*, 209.

128. Celeste Guimarães kindly lent me a copy of this drawing, which was signed by the famous cartoonist Alvarus [Álvaro Cotrim] and dated 1925.

Chapter Two

1. Marcel Gautherot, *Rio de Janeiro* (Munich: Wilhelm Andermann Verlag, 1965), 57; and Angelo Orazil, *Rio de Janeiro and Environs: Travelers's Guide* (Rio de Janeiro: Guias do Brasil, 1939), 485–86.

2. Ferreira Da Rosa, *Rio de Janeiro: Notícias históricas e descritivas da capital do Brasil* (Rio de Janeiro: Anuário do Brasil, 1978), 43–45.

3. "Copacabana, Ipanema, e Leblon parecem destinadas a representar no litoral Atlântico da América do Sul, o papel que Ostende, Biarritz, Deauville, o Lido e Miami representam na Europa e nos Estados Unidos," *Cruzeiro* (Rio de Janeiro), 24 (November 1928): 7; Evelyn Furquim Werneck Lima, "Arquitetura do espectáculo: Teatros e cinemas na formação do espaço público das Praças Tiradentes e Cinelândia, Rio de Janeiro, 1813–1950" (Ph.D. diss., Universidade Federal do Rio de Janeiro, 1997), 235–85.

4. Gabriel de Andrade, "As transformações do Rio de Janeiro," *Jornal do Brasil* (Rio de Janeiro), September 28, 1928, 5, quoted in Lima, "Arquitetura do Espectáculo," 246.

5. Hugh Gibson, *Rio* (Garden City, N.Y.: Doubleday, Doran and Co., 1937), 49–50.

6. Sueann Caulfield, "In Defense of Honor: The Contested Meaning of Sexual Morality in Law and Courtship, Rio de Janeiro, 1920–1940" (Ph.D. diss., New York University, 1994), 74–87. Caulfield describes the royal visit of King Albert and Queen Elizabeth of Belgium to Rio de Janeiro in 1920 and the ways in which the European-influenced urban reforms were used by the government to promote an image of a sophisticated and civilized country.

7. Leonídio Ribeiro, *Homosexualismo e endocrinologia*, with a foreword by Gregório Marañón (Rio de Janeiro: Livraria Francisco Alves Editora, 1938), 109–10.

8. Ibid., 109.

9. Instituto Brasileiro de Geografia e Estatística, *Recenseamento geral do Brasil [1° de setembro de 1940]*, part 16, *Distrito Federal* (Rio de Janeiro: Serviço Gráfico do Instituto Brasileiro de Geografia e Estatística, 1951), 1.

10. José Roberto de Araújo Filho, "A população paulistana," in *A cidade de São Paulo: Estudos de geografia urbana*, ed. Aroldo de Azevedo, vol. 2, *A evolução urbana* (São Paulo: Companhia Editora Nacional, 1958), 169.

11. Susan K. Besse, *Restructuring Patriarchy: The Modernization of Gender Inequality in Brazil, 1914–1940* (Chapel Hill: University of North Carolina Press, 1996), 129, 140–41.

12. Ibid., 29.

13. Ibid., 36–37.

14. See Juandir Freire Costa, *História da psiquiatria no Brasil: Um corte ideológico* (Rio de Janeiro: Editora documentário, 1976).

15. Gilberto Freyre, *The Masters and the Slaves: A Study in the Development of Brazilian Civilization* (Berkeley: University of California Press, 1986).

16. See Nancy Leys Stepan, *"The Hour of Eugenics": Race, Gender, and Nation in Latin America* (Ithaca: Cornell University Press, 1991).

17. The Bloco Operário e Camponês (BOC) failed to challenge the Brazilian oligarchy successfully in the 1928 elections. For an analysis of the relationship between the defeat of the BOC in 1928 and the creation of the discourse about the "Revolution of 1930" from the perspective of the victors, see Edgar de Decca, *1930: O silêncio dos vencidos* (São Paulo: Editora Brasiliense, 1981).

18. Luzardo's proposal to reform Rio de Janeiro's police was in part an attempt to rid the force of opponents of the new regime. When the head of the military police protested Luzardo's plan to centralize the force, Vargas's new chief of police resigned (Michael L. Conniff, *Urban Politics in Brazil: The Rise of Populism, 1925–1945* [Pittsburgh: University of Pittsburgh Press, 1981], 138). Ribeiro, however, continued in his post as the head of the Department of Identification until 1946, a year after the end of the Estado Novo. See Leonídio Ribeiro, *De médico a criminalista: Depoimentos e reminiscências* (Rio de Janeiro: Livraria São José, 1967), 3.

19. Ribeiro, *De médico a criminalista*, 105.

20. Ibid., 108, 116–17. In establishing a uniform system for identifying the population, Ribeiro convinced the government to use fingerprinting as a unique, distinguishing technique. According to a newspaper report quoted by Ribeiro in his memoirs, the purpose of the institute was to set up a system for electoral identification. However, its activities reached beyond that task to include criminal and civil matters, leading to the formation of the Instituto Félix Pacheco, which controlled passports, identification cards, and foreigners residing in Brazil.

21. These articles, which generally repeated the same information, include "Aspectos médico-legais da homossexualidade," *Arquivo de Medicina Legal e Identificação* 5 (1935): 12; "El problema medicolegal del homosexualismo: Contribución a su estudio bajo el punto de vista endocrinológico," *Arquivos de Medicina Legal* (Buenos Aires) (1935): 362; "Homossexualismo e endocrinologia," *Revista Brasileira* (Rio de Janeiro) 5 (1935): 155; "O problema medico-legal do

homossexualismo sob o ponto de vista endocrinológico," *Revista Jurídica* (Rio de Janeiro) 3 (1935): 185; "O problema medico-legal do homossexualismo," *Arquivo da Medicina Legal e Identificação* (Rio de Janeiro) 5 (1936): 145–60; "Aspectos médico-legais da homossexualidade," *Arquivo de Antropologia Criminal* 56 (1936): 425–36; "Homossexualismo e endocrinologia," *Arquivos da Medicina Legal e Identificação* (1937): 167; "Omosessualitá ed endocrinologia," *La Giustizia Penale* (Rome) 44, no. 1 (1938): 527, 758; "Homosexuality: Etiology and Therapy," *Arquivos de Medicina Legal e Identificação* (1938): 8–15; "Etiologia e tratamento da homossexualidade," *Arquivos de Medicina Legal e Identificação* 1 (1938): xcvii–c; "Homossexualité et glandes endocrines," *Arquivos de Medicina Legal e Identificação*, part 1 (1938): 98.

22. The Italian editions, entitled *Omosessualità ed endocrinologia*, were published in Rome by Livraria Città de Casttello and in Milan by Fratelli Bocca (Carlos da Silva La Caz, *Vultos da medicina brasileira* [São Paulo: Aliança Gráfica Industrial, 1977], 4:42).

23. In 1975, the year before his death, Ribeiro published his memoirs. He included in the volume an updated version of a paper entitled "Medical-Social Problems of Homosexuality," which he had originally presented at a conference in Lisbon in 1935. Ribeiro noted the research results of the Kinsey report and acknowledged psychological factors pointed out by Freud that affected homosexual behavior. He even mentioned a newspaper report about a demonstration of five thousand homosexuals in New York's Central Park who were protesting against discrimination, no doubt a reference to a Gay Pride March. Nevertheless, he still insisted on the validity of the theory about the cause of homosexuality that he defended in the 1930s. See Leonídio Ribeiro, *Memórias de um médico legalista* (Rio de Janeiro: Editorial Sul Americana, 1975), 1:83–94.

24. Gonçalves was a *delegado auxiliar*, roughly equivalent to a precinct captain (Ribeiro, *Homosexualismo e endocrinologia*, 105).

25. "Henrique" was probably not a part of the 195-man study, since he was arrested in 1935.

26. This police sweep was not unique. In 1923, for example, Rio Police Chief Franca ordered a "thorough inspection of all hotels and houses of tolerance [brothels] for the purpose of putting a stop to the carnal commerce in minors and the spread of pederasty" (Geminiano da Franca, "Serviço Policial," in Alfredo Pinto Vieira de Mello, *Relatório: Ministro da Justiça e Negocios Interiores* [Rio de Janeiro: Imprensa Nacional, 1920], 75; quoted in Caulfield, "In Defense of Honor," 119).

27. The racial breakdown for males in the Federal District was as follows: total (878,299), white (642,207), mixed race (145,179), black (88,451). The 1920 census did not ask questions about race, and the 1930 census did not take place because of the political upheavals of that year. Therefore, I have used statistics that were collected eight years after Ribeiro's study, which could be another reason why the racial makeup of the group differs from the statistics for the overall population of Rio de Janeiro.

28. See Thomas E. Skidmore, *Black into White: Race and Nationality in Brazilian Thought* (Durham: Duke University Press), 1993.

29. Under the category of race, the census taker was instructed to proceed by first asking the interviewee if he or she was *preta* (black), white (*branca*), or yellow (*amarela*). If a person declared that she or he had a different racial self-identity, it was marked down as *parda* (brown), which was a synonym for *mulato* (Instituto Brasileiro de Geografia e Estatística, *Recenseamento geral do Brasil*, xv). Thus, the census steered people into the three principle categories, and those who wished to identify as white could do so. Given the tendency toward self-whitening, those with very dark skin might also choose to call themselves *pardo*.

30. According to the 1920 census for Rio de Janeiro, out of the 181,152 males between ages sixteen and twenty-nine, only 33,127, or 18.3 percent, were married (Directoria Geral de Estatística, *Recenseamento realizado em 1 de setembro de 1920*, vol. 2, part 1, *População do Rio de*

Janeiro, 1923, 116. In the 1940 census for the Federal District, out of the 198,402 men between ages sixteen and twenty-nine, only 47,045, or 23.7, percent were married (Instituto Brasileiro de Geografia e Estatística, *Recenseamento geral do Brasil*, 6–7).

31. Ribeiro, *Homosexualismo e endocrinologia*, 155–56.

32. Karl Ulrichs coined the concept of a "woman trapped in a man's body" in the 1860s and attributed the condition to the anomalous development of the originally undifferentiated human embryo (Hubert Kennedy, "Karl Heinrich Ulrichs: The First Theorist of Homosexuality," in *Science and Homosexualities*, ed. Vernon A. Rosario [New York: Routledge, 1997], 26–45). See chapter 3, "Control and Cure: The Medicolegal Responses," for further discussion on medical definitions of homosexuality.

33. Edmur de Aguiar Whitaker, Eddi Kraus, Magino Roberto de Oliveira, Joel Botto Nogueira, and Aldo Sinisgalli, "Estudo biográfico dos homosexuais (pederastas passivos) da capital de São Paulo: Aspectos da sua atividade social (costumes, hábitos, 'apelidos,' 'gíria')," *Arquivos de Polícia e Identificação* 2, no. 1 (1938–39): 248–53.

34. Kenneth Welden Rasmussen, "Brazilian Portuguese Words and Phrases for Certain Aspects of Love and Parts of the Body" (Ph.D. diss., University of Wisconsin, 1971), 144–46. In recent years, editors have begun to spell the word *viado* in published texts.

35. Members of Grupo Arco-Iris, interview by author, tape recording, Rio de Janeiro, Brazil, August 4, 1995. I have been told this story since the 1970s, but have never found any written or documented corroboration. Because of its original meaning, it has been suggested that the Disney classic *Bambi* (1942) introduced the term *veado* into Brazilian argot. According to this view, people associated homosexuals with the gentle and feminine personality of the film's innocent cervine star (Richard Parker, *Bodies, Pleasures, and Passions: Sexual Culture in Contemporary Brazil* [Boston: Beacon Press, 1991], 46). However, Leonídio Ribeiro had already documented the use of *veado* as Brazilian slang in 1938 (Ribeiro, *Homosexualismo e endocrinologia*, 224). See also Luiz R. B. Mott, "Os veados são viados, "*Nós Por Exemplo* (Rio de Janeiro), September/October 1994, 13. As Parker points out, popular imagination may have made the connection regardless of the historical accuracy of the supposition.

36. Bernardino de C. A., case no. 1812, Sanatório Pinel, Pirituba, São Paulo.

37. Rasmussen, "Brazilian Portuguese Words and Phrases," 147–8.

38. The term implies that the *bicha* will be receptive, that he desires to be "eaten" (*comido*) or anally penetrated by a "real" man.

39. From an anthropological perspective, Richard Parker has asserted that *bicha*, "[a] word designating a variety of intestinal parasites . . . is also the feminine form of *bicho* (a class of 'unspecified' animals which can range from insects to mammals), and it is this second meaning, with its emphasis on an animal-like femininity, that most clearly catches popular imagination" (Parker, *Bodies, Pleasures, and Passions*, 46).

40. Whitaker et al. "Estudo biográfico dos homosexuais," 254. Whitaker and his colleagues probably did not mention the words *fresco* and *viado* because these terms did not originate from the men they observed, but were exogenous expressions.

41. The earliest listing of the word *bicha* in a standard dictionary appears in a 1940 edition that includes the entry "slang, an effeminate man," as the eighteenth of twenty-one definitions (Laudelino Freire, ed., *Grande e novíssimo dicionário da língua portuguesa* [Rio de Janeiro: A Noite, 1940], 3:1029). As it usually takes some amount of time for jargon to be incorporated into dictionaries, one would think that the term had its origins in the early 1930s if not before. Interestingly enough, the word *veado* is not mentioned in this edition. A 1946 compilation of vocabulary used in the countryside of the state of São Paulo lists *veado* as a "sexually inverted male" (*macho invertido sexual*) (Fausto Teixeira, "Vocabulário do Caipira Paulista," *Revista do*

Arquivo Municipal [São Paulo] 13, no. 61 [1946]: 84, 103). *Vinte e quatro* is listed as another term for *veado*. The alternative definition of *fresco* is "a masculine sexual invert," or *veado*. However, *bicha* is defined as "jaguar" (*onça*) and not as a sexual invert, indicating that the word may have not yet become popularized in the state of São Paulo as a negative term for a homosexual. The listing also defines *bicha* in the plural as vermin or bloodsuckers (ibid., 73).

42. *Trésor de la langue française* (Paris: CNRS, 1975), 461–62.

43. Horácio de Almeida, *Dicionário de termos eróticos e afins* (Rio de Janeiro: Civilização Brasileira, 1981), 44.

44. Other current slang suggests a similar connection between anger, marginality, and prostitution. The adjective *emputecido/a* and the expression *puto/a da vida* both derive from the noun *puta* (prostitute) and mean that a person is very angry. The fame of street transvestites as formidable fighters while dressed as women was one of the reasons cited by one police commissioner for their massive roundup and arrest in the 1970s (Guido Fonseca, interview by author, tape recording, São Paulo, Brazil, March 8, 1995).

45. See Luís Martins, *Noturno da Lapa* (Rio de Janeiro: Editora Brasileira, 1964), and Hernâni de Irajá, *Adeus! Lapa* (Rio de Janeiro: Gráfica Récord Editora, 1967).

46. Richard Graham, "An Interview with Sérgio Buarque de Holanda," *Hispanic American Historical Review* 62, no. 1 (February 1982): 4–7; Sylvan Paezzo, *Memórias de Madame Satã, conforme narração a Sylvan Paezzo* (Rio de Janeiro: Lidador, 1972), 17. While some middle- and upper-class bohemians slummed in Lapa to hear "authentic" songs *do povo* (of the people), most of the Carioca elite preferred to frequent Rio's elegant nightclubs and casinos located in the Zona Sul, the southern beachfront neighborhoods of Copacabana and Leme. The Copacabana Palace Hotel opened the city's first luxury gambling establishment in 1932, followed a year later by the Urca Casino at the foot of Sugarloaf Mountain. A third casino, the Atlântico, was also inaugurated in Copacabana in 1935 (Bororó [Alberto de Castro Simoens da Silva], *Gente da madrugada: Flagrantes da vida noturna* [Rio de Janeiro: Guavira, 1982], 37–38). Carmen Miranda was starring in a musical review at the Urca Casino when she was offered the Broadway theater contract by Lee Shubert that launched her international singing and movie career (Abel Cardoso Júnior, *Carmen Miranda: A cantora do Brasil* [São Paulo: by the author, 1979], 129–33). One commentator described Copacabana of the late 1930s as the "aristocratic neighborhood of the city" with "ostentatious high-rises and princely houses," where evening attire is required in the "gambling palaces and the reception halls" (Francisco Leite, *Flagrantes da "cidade maravilhosa"* [Rio de Janeiro: José Olímpio, 1939], 59–60).

47. Oswald de Andrade, who was not related to Mário, published his comments about "Miss São Paulo" in an article entitled, "Os três sargentos" (The three sergeants) in a literary section, "revista de antropofagia," of the *Diário de São Paulo*, on April 14, 1929, on page 6. The piece was signed Cabo Machado in reference to a sensuous and nationalistic poem, "Cabo Machado" (Corporal Machado), that Mário de Andrade had written in 1926 about a soldier by that name. I wish to thank Jorge Schwartz for this reference.

48. Moacir Werneck de Castro, *Mário de Andrade: Exílio no Rio* (Rio de Janeiro: Rocco, 1989), 83–102. Beatriz Kushnir kindly led me to this source. See chapter 4 for a discussion of the homoerotic subtext in Mário de Andrade's short story, "Federico Paciência," revised many times between 1924 and 1942, published posthumously in 1947 in *Contos novos* (São Paulo: Editora Martins, 1947), and reprinted in Winston Leyland, *My Deep Dark Pain Is Love: A Collection of Latin American Gay Fiction*, trans. E. A. Lacey (San Francisco: Gay Sunshine Press, 1983), 151–63.

49. Alcir Lenharo, *Cantores do rádio: A trajetória de Nora Ney e Jorge Goulart e o meio artístico de seu tempo* (Campinas, São Paulo: Editora da UNICAMP, 1995), 28.

50. Ibid., 27.

51. Most of the information about Madame Satã comes from Paezzo, *Memórias de Madame Satã*; Sérgio Cabral, Millôr Fernandes, Chico Júnior, Paulo Francis, "Madame Satã," *Pasquim* (Rio de Janeiro), no. 95 (April 29, 1971): 2–5; and Elmar Machado, "Madame Satã para o *Pasquim:* 'Enquanto eu viver, a Lapa viverá,'" *Pasquim* (Rio de Janeiro), no. 357 (April 30, 1976): 6–11.

52. Machado, "Madame Satã," 9.

53. Kay Francis [João Ferreira da Paz], interview by author, tape recording, Lapa, Rio de Janeiro, Brazil, November 3, 1994.

54. Quoted in Rogério Durst, *Madame Satã: Com o diabo no corpo* (São Paulo: Editora Brasiliense, 1985), 12.

55. Ibid., 10–11.

56. Paezzo, *Memórias de Madame Satã*, 17.

57. Madame Satã mentions his imitations of Carmen Miranda in 1928, but the "Brazilian bombshell" had only begun her singing career that year. Her first record was released in 1929. However, Carmen Miranda grew up in Lapa, and her mother ran a boardinghouse there. Madame Satã tells the story that he played with Carmen Miranda and her brothers in the streets of Lapa when he was eking out an existence as a pots and pans street vendor. While it is possible that they knew each other and that Madame Satã was aware of her rising career in 1928, it is more likely that Madame Satã confused events or was involved in his own mythmaking. In 1951, Satã returned to the stage in a production where he did, in fact, imitate Carmen Miranda (Durst, *Madame Satã*, 72).

58. Satã enjoyed telling this tale of his first big run-in with the law. Paezzo's account in *Memórias de Madame Satã* is essentially consistent with the two interviews he gave to *Pasquim* in the early 1970s.

59. Paezzo, *Memórias de Madame Satã*, 23–26. I have reduced Paezzo's retelling of this event without modifying the essence of the exchange between João Francisco and the night patrolman. Paezzo himself recreated the incident from interviews he conducted with Satã in preparing his book. I have also changed the spelling of *veado* to *viado* to reflect the popular use of the term.

60. Antônio Correa Dias, the former owner of Colosso Café, where Satã spent much of his time, insisted that while Satã kept order in the bars he frequented, he didn't extort protection money and insisted on paying his bills (Machado, "Madame Satã," 9). However, Satã himself admitted that he protected bars. "I gave protection to the bars and had a lot of money, and a lot of [boys] were after me because they knew that if they were with me they would be with a king" (Cabral, "*Madame Satã*," 3).

Satã recounts numerous examples of police harassment in his memoirs. His arrest and trial records from the 1940s confirm a hostile and retaliatory attitude on the part the police (case no. 6262, delito 29/10/46, 14° Vara Criminal; case no. 2230, delito 04/12/48, 15° Vara Criminal; case no. 481, delito 24/09/49, Archivo Nacional, Rio de Janeiro). I wish to thank Karim Aïnour for sharing these trial documents with me.

According to his file in the Instituto Félix Pacheco, the charges against Madame Satã in twenty-six trials included thirteen assaults, four resisting arrests, two receiving stolen goods, two thefts, one assault on public decency, and arms possession (Machado, "Madame Satã," 6).

61. Paezzo, *Memórias de Madame Satã*, 59.

62. Ibid., 64.

63. Ibid., 64–65.

64. Case no. 6262, delito 29/10/46, 14° Vara Criminal, Arquivo Nacional, Rio de Janeiro.

65. Paezzo, *Memórias de Madame Satã*, 115–16.

66. Ibid., 116.

67. Clive Maia's memoir of his life in prison contains an account of his contact with Madame Satã in the Ilha Grande Penitentiary. Satã maintained a larger-than-life persona behind bars as a powerful and dangerous *bicha* who was not to be crossed (Clive Maia, *Sol Quadrado [Da vida de um ex-presidiário]* [Rio de Janeiro: Irmãos Pongetti, 1962], 177–80).

68. Nestor de Holanda. *Memórias do Café Nice: Subterrâneos da música popular e da vida boêmia do Rio de Janeiro* (Rio de Janeiro: Conquista, 1970), 171.

69. Aguinaldo Silva, "Balada para Madame Satã," *Playguei* (Rio de Janeiro) 1 (November 1981): 25.

70. In 1965, Satã finished his last prison sentence and retired to a small house on Ilha Grande near the penitentiary where he had served so many years. A 1971 interview with the youth culture-based Carioca weekly *Pasquim* brought him back from obscurity and revived his notoriety. His memoirs were published the next year, and he appeared in a play two years later. He died of lung cancer on April 12, 1976, and was buried on Ilha Grande with his white Panama hat and two red roses placed on top of his simple coffin (Durst, *Madame Satã*, 56–70).

71. Suely Robles Reis de Queiroz, *São Paulo* (Madrid: Mapfre, 1992), 162.

72. Ernst von Hesse-Wartegg, *Zwischen Anden und Amazonas*, 2d ed. (Stuttgart: Union Deutsche Verlagsgesellschaft, 1915), 15, quoted in Pasquale Petrone, "São Paulo no século XX," in *A cidade de São Paulo: Estudos de geografia urbana*, ed. Aroldo de Azevedo, vol. 2, *A evolução urbana* (São Paulo: Companhia Editora Nacional, 1958), 113.

73. Warren Dean, *The Industrialization of São Paulo* (Austin: University of Texas Press, 1969), 13.

74. Benedito Lima de Toledo, *Anhangabaú* (São Paulo: Federação das Indústrias do Estado de São Paulo, 1989), 44.

75. Ibid., 65.

76. N. L. Müller, "A área central da cidade," in *A Cidade de São Paulo: Estudos de geografia urbana*, ed. Aroldo de Azevedo, vol. 3, *Aspectos da metrópole paulista* (São Paulo: Companhia Editora Nacional, 1958), 175–80.

77. Inimá Simões, *Salas de cinema em São Paulo* (São Paulo: Secretária Municipal de Cultura de São Paulo, 1990), 48.

78. N. L. Müller argues that the beginnings of this area, which lies immediately outside of the historic triangle of São Paulo on the other side of the Anhangabaú ravine, dates back to the 1870s. The "transition zone" was characterized by residences mixed together with small shops, different workshops, rooms that could be rented by the hour (*rendez-vous*), and *pensões suspeitas* (brothels) (Müller, "A área central da cidade," 175).

79. Lucília Herrmann, "Estudo do desenvolvimento de São Paulo através da análise de um radial—a estrada do café, 1935," *Revista do Arquivo Municipal* 99 (1944): 30.

80. Ibid., 33.

81. Whitaker et al., "Estudo biográfico dos homosexuais," 244–62.

82. Guido Fonseca, a historian of prostitution in São Paulo, relates an incident when Benedito Brasiliense da Silva, frequenting the Praça da República dressed in female attire, was attacked by two soldiers who mistook him for a woman (Guido Fonseca, *História da prostituição em São Paulo* [São Paulo: Editora Resenha Universitária, 1982], 223). The Praça da República is also cited by the students of the Institute of Criminology as a site of homosexual cruising (Whitaker et al., "Estudo biográfico dos homosexuais," 254).

83. Whitaker et al., "Estudo biográfico dos homosexuais," 254.

84. One twenty-year-old waiter arrested in 1937 found an inventive way to have furtive sex

in public bathrooms. When engaging in sexual escapades, he wore specially designed pants that opened on the sides instead of in the front. The laterally folded cloth gave the appearance of pockets. If he wished to engage in anal sex, he merely had to loosen the suspenders and the back half of his pants flipped down to facilitate intercourse. An investigating criminologist photographed this ingenious invention, which the young waiter insisted was merely a question of fashion and served no other purpose (Edmur de Aguiar Whitaker, "O crime e os criminosos à luz da psicologia e da psiquiatria—Estudo acerca de 50 delinquentes—Considerações sobre o problema da delinquência em São Paulo," *Arquivos da Polícia Civil de São Paulo* 3 (1st semester 1942): 435–38.

85. The urinals (*mictórios*) of the Estação da Luz are explicitly mentioned by the students of the Institute of Criminology as one of the "places habitually frequented by pederasts." For a study of homosexual sex in public restrooms in the United States see Lauds Humphrey, *Tearoom Trade: Impersonal Sex in Public Places* (Chicago: Aldine Publishing Company, 1970).

86. In 1940, there were 95,754 movie theater seats in the city of São Paulo. Cinemas sold 19,526,224 tickets that year, which averaged fifteen movies a year per capita (Simões, *Salas de cinema em São Paulo*, 48).

87. Ribeiro, *Homosexualismo e endocrinologia*, 109.

88. *Fazer crochet* may be an adaptation of the French verb *raccrocher*, which means to cruise, pick up, or make a connection. I wish to thank Rudi Bleys for bringing this to my attention.

89. Francis interview, November 3, 1994.

90. Whitaker et al., "Estudo biográfico dos homosexuais," 244–45.

91. Case no. 2230, delito 4/12/48, 15° Vara Criminal, Arquivo Nacional, Rio de Janeiro. Lena Horne, also known as Osvaldo, was accused of assisting Madam Satã in stealing some jewelry in this case.

92. Whitaker et al., "Estudo biográfico dos homosexuais," 257. A picture of Gilda de Abreu published in the article indicates a fastidious application of makeup.

93. Ibid., 247.

94. See Roberto DaMatta, *Carnivals, Rogues, and Heroes: An Interpretation of the Brazilian Dilemma* (Notre Dame: University of Notre Dame Press, 1991), 63–73. DaMatta argues that the opposition street/house (*rua/casa*) separates two mutually exclusive domains that constitute the overarching structure of Brazilian social life.

95. Ibid., 244–57.

96. Lúcio Kowarick and Clara Ant, "One Hundred Years of Overcrowding: Slum Tenements in the City," in *Social Struggles and the City: The Case of São Paulo*, ed. Lúcio Kowarick (New York: Monthly Review Press, 1994), 62–64.

97. Francisco de Assis Carvalho Franco, *Gabinete de Investigações: Relatório apresentado ao Exmo. Snr. Dr. Secretário da Segurança Pública do Estado de São Paulo, 1934* (São Paulo: Typographia do Gabinete de Investigações, 1935), 82. Madame Satã opened a *pensão* in Lapa that he claimed was a residential boardinghouse for women who worked the streets. The police accused Satã of running a bordello. For a general history of prostitution in São Paulo, see Fonseca, *História da prostituição em São Paulo*. For a history of the social space occupied by female prostitutes, see Sarah Feldman, "Segregações espaciais urbanas: A territorialização da prostituição feminina em São Paulo" (master's thesis, Universidade de São Paulo, 1988). Feldman maps the process of spatial segregation of female prostitution in São Paulo from 1924 to the beginning of the 1970s. For a social history of female prostitution in São Paulo, see Margareth Rago, *Os prazeres da noite: Prostituição e códigos da sexualidade feminina em São Paulo, 1890–1930* (Rio de Janeiro: Paz e Terra, 1991).

98. Case no. 1,126, Sanatório Pinel, Pirituba, São Paulo, Arquivo do Estado de São Paulo.

99. Ribeiro, *Homosexualismo e endocrinologia*, 109.

100. Whitaker et al., "Estudo biográfico dos homosexuais, 253.

101. Ibid., 244. The term pederasty was commonly used to refer to homosexuals both by the medical establishment and the people they observed.

102. Ibid., 246, 249.

103. Whitaker, "O crime e os criminosos," 427. Whitaker, who at the time was a professor of juridical psychology at the São Paulo Police School and a medical psychiatrist for the Serviço de Identificação (Identification Service), won the Society of Legal Medicine and Criminology's 1941 Oscar Freire Prize in Criminology for this article.

104. Ibid., 428–29.

105. Whitaker et al., "Estudo biográfico dos homosexuais," 244–48.

106. Francis interview, November 3, 1994. Kay Francis consistently referred to himself in the feminine throughout the interview.

107. Whitaker et al., "Estudo biográfico dos homosexuais," 247–48.

108. Case no. 3571, Sanatório Pinel, Pirituba, São Paulo, Arquivo do Estado de São Paulo. See chapter 3 for a discussion of the role of mental institutions in regimenting what was considered deviant behavior.

109. Whitaker et al., "Estudo biográfico dos homosexuais," 247.

110. The students of the Institute of Criminology reported that those who "lived exclusively from the vice" earned ten or twenty milreis from each sexual encounter and noted that most people they visited lived in poor conditions (Whitaker et al., "Estudo biográfico dos homosexuais," 260).

111. Ibid., 253.

112. Ibid., 247.

Chapter Three

1. Case no. 1126, Napoleão B., Sanatório Pinel, Pirituba, São Paulo, Arquivo do Estado de São Paulo.

2. "Forum Criminal," *Diário de São Paulo*, February 19, 1935, 3.

3. Case no. 1126, Sanatório Pinel.

4. While the archival records provide no explicit proof that Napoleão and João Cândido had a sexual relationship, the circumstantial evidence weighs heavily in that direction.

5. Robert G. Nachman, "Positivism, Modernization, and the Middle Class in Brazil," *Hispanic American Historical Review* 57 (1977): 1–23; Micael M. Herschmann and Carlos Alberto Messeder Pereira, "O imaginário moderno no Brasil," in *A invenção do Brasil moderno: Medicina, educação, e engenharia nos anos 20–30*, ed. Micael M. Herschmann and Carlos Alberto Messeder Pereira (Rio de Janeiro: Rocco, 1994), 9–42.

6. Nancy Leys Stepan, *"The Hour of Eugenics": Race, Gender, and Nation in Latin America* (Ithaca: Cornell University Press, 1991), 39.

7. Leonídio Ribeiro, for example, had a chair in legal medicine and criminology at the Fluminense School of Medicine. He also taught at the medical and law schools in Rio de Janeiro and simultaneously was the director of the Institute of Identification of the Federal District Civil Police, and the head of the Laboratory of Infant Biology. Edmur de Aguiar Whitaker was a psychiatric physician attached to São Paulo police's Identification Service as well as a professor of juridical psychology for the São Paulo Police Academy. Antônio Carlos Pacheco e Silva was professor of clinical psychiatry at both the University of São Paulo and the Paulista medical schools, as well as the director of the Juquery State Mental Hospital and the privately owned Pinel Sana-

NOTES TO PAGES III-I3

torium. Pacheco e Silva was also an active leader in the most important Brazilian eugenics association, the League of Mental Hygiene. See Leonídio Ribeiro, *De médico a criminalista: Depoimentos e reminiscências* (Rio de Janeiro: Livraria São José, 1967), 1–5; Edmur de Aguiar Whitaker, *Manual de psicologia e psicopatiologia judicial* (São Paulo: Serviço Gráfico da Secretaria da Segurança Pública, 1958), 3; Antônio Carlos Pacheco e Silva, *Psiquiatria clínica e forense* (São Paulo: Companhia Editora Nacional, 1940), 354.

8. Talisman Ford, "Passion in the Eye of the Beholder: Sexuality as Seen by Brazilian Sexologists, 1900–1940" (Ph.D. diss., Vanderbilt University, 1995), 32–48. I wish to thank Talisman Ford for sharing her work with me. For a study of the links between Brazilian intellectuals and the state in this period, see Sérgio Miceli, *Intelectuais e classe dirigente no Brasil, 1920–1945* (São Paulo: Difel, 1979).

9. Among the publications that printed these men's articles on homosexuality were *Arquivos de Polícia e Identificação* (São Paulo), *Arquivos da Polícia Civil de São Paulo, Arquivos da Sociedade de Medicina Legal e Criminologia de São Paulo, Arquivos de Medicina Legal e de Identificação* (Rio de Janeiro).

10. Viriato Fernandes Nunes, *As perversões em medicina legal,* tese inaugural da Faculdade de Direito de São Paulo (São Paulo: Irmãos Ferraz, 1928), 5; José Albuquerque, *Da impotência sexual no homem* (Rio de Janeiro: Typ. Coelho, 1928), 85–86; Armando Valente Júnior, "Da responsabilidade moral e legal dos médicos" (Ph.D. diss., Faculdade de Medicina de São Paulo, 1929), 5; Roberto Santos, *Caracteres sexuais neutros e intersexualidade* (Rio de Janeiro: Tipografia Artes Gráficas, 1931), 186–87; Francisco José Viveiros de Castro, *Atentados ao pudor: Estudos sobre as aberrações do instinto sexual,* 3d ed., rev. and enl. (Rio de Janeiro: Editora Freitas Bastos, 1934), 211–18; Afrânio Peixoto, *Sexologia forense* (Rio de Janeiro: Editora Guanabara, 1934), 155–56; Estácio de Lima, *A inversão dos sexos* (Rio de Janeiro: Editora Guanabara, 1935), 125–35; Hernâni de Irajá, *Psicoses do amor: Estudo sobre as alterações do instinto sexual,* 6th ed. (Rio de Janeiro: Freitas Bastos, 1935), 221–30; Leonídio Ribeiro, *Homosexualismo e endocrinologia* (Rio de Janeiro: Livraria Francisco Alves, 1938), 61–62; Aldo Sinisgalli, "Considerações gerais sobre o homosexualismo," *Arquivos de Polícia e Identificação* 2 (1938–40): 305; Pacheco e Silva, *Psiquiatria clínica e forense,* 354; João Carvalhal Ribas, "Oscar Wilde à luz da psiquiatria," *Arquivos da Polícia Civil de São Paulo* 16, no. 2 (2d semester 1948): 172–75.

11. Ribeiro, for example, cites several Brazilian authors who mention same-sex practices among Brazilian indigenous groups (Ribeiro, *Homosexualismo e endocrinologia,* 85–88).

12. Leonídio Ribeiro, *O novo código penal e a medicina legal* (Rio de Janeiro: Jacintho, 1942), 174–81. Ribeiro dedicates six pages of his chapter "Sexual Inversion" to the famous writer and poet who "will remain a part of legal history of all times." See also João Carvalhal Ribas, "Oscar Wilde à luz da psiquiatria," 87–185.

13. Gilberto Freyre, *The Masters and the Slaves: A Study in the Development of Brazilian Civilization* (Berkeley and Los Angeles: University of California Press, 1986), 117–24, 330–32, 413–14.

14. Nunes, *As perversões em medicina legal,* 11.

15. Ribeiro, *Homosexualismo e endocrinologia,* 32.

16. Afrânio Peixoto, introduction to Estácio de Lima's *A inversão dos sexos,* viii. Ironically, Peixoto died in 1947, the year before Alfred Kinsey issued his groundbreaking study, *Sexual Behavior in the Human Male,* which shed new light on homosexuality and offered statistical estimates similar to those suggested by Peixoto.

17. Throughout this period of reconsolidating the influence of the Catholic Church in civil matters, the hierarchy maintained traditional views about women, the family, and sexuality. See Riolando Azzi, "Família, mulher, e sexualidade na Igreja do Brasil, 1930–1964," in *Família,*

mulher, sexualidade, e Igreja na história do Brasil, ed. Maria Luiza Marcílio (São Paulo: Edições Loyola, 1993), 101–34.

18. Ralph Della Cava, "Catholicism and Society in Twentieth-Century Brazil," *Latin American Research Review* 11, no. 2 (1976): 9–19; Scott Mainwaring, *The Catholic Church and Politics in Brazil, 1916–1985* (Stanford: Stanford University Press, 1986), 26–34; José Oscar Beozzo, "A igreja entre a Revolucão de 1930, o Estado Novo e a redemocratização," in *O Brasil republicano*, ed. Boris Fausto, vol. 4, *Economia e cultura* (São Paulo: Difel, 1984), 273–341.

19. Padre Álvaro Negromonte, *A educação sexual (para pais e educadores)* (Rio de Janeiro: Livraria José Olympio, 1953).

20. Stepan, *The Hour of Eugenics*, 41.

21. For a detailed description of the transmission of the eugenics theories to Brazilian physicians between the two world wars see Stepan, *The Hour of Eugenics*, and Jurandir Freire Costa, *História da psiquiatria no Brasil: Um corte ideológico* (Rio de Janeiro: Editora Documentário, 1976).

22. See Renzo Villa, *Il deviante e I suoi segni: Lombrosos e la nascita dell'antropologia criminale* (Milan: Angeli, 1985).

23. Gregório Marañón, "Una clasificación de los homosexuales desde el punto de vista médico-legal," *Arquivos de Medicina Legal e de Identificação* 7, no. 15 (January 1937): 90–100.

24. Gregório Marañón, foreword to Ribeiro's *Homosexualismo e endocrinologia*, 15.

25. Other physicians adopting Marañón's theories of endocrine imbalance included Santos, *Caracteres sexuais neutros e intersexualidade*, 161; Afrânio Peixoto, "Missexualismo," *Arquivos de Medicina Legal e Identificação* 3, no. 6 (February 1933): 67–73; Antônio Bello da Mota, *Homossexualismo em medicina legal*, tese de concurso à cátedra de Medicina Legal da Faculdade de Direito do Estado de Ceará (Rio de Janeiro: Typ. do Jornal do Comércio, 1937), 20–21; Edmur de Aguiar Whitaker, "Contribuição ao estudo dos homosexuais," *Arquivos de Polícia e Identificação* 2, no. 1 (1938–39): 32–35; P. Moncau Júnior, "Pesquisas endocrinólogicas em criminosos," *Arquivos de Polícia e Identificação* 2, no. 1 (1938–39): 92–101; Pacheco e Silva, *Psiquiatria clínica e forense*, 354; Sinisgalli, "Considerações gerais sobre o homosexualismo," 282–303; Sílvio Marone, "Considerações em tôrno de uma nova classificação de missexuais," *Arquivos da Polícia Civil de São Paulo* 10 (December 1945): 103–36.

26. For an analysis of the social background and the professional ties among Brazilian sexologists, see chapter 2, "The Sexology Club: Background, Goals, and Motivations of Brazilian Sexologists," in Ford, "Passion in the Eye of the Beholder," 27–56.

27. Carlos Alberto Messeder Pereira, "*O direito de curar:* Homossexualidade e medicina legal no Brasil dos anos 30," in *A invenção do Brasil moderno: Medicina, educação, e engenharia nos anos 20–30*, ed. Micael M. Herschmann and Carlos Alberto Messeder Pereira (Rio de Janeiro: Rocco, 1994), 109.

28. Efforts by the Brazilian government to control intractable workers began before Vargas came to power in the 1930s. After the 1917 general strike in São Paulo and another strike movement in 1919, employers drew up a blacklist of "undesirable workers" and established the Department for Political and Social Order in 1924 to facilitate the repression of anarchists, socialists, and communists. See Barbara Weinstein, *For Social Peace in Brazil: Industrialists and the Remaking of the Working Class in São Paulo, 1920–1964* (Chapel Hill: University of North Carolina Press, 1996), 53. For details of the growing police repression in Rio de Janeiro during the early years of Vargas's rule, see Michael L. Conniff, *Urban Politics in Brazil: The Rise of Populism, 1925–1945* (Pittsburgh: University of Pittsburgh Press, 1981), 138–42. For the impact of employment passbooks on workers, see also Warren Dean, *The Industrialization of São Paulo* (Austin: University of Texas Press, 1969), 186–92.

29. Ribeiro, *De médico a criminalista*, 237–43.

30. Ribeiro, *Homosexualismo e endocrinologia*, 104–5. That study was among the four projects included in Ribeiro's three-volume work that won him the Lombroso Prize in 1933. After citing European studies that linked biotypes to criminality, Ribeiro presented the statistical results of his study of the thirty-three Afro-Brazilian men charged with criminal offenses. He pointed to the predominance of men with long legs in relationship to the trunks of their bodies. Ribeiro came short of drawing a direct correlation between this physical characteristic and the tendency of black Brazilians to commit violent crime, observing that the alterations due to disturbance in the endocrine glands could be a consequence of infectious diseases contracted in infancy or adolescence.

31. Ibid., 106–7.

32. Ibid., 41, 108.

33. Ibid., photographs between pages 105 and 106.

34. Ibid., photographs between pages 104 and 105.

35. Ibid.

36. Leonídio Ribeiro "O problema médico-legal do homosexualismo sob o ponto de vista endocrinológico," *Revista Jurídica* (Rio de Janeiro) 3 (1935): 146–47.

37. Ribeiro, *Homosexualismo e endocrinologia*, 36.

38. Whitaker, "Contribuição ao estudo dos homosexuais," 32–35. Another study was Moncau's "Pesquisas endocrinológicas em criminosos," which examined eighty-six delinquents, including several "passive pederasts," to determine the endocrinological influences on them, and the research carried out by the students of the São Paulo Institute of Criminology under the direction of Whitaker, which was cited extensively in chapter 2.

39. Nunes, *As perversões em medicina legal*, 25–26.

40. Ibid., 45–47.

41. See the chapter "The Whitening Ideal after Scientific Racism," in Thomas E. Skidmore, *Black into White: Race and Nationality in Brazilian Thought* (Durham: Duke University Press, 1993), 173–218.

42. For a detailed analysis of the role that Ribeiro played as a psychiatric adviser in the case and the ways in which the medicolegal profession constructed the link between sadism, homosexuality, spiritual prophecy, and insanity to justify Febrônio's commitment to a mental institution instead of prison, see Peter Fry, "Febrônio Índio do Brasil: Onde cruzam a psiquiatria, a profecia, a homossexualidade, e a lei," in *Caminhos cruzados: Linguagem, antropologia, e ciências naturais* (São Paulo: Editora Brasiliense, 1982), 65–80.

43. Ribeiro, *Homosexualismo e endocrinologia*, 116.

44. Ibid., 123.

45. Nor was Ribeiro the only medicolegal expert to insist on the link between physical traits and criminality. Murillo de Campos, a psychiatrist who also served as a defense witness, echoed this perspective: "The psycho-sexual tendencies shown in Febrônio's crimes coincided with a physical constitution rich in developmental abnormalities of a eunuchoid nature (large pelvis, gynecomastia, no hair on the trunk or members, etc.)" (ibid., 130). The third member of the defense's expert panel, Heitor Carrilho, then the director of Rio de Janeiro's hospital for the criminally insane, argued that Febrônio should be hospitalized for life instead of receiving the maximum sentence of thirty years for homicide. The judge agreed with him, and Febrônio remained in the Manicômio Judiciário for more than fifty years. Fry recounts a visit to the hospital for the criminally insane to meet Febrônio in 1982 (Fry, "Febrônio Índio do Brasil, 79).

46. Pacheco e Silva, "Psicopatias constitucionais: Estados atípicos de degeneração," in *Psiquiatria clínica e forense*, 346–81. The book won an award from the University of São Paulo

School of Medicine and from the São Paulo Society of Legal Medicine and Criminology. Pacheco e Silva publicly identified with the racial and eugenic notions that denigrated nonwhites. He made a point of inserting his ideas into the political debate of the 1930s. Pacheco e Silva was elected to the Constituent Assembly that wrote the 1934 Constitution. One of the issues vehemently discussed in the assembly was the relationship between race and immigration. Some representatives argued for restricting Asian and other nonwhite immigrants, owing to the sharp increase in the number of Japanese immigrants that had entered Brazil in the 1920s. Pacheco e Silva spoke against nonwhite immigration, using psycho-racial arguments to make his point. He declared emphatically that the "Japanese are extremely subject to certain mental disturbances and that, when mentally ill, they manifest accentuated tendencies to practice crimes" (quoted in Flávio Venâncio Luizetto, *Os constituintes em face da imigração* [master's thesis, Universidade de São Paulo, 1975], 27). Pacheco e Silva's speeches on race, eugenics, immigration, and the need to maintain the purity of the white race can be found in Antônio Carlos Pacheco e Silva, *Direito a saúde: Documentos de atividade parlamentar* (Brazil: n.p., 1934).

47. Pacheco e Silva, "Psicopatias constitucionais," 369–74.

48. Ibid., 374–81. The same case study appeared as an article, "Um interessante caso de homosexualismo feminino," *Arquivos da Sociedade de Medicina Legal e Criminologia de São Paulo* 10 (1939): 69–81. It was also reprinted by the São Paulo Society for Legal Medicine and Criminology as a pamphlet.

49. Sueann Caulfield has uncovered three other cases of women who dressed as men in her review of *Vida Policial*, a weekly police journal from Rio de Janeiro. For her discussion of these "women-men," as they were called, see "Getting into Trouble: Dishonest Women, Modern Girls, and Women-Men in the Conceptual Language of *Vida Policial*, 1925–1927," *Signs: Journal of Women in Culture and Society* 19, no. 11 (autumn 1993): 172–74.

50. Pacheco e Silva, *Psiquiatria clínica e forense*, 361, 365.

51. Ibid., 369.

52. Peixoto, introduction to Estácio de Lima's *A inversão dos sexos*, viii. Peixoto's and Ribeiro's arguments echoed the majority position among intellectuals in the late 1920s and 1930s regarding the way that society should deal with homosexuality. For example, in 1928 Nunes admitted that given developments in science, the harsh punishments imposed on inverts in the past "exceed that which they, given their mental state, deserved and that which society required to defend itself." He pointed to the medical and legal professions along with the assistance of courts and prisons, to control and cure homosexuality and, therefore, assure social tranquility (Nunes, *As perversões em medicina legal*, 45–46).

53. Ribeiro, *Homosexualismo e endocrinologia*, 27. Not all jurists and physicians were willing to abandon the role of the police and the judicial system in containing and controlling the perceived proliferation of homosexuality. In 1933, Professor Rocha Vaz of the School of Medicine in Rio de Janeiro, outlined a strategy of legal and criminal sanctions combined with medical treatment. In a paper presented at a conference of the Society of Medicine and Surgery of Rio de Janeiro, he stated his position clearly: "Don't tolerate homosexuality, but cure it; the problem is resolved with both the police and the doctor" (Rocha Vaz, "Aspectos clínicos da intersexualidade," *Arquivos de Medicina Legal e Identificação* 3, no. 7 [August 1933]: 200).

54. Ribeiro, *Homosexualismo e endocrinologia*, 170.

55. Nunes, *As perversões em medicina legal*, 11–12. I have translated the entire passage into third person plural for more coherent reading.

56. Gastão Ferreira de Almeida, *Os projectos do código criminal brasileiro (de Sá Pereira) e do código dos delictos para a Itália (de Ferri)* (São Paulo: Edições e Publicações Brasil, 1937), 198. See also Ribeiro, *O novo código penal*, 186–87.

57. The conference was sponsored by the Paulista Association of Medicine and the Society

of Legal Medicine and Criminology of São Paulo. See Sinisgalli, "Considerações gerais sobre o homosexualismo," 282–303.

58. Aldo Sinisgalli, "Observações sobre os hábitos, costumes, e condições de vida dos homosexuais (pederastas passivos) de São Paulo, *Arquivos de Polícia e Identificação*, 3 (1938–40): 308.

59. For a contemporaneous critique of the ways the Estado Novo influenced public opinion, see Walter R. Sharp, "Methods of Opinion Control in Present-day Brazil," *Public Opinion Quarterly* 5, no. 1 (March 1941): 3–16

60. Sinisgalli, "Considerações gerais sobre o homosexualismo," 302.

61. Ibid., 303

62. At the sessions of the First Paulista Congress of Psychology, Neurology, Psychiatry, Endocrinology, Identification, Criminology, and Legal Medicine held in July 1938, sponsored by the Paulista Association of Medicine and the São Paulo Society of Legal Medicine and Criminology, the following papers related to homosexuality were presented: P. Moncau Júnior, "Pesquisas endocrinológicas em criminosos"; Edmur de Aguiar Whitaker, Eddi Kraus, Magino Roberto de Oliveira, Joel Botto Nogueira, and Aldo Sinisgalli, "Estudo biográfico dos homossexuais (pederastas passivos) da capital de São Paulo: Aspectos da sua atividade social (Costumes, hábitos, 'apelidos,' 'gíria,'" *Arquivos de Polícia e Identificação* 2, no. 1, (1938–39): 244–60; Aldo Sinisgalli, "Considerações gerais sobre o homosexualismo" and "Observações sobre os hábitos, costumes, e condições de vida dos homosexuais (pederastas passivos) de São Paulo." In addition, at the August 30, 1938, meeting of the São Paulo Society of Legal Medicine and Criminology, Antônio Tavares de Almeida led a discussion about "the penal question of homosexuals," which concluded that "there was a class of homosexuals which needed the special care of the law." At a September 14, 1939, meeting of the association, Antônio Carlos Pacheco e Silva presented the case study "Um interessante caso de homosexualismo feminino."

63. Ferreira de Almeida, *Os projectos do código criminal brasileiro*, 198.

64. José Henrique Pierangelli, *Códigos penais do Brasil: evolução histórica* (Bauru: Editora Jalovi, 1980), 301. The proposed legal reform also suggested a one- to three-year sentence for the "active subject," if a case involved violence or the threat of violence, and two to six years if the victim were fourteen or younger. These provisions modified the 1932 Consolidated Codes by changing the maximum penalty for carnal violence against a minor from four to six years, and lowering the age of consent from twenty-one to fourteen (ibid., 373).

65. Leonídio Ribeiro, commenting on the draft proposal in *O novo código legal*, pointed out that feminine homosexuality was not included in the draft article. Ribeiro attributed this omission to the difficulty of proving the existence of said behavior (*O novo código penal*, 136). More likely, the lack of attention to lesbians had more to do with the virtual silence in the medical and legal literature to sexual relations between women, other than fleeting historical references to Sappho. At the time, as pointed out by Pacheco e Silva in his study "Um interessante caso de homosexualismo feminino," the experts still considered that homosexuality was practiced almost exclusively by men. Lesbians and their sexual activities remained invisible.

66. Ferreira de Almeida, *Os projetos do código criminal brasileiro*, 198.

67. Ribeiro, *Homosexualismo e endocrinologia*, 82.

68. Ribeiro, *O novo código penal*, 186–87.

69. Maria Clementina Pereira Cunha, *O espelho do mundo: Juquery, a história de um asilo* (Rio de Janeiro: Paz e Terra, 1986), 80.

70. For an overview of Franco da Rocha's medicolegal approach to mental illness, see Francisco Franco da Rocha, *Esboço de psiquiatria forense* (São Paulo: Typografia Lammert, 1904).

71. Quoted in Cunha, *O espelho do mundo*, 157.

72. Ibid., 103, 156.

73. Ibid. 175.

74. Case no. 216, Adalberto de O., Sanatório Pinel, Pirituba, São Paulo, Arquivo do Estado de São Paulo.

75. Case no. 760, Sydney da S. F., Sanatório Pinel, Pirituba, São Paulo, Arquivo do Estado de São Paulo.

76. Kenneth P. Serbin, "Priests, Celibacy, and Social Conflict: A History of Brazil's Clergy and Seminaries" (Ph.D. diss., University of California, San Diego, 1993), 304–10. I wish to thank Kenneth Serbin for sharing documents with me.

77. Case no. 139, Rev. Macario S., Sanatório Pinel, Pirituba, São Paulo, Arquivo do Estado de São Paulo.

78. The priest was readmitted nine months later. Curiously, his psychic exam, dated September 1, 1931, stated that Macario had left the sanatorium in December 1930 in "complete remission," implying that the institution considered that Macario's homosexuality or mental illness had been cured. The doctor's new report stated that Macario had begun to manifest psychic disturbances identical to the ones presented the previous year. This situation required his rehospitalization, but the priest insisted that Pinel was not the right place for him. If, in fact, Macario's initial confinement had been his solution to avoiding possible monastic punishment, his first experiences in Pinel convinced him that the sanatorium was not a suitable environment. This time he protested his confinement from the outset, but to no avail. Held for five months, he was released in March 1932, only to be rehospitalized a year later. The medical record indicates that the motivations for his internment were identical to the two previous occasions. His physical health had deteriorated; he was undernourished, depressed, anxious, and insomniac. He was released a year later.

Macario was hospitalized a fourth and final time in January 1937. He was diagnosed with accentuated psychic depression accompanied by insomnia. His physical health, however, was relatively good. His admittance record noted: "In recent times he becomes a bit excited, developing many activities in helping the day laborers he leads, and then he falls into a state of depression, which is the reason he was rehospitalized." Perhaps his continued contact with the young boys he had admittedly desired flung him into bouts of depression. Perhaps his syphilis had reached advanced stages and caused his mental illness. Whatever the causes of his severe despondency, within a year he had lapsed into senility. The medical records do not reveal the reasons surrounding his final release from Pinel on May 31, 1938.

79. Cunha, *O espelho do mundo*, 100. The first documented use of pharmacologic shock to treat homosexuality in the United States took place in Atlanta, Georgia, in 1937. Metrazol, a chemical stimulant, was applied until convulsive shocks were produced, which reportedly eliminated the homosexual desire in the patient. While a preliminary report of the physician's success in "correcting" six homosexuals was published in the *Journal of Nervous and Mental Diseases* in 1940, a subsequent duplicate study reported in 1949 concluded that the pharmacological shock therapy had no effect on homosexual desire. See Jonathan Ned Katz, *Gay American History, Lesbian and Gay Men in the U.S.A., a Documentary History* (New York: Meridian, 1992), 165–67.

80. João Carvalhal Ribas, "Apontamentos de psiquiatria: Curso do Professor A. C. Pacheco e Silva" (Faculdade de Medicina da Universidade de São Paulo, 1938), 392. This document contains the typed class notes of lectures given by Dr. Pacheco e Silva, who held the chair of clinical psychiatry at the University of São Paulo School of Medicine. Both *convulsoterapia* and *insulinoterapia* were recommended for the treatment of schizophrenia.

81. Dr. Antônio Pacheco e Silva, Dr. Pedro Augusto da Silva, and Dr. Júlio de Andrade Silva Júnior, "A insulinoterapia nas formas delirantes da paralisia geral," *Arquivos da Assistên-*

cia Geral a Psicopatas do Estado de São Paulo 2, no. 2 (1937): 461–66. This article was presented to the Section of Neurology and Psychiatry of the Paulista Association of Medicine in November 1937.

82. Katz, *Gay American History*, 164, 170–73.

83. Case no. 3781, João Narciso G., and case no. 3074, Otávio Batista da S., Sanatório Pinel, Pirituba, São Paulo, Arquivo do Estado de São Paulo.

84. Case no. 1990, Armando de S. O. Filho, Sanatório Pinel, Pirituba, São Paulo, Arquivo do Estado de São Paulo.

85. Case no. 2584, Mário B. X., Sanatório Pinel, Pirituba, São Paulo, Arquivo do Estado de São Paulo.

86. Case no. 2479, Octávio B. de O., Sanatório Pinel, Pirituba, São Paulo, Arquivo do Estado de São Paulo.

87. Case no. 3571, Dr. Renato E. de A., Sanatório Pinel, Pirituba, São Paulo, Arquivo do Estado de São Paulo.

88. See Edgard Carone, *O Estado Novo, 1937–1945* (São Paulo: Difel, 1977); Vamireh Chacon, *Estado e povo no Brasil: as experiências do Estado Novo e da democracia populista, 1937–1964* (Rio de Janeiro: J. Olympio, 1977); Eli Diniz, "O Estado Novo: Estrutura de poder, relações de classes," in *O Brasil republicano: Sociedade e política, 1930–1964,* ed. Boris Fausto (São Paulo: Difel, 1981), 3, part 2: 77–120; Nelson Jahr Garcia, *O Estado Novo: Ideologia e propaganda política, a legitimação do estado autoritário perante as classes subalternas* (São Paulo: Loyola, 1982).

89. Lúcia Lippi Oliveira, Mônica Pimenta Velloso, and Ângela Maria de Castro Gomes, *Estado Novo: Ideologia e poder* (Rio de Janeiro: Zahar, 1982).

90. Alcir Lenharo, *Sacralização da política* (Campinas: Papirus, 1986),18.

91. *Educação Física* 73 (1943): 11, quoted in Lenharo, *Sacralização da política*, 78–79.

92. Lenharo, *Sacralização da Política*, 86. For more detailed elaboration of the metaphor of the nation-body, see chapter 3 of Lenharo's study, "The Militarization of the Body."

93. Scientific investigation in Brazil was hampered by the fact that there were few institutions of higher education equipped to carry out such work. While the Instituto Oswaldo Cruz and similar entities conducted specific research projects in tropical medicine or in infectious diseases, they had limited resources. The University of São Paulo, the first modern university capable of conducting scientific research in diverse fields of biology and chemistry as well as the social sciences, was only founded in 1934. See Simon Schwartzman, *A Space for Science: The Development of the Scientific Community in Brazil* (University Park: Pennsylvania State University Press, 1991).

94. Stepan, *The Hour of Eugenics*, 167–70.

95. Celeste Zenha Guimarães, "Homossexualismo: mitologias científicas" (Ph.D. diss., Universidade Estadual de Campinas, 1994), 346–47.

96. Ford, "Passion in the Eye of the Beholder," 162–70, 183–4.

97. "*Psicoses do Amor* de Hernâni de Irajá," *Fon-Fon* (Rio de Janeiro), no. 6 (February 7, 1931): 1.

98. Hernâni Irajá, *Psicoses do amor: Estudos sobre as alterações do instinto sexual*, 9th ed. (Rio de Janeiro: Irmãos Pongetti, 1954), 185.

Chapter Four

1. After the military forced Vargas out of office in 1945, elections were held, bringing General Eurico Dutra, a leading military figure during the Vargas regime, to the presidency. Dutra, who was closely aligned to the United States, encouraged U.S. foreign investment and followed

Washington's Cold War policies by outlawing the only recently legalized Communist Party. In the 1950 elections, Vargas swept back into power, pursuing a nationalist-populist program with the backing of organized labor and sectors of the middle class. Blocked by sectors of the military, opposition political parties, and foreign capital interests, Vargas shocked the nation by committing suicide in the presidential palace in 1954. The following year, Juscelino Kubitschek, campaigning on a platform that included building a new federal capital in the central region of Brazil, won the presidency. His electoral promises, namely, to bring fifty years' development in five years, to inaugurate the new capital of Brasília before he left office, and to offer expanded prosperity through large-scale foreign investment, sparked a period of optimism about the possibilities of national development. In late 1960, the former governor of São Paulo, Jânio Quadros, won the presidential race but resigned from office nine months later when he was not granted broader powers by Congress. After some backstage political maneuvering to prevent the military from vetoing his assumption to the presidency, Vice President João Goulart took office in 1961. By 1963, Goulart's policies shifted increasingly to the left as he relied on organized labor and Communist Party support for his radical nationalist program. In March 1964, a coalition of military leaders, opposition political parties, sectors of the middle class, and the hierarchy of the Catholic Church maneuvered Goulart's ouster in a military takeover. Instead of quickly returning the reins of government to civilian politicians, the generals remained in power until 1985. For a classic interpretation of the political events of this period, see Thomas E. Skidmore, *Politics in Brazil, 1930–1964: An Experiment in Democracy* (New York: Oxford University Press, 1967). On Kubitschek's mark on the political culture of the late 1950s, see Sheldon Maram, "Juscelino Kubitschek and the Politics of Exuberance, 1956–1961," *Luso-Brazilian Review* 27, no. 1 (summer 1990): 31–45. For a "snapshot" view of Rio de Janeiro during the "exuberant" year of 1958, see Joaquim Ferreira dos Santos, *Feliz 1958: O ano que não devia terminar* (Rio de Janeiro: Gráfica Récord Editora, 1997).

2. For detailed data on the socioeconomic status of Brazilian migrants, see Archibald O. Haller, Manoel M. Tourinho, David B. Bills, and José Pastore, "Migration and Socioeconomic Status in Brasil: Interregional and Rural-Urban Variations in Education, Occupational Status, and Income," *Luso-Brazilian Review* 18, no. 1 (summer 1981): 117–38.

3. Carla Bassanezi, *Virando as páginas, revendo as mulheres: Revistas femininas e relações homem-mulher, 1945–1964* (Rio de Janeiro: Civilização Brasileira, 1996), 43–54. A 1968 national survey of twelve hundred Brazilian women conducted by the monthly magazine *Realidade* documented this shift in attitudes about sex, gender roles, and the participation of women in the workforce, politics, and society ("A mulher brasileira, hoje," *Realidade* 1, no. 10 [January 1967]: 20–29).

4. In the context of the homosexual subcultures of Rio de Janeiro and São Paulo in the late 1950s and the 1960s, the notion of an imagined community, borrowed from Benedict Anderson, refers to the development of a sense of connectedness to others who shared a similar socially marginal experience. See Benedict R. O'Gorman Anderson, *Imagined Communities: Reflections on the Origin and Spread of Nationalism* (London: Verso Editions/NLB, 1983). Thus, strong bonds could develop between near strangers who met on the beach, in small parties, or at cultural events, not merely because of sexual attraction but also as a result of a mutual affinity based on their common need to cope in a relatively hostile society. Jeffrey Escoffier points to the "discovery of the social," the ability to imagine oneself within such a world, and the process of socialization into that new universe as important ways that gay men in the United States in the 1950s and '60s overcame countervailing hegemonic antihomosexual discourses. See Jeffrey Escoffier, "Homosexuality and the Sociological Imagination: Hegemonic Discourses, the Circulation of Ideas, and the Process of Reading in the 1950s and 1960s," in *American Homos: Community and Perversity* (Berkeley: University of California Press, 1998), 79–98.

5. Agildo Guimarães, interview by author, tape recording, Rio de Janeiro, Brazil, October 16, 1994.

6. Carlos Miranda, interview by author, tape recording, Rio de Janeiro, Brazil, November 10, 1994.

7. João Antônio Mascarenhas, interview by author, tape recording, Rio de Janeiro, Brazil, June 30, 1995.

8. In *A utopia urbana,* Gilberto Velho's 1970 study of the residents living in an apartment building in Copacabana, the anthropologist asked 220 informants about the reasons why they liked to live in that neighborhood. Velho noted that one respondent, who was open about being a homosexual, stated that he felt less social repression in Copacabana. Among those interviewed in general, there was a clear sense that one "lived better in Copacabana" because there was the possibility of entertainment, pleasure, and happiness (Velho, *A utopia urbana,* 68–69).

9. Marcelo Della Nina, "Jorge Guinle e o Copa: Entrevista a Marcelo Della Nina," in *Copacabana cidade eterna: 100 anos de um mito,* ed. Wilson Coutinho (Rio de Janeiro: Relume Dumará, 1992), 39–44.

10. For a pictorial history of the architectural and social changes of Copacabana in the twentieth century, see Elizabeth Dezouzart Cardoso, Lilian Fessler Vaz, Maria Paula Albernaz, Mario Aizen, and Roberto Moses Pechman, *Copacabana* (Rio de Janeiro: João Fortes Engenharia/Editora Index, 1986).

11. Velho, *A utopia urbana,* 23–25.

12. For a portrayal of Copacabana's bohemian night scene as reflected in the life of singer/composer Dolores Duran, see Maria Izilda Santos de Matos, *Dolores Duran: Experiências boêmias em Copacabana nos anos 50* (Rio de Janeiro: Bertrand Brasil, 1997).

13. For an account of the emergence of bossa nova in Copacabana and Ipanema, see Ruy Castro, *Chega de saudade: A história e as histórias da bossa nova* (São Paulo: Companhia das Letras, 1990).

14. Ângelo, interview by author, tape recording, Rio de Janeiro, July 20, 1995; Sérgio [pseudonym], interview by author, notes, June 26, 1996, Los Angeles, California.

15. José Rodrigues de Sousa, interview by author, tape recording, Rio de Janeiro, Brazil, April 25, 1995.

16. Hélio Fernandes, "Roteiro noturno (de Copacabana) para turistas desprevenidos," *Manchete* (Rio de Janeiro), no. 24 (October 4, 1952): 30.

17. Milton Pedrosa, "Copacabana—cidade independente e semi-nua," *Manchete* (Rio de Janeiro), no. 42 (February 7, 1953): 46.

18. Mascarenhas interview, June 30, 1995.

19. Guimarães interview, October 16, 1994.

20. Miranda interview, November 10, 1994.

21. Fernandes, "Roteiro noturno (de Copacabana)," 28.

22. Mascarenhas interview, June 30, 1995.

23. Darwin Brandão, "Um passeio pelos bares famosos do Rio," *Manchete* (Rio de Janeiro), no. 17 (August 16, 1952): 17.

24. Mascarenhas interview, June 30, 1995.

25. Vítor, interview by author, tape recording, Rio de Janeiro, Brazil, July 9, 1995.

26. Sources: Alcatraz, Rua Francisco Sá, "A house only for dolls [effeminate gay men]," *Última Hora* (Rio de Janeiro), August 15, 1964, 3; Alfredão, "The best gay place in Rio," *O Snob* (Rio de Janeiro) 5, no. 4 (April 30, 1967): 22; Dezon, between R. Sá Ferreira and Almirante Gonçalves, Copacabana, *O Snob* (Rio de Janeiro) 2, no. 15 (October 31, 1964): 21; Stop, Galeria Alaska, Copacabana, where the transvestite shows *International Set* and *Les Girls* started in

1964; Sunset, *O Snob* (Rio de Janeiro) 5, no. 5 (May 31, 1967): 28; Why Not? Rua Francisco Sá, *O Snob* (Rio de Janeiro) 2, no. 15 (November 15, 1964): 21.

27. Miranda interview, November 10, 1994.

28. Nina, "Jorge Guinle e o Copa," 42.

29. Frank Golovitz, "Gay Beach," *One Magazine* 6, no. 7 (July 1958): 8.

30. Miranda interview, November 10, 1994.

31. Rocha interview, November 2, 1994.

32. Miranda interview, November 10, 1994.

33. Ibid. José Rodrigues also remembered emphatically that housewives played a key role in defending the *bichas* on the beaches and helping secure the Bolsa de Valores as their territory (Rodrigues interview, April 25, 1995).

34. João Baptista, interview by author, tape recording, Rio de Janeiro, Brazil, July 20, 1995.

35. Miranda interview, November 10, 1994.

36. Mascarenhas interview, June 30, 1995.

37. Rocha interview, November 2, 1994.

38. João Baptista interview, July 20, 1995.

39. "Ontem, no distrito da Gávea: Quatorze presos rebentaram a grade e tentaram fugir," *Última Hora* (Rio de Janeiro), February 9, 1953, 5.

40. Rocha interview, November 2, 1994.

41. For José Rodrigues, the three public spaces where *bichas* experienced relative freedom in the 1950s were during Carnival, at the beauty pageants, and at the Bolsa de Valores. The other important social realm was the small house parties attended by groups of friends (Rodrigues interview, April 24, 1995).

42. The Biblioteca Nacional, the Brazilian National Library, does not have a collection of *Força e Sáude*, but it does have five issues of *Músculo* from 1953.

43. *Músculo* (Rio de Janeiro) 1, no. 1 (1953): 1.

44. "Apolo brasileiro em Londres," *Manchete* (Rio de Janeiro), no. 15 (August 2, 1952): 28.

45. For a history of the homoerotic content of muscle magazines in the United States, see F. Valentine Hooven III, *Beefcake: The Muscle Magazines of America, 1950–1970* (Köln: Benedikt Taschen, 1995).

46. Several editorials in *Músculo* attack the Liga de Futebol Professional (Professional Soccer League) because of the unequal state financing of different sports, which favored soccer over bodybuilding (See *Músculo* [Rio de Janeiro] 1, no. 3 [April 1953]: 5, 22, and no. 4 [May 1953]: 3).

47. James Kepner, interview by author, notes, October 16, 1995, Los Angeles, California.

48. *Músculo* (Rio de Janeiro) 1, no. 4 (June 1953): 4.

49. *Músculo* (Rio de Janeiro) 1, no. 2 (March 1953): 27.

50. *Músculo* (Rio de Janeiro) 1, no. 3 (April 1953): 36.

51. *Physique Pictorial* (fall 1954): 4–5.

52. In 1952, the station captured 50.2 percent of the capital's listening audience. See Miriam Goldfeder, *Por trás das ondas da Rádio Nacional* (Rio de Janeiro: Paz e Terra, 1980), 39. Goldfeder argues that the listening audience was predominantly composed of lower-middle-class, working-class, and poor women who were brought into the consumer market through the radio programs. By promoting stars such as Emilinha Borba, the mass media reinforced aspirations among these social sectors toward a domestically oriented middle-class consumer culture (ibid., 53). She fails, however, to note the significant role of homosexual men in the fan clubs and auditoriums. For an excellent analysis of radio singers and their relationship to the public that does take account of the role of homosexual men as adoring fans, see chapter 6, "Fan Clubs and Auditorium Programs in 1950s Brazil" in Bryan D. McCann, "Thin Air and the Solid State:

Radio, Culture, and Politics in Brazil, 1930–1955" (Ph.D. diss., Yale University, 1999). I would like to thank Bryan D. McCann for sharing a draft of this chapter of his dissertation with me.

53. These characteristics of the different radio singers became part of their trademark. The unique images and personalities they projected created a galaxy of celebrities with distinct personas from which the listening audience could choose their favorite artist. Rádio Nacional and the magazines *Revista do Rádio* and *Radiolândia* encouraged the cultivation of these images as a way of creating a more intimate relationship between public and performer. For an analysis of images of Marlene, see Goldfeder, *Por trás das ondas do Rádio Nacional*, 73–84. See also *A vida de Marlene: Depoimento* (Rio de Janeiro: Editora Rio Cultura, n.d). For Emilinha Borba, see José Antônio Severo, "Emilinha, ou a volta da Cinderela que acabou Rainha do Brasil," *Revista Realidade* 6, no. 72 (March 1972): 122–30, and Goldfeder, *Por trás das ondas da Rádio Nacional*, 48–73. For Nora Ney, see Lenharo, *Cantores do rádio*.

54. Lenharo, *Cantores do rádio*, 142.

55. Alcir Lenharo, interview by author, tape recording, Campinas, São Paulo, April 15, 1995. See also Marta Avancini, "Na Era de Ouro das cantoras do rádio," *Luso-Brazilian Review* 30, no. 1 (summer 1993): 85–93.

56. During the interview with Alcir Lenharo, I posited that perhaps gay men identified with a given singer because of the pain and suffering that she endured or because of the kinds of songs that she sang. He rejected this hypothesis, pointing out that both Marlene and Emilinha had a broad repertoire of songs that didn't characterize them as women who led a tragic or suffering life. Thus, a correlation between the social marginalization of a homosexual audience and their identification with the life and suffering of a star, a theory developed about gay fan support for Judy Garland, doesn't seem to fit Brazil in the 1950s.

57. João Baptista interview, July 20, 1995.

58. Lenharo interview, April 15, 1995.

59. In 1995, gay men in their sixties still lived the rivalry, taking sides as to who was the real queen of radio and the best singer of the 1950s. Several interviewees even solicited my opinions regarding who was my favorite of the two.

60. Carlos Ricardo da Silva, interview by author, tape recording, São Paulo, Brazil, November 26, 1994; Luiz Amorim, interview by author, tape recording, São Paulo, Brazil, September 11, 1994.

61. Lenharo interview, April 14, 1995.

62. Sarah Feldman, "Segregações espaciais urbanas: A territorialização da prostituição feminina em São Paulo" (master's thesis, Universidade de São Paulo, 1988), 87–95.

63. Lenharo interview, April 15, 1995.

64. In the late 1970s and early 1980s when Barbosa da Silva's work was rediscovered by a new generation of gay academics, one author argued that his thesis had disappeared from the university's collection as a result of institutional homophobia. See Reginaldo Prandi, "Homossexualismo: Duas teses acadêmicas," *Lampião da Esquina* 1, no. 11 (April 1979): 17. Barbosa da Silva believes that the copy of his work, which should have been filed with the Escola de Sociologia e Política in São Paulo, was likely lost owing to the turbulent political conditions at the school around the time of the 1964 military coup (José Fábio Barbosa da Silva, telephone interview by author, notes, Los Angeles, April 8, 1998).

65. José Fábio Barbosa da Silva, "Homossexualismo em São Paulo: Estudo de um grupo minoritário" (master's thesis, Escola de Sociologia e Política de São Paulo, 1960). I wish to thank Fábio Barbosa da Silva for sharing the only copy of his thesis with me. A chapter of his work was published as "Aspectos sociológicos do homossexualismo em São Paulo," *Sociologia* 21, no. 4 (October 1959): 350–60.

66. Raul Pompéia, *O Ateneu* (São Paulo: Editora Ática, 1991). Pompéia's 1888 novel about life in a boarding school in Rio de Janeiro describes adolescent sexual affairs among the boys. Selections of the novel appear in *My Deep Dark Pain Is Love: A Collection of Latin American Gay Fiction*, ed. Winston Leyland, trans. E. A. Lacey (San Francisco: Gay Sunshine Press, 1983), 343–83. See also Ricardo Noblat, "Playboy entrevista Gilberto Freyre," *Playboy* 5 (March 1980): 29–30; Richard Parker, *Bodies, Pleasures, and Passions: Sexual Culture in Contemporary Brazil* (Boston: Beacon Press, 1991), 122–28; Peter Fry, *Para inglês ver: Identidade e política na cultura brasileira* (Rio de Janeiro: Zahar, 1982), 92–93. Jeffrey Needell generously obtained a copy of Freyre's *Playboy* interview for me.

67. Barbosa da Silva, "Homossexualismo em São Paulo," tables 1 and 2.

68. Ibid., 34, 35.

69. Ibid., 13.

70. Ibid., 11–12.

71. Ibid.

72. Barbosa da Silva, "Aspectos sociológicos do homossexualismo em São Paulo," 357.

73. Ibid., 358.

74. Quoted from Néstor Perlongher, "Transformações no espaço urbano: O gueto *gay* paulistano entre 1959 e 1984," in *O negócio do michê: Prostituição viril em São Paulo* (São Paulo: Brasiliense, 1987), 78.

75. Silva interview, November 26, 1994.

76. Perlongher, *O negócio do michê*, 79. Perlongher's mapping of homosexual space in São Paulo proved invaluable in developing the material for this section.

77. Barbosa da Silva lists Paribar as one of the favorite locations for homosexual cruising (Barbosa da Silva, "Aspectos sociológicos dos homossexualismo em São Paulo," 352). Clóvis recalls that Barbazul "was more refined, more conventional people with suits and ties," while Arpège was a bar where you stood when you had drinks (Perlongher, *O negócio do michê*, 73–74). Paribar, Barbazul, and Arpège, along with Mirim, are mentioned by Bento Prado Júnior as bars frequented by young Paulista intellectuals who congregated in the area in the mid-1950s (Bento Prado Júnior, "A biblioteca e os bares na década de 50," *Folhetim: Folha de São Paulo* [January 22, 1988]: 20).

78. Prado, "A biblioteca e os bares," 20–21.

79. José Fábio Barbosa da Silva, notes for research on homosexuality in São Paulo, unpublished material in possession of James N. Green, 1959–60, 7; Edward MacRae, "Gueto," *Novos Estudos Cebrap* (São Paulo) 2, 1 (April 1983): 54.

80. Darcy Penteado, interview by Edward MacRae, tape recording, São Paulo, Brazil, June 13, 1980. I would like to thank Edward MacRae for sharing this interview with me.

81. Perlongher, *O negócio do michê*, 78.

82. Antônio Bivar, "O paraíso gay, São Paulo, é claro," *Especial* (São Paulo), February 1980, 26.

83. Max Jurth, "L'homophilie au Brésil," *Arcadie* 83 (November 1960): 654–665. In the 1950s, groups that worked to educate the public about homosexuality and to provide support to individuals called themselves homophile organizations. The gay liberation movement that developed in 1969 preferred other language to express a more radical and politicized approach and rejected the term homophile, which then fell into misuse. For a history of Arcadie see Jacques Girard, *Le mouvement homosexuel en France, 1945–1980* (Paris: Editions Syros, 1981).

84. An irony about the Municipal Library that Jurth failed to note was the fact that it was named after Mário de Andrade, whose homosexuality still remains a taboo topic for Brazil's literary establishment.

85. In this volume, Marone, who relied on theories of homosexuality promoted by Ribeiro, Marañón, and Peixoto, argued that the effeminate characteristics in some figures painted by Raphael proved that all people were a mixture of both sexes. See Sílvio Marone, *Missexualidade e arte* (São Paulo: n.p., 1947).

86. Daniel Franco, "O homossexual brasileiro nas últimas três décadas," *Jornal do Gay: Noticiário do Mundo Entendido* (São Paulo) 2 (1978): 21.

87. Jorge Jaime, *Homossexualismo masculino* (Rio de Janeiro: Editora "O Constructor," 1953). Jurth pointed out, though, that it could not be found in the São Paulo public library ("L'homophilie au Brésil," 657).

88. Jaime, *Homossexualismo masculino*, 13.

89. Ibid., 17–18.

90. Ibid., 24.

91. Jurth, "L'homophilie au Brésil," 657.

92. Jaime, *Homossexualismo masculino*, 59. This proposal to permit homosexuals the right to marry impressed Max Jurth when he reported on the importance of Jaime's work, although the French homophile leader dismissed the idea as utopian.

93. Ibid., 59, 60, 61, 63.

94. Ibid., 85.

95. Jorge Jaime, *Monstro que chora* (Rio de Janeiro: Livraria Império, 1957).

96. Jaime, *Monstro que chora*, 132. Tasca, Follies, Posto 5, OK, and Bolero were nightclubs or café restaurants frequented by Carioca homosexuals. Mercadinho Azul was a small shopping mall that had a public restroom that was a favorite cruising spot (Sérgio interview, June 26, 1996).

97. Franco, "O homossexual brasileiro nas últimas três décadas," 21.

98. Mário de Andrade, *Contos novos* (São Paulo: Editora Martins, 1947). An English translation was published in Leyland, *My Deep Dark Pain Is Love*, 151–63.

99. Paulo Hecker Filho, *Internato* ([Porto Alegre?]: Edição Fronteira, 1951). An English translation of this novella entitled "Boarding-School" appears in Leyland, *My Deep Dark Pain Is Love*, 245–66.

100. "Boarding-School," 265.

101. Ibid., 266.

102. Ibid., 28.

103. Anuar Farah, interview by author, tape recording, Rio de Janeiro, July 31, 1995.

104. Barbosa da Silva, "Homossexualismo em São Paulo," 29.

105. Silva interview, November 26, 1994; Amorim interview, September 11, 1994; Guimarães interview, October 16, 1994; Carmen Dora Guimarães, "O homossexual visto por entendidos" (master's thesis, Rio de Janeiro, Museu Nacional, 1977).

106. Jaime, *Homossexualismo masculino*, 70. Jaime described Robert as a "passive pederast" and justified publishing a series of letters written by homosexuals "[so that] we can know how they think and act as Urnings, how they react to life, what are their points of view, their peculiar slang."

107. In the United States, the term "gay" was employed in a similar fashion as a code word as early as the 1920s and then later took on an additional connotation as a marker for homosexual men based on their sexual interests rather than effeminacy. See George Chauncey, *Gay New York: Gender, Urban Culture, and the Making of the Gay Male World, 1890–1940* (New York: Basic Books, 1994), 14–21. Most anthropologists who have written on homosexuality in Brazil date the use of the term to the 1960s. See Guimarães, "O homossexual visto por entendidos," 130; Fry, *Para inglês ver*, 93; Perlongher, *O negócio do michê*, 78. The documents cited in this chapter indicate that the slang term *entendido* was already in use in the immediate post–World

War II period, leading one to deduce that it was possibly coined as early as the Estado Novo (1937–45). The term *entendido* has also been used in Venezuela, Peru, and Argentina, suggesting a Latin American borrowing. Significantly, Robert used the word *entendido*, a term indigenous to Brazil, instead of the Portuguese word *alegre* (happy, gay), which would have been the direct translation of the word used in the United States at the time. In Brazil, *alegre* had been linked to female prostitution at the turn of the century. Brazilian journalists in the 1960s and '70s, who were familiar with the English term gay, translated it as *alegre* and used it to mean homosexual. See, for example, Paulo Tavares, "Os alegres enxutos," *Manchete* (Rio de Janeiro), no. 517 (March 17, 1962): 60–63. See also Gasparino Damata. "Nossos alegres rapazes da banda," *Pasquim* (Rio de Janeiro), no. 436 (November 4, 1977): 6; "Ipanema: Os alegres rapazes da banda," *Manchete* (Rio de Janeiro), no. 1508 (March 14, 1981): 50–54. In both articles, the journalists described homosexuals as gay boys (*rapazes alegres*). This expression was a double play on words. It referred to the Carnival street groups (*bandas*), in which many drag queens, transvestites, and gay men participated, and also alluded to the pioneering gay-themed Broadway show *The Boys in the Band* (1968). By adding the adjective *alegre*, the authors communicated the homosexual content of the *banda* for those who were "in the know" (*entendido*) or those familiar with English cultural references to homosexuality. The turn-of-the-century use of the term *a vida alegre* (the gay life) as an expression describing female prostitution does seem to have survived in midcentury slang.

108. Jaime, *Homossexualismo masculino*, 74–75.

109. Ibid., 72.

110. Ibid., 70. Portuguese grammar permits the speaker or writer to drop the gendered pronoun, as Robert did in this case.

111. Ibid., 71.

112. Guimarães interview, October 16, 1994.

113. *O Snob* (Rio de Janeiro) 1, no. 1 (July 10, 1963). A complete collection of *O Snob* is housed at the Edgard Leuenroth Archive, UNICAMP, Campinas, Brazil. Unfortunately, there is no original copy of the first issue, only a reprint for the sixth anniversary edition in 1968.

114. Guimarães interview, October 16, 1994.

115. These included *O Vedete* (Campos, State of Rio de Janeiro) [1962?]; *Terceira Força* (Rio de Janeiro) 1963; *Zona Norte* (Rio de Janeiro) 1963; *Vagalume* (Rio de Janeiro) 1964; *O Mito* (Niterói) (1966); *Subúrbio a Noite* (Rio de Janeiro) [1966?]; *Cinelândia a Noite* (Rio de Janeiro) 1966; *O Bem* (Rio de Janeiro) 1966; *Edifício Avenida Central* (Rio de Janeiro) 1966; *O Show* (Rio de Janeiro) 1966; *O Estábulo* (Niterói) 1966; *Sophistique* (Campos) 1966; *Mais* (Belo Horizonte); *Fatos e Fofocas* (Salvador, Bahia) 1966; *Charme* (Rio de Janeiro) 1966; *O Pelicano* (Rio de Janeiro) 1966; *Le Carrillon* (Rio de Janeiro) 1966; *Chic* (Rio de Janeiro) 1966; *Sputnik* (Rio Grande do Sul) 1967; *Os Felinos* (Niterói) 1967; *Gay* (Salvador, Bahia) 1967; *Gay Society* (Salvador, Bahia) 1967; *Zéfiro* (Salvador, Bahia) 1967; *Baby* (Salvador, Bahia) 1967; *O Núcleo* 1967; *Le Femme* (Rio de Janeiro) 1968; *Centauro* (Rio de Janeiro) 1968; *O Vic* (Rio de Janeiro) 1968; *O Badalo* (Rio de Janeiro) 1968; *O Grupo* (Rio de Janeiro) 1968; *Opinião* (1968); *Darling* (Rio de Janeiro) 1968; *O Tiraninho* (Salvador, Bahia); *Ello* (Salvador, Bahia); *La Saison* (Rio de Janeiro); *Gay Press Magazine* (Rio de Janeiro); *20 de Abril* (Rio de Janeiro), *Little Darling* (Salvador, Bahia) 1970. For a brief account of the homecraft publications from Salvador, Bahia, see Peter Fry, "História da imprensa baiana," *Lampião da Esquina* (Rio de Janeiro) 1, no. 4 (August 25, 1978): 4. José Fábio Barbosa da Silva noted that an ephemeral publication had also appeared in São Paulo while he was doing his research in 1959 and 1960. Although he did not give details as to the nature of the newsletter other than to note that it published comments on the members

of the subgroup, he argued that it reflected a significant development in the organization of this minority. He further speculated that it might portend the future publication of lists of bars, hotels, or other specialized services for homosexuals (Barbosa da Silva, "Considerações finais," in "Homossexualismo em São Paulo," 5).

116. *O Snob* (Rio de Janeiro) 1, no. 1 (July 10, 1963): 1.

117. *O Snob* (Rio de Janeiro) 1, no. 8 (September 30, 1963): 3.

118. Délcio Monteiro de Lima, *Os homoeróticos* (Rio de Janeiro: Livraria Francisco Alves Editora, 1983), 59–61, 105–6.

119. *O Snob* (Rio de Janeiro) 2, no. 12 (September 15, 1964): 1.

120. "Gay Is Good" was inspired by "Black Is Beautiful," a phrase affirming the value of Afro-American culture, style, and physical appearance. "Gay Is Good," however, did not emphasize the effeminate homosexual, as did the *bonecas* of *O Snob*. Rather it universalized different identities under the umbrella term "gay."

121. Ramalhete [pseudonym], interview by author, tape recording, Rio de Janeiro, February 15, 1995.

122. Ibid.

123. Rodrigues interview, April 25, 1995.

124. In Teresa Adada Sell's study of the formation of homosexual identity conducted in the 1980s, informants reported that when "hetero" men had sex with homosexuals, they didn't like to be seen with their sexual partner after the encounter took place, indicating a reluctance on the part of "real" men to being identified with same-sex erotic liasions. See Teresa Adada Sell, *Identidade homossexual e normas sociais (histórias de vida)* (Florianópolis: Editora da UFSC, 1987), 154. In studying Spanish-speaking Latin America, Stephen O. Murray has noted a similar reluctance of "real" men to let their peers know of their sexual involvement with other men for fear of social stigmatization. See Stephen O. Murray, "Machismo, Male Homosexuality, and Latin Culture," in *Latin American Male Homosexualities*, ed. Stephan O. Murray, (Albuquerque: University of New Mexico Press, 1995), 49–70. I tend to agree with Murray's analysis.

125. Guimarães interview, October 16, 1994.

126. Ibid.

127. Rodrigues interview, April 25, 1995.

128. Gasparino Damata [Gasparino da Mata e Silva], *Os solteirões* (Rio de Janeiro: Pallas, 1975).

129. *O Snob* (Rio de Janeiro) 2, no. 3 (February 29, 1964): 1.

130. *O Snob* (Rio de Janeiro) 2, no. 12 (September 15, 1994): 1.

131. Farah interview, July 31, 1995.

132. Guimarães interview, October 16, 1994; Miranda interview, November 10, 1994; Rocha interview, November 2, 1994; Rodrigues interview, April 25, 1995; Ramalhete interview, February 15, 1995.

133. Hélio Fonseca, interview by author, tape recording, Niterói, state of Rio de Janeiro, Brazil, July 25, 1995.

134. *O Snob* (Rio de Janeiro) 7, no 2 (May/June 1969): 16.

135. Fonseca interview, July 25, 1995.

136. Dora Guimarães, "O homossexual visto por entendidos," 130.

137. Edward MacRae, *A construção da igualdade: Identidade sexual e política no Brasil da "abertura"* (Campinas: Editora da UNICAMP, 1990), 52.

138. Fry, *Para inglês ver*, 93.

139. Perlongher, *O negócio do michê*, 78.

140. MacRae, *A construção da igualdade*, 52.

141. *O Snob* (Rio de Janeiro) 5, no. 10 (August 31, 1967): 1.

142. Jaime Snoek, "Eles também são da nossa estripe: Considerações sobre a homofilia." *Revista Vozes* 9 (September 1967): 792.

143. Ibid., 795.

144. Ibid., 803. Snoek repeated his arguments about toleration of homosexuality in a paper presented in the Second Brazilian Catholic Congress on Medicine, held in January 1967. See Jaime Snoek, "Emancipação dos homossexuais e valores positivos da homossexualidade," in *Católicos e Medicina Hoje: Anais do II Congresso Católico Brasileiro de Medicina*, ed. A. G. Mattos (São Paulo: n.p., 1967).

145. Dom Marcos Barbosa, "Bazares e feiras," *Jornal do Brasil* (Rio de Janeiro), September 26, 1969, 1. The priest elliptically referred to Snoek by mentioning "certain (Dutch?) theologians," alluding to the fact that the professor of theology had been born in Holland although he had been a naturalized Brazilian since 1963. The official church position on homosexuality did not waiver even among sectors of the Brazilian Catholic hierarchy who played an important role in criticizing the economic policies and human rights abuses of the military dictatorship in the 1970s. The National Council of Brazilian Bishops, for example, reiterated the Vatican teaching that while homosexual tendencies should not be considered a sin, individuals with such desires should either marry and have children or remain celibate. See Ney Flávio Meirelles, "CNBB recomenda que homossexuais casem ou mantenham abstinência," *Jornal do Brasil* (Rio de Janeiro), October 31, 1986, 1.

146. *O Snob* (Rio de Janeiro) 7, no. 1 (March 31, 1969): 1.

147. *O Snob* (Rio de Janeiro) 3, no. 12 (August 15, 1965): 12; 5, no. 8 (July 15, 1967); 5, no. 10 (August 31, 1967): 12.

148. *O Snob* (Rio de Janeiro) 6, no. 4 (April 30, 1968): 1.

149. *O Snob* (Rio de Janeiro) 6, no. 6 (June 30, 1968): 3.

150. *O Snob* (Rio de Janeiro) 6, no. 7 (July 31, 1968): 13.

151. *O Snob* (Rio de Janeiro) 7, no. 1 (March 31, 1969): 2. These slogans were not as far-fetched as one would imagine. Eleven years later, the gay and lesbian rights groups of São Paulo organized a march of a thousand people through the streets of the downtown area protesting police commissioner Richetti's dragnet of homosexuals, transvestites, and prostitutes in the city's center. Among the more popular slogans during the march was "Down with Repression, More Love and More Desire."

152. The term "gay" was used by members of *O Snob* in the first issues of the publication (*O Snob* [Rio de Janeiro] 1, no. 11 [October 31, 1963]). By 1967, it was commonly employed as a synonym for *entendido* or homosexual.

153. Guimarães interview, October 16, 1994; Farah interview, July 31, 1995; Fonseca interview, July 25, 1995.

154. *O Snob* (Rio de Janeiro) 6, no. 12 (December 31, 1968): 1; Guimarães interview, October 16, 1994. Agildo, Riva, Carlos, Hélio, and Anuar, along with others, joined efforts in the early 1980s to achieve Agildo's dream of forming a Shangri-lá. Working with the Turma OK, which had been founded in 1959, but had lain dormant from 1965 to 1976, they helped to open a center in 1982 in the Lapa neighborhood. The group organizes parties, drag shows, and other social events for diverse groups of homosexuals of all ages, social classes, and sexual identities (Farah interview, July 31, 1995).

155. Fonseca interview, July 25, 1995.

156. Guimarães interview, October 16, 1994.

Chapter Five

1. Hugh Gibson, *Rio de Janeiro* (Garden City, N.Y.: Doubleday, Doran and Company, 1937), x–xi.

2. Edmur de Aguiar Whitaker, Eddi Kraus, Magino Roberto de Oliveira, and Aldo Sinisgalli, "Estudo biográfico dos homossexuais (pederastas passivos) da capital de São Paulo: Aspectos da sua atividade social (São Paulo), costumes, hábitos, 'apelidos', 'gíria')," *Arquivos de Polícia e Identificação* 2, no. 1 (1938–39): 253.

3. See Mikhail Bakhtin, *Rabelais and His World*, trans. Helene Iswolsky (Bloomington: Indiana University Press, 1984). Roberto Da Matta has developed his analysis on Brazilian Carnival in different articles and books. These include: "O Carnaval como um rito de passagem," in *Ensaios de antropologia estrutural* (Petrópolis: Editora Vozes, 1973), 121–68; *Carnavais, malandros, e heróis: Para uma sociologia do dilema brasileiro* (Rio de Janeiro: Zahar Editores, 1978); the English translation is *Carnivals, Rogues, and Heroes: An Interpretation of the Brazilian Dilemma*, trans. John Drury (Notre Dame: University of Notre Dame Press, 1991); *Universo do Carnaval: Imagens e reflexões* (Rio de Janeiro: Edições Pinakotheke, 1981); "Carnival in Multiple Planes," in *Rite, Drama, Festival, Spectacle: Rehearsals toward a Theory of Cultural Performance*, ed. John J. MacAloon (Philadelphia: Institute for the Study of Human Issues, 1984), 208–40; "*Carnaval* as a Cultural Problem: Towards a Theory of Formal Events and their Magic," Working Paper no. 79, Helen Kellogg Institute for International Studies, Notre Dame, Ind., September 1986.

4. Victor Turner makes a similar argument in "Carnaval in Rio: Dionysian Drama in an Industrializing Society," in *The Anthropology of Performance* (New York: PAJ Publications, 1986), 123–38.

5. Sandra Lauderdale Graham, *House and Street: The Domestic World of Servants and Masters in Nineteenth-Century Rio de Janeiro* (Cambridge: Cambridge Latin American Studies, 1988).

6. Maria Clementina Pereira Cunha, "E viva o Zé Pereira! O Carnaval carioca como teatro de conflitos, 1880–1920," paper delivered at the 1997 meeting of the Latin American Studies Association, Guadalajara, Mexico, April 1997, 5.

7. Kay Francis [João Ferreira da Paz], interview by author, tape recording, Lapa, Rio de Janeiro, Brazil, November 3, 1994.

8. David Bergman, ed., *Camp Grounds: Style and Homosexuality* (Amherst: University of Massachusetts Press, 1993), 4–5.

9. Martha Gil-Montero, *Brazilian Bombshell: The Biography of Carmen Miranda* (New York: Donald I. Fine, 1989) 152–53.

10. For the best overall history of Carnival in Rio de Janeiro, see Eneida Moraes, *História do Carnaval carioca*, new edition, revised and expanded by Haroldo Costa (Rio de Janeiro: Gráfica Récord Editora, 1987). See also Maria Isaura Pereira de Queiroz, *Carnaval brasileiro: O vivido e o mito* (São Paulo: Editora Brasiliense, 1992).

11. "Do entrudo à passarela, 419 anos de folia," *O Globo*, October 8, 1989, 22; Maria Helena Linhares, "O Carnaval de antigamente (primeira parte): Há quatro séculos nascia o gosto brasileiro pelas folias, *Estado de Minas* January 30, 1986, 8.

12. Noélia Pelegrin de Oliveira, "O Carnaval começou com um rei para acabar na rua," *Folha de São Paulo*, February 23, 1979, 39.

13. The Commission of Tourism began awarding prizes for the best costumes in 1935 (Clóvis Bornay, interview by author, tape recording, Rio de Janeiro, Brazil, May 25, 1995).

14. Luiz Edmundo, *O Rio de Janeiro do meu tempo* (Rio de Janeiro: Imprensa Nacional, 1938), 779–825; Moraes, *História do Carnaval carioca*, 113, 124–27.

15. Pelegrin de Oliveira, "O Carnaval começou com um rei," 39. The refrain to this samba

song, composed by Donga [Ernesto dos Santos] expresses a comic irony about the corruption of public officials: "The Chief of Police / Over the telephone / Sent word to me / That at the Carioca / There is a roulette / Where everyone can play . . . "

16. Edison Carneiro, *A sabedoria popular* (Rio de Janeiro: Ministério da Educação e Cultura, Instituto Nacional do Livro, 1957), 113–22.

17. Luis D. Gardel, *Escolas de Samba: An Affectionate Descriptive Account of the Carnival Guilds of Rio de Janeiro* (Rio de Janeiro: Livraria Kosmos Editora, 1967), 73–85.

18. For an engaging portrayal of modern Carnival in Brazil, see Alma Guillermoprieto, *Samba* (New York: Vintage Books, 1991).

19. Jota Efegê [João Ferreira Gomes], *Figuras e coisas do Carnaval carioca* (Rio de Janeiro: FUNARTE, 1982), 87–88.

20. Madame Satã, "Madame Satã," interview by Sérgio Cabral, Millôr Fernandes, Chico Júnior, and Paulo Francis, *Pasquim*, no. 95 (April 29, 1971): 3.

21. Ibid. In the *Pasquim* interview with Madame Satã in 1971 he identified himself as a *viado*, in much the same way that many gay and lesbian activists have recently adopted the term "queer" as a political identity to subvert and to empty the word of a negative connotation.

22. Maraca Figueiredo, *Cordão da Bola Preta: Boêmia carioca* (Rio de Janeiro: Comércio e Representações Bahia Ltda., 1966), 26, 73. The Cordão da Bola Preta is one of Rio de Janeiro's traditional Carnival clubs. Founded by a group of bohemian Cariocas in 1918, the club launched Carnival festivities on Saturday morning. The Cordão de Bola Preta became a social club, with bylaws, a headquarters, and a leadership body that organized social events through the year. The term *cordão*, a snakelike line formed during Carnival celebrations where people weave through the crowd of dancing revelers, is translated in a broader sense as a "club" to reflect the diverse functions of this association. The history of the Carnival club, written by a longtime member, is a collection of favorable memories of the group's revels during pre-Lenten festivities.

23. Francisco José Viveiros de Castro, *Atentados ao pudor: Estudos sobre as aberrações do instinto sexual*, 3d ed. rev. and enl. (Rio de Janeiro: Livraria Editora Freitas Bastos, 1934), 221–22.

24. Sylvan Paezzo, *Memórias de Madame Satã, conforme narração a Sylvan Paezzo* (Rio de Janeiro: Lidador, 1972), 59.

25. *Jornal do Brasil* (Rio de Janeiro), March 4, 1938, 13.

26. Indirect evidence links homosexuality and the theaters surrounding Praça Tiradentes. According to Nestor de Holanda, the word *bói* was a slang term for homosexual. Derived from the English word "boy," it came from the fact that the majority of the male members of the chorus (*coristas*) of the Praça Tiradentes theater reviews were homosexuals. Nestor de Holanda, *Memórias do café Nice: Subterrâneos da música popular e da vida boêmia do Rio de Janeiro* (Rio de Janeiro: Conquista, 1970), 38.

27. Neyde Veneziano, *O teatro de revista no Brasil: dramaturgia e convenções* (Campinas: Editorial da UNICAMP, 1991), 50–51; Alcir Lenharo, *Cantores do rádio: A trajetória de Nora Ney e Jorge Goulart e o meio artístico de seu tempo* (Campinas, São Paulo: Editora da UNICAMP, 1995), 49.

28. The ball was held in the João Caetano Theater, which faced Praça Tiradentes. See "A antiga lenda é revivida por muitos, todos os anos no João Caetano," *Manchete* (Rio de Janeiro), no. 306 (March 1, 1958): 26.

29. Riva Rocha, interview by author, tape recording, Rio de Janeiro, Brazil, November 2, 1994; Carlos Miranda, interview by author, tape recording, Rio de Janeiro, Brazil, November 10, 1994.

30. A survey of the photo archive of *Manchete* magazine between 1952 and 1969 uncovered this dissonance between the images that appeared in the weekly and the actual composition of

these balls. While the editors chose to feature men dressed as women in their coverage of the event, other photographs taken inside the theaters reveal that the majority of celebrants, almost all men, dressed in masculine attire.

31. Lilian Newlands, "Elvira Pagã, a primeira Rainha do Carnaval," *Jornal do Brasil* (Rio de Janeiro), January 15, 1984, 4.

32. "A antiga lenda é revivida por muitos," 26.

33. *Jornal do Brasil* (Rio de Janeiro), March 4, 1938, 13. The caption read "Outro rancho: O 'Quem são eles?'"

34. Evaraldo de Barros, "As 'falsas baianas' do Carnaval carioca," *Última Hora* (Rio de Janeiro), February 14, 1953, 8.

35. See Moraes, *História do Carnaval carioca*, 243–55.

36. Barros, "As 'falsas baianas' do Carnaval carioca," 8.

37. Ibid.

38. José Rodrigues, interview by author, tape recording, Rio de Janeiro, April 25, 1995.

39. Sérgio Roberto, "Noite dos Artistas: 4000 pessoas brincando," *Manchete* (Rio de Janeiro), no. 44 (February 21, 1953): 36–37.

40. "Desfile de fantasias no Baile dos Artistas," *Manchete* (Rio de Janeiro), no. 98 (March 6, 1954): 35.

41. "A antiga lenda é revivida por muitos," 26.

42. Jânio Freitas, "A extravagante exibição do João Caetano," *Manchete* (Rio de Janeiro), no. 201 (February 25, 1956): 28.

43. Clarice Lispector, "Clóvis Bornay," *Manchete* (Rio de Janeiro), no. 879 (February 22, 1969): 48–49.

44. Ibid., 49.

45. Ibid., 37.

46. "Aelson, o costureiro do Carnaval," *Manchete* (Rio de Janeiro), no. 202 (March 3, 1956): 32.

47. In 1966, Agildo Guimarães, writing about the "elites of the *mundo entendido*" (gay world), commented about a dress rehearsal at the Golden Room of the Copacabana Palace Hotel, where he mentioned the city's most important hairdressers, designers, and Carnival figures, including Aelson, Evandro Castro Lima, and Clóvis Bornay" (*O Snob* [Rio de Janeiro] 4, no. 9 [September 7, 1966]: 17).

48. Luis Gutemberg, "O baile proibido," *Manchete* (Rio de Janeiro), no. 255 (March 9, 1957): 56–57.

49. Júlio Bartolo, "Uma noite di-vi-na com elas e elas," *Manchete* (Rio de Janeiro), no. 1348 (February 18, 1978): 83.

50. "O Baile do Arco-Íris," *Manchete* (Rio de Janeiro), no. 306 (March 1, 1958): 25.

51. Da folia ao exagero: Excessos que mancham o Carnaval carioca," *Última Hora* (Rio de Janeiro), February 20, 1958, 10.

52. Rock Hudson and Sara Davidson, *Rock Hudson: His Story* (New Work: William Morrow and Company, 1986), 89–109; Jerry Openheimer and Jack Vitek, *Idol: Rock Hudson: The True Story of an American Film Hero* (New York: Villard, 1986), 55–67.

53. The daily *Última Hora* provided extensive coverage of Rock Hudson's visit to Rio, speculating endlessly about the possible romantic liaisons that might develop between the Hollywood star and any number of Brazilian beauties.

54. For a discussion of Hudson's Hollywood-driven masculine representation in the 1950s, see Richard Meyer, "Rock Hudson's Body," in *Inside/Out: Lesbian Theories, Gay Theories*, ed. Diana Fuss (New York: Routledge, 1991), 259–88.

55. Álvaro and Vicente Marzullo, two brothers who worked as secretaries for Walter Pinto, the "Ziegfeld of Praça Tiradentes," proposed the Carnival ball for men dressed in drag. Pinto's business ventures had not gone well that year, and the brothers thought that the event could attract a large crowd and prove financially successful. Álvaro suggested calling it the Baile dos Garotos Enxutos (Ball of the Shapely Boys). Vincent preferred to simply call it Baile dos Enxutos, which became its official name. They promoted the ball as featuring elegantly costumed men dressed in drag, and the attendance exceeded their expectations. Sheila Kaplan, "A 'explosão gay' na festa carioca atrai mais turistas," *O Globo* (Rio de Janeiro), March 1, 1984, 4.

56. "A terceira força no Carnaval carioca," *Manchete, Edição Especial* (Rio de Janeiro), no. 356 (February 1959): 64.

57. Ibid., 68.

58. "Eles não usam *black tie.*" *Manchete* (Rio de Janeiro), no. 463 (March 4, 1961): 66–69.

59. *Última Hora*, for example, ran advertisements in 1961 printed in large block letters announcing the Baile dos Enxutos at the Teatro Recreio on Carnival Saturday, Sunday, Monday, and Tuesday (*Última Hora* [Rio de Janeiro], February 10, 1961).

60. These ads ran the Wednesday and Thursday before Carnival as well as on the Friday and Saturday, two days when the balls took place (*Última Hora* [Rio de Janeiro], February 28, 1962, 10).

61. Paulo Tavares, "Os alegres enxutos," *Manchete* (Rio de Janeiro), no. 517 (March 17, 1962): 60–63.

62. Official prohibitions of specific Carnival activities had a long tradition in Brazil. In the seventeenth century, for example, the Portuguese crown outlawed the use of masks during street festivities (Moraes, *História do Carnaval carioca*, 17). Many times the restrictions were ignored or only intermittently enforced. Each year the chief of police would issue a series of regulations for that year's Carnival. In this way the police retained the right to enforce the prohibitions and could do so discriminately when they didn't approve of a given type of conduct. Among other items outlawed in 1962 were the use of perfumed ether (*lança-perfume*) and the wearing of "transvestite costumes" in clubs, bars, or other houses of entertainment ("Cariocas já em pleno reinado carnavalesco," *Última Hora* [Rio de Janeiro], March 3, 1962, 2). The police regulation published in the newspapers read: "Não será permitida a utilização de fantasias de 'travesti.'"

63. Tavares, "Os alegres enxutos," 60; "'Enxutos' tiveram seu baile," *Última Hora* (Rio de Janeiro), March 7, 1962, 8

64. Agildo Guimarães, interview by author, Tape recording, Rio de Janeiro, Brazil, October 16, 1994.

65. Ângelo, interview by author, tape recording, Rio de Janeiro, Brazil, July 20, 1995.

66. "Borrachada comandou 'Baile dos Enxutos,'" *Última Hora* (Rio de Janeiro), February 12, 1964, 6. Rio de Janeiro's chief of police, Colonel Gustavo Borges, waged a fruitless battle to prohibit kissing during that Carnival season. His regulation received the support of several judges, one of whom stated that "kisses on the mouth during Carnival are not kisses, they are manifestations of lasciviousness that are unfortunately exploited by some magazines." A host of artists, singers, and public personalities opposed the ban, and it was widely ignored during Carnival revelry. See "Carnaval na base do beijo prohibido," *Última Hora* (Rio de Janeiro), February 12, 1964, 5; "Borges vai prender quem beijar na boca," *Última Hora* (Rio de Janeiro), February 6, 1964, 2.

67. "Delegacia especializada de vigilância e capturas," *Última Hora* (Rio de Janeiro), March 8, 1962, 12; "Carnaval em plena cinzas: 'Enxutos' e 'chave' saem 4ᵃ feira," *Última Hora* (Rio de Janeiro), February 13, 1964, 1; "Pancadaria, enxutos, e pouca gente animada no 'Baile dos Artista,'" *Última Hora* (Rio de Janeiro), February 3, 1964, 7. The name of the informally or-

ganized *bloco* (Carnival street group) was "O que é que eu vou dizer em casa." The March 8, 1962, story included a photograph of a man dressed as a *baiana* and a group of drag queens leaving the police station. On February 13, 1964, this parade was announced on the front page of *Última Hora* with a photograph of a man dressed as an Indian in a skimpy skirt leaving police detention. The caption stated that the majority were *travestis* detained at the Baile dos Enxutos.

68. "O Carnaval dos 'excêntricos': 'Travesti' elegante, e curioso," *Última Hora* (Rio de Janeiro), February 19, 1958, 14.

69. Maria Antônio, "Carnaval em Copacabana," *Última Hora* February 16, 1961, 8.

70. See Roberto M. Moura, *Carnaval: Da Redentora à Praça do Apocalipse* (Rio de Janeiro: Jorge Zahar Editor, 1986), 17. The Portuguese lyrics are:

> Olha a cabeleira de Zezé,
> Será que ele é? Será que ele é? [bicha]
> Olha a cabeleira de Zezé,
> Será que ele é? Será que ele é? [bicha]
> Será que ele é bossa nova? Será que ele é Maomé?
> Parece que ele é transviado
> Mas isso não sei se ele é.
> Corte o cabelo dele. Corte o cabelo dele.

71. João Batista, interview by author, tape recording, Rio de Janeiro, Brazil, July 20, 1995; Ângelo interview, July 20, 1995.

72. Lenharo, *Cantores do rádio*, 200.

73. "Enxutos e bonecas: A grande guerra," *Manchete* (Rio de Janeiro), no. 724 (March 5, 1966): 56.

74. "'Boneca' lidera bloco de cinzas," *Última Hora* (Rio de Janeiro), February 24, 1966, 8.

75. Zuenir Ventura captures this optimism in his account of the events of 1968, *1968: A ano que não terminou* (Rio de Janeiro: Nova Fronteira, 1988).

76. "Soares levou bonecas de luxo ao seu baile," *Última Hora* (Rio de Janeiro), February 28, 1968, 1.

77. Ibid.

78. *Última Hora* (Rio de Janeiro), February 11, 1969, 10; February 12, 1969, 8; February 13, 1969, 8; February 14, 1969, 8.

79. Leonard Greenwood, "Sex, Samba Disputes Cloud Carnival for Rio," *Los Angeles Times*, February 8, 1970, 4; Alfredo Buzaid, "Censura prévia para livros e periódicos," *Última Hora* (Rio de Janeiro), February 12, 1970, 1.

80. "Travesti bem comportado poderá entrar nos bailes," *Comércio Mercantil* (Rio de Janeiro), October 27, 1971, 3.

81. M. Helena, Dispatch to *Veja*, August 17, 1972.

82. The event was moved to a privately organized venue the next year. One of the male participants in the contest argued that the ban had nothing to do with homosexuality, but rather was part of a larger policy of the Division of Tourism in Rio de Janeiro to eliminate the Municipal's Gala Ball altogether (Tarlis Baptista and Thea Sequerra, "Carnaval: Os cassados da passarela," *Manchete* [Rio de Janeiro], no. 1089 [March 3, 1973]: 24–26).

83. "Façanha quer volta dos "Enxutos," *Jornal do Brasil* (Rio de Janeiro), October 23, 1972): 13.

84. "Enxutos: As bonecas são um luxo," *Manchete* (Rio de Janeiro), no. 1091 (March 17, 1973): 74–75.

85. "Bonecas: Divinas e maravilhosas," *Manchete* (Rio de Janeiro), no. 1142 (March 9, 1974): 78–82.

86. "Baile do São José: Mais de mil bonecas no salão," *Manchete* (Rio de Janeiro), no. 1247 (March 13, 1976): 54–58.

87. One final intervention by government censors took place in 1978. Officials shut down the drag ball at Cine São José at the last moment, forcing costumed celebrants to join the Paulistinha street drag show in the nearby neighborhood ("Bonecas ao luar," *Manchete* [Rio de Janeiro], no. 1348 [February 18, 1978]: 76–81).

88. Rocha interview, November 2, 1994.

89. "Coccinelli mostrou no Copa 99% do que a tornou mulher," *Última Hora* (Rio de Janeiro), March 12, 1963, 3; Stanislaw Ponte Preta [Sérgio Porto], "Coccinelli—badalando, badalando, badalando," *Última Hora* (Rio de Janeiro), March 19, 1963, 10. Coccinelli was not the first foreign transvestite to become famous in Brazil. Both Walter Pinto, the "Ziegfeld of Praça Tiradentes" and Carlos Machado, who mounted extravagant shows with Carnival themes at the city's top nightclubs, had used Ivan Monteiro Damião, or Ivana, a French cross-dressing dancer with Portuguese parents, in their shows in the 1950s. Ivo Serra, "Ivana—a grande dúvida," *Manchete* (Rio de Janeiro), no. 75 (September 26, 1953): 22–23.

90. "Ex-'travesti' Coccinelli é mulher mesmo: Espera bebê," *Última Hora* (Rio de Janeiro), March 13, 1963, 1.

91. Thor Carvalho, "'Elas' são assim," *Última Hora* (Rio de Janeiro), June 18, 1964, 6.

92. Eli Halfoun, "Agora para Paulista," *Última Hora Revista* (Rio de Janeiro), August 12, 1964, 3.

93. Manequim, "Les Girls," *O Snob* (Rio de Janeiro) 3, no 2 (January 31, 1965): 6.

94. *O Snob* (Rio de Janeiro) 3, no. 8 (May 30, 1965): 23; 3, no. 10 (June 30, 1965): 11; 3, no. 14 (September 18, 1965): 9; 3, no. 20 (November 30, 1965): 16; 5, no. 3 (March 31, 1967): 7; 5, no. 5 (May 31, 1967): 27; 5, no. 9 (July 31, 1967): 5.

95. Serra, "Ivana—a grande dúvida," 22.

96. Others followed Rogéria's international trajectory. Valéria, for example, who had also appeared in the show where Rogéria got her start in 1964, later went to Paris to perform in nightclubs. She returned to Rio in 1973 to continue starring in shows and become a toast of the town, even having her portrait painted by the renowned artist Di Cavalcanti ("Charme e taleno na arte de Valéria," *Folha de São Paulo*, December 9, 1973, 10.

97. In December 1964, Manequim, one of *O Snob*'s journalists, interviewed Rogéria when she was still only one of several performers in the show *Les Girls* and not a famous personality. She stated that she was born on May 25, 1943, in Novo Friburgo, Rio de Janeiro, which would have made her twenty-one at the time. (*O Snob* [Rio de Janeiro] 2, no. 19 [December 31, 1964]: 25). In July 1967, Manequim, again on assignment for *O Snob*, interviewed Rogéria once more. She was now a nationally famous figure and, like many celebrities, had shaved a year off her life, reporting that she had been born in 1944 (*O Snob* [Rio de Janeiro] 5, no. 8 [15 July 1967] 2). In October 1973, having returned from Paris as an international star, Rogéria informed the editors of *Pasquim* that she was born in 1946, and was twenty-seven at the time of the interview (*Pasquim* [Rio de Janeiro], no. 223 [October 9, 1973]: 4–7).

98. *O Snob* (Rio de Janeiro) 5, no. 8 (July 15, 1967): 2.

99. Ibid.

100. "Rogéria," *Pasquim*, 4.

101. Glória Kalil, "Loura, provocante, sensual: Astrolfo Barroso Pinto, ou melhor … Rogéria," *Nova* 13 (October 1974): 72–75.

102. "Rogéria," *Pasquim*, 7.

103. Ibid.

104. Alcir Lenharo, interview by author, tape recording, Campinas, Brazil, April 15, 1985.

See also the example of successful hairdressers in Marilda Varejão and Narceu de Almeida, "Quase tudo que você sempre quis saber sobre o homossexualismo e nunca ousou perguntar," *Manchete* (Rio de Janeiro), no. 1234 (December 13, 1975): 16–19; and Narceu de Almeida, Marilda Varejão, Nello Pedra Gandara, Ruth de Aquino Araújo, Cláudio Segovick, João de Albuquerque, "Homossexualismo: A hora da verdade," *Manchete*, no. 1231 (November 22, 1975): 18–23.

105. *O Snob* (Rio de Janeiro) 3, no. 19 (December 31, 1964); 5, no. 8 (July 15, 1967); 6, no. 1 (January 1968).

106. *O Snob* (Rio de Janeiro) 5, no. 4 (April 30, 1967); 6, no. 1 (January 1968): 16. Despite the popularity of these drag shows in Brazil's major cities, there was not universal acceptance of this new form of entertainment. During a tour through small towns in the southernmost state of Rio Grande do Sul, Marquesa's production of *Les Girls* met hostile opposition. In the small town of Jaguarão, the show had to be postponed because the orchestra had been delayed. Spurred on by the adolescent boys of the town, the entire auditorium began to attack the cast, who sought shelter in the home of a citizen of the town in order to avoid being stoned. In another small town on the border with Uruguay, the local priest opposed the show, although the population ignored his prohibitions and attended the performance (*O Snob* [Rio de Janeiro] 6, no. 1 [January 1968]: 15).

107. *O Snob* (Rio de Janeiro) 6, no. 12 (December 31, 1968): 1.

108. Moura points to 1967 as the date when the "courtship" of the middle class and the samba schools began. See Moura, *Carnaval*, 23–24. Costa dates the arrival of the middle class as early as 1963, when the increase in ticket prices to watch the samba schools encouraged many to participate in the parade itself. It was more economical to have a costume made, and "for a modest price, there was beer, samba and flirting" (Haroldo Costa, "Trinta anos depois . . . ," in Moraes, *História do Carnaval carioca*, 245).

109. Ângelo interview, July 20, 1995.

110. Rodrigues interview, April 25, 1995.

111. Moura, *Carnaval*, 30–33.

112. Although the government prohibited men dressed as women from parading with a school in 1969, threatening to disqualify the entire entry if someone did, the ban only lasted a year (ibid., 27).

113. Ramalhete, interview by author, tape recording, Rio de Janeiro, February 15, 1995.

114. João Baptista interview, July 20, 1995.

115. Bornay interview, May 25, 1995. See also Richard G. Parker, "The Carnivalization of the World," in *Bodies, Pleasures, and Passions: Sexual Culture in Contemporary Brazil* (Boston: Beacon Press, 1991), 136–64.

Chapter Six

1. For accounts of the political events of 1968, see Fernando Gabeira, *Carta sobre a anistia: A entrevista do Pasquim, conversação sobre 1968* (Rio de Janeiro: Editora Codecri, 1979); Zuenir Ventura, *O ano que não terminou* (Rio de Janeiro: Nova Fronteira, 1988); and Fernando Perrone, *Relato de guerra: Praga, São Paulo, Paris* (São Paulo: Busca Vida, 1988). For an analysis of the political debates that impelled the student movement in the first years of the dictatorship, see João Roberto Martins Filho, *Movimento estudantil e ditadura militar, 1964–68* (Campinas, São Paulo: Papirus, 1987).

2. Documentation of the extensive violation of human rights by the military dictatorship has been collected in Arquidiocese de São Paulo, *Brasil nunca mais* (Petrópolis: Vozes, 1985).

3. Janet Lever, *Soccer Madness* (Chicago: University of Chicago Press, 1983), 69.

4. Murilo Melo Filho, "O governo garante um clima de tranquilidade e trabalho: O mundo em guerra o Brasil em paz," *Manchete* (Rio de Janeiro), no. 1035 (February 19, 1972): 20–21.

5. Maria Helena Moreira Alves, *State and Opposition in Military Brazil* (Austin: University of Texas Press, 1985), 106–14.

6. Ibid.

7. Alfredo Buzaid, "Censura prévia para livros e periódicos," *Última Hora* (Rio de Janeiro), February 12, 1970, 1. On government restrictions on the press, see Peter T. Johnson, "Academic Press Censorship under Military and Civilian Regimes: The Argentine and Brazilian Cases, 1964–1975," *Luso-Brazilian Review* 15, no. 1 (summer 1978): 3–25; Paoli Marconi, *A censura política na imprensa brasileira, 1968–1978* (São Paulo: Global, 1980); and Anne-Marie Smith, *A Forced Agreement: Press Acquiescence to Censorship in Brazil* (Pittsburgh: University of Pittsburgh Press, 1997). For its influence on literary production, see Silviano Santiago, "Repressão e censura no campo da literatura e das artes na década de 70," *Encontros com a civilização brasileira* 17 (November 1979): 187–95; and Tânia Pellegrini, *Gavetas vazias: Ficção e política nos anos 70* (São Carlos, São Paulo: Mercado de Letras, 1996).

8. An insightful analysis of the process of liberalization under President Geisel can be found in Bernardo Kucinski, *Abertura, a história de uma crise* (São Paulo: Brasil Debates, 1982).

9. James N. Green, "Liberalization on Trial: The Brazilian Workers' Movement," North American Congress on Latin America, *Report on the Americas* 13, no. 3 (May / June 1979): 15–25; José Álvaro Moises, "What Is the Strategy of the 'New Syndicalism'?" *Latin American Perspectives* 9 (fall 1982): 55–73; Margaret Keck, "Update on the Brazilian Labor Movement," *Latin American Perspectives* 11 (winter 1984): 27–36.

10. Sonia Alvarez has written the most complete history of the women's movement in this period. See Sonia E. Alvarez, *Engendering Democracy in Brazil: Women's Movements in Transition Politics* (Princeton: Princeton University Press, 1990). See also Michael George Hanchard, *Orpheus and Power: The Movimento Negro of Rio de Janeiro and São Paulo, 1945-1988* (Princeton: Princeton University Press, 1994).

11. Alvarez, *Engendering Democracy in Brazil*, 82.

12. Ibid., 84–96.

13. Ibid., 109.

14. For different interpretations of the Brazilian gay movement's early years, see João S. Trevisan, *Perverts in Paradise* (London: GMP Publishers, 1986), 133–54; Edward MacRae, *A construção da igualdade: Identidade sexual e política no Brasil da "abertura"* (Campinas: Editora da Universidade Estadual de Campinas UNICAMP, 1990); and James N. Green, "The Emergence of the Brazilian Gay Liberation Movement, 1977–81," *Latin American Perspectives* 21, no. 1 (winter 1994): 38–55. For a study of Somos's correspondence with various individuals, see Pedro de Souza, "Confidências da carne: O público e o privado na enunciação da sexualidade" (Ph.D. diss., Universidade Estadual de Campinas, 1993).

15. Among the best works in English on the period of the military dictatorship (1964–85) and the process of democratization are Alves, *State and Opposition in Military Brazil*, and Thomas E. Skidmore, *The Politics of Military Rule in Brazil, 1964–85* (New York: Oxford University Press, 1988).

16. Carlos Ricardo da Silva, interview by author, tape recording, São Paulo, November 26, 1994.

17. Nestor Perlongher, *O negócio do michê: Prostituição viril em São Paulo* (São Paulo: Editora Brasiliense, 1987), 78–79.

18. Comar Diniz, interview by author, tape recording, Rio de Janeiro, Brazil, November 2, 1994.

19. Hélio Fonseca, interview by author, tape recording, Niterói, State of Rio de Janeiro, Brazil, July 25, 1995.

20. Carlos Jáuregui, *La homosexualidad en la Argentina* (Buenos Aires: Ediciones Tarso, 1987), 167–74; and Azelmar Acevedo, *Homosexualidad: Hacia la destrucción de los mitos* (Buenos Aires: Ediciones Del Ser, 1985), 218–19, 235–37.

21. Haroldo Costa argues this point in his updated version of Eneida's classic history of Carioca Carnival. See Haroldo Costa, "Trinta anos depois . . . ," in *História do Carnaval carioca, revista e ampliada por Haroldo Costa,* ed. Eneida Moraes (Rio de Janeiro: Gráfica Récord Editora, 1987), 247.

22. "Mineiro quer Dener fora da TV," *Jornal do Brasil* (Rio de Janeiro), April 19, 1972, 26.

23. In 1973, the Ministry of Tourism, which sponsored the Municipal Theater's Gala Ball, where the luxury costume contest was held, canceled the male competition. At the time, it was widely understood that the reason for this measure was the high-profile participation of homosexuals in the event.

24. On Rio de Janeiro: Caê [Jorge Luis Pinto Rodrigues], interview by author, tape recording, Rio de Janeiro, July 9, 1996; João Antônio, *Ó Copacabana! Ó Copacabana!* (Rio de Janeiro: Civilização brasileira, 1978), 47–50. On São Paulo: Antônio Bivar, "Revolução sexual a paulista," *Ele-Ela* 9, no. 96 (April 1977): 50.

25. Celso Ricardo, interview by author, tape recording, São Paulo, Brazil, June 17, 1995. For outsiders' accounts of gay life in Rio de Janeiro and São Paulo in this period, see Dennis Altman, "Down Rio Way," in *The Christopher Street Reader,* ed. Michael Denneny, Charles Ortleb, Thomas Steele (New York: Putnam, 1983), 214–19; and Frederick Whitam, "*Os Entendidos:* Gay Life in São Paulo in the Late 1970s," in *Latin American Male Homosexualities,* ed. Stephen O. Murray (Albuquerque: University of New Mexico Press, 1995), 231–40.

26. Caê, who preferred to dance at Zig-Zag in the early 1970s because it had less restrictive club policies, remembered that he was once told by the waiter at Sótão that he could not kiss his boyfriend while in the discotheque (Caê [Jorge Luiz Pinto Rodrigues], interview by author, tape recording, Rio de Janeiro, Brazil, July 9, 1995).

27. John McCarthy, interview by author, tape recording, Rio de Janeiro, July 9, 1995.

28. Veriano Terto Júnior conducted a study of homosexual sex in Rio de Janeiro's movie theaters in the 1980s that describes in detail the sexual and social interactions that took place there. See Veriano Terto Júnior, "No escurinho do cinema . . . : Socialidade orgiástica nas tardes cariocas" (master's thesis, Pontífica Universidade Católica do Rio de Janeiro, 1989).

29. "O prostituto," *Veja* 115 (November 18, 1970): 30.

30. At the Primor, a male usher, nicknamed "Geralda" by homosexual moviegoers, acted as a passive accomplice in the sexual adventures that took place there by ignoring the behavior of the patrons (see "O prostituto," 30). Likewise Terto documented the silent consent that movie house employees gave to the homosexual activities taking place in the Carioca cinema he studied (Veriano Terto Júnior, interview by author, tape recording, Rio de Janeiro, Brazil, July 24, 1995). Celso Ricardo, who worked for one of the major cinema chains in São Paulo, confirmed the fact that cinema owners relied on the box office income that men engaging in homosexual sex provided (Ricardo interview, June 17, 1995).

31. José Saffioti Filho, "Os acordes da liberação gay," *Manchete* (Rio de Janeiro), no. 1325 (September 10, 1977): 91.

32. Carlos Nelson F. dos Santos, "Bichas e entendidos: A sauna como lugar de confronto"

(Rio de Janeiro, 1976), 2. Dos Santos conducted an anthropological study of one such sauna in Rio de Janeiro in the early 1970s.

33. Ricardo interview, June 17, 1995.

34. Alice, interview by author, tape recording, São Paulo, Brazil, June 22, 1995.

35. "Travestis são presos de biquinis," *Jornal do Brasil* (Rio de Janeiro), September 18, 1972, 22.

36. Allen Young, an American journalist and early gay liberation activist, came out while visiting Rio de Janeiro in 1964. On a return trip in 1972, he reported the changes in the subculture, pointing to "gay freaks" who "didn't feel 100 percent free to tell their straight friends, but they said they didn't care if their straight friends knew." See Allen Young, "Gay Gringo in Brazil," in *The Gay Liberation Book,* ed. Len Richmond and Gary Noguera (San Francisco: Ramparts Press, 1973), 63. One magazine reported the near lynching of two men who had kissed each other on Ipanema Beach in 1976 ("Um gay power à brasileira, *Veja,* August 24, 1977, 67.

37. By far the best study of Brazilian *travestis* is Don Kulick, *Travesti: Sex, Gender, and Culture among Brazilian Transgendered Prostitutes* (Chicago: University of Chicago Press, 1998). Kulik studied *travestis* from Salvador, Bahia, in the 1990s, but his observations about the practices and identity construction are consistent with the historical material I have found about *travestis* in Rio de Janeiro and São Paulo in the 1970s.

38. Cf. Paulo Roberto Ottoni, "A prostituição masculina homossexual e o 'Travesti'" (Campinas, 1981); Hélio R. S. Silva, *Travesti: A invenção do feminino* (Rio de Janeiro: Relume Dumará, 1993); Andrea Cornwall, "Gendered Identities and Gender Ambiguity among *Travestis* in Salvador, Brazil," in *Dislocating Masculinity: Comparative Ethnographies,* ed. Andrea Cornwall and Nancy Lindisfarne (London: Routledge, 1994), 111–32; and Rogério Botelho de Mattos and Miguel Ângelo Campos Ribeiro, "Territórios da prostituição nos espaços públicos da área central do Rio de Janeiro" (manuscript, 1994).

39. Zilda Brandão, "Cuidado: Travestis invadem a cidade," *Última Hora,* August 2, 1975, 8; "Travesti, presença crescente na cidade," *Folha de São Paulo,* August 16, 1976, 26; "Mais 28 travestis detidos pelo Deic," *Notícias Populares* (São Paulo), October 8, 1977; and Ramão Gomes Portão, "Polícia declara guerra aos travestis paulistanos," *Folha da Tarde* (São Paulo), January 31, 1977, 13.

40. Over half of the three hundred *travestis* detained between December 1976 and January 1977 used hormones to enlarge their breasts. See Departamento das Delegacias Regionais de Polícia da Grande São Paulo, Degran, Delegacia Quarto Distrito Policial, "Termo de Declarações" (personal archive, Guido Fonseca, December 1976 to January 1977).

41. Brazilian male prostitution in France was prevalent enough that the word *brazilien* became a French term for a *travesti* in the 1980s.

42. The story of one such *travesti,* who ends up in a Roman prison where he is interviewed by a former member of the Red Brigades, provides a compelling account of the lives of these sex workers. See Fernanda Farias de Albuquerque and Maruizio Jannelli, *A princesa,* trans. Elisa Byington (Rio de Janeiro: Nova Fronteira, 1995).

43. "Polícia diz que Cinelândia à noite seguiu sua vocação," *Jornal do Brasil* (Rio de Janeiro), March 3, 1972, 15.

44. Guido Fonseca, interview by author, tape recording, São Paulo, Brazil, March 8, 1995; see also José Henrique Pierangelli, ed., *Códigos penais do Brasil: Evolução histórica* (Bauru, São Paulo: Javoli, 1980), 596.

45. Guido Fonseca interview, March 8, 1995.

46. Guido Fonseca, *História da prostituição em São Paulo* (São Paulo: Editora Resenha Universitária, 1982), 226.

47. "Termo de Declarações," December 1976 to January 1977.

48. Guido Fonseca interview, March 8, 1995.

49. Brandão, "Cuidado: Travestis invadem a cidade," 8.

50. Adauto B. Alves, interview by author, tape recording, Curitiba, Paraná, January 21, 1995.

51. Guido Fonseca, interview, 8 March 1995.

52. For a fictional portrayal of this relationship set in Rio de Janeiro in the early 1960s, see "A Desforra," in Gasparino Damata [Gasparino da Mata e Silva], *Os solteirões* (Rio de Janeiro: Pallas, 1976): 129–58. This short story has been published as "Revenge" in *Now the Volcano: An Anthology of Latin American Gay Literature*, ed. Winston Leyland (San Francisco: Gay Sunshine Press, 1979), 98–126.

53. Sérgio Martins and Jaime Srur, "A passarela dos caubóis," *Última Hora* (Rio de Janeiro), November 7, 1970, 5; "A vida continua," *Veja* 119 (November 25, 1970), 32–33; "Homossexuais são detidos em São Paulo," *Jornal do Brasil* (Rio de Janeiro), October 6, 1971, 6.

54. "O prostituto," 30.

55. "A vida continua," 33.

56. Sérgio José Alves de Almeida, "Michê" (master's thesis, Pontifícia Universidade Católica de São Paulo, 1984), 128.

57. Perlongher, *O negócio do michê*, 246–51.For other examples of the dangers associated with picking up a male hustler, see Armando Pereira, *Sexo e prostituição* (Rio de Janeiro: Gráfica Récord Editora, 1967), 112–16.

58. Cf. Edward MacRae, *A construção da igualdade*, 52–53; and João S. Trevisan, *Perverts in Paradise*, 116–22.

59. A history of Teatro Oficina can be found in David George, *The Modern Brazilian Stage* (Austin: University of Texas Press,1992), 55–73.

60. According to João S. Trevisan, Caetano Veloso "said explicitly on many occasions that he did not have sex with men," although rumors abounded (Trevisan, *Perverts in Paradise*, 117). When asked about these denials in a 1987 interview for a New York gay magazine, Caetano Veloso stated: I have never denied having a gay experience. But I am married, you know, and I don't think it's dignified to talk specifically about your sex life in public" (David Andrusia, "Caetano Veloso, the Most Popular Singer/Songwriter in Brazil, Talks About Music, Sexuality, AIDS, and Creating a New Pop Nationality." *New York Native* 222 [July 20, 1987]: 38). For a discussion of *tropicalismo* and its impact on Brazilian culture in the late 1960s, see Heloísa Buarque de Hollanda, *Impressões de viagem: Cpc, vanguarda, e desbunde, 1960–1970* (Rio de Janeiro: Rocco, 1992), 53–87; and Christopher John Dunn's "The Relics of Brazil: Modernity and Nationality in the Tropicalista Movement" (Ph.D. diss., Brown University, 1996) and "The Tropicalista Rebellion: A Conversation with Caetano Veloso," *Transition: An International Review* 6, no. 2, issue 70 (summer 1996): 116–38. I would like to thank Christopher Dunn for sharing his work with me.

61. This shift in gender identity and tolerance for androgynous behavior among Brazilian youth was documented in a research project conducted in the early 1980s. Lázaro Sanches de Oliveira interviewed seven hundred Carioca university students to see how they identified with traditional gender roles. Using Sandra Lipsitz Bem's Sex-Role Inventory, Oliveira found that 26 percent of the respondents possessed characteristics culturally associated with both masculine and feminine behavior and another 19 percent assumed characteristics that were considered neither masculine nor feminine according to social norms. The researcher noted that this "androgynous" identity, while perhaps slanted because the sampling was restricted to students, nevertheless reflected a shift away from traditional gender role identification. The study re-

ceived an award from the Federal Council of Psychology in 1982 (Lázaro Sanches de Oliveira, *Masculindidade, feminilidade, androginia* [Rio de Janeiro: Aciamé, 1983], 52–53). Sympathy toward androgynous performers, however, did not necessarily translate into a positive view of homosexuality, as several research surveys of the period indicate. In 1975, the weekly picture magazine *Manchete* conducted a poll of two hundred people in Rio de Janeiro and São Paulo in which 79 percent considered homosexuality an abnormality and 82 percent thought that homosexuals should undergo medical treatment to cure their condition (Narceu de Almeida, Marilda Varejão, Nello Pedra Gandara, Ruth de Aquino Araújo, Cláudio Segovick, João de Albuquerque," Homossexualismo: A hora da verdade," *Manchete* [Rio de Janeiro], no. 1231 [November 22, 1975]: 18, 21). Five years later, the Paulista Marketing Research Institute carried out a more extensive national survey of the "sexual habits and attitudes of Brazilians." Of the 4,860 people interviewed or asked to complete questionnaires, 69 percent responded. The response level of those between the ages of eighteen and twenty-three was significantly greater than the entire sampling, thus skewing the results to "reinforce the opinions of youth who are more liberated and active" (Antônio Leal de Santa Inez, ed., *Pesquisa acerca dos hábitos e atitudes sexuais dos brasileiros* [São Paulo: Editora Cultrix, 1983], 18). In spite of this bias, social attitudes about homosexuality remained similar to the results of the 1975 *Manchete* poll, with 70 percent of those interviewed from Rio de Janeiro and São Paulo opposed to homosexuality (ibid., 30).

62. Some of Lennie Dale's reminiscences about his work can be found in two interviews: "Lennie Dale Confessa, sob Protestos Gerais," *Lampião da Esquina* (Rio de Janeiro) 1, no. 2 (June 25, 1978): 6–7; and "Lennie—Pó de guaraná, ginseng, drugs, sex, and rock and roll!" *Pasquim* (Rio de Janeiro), no. 616 (April 16, 1981): 8–10. The name Dzi Croquettes has been attributed to a borrowing from a San Francisco gay theater troupe, the Cockettes, whose outrageous performances subverted gender constructs in the early 1970s. See Trevisan, *Perverts in Paradise*, 119. Rosemary Lobert, citing founding members of the group, asserts that the members only had a vague notion of San Francisco performers, and in fact played with Brazilianized pronunciation of the English word "the" (dzi) and *croquette*, a meat-filled fried dough, consumed as a snack. See Rosemary Lobert, "A palavra mágica Dzi: Uma resposta difícil de se perguntar" (master's thesis, Universidade Estadual de Campinas, 1979), 7. Whether or not the group's name was a variation of the Cockettes, it is interesting to note the similarity in the two groups' playful transformations of gender roles.

63. Lobert, "A palavra mágica Dzi," 31–32.

64. Ibid., 33.

65. "Travesti sem bichismo" is from A. Savah, *Roteiro* (São Paulo), May 19, 1973; "Travesti sem cara de homossexual" is from "Giba Um," *Última Hora* (São Paulo), July 1, 1973; both quoted in Lobert, *A palavra mágica Dʒi*, 218.

66. Ibid., 218.

67. Cf. Denise Pires Vaz, *Ney Matogrosso: Um cara meio estranho* (Rio de Janeiro: Rio Fundo, 1992).

68. Roberto Moura, "O canto do eterno feminino," *Pasquim* (Rio de Janeiro), no. 243 (February 26, 1974): 19.

69. "Ney Matogrosso fala sem make-up," *Interview* (São Paulo) 5 (May 1978): 5.

70. Ibid.

71. Between 1970 and 1978, college enrollment almost tripled, increasing from 456,134 to 1,267,599. See Cláudio de Moura Castro, "What Is Happening in Brazilian Education," in *Social Change in Brazil, 1945–1985: The Incomplete Transition*, ed Edmar L. Bacha and Herbert S. Klein (Albuquerque: University of New Mexico Press, 1989), 269. This growth in the student

population, combined with increased consumption possibilities for the middle class, encouraged a boom in literature and theater. Homosexual-themed works were a part of this phenomenon.

72. Luis Canales, "O homossexualismo como tema no moderno teatro brasileiro," *Luso-Brazilian Review* 18, no. 1 (summer 1981): 174–76; and Melissa A. Lockhart, "Walmir Ayala," in *Latin American Writers on Gay and Lesbian Themes: A Bio Critical Sourcebook*, ed. David William Foster (Westport, Conn.: Greenwood Press, 1994), 46–47.

73. Canales, "O homossexualismo com tema no moderno teatro brasileiro," 177; and Melissa A. Lockhart, "Nelson Rodrigues," in *Latin American Writers on Gay and Lesbian Themes*, 372–73. Cf. Trevisan, *Perverts in Paradise*, 114–15.

74. Sylvio Lamenha, "Gay Power," *Já* (Rio de Janeiro), no. 7 (July 27, 1971): 8.

75. Canales, "O homossexualismo como tema no moderno teatro brasileiro," 178–80.

76. Gasparino Damata, *Histórias do amor maldito* (Rio de Janeiro: Gráfica Récord Editora, 1967).

77. See, for example, the short story "O Voluntário" in Damata, *Os solteirões*, 65–127.

78. Aguinaldo Silva, *Primeira carta aos andróginos* (Rio de Janeiro: Pallas, 1975); Darcy Penteado, *A meta* (Sao Paulo: Símbolo, 1976).

79. Bivar, "Revolução sexual à paulista," 50.

80. A survey of all of *Jornal do Brasil*'s coverage of homosexuality from 1965 (when the publisher organized an in-house index) to 1978 reveals that much more emphasis was given to news from abroad than to homosexuals in Brazil. This may have been due to censorship, either government-induced or self-imposed. There is a dramatic increase in the number of articles covering national news items from 1977 on, reflecting the relaxation of military rule in the country and the expanded space for a discussion about the subject. Other newspapers, such as *Notícias Populares*, which published sensationalist, pejorative articles about homosexuality during the same period, carried little coverage of the international movement.

81. "Um novo poder nas ruas da California," *Jornal da Tarde*, December 4, 1969; "Marcha de homossexuais dá briga," *O Globo* (Rio de Janeiro), August 31, 1970, 5; "Grupo de homossexuais italianos lançará revista," *Jornal do Brasil* (Rio de Janeiro), June 18, 1971, 9; "Homossexuais protestam em Nova Iorque," *Jornal do Brasil* (Rio de Janeiro), June 29, 1971.

82. "O direito de não ser maldito," *Jornal do Brasil, Revista Domingo* (Rio de Janeiro), May 28, 1972, 2; "Associação psiquiátrica dos EUA exclui o homossexualismo do índice de distúrbios mentais," *Jornal do Brasil* (Rio de Janeiro), December 16, 1973, 16; "Homossexuais exigem liberdade," *Jornal do Brasil* (Rio de Janeiro), April 5, 1973, 8.

83. The *imprensa alternativa* (alternative press) was usually published by students and leftist intellectuals without major capital investment as a vehicle to articulate political, social, and cultural criticism of capitalism, the dictatorship, and the status quo. Some editorial staffs were linked to underground leftist organizations that used the tenuous legal status of these papers to promote their political perspectives and targeted the working class. Others functioned as collectives or had editorial boards with diverse political viewpoints. Some papers, while critical of the government, focused more on countercultural issues. See Bernardo Kucinski, *Jornalistas e revolucionários nos tempos da imprensa alternativa* (São Paulo: Página Aberta, 1991).

84. *Já* (Rio de Janeiro) 1 (June 1, 1971) to 11 (August 25, 1971). The expression "gay power" was commonly used by the Brazilian press in the early 1970s as the catchall phrase to describe the gay and lesbian movement in the United States and Europe. While this term fell quickly out of favor in the United States as gay liberation fronts and other radical organizations fell apart in the first few years of the 1970s, the expression "gay power" continued to be employed in Brazil until the late 1970s.

85. *Já* (Rio de Janeiro) 11 (August 25, 1971): 10–11. In the mid-1960s, Thor Carvalho,

Maurício de Paiva, and especially Eli Halfoun, social columnists for *Última Hora*, reported on drag shows and other events of the homosexual subculture in Rio de Janeiro. The tone of the articles was of a person "in the know" but not necessarily *entendido*. The "Gay Power" columnist clearly positioned himself as a gay man and the thrust of the articles, in line with gay liberationist ideas, projected a self-affirmation of homosexuality.

86. Aguinaldo Silva, "Rogéria: Minhas memórias de alcova abalariam o Brasil," *Pasquim* (Rio de Janeiro), no. 107 (July 22, 1971): 6, 7.

87. See José Luiz Braga, *O Pasquim e os anos 70: Mais pra epa que para oba* (Brasília, D.F.: Editora Universidade de Brasília, 1991).

88. "Rogéria," *Pasquim* (Rio de Janeiro), no. 223 (October 9, 1973): 4–7; Jaguar, "Noite deslumbrante no Carlos Gomes," *Pasquim*, no. 272 (September 17, 1974): 6–7; Jaguar, "Miss Boneca Pop 75," *Pasquim*, no. 318 (August 1, 1975): 16–17.

89. Sérgio Cabral, Millôr Fernandes, Chico Júnior, and Paulo Francis, "Madame Satã," *Pasquim* (Rio de Janeiro), no. 95 (April 29, 1971): 2–5; Elmar Machado, "Madame Satã para o *Pasquim* 'Enquanto eu viver, a Lapa viverá,'" *Pasquim*, no. 357 (April 30, 1976): 6–11.

90. Braga, *O Pasquim e os anos 70*, 26.

91. "Todo paulista que não gosta de mulher é bicha," *Pasquim* (Rio de Janeiro), no. 105 (July 8, 1971): 3.

92. The homophobic coverage of *Pasquim* is insightfully criticized in a 1977 article written by José Castello Branco. See "A homossexualidade do Pasquim," *O Beijo* (Rio de Janeiro) 2 (December 1977): 3–4.

93. João S. Trevisan, "Demissão, processo, perseguições: Mas qual é o crime de Celso Curi?" *Lampião da Esquina*, no. o (April 1978): 6.

94. In order to have access to the people mentioned in Curi's column, readers sent a stamped letter to the journalist, who then sent it on to the individual who had advertised, thus protecting the anonymity of both parties ("Coluna do meio," *Última Hora* [São Paulo], March 3, 1976, 11).

95. *Entender* (São Paulo) 1, no. 1 (July 24, 1977).

96. "Um gay power à brasileira," *Veja*, August 24, 1977, 66–67.

97. Calvacanti J. Kosinski, "Homossexual: Onde está a diferença," *Isto É*, October 1976, 114–17; Bivar, "Revolução sexual à paulista," 50–57; Vera Nóbrega, "A explosão do homossexualismo," *Nova* (August 1977): 84–87; "Um gay power à brasileira," *Veja*, August 24, 1977, 66–70; Saffioti Filho, "Os acordes da liberação gay," 89–90; Jairo Ferreira, "A identidade de uma minoria," *Folha de São Paulo*, October 3, 1977, 26; Joaquim Ferreira Dos Santos, "A imprensa gay," *Pasquim* (Rio de Janeiro), no. 436 (November 4, 1977): 4–5; "Brasil/Gay: Somos onze milhões," *Última Hora* (Rio de Janeiro), December 3, 1977, 6; "Os 'gays' saíram à luz," *Isto É*, December 28, 1977, 8–15.

98. Lélia Míccolis, "Snob, Le Femme . . . os bons tempos da imprensa gay," *Lampião da Esquina* (Rio de Janeiro) 3, no. 28 (September 1980): 7.

99. *Gente Gay* (Rio de Janeiro) 8 (July 30, 1977): 3–5.

100. *Gente Gay* (Rio de Janeiro) 3 (February 15, 1977).

101. Anuar Farad, interview by author, tape recording, Rio de Janeiro, Brazil, July 31, 1995.

102. *Entender* (São Paulo), no. o (June 24, 1977) to no. 5 (December 1977); *Mundo Gay* (São Paulo) 1, no. 1 (October 15, 1977) to no. 3 (December 1, 1977).

103. Peter Fry, "Da hierarquia à igualdade: A construção histórica da homossexualidade no Brasil," in *Para inglês ver: Identidade e política na cultura brasileira* (Rio de Janeiro: Zahar Editores, 1982), 94–95. See also three papers by Carmen Dora Guimarães: "O homossexual face à norma familiar: Desvios e convergências," (paper presented at the sixth annual meeting of the Grupo de Trabalho sobre Processos de Reprodução da População, CLASCO, Teresópolis,

1980); "Um discurso de retorno: A reconstrução da identidade homossexual," (paper presented at the thirteenth annual meeting of the Associação Brasileira de Antropologia, São Paulo, 1982); and "Casos e Acasos," *Anais Quarto Encontro Nacional Estudos Populacionais* 1 (1984): 575–86; as well as Edward MacRae, "A homossexualidade," in *Macho, masculino, homem* (Porto Alegre: L & PM Editores, 1986), 66–69.

104. Perlongher, *O negócio do michê*, 78.

105. Edward MacRae, "Homosexual Identities in Transitional Brazilian Politics," in *The Making of Social Movements in Latin America: Identity, Strategy, and Democracy*, ed. Arturo Escobar and Sonia E. Alvarez (Boulder: Westview Press, 1992), 190.

106. Ramalhete, interview by author, tape recording, Rio de Janeiro, Brazil, February 15, 1995.

107. "Homossexualismo," *Realidade* 3, no. 26 (May 1968): 115. Letters to the editor of *Realidade* ranged from disgust to praise for the treatment of the subject. One reader considered homosexuality to be a "contagious disease that is propagating at an alarming rate," while another characterized it as "sad, immoral, disgusting, undesirable, indecent, and improper." Making a reference to the title of the publication, the reader continued that "not all reality should be told to the public especially by a magazine that circulates in households with good moral upbringing." Others praised the article for its compassionate treatment of the subject, while still others considered the report's portrayal of homosexuality stereotypical and based on outmoded theories. Significantly, several who responded to the article declared that they were homosexual and their names and city of residency appeared below their comments (letters from *Realidade* 3, no. 27 [June 1968]: 6; no. 28 [July 1968]: 4–6).

108. See Flávio Gikovate, "Doença, decadência, ou amor," *Aqui*, October 1977, 26. A 1982 study that examined the literature from the fields of juridical psychology, forensic psychiatry, and legal medicine used by the Schools of Law, Psychology, and Medicine of the University of São Paulo found that material on homosexuality in textbooks used at the time dated from the 1940s and 1950s and had been reprinted without any alterations in the content. Homosexuality was still considered "pathological," "a mental disorder," a "sexual perversion," or a "deviation." See Ricardo Cury, "As ciências da saúde mental, direito, e homossexualismo," *Resumos da 34º Reunião Anual da Sociedade Brasileira para o Progresso da Ciência* (Campinas: SPBC, July 1982), 890. Examples of the repetition of the medicolegal discourse of the 1930s and '40s are Isabel Adrados, "Estudo da homossexualidade mediante o teste de Rorschach," *Arquivo Brasileiro de Psicotécnica* 16 (March 1964): 65–74; Laertes Moura Ferrão, "Homossexualidade e defesas maníacas," *Revista Brasileira de Psicanálise* 1, no. 1 (1967): 85–93; José A. Gaiarsa, "O terceiro sexo," in *A juventude diante do sexo* (São Paulo: Brasiliense, 1967) 283–97; Luiz Ângelo Dourado, *Homossexualismo masculino e feminino e delinquência* (Rio de Janeiro: Zahar, 1967); Antônio Carlos Pacheco e Silva Filho, "As origens psicológicas da homossexualidade masculina" (Ph.D. diss, Faculdade de Medicina da Universidade de São Paulo, 1971); Sérgio Nogueira Ribeiro, *Crimes passionais e outros temas*, 2d ed. (Rio de Janeiro: Editora Itambé, 1975), 47–53; Armando C. Rodrigues and Luiz M. Paiva, "Transexualismo, transvestismo, homossexualismo," *Arquivos da Polícia Civil de São Paulo*, 26 (July-December 1976): 7–39; Délcio Monteiro de Lima, *Comportamento sexual do brasileiro* (Rio de Janeiro: Livraria Francisco Alves Editora, 1976), 135–75; Vitorino Castelo Branco, *O Advogado diante dos crimes sexuais* (São Paulo: Sugestões Literárias, 1977): 391, 413–14; Pérsivo Cunha, *Sexologia forense* (São Paulo: Sugestões Literárias, 1977); Genival Veloso de França, *Medicina legal* (Rio de Janeiro: Guanabara Koogan, 1977); Antônio F. Almeida Júnior and J. B. Costa Júnior, "Atos libidinosos e atos obsenos," in *Lições de medicina legal* (São Paulo: Companhia Editora Nacional, 1978), 332–38; José Cândido Bastos, "Homossexualidade masculina," *Jornal Brasileiro de Psiquiatria* 28, nos. 1–4 (1979): 7–11.

109. Agildo Guimarães, interview by author, tape recording, Rio de Janeiro, Brazil, October 16, 1994.

110. Trevisan, *Perverts in Paradise*, 135.

111. Hiro Okita, *Homossexualismo: Da opressão à libertação* (São Paulo: Proposta, 1981), 63−73.

112. Aguinaldo Silva, "Compromissos, queridinhas? Nem morta!" *Lampião da Esquina* 3, no. 26 (July 1980): 10−11.

113. Daniel documented his criticisms of the left in a memoir written while in exile in Paris: Herbert Daniel, *Passagem para o próximo sonho* (Rio de Janeiro: Editora Codecri, 1982). He later returned from exile and ran for Federal Congress on the Green Party ticket. He continued as an AIDS activist in the late 1980s and early 1990s until his death from AIDS in 1992.

114. Gabeira chronicled his journey from journalist to urban guerrilla to proponent of feminism and gay rights in a trilogy of memoirs: *O que é isso companheiro?* (Rio de Janeiro: Editora Codecri, 1979); *O crepúsculo do macho: Depoimento* (Rio de Janeiro: Editora Codecri, 1981); *Entradas e bandeiras* (Rio de Janeiro: Editora Codecri, 1981).

115. "A jaula da bicha está aberta," *Bagaço* (Rio de Janeiro), 1976, 17.

116. "Polícia acaba com Dia do Homossexual," *Última Hora* (Rio de Janeiro), July 5, 1976, 6.

117. João Antônio Mascarenhas, interview by author, tape recording, Rio de Janeiro, June 30, 1995. Other accounts of this period have underplayed the extremely significant role Mascarenhas played in the 1970s and '80s in providing leadership to the movement. Among the newspaper and magazine articles covering Leyland's visit are Joana Angélica, "Winston Leyland: A literatura e a arte de homossexuais têm estilo próprio?" *O Globo* (Rio de Janeiro), September 9, 1977, 26; Elice Munerato and Myriam Campello, "Convite aos homossexuais," *Isto É*, September 21, 1977, 60−61; Ferreira, "A identidade de uma minoria," 26; "Os gays estão se conscientizando," *Pasquim* (Rio de Janeiro), no. 436 (November 4, 1977): 4−5.

118. "Saindo do Gueto," *Lampião da Esquina* 0 (April 1978): 2.

119. "Os 'gays' saíram à luz," 14.

120. *Lampião*'s editors also encouraged the publication and distribution of many titles about homosexuality through a mail-order service that promoted gay writers. One example was Francisco Bittencourt's *A bicha que ri* (Rio de Janeiro: Esquina Editora, 1981), a collection of anecdotes and jokes that captured elements of gay urban humor. For a history of *Lampião da Esquina* and its relationship to the rise of the gay and lesbian movement based on oral histories, see Cláudio Roberto da Silva, "Reinventando o sonho: História oral de vida política e homossexualidade no Brasil contemporâneo" (master's thesis, Universidade de São Paulo, 1998).

121. Quoted in Trevisan, "Demissão, processo, perseguições," 6.

122. In the 1980s, during the movement's second wave, the cumbersome word *homossexual* was replaced by the English term "gay." This was not merely a matter of literary economy. For many, the term "gay" was devoid of pejorative baggage. For others, the word had a chic, international tone. Moreover, the international movement had become a reference point by the late 1980s for all organizations, as nationalistic, anti-imperialist sentiments faded.

123. Eduardo Dantas, "Negros, mulheres, homossexuais, e índios nos debates da USP," *Lampião da Esquina* 2, no. 10 (March 1979): 9−10.

124. Criticism of the left by members of Somos was documented in a roundtable discussion held in March 1979 soon after the debate at the University of São Paulo. See Flávio Aguiar, "Homossexualidade e repressão," in *Sexo e poder,* ed. Guido Mantega (São Paulo: Editora Brasiliense, 1979), 139−55. An interview with members of Somos and a left-wing journal conducted several months later also reveals the tensions between this incipient movement and sectors of the Brazil-

ian left. See Elisabeth Marie and Jim Green, "Depois da fuga, saímos ao sol," *Versus* 34 (October 1979): 30-32.

125. Some of the academic articles, masters' theses, and doctoral dissertations that studied homosexuality in a positive light include Pedro J. Daguer, "Transexualismo masculino" (master's thesis, Universidade Federal do Rio de Janeiro, 1977); Carmen Dora Guimarães, "O homossexual visto por entendidos" (master's thesis, Museu Nacional da Universidade Federal do Rio de Janeiro, 1977); Aracy A. L. Klabin, "Aspectos jurídicos do transexualismo" (Faculdade de Direito da Universidade de São Paulo, 1977); Maria Júlia Lembruger, "Cemitério dos vivos" (master's thesis, Museu Nacional da Universidade Federal do Rio de Janeiro, 1979); Lobert, "A palavra mágica Dzi" ; Filipina Chinelli, "Acusação e desvio em uma minoria," in *Desvio e divergência: Uma crítica da patologia social,* ed., Gilberto Velho (Rio de Janeiro: Zahar Editores, 1981), 125-44; Regina Maria Enderman, "Reis e rainhas do desterro: Um estudo de caso" (master's thesis, Universidade Federal de Santa Catarina, Florianópolis, 1981); Gilberto Velho, "Estigma e comportamento desviante em Copacabana," in *Desvio e divergência,* 116-24; Mára L. Faury, *Uma flor para os malditos: A homossexualidade na literatura* (Campinas: Papirus, 1983); Almeida, "Michê";" Carlos Alberto Messender Pereira, "Desvio e / ou reprodução, O estudo de um 'caso,'" in *Testemunha ocular: Textos de antropologia social do cotidiano* (São Paulo: Editora Brasiliense, 1984), 107-33; Gilberto Velho, "A busca de coerência: Coexistência e contradições entre códigos em camadas médias urbanas," in *Cultura da psicanálise,* ed., Sérvulo A. Figueira (São Paulo: Editora Brasiliense, 1985), 169-77; Maria Lina Leão Teixeira, "Transas de um povo de santo: Um estudo sobre as identidades sexuais" (master's thesis, Universidade Federal do Rio de Janeiro, 1986); Rommel Mendes Leite, "Acasos, casos, e ocasos: O relacionamento homossexual masculino e a ideologia sexual dominante" (master's thesis, Universidade Federal do Ceará, Fortaleza, 1986); Edward MacRae, "A construção da igualdade: Identidade sexual e política no Brasil da abertura" (Ph.D. diss., Universidade de São Paulo, 1986); Neuza Maria Oliveira, "As monas da Casa Amarela: Os travestis no espelho da mulher" (master's thesis, Universidade Federal da Bahia, 1986); Nestor Perlongher, "O negócio do michê" (master's thesis, Universidade Estadual de Campinas, 1986); Lindinalva Laurindo Silva, "Aids e homossexualidade em São Paulo" (master's thesis, Pontifícia Universidade Católica de São Paulo, 1986); Tereza Adada Sell, "Identidade homossexual e normas sociais: Histórias de vida" (master's thesis, Universidade de São Paulo, 1987); Ricardo Calheiro Pereira, "O desperdício do sêmen: Um estudo do erotismo entre rapazes" (master's thesis, Universidade Federal da Bahia, 1988); Antônio Ribeiro Dantas, "A representação da homossexualidade: A 'leitura' da imprensa escrita" (master's thesis, Universidade Federal do Rio Grande do Norte, 1989); Hélio R. S. Silva, "O travesti: A invenção do feminismo" (master's thesis, Museu Nacional da Universidade Federal do Rio de Janeiro, 1989); Terto, "No escurinho do cinema."

126. See, for example, Flávio Gikovate, *O instinto sexual* (São Paulo: Editora MG, 1980); Lúcia Figueiroa, "O diagnóstico de homossexualidade: Modificações ocorridas no novo código," *Jornal Brasileiro de Psiquiatria* 31, no. 1 (1982): 19-23; Luiz Carlos Machado, *Descansa em paz, Oscar Wilde* (Rio de Janeiro: Editora Codecri, 1982); Marta Suplicy, *Conversando sobre sexo* (Rio de Janeiro: Editora Vozes, 1983); Marilena Chaui, *Repressão sexual, essa nossa (des)conhecida* (São Paulo: Editora Brasiliense, 1984); and E. Christian Gauderer, "Homossexualidade masculina e lesbianismo," *Jornal de Pediatria* 56, no. 3 (1984): 236-42.

127. Allen Young, "Brazilian Journalists Rally around Gay Newspaper," *Gay Community News,* March 1979, 5.

128. Comissão de Homossexuais Pro-1° de Maio, "Contra a intervenção nos sindicatos de São Paulo, contra a discriminação do trabalhador / a homossexual," Mimeo, São Paulo, 1980.

129. The DOPS was only one of several surveillance operations by the military regime. The

files of the other repressive apparatuses have yet to be opened to the public for review. They may very well hold material about the gay and lesbian movement. The voluminous DOPS files do contain a few minor references to Somos and *Lampião*, including a newspaper clipping about the University of São Paulo debate that marked the public "coming out" of Somos in February 1979. The names of Darcy Penteado and other debate participants mentioned in the article are duly marked with red and blue pencils, indicating that the information also appears in their individual files (Delegacia de Ordem Política e Social, São Paulo, "Jornal Lampião" ref. Seminário na USP, 50-J-0-6153, Arquivo do Estado de São Paulo). Darcy Penteado is also cited elsewhere for speaking at the Legislative Assembly against the June 1980 wave of police arrests in downtown São Paulo, although there is no mention about the June 13 protest march (Delegacia de Ordem Política e Social, São Paulo, Darcy Penteado, 21-Z-14-9336, Arquivo do Estado de São Paulo). Another record notes the book-signing party for Hiro Okita's *Homossexualismo: Da opressão à libertação* (Homosexuality: From oppression to liberation), sponsored by the Homossexual Faction of the Convergência Socialista (Socialist Convergence), a caucus within the left-wing party that participated in the gay and lesbian movement (Delegacia de Ordem Política e Social, São Paulo, "Homossexualismo: Da oppressão à libertação," 20-c-44-11158, Arquivo do Estado de São Paulo).

130. For different interpretations of the history of the gay and lesbian movement in Brazil, including its relationship to AIDS activism in the 1980s and '90s, see Okita, *Homossexualismo: Da opressão à libertação;* Outra Coisa—Ação Homossexualista, *O bandeirante destemido: Um guia gay de São Paulo* (São Paulo: privately printed, 1981); Edward MacRae, "Os respeitáveis militantes e as bichas loucas," in *Caminhos Cruzados: Linguagem, antropologia, e ciências naturais* (São Paulo: Editora Brasiliense, 1982), 99–111; Leila Míccolis and Herbert Daniel, *Jacarés e lobisomens: Dois ensaios sobre a homossexualidade* (Rio de Janeiro: Achiamé, 1983); Rita Colaço, *Uma conversa informal sobre homossexualismo* (Duque de Caxias, Rio de Janeiro: by the author, 1984); Wilson Santos and Grupo Adé Dudu, "A participação dos homossexuais no movimento negro brasileiro," (Salvador, Bahia: mimeograph, 1994); Trevisan, *Perverts in Paradise*, 133–54; MacRae, *A construção da igualdade;* Tereza Christina Vallinoto, "A construção da solidariedade: Um estudo sobre a resposta coletiva à AIDS" (master's thesis, Escola Nacional de Saúde Pública da Fundação Oswaldo Cruz, 1991); MacRae, "Homosexual Identities in Transitional Brazilian Politics"; Herbert Daniel and Richard Parker, *Sexuality, Politics, and AIDS in Brazil: In Another World?* (London: Falmer Press, 1993); "A história do 'EBHO': Encontro Brasileiro de Homosexuais," part 2, *Boletim do Grupo Gay da Bahia* 13, no. 27 (August 1993): 7; Eduardo Toledo, interview with author, tape recording, São Paulo, September 18, 1993; Cristina Luci Câmara da Silva, "Triângulo Rosa: A busca pela cidadania dos 'homossexuais" (master's thesis, Universidade Federal do Rio de Janeiro, 1993); Green, "The Emergence of the Brazilian Gay Liberation Movement, 1977–81," and "A Comparative Analysis of the Argentine and Brazilian Gay Rights Movement of the 1970s" (paper presented at the annual meeting of the Latin American Studies Association, Atlanta, Georgia, March 1994); Richard Parker, *A construção da solidariedade: AIDS, sexualidade, e política no Brasil* (Rio de Janeiro: Relume-Dumará / ABIA / IMS / UERJ, 1994); Miriam Martinho, "Brazil," in *Unspoken Rules: Sexual Orientation and Women's Human Rights*, ed. Rachel Rosenbloom (San Francisco: International Gay and Lesbian Human Rights Commission, 1995), 18–22; Luiz R. B. Mott, "The Gay Movement and Human Rights in Brazil," in *Latin American Male Homosexualities*, ed. Stephen O. Murray (Albuquerque: University of New Mexico Press, 1995), 221–30; Elaine Marques Zanatta, "Documento e identidade: O movimento homossexual no Brasil na década de 80," *Cadernos AEL Arquivos e Memória* 5 / 6 (1996–97): 193–220; João Antônio de Souza Mascarenhas, *A tríplice conexão: Machismo, conservadorismo político, e falso moralismo* (Rio de Janeiro: 2AB Editora, 1997); Silva, "Reinventando

o sonho," 1998; James N. Green, "More Love and More Desire: The Building of the Brazilian Movement," in *The Global Emergence of Gay and Lesbian Politics: National Imprints of a World-wide Movement*, ed. Barry Adam, Jan Willem Duyvendak, and André Krouwel (Philadelphia: Temple University Press, 1999), 91–109, and "Desire and Militancy: Lesbians, Gays, and the Brazilian Workers' Party," in *Different Rainbow: Same-Sex Sexuality and Popular Struggles in the Third World*, ed. Peter Drucker (London: Gay Men's Press, 1999).

Conclusion

1. Gigi Bryant, "Da Arte de Caçar," chapter 7, "Country Club Gay," *O Snob* 2, no. 10 (August 15, 1964): 6.

BIBLIOGRAPHY

1. Medical Records

Case no. 139, Rev. Macario S., Sanatório Pinel, Pirituba, São Paulo. Arquivo do Estado de São Paulo.

Case no. 216, Adalberto de O., Sanatório Pinel, Pirituba, São Paulo. Arquivo do Estado de São Paulo.

Case no. 760, Sydney da S. F., Sanatório Pinel, Pirituba, São Paulo. Arquivo do Estado de São Paulo.

Case no. 1126, Napoleão B., Sanatório Pinel, Pirituba, São Paulo. Arquivo do Estado de São Paulo.

Case no. 1812, Bernardino de C. A., Sanatório Pinel, Pirituba, São Paulo. Arquivo do Estado de São Paulo.

Case no. 1990, Armando de S. O. Filho, Sanatório Pinel, Pirituba, São Paulo. Arquivo do Estado de São Paulo.

Case no. 2479, Octávio B. de O, Sanatório Pinel, Pirituba, São Paulo. Arquivo do Estado de São Paulo.

Case no. 2584, Mário B. X., Sanatório Pinel, Pirituba, São Paulo. Arquivo do Estado de São Paulo.

Case no. 3074, Otávio B. da S., Sanatório Pinel, Pirituba, São Paulo. Arquivo do Estado de São Paulo.

Case no. 3571, Dr. Renato E. de A, Sanatório Pinel, Pirituba, São Paulo. Arquivo do Estado de São Paulo.

Case no. 3781, José Narciso G. Sanatório Pinel, Pirituba, São Paulo. Arquivo do Estado de São Paulo.

2. Police and Trial Records

Case 7H.163, 028C, 1890. Arquivo Nacional, Rio de Janeiro.

Case MV.18, 029, 1891. Arquivo Nacional, Rio de Janeiro.

Case T7.492, 039, 1905. Arquivo Nacional, Rio de Janeiro.

Case T8.2021, 040 1906. Arquivo Nacional, Rio de Janeiro.

Case no. 6262, delito 29/10/46, 14° Vara Criminal. Arquivo Nacional, Rio de Janeiro.

Case no. 2230, delito 04/12/48, 15° Vara Criminal. Arquivo Nacional, Rio de Janeiro.

Case no. 481, delito 24/09/49, Vara Criminal. Arquivo Nacional, Rio de Janeiro.

Delegacia de Ordem Política e Social, São Paulo. "Jornal Lampião," ref. Seminário na USP, 50-J-0-6153. Arquivo do Estado de São Paulo.

Delegacia de Ordem Política e Social, São Paulo. Darcy Penteado, 21-Z-14-9336. Arquivo do Estado de São Paulo.

Delegacia de Ordem Política e Social, São Paulo. "Homossexualismo: Da opressão à libertação," 20-c-44-11158. Arquivo do Estado de São Paulo.

Departamento das Delegacias Regionais de Polícia da Grande São Paulo, Degran, Delegacia Quarto Distrito Policial. "Termo de Declarações." Personal archive, Guido Fonseca, December 1976 to January 1977.

3. Interviews

Alice. Interview by author, June 19, 1995, São Paulo, Brazil. Tape recording.

Alves, Adauto Belarmino. Interview by author, January 21, 1995, Curitiba, Paraná, Brazil, and July 18, 1995, Rio de Janeiro, Brazil. Tape recording.

Amorim, Luiz. Interview by author, September 11, 1994, São Paulo, Brazil. Tape recording.

Ângelo. Interview by author, July 20, 1995, Rio de Janeiro, Brazil. Tape recording.

Barbosa da Silva, José Fábio. Telephone interview by author, April 8, 1998, Los Angeles. Notes.

Bornay, Clóvis. Interview by author, May 25, 1995, Rio de Janeiro, Brazil. Tape recording.

Caê [Jorge Luiz Pinto Rodrigues]. Interview by author, July 9, 1995, Rio de Janeiro, Brazil. Tape recording.

Celso Ricardo. Interview by author, June 17, 1995, São Paulo, Brazil. Tape recording.

Diniz, Comar. Interview by author, November 2, 1994, Rio de Janeiro, Brazil. Tape recording.

Farah, Anuar. Interview by author, July 31, 1995, Rio de Janeiro, Brazil. Tape recording.

Fernandes, Marisa. Interview by author, June 25, 1995, Rio de Janeiro, Brazil. Tape recording.

Fonseca, Guido. Interview by author, March 8, 1995, São Paulo, Brazil. Tape recording.

Fonseca, Hélio. Interview by author, July 25, 1995, Niterói, State of Rio de Janeiro. Tape Recording.

Francis, Kay [João Ferreira da Paz]. Interview by author, November 3, 1994, Lapa, Rio de Janeiro, Brazil. Tape recording.

Grupo Arco-Iris. Interview by author, August 4, 1995, Rio de Janeiro, Brazil. Tape recording.

Guimarães, Agildo. Interview by author, October 16, 1994, Rio de Janeiro, Brazil. Tape recording.

João Baptista. Interview by author, July 20, 1995, Rio de Janeiro, Brazil. Tape recording.

Kepner, James. Interview by author, October 16, 1995, Los Angeles, California. Notes.

Lenharo, Alcir. Interview by author, April 15, 1995, Campinas, Brazil. Tape recording.

Mascarenhas, João Antônio de Souza. Interview by author, June 30, 1995, Rio de Janeiro, Brazil. Tape recording.

McCarthy, John. Interview by author, July 9, 1995, Rio de Janeiro, Brazil. Tape recording.

Miranda, Carlos. Interview by author, November 10, 1994, Rio de Janeiro, Brazil. Tape recording.

Mott, Luiz R. B. Interview by author, May 17, 1995, Salvador, Bahia, and 25 June 1995, Rio de Janeiro, Brazil. Tape recording.

Penteado, Darcy. Interview by Edward MacRae, June 13, 1980, São Paulo, Brazil. Tape recording.

Ramalhete [pseudonym]. Interview by author, February 15, 1995, Rio de Janeiro, Brazil. Tape recording.

Reis, Toni. Interview by author, January 20, 1995, Curitiba, Paraná, Brazil. Tape recording.

Rocha, Riva. Interview by author, November 2, 1994, Rio de Janeiro, Brazil. Tape recording.

Rodrigues de Souza, José. Interview by author, April 25, 1995, Rio de Janeiro, Brazil. Tape recording.

Sérgio [pseudonym]. Interview by author, June 26, 1996, Los Angeles, California. Notes.

Silva, Carlos Ricardo da. Interview by author, November 26, 1994, São Paulo, Brazil. Tape recording.

Silva, Wilson da. Interview by author, June 25, 1995, Rio de Janeiro, Brazil. Tape recording.

Terto, Veriano Júnior. Interview by author, July 24, 1995, Rio de Janeiro, Brazil. Tape recording.

Toledo, Eduardo. Interview by author, September 18, 1993, São Paulo, Brazil. Tape recording.

Vítor. Interview by author, July 9, 1995, Rio de Janeiro, Brazil. Tape recording.

4. Serial Collections

Baby (Salvador) 1, nos. 1–4 (1969).

Celso Curi. "Coluna do Meio." *Última Hora* (São Paulo), February 5, 1976, to December 1, 1977.

O Centro (Rio de Janeiro), 1967.

Darling (Salvador) 1, nos. 1–6 (1968).

Entender (São Paulo), no. o (June 24, 1977) to no. 5 (December 1977).

Le Femme (Rio de Janeiro) 1, no 1 (1968) to 2, no. 6 (1969).

Gay Society (Salvador) 1, nos. 3–6 (1968).

Gente Gay (Rio de Janeiro), no. 1 (December 24, 1976) to no. 14 (August 15, 1978).

Já (Rio de Janeiro), no. 1 (June 1, 1971) to no. 11 (August 25, 1971).

Lampião da Esquina (Rio de Janeiro), no. o (April 1978) to no. 37 (June 1981).

O Malho (Rio de Janeiro), no. 1 (1902) to no. 130 (1905).

Mundo Gay (São Paulo) 1, no. 1 (October 15, 1977) to no. 3 (December 1, 1977).

Músculo (Rio de Janeiro) 1, no. 1 (February 1953) to no. 5 (June 1953).

Physique Pictorial (Chicago), 1954.

O Snob (Rio de Janeiro) 1, no. 1 (July 10, 1963), to 7, no. 2 (May/June 1969).

Le Sophistique (Campos) 1, no. 2 (December 1966).

5. Government Records and Documents

Arquivo da Cidade do Rio de Janeiro. Códices 15.4.29, page 29, April 9, 1870.

Arquivo da Cidade do Rio de Janeiro. Códices 15.4.29, page 14, no. 5841, August 26, 1878.

Arquivo da Cidade do Rio de Janeiro. Códices 15.4.29, page 15, September 10, 1878.

Directoria Geral de Estatística. *Recenseamento geral da República dos Estados Unidos do Brazil em 31 de Dezembro de 1890, Distrito Federal.* Rio de Janeiro: Imprensa Nacional, 1895.

————. *Sexo, raça, e estado civil, nacionalidade, filiação, culto, e analphabetismo da população recenseada em 31 de dezembro de 1890.* Rio de Janeiro: Imprensa Nacional, 1898.

————. *Recenseamento do Rio de Janeiro realisado em 20 de Setembro de 1906.* Rio de Janeiro: Imprensa Nacional, 1907.

————. *Recenseamento do Brazil realizado em 1 de Setembro de 1920, população do Rio de Janeiro (Distrito Federal).* Rio de Janeiro: Imprensa Nacional, 1923.

Franco, Francisco de Assis Carvalho. *Gabinete de Investigações: Relatório apresentado ao Exmo.*

Snr. Dr. Secretário da Segurança Pública do Estado de São Paulo, 1934. São Paulo: Typografia do Gabinete de Investigações, 1935.

Instituto Brasileiro de Geografia e Estatística. *Recenseamento geral do Brasil (1º de Setembro de 1940).* Part 16, *Distrito Federal.* Rio de Janeiro: Serviço Gráfico do Instituto Brasileiro de Geografia e Estatística, 1951.

————. *Recenseamento geral do Brasil (1º de Julho de 1950): Sinopse preliminar do censo demográfico.* Rio de Janeiro: Serviço Gráfico do Instituto Brasileiro de Geografia e Estatística, 1951.

U.S. Congress, House, Senate. Committee on Foreign Relations and International Relations. *Country Reports on Human Rights Practices for 1993.* Report prepared by the Department of State. 103d Cong., 2d sess. Joint Comm. Print, 1994.

————. *Country Report on Human Rights Practices for 1995.* Report prepared by the Department of State. 104th Cong., 2d sess. Joint Comm. Print, 1996.

————. *Country Report on Human Rights Practices for 1996.* Report prepared by the Department of State. 105th Cong., 1st sess. Joint Comm. Print, 1997.

6. Books and Articles

Abreu, Mauricio de Almeida. *Evolução urbana do Rio de Janeiro.* 2d ed. Rio de Janeiro: Iplan-Rio / Zahar Editores, 1988.

Acevedo, Azelmar. *Homosexualidad: Hacia la destrucción de los mitos.* Buenos Aires: Ediciones Del Ser, 1985.

Adam, Barry D. "In Nicaragua: Homosexuality without a Gay World." In *If You Seduce a Straight Person, Can You Make Them Gay? Issues in Biological Essentialism versus Social Constructionism in Gay and Lesbian Identities,* ed. John P. DeCecco and John P. Elia, 171–80. New York: Harrington Park Press, 1993.

Adrados, Isabel. "Estudo da homossexualidade mediante o teste de Rorschach." *Arquivo Brasileiro de Psicotécnica* 16 (March 1964): 65–74.

"Aelson, o costureiro do carnaval." *Manchete* (Rio de Janeiro), no. 202 (March 3, 1956): 32.

Aguiar, Flávio. "Homossexualidade e repressão." In *Sexo e poder,* ed. Guido Mantega, 139–55. São Paulo: Editora Brasiliense, 1979.

Albuquerque, Fernanda Farias de, and Maurizio Jannelli. *A princesa.* Trans. Elisa Byington. Rio de Janeiro: Nova Fronteira, 1995.

Albuquerque, José. *Da impotência sexual no homem.* Rio de Janeiro: Typografia Coelho, 1928.

Alcoforado, Maria Letícia Guedes. "Bom-Crioulo de Adolfo Caminha e a França." *Revista de Letras* (São Paulo) 28 (1988): 85–93.

Almeida, Antônio F. Júnior, and J. B. Costa Júnior. "Atos libidinosos e atos obscenos." In *Lições de medicina legal,* 332–338. São Paulo: Companhia Editora Nacional, 1978.

Almeida, Gastão Ferreira de. *Os projetos do código criminal brasileiro (de Sá Pereira) e do código dos delitos para a Itália (de Ferri).* São Paulo: Edições e Publicações Brasil, 1937.

Almeida, Horácio de. *Dicionário de termos eróticos e afins.* Rio de Janeiro: Civilização Brasileira, 1981.

Almeida, Narceu de, Marilda Varejão, Nello Pedra Gandara, Ruth de Aquino Araújo, Cláudio Segovick, and João de Albuquerque. "Homossexualismo: A hora da verdade." *Manchete* (Rio de Janeiro), no. 1231 (November 22, 1975): 18–23.

Almeida, Sérgio José Alves de. "Michê." Master's thesis, Pontifícia Universidade Católica de São Paulo, 1984.

Altman, Dennis. "Down Rio Way." In *The Christopher Street Reader*, ed. Michael Denneny, Charles Ortleb, Thomas Steele, 214–19. New York: Putnam, 1983.

Alvarez, Sonia E. *Engendering Democracy in Brazil: Women's Movements in Transition Politics*. Princeton: Princeton University Press, 1990.

Alves, Maria Helena Moreira. *State and Opposition in Military Brazil*. Austin: University of Texas Press, 1985.

Amado, Gilberto. *Mocidade no Rio e primeira viagem à Europa*. 2d ed. Rio de Janeiro: Livraria José Olímpio Editora, 1958.

Amnesty International, USA. *Breaking the Silence: Human Rights Violations Based on Sexual Orientation*. New York: Amnesty International Publications, 1994.

Anderson, Benedict R. O'Gorman. *Imagined Communities: Reflections on the Origin and Spread of Nationalism*. London: Verso Editions / NLB, 1983.

Andrade, Mário de. "Frederico Paciência," In *Contos novos*. São Paulo: Editora Martins, 1947. Reprinted in *My Deep Dark Pain Is Love: A Collection of Latin American Gay Fiction*, ed. Winston Leyland, trans. E. A. Lacey, 151–70. San Francisco: Gay Sunshine Press, 1983.

Andrade, Oswald de. "Os Três Sargentos." *Diário de São Paulo*, April 14, 1929, 6.

Andrews, George Reid. *Blacks and Whites in São Paulo Brazil, 1888–1988*. Madison: University of Wisconsin Press, 1991.

Andrusia, David. "Caetano Veloso, the Most Popular Singer / Songwriter in Brazil, Talks about Music, Sexuality, AIDS, and Creating a New Pop Nationality." *New York Native* 222 (July 20, 1987): 37–38.

Angélica, Joana. "Winston Leyland: A literatura e a arte de homossexuais têm estilo próprio?" *O Globo* (Rio de Janeiro), September 9, 1977, 26.

Antelo, Raúl. *João do Rio: O dândi e a especulação*. Rio de Janeiro: Livrarias Taurus-Timbre Editores, 1989.

"A antiga lenda é revivida por muitos, todos os anos no João Caetano." *Manchete* (Rio de Janeiro), no. 306 (March 1, 1958): 26.

Antônio, Maria. "Carnaval em Copacabana," *Última Hora* (Rio de Janeiro), February 16, 1961, 8.

"Apolo brasileiro em Londres." *Manchete* (Rio de Janeiro), no. 15 (August 2, 1952): 28.

Araújo, Rosa Maria Barboza de. *A vocação do prazer: A cidade e a família no Rio de Janeiro republicano*. Rio de Janeiro: Rocco, 1995.

Araújo, Vicente de Paula. *A bela época do cinema brasileiro*. São Paulo: Editora Perspectiva, 1976.

Araújo Filho, José Roberto de. "A população paulistana." In *A cidade de São Paulo: estudos de geografia urbana*, vol. 2, *A evolução urbana*, 167–247, ed. Aroldo de Azevedo. São Paulo: Companhia Editora Nacional, 1958.

Argüelles, Lourdes, and B. Ruby Rich. "Homosexuality, Homophobia, and Revolution: Notes toward an Understanding of the Cuban Lesbian and Gay Male Experience." *Signs: Journal of Women in Culture and Society* 9, no. 4 (summer 1984): 683–99.

Arquidiocese de São Paulo. *Brasil nunca mais*. Petrópolis: Vozes, 1985.

"Associação Psiquiátrica dos EUA exclui o homossexualismo do índice de distúrbios mentais." *Jornal do Brasil* (Rio de Janeiro), December 16, 1973, 16.

Aufterherde, Patricia. "True Confessions: The Inquisition and Social Attitudes in Brazil at the Turn of the Seventeenth Century." *Luso-Brazilian Review* 10, no. 2 (1973): 208–40.

Augusto, Sérgio. "Hollywood Looks at Brazil: From Carmen Miranda to *Moonraker*." In *Brazilian Cinema*, ed. Randal Johnson and Robert Stam, 351–61. New York: Columbia University Press, 1995.

Avancini, Marta. "Na Era de Ouro das cantoras do rádio." *Luso-Brazilian Review* 30, no. 1 (summer 1993): 85–93.

Azzi, Riolando. "Família, mulher, e sexualidade na Igreja do Brasil, 1930–1964." In *Família, mulher, sexualidade, e Igreja na história do Brasil*, ed. Maria Luiza Marcílio, 101–34. São Paulo: Edições Loyola, 1993.

"Baile do São José: Mais de mil bonecas no salão." *Manchete* (Rio de Janeiro), no. 1247 (March 13, 1976): 54–58.

Bakhtin, Mikhail. *Rabelais and His World*. Trans. Helene Iswolsky. Bloomington: Indiana University Press, 1984.

Bao, Daniel. "Invertidos Sexuales, Tortilleras, and Maricas Machos: The Construction of Homosexuality in Buenos Aires, Argentina, 1900–1950." In *If You Seduce a Straight Person, Can You Make Them Gay? Issues in Biological Essentialism versus Social Constructionism in Gay and Lesbian Identities*, ed. John P. DeCecco and John P. Elia, 183–219. Binghamton, N.Y.: Harrington Park Press, 1993.

Baptista, Tarlis, and Thea Sequerra. "Carnaval: Os cassados da passarela." *Manchete* (Rio de Janeiro), no. 1089 (March 3, 1973): 24–26.

Barbosa, Dom Marcos. "Bazares e feiras." *Jornal do Brasil*, September 26, 1969, 1.

Barbosa da Silva, José Fábio. "Aspectos sociológicos do homossexualismo em São Paulo." *Sociologia* 21, no. 4 (October 1959): 350–60.

———. "Homossexualismo em São Paulo: Estudo de um grupo minoritário." Master's thesis, Escola de Sociologia e Política de São Paulo, 1960.

———. Notes for research on homosexuality in São Paulo. Unpublished material in possession of James N. Green, 1959–60.

Barreto, Lima. *Recordações do escrivão Isaías Caminha*. Rio de Janeiro: Livraria Garnier, 1989.

———. *Um longo sonho do futuro: Diários, cartas, entrevistas, e confissões dispersas*. Rio de Janeiro: Graphic Editorial, 1993.

Barros, Evardado de, "As 'falsas baianas' do carnaval carioca." *Última Hora* (Rio de Janeiro), February 14, 1953, 8.

Bartolo, Júlio. "Uma noite di-vi-na com elas e elas." *Manchete* (Rio de Janeiro), no. 1348 (February 18, 1978): 83–84.

Bassanezi, Carla. *Virando as páginas, revendo as mulheres: Revistas femininas e relações homem-mulher, 1945–1964*. Rio de Janeiro: Civilização Brasileira, 1996.

Bastos, José Cândido. "Homossexualidade masculina." *Jornal Brasileiro de Psiquiatria*. 28, nos. 1–4 (1979): 7–11.

Beattie, Peter M. "Asking, Telling, and Pursuing in the Brazilian Army and Navy in the Days of *Cachaça*, Sodomy, and the Lash, 1860–1916." In *Sex and Sexuality in Latin America*, ed. Donna J. Guy and Daniel Balderston, 65–85. New York: New York University Press, 1997.

Belini, Lígia. *A coisa obscura: Mulher, sodomia, e inquisição no Brasil colonial*. São Paulo: Editora Brasiliense, 1987.

Bell, David, and Gill Valentine, ed. *Mapping Desire: Geographies of Sexualities*. London: Routledge, 1995.

Bello, José Maria. *A History of Modern Brazil, 1889–1964*. Stanford: Stanford University Press, 1966.

Bello da Mota, Antônio. *Homossexualismo em medicina legal*. Tese de concurso à cátedra de Medicina Legal da Faculdade de Direito do Estado de Ceará. Rio de Janeiro: Typografia do Jornal do Comércio, 1937.

Benchimol, Jaime Larry. *Pereira Passos, um Haussmann tropical: A renovação urbana da cidade do Rio de Janeiro no início do século XX*. Rio de Janeiro: Secretaria Municipal de Cultura,

Turismo, e Esportes, Departamento Geral de Documentação e Informação Cultural, Divisão de Editoração, 1992.

Beozzo, José Oscar. "A igreja entre a Revolução de 1930, o Estado Novo e a redemocratização." In *O Brasil republicano*, ed. Boris Fausto, vol. 4, *Economia e cultura*, 273–341. São Paulo: Difel, 1984.

Bergmann, Emelie L., and Paul Julian Smith, ed. *Entiendes? Queer Readings, Hispanic Writings*. Durham: Duke University Press, 1995.

Berman, David, ed. *Camp Grounds: Style and Homosexuality*. Amherst: University of Massachusetts Press, 1993.

Besse, Susan K. *Restructuring Patriarchy: The Modernization of Gender Inequality in Brazil, 1914–1940*. Chapel Hill: University of North Carolina Press, 1996.

Birman, Patrícia. *Fazer estilo criando gêneros: Possessão e diferenças de gênero em terreiros de umbanda e candomblé no Rio de Janeiro*. Rio de Janeiro: Relume Dumará, EdUERJ, 1995.

Bittencourt, Francisco. *A bicha que ri*. Rio de Janeiro: Esquina Editora, 1981.

Bivar, Antônio. "Revolução sexual à paulista." *Ele-Ela* 96 (April 1977): 50–57.

———. "O paraíso gay, São Paulo, é claro." *Especial* (São Paulo), February 1980, 26.

Bjorn, Kristen. *Carnival in Rio*. Kristen Bjorn Productions, Miami Beach, 1989.

———. *Tropical Heat Wave*. Kristen Bjorn Productions, Miami Beach, 1990.

———. *Jungle Heat*. Kristen Bjorn Productions, Miami Beach, 1993.

———. *Paradise Plantation*. Kristen Bjorn Productions, Miami Beach, 1994.

———. *A World of Men*. Kristen Bjorn Productions, Miami Beach, 1995.

———. *Amazon Adventure*. Kristen Bjorn Productions, Miami Beach, 1996.

Bland, John Otway Percy. *Men, Manners, and Morals in South America*. New York: Charles Scribner's Sons, 1920.

Bleys, Rudi C. *The Geography of Perversion: Male-to-Male Sexual Behavior outside the West and the Ethnographic Imagination, 1750–1918*. New York: New York University Press, 1995.

"'Boneca' lidera bloco de cinzas." *Última Hora* (Rio de Janeiro), February 24, 1966, 8.

"Bonecas ao luar." *Manchete* (Rio de Janeiro), no. 1348 (February 18, 1978): 76–81.

"Bonecas: divinas e maravilhosas." *Manchete* (Rio de Janeiro), no. 1142 (March 9, 1974): 78–82.

Borges, Dain. *The Family in Bahia, Brazil, 1870–1945*. Stanford: Stanford University Press, 1992.

"Borges vai prender quem beijar na boca." *Última Hora* (Rio de Janeiro), February 6, 1964, 2.

Bororó [Alberto de Castro Simoens da Silva]. *Gente da madrugada: Flagrantes da vida noturna*. Rio de Janeiro: Guavira, 1982.

"Borrachada comandou 'baile dos enxutos.'" *Última Hora* (Rio de Janeiro), February 12, 1964, 6.

Botelho, Abel. *O Barão de Lavos (pathologia social)*. Porto: Imprensa Moderna, 1908.

Braga, José Luiz. *O Pasquim e os anos 70: Mais pra epa que para oba*. Brasília, D.F.: Editora Universidade de Brasília, 1991.

Brandão, Darwin. "Um passeio pelos bares famosos do Rio." *Manchete* (Rio de Janeiro), no. 17 (August 16, 1952): 17.

Brandão, Zilda. "Cuidado: Travestis invadem a cidade." *Última Hora* (São Paulo), August 2, 1975, 8.

"Brazil / Gay: "Somos onze milhões." *Última Hora* (Rio de Janeiro), December 3, 1977, 6.

Brenna, Giovanna Rosso Del, ed. *O Rio de Janeiro de Pereira Passos: Uma cidade em questão II*. Rio de Janeiro: Editora Index, 1985.

Bretas, Marcos Luiz. *Ordem na Cidade: O exercício cotidiano da autoridade policial no Rio de Janeiro, 1907–1930*. Rio de Janeiro: Rocco, 1997.

Brooke, James. "In Live-and-Let-Live Land, Gay People are Slain." *New York Times*, August 12, 1993, 3.

Burns, E. Bradford. *A History of Brazil*. 3d ed. New York: Columbia University Press, 1993.

Buzaid, Alfredo. "Censura prévia para livros e periódicos." *Última Hora* (Rio de Janeiro), February 12, 1970, 1.

Cabo Machado [Oswald de Andrade]. "Os três sargentos." *Diário de São Paulo*, April 14, 1929, 6.

Cabral, Sérgio, Millôr Fernandes, Chico Júnior, and Paulo Francis. "Madame Satã." *Pasquim* (Rio de Janeiro), no. 95 (April 29, 1971): 2–5.

Caminha, Adolfo. "Um livro condenado." *A Nova Revista* (Rio de Janeiro) 2 (February 1896): 40–42.

———. *Bom-Crioulo: The Black Man and the Cabin Boy*. Trans. E. A. Lacey. San Francisco: Gay Sunshine Press, 1982.

———. *Bom-Crioulo*. Rio de Janeiro: Prefeitura da Cidade do Rio de Janeiro, Secretaria Municipal de Cultura, Turismo e Esportes, Departamento Geral de Documentação e Informação Cultural, 1991.

Canales, Luis. "O Homossexualismo como tema no moderno teatro brasileiro," *Luso-Brazilian Review* 18, no. 1 (summer 1981): 173–81.

Cardoso, Abel Júnior. *Carmen Miranda: A cantora do Brasil*. São Paulo: by the author, 1979.

Cardoso, Elizabeth Dezouzart, Lilian Fessler Vaz, Maria Paula Albernaz, Mario Aizen, and Roberto Moses Pechman. *Copacabana*. Rio de Janeiro: João Fortes Engenharia/Editora Index, 1986.

"Cariocas já em pleno reinado carnavalesco." *Última Hora* (Rio de Janeiro), March 3, 1962, 2.

"O Carnaval dos 'excêntricos': 'Travesti' elegante e curioso." *Última Hora* (Rio de Janeiro), February 19, 1958, 14.

"Carnaval em plena cinzas: 'Enxutos' e 'chave' saem 4ª feira." *Última Hora* (Rio de Janeiro), February 13, 1964, 1.

"Carnaval na base do beijo proibido." *Última Hora* (Rio de Janeiro), February 12, 1964, 5.

Carneiro, Edison. *A sabedoria popular*. Rio de Janeiro: Ministério da Educação e Cultura, Instituto Nacional do Livro, 1957.

Carone, Edgard. *O Estado Novo, 1937–1945*. São Paulo: Difel, 1977.

Carrier, Joseph. *De Los Otros: Intimacy and Homosexuality among Mexican Men*. New York: Columbia University Press, 1995.

Carvalho, José Murilo de. *Os bestializados: O Rio de Janeiro e a república que não foi*. São Paulo: Editora Schwarcz, 1987.

Carvalho, Lia de Aquino. *Habitações populares*. Rio de Janeiro: Prefeitura da Cidade do Rio de Janeiro, Secretaria Municipal de Cultura, Departamento Geral de Documentação e Informação Cultural, Divisão de Editoração, 1995.

Carvalho, Tamara Teixeira de. "Caminhos do desejo: Uma abordagem antropológica das relações homoeróticas femininas em Belo Horizonte." Master's thesis, Universidade Estadual de Campinas, 1995.

Carvalho, Thor. "'Elas' são assim." *Última Hora* (Rio de Janeiro), June 18, 1964, 6.

Castelo Branco, José. "A homossexualidade do Pasquim." *O Beijo* (Rio de Janeiro) 2 (December 1977): 3–4.

Castelo Branco, Vitorino. *O advogado diante dos crimes sexuais*. São Paulo: Sugestões Literárias, 1977.

Castro, Cláudio de Moura. "What Is Happening in Brazilian Education." In *Social Change in Brazil, 1945–1985: The Incomplete Transition*, ed. Edmar L. Bacha and Herbert S. Klein, 263–309. Albuquerque: University of New Mexico Press, 1989.

Castro, Elias Ribeiro. "No limiar do permitido: Uma introdução ao espírito carnavalesco do romance de Adolfo Caminha." Universidade de São Paulo, 1997.

Castro, Moacir Werneck de. *Mário de Andrade: exílio no Rio.* Rio de Janeiro: Rocco, 1989.

Castro, Ruy. *Chega de saudade: A história e as histórias da bossa nova.* São Paulo: Companhia das Letras, 1990.

Caulfield, Sueann. "Getting into Trouble: Dishonest Women, Modern Girls, and Women-Men in the Conceptual Language of *Vida Policial,* 1925–1927." *Signs: Journal of Women in Culture and Society* 19, no. 11 (autumn 1993): 146–76.

———. "In Defense of Honor: The Contested Meaning of Sexual Morality in Law and Courtship, Rio de Janeiro, 1920–40." Ph.D. diss., New York University, 1994.

———. "The Birth of Mangue: Race, Nation, and the Politics of Prostitution in Rio de Janeiro, 1850–1942." In *Sex and Sexuality in Latin America,* ed. Donna J. Guy and Daniel Balderston, 86–100. New York: New York University Press, 1997.

Chacon, Vamireh. *Estado e povo no Brasil: As experiências do Estado Novo e da democracia populista, 1937–1964.* Rio de Janeiro: Livraria José Olímpio Editora, 1977.

Chalhoub, Sidney. *Trabalho, lar e botequim: O cotidiano dos trabalhadores no Rio de Janeiro da belle époque.* São Paulo: Editora Brasiliense, 1986.

"Charme e talento na arte de Valéria." *Folha de São Paulo,* December 9, 1973, 10.

Chaui, Marilena. *Repressão sexual, essa nossa (des)conhecida.* São Paulo: Editora Brasiliense, 1984.

Chauncey, George. *Gay New York: Gender, Urban Culture, and the Making of the Gay Male World, 1890–1940.* New York: Basic Books, 1994.

Chinelli, Filipina. "Acusação e desvio em uma minoria." In *Desvio e divergência: Uma crítica da patologia social,* ed. Gilberto Velho, 125–44. Rio de Janeiro: Zahar Editores, 1981.

Coaracy, Vivaldo. *Memórias da cidade do Rio de Janeiro.* 3d ed. Belo Horizonte: Itatiaia, 1988.

"Coccinelli mostrou no Copa 99% do que a tornou mulher." *Última Hora* (Rio de Janeiro), March 12, 1963, 3.

Colaço, Rita. *Uma conversa informal sobre homossexualismo.* Duque de Caxias, Rio de Janeiro: by the author, 1984.

Comissão de Homossexuais Pro-1° de Maio. "Contra a intervenção nos sindicatos de São Paulo, contra a discriminação do trabalhador/a homossexual." São Paulo, 1980. Mimeographed.

Conniff, Michael. *Urban Politics in Brazil: The Rise of Populism, 1925–1945.* Pittsburgh: University of Pittsburgh Press, 1981.

Conrad, Robert Edgar. *Children of God's Fire: A Documentary History of Black Slavery in Brazil.* Princeton: Princeton University Press, 1984.

"Copacabana, Ipanema, e Leblon parecem destinadas a representar no litoral atlântico da América do Sul, o papel que Ostende, Biarritz, Deauville, o Lido e Miami representam na Europa e nos Estados Unidos." *Cruzeiro,* November 24, 1928, 7.

Cornwall, Andrea. "Gendered Identities and Gender Ambiguity among *Travestis* in Salvador, Brazil." In *Dislocating Masculinity: Comparative Ethnographies,* ed. Andrea Cornwall and Nancy Lindisfarne, 112–32. London: Routledge, 1994.

Corrêa, Mariza. "Repensando a família patriarcal brasileira [notas para o estudo das formas de organização familiar no Brasil]." In *Colcha de retalhos: Estudos sobre a família no Brasil,* ed. Mariza Corrêa, 13–38. São Paulo: Editora Brasiliense, 1982.

Costa, Emília Viotti da. *The Brazilian Empire: Myths and Histories.* Chicago: University of Chicago Press, 1985.

Costa, Haroldo. "Trinta anos depois . . . " In *História do Carnaval carioca,* by Eneida Moraes, new edition, revised and expanded by Haroldo Costa. Rio de Janeiro: Gráfica Récord Editora, 1987.

Costa, Juandir Freire. *História da psiquiatria no Brasil: Um corte ideológico.* Rio de Janeiro: Editora Documentário, 1976.

――――. *Ordem médica e norma familiar.* Rio de Janeiro: Edições Graal, 1979.

Cunha, Maria Clementina Pereira. *O espelho do mundo: Juquery, a história de um asilo.* Rio de Janeiro: Paz e Terra, 1986.

――――. "E viva o Zé Pereira! O Carnaval carioca como teatro de conflitos, 1880–1920." Paper delivered at a meeting of the Latin American Studies Association, Guadalajara, Mexico, April 1997.

Cunha, Pérsivo. *Sexologia forense.* São Paulo: Sugestões Literárias, 1977.

Cury, Ricardo. "As ciências da saúde mental, direito, e homossexualismo." In *Resumos da 34ª Reunião Anual da Sociedade Brasileira para o Progresso da Ciência,* 890. Campinas: SPBC, 1982.

"Da folia ao exagero: Excessos que mancham o Carnaval carioca." *Última Hora* (Rio de Janeiro), February 20, 1958, 10.

Daguer, Pedro J. "Transexualismo masculino." Master's thesis, Universidade Federal do Rio de Janeiro, 1977.

Damata, Gasparino [Gasparino da Mata e Silva]. *Histórias do amor maldito.* Rio de Janeiro: Gráfica Récord Editora, 1967.

――――. *Os solteirões.* Rio de Janeiro: Pallas, 1976.

――――. "Nossos alegres rapazes da banda." *Pasquim* (Rio de Janeiro), no. 436 (November 4, 1977): 6.

Da Matta, Roberto. "O Carnaval como um rito de passagem." Chap. in *Ensaios de antropologia estrutural.* Petrópolis: Editora Vozes, 1973.

――――. *Universo do Carnaval: Imagens e reflexões.* Rio de Janeiro: Edições Pinakotheke, 1981.

――――. "Carnival in Multiple Planes." In *Rite, Drama, Festival, Spectacle: Rehearsals toward a Theory of Cultural Performance,* ed. John J. MacAloon, 208–40. Philadelphia: Institute for the Study of Human Issues, 1984.

――――. "*Carnival* as a Cultural Problem: Towards a Theory of Formal Events and Their Magic." Working Paper no. 79. Helen Kellogg Institute for International Studies, Notre Dame, Ind., September 1986.

――――. *Carnavals, Rogues, and Heroes: An Interpretation of the Brazilian Dilemma.* Trans. John Drury. Notre Dame: University of Notre Dame Press, 1991.

Damazio, Sylvia F. *Retrato social do Rio de Janeiro na virada do século.* Rio de Janeiro: EdUERJ, 1996.

Daniel, Herbert. *Passagem para o próximo sonho.* Rio de Janeiro: Editora Codecri, 1982.

Daniel, Herbert, and Richard Parker, *Sexuality, Politics, and AIDS in Brazil: In Another World?* London: Falmer Press, 1993.

Daniel, Marc. "Historie de la législation pénale française concernant l'homosexualité." *Acadie* (Paris) 96:618–27; 97:10–29.

Dantas, Antônio Ribeiro. "A representação da homossexualidade: A 'leitura' da imprensa escrita." Master's thesis, Universidade Federal do Rio Grande do Norte, 1989.

Dantas, Eduardo. "Negros, mulheres, homossexuais, e índios nos debates da USP." *Lampião da Esquina* 2, no. 10 (March 1979): 9–10.

Dean, Warren. *The Industrialization of São Paulo.* Austin: University of Texas Press, 1969.

Decca, Edgar de. *1930: O silêncio dos vencidos.* São Paulo: Editora Brasiliense, 1981.

Define, Jacomino. "A Rua do Ouvidor." *Kosmos* (Rio de Janeiro) 2, no. 1 (February 1905): 37–39.

Degler, Carl N. *Neither Black nor White: Slavery and Race Relations in Brazil and the United States.* Madison: University of Wisconsin Press, 1971.

"Delegacia especializada de vigilância e capturas." *Última Hora* (Rio de Janeiro), March 8, 1962, 12.

Della Cava, Ralph. "Catholicism and Society in Twentieth Century Brazil." *Latin American Research Review* 11, no. 2 (1976): 7–50.

D'Emilio, John. *Sexual Politics, Sexual Communities: The Making of a Homosexual Minority in the United States, 1940–1970*. Chicago: University of Chicago Press, 1983.

"Desfile de fantasias no Baile dos Artistas," *Manchete* (Rio de Janeiro), no. 98 (March 6, 1954): 35.

Diccionário da lingua portugueza recopilado dos vocabulários impressos até agora e nesta segunda edição novamente emendado e muito accrescentado por Antonio de Maraes Silva Antural do Rio de Janeiro offerecido ao muito alto e muito poderoso Principe Regente N. Senhor. Tomo Segundo F–Z. Lisbon: Lacédina, 1813.

Dignidade, Grupo de Conscientização e Emancipação Homossexual. *News from Brazil*, no. 2 (June 1994).

Diniz, Eli. "O Estado Novo: Estrutura de poder, relações de classes." In *O Brasil republicano: Sociedade e política, 1930–1964*, ed. Boris Fausto, 3, part 2: 77–120. São Paulo: Difel, 1981.

"O direito de não ser maldito." *Jornal do Brasil, Revista Domingo* (Rio de Janeiro), May 28, 1972, 2.

Dos Santos, Carlos Nelson F. "Bichas e entendidos: A sauna como lugar de confronto." Rio de Janeiro, 1976.

Dos Santos, Joaquim Ferreira. "A imprensa gay." *Pasquim* (Rio de Janeiro), no. 436 (November 4, 1977): 4–5.

Dourado, Luiz Ângelo. *Homossexualismo masculino e feminino e delinquência*. Rio de Janeiro: Zahar Editores, 1967.

Dunbar, John, Marvin Brown, and Sophie Vuorine. "Attitudes toward Homosexuality among Brazilian and Canadian College Students." *Journal of Social Psychology* 90 (1973): 173–83.

Dunn, Christopher John. "The Relics of Brazil: Modernity and Nationality in the Tropicalista Movement." Ph.D. diss., Brown University, 1996.

———. "The Tropicalista Rebellion: A Conversation with Caetano Veloso." *Transition: An International Review* 6, no. 2, issue 70 (summer 1996): 116–38.

Durst, Rogério. *Madame Satã: Com o diabo no corpo*. São Paulo: Editora Brasiliense, 1985.

Dynes, Wayne R. "Portugayese." In *Latin American Male Homosexualities*, ed. Stephen O. Murray, 256–263. Albuquerque: University of New Mexico Press, 1995.

Edmundo, Luiz. *O Rio de Janeiro do meu tempo*. Rio de Janeiro: Imprensa Nacional, 1938.

"Eles não usam black tie." *Manchete* (Rio de Janeiro), no. 463 (March 4, 1961): 66–69.

Elisabeth, Marie, and Jim Green, "Depois da fuga, saímos ao sol." *Versus* 34 (October 1979): 30–32.

Enderman, Regina Maria. "Reis e rainhas do desterro: Um estudo de caso." Master's thesis, Universidade Federal de Santa Catarina, Florianópolis, 1981.

Engel, Magali. *Meretrizes e doutores: Saber médico e prostituição no Rio de Janeiro, 1840–1890*. São Paulo: Editora Brasiliense, 1988.

"Do entrudo à passarela, 419 anos de folia." *O Globo* (Rio de Janeiro), October 8, 1989, 22.

"Enxutos: As bonecas são um luxo" *Manchete* (Rio de Janeiro), no. 1091 (March 17, 1973): 74–75.

"Enxutos e bonecas: A grande guerra." *Manchete* (Rio de Janeiro), no. 724 (March 5, 1966): 56.

"'Enxutos' tiveram seu baile." *Última Hora* (Rio de Janeiro), (March 7, 1962): 8.

Escoffier, Jeffrey. *American Homos: Community and Perversity*. Berkeley: University of California Press, 1998.

Esteves, Martha de Abreu. *Meninas perdidas: Os populares e o cotidiano do amor no Rio de Janeiro da belle époque.* Rio de Janeiro: Paz e Terra, 1989.

"Ex-'travesti' Coccinelli é mulher mesmo: Espera bebê." *Última Hora* (Rio de Janeiro), March 13, 1963, 1.

"Façanha quer volta dos "enxutos." *Jornal do Brasil* (Rio de Janeiro), October 23, 1972, 13.

Fantásio [pseudonym]. "O namoro no Rio de Janeiro." *Kosmos* (Rio de Janeiro) 3, no. 7 (July 1906): 43–45.

Faria, Eduardo de. *Novo diccionario da lingua portugueza.* Vol. 3. Lisbon: Typografia Lisbonense, 1849.

Faria, Gentil Luiz de. *A presença de Oscar Wilde na belle-époque literária brasileira.* São João do Rio Preto, São Paulo: Pannartz, 1988.

Faury, Mára L. *Uma flor para os malditos: A homossexualidade na literatura.* Campinas: Editora Papirus, 1983.

Fausto, Boris. *História do Brasil.* São Paulo: EDUSP, 1994.

Feldman, Sara. "Segregações espaciais urbanas: A territorialização da prostituição feminina em São Paulo." Master's thesis, Universidade de São Paulo, 1988.

Fernandes, Hélio. "Roteiro noturno (de Copacabana) para turistas desprevenidos." *Manchete* (Rio de Janeiro), no. 24 (October 4, 1952): 30.

Ferrão, Laertes Moura. "Homossexualidade e defesas maníacas." *Revista Brasileira de Psicanálise* 1, no. 1 (1967): 85–93.

Ferraz de Macedo, Francisco. *Da prostituição em geral e em particular em relação ao Rio de Janeiro.* Medical thesis, Faculdade de Medicina da Universidade do Rio de Janeiro, 1872.

Ferreira, Jairo. "A identidade de uma minoria." *Folha de São Paulo*, October 3, 1977, 26.

Fey, Ingrid Elizabeth. "First Tango in Paris: Latin Americans in Turn-of-the-Century France, 1880 to 1920." Ph.D. diss., University of California, Los Angeles, 1996.

Figueiredo, Maurício. *Cordão da Bola Preta: Boêmia carioca.* Rio de Janeiro: Comércio e Representações Bahia, 1966.

Fonseca, Guido. *História da prostituição em São Paulo.* São Paulo: Editora Resenha Universitária, 1982.

Fontaine, Pierre-Michel, ed. *Race, Class, and Power in Brazil.* Los Angeles: Center for Afro-American Studies, 1985.

Ford, Talisman. "Passion in the Eye of the Beholder: Sexuality as Seen by Brazilian Sexologists, 1900–1940." Ph.D. diss., Vanderbilt University, 1995.

Foster, David William. *Gay and Lesbian Themes in Latin American Writing.* Austin: University of Texas Press, 1991.

———, ed. *Latin American Writers on Gay and Lesbian Themes: A Bio-Critical Sourcebook.* Westport, Conn.: Greenwood Press, 1994.

Foster, David William, and Roberto Reis, ed. *Bodies and Biases: Sexualities in Hispanic Cultures and Literatures.* Minneapolis: University of Minnesota Press, 1996.

Foucault, Michel. *The History of Sexuality: An Introduction.* Vol. 1. Trans. Robert Hurley. New York: Vintage Books, 1990.

Franca, Geminiano da. "Serviço Policial." In *Relatório, Ministro da Justiça, e Negocios Interiores*, by Alfredo Pinto Vieira de Mello. Rio de Janeiro: Imprensa Nacional, 1920, 75.

França, Genival Veloso de. *Medicina legal.* Rio de Janeiro: Guanabara Koogan, 1977.

Franco, Daniel. "O homossexual brasileiro nas últimas três décadas." *Jornal do Gay: Noticiário do Mundo Entendido.* (São Paulo), no. 2 (1978): 20–23.

Franco da Rocha, Francisco. *Esboço de psiquiatria forense.* São Paulo: Typografia Laemmert, 1904.

Freire, Laudelino, ed. *Dicionário da língua portuguesa.* Vol. 3. Rio de Janeiro: A Noite Editora, 1941.

Freitas, Jânio. "A extravagante exibição do João Caetano." *Manchete* (Rio de Janeiro), no. 201 (February 25, 1956): 28–29.

Freyre, Gilberto. *The Masters and the Slaves: A Study in the Development of Brazilian Civilization*. Berkeley: University of California Press, 1986.

———. *Order and Progress: Brazil from Monarch to Republic*. Berkeley: University of California Press, 1986.

Fry, Peter. "História da imprensa baiana." *Lampião da Esquina* (Rio de Janeiro) 1, no. 4 (August 25, 1978): 4.

———. "Febrônio Índio do Brasil: Onde cruzam a psiquiatria, a profecia, a homossexualidade, e a lei." In *Caminhos cruzados: Linguagem, antropologia, e ciências naturais*, 65–80. São Paulo: Editora Brasiliense, 1982.

———. "Léonie, Pombinha, Amaro, e Aleixo: Prostituição, homossexualidade, e raça em dois romances naturalistas." In *Caminhos Cruzados: Linguagem, antropologia, e ciências naturais*, 33–51. São Paulo: Editora Brasiliense, 1982.

———. "Da hierarquia a igualdade: A construção histórica da homossexualidade no Brasil." In *Para inglês ver: Identidade e política na cultura brasileira*, 87–115. Rio de Janeiro: Zahar Editores, 1982.

———. "Male Homosexuality and Spirit Possession in Brazil." *Journal of Homosexuality* 11, nos. 3–4 (summer 1986): 137–54.

———. "Male Homosexuality and Afro-Brazilian Possession Cults." In *Latin American Male Homosexualities*, ed. Stephen O. Murray, 193–220. Albuquerque: University of New Mexico Press, 1995.

Fry, Peter, and Edward MacRae. *O que é homossexualidade*. São Paulo: Editora Brasiliense, 1983.

Gabeira, Fernando. *Carta sobre a anistia: A entrevista do Pasquim, conversação sobre 1968*. Rio de Janeiro: Editora Codecri, 1979.

———. *O que é isso companheiro?* Rio de Janeiro: Editora Codecri, 1979.

———. *O crepúsculo do macho: Depoimento*. Rio de Janeiro: Editora Codecri, 1981.

———. *Entradas e bandeiras*. Rio de Janeiro: Editora Codecri, 1981.

Gaiarsa, José A. *A juventude diante do sexo*. São Paulo: Editora Brasiliense, 1967.

Garcia, Nelson Jahr. *O Estado Novo, ideologia e propaganda política: A legitimação do estado autoritário perante as classes subalternas*. São Paulo: Loyola, 1982.

Gardel, Luis D. *Escolas de Samba: An Affectionate Descriptive Account of the Carnival Guilds of Rio de Janeiro*. Rio de Janeiro: Livraria Kosmos Editora, 1967.

Gauderer, E. Christian. "Homossexualidade masculina e lesbianismo." *Jornal de Pediatria* 56, no. 3 (1984): 236–42.

Gautherot, Marcel. *Rio de Janeiro*. Munich: Wilhelm Andermann Verlag, 1965.

"Um gay power à brasileira." *Veja*, no. 468 (August 24, 1977): 66–70.

"Os gays estão se conscientizando," *Pasquim* (Rio de Janeiro), no. 436 (November 4, 1977): 4–5.

"Os 'gays' saíram à luz." *Isto É*, December 28, 1977, 8–15.

George, David. *The Modern Brazilian Stage*. Austin: University of Texas Press, 1992.

Gibson, Hugh. *Rio de Janeiro*. Garden City, N.Y.: Doubleday, Doran and Company, 1937.

Gikovate, Flávio. "Doença, decadência, ou amor." *Aqui*, October 1977, 26–27.

———. *O instinto sexual*. São Paulo: Editora MG, 1980.

Gil-Montero, Martha. *Brazilian Bombshell: The Biography of Carmen Miranda*. New York: Donald I. Fine, 1989.

Girard, Jacques. *Le mouvement homosexuel en France, 1945–1980*. Paris: Editions Syros, 1981.

Goldfeder, Miriam. *Por trás das ondas da Rádio Nacional*. Rio de Janeiro: Paz e Terra, 1980.

Golovitz, Frank. "Gay Beach." *One Magazine* 6, no. 7 (July 1958): 8.

Gomes, Danilo. *Uma rua chamada Ouvidor*. Rio de Janeiro: Prefeitura da Cidade do Rio de Janeiro, 1980.

———. *Antigos cafés do Rio de Janeiro*. Rio de Janeiro: Livraria Kosmos Editora, 1989.

Gomes, Júlio. *A homossexualidade no mundo*. Lisbon: by the author, 1979.

Gomes, Renato Cordeiro. *João do Rio: Vielas do vício, ruas da graça*. Rio de Janeiro: Relume Dumará, 1996.

Graham, Richard. "An Interview with Sérgio Buarque de Holanda." *Hispanic American Historical Review* 62, no. 1 (February 1982): 3–17.

Graham, Sandra Lauderdale. *House and Street: The Domestic World of Servants and Masters in Nineteenth-Century Rio de Janeiro*. Cambridge: Cambridge Latin American Studies, 1988.

Green, James N. "Liberalization on Trial: The Brazilian Workers' Movement." *North American Congress on Latin America Report on the Americas* 13, no. 3 (May/June 1979): 15–25.

———. "A Comparative Analysis of the Argentine and Brazilian Gay Rights Movement of the 1970s." Paper presented at a meeting of the Latin American Studies Association, Atlanta, Georgia, March 1994.

———. "The Emergence of the Brazilian Gay Liberation Movement, 1977–81." *Latin American Perspectives* 21, no. 1 (winter 1994): 38–55.

———. "Desire and Militancy: Lesbians, Gays, and the Brazilian Workers' Party." In *Different Rainbow: Same-Sex Sexuality and Popular Struggles in the Third World*, ed. Peter Drucker. London: Gay Men's Press, 1999.

———. "More Love and More Desire: The Building of the Brazilian Movement." In *The Global Emergence of Gay and Lesbian Politics: National Imprints of a Worldwide Movement*, ed. Barry Adam, Jan Willem Duyvendak, and André Krouwel, 91–109. Philadelphia: Temple University Press, 1999.

Greenberg, David F. *The Construction of Homosexuality*. Chicago: University of Chicago Press, 1988.

Greenwood, Leonard. "Sex, Samba Disputes Cloud Carnival for Rio." *Los Angeles Times*, February 8, 1970, 4.

Grootendorst, Sapê. "Literatura gay no Brasil: Dezoito escritores brasileiros falando da temática homo-erótica." University of Utrecht, 1993.

"Grupo de homossexuais italianos lançará revista." *Jornal do Brasil* (Rio de Janeiro), June 18, 1971, 9.

Grupo Gay da Bahia. "Grupos de extermínio de homossexuais no Brasil." Salvador: Grupo Gay da Bahia, n.d.

———. "Violação dos direitos humanos e assassinato de homossexuais no Brasil—1997." *Boletim do Grupo Gay da Bahia*, no. 37 (January/February 1998).

Gruzinski, Serge. "Las cenizas del deseo: Homosexuales novohispanos mediados del siglo XVII." In *De la santidad a la perversión, o de porqué no se cumplía la ley de Dios en la sociedad novohispana*, ed. Sergio Ortega, 255–81. Mexico City: Enlace/Historia, 1985.

Guillermoprieto, Alma. *Samba*. New York: Vintage Books, 1991.

Guimarães, Carmen Dora. "O homossexual visto por entendidos." Master's thesis, Museu Nacional, Rio de Janeiro, 1977.

———. "O homossexual face à norma familiar: Desvios e convergências." Paper presented at the sixth annual meeting of the Grupo de Trabalho sobre Processos de Reprodução da População, CLASCO, Teresópolis, 1980.

———. "Um discurso de retorno: A reconstrução da identidade homossexual." Paper presented at the thirteenth annual meeting of the Associação Brasileira de Antropologia, São Paulo, 1982.

————. "Casos e Acasos," *Anais Quarto Encontro Nacional Estudos Populacionais* 1 (1984): 575–86.

Guimarães, Celeste Zenha. "Homossexualismo: Mitologias científicas." Ph.D. diss., Universidade Estadual de Campinas, 1994.

Gutemberg, Luis. "O Baile Proibido." *Manchete* (Rio de Janeiro), no. 255 (March 9, 1957): 56–57.

Guy, Donna J. "Future Directions in Latin American Gender History." *Americas* 51, no. 1 (July 1994): 1–9.

Hahner, June E. *Poverty and Progress: The Urban Poor in Brazil, 1870–1920.* Albuquerque: University of New Mexico Press, 1986.

Halfoun, Eli, "Agora para Paulista." *Última Hora Revista* (Rio de Janeiro), August 12, 1964, 3.

Haller, Archibald O., Manoel M. Tourinho, David B. Bills, and José Pastore. "Migration and Socioeconomic Status in Brasil: Interregional and Rural-Urban Variations in Education, Occupational Status, and Income." *Luso-Brazilian Review* 18, no. 1 (summer 1981): 117–38.

Hanchard, Michael George. *Orpheus and Power: The Movimento Negro of Rio de Janeiro and São Paulo, 1945–1988.* Princeton: Princeton University Press, 1994.

Hecker Filho, Paulo. *Internato.* [Porto Alegre?]: Edição Fronteira, 1951. Reprinted as "Boarding-School," in *My Deep Dark Pain Is Love: A Collection of Latin American Gay Fiction,* ed. Winston Leyland, trans. E. A. Lacey (San Francisco: Gay Sunshine Press, 1983), 245–66.

Heilborn, Maria Luisa. "Dois é par: Conjugalidade gênero e identidade sexual em contexto igualitário." Ph.D. diss., Museu Nacional, Universidade Federal do Rio de Janeiro, 1992.

Herrmann, Lucília. "Estudo do desenvolvimento de São Paulo através da análise de um radial— a estrada do café, 1935." *Revista do Arquivo Municipal* (São Paulo) 99 (1944): 7–45.

Herschmann, Micael M., and Carlos Alberto Messeder Pereira. "O imaginário moderno no Brasil." In *A invenção do Brasil moderno: Medicina, educação, e engenharia nos anos 20–30,* ed. Micael M. Herschmann and Carlos Alberto Messeder Pereira, 9–42. Rio de Janeiro: Rocco, 1994.

Hidalgo, Hilda A., and Elia Hidalgo Christensen. "The Puerto Rican Lesbian and the Puerto Rican Community." *Journal of Homosexuality* 2, no. 2 (winter 1976–77): 109–21.

Higgs, David. "Rio de Janeiro." In *Queer Sites: Gay Urban Histories Since 1600,* ed. David Higgs, 138–63. London: Routledge, 1999.

"A história do 'EBHO': Encontro brasileiro de homossexuais." Part 2. *Boletim do Grupo Gay da Bahia* 13, no. 27 (August 1993): 7.

Holanda, Nestor de. *Memórias do café Nice: Subterrâneos da música popular e da vida boêmia do Rio de Janeiro.* Rio de Janeiro: Conquista, 1970.

Hollanda, Heloísa Buarque de. *Impressões de viagem: Cpc, vanguarda, e desbunde, 1960–1970.* Rio de Janeiro: Rocco, 1992.

Holloway, Thomas H. *Policing Rio de Janeiro: Repression and Resistance in a Nineteenth-Century City.* Stanford: Stanford University Press, 1993.

"Homossexuais exigem liberdade." *Jornal do Brasil* (Rio de Janeiro), April 5, 1973, 8.

"Homossexuais protestam em Nova Iorque." *Jornal do Brasil* (Rio de Janeiro), June 29, 1971.

"Homossexuais são detidos em São Paulo." *Jornal do Brasil* (Rio de Janeiro), October 6, 1971, 6.

"Homossexualismo." *Realidade* 3, no. 26 (May 1968): 112–22.

Hooven, F. Valentine III. *Beefcake: The Muscle Magazines of America, 1950–1970.* Cologne: Benedikt Taschen, 1995.

Howes, Robert. Introduction to *Bom-Crioulo: The Black Man and the Cabin Boy,* by Adolfo Caminha, trans. E. A. Lacey. San Francisco: Gay Sunshine Press, 1982.

————. "The Literatures of Outsiders: The Literature of the Gay Community in Latin America." In *Latin American Masses and Minorities: Their Images and Realities*, Seminar on the Acquisition of Latin American Library Materials, 30: 288–304. Madison: SALALM Secretariat, University of Wisconsin, 1987.

————. "Literature of the Contemporary Brazilian Gay Community: A Review." In *Modernity and Tradition: The New Latin American and Caribbean Literature, 1956–1994*, Seminar on the Acquisition of Latin American Library Materials, 126–138. Austin: SALALM Secretariat, Benson Latin American Collection, the General Libraries, University of Texas, 1996.

Hudson, Rock, and Sara Davidson. *Rock Hudson: His Story.* New York: William Morrow, 1986.

Humphrey, Lauds. *Tearoom Trade: Impersonal Sex in Public Places.* Chicago: Aldine Publishing, 1970.

"Internacional baile das bonecas." *Última Hora* (Rio de Janeiro), February 4, 1966, 7.

Irajá, Hernâni de. *Psicoses do amor: Estudo sobre as alterações do instinto sexual.* 6th ed. Rio de Janeiro: Freitas Bastos, 1935.

————. *Adeus! Lapa.* Rio de Janeiro: Gráfica Récord Editora, 1967.

"Ipanema cria Banda Carmen Miranda." *O Globo* (Rio de Janeiro), December 15, 1984, 12.

"Ipanema: Os alegres rapazes da Banda." *Manchete* (Rio de Janeiro), no. 1508 (March 14, 1981): 50–54.

Jaguar. "Noite deslumbrante no Carlos Gomes." *Pasquim* (Rio de Janeiro), no. 272 (September 17, 1974): 6–7.

————. "Miss Boneca Pop 75." *Pasquim* (Rio de Janeiro), no. 318 (August 1, 1975): 116–17.

Jaime, Jorge. *Homossexualismo masculino.* Rio de Janeiro: Editora "O Constructor," 1953.

————. *Monstro que chora.* Rio de Janeiro: Livraria Império, 1957.

"A jaula da bicha esta aberta." *Bagaço* (Rio de Janeiro) 1976.

Jáuregui, Carlos. *La homosexualidad en la Argentina.* Buenos Aires: Ediciones Tarso, 1987.

João Antônio. *Ó Copacabana!* Rio de Janeiro: Civilização Brasileira, 1978.

Johnson, Peter T. "Academic Press Censorship under Military and Civilian Regimes: The Argentine and Brazilian Cases, 1964–1975." *Luso-Brazilian Review* 15, no. 1 (summer 1978): 3–25.

Jota Efegê [João Ferreira Gomes]. *Figuras e coisas do carnaval carioca.* Rio de Janeiro: FUNARTE, 1982.

Jurth, Max. "L'homophilie au Brésil." *Arcadie* 83 (November 1960): 654–65.

Kalil, Glória. "Loura, provocante, sensual: Astrolfo Barroso Pinto, ou melhor . . . Rogéria." *Nova* 13 (October 1974): 72–75.

Kaplan, Sheila. "A 'explosão gay' na festa carioca atrai mais turistas." *O Globo* (Rio de Janeiro), March 1, 1984, 4

Katz, Jonathan Ned. *Gay American History: Lesbian and Gay Men in the U.S.A., a Documentary History.* Rev. ed. New York: Meridan, 1992.

Keck, Margaret. "Update on the Brazilian Labor Movement." *Latin American Perspectives* 11 (winter 1984): 27–36.

Kennedy, Hubert. "Karl Heinrich Ulrichs: The First Theorist of Homosexuality." In *Science and Homosexualities*, ed. Vernon A. Rosario, 26–45. New York: Routledge, 1997.

Klabin, Aracy A. L. "Aspectos jurídicos do transexualismo." Faculdade de Direito da Universidade de São Paulo, 1977.

K. Lixto [pseudonym]. "Caricatura." *O Malho* (Rio de Janeiro) 2, no. 20 (March 28, 1903): 14.

Kosinski, Calvacanti J. "Homossexual: Onde está a diferença." *Isto É*, October 1976, 114–17.

Kovarick, Lúcio, and Clara Ant. "One Hundred Years of Overcrowding: Slum Tenements in the City." In *Social Struggles and the City: The Case of São Paulo,* ed. Lúcio Kowarick, 60–76. New York: Monthly Review Press, 1994.

Kucinski, Bernardo. *Abertura, a história de uma crise.* São Paulo: Brasil Debates, 1982.

———. *Jornalistas e revolucionários nos tempos da imprensa alternativa.* São Paulo: Página Aberta, 1991.

Kulick, Don. *Travesti: Sex, Gender, and Culture among Brazilian Transgendered Prostitutes.* Chicago: University of Chicago Press, 1998.

Kushnir, Beatriz. *Baile de máscaras: Mulheres judias e prostituição, as polacas e sua associações de ajuda mútua.* Rio de Janeiro: Imago Editora, 1997.

La Caz, Carlos da Silva. *Vultos da medicina brasileira.* Academia Nacional de Medicina, vol. 4. São Paulo: Aliança Gráfica Industrial, 1977.

Lamenha, Sylvio. "Gay Power." *Já* (Rio de Janeiro), no. 7 (July 27, 1971): 8.

Lancaster, Roger N. *Life Is Hard: Machismo, Danger, and Intimacy of Power in Nicaragua.* Berkeley: University of California Press, 1992.

Landes, Ruth. "A Cult Matriarchate and Male Homosexuality." *Journal of Abnormal and Social Psychology* 34 (1940): 386–97.

———. *The City of Women.* Albuquerque: University of New Mexico Press, 1994.

Leal, Ferreira. *Um homem gasto: Episódio da história social do XIX século. Estudo naturalista por L.L.* 2d ed. Rio de Janeiro: Matheus, Costa, 1885.

Leiner, Marvin. *Sexual Politics in Cuba: Machismo, Homosexuality, and AIDS.* Boulder: Westview Press, 1994.

Leite, Francisco. *Flagrantes da "cidade maravilhosa."* Rio de Janeiro: Livraria José Olímpio Editora, 1939.

Leite, Rommel Mendes. "Acasos, casos, e ocasos: O relacionamento homossexual masculino e a ideologia sexual dominante." Master's thesis, Universidade Federal do Ceará, Fortaleza, 1986.

Lembruger, Maria Júlia. "Cemitério dos vivos." Master's thesis, Museu Nacional da Universidade Federal do Rio de Janeiro, 1979.

Lenharo, Alcir. *Sacralização da política.* Campinas: Editora Papirus, 1986.

———. *Cantores do rádio: A trajetória de Nora Ney e Jorge Goulart e o meio artístico de seu tempo.* Campinas, São Paulo: Editora da UNICAMP, 1995.

"Lennie Dale confessa, sob protestos gerais," *Lampião da Esquina* (Rio de Janeiro) 1, no. 2 (June 25, 1978): 6–7.

"Lennie—Pó de guaraná, ginseng, drugs, sex and rock and roll!" *Pasquim* (Rio de Janeiro), no. 616 (April 16, 1981): 8–10.

Lesser, Jeffrey. *Welcoming the Undesirables: Brazil and the Jewish Question.* Berkeley: University of California Press, 1995.

Lever, Janet. *Soccer Madness.* Chicago: University of Chicago Press, 1983.

Leyland, Winston, ed. *Now the Volcano: An Anthology of Latin American Gay Literature.* San Francisco: Gay Sunshine Press, 1979.

———. *My Deep Dark Pain Is Love: A Collection of Latin American Gay Fiction.* Trans. E. A. Lacey. San Francisco: Gay Sunshine Press, 1983.

Ligiéro, Zeca. "Carmen Miranda: An Afro-Brazilian Paradox." Ph.D. diss., New York University, 1998.

Lima, Délcio Monteiro de. *Comportamento sexual do brasileiro.* Rio de Janeiro: Livraria Francisco Alves Editora, 1976.

———. *Os homoeróticos.* Rio de Janeiro: Livraria Francisco Alves Editora, 1983.

Lima, Estácio de. *A inversão dos sexos.* Rio de Janeiro: Editora Guanabara, 1935.

Lima, Evelyn Furquim Werneck. "Arquitetura do espetáculo: Teatros e cinemas na formação do espaço público das Praças Tiradentes e Cinelândia, Rio de Janeiro, 1813–1950." Ph.D. diss., Universidade Federal do Rio de Janeiro, 1997.

Lima, Herman. *História da caricatura no Brasil.* Vol. 3. Rio de Janeiro: Livraria José Olímpio Editora, 1963.

Linhares, Maria Helena. "O Carnaval de antigamente." Part 1, "Há quatro séculos nascia o gosto brasileiro pelas folias." *Estado de Minas,* January 30, 1986, 8.

Lispector, Clarice. "Clóvis Bornay." *Manchete* (Rio de Janeiro), no. 879 (February 22, 1969): 48–49.

Lobert, Rosemary. "A palavra mágica Dzi: Uma resposta difícil de se perguntar." Master's thesis, Universidade Estadual de Campinas, 1979.

Lockhart, Melissa A. "Nelson Rodrigues." In *Latin American Writers on Gay and Lesbian Themes: A Bio-Critical Sourcebook,* ed. David William Foster, 370–74. Westport, Conn.: Greenwood Press, 1994.

———. "Walmir Ayala." In *Latin American Writers on Gay and Lesbian Themes: A Bio-Critical Sourcebook,* ed. David William Foster, 46–48. Westport, Conn.: Greenwood Press, 1994.

Luizetto, Flávio Venâncio. *Os constituintes em face da imigração.* Master's thesis, Universidade de São Paulo, 1975.

Lumsden, Ian. *Homosexuality: Society and the State in Mexico.* Toronto: Canadian Gay Archives, 1991.

———. *Machos, Maricones, and Gays: Cuba and Homosexuality.* Philadelphia: Temple University Press, 1996.

Lutz, Gualater Adolpho. *Auto-acusação, homossexualismo, e transvestismo: Contribuição à prática da criminologia psicanalítica.* Medical thesis, Faculdade Nacional de Medicina, Universidade do Brasil, Rio de Janeiro, 1939.

Macaulay, Neill. *Dom Pedro: The Struggle for Liberty in Brazil and Portugal, 1798–1834.* Durham: Duke University Press, 1986.

Macedo, Joaquim Manuel de. *Memórias da rua do Ouvidor.* Brasília: Editora Universidade de Brasília, 1988.

Machado, Elmar. "Madame Satã para o *Pasquim* 'Enquanto eu viver, a Lapa viverá.'" *Pasquim* (Rio de Janeiro), no. 357 (April 30, 1976): 6–11.

Machado, Luiz Carlos. *Descansa em paz, Oscar Wilde.* Rio de Janeiro: Editora Codecri, 1982.

MacRae, Edward. "Os respeitáveis militantes e as bichas loucas." In *Caminhos cruzados: Linguagem, antropologia, e ciências naturais,* 99–111. São Paulo: Editora Brasiliense, 1982.

———. "Gueto." *Novos Estudos Cebrap* (São Paulo) 2, 1 (April 1983): 53–60.

———. "A homossexualidade." In *Macho, masculino, homem,* 64–71. Porto Alegre: L & PM Editores, 1986.

———. *A construção da igualdade: Identidade sexual e política no Brasil da "abertura."* Campinas: Editora da UNICAMP, 1990.

———. "Homosexual Identities in Transitional Brazilian Politics." In *The Making of Social Movements in Latin America: Identity, Strategy, and Democracy,* ed. Arturo Escobar and Sonia E. Alvarez, 185–203. Boulder: Westview Press, 1992.

Magalhães, Raimundo Júnior. *Olavo Bilac e sua época.* Rio de Janeiro: Companhia Editora Americana, 1974.

———. *A vida vertiginosa de João do Rio.* Rio de Janeiro: Civilização Brasileira, 1978.

Maia, Clive. *Sol Quadrado: Da vida de um ex-presidiário.* Rio de Janeiro: Irmãos Pongetti, 1962.

Mainwaring, Scott. *The Catholic Church and Politics in Brazil, 1916–1985.* Stanford: Stanford University Press, 1986.

"Mais 28 travestis detidos pelo Deic." *Notícias Populares* (São Paulo), October 8, 1977.

"A Maison Moderne." *O Malho* (Rio de Janeiro) 3, no. 95 (9 July 1904): 10.

Maluco, Capadócio [pseudonym]. *O menino do Gouveia.* Contos Rápidos no. 6. Ilha de Vênus: Editora Cupido e Companhia, [1914].

Manta, Ignácio de Lyra Neves. *A arte e a neurose de João do Rio.* Rio de Janeiro: Francisco Alvarez, 1977.

Mantega, Guido, ed. *Sexo e poder.* São Paulo: Editora Brasiliense, 1979.

Maram, Sheldon. "Juscelino Kubitschek and the Politics of Exuberance, 1956–1961," *Luso-Brazilian Review* 27, no. 1 (summer 1990): 31–45.

Marañón, Gregório. "Una clasificación de los homosexuales desde el punto de vista médico-legal." *Arquivos de Medicina Legal e de Identificação* 7, no. 15 (January 1937): 90–100.

———. Foreword to *Homosexualismo e endocrinologia,* by Leonídio Ribeiro. Rio de Janeiro: Livraria Francisco Alves Editora, 1938.

"Marcha de homossexuais dá briga." *O Globo* (Rio de Janeiro), August 31, 1970.

Marconi, Paolo. *A censura política na imprensa brasileira, 1968–1978.* São Paulo: O Global, 1980.

Marone, Sílvio. "Considerações em tôrno de uma nova classificação de missexuais." *Arquivos da Polícia Civil de São Paulo* 10 (December 1945): 103–36.

———. *Missexualidade e arte.* São Paulo: n.p., 1947.

Martinho, Miriam. "Brazil." In *Unspoken Rules: Sexual Orientation and Women's Human Rights,* ed. Rachel Rosenbloom, 18–22. San Francisco: International Gay and Lesbian Human Rights Commission, 1995.

Martins, Luís. *Noturno da Lapa.* Rio de Janeiro: Editora Brasileira, 1964.

Martins, Sérgio, and Jaime Srur. "A passarela dos caubóis." *Última Hora* (Rio de Janeiro), November 7, 1970, 5.

Martins Filho, João Roberto. *Movimento estudantil e ditadura militar, 1964–68.* Campinas, São Paulo: Editora Papirus, 1987.

Mascarenhas, João Antônio de Souza. *A tríplice conexão: Machismo, conservadorismo político, e falso moralismo.* Rio de Janeiro: 2AB Editora, 1997.

Matos, Maria Izilda Santos de. *Dolores Duran: Experiências boêmias em Copacabana nos anos 50.* Rio de Janeiro: Bertrand Brasil, 1997.

Mattos, Rogério Botelho de, and Miguel Ângelo Campos Ribeiro. "Territórios da prostituição nos espaços públicos da área central do Rio de Janeiro." Rio de Janeiro, 1994.

Maurício, Augusto. *Algo do meu velho Rio.* Rio de Janeiro: Livraria Editora Brasiliana, 1966.

McCann, Bryan D. "Thin Air and the Solid State: Radio, Culture, and Politics in Brazil, 1930–1955." Ph.D. diss., Yale University, 1999.

Meade, Teresa A. *"Civilizing" Rio: Reform and Resistance in a Brazilian City, 1889–1930.* University Park: Pennsylvania State University Press, 1997.

Meirelles, Ney Flávio. "CNBB recomenda que homossexuais casem ou mantenham abstinência." *Jornal do Brasil,* October 31, 1986, 1.

Mello e Souza, Antônio Candido de. "The Brazilian Family." In *Brazil: Portrait of Half a Continent,* ed. T. Lynn Smith, 291–312. New York: Dryden Press, 1951.

Melo Filho, Murilo. "O governo garante um clima de tranqüilidade e trabalho: O mundo em guerra; o Brasil em paz." *Manchete* (Rio de Janeiro), no. 1035 (February 19, 1972): 20–21.

Menezes, Lená Medeiros de. *Os estrangeiros e o comércio do prazer nas ruas do Rio, 1890–1930.* Rio de Janeiro: Arquivo Nacional, 1992.

Meyer, Richard. "Rock Hudson's Body." In *Inside/Out: Lesbian Theories, Gay Theories*, ed. Diana Fuss, 259–88. New York: Routledge, 1991.

Miceli, Sérgio. *Intelectuais e Classe Dirigente no Brasil, 1920–1945*. São Paulo: Difel, 1979.

Míccolis, Lélia. "*Snob, Le Femme* . . . os bons tempos da imprensa gay." *Lampião da Esquina* (Rio de Janeiro) 3, no. 28 (September 1980): 6–7.

Míccolis, Leila, and Herbert Daniel. *Jacarés e lobisomens: Dois ensaios sobre a homossexualidade*. Rio de Janeiro: Achiamé, 1983.

"Mineiro quer Dener fora da TV." *Jornal do Brasil*, April 19, 1972, 26.

Misse, Michel. *O estigma do passivo sexual: Um símbolo de estigma no discurso cotidiano*. Rio de Janeiro: Achiamé, 1979.

Moises, José Álvaro. "What Is the Strategy of the 'New Syndicalism'?" *Latin American Perspectives* 9 (fall 1982): 55–73.

Moncau, P. Júnior. "Pesquisas endocrinólogicas em criminosos." *Arquivos de Polícia e Identificação* 2 (1938–39): 92–101.

Moraes, Eneida. *História do Carnaval carioca*. New edition, revised and expanded by Haroldo Costa. Rio de Janeiro: Gráfica Récord Editora, 1987.

Moreno, Antônio do Nascimento. "A personagem homossexual no cinema brasileiro." Master's thesis, Universidade Estadual de Campinas, 1995.

Mott, Luiz R. B. "Relações raciais entre homossexuais no Brasil colonial." *Revista Brasileira de História* 10 (1985): 89–102.

——. "Escravidão e homossexualidade." In *História e sexualidade no Brasil*, ed. Ronaldo Vainfas, 19–40. Rio de Janeiro: Edições Graal, 1986.

——. *O lesbianismo no Brasil*. Porto Alegre: Mercado Aberto, 1987.

——. "Pagode português: A subcultura gay em Portugal nos tempos inquisitoriais." *Revista Ciência e Cultura* 40 no. 20 (1988): 120–39.

——. *O sexo proibido: Virgens, gays, e escravos nas garras da inquisição*. Campinas: Editora Papirus, 1989.

——. "Os veados são viados." *Nós por Exemplo* (Rio de Janeiro) 3, no. 16 (September/October 1994): 13.

——. "The Gay Movement and Human Rights in Brazil." In *Latin American Male Homosexualities*, ed. Stephen O. Murray, 221–30. Albuquerque: University of New Mexico Press, 1995.

——. *Epidemic of Hate: Violations of the Human Rights of Gay Men, Lesbians, and Transvestites in Brazil*. San Francisco: Grupo Gay da Bahia/International Gay and Lesbian Human Rights Commission, 1996.

Moura, Roberto M. "O canto do eterno feminino." *Pasquim* (Rio de Janeiro), no. 243 (February 26, 1974): 19.

——. *Carnaval: Da redentora à Praça do Apocalipse*. Rio de Janeiro: Zahar Editores, 1986.

——. *Tia Ciata e a Pequena África no Rio de Janeiro*. Rio de Janeiro: Prefeitura da Cidade do Rio de Janeiro, Secretaria Municipal de Cultura, Departamento Geral de Documentação e Informação Cultural, Divisão de Editoração, 1995.

"A mulher brasileira, hoje." *Realidade* 1, no. 10 (January 1967): 20–29.

Müller, N. L. "A área central da cidade." In *A cidade de São Paulo: Estudos de geografia urbana*, vol. 3, *Aspectos da metrópole paulista*, ed. Aroldo de Azevedo, 121–82. São Paulo: Companhia Editora Nacional, 1958.

"O mundo gay rasga as fantasias." *Veja*, no. 19 (May 12, 1993): 52–53.

Munerato, Elice, and Myriam Campello, "Convite aos homossexuais." *Isto É*, September 21, 1977, 60–61.

Murray, Stephen O. "Machismo, Male Homosexuality, and Latin Culture." In *Latin American Male Homosexualities*, ed. Stephen O. Murray, 49–70. Albuquerque: University of New Mexico Press, 1995.

———, ed. *Latin American Male Homosexualities*. Albuquerque: University of New Mexico Press, 1995.

Nachman, Robert G. "Positivism, Modernization, and the Middle Class in Brazil." *Hispanic American Historical Review* 57 (1977): 1–23.

Negromonte, Padre Álvaro. *A educação sexual (para pais e educadores)*. Rio de Janeiro: Livraria José Olímpio Editora, 1953.

Needell, Jeffrey D. "The *Revolta contra Vacina* of 1904: The Revolt against 'Modernization' in *Belle-Époque* Rio de Janeiro." *Hispanic American Historical Review* 67, no. 2 (May 1987): 233–69.

———. *A Tropical Belle Époque: Elite Culture and Society in Turn-of-the-Century Rio de Janeiro*. Cambridge: Cambridge University Press, 1987.

———. "Identity, Race, Gender, and Modernity in the Origins of Gilberto Freyre's *Ouvre*." *American Historical Review* 100, no. 1 (February 1995): 51–77.

Neto, [Henrique Maximiliano] Coelho. "Os Sertanejos." *A Notícia* (Rio de Janeiro), November 29, 1908, 3.

Newlands, Lilian. "Elvira Pagã, a primeira rainha do Carnaval." *Jornal do Brasil* (Rio de Janeiro), January 15, 1984, 4.

"Ney Matogrosso fala sem make-up." *Interview* (São Paulo) 5 (May 1978): 5–7.

Nina, Marcelo Della. "Jorge Guinle e o Copa: Entrevista a Marcelo Della Nina." In *Copacabana cidade eterna: 100 anos de um mito*, ed. Wilson Coutinho, 39–44. Rio de Janeiro: Relume Dumará, 1992.

Noblat, Ricardo. "Playboy entrevista Gilberto Freyre." *Playboy* 5 (March 1980): 27–37.

Nóbrega, Regina. "Tudo começou com 'seu' Paschoal." *Lampião da Esquina* 3, no. 36 (May 1981): 15.

Nóbrega, Vera. "A explosão do homossexualismo." *Nova*, August 1977, 84–87.

"Um novo poder nas ruas da California." *Jornal da Tarde* (December 4, 1969).

Nunes, Viriato Fernandes. *As perversões em medicina legal*. Tese inaugural da Faculdade de Direito de São Paulo. São Paulo: Irmãos Ferraz, 1928.

Okita, Hiro. *Homossexualismo: Da opressão à libertação*. São Paulo: Proposta, 1981.

Oliveira, Lázaro Sanches de. *Masculinidade, feminilidade, androginia*. Rio de Janeiro: Aciamé, 1983.

Oliveira, Lúcia Lippi, Mônica Pimenta Velloso, and Angela Maria de Castro Gomes. *Estado Novo: Ideologia e poder*. Rio de Janeiro: Zahar Editores, 1982.

Oliveria, Neuza Maria. "As monas da Casa Amarela: Os travestis no espelho da mulher." Master's thesis, Universidade Federal da Bahia, 1986.

"Ontem, no distrito da Gávea: Quatorze presos rebentaram a grade e tentaram fugir." *Última Hora* (Rio de Janeiro), February 9, 1953, 5.

Openheimer, Jerry, and Jack Vitek. *Idol: Rock Hudson, the True Story of an American Film Hero*. New York: Villard, 1986.

Orazil, Angelo. *Rio de Janeiro and Environs: Travelers's Guide*. Rio de Janeiro: Guias do Brasil, 1939.

Ottoni, Paulo Roberto. "A prostituição masculina homossexual e o 'Travesti.'" Campinas, 1981.

Outra Coisa / Ação Homossexualista. *O bandeirante destemido: Um guia gay de São Paulo*. São Paulo: Privately printed, 1981.

"Outro rancho: 'O quem são eles.'" *Jornal do Brasil* (Rio de Janeiro), March 4, 1938, 13.

Pacheco e Silva, Antônio Carlos. *Direito à saúde: Documentos de atividade parlamentar*, Brazil: n.p., 1934.

———. *Psiquiatria clínica e forense*. São Paulo: Companhia Editora Nacional, 1940.

Pacheco e Silva, Antônio Carlos, and Olyntho de Mattos. "Um interessante caso de homossexualismo feminino." *Arquivos da Sociedade de Medicina Legal e Criminologia de São Paulo* 10 (1939): 69–81.

Pacheco e Silva, Antônio Carlos, Pedro Augusto da Silva, and Júlio de Andrade Silva Júnior. "A insulinoterapia nas formas delirantes da paralisia geral." *Arquivos da Assistência Geral a Psicopatas do Estado de São Paulo* 2, no. 2 (1937): 461–66.

Pacheco e Silva Filho, Antônio Carlos. *As origens psicológicas da homossexualidade masculina*. Ph.D. diss, Faculdade de Medicina da Universidade de São Paulo, 1971.

Paezzo, Sylvan. *Memórias de Madame Satã, conforme narração a Sylvan Paezzo*. Rio de Janeiro: Lidador, 1972.

Page, Joseph A. *The Brazilians*. Reading, Mass.: Addison-Wesley, 1995.

Paiva, Salvyano Cavalcanti de. *Viva o rebolado! Vida e morte do teatro de revista brasileiro*. Rio de Janeiro: Nova Fronteira, 1991.

Pamplona, Marco A. *Riots, Republicanism, and Citizenship: New York City and Rio de Janeiro City during the Consolidation of the Republican Order*. New York: Garland, 1996.

"Pancadaria, enxutos, e pouca gente animada no 'Baile dos Artists.'" *Última Hora* (Rio de Janeiro), February 3, 1964, 7.

Parker, Richard. *Bodies, Pleasures, and Passions: Sexual Culture in Contemporary Brazil*. Boston: Beacon Press, 1991.

———. "After AIDS: Changes in (Homo)sexual Behaviour." In *Sexuality, Politics, and AIDS in Brazil*, ed. Herbert Daniel and Richard Parker, 97–114. London: Falmer Press, 1993.

———. *A construção da solidariedade: AIDS, sexualidade, e política no Brasil*. Rio de Janeiro: Relume-Dumará; ABIA: IMS, UERJ, 1994.

———. "Changing Brazilian Constructions of Homosexuality." In *Latin American Male Homosexualities*, ed. Stephen O. Murray, 241–55. Albuquerque: University of New Mexico Press, 1995.

———. *Beneath the Equator: Culture of Desire, Male Homosexuality, and Emerging Gay Communities in Brazil*. New York: Routledge, 1999.

Pedrosa, Milton. "Copacabana—cidade independente e semi-nua." *Manchete* (Rio de Janeiro), no. 42 (February 7, 1953): 46–47.

Peixoto, Afrânio. "Missexualismo." *Arquivos de Medicina Legal e Identificação*. 3, no. 6 (February 1933): 67–73

———. *Sexologia Forense*. Rio de Janeiro: Editora Guanabara, 1934.

Pelegrin de Oliveira, Noélia. "O Carnaval começou com um rei para acabar na rua." *Folha de São Paulo*, February 23, 1979, 39.

Pellegrini, Tânia. *Gavetas vazias: Ficção e política nos anos 70*. São Carlos, São Paulo: Mercado de Letras, 1996.

Penna, Lincoln de Abreu. *Uma história da República*. Rio de Janeiro: Nova Fronteira, 1989.

Penteado, Darcy. *A meta*. São Paulo: Símbolo, 1976.

Pereira, Armando. *Sexo e prostituição*. Rio de Janeiro: Gráfica Récord Editora, 1967.

Pereira, Carlos Alberto Messeder. "Desvio e / ou reprodução: O estudo de um 'caso.'" In *Testemunha ocular: Textos de antropologia social do cotidiano*, 107–33. São Paulo: Editora Brasiliense, 1984.

———. "*O direito de curar:* Homossexualidade e medicina legal no Brasil dos anos 30." In *A invenção do Brasil moderno: Medicina, educação, e engenharia nos anos 20–30*, ed. Micael M. Herschmann and Carlos Alberto Messeder Pereira, 88–129. Rio de Janeiro: Rocco, 1994.

Pereira, Cristiana Sunetinni. "Um gênero alegre: Imprensa e pornografia no Rio de Janeiro, 1898–1916." Master's thesis, Universidade Estadual de Campinas, 1997.

Pereira, Ricardo Calheiro. "O desperdício do sêmen: Um estudo do erotismo entre rapazes." Master's thesis, Universidade Federal da Bahia, 1988.

Perlongher, Néstor. *O negócio do michê: Prostituição viril em São Paulo*. São Paulo: Editora Brasiliense, 1987.

Perrone, Fernando. *Relato de guerra: Praga, São Paulo, Paris*. São Paulo: Busca Vida, 1988.

Petrone, Pasquale. "São Paulo no século XX." In *A cidade de São Paulo: estudos de geografia urbana*, ed. Aroldo de Azevedo, vol. 2, *A evolução urbana*, 101–65. São Paulo: Companhia Editora Nacional, 1958.

Pierangelli, José Henrique, ed. *Códigos penais do Brasil: Evolução histórica*. Bauru, São Paulo: Javoli, 1980.

Pires de Almeida, José Ricardo. *Homosexualismo (a libertinagem no Rio de Janeiro): Estudo sobre as perversões do instinto genital*. Rio de Janeiro: Laemmert, 1906.

"Polícia acaba com dia do homossexual." *Última Hora* (Rio de Janeiro), July 5, 1976, 6.

Pompéia, Raul. *O Ateneu*. São Paulo: Editora Ática, 1991. Selections reprinted in *My Deep Dark Pain Is Love: A Collection of Latin American Gay Fiction*, ed. Winston Leyland, trans. E. A. Lacey, 343–83 (San Francisco: Gay Sunshine Press, 1983).

Ponte Preta, Santislaw [Sérgio Porto]. "Coccinelli—badalando, badalando, badalando." *Última Hora* (Rio de Janeiro), March 19, 1963, 10.

"Polícia diz que Cinelândia à noite seguiu sua vocação." *Jornal do Brasil* (Rio de Janeiro), March 3, 1972, 15.

Portão, Ramão Gomes. "Polícia declara guerra aos travestis paulistanos." *Folha da Tarde* (São Paulo), January 31, 1977, 13.

Portinari, Denise. *O discurso da homossexualidade feminina*. São Paulo: Editora Brasiliense, 1989.

Prado, Bento Júnior. "A biblioteca e os bares na década de 50." *Folhetim: Folha de São Paulo*, January 22, 1988, 20–21.

Prandi, Reginaldo. "Homossexualismo: Duas teses acadêmicas." *Lampião da Esquina* 1, no. 11 (April 1979): 17.

Preti, Dino. *A linguagem proibida: Um estudo sobre a linguagem erótica*. São Paulo: T. A. Queiroz, 1983.

"O prostituto." *Veja*, no. 115 (November 18, 1970): 30.

"*Psicoses do Amor* de Hernâni de Irajá." *Fon-Fon* (Rio de Janeiro), no. 6 (February 7, 1931): 1.

Queiroz, Luiz Gonzaga Morando. "Transgressores e transviados: A representação do homossexual nos discursos médicos e literários no final do século XIX, 1870–1900." Master's thesis, Universidade Federal de Minas Gerais, 1992.

Queiroz, Maria Isaura Pereira de. *Carnaval brasileiro: O vivido e o mito*. São Paulo: Editora Brasiliense, 1992.

Queiroz, Suley Robles Reis de. *São Paulo*. Madrid: Mapfre, 1992.

Rago, Margareth. *Os prazeres da noite: Prostituição e códigos da sexualidade feminina em São Paulo, 1890–1930*. Rio de Janeiro: Paz e Terra, 1991.

Ramírez, Rafael L. *Dime capitán: Reflexiones sobre la masculinidad*. Río Piedras: Ediciones Huracán, 1993.

Rasmussen, Kenneth Welden. "Brazilian Portuguese Words and Phrases for Certain Aspects of Love and Parts of the Body." Ph.D. diss., University of Wisconsin, 1971.

"Reclamando Nossos Direitos." *Jornal Folha de Parreira* (Curitiba) 3, no. 25 (May 1995): 2.

Ribas, João Carvalhal. "Apontamentos de psiquiatria: Curso do Professor A.C. Pacheco e Silva." Faculdade de Medicina da Universidade de São Paulo, 1938.

————. "Oscar Wilde à luz da psiquiatria." *Arquivos da Polícia Civil de São Paulo* 16, no. 2 (2d semester 1948): 87–185.

Ribeiro, Leonídio, "Aspectos médico-legais da homosexualidade." *Arquivos de Medicina Legal e Identificação* (Rio de Janeiro) 5 (1935): 12.

————. "Homosexualismo e endocrinologia." *Revista Brasileira* (Rio de Janeiro) 5 (1935): 155.

————. "El problema medicolegal del homosexualismo: Contribución a su estudio bajo el punto de vista endrocrinológico." *Archivos de Medicina Legal* (Buenos Aires) (1935): 362.

————. "O problema medico-legal do homosexualismo sob o ponto de vista endocrinológico." *Revista Jurídica* (Rio de Janeiro) 3 (1935): 185.

————. "Aspectos medico-legais da homosexualidade." *Arquivo de Antropologia Criminal* (Rio de Janeiro) 56 (1936): 425–36.

————. "O problema medico-legal do homosexualismo." *Arquivos da Medicina Legal e Identificação* (Rio de Janeiro) 5 (1936): 145–60.

————. "Homosexualismo e endocrinologia." *Arquivos da Medicina Legal e Identificação* (Rio de Janeiro) (1937): 167.

————. "Etiologia e tratamento da homosexualidade." *Arquivos de Medicina Legal e Identificação* (Rio de Janeiro), part 1 (1938): xcvii—c.

————. "Homosexuality: Etiology and Therapy." *Arquivos de Medicina Legal e Identificação* (Rio de Janeiro), part 1 (1938): 8–15.

————. "Homossexualité et glandes endocrines." *Arquivos de Medicina Legal e Identificação* (Rio de Janeiro), part 1 (1938): 98.

————. *Homosexualismo e endocrinologia.* With a foreword by Gregório Marañón. Rio de Janeiro: Livraria Francisco Alves Editora, 1938.

————. "Omosessualitá e endocrinologia." *La Giustizia Penale* (Rome) 44, no. 1 (1938): 527, 758.

————. *O novo código penal e a medicina legal.* Rio de Janeiro: Jacintho, 1942.

————. *De médico a criminalista: Depoimentos e reminiscências.* Rio de Janeiro: Livraria São José, 1967.

————. *Memórias de um médico legista.* Vol. 1. Rio de Janeiro: Editorial Sul Americana, 1975.

Ribeiro, Saboia. *Roteiro de Adolfo Caminha.* Rio de Janeiro: Livraria São José, 1957.

Ribeiro, Sérgio Nogueira. *Crimes passionais e outros temas.* 2d ed. Rio de Janeiro: Editora Itambé, 1975.

Rio, João do [Paulo Barreto]. "Impotência." *A Cidade do Rio* (Rio de Janeiro), August 16, 1899, 2.

————. *As religiões do Rio.* Paris: Garnier, 1904.

————. "A fisionomia dos jardins." *Gazeta de Notícias* (Rio de Janeiro), July 20, 1907, 2.

————. *A alma encantadora das ruas.* 1908. Rio de Janeiro: Secretaria Municipal de Cultura, Departamento Geral de Documentação e Informação Cultural, Divisão de Editoração, 1995.

Roberto, Sérgio. "Noite dos artistas: 4000 pessoas brincando." *Manchete* (Rio de Janeiro), no. 44 (February 21, 1953): 32–36.

Rocco, Pat. *Marco of Rio.* Bizarre Productions, Los Angeles, 1970.

Rocha, Oswaldo Porto. *A era das demolições: Cidade do Rio de Janeiro, 1870–1920.* Rio de Janeiro: Prefeitura da Cidade do Rio de Janeiro, Secretaria Municipal de Cultura, Departamento Geral de Documentação e Informação Cultural, Divisão de Editoração, 1995.

Rodrigues, Armando C., and Luiz M. Paiva. "Transexualismo, transvestismo, homossexualismo." *Arquivos da Polícia Civil de São Paulo* 26 (July–December 1976): 7–39.

Rodrigues, João Carlos. *João do Rio: Catálogo bibliográfico, 1899–1921.* Rio de Janeiro: Prefeitura da Cidade do Rio de Janeiro, Secretaria Municipal de Cultura, Departamento Geral de Documentação e Informação Cultural, Divisão de Editoração, 1994.

———. *João do Rio: Uma biografia.* Rio de Janeiro: Topbooks, 1996.

"Rogéria." *Pasquim* (Rio de Janeiro), no. 223 (October 9, 1973): 4–7.

Rosa, Ferreira da. *Rio de Janeiro: Notícias históricas e descritivas da capital do Brasil.* Rio de Janeiro: Anuário do Brasil, 1978.

Rosario, Vernon A. *The Erotic Imagination: French Histories of Perversity.* New York: Oxford University Press, 1997.

Ruiz, Roberto. *O teatro de revista no Brasil: Do início à primeira guerra mundial.* Rio de Janeiro: INACEN, 1988.

Saffioti Filho, José. "Os acordes da liberação Gay." *Manchete* (Rio de Janeiro), no. 1325 (September 10, 1977): 88–93.

"Saindo do Gueto." *Lampião da Esquina* 0 (April 1978): 2.

Salessi, Jorge. "The Argentine Dissemination of Homosexuality." In *Entiendes? Queer Readings, Hispanic Writings,* ed. Emilie L. Bermann and Paul Julian Smith, 49–91. Durham: Duke University Press, 1995.

———. *Médicos, maleantes, y maricas: Higiene, criminología, y homosexualidad en la construcción de la nación Argentina, Buenos Aires, 1871–1914.* Rosario: Beatriz Viterbo, 1995.

Santa Inez, Antônio Leal de, ed. *Pesquisa acerca dos hábitos e atitudes sexuais dos brasileiros.* São Paulo: Editora Cultrix, 1983.

Santiago, Silviano. "Repressão e censura no campo da literatura e das artes na década de 70." *Encontros com a Civilização Brasileira* 17 (November 1979): 187–95.

Santos, Carlos Nelson F. dos. "Bichas e entendidos: A sauna como lugar de confronto." Rio de Janeiro, 1976.

Santos, Joaquim Ferreira dos. *Feliz 1958: O ano que não devia terminar.* Rio de Janeiro: Gráfica Récord Editora, 1997.

Santos, Roberto. *Caracteres sexuais neutros e intersexualidade.* Rio de Janeiro: Tipografia Artes Gráficas, 1931.

Satã, Madame. "Madame Satã." Interview by Sérgio Cabral, Millôr Fernandes, Chico Júnior, and Paulo Francis. *Pasquim* (Rio de Janeiro), no. 95 (April 29, 1971): 2–5.

Schifter, Jacobo. *La formación de una contracultura. Homosexualismo y SIDA en Costa Rica.* San José, Costa Rica: Editorial Cuaycán, 1989.

———. *Lila's House: Male Prostitution in Latin America.* New York: Harrington Park Press, 1998.

Schneider, Ronald M. *"Order and Progress": A Political History of Brazil.* Boulder: Westview Press, 1991.

Schwartzman, Simon. *A Space for Science: The Development of the Scientific Community in Brazil.* University Park: Pennsylvania State University Press, 1991.

Scliar, Salomão. "Tipos de Carnaval." *Manchete* (Rio de Janeiro), no. 44 (February 21, 1953): 30–31.

Secco, Carmen Lúcia Tindó. *Morte e prazer em João do Rio.* Rio de Janeiro: Livraria Francisco Alves Editora / Instituto Estadual do Livro, 1978.

Sell, Teresa Adada. *Identidade homossexual e normas sociais (histórias de vida).* Florianópolis: Editora da UFSC, 1987.

Serbin, Kenneth P. "Priests, Celibacy, and Social Conflict: A History of Brazil's Clergy and Seminaries." Ph.D. diss., University of California, San Diego, 1993.

Serra, Ivo. "Ivana—a grande dúvida." *Manchete* (Rio de Janeiro), no. 75 (September 26, 1953): 22–23.

Sevcenko, Nicolau. *A revolta da vacina: Mentes insanas em corpos rebeldes.* São Paulo: Editora Brasiliense, 1984.

Severo, José Antônio "Emilinha, ou a volta da Cinderela que acabou Rainha do Brasil." *Revista Realidade* 6, no. 72 (March 1972), 122–30.

Sharp, Walter R. "Methods of Opinion Control in Present-day Brazil." *Public Opinion Quarterly* 5, no. 1 (March 1941): 3–16.

Silva, Aguinaldo. "Rogéria: Minhas memórias de alcova abalariam o Brasil." *Pasquim* (Rio de Janeiro), no. 107 (July 22, 1971): 6.

———. *Primeira carta aos andróginos.* Rio de Janeiro: Pallas, 1975.

———. "Compromissos, queridinhas? Nem morta!" *Lampião da Esquina* 3, no. 26 (July 1980): 10–11.

———. "Balada para Madame Satã." *Pleiguei* (Rio de Janeiro) 1 (November 1981): 24–26.

Silva, Cláudio Roberto da. "Reinventando o sonho: História oral de vida política e homossexualidade no Brasil contemporâneo." Master's thesis, Universidade de São Paulo, 1998.

Silva, Cristina Luci Câmara da. "Triângulo Rosa: A busca pela cidadania dos homossexuais." Master's thesis, Universidade Federal do Rio de Janeiro, 1993.

Silva, Hélio R. S. *Travesti: A invenção do feminino.* Rio de Janeiro: Relume Dumará, 1993.

Silva, Lindinalva Laurindo. "Aids e homossexualidade em São Paulo." Master's thesis, Pontifícia Universidade Católica de São Paulo, 1986.

Simões, Inimá. *Salas de cinema em São Paulo.* São Paulo: Secretaria Municipal de Cultura de São Paulo, 1990.

Sinisgalli, Aldo. "Considerações gerais sobre o homossexualismo." *Arquivos de Polícia e Identificação* (São Paulo) 3 (1938–40): 282–303.

———. "Observações sobre os hábitos, costumes, e condições de vida dos homossexuais (pederastas passivos) de São Paulo." *Arquivos de Polícia e Identificação* (São Paulo) 3 (1938–40): 304–9.

Skidmore, Thomas E. *Politics in Brazil, 1930–1964: An Experiment in Democracy.* New York: Oxford University Press, 1967.

———. *The Politics of Military Rule in Brazil, 1964–85.* New York: Oxford University Press, 1988.

———. *Black into White: Race and Nationality in Brazilian Thought.* Durham: Duke University Press, 1993.

Smith, Anne-Marie. *A Forced Agreement: Press Acquiescence to Censorship in Brazil.* Pittsburgh: University of Pittsburgh Press, 1997.

Snoek, Jaime. "Eles também são da nossa estripe: Considerações sobre a homofilia." *Revista Vozes* 9 (September 1967): 792–802.

———. "Emancipação dos homossexuais e valores positivos da homossexualidade." In *Católicos e Medicina Hoje: Anais do II Congresso Católico Brasileiro de Medicina,* ed. A. G. Mattos. São Paulo, 1967.

"Soares levou bonecas de luxo ao seu baile." *Última Hora* (Rio de Janeiro), February 28, 1968, 1.

Soares, Luiz Carlos. *Rameiras, ilhoas, polacas . . . a prostituição no Rio de Janeiro do século XIX.* São Paulo: Editora Ática, 1992.

Soihet, Rachel. *Condição feminina e formas de violência: Mulheres pobres e ordem urbana, 1890–1920.* Rio de Janeiro: Forense Universitária, 1989.

Souza, Iara Lis F. Stto. Carvalho. "Pátria Coroada: O Brasil como corpo político autônomo, 1780–1863." Ph.D. diss., Universidade Estadual de Campinas, 1997.

Souza, Pedro de. "Confidências da carne: O público e o privado na enunciação da sexualidade." Ph.D. diss., Universidade Estadual de Campinas, 1993.

Spagnol, Antônio Sérgio. "O desejo marginal: Violência nas relações homossexuais na cidade de São Paulo." Master's thesis, Universidade de São Paulo, 1996.

Stepan, Nancy Leys. *Beginnings of Brazilian Science: Oswaldo Cruz, Medical Research, and Policy, 1890–1920.* New York: Science History Publications, 1981.

———. *"The Hour of Eugenics": Race, Gender, and Nation in Latin America.* Ithaca: Cornell University Press, 1991.

Suplicy, Marta. *Conversando sobre sexo.* Rio de Janeiro: Editora Vozes, 1983.

Tavares, Paulo. "Os alegres enxutos." *Manchete* (Rio de Janeiro), no. 517 (March 17, 1962): 60–63.

Taylor, Clark C. "Legends, Syncretism, and Continuing Echoes of Homosexuality from Pre-Columbian and Colonial México." In *Latin American Male Homosexualities*, ed. Steve O. Murray, 80–99. Albuquerque: University of New Mexico Press, 1995.

Teixeira, Fausto. "Vocabulário do caipira paulista." *Revista do Arquivo Municipal* (São Paulo) 13, no. 61 (1946): 67–104.

Teixeira, Maria Lina Leão. "Transas de um povo de santo: Um estudo sobre as identidades sexuais." Master's thesis, Universidade Federal do Rio de Janeiro, 1986.

"A terceira força no Carnaval carioca." *Manchete, Edição Especial* (Rio de Janeiro), no. 356 (February 1959): 64–68.

Terto, Veriano Júnior. "No escurinho do cinema . . . : Socialidade orgiástica nas tardes cariocas." Master's thesis, Pontifícia Universidade Católica do Rio de Janeiro, 1989.

"Todo paulista que não gosta de mulher é bicha." *Pasquim* (Rio de Janeiro), no. 105 (July 8, 1971): 3.

Toledo, Benedito Lima de. *Anhangabaú.* São Paulo: Federação das Industrias do Estado de São Paulo, 1989.

"Travesti, presença crescente na cidade." *Folha de São Paulo*, August 16, 1976, 26.

"Travestis são presos de biquinis." *Jornal do Brasil* (Rio de Janeiro), September 18, 1972, 22.

Trésor de la langue française. Paris: CNRS, 1975.

Trevisan, João S. "Demissão, processo, perseguições. Mas qual é o crime de Celso Curi?" *Lampião da Esquina* (Rio de Janeiro), no. 0 (April 1978): 6–8.

———. *Perverts in Paradise.* Trans. Martin Foreman. London: GMP Publishers, 1986.

Trexler, Richard. *Sex and Conquest: Gendered Violence, Political Order, and the European Conquest of the Americas.* Ithaca: Cornell University Press, 1995.

Turner, Victor. "Carnaval in Rio: Dionysian Drama in an Industrializing Society." In *The Anthropology of Performance.* New York: PAJ Publications, 1986.

Valente, Armando Júnior. "Da responsabilidade moral e legal dos médicos." Ph.D. diss., Faculdade de Medicina de São Paulo, 1929.

Vallinoto, Tereza Christina. "A construção da solidariedade: Um estudo sobre a resposta coletiva à AIDS." Master's thesis, Escola Nacional de Saúde Pública da Fundação Oswaldo Cruz, 1991.

Varejão, Marilda, and Narceu de Almeida. "Quase tudo que você sempre quis saber sobre o homossexualismo e nunca ousou perguntar." *Manchete* (Rio de Janeiro), no. 1234 (December 13, 1975): 16–19.

Vaz, Denise Pires. *Ney Matogrosso: Um cara meio estranho.* Rio de Janeiro: Rio Fundo, 1992.

Vaz, Rocha. "Aspectos clínicos da intersexualidade." *Arquivo de Medicina Legal e Identificação* (Rio de Janeiro) 3, no. 7 (August 1933): 190–202.

Velho, Gilberto. "Estigma e comportamento desviante em Copacabana." In *Desvio e divergência: Uma crítica da patologia social*, ed. Gilberto Velho, 116–24. Rio de Janeiro: Zahar Editores, 1981.

————. *A utopia urbana: Um estudo de antropologia social.* 4th ed. Rio de Janeiro: Zahar Editores, 1982.

————. "A busca de coerência: Coexistência e contradições entre códigos em camadas médias urbanas." In *Cultura da psicanálise,* ed. Sérvulo A. Figueira, 169–77. São Paulo: Editora Brasiliense, 1985.

Venciguerra, Márcio, and Maurício Maia. *O pecado de adão: Crimes homossexuais no eixo Rio—São Paulo.* São Paulo: Ícone, 1988.

Veneziano, Neyde. *O teatro de revista no Brasil: Dramaturgia e convenções.* Campinas: Editorial da UNICAMP, 1991.

Ventura, Zuenir. *O ano que não terminou.* Rio de Janeiro: Nova Fronteira, 1988.

"A vida continua." *Veja,* no. 119 (November 25, 1970): 32–33.

A vida de Marlene: Depoimento. Rio de Janeiro: Editora Rio Cultura, n.d.

Villa, Renzo. *Il deviante e i suoi segni: Lombrosos e la nascita dell'antropologia criminale.* Milan: Angeli, 1985.

Viveiros de Castro, Francisco José. *Atentados ao pudor: estudos sobre as aberações do instinto sexual.* 3d ed., rev. and enl. Rio de Janeiro: Libraria Editora Feitas Bastos, 1934.

Wafer, Jim. *The Taste of Blood: Spirit Possession in Brazilian Candomblé.* Philadelphia: University of Pennsylvania Press, 1991.

Weinstein, Barbara. *For Social Peace in Brazil: Industrialists and the Remaking of the Working Class in São Paulo, 1920–1964.* Chapel Hill: University of North Carolina Press, 1996.

Whitaker, Edmur de Aguiar. "Contribuição ao estudo dos homossexuais." *Arquivos de Polícia e Identificação* (São Paulo) 2, no. 1 (1938–39): 32–35.

————. "O crime e os criminosos à luz da psicologia e da psiquiatria—Estudo acerca de 50 delinqüentes—Considerações sobre o problema da delinqüência em São Paulo." *Arquivos da Polícia Civil de São Paulo* 3 (1st semester 1942): 426–38.

————. *Manual de psicologia e psicopatologia judicial.* São Paulo: Serviço Gráfico da Secretaria da Segurança Pública, 1958.

Whitaker, Edmur de Aguiar, Eddi Kraus, Magino Roberto de Oliveira, and Aldo Sinisgalli, "Estudo biográfico dos homosexuais (pederastas passivos) da Capital de São Paulo: Aspectos da sua atividade social, costumes, hábitos, 'apelidos,' 'gíria'." *Arquivos de Polícia e Identificação* 2, no. 1 (1938–39): 244–60.

Whitam, Frederick. "*Os Entendidos:* Gay Life in São Paulo in the late 1970s." In *Latin American Male Homosexualities,* ed. Stephen O. Murray, 231–40. Albuquerque: University of New Mexico Press, 1995.

Woll, Allen L. *The Latin Image in American Film.* Los Angeles: UCLA Press, 1977.

Worcester, Donald E. *Brazil: From Colony to World Power.* New York: Charles Scribner's Sons, 1973.

Young, Allen. "Gay Gringo in Brazil." In *The Gay Liberation Book,* ed. Len Richmond and Gary Noguera, 60–67. San Francisco: Ramparts Press, 1973.

————. "Brazilian Journalists Rally around Gay Newspaper." *Gay Community News,* March 1979, 5.

Zanatta, Elaine Marques. "Documento e identidade: O movimento homossexual no Brasil na década de 80." *Cadernos AEL Arquivos e Memória* 5/6 (1996–97): 193–220.

INDEX